Roman British Pottery.

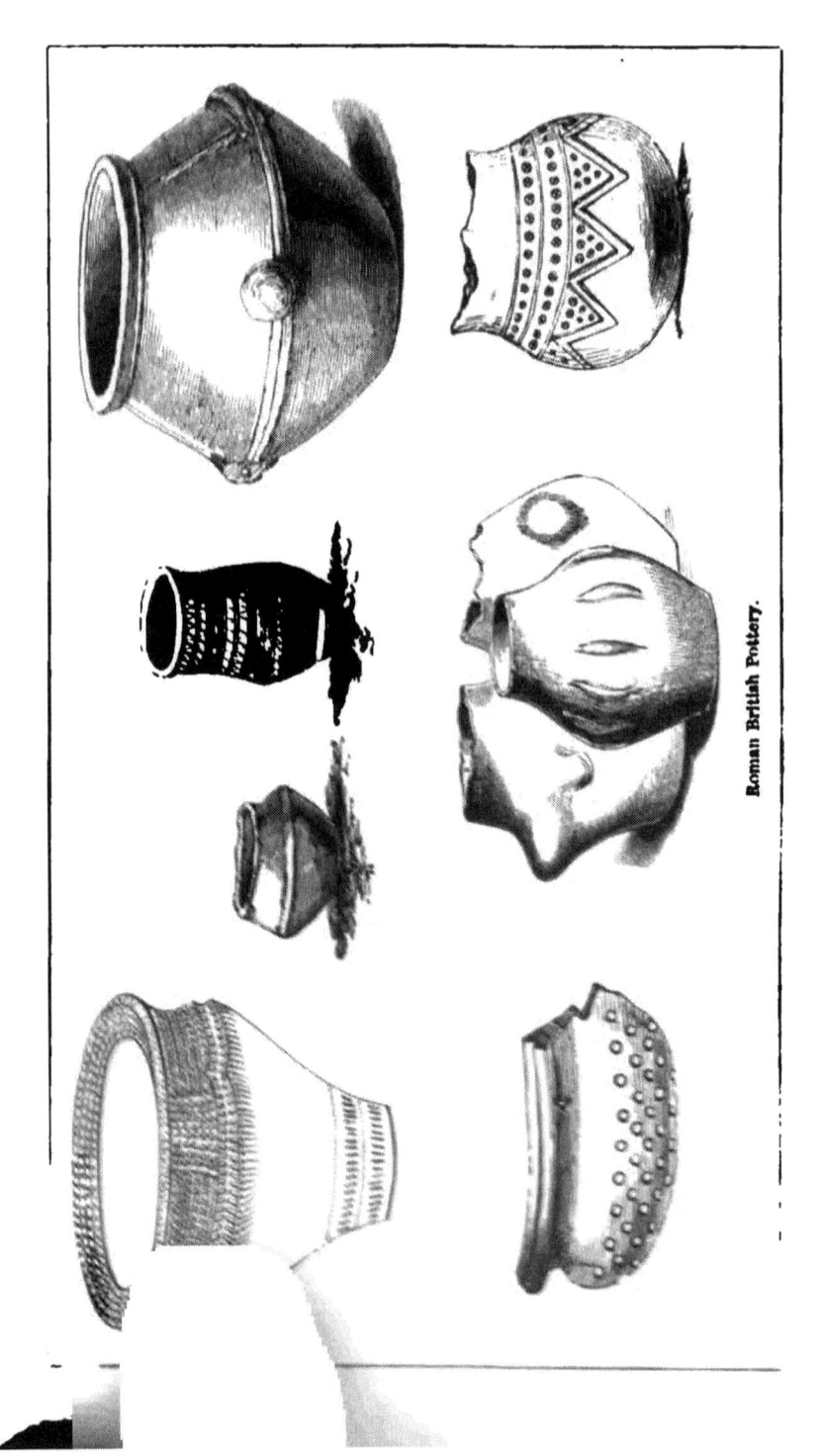

THE CELT, THE ROMAN, AND THE SAXON:

A HISTORY OF THE EARLY INHABITANTS OF BRITAIN,

DOWN TO THE CONVERSION OF THE ANGLO-SAXONS TO CHRISTIANITY.

ILLUSTRATED BY THE ANCIENT REMAINS BROUGHT TO LIGHT BY RECENT RESEARCH.

BY

THOMAS WRIGHT, Esq.,

M.A., F.S.A., H.S.S.L.,

AND CORRESPONDING MEMBER OF THE NATIONAL INSTITUTE OF FRANCE
(*Académie des Inscriptions et Belles Lettres*).

WITH NUMEROUS ENGRAVINGS ON WOOD.

SIXTH EDITION.

LONDON:
KEGAN PAUL, TRENCH, TRÜBNER, & CO. L??
PATERNOSTER HOUSE, CHARING CROSS ROAD.
1902.

TO

THE RIGHT HONOURABLE

The Earl of Powys

THIS VOLUME

ON THE EARLIER HISTORY OF OUR FOREFATHERS

IS MOST RESPECTFULLY DEDICATED BY

THE AUTHOR.

PREFACE.

THERE is hardly a corner in our island in which the spade or the plough does not, from time to time, turn up relics of its earlier inhabitants, to astonish and to excite the curiosity of the observer, who, when he looks to an ordinary history of England, finds that the period to which such remains belong is passed over with so little notice, that he is left with no more information on the subject of his research than he possessed before he opened the book. There is, in fact, no popular history of what is termed by antiquaries the Primeval Period, and those who are placed in the position just mentioned, if they happen not to possess a library of expensive publications, or to have the opportunity of consulting with those who have made archæology their study, are at present obliged to remain satisfied with uncertain conjectures, and are thus led, in the absence of the requisite elementary knowledge, to form theories of their own which are far removed from the truth. It was in the wish to supply a want thus very extensively felt that the following volume originated. Its object is to give a sketch of that part of our history which is not generally treated of, the period before Britain became Christian England—the period, indeed, which, in the absence of much documentary evidence, it is the peculiar province of the antiquary to illustrate. Every article which, as just stated, is turned up by the spade or the plough, is a record of that history, and it is by comparing them together, and subjecting them to the assay of science, that we make them tell their story. I have attempted in the following pages to show what light the still imperfect discoveries of the antiquary have thrown upon the condition of this island, during centuries which present little more than a blank in our ordinary annals.

The studies of the antiquary are not so dry or so useless as many have been led to suppose, and it is clear that this is beginning to be generally understood by the widely increased popularity which they have gained during the last few years. His science, however, is as yet but very imperfectly developed, but the difficulties which stood in the way of its advance are now in a great measure cleared away, and we may hope that it is making a steady and satisfactory progress. The great obstacle with which the student has had to contend was, the want of examples brought together for comparison, which led him continually to make assumptions that had no foundation, and to appropriate incorrectly, the consequences of which are visible in almost every work touching on the primeval antiquities of Britain that has appeared until the last few years. This obstacle is now rapidly giving way before the increasing facility of communicating knowledge, the formation of local museums, and the greater number of good books on the subject. But there is another danger against which the student in British archæology is to be especially warned; the old scholars failed in not following a sufficiently strict course of comparison and deduction; but some of the new ones run into the opposite extreme of generalizing too hastily, and they thus form systems specious and attractive in appearance, but without foundation in truth. Such I am convinced is the system of archæological periods which has been adopted by the antiquaries of the north, and which a vain attempt has been made to introduce into this country. There is something we may perhaps say poetical, certainly imaginative, in talking of an age of stone, or an age of bronze, or an age of iron, but such divisions have no meaning in history, which cannot be treated as a physical science, and its objects arranged in genera and species. We have to do with races of mankind, and we can only arrange the objects which come under our examination according to the peoples to whom they belonged, and as they illustrate their manners and history. In fact, the divisions alluded to are in themselves, I believe, incorrect, and so far is the discovery of implements of stone, or of bronze, or of iron, in themselves a proof of any particular age, that we often find them together. It is true that there may have been a period when society was in so barbarous a state, that sticks or stones were the only implements with which men knew how to furnish themselves; but I doubt if the antiquary has yet found any evidence of such a period. Stone implements are certainly found with articles of metal, and it may fairly be doubted if the stone implements in general, found either in these islands or in the north, belong to a period antecedent, or much antecedent, to that in which metals were in common use. In the early period to which the present volume refers, intercommunication was slow and difficult, and an individual in any obscure village could not, as at present, send off by post to any distant town and get immediately the material he wanted in any given quantity. It was thus necessary to use such materials as came to hand, and there is no possible reason why one man should not possess a weapon or a tool formed of stone, while his richer or more fortunate contemporary had one of iron or of bronze. This latter is the metal found almost exclusively in what seem to be the earliest sepulchral interments; but we are not sufficiently acquainted with the manners and sentiments of the people to whom they belonged, to say that there was not some particular reasons why the deceased preferred articles of bronze to those of other metals. Perhaps it was looked upon as more precious. What was the origin of bronze but the attempt to harden copper in countries where iron was not known, or could not be procured? it is a mixed metal, and it is absurd to suppose that its use could have preceded that of iron in countries where the latter metal was abundant. We must also bear in mind that iron undergoes much more rapid decomposition; and if even in interments of the Anglo-Saxon period we very often find scarcely a trace remaining of what we know were articles composed of that metal, what must be the case with regard to similar interments made six or seven hundred years earlier, or possibly at a still more remote period?

I have thought it necessary to make these observations, because it will be seen, that in the following manual I have altogether discarded this vague system of metallic periods. I have treated antiquities simply according to the races to which they belonged. In fact, I have attempted to make archæology walk hand-in-hand with history.[*]

I feel conscious, at the same time, that my attempt must be, in many respects, an imperfect one, and that I have good reason for appealing to the indulgence of my readers. My object was to supply the want of a manual of British archæology, where there was really no such work existing, and it has been the occupation of leisure moments under many disadvantages. If it

---

[*] After this preface was written, I delivered at the meeting of the British Association a Paper on this subject of Primeval Antiquities, which was printed in the Transactions of the Ethnological Society of London, in which I had examined a little more carefully into the arguments which had been for and against. I have yielded to the suggestion of friends to give this paper, slightly revised, as the first chapter in my book in the present edition.

PREFACE.

help to render the science more popular, and to call the attention of Englishmen more generally to the memorials of the past history of their country, my object will be fully accomplished. Those who wish to pursue the subject further must study the objects themselves, and refer to some of the larger and more expensive works which may be found in public libraries. To place such objects and works within the reach of people in general is the chief purpose of local museums and societies. A great mass of valuable material for the illustration of the antiquities of the period under our present consideration, will be found scattered through the volumes of the Archæologia of the Society of Antiquaries of London; but the unexperienced antiquary must pay more attention to the plates than to the descriptions. The best collection of antiquarian materials we possess at present is the Collectanea Antiqua by Mr Roach Smith, which, however, is already becoming rare. Many good papers on primeval antiquities, by Mr Roach Smith and others, will also be found in the volumes of the Journal of the British Archæological Association, and in the Archæological Journal published by the Archæological Institute. Other valuable works for reference, but of a less general character, will be pointed out in the notes to the following pages.

The value of a work on antiquities depends much on its pictorial illustrations, for it is evident that descriptions of the objects without engravings would be very vague and unsatisfactory. I have endeavoured in the present work to give engravings of such objects as represent the classes, or peculiar types, with which it is necessary that the student in archæology should make himself acquainted. In doing this, I have to acknowledge the kind and ready assistance of one or two friends, to whom the antiquarianism of this country owes much of its progress at the present day; and, although by far the greater part of the illustrations were engraved expressly for this work, and are due to the skilful pencil of Mr Fairholt, I have availed myself of the offers of Dr Bruce of Newcastle, to lend me some of the cuts from his excellent work on the Roman Wall, and of Mr Roach Smith, who similarly placed at my disposal the cuts of his Collectanea, of his work on the antiquities of Richborough, Reculver, and Lymne, and of his still more recent work on Roman London.

A new edition of this work having been called for, I have only here to add a few words to the foregoing remarks. A volume like this, containing so many facts brought together from different sources, could hardly be expected to be free from errors. I have done my best to discover and correct these in the new edition, and the text has not only been revised throughout, but many additions have been made, chiefly arising out of discoveries made since the appearance of the former edition, and among these additions are a considerable number of new illustrative engravings.

THOMAS WRIGHT.

BROMPTON, *December*, 1874.

CONTENTS.

CHAPTER I.

On the True Assignation of the Bronze Weapons, etc., supposed to indicate a Bronze Age in Western and Northern Europe—Stone, the earliest known material used for Weapons—The Stone Age, Bronze Age, and Iron Age of the Northern Antiquaries 1

CHAPTER II.

Ethnological Views—Political Movements in Gaul—Cæsar's first and second Invasions—Cassivellaunus—The Britons, as described by Cæsar, Strabo, and Diodorus—Cunobeline and his Sons—Expedition of Claudius—Conquests of the earlier Propretors—Caractacus—Cartismandua and Venusius—Invasion of Mona—Insurrection of Boadicea—War with the Brigantes—Campaigns of Agricola—Total Subjection of the Island to Rome—Enumeration of the British Tribes—Hibernia—Manners of the Britons, as described by Ancient Writers—The Druids 23

CHAPTER III.

British Antiquities—Barrows—Cromlechs, and Sepulchral Chambers—Circles; Stonehenge—Other Monuments of Stone—Various descriptions of British Barrows—Their contents—Pottery—Instruments of Stone—Instruments of Metal—Other articles—Their value as illustrative of History—The British Coinage—Earthworks, and supposed sites of Towns and Villages 70

CHAPTER IV.

Britain at the beginning of the Second Century—Towns enumerated by Ptolemy—Hadrian—The Wall—Lollius Urbicus; the Wall of Antoninus—Rebellion of the Soldiery in Britain—Albinus contends for the Purple—Campaigns of Severus, who dies at Eburacum (*York*)—The Caledonians—Carausius usurps the Purple—Allectus—Britain restored to the Empire by Constantius—Constantine the Great—Revolt of Magnentius—The Picts and Scots 120

CONTENTS.

CHAPTER V.

A Journey through Roman Britain—Londinium—Great Road from Londinium to Segontium—Verulamium; Uriconium, &c.—Direct Northern Road from Londinium; Durobrivæ, Lindum, Danum, Eburacum, Isurium—Passage of the two Walls—Stations on the Wall—Branch to Luguballium and Blatum Bulgium—Eastern Road; Camulodunum, Camboricum—From Londinium to Calleva—Branch to Corinium and Glevum; Isca and Maridunum—From Glevum by Magna to Deva, and thence through Coccium to the North—Cross Roads—Salinæ and other Towns—The Western Road, from Calleva to Sorbiodunum, Durnovaria, and Isca Dumnoniorum—Aquæ Solis—The *trajectus* to Wales, and the Sarn Helen—The Road on the Southern Coast; Venta Belgarum, Clausentum, Portus Magnus, Regnum, Anderida, Portus Lemanis . . . 145

CHAPTER VI.

A Roman Town in Britain—Its Walls, Towers, and Gates—Materials, and Modes of Construction—The Houses—Their Plan and Arrangement—The Tessellated Pavements and Frescoed Walls—Method of Warming the Houses; the Hypocausts—the Baths—Windows and Roofs—Distribution of the Houses in Streets—Public Buildings; Temples, Basilicæ, Theatres, Amphitheatres—The Suburbs and Burial-places—Sanitary Arrangements; Sewers, Rubbish-pits—The Language of Britain . . 171

CHAPTER VII.

The Country—Roman Roads and their Construction—Milliaria; the Roman Mile—Bridges—Roman Villas; Woodchester, Bignor, &c.—Tessellated Pavements, and the Subjects represented on them—Rustic Villages—Agriculture and Farming—Country Life; the Chase—British Dogs . 221

CHAPTER VIII.

Manufactures of the Romans in Britain—Pottery—The Upchurch Ware—Dymchurch—The Potteries at Durobrivæ—The Samian Ware—Romano-Salopian Wares—Other Varieties—Terra-cottas—Roman Glass—Kimmeridge Coal Manufacture—Mineral Coal—Metals—The Roman Ironworks in Britain; Sussex, the Forest of Dean, &c.—Tin and Lead—Other Metals—Bronze—The Arts; Sculpture—Medicine; the Oculists' Stamps—Trades; a Goldsmith's Sign 259

CHAPTER IX

Ethnological Character of the Roman Population of Britain—Countries from which it was derived—The Auxiliary Troops—Names and Birthplaces of Individuals—Traces of Languages; Inscribed Pottery; the Roundels found at Colchester—Debased Latinity—Remains of the British Population 306

CHAPTER X.

Religious Worship of the Romans in Britain—Roman chief Deities; Jupiter, Mars, Apollo, Minerva, Ceres, &c.—The eight Deities—Lesser Deities; Silvanus, Æsculapius—Grecian and Eastern Deities; the Tyrian Hercules, Mithras, Serapis—The Nymphs and Genii, Fortune, and Deified Personifications—Deities of the Auxiliary Races; the Deæ Matres, Viteres, or Vitris, Belatucadrus, Cocidius, Mogontis, &c.—Did Christianity prevail or exist in Roman Britain? 3:8

CONTENTS.

CHAPTER XI.

PAGE

Modes of Sepulture in Roman Britain—Cremation and Urn-Burial—Modes of Interment—Burial of the Body entire—Sarcophagi—Coffins of Baked Clay, Lead, and Wood—Barrows—Sepulchral Chambers—Inscriptions and their Sentiments—Various Articles deposited with the Dead—Fulgor Divom 357

CHAPTER XII.

Domestic Life among the Romans in Britain as Illustrated by their Remains—Dress and Personal Ornaments—The Toilette—The Household; Furniture and Utensils—Female Occupations—Cutlery — Styli — Scales — Ornamental Articles—Weapons, &c. 391

CHAPTER XIII.

The Roman Province—Its Divisions and Officers—The Military Force—Centurial and other Inscriptions—Towns and their Municipal Constitution—The Coinage—Roman Coins relating to Britain—Spurious Coinage—Different methods of Hoarding Money 416

CHAPTER XIV.

Declining State of the Roman Empire after the age of Julian—Theodosius sent to Britain—Revolt and Career of Maximus—Stilicho—Marcus and Gratian revolt in Britain—The Usurper Constantine—Honorius—Britain independent of the Empire and harassed by the Northern Barbarians—The Britons receive assistance from Rome — The last Roman Legion withdrawn—The Angles and Saxons come in—The Angles settle in Northumbria—The Jutes in Kent—Hengest and Horsa—Ælla in Sussex—Cerdic arrives in Hampshire—Essex and the Angles—Mission of St Augustine and Conversion of the Anglo-Saxons to Christianity . . 440

CHAPTER XV.

Anglo-Saxon Antiquities—Barrows or Graves, and the general Character of their Contents—Arms—Personal Ornaments; Fibulæ, &c.—Anglo-Saxon Jewellery — Pottery — Glass— Other Articles found in the Barrows Bowls, Buckets, &c.—Coins—Early Anglo-Saxon Coinage . . . 465

CHAPTER XVI.

Anglo-Saxon Settlement—Division of the Land—Population of the Country and of the Towns—Continuance of the Roman Municipalities—Traces of Municipal Privileges in the Anglo-Saxon Towns; Canterbury, Rochester, Dover, Exeter, London 505

CHAPTER XVII.

Celtic Establishments—Strath-Cluyd, Cornwall, Wales—Early Sepulchral Inscriptions found in the two latter Countries 525

APPENDIX I.—The Itineraries and Lists of Towns:
    Itinerary of Antoninus 531
    Itinerary of Richard of Cirencester 533
    The Ravenna List of Towns 536

APPENDIX II.—Roman Potters' Marks 541

LIST OF PLATES.

ROMAN BRITISH POTTERY	to face Title
MAP OF BRITAIN UNDER THE ROMANS	to face Appendix
STONEHENGE, FROM THE W.N.W.	to face page 80
RUINS OF THE GATE AT LYMNE	,, 174
PART OF THE WALLS OF A TOWN	,, 180
FOUNDATIONS OF ROMAN HOUSES AT ALDBOROUGH	,, 192
THE PROCESS OF FRESCO-PAINTING	,, 203
HYPOCAUST IN THE ROMAN VILLA AT WOODCHESTER	,, 236
CORNER OF THE CRYPTOPORTICUS, ROMAN VILLA AT BIGNOR	,, 243
TESSELLATED PAVEMENTS AT WROXETER, NO. 1	,, 249
,, ,, ,, NO. 2	,, 250
ROMAN POTTERY FROM CASTOR AND THE UPCHURCH MARSHES	,, 260
CASTOR, NORTHAMPTONSHIRE (*Durobrivæ*)	,, 263
ROMAN POTTERY KILN, AT SIBSON	,, 263
ROMAN POTTER'S KILN AT CASTOR (*Durobrivæ*)	,, 267
GROUP OF SAMIAN WARE FOUND IN ENGLAND	,, 273
ROMAN TOMBS	,, 363
ANGLO-SAXON WEAPONS, ETC.	,, 470
ANGLO-SAXON FIBULÆ	,, 478
ANGLO-SAXON JEWELLERY	,, 486

THE BRITONS.

CHAPTER I.

On the True Assignation of the Bronze Weapons, etc., supposed to indicate a Bronze Age in Western and Northern Europe—Stone, the earliest known material used for Weapons—The Stone Age, Bronze Age, and Iron Age of the Northern Antiquaries.

WITHIN a few years there has come into existence, I will not say a new science, but certainly a new and very extraordinary field for scientific inquiry. Not long ago, antiquaries limited their knowledge of the remains of human industry in this part of the world to a few generations, at most, before the date when we are made acquainted with its inhabitants by the Roman historians, and everybody was satisfied with the biblical account, that mankind had existed upon this earth somewhat more than six thousand years. It is but recently that we were all surprised by the announcement that flint implements, which had evidently been formed by man's hand, had been found in the geological formation known by the name of drift. As soon as this discovery became an accepted fact, and more general attention was called to the subject, it was discovered that these flint implements, instead of being rare (as we might perhaps have expected), were, in many parts where the drift was examined, so abundant as to imply the evidence of a considerable population at a period of course preceding the formation of the drift itself. These implements present a great uniformity in shape, and to some degree in size,—at all events there are only two or three varieties,—and it is remarkable that, while the fossil bones of various animals are found in the same drift, there has been as yet no authentic discovery of human bones; yet there appears to be no room for doubt that these implements are really the work of man. Of course, according to the opinions of geologists on the age of the drift, this discovery would carry back the existence of man on earth to an immense distance beyond the biblical date, and it leaves us for speculation and theory a period of far greater extent than the whole historical period.

The question of the Antiquity of Man became thus an attractive, and even an exciting, study. It happened that the northern—the Scandinavian—antiquaries, whose peculiar fault, if any, is a spirit of too hasty generalising, had already started an ingenious theory in relation to these pre-historic times, according to which these were divided into three periods or ages, distinguished by the names of stone age, bronze age, and iron age. During the first of these periods, it is supposed that metal was unknown to man, and that stone was the best material he had for the manufacture of weapons or of other implements for cutting or hammering; the second was characterised by the use of bronze as the only metal; in the third, bronze had been superseded for these purposes by iron. This system of periods was eagerly embraced by the new school of pre-historic antiquaries, who have even refined upon it and divided at least the first two periods into subdivisions.

It is this dark and mysterious pre-historic period which has furnished the subject treated in a handsome volume published by Sir John Lubbock,* which treats successively on the system of periods or ages just mentioned, on the tumuli of the pre-historic times, on the lake-habitations, shell-mounds, and caves, on the more general subject of the Antiquity of Man himself, and on the manners of modern savages, which the author employs very judiciously to illustrate those of the savages of pre-historic ages, for absolute savages at all times bear a certain resemblance to one another. I will only add, as to the book itself, that it is a well-written and well-arranged work, characterised equally by purity of language and by its singular clearness and perspicuity, while it presents a view of the whole subject which surprises us by its comprehensiveness, without wearying us with what too often constitutes comprehensiveness, a close dry mass of enumerations of facts. I take Sir John Lubbock's work only from one point of view—so far as its talented author treats of the system of periods—a system which

---

* 'Prehistoric Times, as illustrated by Ancient Remains, and the Manners and Customs of Modern Savages.' By Sir John Lubbock, Bart., F.R.S. 8vo. Williams and Norgate. 1865.

it is tolerably well known that I, in common with antiquaries of some eminence in their science, reject altogether, and look upon as a mere delusion, and some parts of the first chapters of my friend's book are aimed at me; that is, they are directed against opinions which I have expressed and which are here rightly put into my mouth, and I am glad of the opportunity of explaining my reasons rather more fully. It will be understood by everybody that whatever strictures I have to make are directed, not against Sir John Lubbock's writings, but against the opinions of the school of pre-historic archæologists which he has adopted, and which are here stated more fairly and distinctly than in any other work with which I am acquainted.

I am by no means inclined to impugn hastily the general conclusions at which men of science seem now arriving upon the great question of the antiquity of man—it is a subject in regard to which I look forward with anxious interest to the increase of our knowledge, certain that the ultimate result must be truth. *Magna est veritas, et prævalebit.* But I complain of the treatment which the science of archæology has hitherto received at their hands. There was a cry some time ago—and nobody joined in it more heartily than myself—that a close alliance should exist between archæology and geology; but this was to have been a fair and equal alliance, in which the geologist should accept the conclusions of archæology on the same footing as the archæologist is expected to receive the opinions of the geologist. Instead of this, the geologist seems to have considered that the science he had thus to give his hand to is a vague and uncertain one,—he has created a sort of archæology of his own, made in the first place to suit his own theories, and he takes only the advice of those who will give him an opinion which is in accordance with a foregone conclusion, and this is often quite contrary to the teachings of archæological science. Archæology, as a science, has now reached too high a position to be treated with so little respect. But let us go on to the more especial subject now before me.

Sir John Lubbock alleges that 'Mr Wright sees nothing in Great Britain which can be referred to ante-Roman times' (p. 35); and upon this he remarks (p. 36), 'But if we are to refer not only the bronze implements, but also those of stone, to the Roman period, what implements, we may ask, does Mr Wright suppose were used by the ancient Britons before the arrival of Cæsar? It would be more reasonable to deny the existence of ancient Britons at once, than thus to deprive them, as it were, of all means of obtaining subsistence.' What I have said on this subject must have been strangely misunderstood, or I may have explained myself badly; for I am entirely unconscious of having ever uttered an opinion which could bear the interpretation here given to it. I have said, and I still say, that I do not believe we have many—perhaps any—monuments of importance much older than the Roman period, and that such ancient remains as are supposed to be older than the Roman period bear no characteristics which would enable us to ascribe them to any particular date. I have never pretended to deprive the Britons of the use of stone,—it would not be in my power; but I say that stone was also in use for the same purpose in Roman and Saxon times, and that the mere presence of a stone implement does not prove that the deposit was British any more than Roman. Stone, of various kinds, is a very ready and convenient material for purposes such as the stone implements of antiquity evidently served, and it is found in use in Western Europe even in the middle ages. Stone implements have often been found on Roman sites in this island; they have been found in Saxon graves in Kent, and I have myself found flint flakes, evidently placed there by the hand of man, in Saxon graves in the Isle of Wight, perfectly resembling those of which the geologists have talked so much of late. The Abbé Cochet found similar flint flakes in Roman graves in Normandy, so arranged as to leave no doubt that they were placed there intentionally.

Sir John, indeed, acknowledges that implements in stone were in use in Roman times, but it was not so much a difference between the poor and the rich, as he puts it (the structure of society was altogether different from that of modern times), as between different localities. It would be very wrong to suppose that the social condition of Britain under the Romans was uniform in cultivation and condition throughout the province. There were no doubt 'savages' in wild and retired parts of the island, as there have been in much more recent times, and communication between distant localities, except on the lines of the great roads, was slow and precarious. People must thus have been frequently exposed to the inconvenience of falling short of metals, which, moreover, were probably always expensive, and then they would be obliged to have recourse to stones, the use of which would thus be habitual. People, under this state of society, could not go to obtain their flint implements at distant manufactories, but must either have made them individually for themselves, or, at the most, there may have been a man in each village or rural district who was more skilful in making them than his neighbours, and supplied them to those who were able or willing to purchase. In this manner there must have been, throughout the land, at the same time, a vast variety in the form and style of flint implements, according to local taste or individual caprice, so that it would be absurd to consider difference of form and character as a proof of difference of date. In primitive times diversity, and not uniformity, was usually the rule, and sometimes this difference of form and design became almost a family distinction. Among the Anglo-Saxons, long after they had risen above the character of savages, the different tribes were distinguished by different forms of personal ornaments, and we know that in much later times the clans of the Scottish highlanders have been similarly distinguished by the patterns of their plaids.

But, enough of stone for the present—let us proceed to bronze, which forms the grand corner-stone of the edifice of this system of periods. We may, perhaps, consider as the most important of these objects of bronze the swords, because they present a greater number of peculiarities of form than any of the other classes, and the circumstances connected with their discovery seem at a first glance of the subject to suggest more difficulty in identifying them with the Romans; I shall, therefore, take them as the special object of investigation, but the arguments I shall use with regard to them apply with still more force to the other objects made of the same metal. I give four examples of these swords in the cut No. 1, three of which are taken from Sir John Lubbock's 'Pre-historic Times,' as the readiest and most convenient book to quote. It will be seen that there are here three forms of blades, of which figs. 2 and 3 are what are commonly called leaf-shaped, the blade of fig. 1 tapers from the hilt to the point, while the two edges of the blade in fig. 4 are nearly parallel. They are all distinguished by the peculiarity of being ribbed. The swords, as will be seen, present two descriptions of handles, which were either of the same material as the blade and rivetted to it, or of material of a more perishable nature, and attached to the blades in the same manner as our old knife-handles. These swords, it must be agreed, do not present any varieties of forms which might be

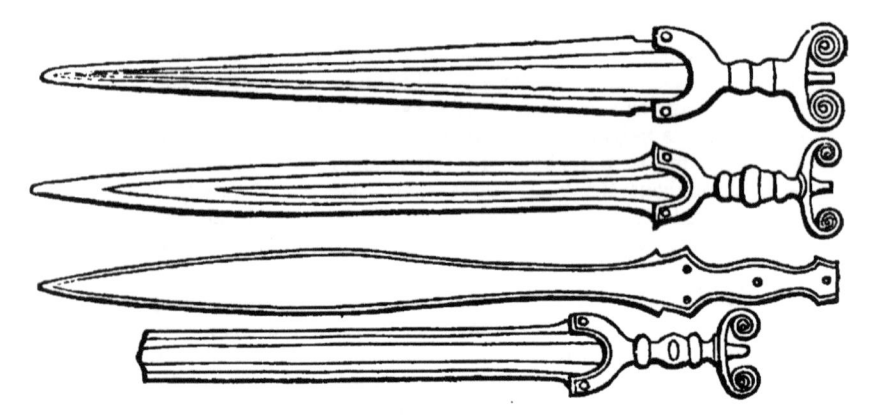

No. 1. Examples of Bronze Swords.

supposed to have originated among different peoples unacquainted with one another, but they are perfectly identical in character, yet they have been found in almost all parts of Europe. Of the four examples here given, No. 1 was found in the valley of the Somme in France; 2, in the lake of Neufchatel in Switzerland; 3, in Sweden; and 4, in some part of Scandinavia, but I am not aware of the exact locality.* No one could doubt for a moment the identity in form of the handles of figs. 1, 2, and 4.

Sir John asserts that 'bronze weapons are *never found associated* with coins, pottery, or other relics of Roman origin;' he then proceeds to quote a statement of mine to the effect that on all the sites of ruined Roman towns these other objects are found scattered about rather abundantly; and he adds somewhat triumphantly, 'We may assume, then, on the authority of Mr Wright himself, that, if all these bronze arms were really of Roman origin, many of them would have been found from time to time in conjunction with other Roman remains.' I can admit of no such assumption as arising from the facts I have stated; and I am sorry to be obliged to say that this remark only shows that my friend, in common with the advocates of this system of periods generally, is but imperfectly acquainted with the archæological conditions of the question. The reason we do not find bronze swords under the circumstances which he

* In the noble museum of my friend Mr Joseph Mayer, in Liverpool, there is one of these leaf-shaped bronze swords, which was found in Hungary; it came from the collection of the late Count Pulszky.

insists upon, is a very simple one, easily explained, and applies to iron swords equally with bronze swords. The Romans did not bury their weapons with the dead, and they took great care of them, especially of the sword, while alive. Even in the last struggles of the empire, when the Romans must sometimes have been obliged to leave their weapons behind them, the barbarians, among whom we know that a sword was an object of inestimable value, took very good care to carry them away. The consequence of this is that a Roman sword in iron is one of the rarest objects of antiquarian discovery. I remember, within my own observation, hardly a single instance of one having been found in Roman Britain, and not above two swords supposed to have been found here, and it is my impression that the bronze handle of one of the latter presented a considerable resemblance, in its style of ornament, to those of some of the bronze swords found in Scandinavia. During the whole of our excavations at Wroxeter, which have filled a considerable museum with articles of Roman fabrication, we have never met with the smallest fragment of a Roman sword, nor do I remember a single instance of such a find on any site of a Roman town or villa in this island. In one or two cases in the West of England, as in the very remarkable discoveries at Hod Hill in Dorsetshire,* bundles of unfinished iron blades, which looked like swords, have been discovered under circumstances which appeared to me to show that they had been government stores on their way to some imperial manufactory where the finish was to be given to them; other antiquaries thought they were not swords at all, and I think they may be right; but it is a very remarkable circumstance that among the Roman antiquities found at Hod Hill there was one undoubted iron sword-blade, and this was in every respect *an exact copy* of one of the swords in bronze, of which we are now speaking, a proof beyond doubt that the latter were at that time well known.† This Roman sword-blade is represented in the cut annexed (No. 2), and will be seen to possess the characteristic leaf-shape, with the ribs, and the holes for the rivets, by which the handle was fixed on.

* See Roach Smith's 'Collectanea Antiqua,' vol. vi. p. 1.
† I may remark that, to my knowledge, one or two examples have been found in this island of the so-called 'celt' cast in iron, instead of bronze, but of course the casting in bronze was the easier process. It is a proof, however, that, when these implements were made, iron and bronze were both in use. In my friend Mr Roach Smith's museum, now in the British Museum, there was a remarkable Roman spear-head, *of the bronze type*, but of iron; it was found in the Somme at Abbeville.

No. 2. Blade of a Roman Sword.

The fact of no Roman swords in iron being found, would be rather in favour of the bronze swords being Roman. Again, Sir John Lubbock gives as one of his arguments against me the fact that the bronze and iron swords and other implements are not found mixed together in the same locality. It seems to me that this is exactly what we might expect, especially in the case of the swords. These, as I have just observed, were valuable articles, and were probably, at least in the provinces, in the possession of few individuals, except the military. The inhabitants of a lacustrine village, for instance, were not likely to be in possession of a sword, unless they had stolen it, and whence would they steal it? From some soldier belonging to the nearest military post. I am sure that Sir John Lubbock will allow that it has never been the custom to arm any corps of troops with a variety of weapons—if their swords were bronze. they were all bronze, if iron, all iron. The discovery, therefore, of weapons in any particular place would only necessarily show that it was the weapon with which the detachment of Roman troops stationed in that neighbourhood—or, at least, nearest to it—were armed. But I think that it is stated rather rashly that bronze swords are not found with iron swords; for in the very rare instances of the discovery of Roman iron swords found in Britain, in, I believe, almost a majority of cases, they have been found associated with bronze swords. A few years ago a Roman sword in a bronze scabbard, the blade appearing from the rust to be of iron, was dredged up from the Thames, along with a very fine specimen of the well-known bronze leaf-shaped sword, and a large stone celt, all which were in the museum of the late Lord Londesborough;* and a similar iron sword in a bronze scabbard was found together with a bronze sword in the river below Lincoln, at a spot where a bronze circular shield had previously been found.† The discovery, in one or two instances, of a mass of bronze implements, with no mixture of iron, leads

---

* The iron sword is engraved and described in Roach Smith's 'Collectanea Antiqua,' vol. iii. p. 67.
† Roach Smith, ib. p. 68.

only to the conclusion that they had formed the stock-in-trade of some dealer in bronze implements, or that they had been a consignment of such articles lost on the way. But of this I shall say more.

I must, however, state generally that the archæological fact is that, instead of our *not* finding the bronze swords in juxta-position with Roman remains, in every case where they have been found in Britain or Gaul, where the details of the discovery have been carefully observed, it has occurred under circumstances which lead to the strongest presumption of their being Roman. A bronze sword, of the usual leaf-shaped type, is stated to have been found at the Roman station of Ardòch in Scotland, on the wall of Antoninus, and there appears no reason to doubt the accuracy of the statement.* But, to come farther south, it is well known to the archæologist that the great treasury of the antiquities of Roman London—and of mediæval London also—is the mud of the river Thames, and within the limits of the town I believe that no object has been found that could claim an earlier date than Roman. This is just the place where objects of all kinds would be deposited by accidents, such as boats upsetting in the transit, people falling in and being drowned, and the dropping into the water of objects of various kinds which would sink by their weight. Now swords have been found in the Thames at London, and I should underrate the number in saying a few, but they were nearly all of bronze, and leaf-shaped in form, which might almost be taken to show that this bronze sword was most in fashion among the Romans in London. Certain it is, that my friend Mr Roach Smith, who has examined these Roman antiquities of London more extensively and deeply than anybody else, and whom I have no hesitation in saying that I regard as the first authority on the antiquities of the Roman period in England or even on the continent, is convinced, equally with me, that the bronze swords are of Roman manufacture or origin.† Discoveries of the axes, chisels, and other implements of bronze, have been much more frequent, and in positions which speak still more strongly of their Roman character. Thomas Hearne, who first called attention to these objects more than a century ago, took it for

---

* Stuart's 'Caledonia Antiqua,' second edit. pl. v., where this sword is engraved. I make the remark, because Sir John Lubbock expresses a doubt upon it :—'Yet Mr Wright himself has only been able to give me one *doubtful* instance of this kind' (p. 12).

† See, for some remarks on this subject, his 'Catalogue of London Antiquities,' p. 80.

granted that they were Roman, but he unfortunately gave it as his opinion that they represented the Roman *celtis* (a technical word for a sort of chisel), and, in the low ebb at which archæological knowledge has stood from his time down to the present generation, antiquaries seem to have blindly fallen into the mistake that the name *celt* (*celtis*) was equivalent to *Celtic*, and that it meant that they belonged to the ancient Britons. In this blunder solely, I believe, originated the notion that these 'celts' are not Roman.

Let us now cross the Channel to our neighbours, and see what is the case in Gaul. France has undoubtedly produced by far the ablest, the soundest, and the most judicious antiquaries of modern times; and I believe that they have all regarded the bronze swords, equally with the other bronze implements, as Roman. I will quote the authority of Monsieur de Caumont, to which I am sure that nobody who knows anything of archæology will object. In his *Cours d'Antiquités Monumentales*, De Caumont, in speaking of these so-called 'celts,' says, 'But we find also very frequently these bronze axes in places covered with Roman ruins; I have acquired the certainty of this by my own observations and by the information I have collected in my travels.' * Again, the same distinguished scholar, in speaking of the bronze swords, after noticing the opinion of a previous writer who thought that the Gauls had derived the use of these swords from the Greeks, goes on to say, 'At all events, I must not conceal from you the fact that the bronze swords have been found sometimes along with objects of Roman manufacture, which would seem to announce a different origin.' †

I will go back a little farther among the antiquaries of France to produce not only opinions, but facts, such as I think ought to set the whole question at rest. At the beginning of the present century flourished the able antiquary Antoine Mongez, one of the most celebrated members of the Institute of France, a man distinguished for his science and learning, and for his judicious use of them. On the 16th of Prairial, an 9 (for we are still in the days of the Republic), according to our reckoning the 5th of June, 1801, the 'citoyen' Mongez read at

---

* Mais on trouve aussi *très fréquemment* des haches en bronze dans des emplacements couverts de ruines Romaines; j'en ai acquis la certitude par moi-même et par les renseignements que j'ai recueillis dans mes voyages.—*De Caumont, Cours d'Antiquités Monumentales*, tom. i. p. 232.

† Toutefois je ne dois pas vous laisser ignorer que les épées en bronze ont été trouvées parfois avec des objets de fabrique Romaine, ce qui paroîtrait annoncer une autre origine.—*Ib.*, p. 239.

the Institute, before what was then called the Class of Literature and Fine Arts, but which is now represented by the Académie des Inscriptions et Belles Lettres, a memoir on an ancient bronze sword, which had been found with the skeleton of a man and horse, in a turbary (*tourbière*) near Corbie, at Hailly, in the valley of the Albert, a tributary of the Somme. In this memoir, which is published in the volume of the papers read before the class,* this sword is described, and figured in an engraving; it is the sword represented in fig. 1, in our cut No. 1, and is entirely of bronze, blade and handle. The object of Mongez was chiefly to analyse the bronze of which this sword was made; but he also enters into the question of what manufacture it might be, and, after careful discussion, he arrives at the conclusion that these bronze swords were all Roman. On the 8th Frimaire, an 10 of the Republic, or the 29th of November, 1801, in our reckoning, M. Mongez read another paper on three bronze swords which had been recently found near Abbeville, and which resembled the other so closely that he thought it unnecessary to have them engraved.† Mongez reconsidered the question, and again pronounced them Roman—*je les crois Romaines.*

After Mongez had read his Memoires on the bronze swords before the Institute, his opinion received a singularly remarkable confirmation in a more exact and complete account of the circumstances of the discoveries, which he obtained from a very zealous and able antiquary of Abbeville, M. Traullé. The bronze sword, as just stated, was found in the turbary at Heilly along with the skeletons of a man and a horse, and by the sword were four brass coins of the Emperor Caracalla, who, as is well known, reigned from A.D. 211 to 217.‡ This sword, therefore, was that of a Roman cavalry soldier, not older, and perhaps a little later, than this reign, who had sunk in the bog to which the turbary had succeeded. The history of two of the other swords, found in a turbary at Pequigny, near Abbeville, was, if anything, still more curious. A large boat was found, which had evidently sunk, and in it were several skeletons. One of these had on his head a bronze casque, or helmet, accompanied with the remains of the other accoutrements of a soldier. The bronze sword lay by his side, and with it some Roman coins, some of which, if not all, were middle brass of the Emperor Maxentius, who reigned from 306 to 312.§ Another

* 'Mémoires de l'Institut Nationale des Science et Arts.'—Littérature et Beaux Arts, tom. v. p. 187.
† Ib., p. 496.   ‡ Ib., note on p. 193.   § Ib., note on p. 501.

similar sword was found in the turbary outside the boat, which would appear to have been sunk in a skirmish after some of its crew had been killed in it. We learn here that Roman soldiers, in the wars and troubles which agitated Gaul in the third and fourth centuries after Christ, were armed with these bronze swords, which some have so ingeniously supposed to have been brought into this island by the Phœnicians, some seventeen or eighteen hundred years before the Christian era. From the time of Mongez, the French antiquaries have generally regarded the bronze swords as Roman.

I have thus crept on from one little, though significant, fact to another, until it seems to me tolerably clear that they all point to one conclusion, that the bronze swords found so often in different parts of western and northern Europe are Roman; that is, that they were all either of Roman manufacture, or, at the least, copied from Roman models. I consider that this evidence is sufficiently strong, but still it will be worthy of inquiry, whether it be confirmed by pictorial delineations on Roman monuments. I have no doubt that with a little labour we might bring together a mass of corroborative evidence of this description which would be quite irresistible, but I regret to say that pressing engagements of a different character will not at present allow me to undertake that labour myself to its full extent. I think, however, that I can produce a few very satisfactory examples of it—and I will only take them in two classes of such monuments.

First, as to the sculptures on stone, the figure of a Roman soldier, generally on horseback, is a common adjunct to sepulchral inscriptions found in the Roman cemeteries. Unfortunately, the soldier usually has his sword by his side in its sheath, and although the shape of the sheath would lead us to believe that they did hold blades of the different known forms of the bronze swords, yet we cannot insist upon it. If the sheath were made of the form of the blade of a leaf-shaped sword, of course the blade could not be drawn out; it is therefore represented in one uniform shape, distinguished only from any ordinary scabbard by being short. However, I feel convinced that I have seen one or two of these sculptures in which the Roman soldier held the sword drawn, and in which it was clearly leaf-shaped; but I cannot at this moment put my hands upon them. If any one, however, will take the trouble to look over the plates of that readiest of all books of reference, the père Montfaucon's *Antiquité Expliquée*, he must, I think, be convinced of the absurdity of denying that these swords are

Roman. In the sculptures on the arch of Constantine at Rome, about contemporary with the bronze swords found near Abbeville, and described by Mongez, the Roman soldiers are evidently armed with the leaf-shaped swords, as well as with the other forms shown in our cut No. 1, a circumstance which brings into immediate relation the forms and the metal.*

But I will go farther from Italy, and give examples from an important work very recently printed,—I mean the *Exploration scientifique de l'Algerie*, published at the expense of the French government,—which are represented on Roman monuments in another part of the world. In the archæological part, the work of M. Delamare, engravings are given of a number of Roman monuments of various kinds found at the town of Constantine in the province of Algeria, the Roman Constantina, representing the still older Numidian town of Cirta. Most of these sculptures are rather rude, and belong probably to the time of the emperor from whom the town took its second name. On one of them,† we have a representation in sculpture of the accoutrements of a soldier, with the figure of a sword on

Fig. 1.   Fig. 2.   Fig. 3.
No. 3. Roman Swords from Algeria.

---

* I will merely refer to this great work, tom. iv. plate vii. fig. 3, for a Roman soldier from a sculpture at Narbonne, with the leaf-shaped sword by his side; to pl. xxiv., where there are several of our swords a little varied in ornament; to pl. lii., representing a combat in which the Romans have their swords in their scabbards, but the handles seem clearly to represent the scroll-formed ornament represented in our cut No. 1; to pl. lxix. and lxx., where the swords are the same represented in our cut, though not leaf-shaped; and to the Supplement, tom. iv. pl. xv. and pl. xxx. In the work itself, tom. iv. pl. xiii., the Etruscan soldiers are represented as armed with the leaf-shaped sword. In fact, it was the Italian sword, derived, no doubt, from the Greeks.

† Represented in plate 156, fig. 3, of the work in question.

14   THE BRITONS.   [CHAP. I.

each side—the swords are represented in our cut No. 3, figs. 1 and 2. Another sculptured monument, found also at Constantine,* contains several figures of swords, one of which I give in the same cut, fig. 3. One of these swords is distinctly leaf-shaped, and they are all characterised, as clearly as such things are usually drawn in these rude Roman sculptures, by the ribs which are found on the bronze swords. The handles are clearly intended to be represented as fastened on in the same way as those of the bronze swords, and fig. 3 is no doubt intended to represent the same termination of the hilt as is shown in figs. 1, 2, and 4, of our cut No. 1. In the other two, this termination is replaced by a ball, but the rest of the handles are quite identical.

I will next proceed to a class of monuments of, if possible, still greater importance in the discussion of our subject, the Roman coinage. The coins of what are called by numismatists the consular series, are remarkable for the interesting illustrations they give us of Roman costume and Roman manners, and are, on that account, well worthy of the study of the antiquary. Examples of swords are found on coins of the Servilia, Carisia, Plætoria, Terentia, and Minutia families, which evidently represent the ordinary forms of the bronze swords which we are discussing. I give as an example a well-known coin of the Servilia *gens*.† The obverse represents the head of the goddess Flora, with the inscription FLORA . PRIMVS, meaning that in giving the Floralia that year, the member of this family in whose honour the coin was struck, and whose name is given on the reverse as C . SERVEIL . C . F. ;

No. 4. Coin of C. Servilius.

i.e., Caius Servilius, the son of Caius, stood first. On this reverse we see two military figures, standing face to face, with drawn swords, and these plainly have the same ribbed leaf-shaped blades which are represented in our cut No. 1. The man in whose honour this coin was struck was a contemporary of Julius Cæsar. The second example of these coins I give belongs to the Minucia family, and to a member of that family named in the

---

* Ib., plate 128, figs. 7 and 8.
† It is copied from a beautiful example of the coin in the cabinet of my friend Mr C. Roach Smith.

inscription Q . THERM . MF, Quintus Thermus, the son of Marcus.* Three men are here engaged in combat, one apparently a Roman protecting a fallen comrade against his foe, whose difference of costume probably denotes a foreigner.† The swords of the two Romans are evidently identical in form with that represented by fig. 4, in our cut No. 1. Thus an examination of this best of all evidence, the coinage, leaves us no room for doubting that the characteristic sword of republican Rome was actually this same sword to which the pre-historic archæologists have been ascribing such a remote date in our islands.

No. 5. Coin of Quintus Thermus.

In these coins we trace, curiously enough, all the forms of weapons of bronze found in this country. The spear-heads, drawn small, are like spear-heads in general, but nobody doubts that the Roman spear-head was made of bronze. We trace here the figures of the round bronze shields formed of concentric circles, which the pre-historic antiquaries ascribe to the Britons of the ante-Roman period, and of which a good example is seen in the hands of one of the soldiers holding the leaf-shaped swords, in our cut No. 4 ; and in some examples the concentric circles are more numerous, and resemble still more closely those found in Britain. But there is another object on which the light thrown by these coins is still more remarkable. A curious broad-bladed dagger, of bronze, is not unfrequently found in early barrows in this country, the blade ribbed, and evidently belonging to the same period as the bronze swords. I give, from Sir John Lubbock, an example found in Ireland (cut No. 6), which will

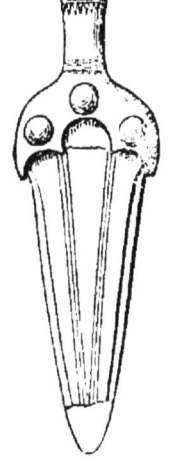

No. 6. Bronze Dagger.

* It is here engraved from a coin in the British Museum.
† Julius Cæsar made his first campaign under Marcus Minucius Thermus, and fought with distinction at the taking of Mytelene, on which occasion he saved the life of a Roman citizen, and received from Thermus a civic crown as his reward. It is understood that this act of Cæsar is commemorated in this coin of Quintus Thermus, the son of Marcus.

afford a general idea of the form of these daggers, which used to be called British. I was always inclined to ascribe them to rather an early date; that is, to a period very little before Cæsar's time, or at least early under the Roman domination, not because I thought they could not be Roman, but because, as the Romans did not bury their arms with the dead, it seemed reasonable enough to suppose that barrows in which they are found are older than the final and entire establishment of Roman customs and laws. But the Roman consular coins, on which daggers identical in character, broad-bladed and ribbed, and with the same handles, occur frequently. I give in cut No. 7, a very curious example.* It is a coin of Junius Brutus, who slew Julius Cæsar. On the obverse we have the name L . PLAET . CEST; *i.e.*, Lucius Plætorius Cestianus, one of the officers of Brutus, by whose order the coin was struck, and who gives to his chief the title BRVT . IMP; *i.e.*, Brutus imperator. On the reverse, we see the terrible emblems, the *pileus* or cap of liberty in the middle, two daggers, and the word EID . MAR, *Eidus* (the archaic form of *Idus*) *Martiæ*, the day on which the deed was done. We see at a glance that the dagger with which Cæsar was slain was identical in every particular with those found in the tumuli of Britain which some antiquaries are now ascribing to the remote age of Phœnician colonies!

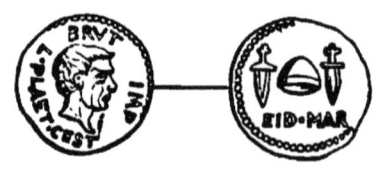

No. 7. Coin of Brutus.

Thus we see that the bronze swords, the bronze shields, the bronze spears, the bronze daggers, which have been found in Britain, are all Roman in character. The so-called 'celts,' chisels, etc., bear the same character with the weapons, and are sometimes found with them, and probably continued in use later. It is my firm conviction that not a bit of bronze which has been found in the British islands belongs to an older date than that at which Cæsar wrote that the Britons obtained their bronze from abroad, meaning, of course, from Gaul, *ære utuntur importato*. In fact, these objects in bronze were Roman in character, and in their primary origin.

And who has ever brought forward any evidence to show that the Romans did not use bronze for their weapons? Pliny

* Engraved from one in the British Museum.

tells us that, in the treaty which concluded the war between Porsena and the Romans after the expulsion of the Tarquins, that is, about five hundred years before Christ, it was expressly stipulated that the Romans thenceforth should use iron for nothing but agricultural purposes.* Our acquaintance with the condition of that time is not sufficiently minute to enable us to judge what was the cause or the object of this stipulation, but it seems clear that swords were not made of iron, and they must therefore have been made of bronze. This stipulation continued in force during some three centuries, and it was only after the second Punic war, we are told, that the Romans began to adopt the form and material of the sword as it was in use among the Spaniards. Polybius tells a curious anecdote relating to the great victory obtained by the Romans over the Gauls during the consulate of Caius Flaminius, a little more than two hundred years before Christ. He informs us that the Gauls were armed with long pointless swords, which they used only in striking the enemy, while the Romans used short, stiff, pointed swords, with which they stabbed at the face and person. When the Gauls struck hard, the blade of the sword became so much bent that the soldier had to straighten it with his foot before he could strike another blow. The Roman officers, having observed this, directed the soldiers to close upon the ranks of the Gauls, and thrust vigorously at their bodies and faces, before the latter had time to recover the use of their swords, and by this manœuvre the great inequality of numbers was partly compensated.† We cannot doubt, from this description, that the swords of the Gauls were made of iron, and that their liability to bend arose from the circumstance that that people did not yet possess the art of tempering it; while the account of the Roman swords answers exactly to the short pointed bronze weapons of which we are speaking. We have a rather similar anecdote, of a later date, which brings us nearer home. Tacitus tells us that, in the great battle in which Agricola defeated the Caledonians under Galgacus, the Britons were armed with immense swords, that is, of course, long ones, and small bucklers; while the Roman auxiliaries, consisting of three cohorts of Batavi and two of Tungri, who were chiefly put forward in the engagement, were armed with short pointed swords (*mucrones*). The result was the same

---

* In fœdere quod expulsis regibus populo Romano dedit Porsena nominatim comprehensum invenimus, ne ferro nisi in agricultura uterentur.—Pliny, 'Hist. Nat.,' lib. xxxiv. c. 39.
† Polybii Histor., lib. ii. c. 33.

as that just described: the Roman auxiliaries closed upon the Caledonii, who, unprepared for this to them new mode of fighting, were defeated with great slaughter.* These anecdotes point very distinctly to the bronze swords of which we are speaking. We are thus tracing the use of bronze swords very near to the time, or quite to the time, when the leaf-shape and other forms are seen on the consular coins, so that we are quite justified in supposing that those represented swords of bronze. I know nothing in the Latin classical writers contradictory to this view of the subject. Even Virgil, the fashionable court poet, and the least likely of any to give evidence on my side of the question, was certainly well aware of the use of bronze in the manufacture of arms. The armour was of bronze—that of Mazentius was triple in thickness ('*ære cavum triplici,*' *Æn.*, x. 784), like the triple bronze which surrounded the breast of the brave man in Horace ('*æs triplex circa pectus erat,*' *Carm.*, lib. i. od. 3); the helmet was of bronze ('*ære caput fulgens,*' *Æn.*, x. 869); the shield was of bronze ('*ærei clypei,*' *Æn.*, xii. 541, and '*ærea scuta,*' *Æn.*, x. 313); the battle-axe was of bronze ('*et æratam quatiens Tarpeia securim,*' *Æn.*, xi. 656). In one instance, Virgil speaks even of bronze swords,—

'Æratæque micant peltæ, micat æreus ensis.'—*Æn.*, vii. 743.

It is true, that these bronze swords are put into the hands of a people foreign to Italy, but it is not stated that they were peculiar to that people. Virgil, further, uses the word *æs* for arms generally. Æneas, describing his flight from Troy, with his father on his shoulder, says,—

'Genitorque per umbram
Prospiciens, "Nate," exclamat, "fuge, nate; propinquant,—
Ardentes clypeos atque æra micantia cerno."'—*Æn.*, ii. 734.

More than once Virgil uses the word *æratus* as a general epithet for troops (see *Æn.*, vii. 703, and ix. 463); in the latter passage, the 'bronze-armed battalions' are described as marching into battle,—

'Turnus in arma viros, armis circumdatus ipse,
Suscitat, æratasque acies in prælia cogit
Quisque suas.'

For the spear, we might quote Ovid's *hasta æratæ cuspidis* (*Metam.*, v. 9), or the line of Tibullus (lib. i. eleg. xi. l. 25),—

'At novis ærata, Lares, depellite tela.'

In fact, when the Roman thought of arms and accoutrements of

---

* Taciti Agricola, c. 36.

war, *æs*, or bronze, appears to have been the metal which came uppermost to his mind.

I confess that I see little weight in the argument which has been drawn from the secondary use of the word *ferrum* as synonymous with *gladius* or *ensis*, a sword. It can only prove that there were swords made of iron among the Romans at the time when the word was thus used; probably the sword of iron was then considered the more fashionable—the more aristocratic. At all events, it would be becoming more distinctive. Iron was then the newest, and probably the most esteemed, material. We must not forget that, as we have just seen, on one hand the word *æs* was used for arms in general, not for a particular arm, and therefore, when iron was employed for swords, it would be more distinctive of the particular weapon; and that, on the other hand, from the time when money had begun to be coined among the Romans, *æs*, as the material of which it was made, was used in a secondary sense to signify money.

When Sir John Lubbock (p. 35) says that I 'lay much stress on the fact that the bronze weapons have generally been found near Roman stations and Roman roads,' he has applied to the weapons what I had said of a rather different object. During ages when travelling was neither quick nor safe, and people seldom took long journeys unnecessarily, they had to depend for many even of the necessaries of life upon men who carried them round for sale periodically, and a multitude of people gained their living as itinerant traders and manufacturers. It was a practice general throughout the middle ages, no doubt derived from the Romans, and the very utility of such dealers formed their protection against injury and interruption. We find abundant traces of this practice, curiously enough, in relation to the bronze swords and hatchets. These consist in discoveries of deposits, usually of an earthen vessel for melting bronze, of which there is sometimes a residuum at the bottom, of moulds for casting the implements, and generally of some broken swords or other bronze implements, no doubt intended to be melted down for metal, and of similar articles entire, constituting stock in trade. Now my remark was, that these tools and stock of itinerant bronze manufacturers are almost always found near a Roman road, or in the neighbourhood of a Roman station, and that therefore we are justified in considering them as Roman subjects, who had travelled along the Roman roads, and rested at those spots for personal or local reasons which are unknown to us. Discoveries of such deposits have been very numerous in

Britain, Gaul, Switzerland, and Germany. I am not aware if they have been found on the other confines of the empire. One of these, consisting of a quantity of bronze celts, both entire and broken, was found near the foot of the Wrekin in Shropshire, not far from the great Roman road, the Watlingstreet; another, among which there were fragments of a bronze sword, at Sittingbourne, on the Kentish portion of the Watlingstreet; a third, consisting of bronze punches, chisels, and other implements, with several pieces of unused metal, one of which was evidently the residuum of the melting-pot, at Attleborough in Norfolk, on the Roman road between Thetford and Norwich; a fourth, consisting of sixty bronze chisels, etc., with a portion of a bronze sword and a piece of bronze which again appeared to be the residue from melting, all contained in an earthen pot, at Weston in Yorkshire, on the road from Old Malton (where there are the remains of a Roman town) to York. It is not necessary to enumerate any further examples. Sir John Lubbock seeks to explain the position of these finds by supposing that the Roman roads were laid upon older British roads, but this is an objection to which I cannot listen until he brings me the slightest substantial evidence that such was the case. To me, these 'finds' alone are sufficient to explain a fact which Sir John hardly, or only feebly, denies, the identity of forms, and not mere similarity, of all these bronze swords, in whatever part of Europe they are found. I cannot imagine that any one will believe that this identity of form is the result of chance, but they must have been derived from one general centre; and, when we consider the radius through which they are scattered, it was only the Roman empire that could have supplied such a centre. It is nonsense to suppose that, brought into Britain at a remote and obscure period by the Phœnicians, they could have spread in this manner. The whole mystery, then, is dispelled by the proceedings of these itinerant manufacturers, who must have been very numerous, and who went not only to the limits of the Roman province, but, no doubt, penetrated into the surrounding countries, and made weapons for their inhabitants. It was, for these, the easiest way of obtaining weapons. Swords were so rare, and so valued, among the Scandinavians and Teutons, that they believed them to have been forged by the gods; and I beg to state that the arms which the gods forged were made of iron.* There are

---

* It may be remarked, on this subject, that even in the early Anglo-Saxon cemeteries in this island, which belong to the period immediately following the Romans, only one warrior here and there is found with a

many reasons, into which I will not now enter, for believing
that it was a subject of honour and glory, among the different
branches of the Teutonic race, for a man to possess a sword;
and here the 'barbarian' had a chance of getting a sword to
wear by his side at not so great an expense of wealth and trouble
as if it had been made by the gods, and he no doubt profited
largely by it. And ·then, the 'barbarians,' contrary to the
Roman practice, buried their weapons with the dead, in consequence of which we find in their graves a sufficiency of those
weapons to fill our museums, while we only pick up one now
and then within the bounds of the Roman empire. Such is the
case with Ireland, where, by the way, it has been somewhat
too hastily asserted that the Roman arms never penetrated,
seeing that we know little of the *history* of our islands under the
Romans,—that Juvenal, speaking as of a fact generally known,
asserts,—

> 'Arma quidem ultra
> Litora Juvernæ promovimus,'—

and that Roman antiquities are now found in Ireland. Such is
the case with Scandinavia, and also of the other countries of
Europe bordering upon the Roman provinces. It has been
alleged that some of the ornamentation of the Scandinavian
bronze-work is not Roman in its character, which is true—but
why? It is not probable that an enterprising people like the
Scandinavians would be satisfied to remain long dependent on
the precarious supplies, as they must have been at such a distance, of wandering merchants, and they would soon learn to
imitate what they had seen done by others. Roman ornamentation and design, in their hands, would soon undergo degradation until it took a character of its own, just as it did among
the Anglo-Saxons, and among the Germans, and indeed among
all the other non-Roman peoples into whose hands it fell. I
have always held the belief that the mass of the Scandinavian
ornamented bronze is nothing more than the development of

---

sword, while most of them were buried with spears. This would show
that the sword was comparatively rare among the Anglo-Saxons, that only
one individual here and there possessed one, or that they were considered
too precious to be buried. Yet the common poetical phrase for being killed
in battle was *sweordum aswefede*, 'put to sleep with swords.' In fact, the
name of the more valuable of the weapons was employed to represent them
all, just as among the Romans the name of the more valued metal for
making a sword, *ferrum*, was used to signify all swords, and then used for
weapons in general, because the sword was considered the most excellent.
We still talk of putting the enemy 'to the sword,' omitting altogether the
mention of muskets, rifles, lances, revolvers, etc., etc.

Roman popular art under the influence of barbaric taste; and I think this will hardly be denied by any one who is familiarly acquainted with the forms and spirit of Roman art.

But it is time to conclude these remarks. I will only repeat the belief, on which I have always insisted, that in this part of the world the use of bronze did not precede that of iron, and I believe that I am fully supported in this view by the opinion of our great metallurgist, my friend Dr Percy. At the time of Cæsar's invasion, as that great warrior and statesman declares deliberately, the only bronze known to the Britons was imported; of course from Gaul, and it could not have come in large quantities. The Britons could not have made bronze themselves, for I am satisfied, by my own researches among our ancient mines, that no copper was obtained in this island until it was found by the Romans. I am informed that, instead of being easy, the process of mining copper and tin, and preparing bronze, is very complicated and difficult; whereas the smelting of iron is extremely easy, and in some parts of our island, as in the forest of Dean, the iron ore presented itself on the surface, and in a form which could not fail to draw the attention of men who knew anything about metals. I confess that I only look upon the modern myth of the colonisation of this island by the Phœnicians as unworthy the consideration of a serious antiquary. It is based upon speculations which have no historical foundation. In these new questions which are agitated by men of science, we must enter upon the study of the remote period of archæology of which we have no practical knowledge, with a very profound knowledge of the subsequent historic period; whereas this new school of antiquaries prefer contemplating altogether the doubtful period speculatively from the utterly unknown period which preceded it, to going back to it from the known period which followed. Indeed, I fear that far too much of prehistoric archæology, as it has been hitherto presented to us, rests only upon a want of knowledge of what is historic.

CHAPTER II.

Ethnological Views—Political Movements in Gaul—Cæsar's first and second Invasions—Cassivellaunus—The Britons, as described by Cæsar, Strabo, and Diodorus—Cunobeline and his Sons—Expedition of Claudius—Conquests of the earlier Prætors—Caractacus—Cartismandua and Venusius—Invasion of Mona—Insurrection of Boadicea—War with the Brigantes—Campaigns of Agricola—Total Subjection of the Island to Rome—Enumeration of the British Tribes—Hibernia—Manners of the Britons, as described by ancient writers—The Druids.

According to the system now generally adopted by ethnologists, Europe was peopled by several successive migrations, or, as they have been technically named, waves of population, all flowing from one point in the east. Of these the two principal were the Celts and the Teutons or Germans, both branches of the same great race, which has been popularly termed the Japhetan, because, according to the Scriptural account, the various peoples which belonged to it were all descended from Japhet. The Celts came first in point of time, and, making their way apparently through the districts bordering on the Mediterranean, they spread over all Western Europe. The German nations, entering Europe from the shores of the Black Sea, advanced through its central parts, till, coming in contact with the Celts, they gradually drove them forwards to the west and south-west. The Germans themselves were urged westward by a new migration which was pressing upon them from behind, that of the Sclavonic or Sarmatian race, which, as early as the time of the Greek historian Herodotus, that is, in the middle of the fifth century before Christ, had already established itself on the eastern borders of Europe.

Of the successive movements of these nations, and the mutual struggles which ended in their location in the positions they occupied when we first became acquainted with them, history has preserved no record. The early Greek writers knew little of Western Europe, and Herodotus could only inform us that the western extremity was occupied by a people whom he terms the Cynetæ, and that all the countries next to them were said to be inhabited by the Celtæ or Celts; and he had an indistinct notion of the British Isles, under the general term of Cassiterides, or the tin islands, as the grand source from which the Phœnicians derived their supply of that metal. The philosopher Aristotle, who lived a hundred years later, or about three centuries and a half before Christ, speaks more definitely and distinctly of the ocean without the Pillars of Hercules (the Straits of Gibraltar), in which he tells us there were 'two islands, which are very large, Albion and Ierne, called the Britannic, which lie beyond the Celtæ.' This is the earliest mention of our islands by their names. Another Greek historian, Polybius, who wrote very little more than a hundred and fifty years before the Christian era, adds nothing to our knowledge on this subject, but he speaks of the method in which the tin was obtained and prepared in the 'Britannic Isles,' as of a matter with which he was well acquainted, and which was then a subject of so much interest that he wrote a separate treatise upon it, now unfortunately lost. All that we learn from these few and scanty notices is, that from a very early period of the history of the world, the merchants of Phœnicia obtained their supply of tin (an article in use as far back as the time of Homer) from Britain. As this metal is found chiefly in Cornwall and the Scilly Islands, the parts of Britain which would first present themselves to navigators from the Phœnician port on the coast of Spain, Gadeira or Gades (the modern Cadiz), we are justified in believing that these and the south of Ireland were the only districts visited by that people, who, as we are further assured, kept their knowledge a profound secret, in order that they might with greater ease monopolise a lucrative branch of commerce. The geographer Strabo tells us that the Romans long attempted in vain to discover the place from whence the Phœnicians obtained their tin, to which at this time were added lead and perhaps copper, and that on one occasion a Phœnician captain, perceiving that he was followed and watched by Roman vessels, ran his own ship intentionally on the rocks rather than let the secret be discovered, and, escaping with his crew on a raft, was rewarded by his own government for his patriotism. It was not till a Roman named Publius Crassus, who is supposed to be the commander sent by Cæsar at the end of his first campaign in Gaul to reduce the Gallic tribes on the shores of the British Channel, discovered the trade of the Phœnicians with Britain, that the Romans became acquainted with the route by which their merchants reached Britain by sea, and with the ease with which the tin was dug up, it being then found at a very small depth under the surface of the ground. Previous to this, however, two other commercial states had established an intercourse with the tin district of Britain. The Carthaginian Himilco, sent by his government on a voyage of discovery between the years 362 and 350 before the Christian era, visited the tin islands, which he calls Œstrymnides, near Albion, and two days' sail from Ierne, by which he is supposed to mean some of the isles on the Cornish coast; and the Phocean colonies of Massilia and Narbona carried on the same commerce overland. We are informed by another Greek writer, Diodorus Siculus, that the tin was conveyed from the district in which it was found to an island 'in front of Britain,' named Ictis, apparently the Isle of Wight, where it was purchased by native merchants, who transported it to Gaul, and it was then carried overland on pack-horses a journey of thirty days to the mouth of the Rhone. Everything, however, relating to this distant region, almost unconnected with the world as then known, was wrapped in mystery; and Scipio could obtain no satisfactory answer to the anxious inquiries concerning Britain which he made among the merchants of the great cities of Massilia, Narbona, and Corbelo. The veil was at length drawn aside by the ambition of Julius Cæsar.

At this time the movement of the German race towards the west was proceedingly rapidly, and the Celtic populations of Gaul and Britain would probably have been soon crushed beneath the invasion, had not the Romans stepped in to arrest its progress. Perhaps the northern parts of Gaul were already extensively peopled by tribes of German extraction, and there are reasons for believing that the Belgæ were themselves a Teutonic race,* a circumstance which would explain some difficulties in the history of Western Europe at this period.

The mass of the Celtic population, as we learn from Cæsar, were serfs, without civil influence or even civil rights; the mere

---

* Cæsar tells us distinctly, that the Belgæ differed in language, customs, and laws, from the Celtæ, equally with the Aquitani: 'Gallia est omnis divisa in partes tres; quarum unam incolunt Belgæ, aliam Aquitani, tertiam qui ipsorum lingua Celtæ, nostra Galli, adpellantur. Hi omnes lingua, institutis, legibus inter se differunt.' This statement, combined with various circumstances of their history, lead me to believe that the Belgæ were of German origin; and I confess that the arguments of Dr Prichard and others, to the contrary, seem to me unsatisfactory.

slaves of the superior orders. The latter were divided into two very distinct classes—the Druids and the knights (*milites*); or in other words, the priests and the chiefs of clans or military leaders. The former, who resembled the Brahminical class in India, combined with the sacerdotal profession the functions of judges and legislators, and during the course of ages they seem gradually to have usurped the supreme powers in the state, and to have reduced the military chiefs to a state of political subjection. These, however, had not entirely forgotten their ancient independence, and the spirit of resistance appears to have been stirred up and encouraged by the example of the Teutonic tribes who were now mixing with them, and who were far less priest-ridden, for Cæsar tells us that they had no Druids. The whole of Gaul became thus divided into two great political factions, some of the tribes uniting in support of the Druidic influence, while others took part with the military chiefs. The western Celtæ—among whom were the Carnutes, in whose territory (the modern Chartres) stood the sacred grove, the head seat of Druidic worship in Gaul, with the people of Brittany, of whose devotion to the religion of their race so many rude monuments still remain—all supported the Druidic faction, of which the Hedui, who inhabited the modern Burgundy, took the lead. The Belgæ, as might be expected, with the northern tribes, supported the other faction, at the head of which were the Sequani, whose capital was Vesontio (the modern Besançon). Hard pressed by the Druid faction, the tribes who supported the military chiefs had called to their assistance the Germans under Ariovistus, while, to resist these terrible invaders, the Hedui appealed for protection to Rome. To Cæsar this was a welcome proposal; he came with his legions, drove the Germans back over the Rhine, and then taking advantage of the political divisions among the nations of Gaul, proceeded to reduce it to a Roman province. The Gauls, too late, threw aside their mutual animosities in order to resist their common enemy, and when Cæsar thought that they were cut off from all foreign aid by the ocean behind them, he found that they were drawing powerful reinforcements from Britain. The Belgæ, who surpassed all the other nations of Gaul in valour and conduct, were the last to yield to the military genius of the Roman commander, and to the steady discipline of his cohorts. When he at length reached their coast, and saw from the heights between Boulogne and Calais the white cliffs of Albion, he resolved to carry his arms into the island which had so long been an object of curiosity to his countrymen, and ascertain the resources which might be used to assist those whom he had made their foes.

Britain contained at this time nearly the same political elements as Gaul. The basis of its population was the same Celtic race which there held with the Druidic faction; and the supremacy of the Druids or priestly order seems to have been established more firmly in Britain even than in Gaul. We are not able to say with any certainty if any, or how much, of the population of the western parts of our island derived its origin from the Aquitanian or Basque race, but we know that the Belgæ had taken possession of the richest parts of South Britain, and that these settlers were in close alliance with their brethren on the other side of the Straits, while the Celtic Veneti of Gaul, a seafaring tribe, maintained their old commercial intercourse with the Celts of Britain. We are ignorant of the extent to which the division between the Druids and the military chiefs had been introduced into this island, but we know that the British tribes in the time of Cæsar were no strangers to civil strife.

As the season was far advanced, the Roman commander saw that no time was to be lost, and he called together the merchants from different parts of the coast, in the hopes of obtaining from them the necessary information relating to the country which he was about to invade. But they seemed to have conspired together to deceive him, and when he questioned them, they could tell him neither the extent of the island, nor the number or character of the natives who inhabited it, nor even the harbours in which a fleet might anchor. Nevertheless, they sent intelligence to the Britons of the designs of invasion and conquest which Cæsar had not concealed. Several of the British states, thus warned, despatched messengers to Cæsar, offering to submit to the government of the Roman people and to give hostages for their fidelity. These he sent back with liberal promises, and they were accompanied by Commius, whom the Roman commander had made king over the vanquished Attrebates of Gaul, and who was directed to visit as many of the states as he could, and to exhort them to submit to the Romans. The real object of the British envoys was perhaps to gain information, as Cæsar was still as ignorant as ever of the country and its coasts. He, therefore, sent one of his officers, Caius Volusenus, with a war-galley, to survey the British coasts, while he assembled his troops in the country of the Morini (the Pas-de-Calais), and ordered the ships which had been employed in the preceding year against the Veneti to repair to the Portus Iccius, a naval station afterwards called Gessoriacum (Boulogne).

Satisfied with the imperfect survey of Volusenus, Cæsar embarked at the Portus Iccius before daybreak in an autumn morning, carrying with him, in about eighty vessels of burden, his favourite legion, the tenth, in the courage and devotion of which he placed the utmost confidence, and the seventh. His cavalry was directed to follow in eighteen vessels which were stationed in a port about eight miles from that in which Cæsar embarked. About ten o'clock in the forenoon the Roman fleet reached the coast of Britain, here formed of low cliffs, which were lined with British warriors prepared for battle. After waiting in vain for the arrival of his cavalry until three o'clock in the afternoon, Cæsar took advantage of a favourable wind and tide, and running on about seven miles further, brought his vessels to an open and level strand, which was more favourable for the landing of his troops. The latter were seized with alarm at the novel and formidable appearance of the multitude of Britons who had hurried forwards to meet them, and were drawn up in hostile array on the shore, and, unacquainted with the depth of the water, they were unwilling to leave their ships. At length, after much hesitation, the standard-bearer of the tenth legion, calling on his fellow-soldiers to follow, jumped into the sea. It was some time before the Roman soldiers could gain the ground; for the depth of their ships had obliged them to anchor at a considerable distance from the shore, and they had to struggle through deep water, in which they were oppressed by the weight of their arms and accoutrements; while their enemies, lighter and more agile, rode into the water with their horses, and attacked them, as they attempted to form, in small parties, or overwhelmed them with a shower of missiles from the beach. As soon, however, as the soldiers obtained a firm footing, the Britons who had shown no want of courage in the previous confused engagement, yielded to superior discipline, and fled, making their escape with the less loss because the invaders were destitute of cavalry.

Thus did the Romans, for the first time, place their feet on that distant island whose name had hitherto belonged rather to the poet than to the historian. It is not easy to explain the subsequent conduct of the Britons, except by the entire want of union among the various tribes which were scattered over the island. Their chiefs, instead of making any further attempt to retrieve their first defeat, or appealing to the other tribes to join them in resisting the invaders, sent messengers to Cæsar with excuses for the resistance they had already made, promising obedience in future, and offering hostages. Commius, the chief of the Attrebates, came with these messengers; he had been seized on his arrival in Britain, and thrown into chains; but the chiefs now gave him his liberty, throwing the blame of his detention on the multitude, and promising to make amends for their imprudent hostility. Cæsar readily granted them peace, demanding a certain number of hostages, part of whom were immediately delivered; and the chiefs dismissed their followers, and repaired, in considerable numbers, to Cæsar's camp. The insincerity of their submission was, however, soon proved. Cæsar had been four days in Britain before his cavalry could put to sea from the coast of Gaul, and then, although a favourable wind brought them within sight of the camp, the weather became so stormy that they were driven back to the ports they had left. The storm increased during the night, dragged the transports from their anchors, and drove the whole fleet on the shore, where most of the Roman ships were destroyed, or more or less damaged. This accident, and the dismay into which it threw Cæsar's army, encouraged the British chiefs to form a new confederacy, with the design of attacking the camp, from which, under various pretences, they gradually withdrew. The Romans busied themselves with refitting their fleet, and were not aware of the designs of the Britons, till one day the seventh legion went out, as usual, to forage, and they had not been long absent, when the guards at the gate of the camp reported that there was an unusual cloud of dust in the direction which they had taken. Cæsar, hurrying with other troops to the assistance of his foragers, found that the latter were surrounded by a multitude of armed Britons, who had rushed upon them from the woods, and that they were defending themselves with difficulty against the attacks of the horsemen and charioteers. The assailants were now repulsed; but Cæsar found it necessary to draw off his men, and make good his retreat to the camp, where the Britons, who considered this engagement as a victory, determined to attack him; and they sent messengers in all directions to call the neighbouring chiefs to their standard. A continuance of stormy weather prevented the attack for several days during which Cæsar, warned of their design, made every preparation for defence, the result of which was a new and severe defeat of the Britons, who were pursued with slaughter by a small body of cavalry which attended upon the Attrebatian Commius. The same day, the chiefs sent again to demand peace, which Cæsar, anxious to return to Gaul before the setting-in of the equinoctial gales, granted, after exacting double the number of hostages which he had previously required. He then embarked his troops, and reached the country of the Morini in safety, from whence the intelligence sent him by his friends recalled him to Italy. But, before his departure, he gave directions for fitting out a great number of ships, of a shape better adapted for landing his troops on the shores of Britain, announcing that it was his intention to return to the island in the ensuing spring.

The officers and troops left in Gaul showed their zeal in the completeness with which they executed the orders of their great commander; and when Cæsar returned to them, in the year 64 B.C., he found everything ready for the transport of his troops, his horses, and his provisions. The former consisted of five legions, with two thousand cavalry. These were embarked in upwards of eight hundred ships, and the appearance of this numerous fleet so alarmed the Britons, that they deserted the coast, and retired to the less accessible parts of the country. The Romans, on this occasion, landed in or near the same spot as in the year preceding; and Cæsar chose a place for his camp on the shore. Some prisoners, taken in the course of the same afternoon, having given information of the spot where the Britons were assembled, he marched against them at night, leaving ten cohorts and three hundred horse to guard the ships. He found the Britons posted in a woody district, about twelve Roman (perhaps sixteen English) miles from his camp, on the banks of a river supposed to be the Stour; and as he approached (I now use his own words), they 'came down to the river to meet him, with their horsemen and chariots, and attempted, from elevated ground, to begin the battle, and repel our troops. But our horse soon drove them back, and they took refuge in the woods, where they had a place singularly strong both by nature and art, and which, to all appearances, had been constructed by them as a stronghold during their civil wars; for every approach to it was effectually blocked up with felled trees. Some few of their troops, however, continued to skirmish from the woods, and prevented our men from entering their fortress. But the soldiers of the seventh legion locked their shields together, so as to form what is called the *testudo*, and, mounting over a mound thrown up against the defences, took the place, and expelled the Britons from the woods, without experiencing much loss themselves.'

Cæsar was prevented from following up this success by the intelligence of another disaster which had befallen his fleet, through a violent storm on the second night after his arrival. He returned in haste to his camp, found that the damage done to his fleet had not been exaggerated by the messengers who brought him intelligence of it, and gave immediate directions for repairing the shattered ships. 'He now resolved, notwithstanding the difficulty of the task, to haul up all his ships, and inclose them in one line of fortification with the camp. This labour occupied about ten days; and the work was not intermitted during the night. The vessels were thus drawn up, and a camp strongly fortified; after which, leaving the same force to guard the fleet, he recommenced his march in the same direction as before.' Cæsar found that the Britons had employed the time which he had lost by the disaster of his fleet, in composing their differences and uniting against him; for when he landed in Britain, the different tribes were engaged in mutual hostilities: perhaps it was a struggle between the Belgian settler and the aboriginal Celt:[*] and the chief of the latter is named by Cæsar, Cassivellaunus or Cassibellaunus. This chief, who seems to have been of the British race, and whose territory is supposed to have been the present county of Hertford, had been gradually reducing under his sway the tribes around him. We learn, incidentally, that some of the chiefs, whose rights he had usurped, had fled to Gaul, and there made their complaint to Cæsar, and implored his protection. This was the case with Mandubratius, the young chief of the Trinobantes, a people occupying the modern county of Essex, and considered, at the time of Cæsar's invasion, as the principal tribe of this part of the island. The kingdom of the Trinobantes had been seized by Cassivellaunus, who murdered its king, Imanuentius, the father of Mandubratius, and the latter only escaped a similar fate by flight.

The different tribes of the south-eastern parts of the island, as we have just said, now joined in a temporary league against the invaders: and it is a proof of the general estimation of the talents of Cassivellaunus, that they agreed in selecting him

[*] It may perhaps be considered, in favour of this supposition, that the chiefs who were oppressed by Cassivellaunus fled to the continent to seek assistance, instead of applying to the native tribes of the interior.

for their leader. In consequence of this confederacy, when Cæsar marched back to the position from which he had been called by the disaster of his fleet, he found the enemy collected in much greater numbers than before, to oppose his further progress. The Roman legions and their auxiliaries were now exposed to constant attacks, in the course of which they lost many men; for the woods, which appear to have covered or skirted the country through which Cæsar marched, gave a secure shelter to the Britons, and they were thus enabled to harass the Romans by sudden and unexpected attacks, and, when repulsed, to retreat without loss, as the heavy-armed legionaries would seldom overtake them in their flight. 'In all these skirmishes,' Cæsar tells us, 'so immediately under our eyes, and close to the camp, it was evident that the weight of our men's armour prevented them from pursuing the enemy when they retreated, or advancing far from their own colours. In short, their accoutrements were ill-adapted for contending with such an enemy as they had now to deal with; and the cavalry, in particular, were much exposed on the field of battle; for the Britons would often make a feigned retreat, and allure them to separate from the legions, after which they would leap from their chariots, and take the cavalry at a disadvantage. . . . Moreover, the Britons never advanced in one body, but fought in small parties, stationed at intervals, so that one squadron relieved another, and our men, who had been contending against those who were exhausted, suddenly found themselves engaged with a fresh body, who had taken their places. The next day, the enemy posted themselves on the hills, at some distance from the camp, and only appeared a few at a time; and they were also less disposed to attack our cavalry than they had been the day before. About noon, Cæsar sent out Caius Trebonius, the lieutenant, with three legions and all the cavalry, to forage; upon which the enemy assembled from all sides, and surrounded the foragers, who were unable to leave their colours, or separate from the legions. Our men now made a general attack upon them, and put them to flight and pursued them without interruption, as long as the legions kept in sight to give the cavalry confidence of support whilst they drove the Britons before them. In this manner, they did not allow them time to rally, or halt, or leap from their chariots, according to their usual custom. In consequence of this defeat, the British reinforcements, which were arriving from all sides, again disbanded, and from that time the enemy never again came to a general engagement. Cæsar, now knowing their intentions, led his army towards the Thames, in order to invade the territories of Cassivellaunus. The river could only be passed, on foot, in one place, and that with difficulty. When he arrived on its banks, he perceived a large force drawn up on the other side to oppose him; the bank, moreover, was planted with sharp stakes, and others of the same kind were fixed in the bed of the river beneath the water. Cæsar gained intelligence of this from prisoners and deserters. He accordingly sent the cavalry in advance, and brought up the infantry immediately in the rear. So great were the ardour and impetuosity of the soldiers, that, whilst their heads alone appeared above the water, the enemy, unable to sustain their attack, abandoned the bank and fled precipitately. Cassivellaunus, as we have before observed, abandoned all idea of fighting, and dismissed the greater part of his forces, retaining only about four thousand men in chariots. With these he watched our march, and, retiring out of our way, lay in wait for us among the woods and difficult passes. Meanwhile, he cleared the whole country through which our road lay, both of men and cattle; and when our foragers went out to get provisions and waste the country, his knowledge of the ways enabled him to assail them with all his chariots; this caused much danger to our cavalry, and prevented them from going far from the main body.'

One defeat was sufficient to break the ill-consorted alliance which Cassivellaunus had formed against the Romans; and the superiority of the latter once demonstrated, the different tribes who had been oppressed by that chieftain seem to have thrown the blame of their resistance on his influence, making a merit of their personal hostility towards him, and seeking an alliance with the invaders. First came messengers from the Trinobantes of Middlesex and Essex, who offered to submit to the Romans on condition that they should espouse the cause of their young chief Mandubratius, and restore him to the sovereignty of their tribe, which Cassivellaunus had usurped. The treaty was soon arranged; Mandubratius, who happened to be in Cæsar's camp, was sent back to rule his tribe as a Roman tributary; and the Trinobantes, according to agreement, gave forty hostages, and supplied the Roman army with corn. The examples of the Trinobantes was immediately followed by the Cenimagni, the Segontiaci, the Ancalites, the Bibroci, and the Cassi. The first of these tribes lay to the north of the Trinobantes, in the present county of Suffolk; the Segontiaci occupied the greater part of the present counties of Hampshire and Berkshire; the Bibroci inhabited a thickly-wooded country containing the celebrated forest of Anderida—including a small part of Hampshire and Berkshire, and stretching through the modern counties of Sussex and Surrey into the eastern parts of Kent; the position of the Ancalites is less certain, but they, perhaps, lay on the north of Berkshire and on the western borders of Middlesex; and if the Cassi were the same tribe that was called by Ptolemy the Catyeuchlani, as is supposed, they formed the link between these other tribes and the Trinobantes, stretching through the modern counties of Hertford, Bedford, and Buckingham. The envoys of these tribes informed Cæsar, 'that the town of Cassivellaunus was not far off, surrounded by woods and marshes, and occupied by a large number of men and cattle. The Britons call by the name of town a place in the fastnesses of the woods surrounded by a mound and trench, and calculated to afford them a retreat and protection from hostile invasion.* Cæsar immediately marched to this place, which he found extremely strong, both by nature and art; nevertheless, he assailed it at once in two different quarters. The enemy stood their ground for a time, but at length gave way before the onset of our men, and abandoned the town by the opposite side. A great number of cattle were found there, and many of the enemy were slain or taken prisoners in the pursuit.'

It will be seen by reference to a map that Cæsar had now received the submission of a very large tract of country, extending from sea to sea, and completely surrounding the country of the Cantii, in which he had first landed. All these tribes seem to have bargained for protection against Cassivellaunus, and it is probable that they had been all more or less brought under his rule. This had been the case also with Cantium, or Kent, which was then ruled by four kings, or chiefs, whom Cæsar calls Cingetorix, Carvilius, Taximagulus, and Segonax. When Cæsar marched across the Thames, Cassivellaunus, driven from his own country, seems to have formed the project of cutting him off from the coast, and, marching into Kent, he sent to the four Kentish chiefs just mentioned his orders to assemble their forces immediately, and

---

* Oppidum autem Britanni vocant, quum sylvas impeditas vallo atque fossa munierunt, quo, incursionis hostium vitandæ causâ, convenire consueverunt. Eo proficiscitur cum legionibus: locum reperit egregia natura atque opere munitum.—Cæsar, Bell. Gall. lib. v. c. 17.

join him in surprising the naval camp of the Romans. This attack was, like so many others, unsuccessful; the assailants were beaten from the camp with considerable slaughter, and a young chief of consideration, named Lugotorix, was taken prisoner. This action convinced Cassivellaunus that it was in vain to contend with his irregular warriors against the discipline of the Roman veterans; and now, finding that even his own subjects were disaffected to him and had made their peace with the invaders, he also, through the intermediation of the Attrebatian Commius, offered to submit. His proposals were accepted, for Cæsar was now anxious, for various reasons, to return to Gaul; and having agreed upon a tribute which the Britons were to pay annually to the Roman people, and given his injunction to Cassivellaunus not to make war upon Mandubratius or the Trinobantes, who were naturally supposed to have incurred his hatred by their being the first to submit, Cæsar led his legions back to Gaul, carrying with him hostages which he had taken from the British chiefs as pledges for their fulfilment of the terms of the treaty.

Such is Cæsar's account of his exploits in Britain, which have every appearance of being truthful, although we have no other authority by which to test them. His descriptions are much too indefinite to enable us to trace with any certainty the line of his march, and it is but a waste of time with so few data to attempt to fix the sites of his camps or battle-fields. There can be little doubt that the Romans landed somewhere on the line of coast between Folkestone and Sandwich, but as that coast is known to have undergone great changes since that period, it would be unsafe to rely on his description at the present day.* The river on the banks of which he found the Britons posted is supposed to have been the Stour. We can hardly doubt that his subsequent march lay along the edge of the Weald, perhaps along the vale of Maidstone. The place at which the Romans crossed the Thames was fixed by a tradition which existed in the time of Bede, when the stakes, said to have been those which defended the river, remained,† at a place now

---

* The theory has recently been sustained with some ingenuity, that the Romans did not start for this expedition from the country of the Morini, but from the mouth of the river Somme, and that the Romans landed in the neighbourhood of Pevensey; but I do not believe that Cæsar's narrative will bear this interpretation. See my remarks on this subject in the 'Wanderings of an Antiquary,' pp. 102, 103 (London, 1854).

† Traditions, even of the time of Bede, are not of much value, unless well supported by other circumstances. The words of this writer, after

called Cowey Stakes, near Chertsey, in Surrey. The stronghold of Cassivellaunus, which the Roman soldiers carried by storm, has been conjectured with much less probability to have stood on the spot afterwards occupied by the Roman city of Verulamium (near St Alban's). Other sites have been suggested, but we willingly pass over such vague and useless conjectures to confine ourselves as much as possible to known, or more apparent, facts.

Cæsar's expedition to Britain was looked upon as one of the most remarkable events of the time, and from this moment the distant western island was a common theme for poetry and declamation. The victorious commander was looked upon as one who had carried the Roman arms into a new world—*penitus toto divisos orbe Britannos*—and his countrymen listened eagerly to the account brought home by their armies of these hitherto unknown peoples. Cæsar evidently gained the best information he could on the manners of the Britons, and his brief description of the island and its inhabitants is apparently given at least with good faith. He knew that the island was in its general form triangular, and he was sufficiently well informed of the comparative proportions of its different sides. He knew that another island, which he reckoned to be half the size of Britain, and which he called Hibernia (Ireland), lay to the west of Britain, and he placed between these an isle named Mona (Anglesea or Man). He speaks more doubtfully of other islands, of smaller dimensions, with a more northerly position. The inhabitants of the interior of Britain, according to the traditional information gained by Cæsar, were the original inhabitants of the island, while the south-eastern coasts were inhabited by Belgic colonies, who, as he informs us, had given to the different petty states (*civitates*) of Britain the name of

giving the account from Cæsar of the fortifying of the river with stakes, are, 'the remains of which stakes are to be seen there to this day; and it appears to the observer as though the several stakes—each about the thickness of man's thigh, and cased with lead—were fixed immoveably in the bed of the river,'—(*quarum vestigia sudium ibidem usque hodie visuntur, et videtur inspectantibus quod singulæ earum admodum humani femoris grossæ et circumfusæ plumbo immobiliter hæreant in profundum fluminis infixæ.* Bedæ Hist. Eccl. i. 3.) Bede's account of these stakes is probably correct; but, as it is not likely that in the hurry of a sudden defence, like that against Cæsar's march, the Britons would have the time to erect posts of this magnitude, and case them with lead, we are justified in supposing that the stakes existing in Bede's time were a Roman work of a later period connected in some way with the navigation or fishery of the Thames, which we cannot now explain, and that they had nothing to do with Cæsar's passage of the river.

those from which they came. This statement is corroborated by the list of British tribes given by subsequent writers, in which the Hedui of Somersetshire, the Morini of Dorset, the Senones of Hampshire, the Rhemi (another name of the Bibroci) of Berkshire and Surrey, the Attrebates, stretching from the former county into Hampshire, the Cimbri of the borders of Devon, had all their representatives in Gaul. The people of Cantium (Kent) were the most civilized of all the British tribes, and in their manners bore a strong resemblance to their Gallic neighbours. The maritime districts were essentially corn countries, for it was the Belgic settlers who introduced agriculture; the wild tribes of the interior did not cultivate the earth, but they lived on milk and flesh, and clothed themselves with skins. All the Britons, we are assured by Cæsar, stained themselves with a blue dye made from woad, to give them a more terrible appearance in battle; and they wore their hair long, and shaved every part of the body but the head and upper lip. A sentiment of national pride has led many writers to doubt the truth of Cæsar's account of the prevalence of polygamy among the Britons, and he was probably speaking only of the maritime districts when he tells us with a tone of wonder of their numerous population, and of the frequency of buildings which resembled those of the Gauls. Cattle were very abundant. But the Britons had no money, using in place of it pieces of brass or iron rings, reduced to certain standard weight.*
White *plumbum* (tin) was procured in the midland districts, and iron was found, though not very abundant, in the parts bordering on the sea.† Brass, Cæsar tells us, was imported from abroad. The island produced timber of every kind, except beech and fir.

Such was Britain as known to Julius Cæsar. Two nearly contemporary writers, Strabo the geographer, and the historian Diodorus Siculus, have supplied us with some information omitted by him, and probably obtained from subsequent communications with the island. These authors describe the island as being for the most part flat and woody, having however, 'many strong places on hills.' The produce, they tell us, consisted of corn and cattle, gold, silver, and iron, with skins,

---

* 'Utuntur aut ære aut annulis ferreis ad certum pondus examinatis pro nummo.'—Cæsar, Bell. Gall. lib. v. c. 10.

† Cæsar may perhaps be supposed to have taken Cornwall for a midland district, as it was far from the country in which he was engaged. His iron district was perhaps the weald of Sussex and Kent.

slaves, and dogs of a superior breed for the chase. The British dogs were widely celebrated, and so strong and fierce that the Gauls are said to have used them in war. The aboriginal Britons are described as being tall of stature, and corpulent, but not well made. According to Strabo, although they used milk in great abundance, they were not acquainted with the art of making cheese, and they were total strangers to gardening and agriculture. Diodorus describes them as practising agriculture, gathering the corn and storing it up in the stalk in thatched houses, out of which 'they plucked the old ears from day to day, and used them to make their food.' Their houses, we are told, were mere temporary establishments, formed in the forests by enclosing a space with felled trees, within which they made huts of reeds and logs, and sheds for their cattle, 'not intended to remain long' (οὐ πρὸς πολὺν χρόνον). Cæsar as we have seen alludes to the tin (*plumbum album*, as it is named also by Pliny), which appears to have been the principal export of Britain in those remote ages; and Strabo tells us that 'the inhabitants of Britain who live near the Belerian promontory (the Land's End, Cornwall), are peculiarly hospitable, and, from the great resort of foreigners, more polished in manners than the others. They prepare the tin, and show much skill in working the earth which produces it. This being of a stony nature and having earthy veins in every direction, they work their way into these veins, and so by means of water separate the fragments. These they bruise into small pieces, and convey to an island which lies in front of Britain, called Ictis [Wight? or perhaps an island on the Cornish coast]; for at the great ebb of the tide the channel becomes dry, and they carry over the tin in large quantities on waggons. From Ictis the tin is purchased by native merchants, and transported to Gaul.' The same writer tells us that ivory bracelets, necklaces, vessels of glass, and such like small wares, were usually imported from Gaul into Britain.

In comparing these writers, we have some difficulty in separating the characteristics of the maritime states from those which applied only to the tribes of the interior; but it seems clear that the island was then inhabited by two very distinct races, differing no doubt in language as well as in manners. The country extending along the coast from the mouth of the Humber to Devonshire, and stretching inwardly perhaps through the modern counties of Hertford, Buckingham, and Berkshire, was possessed by tribes who had passed over from the

Continent, and driven the aboriginal inhabitants into the interior. They were distinguished by a much higher civilization, especially in Kent, which had probably been settled more recently than the others, and although they had no towns properly so called, they had permanent dwellings, and were extensively employed in cultivating the land. The primitive Britons wandered over the interior of the island, driving their herds and flocks from pasture to pasture, having no fixed habitation, but throwing up temporary dwelling-places for security for themselves and their cattle—in fact, living precisely in the same manner as the wild Irish three centuries ago. In a few places accidental circumstances led the natives to adopt a more settled mode of life, and to become less barbarous. This was especially the case in Cornwall, where, from a remote period, the trade in the metals produced so abundantly in that district had, as Strabo says, brought them into a continued intercourse with merchants from foreign lands, but chiefly, it would appear, from Gaul.

During the long period of a century, from the time of Cæsar to that of Claudius, we have scarcely any information relating to the island of Britain. We have seen that, before Cæsar left its shores, all the tribes in the south-east from the Iceni or Cenimagni of Suffolk to the inhabitants of Hampshire, had agreed to acknowledge the supremacy of Rome. Among the chiefs of these tribes there appears to have arisen a sudden emulation of imitating Roman forms and manners—a sort of pride, as we might say, of wearing the livery of their masters. Britons now were seen not unfrequently in Rome, and travellers from Italy probably made their way through Gaul to visit the distant home of the strangers whose appearance in the south must always have excited curiosity. The feeling of eagerness for what was called friendship with Rome seems to have soon spread into other parts of the island, and when Strabo was writing his Geography, British ambassadors were in Rome, bowing to the throne of Augustus. 'At present,' he says, 'some of their princes have sent ambassadors to cultivate the friendship of Augustus Cæsar, and have deposited offerings in the Capitol, thus bringing the whole island to be in friendly connection with the Romans.' *

* Strabo's account is fully confirmed by an inscription in honour of Augustus, found at Angora, in Asia Minor, in which, among the public acts of this emperor's reign, the submission of the British princes is mentioned. The Latin text of this inscription, which is completed from

Among the various arts now imported from Rome was that of coining money. No evidence has yet been discovered to make us doubt the truth of Cæsar's statement that, when he visited the island, the Britons had no coinage; but soon after that event mints were established in Britain, and we find numerous coins, many of which bear inscriptions in Roman characters. Most of these inscriptions evidently give us the names of British chiefs who, since their 'friendship' with Rome, assumed the title of *reges*, and they adopted the formula of the coinage of Augustus, CÆSAR DIVI FILIUS. The history of this coinage is still very obscure, but the earlier examples seem to make us acquainted with two distinct families of chiefs, both of which are connected with the different tribes who submitted to Cæsar. The power which in Cæsar's time had been held by Cassivellaunus, appears to have descended to a prince named Tasciovanus, who was father of the (we may say) celebrated Cunobelinus or Cunobeline.* The latter, we know, had three sons, Adminius, Caratacus or Caractacus, and Togodumnus. Another, and apparently contemporary (or nearly contemporary), family of British kings, named Eppillus (or Ippillus), Veric, Viric, or Beric, and a name of which only the first syllable Tinc is known, are described on a number of coins as sons of a British chief named Comius.† There is no necessity for believing that the latter was the Commius whose name occurs in Cæsar's transactions with the British chiefs. The coinage of Tasciovanus and of Cunobeline was very numerous, and it furnishes us with another piece of very important information, for it appears from the inscriptions on it that after the Britons had become more intimately acquainted with their Roman allies they began to imi-

the parallel Greek text, is, Britannorum reges, Damno, Bellaunos, et Timan, Sicambrorum Maelo, Marcomannorum Suebo, fidem petierunt meam (the kings of the Britons, Damno, Bellaunos, and Timan, of the Sicambri Maelo, and of the Marcomanni Suebo, submitted to me).

* The legend on the coins of Cunobeline is CUNOBELINUS TASCIOVANI F REX, in one or two instances complete, but in general more or less abbreviated. I believe that it was Mr Birch who pointed out the simple and natural explanation that F stood for the Latin *filius*. Mr Beale Poste has given, in a series of papers in the Journal of the British Archæological Association, a very different explanation of this and the whole series of the British coinage, supported by an ingenious train of argument, which, however, appears to me neither convincing nor satisfactory, as being founded too much on assumptions and suppositions. Like every other branch of archæology or historical inquiry which is very imperfectly known, the coins of the ancient Britons furnish a wide field for speculative theory.

† The legends on the most perfect specimens are, EPPILLUS COMI F, VERIC COM F REX, and TINC COM F REX.

tate them in building stationary towns. The coins of Tasciovanus were struck at Verlamium, as it is spelt on the coins, which was no doubt the capital of that prince; his son Cunobeline fixed his chief residence at Camulodunum (Colchester, in Essex), on the borders of the Iceni, who acknowledged his power, the name of which also is impressed on his money.* The coins of the sons of Comius bear no indication of the place where they were minted, but it seems probable from the localities in which they have been found, that Eppillus ruled in Kent, and that Veric and Tinc . . . . . . were joint or rival chiefs (or perhaps one succeeded the other), in Sussex and Hampshire.

During the reigns of Augustus and Tiberius, making together a period of nearly eighty years, the British states which had submitted to Julius Cæsar were left in that position of friendship or alliance with Rome which we have already described, and history tells us nothing of their condition or of the actions of their chiefs. We know that Cunobelinus, who has been made familiar to every English ear by Shakespeare under the name of Cymbeline, was living in the time of the latter of the two emperors just mentioned, but the stories of that chief's intercourse with Augustus, resting on no very early authority, are evidently monkish fables. The very numerous coinage of Cunobeline, and its superior execution, show that he was a powerful and distinguished prince; yet war and sedition prevailed among the tribes under his command, and in his latter years, the rivalry among his own sons arose to such a height that he was obliged to banish one of them, Adminius, from his court. Adminius, with a few of his adherents, hurried to Rome, and claimed the protection of Caligula, who had now succeeded to the imperial throne. The British refugees were received as vassals of the Empire, and were exhibited in triumph to the Romans, and Caligula having placed himself at the head of an army, marched to the coast of Gaul with the declared intention of restoring Adminius and reducing Britain to a province. But this vaunted expedition ended ingloriously; instead of passing

---

* It has been conjectured, that one or two legends, not yet understood, may be names of towns. A coin bearing the name TASCIO (for Tasciovanus or Tasciovani) has SEGO on the reverse, which some interpret as Segontium, the name of a town, while others make it Segonax, the name of a chief, perhaps a son of Tasciovanus. It has, in a similar manner, been suggested that CALLE, VRICON, SOLIDO, and CUN, found on coins most of which appear to have belonged to Tasciovanus and Cunobelin, indicate towns named Callova, Uriconium, Solidunum, and Cunetio. In the first of these, the word REX, joined with CALLE, seems to prove that it is the name of an individual; and the others are far from certain.

over into Britain, the Roman soldiers were ordered to gather shells on the beach, and they were then led back to Rome to triumph in what were called the 'spoils of the ocean.'

In the mean while, Britain seems to have been more and more disturbed with civil strife. As far as we can understand by a comparison of the slight notices preserved by the Roman annalists, with the yet imperfectly explained British coins, the sons of Cunobeline, who was now dead, were oppressing the sons of Comius. One of the latter, called by Dio Cassius, Bericus, probably the Veric of the coins, was compelled to fly from the island, and took refuge at the court of Claudius, to whom he explained the state of Britain and the facility with which, at that moment, it might be conquered. We are told that the Britons sent to Rome to demand that the fugitives should be delivered up, and that the refusal was accompanied with recriminations on the irregularity with which the islanders had of late paid their tribute. Claudius, anxious to deserve a triumph by some military exploit, listened willingly to the representatives of the fugitive chief, and found an excuse for hostilities in the complaints of the Britons. An army was collected in the spring of the year 43, under the command of a senator of distinction, named Aulus Plautius; but the legions mutinied at the prospect of an expedition which seemed to expose them to the perils of the unknown ocean, and it was not until after much labour and anxiety that their fears were calmed, and they were persuaded at length to embark. They landed on the shores of Britain in the autumn of the same year. The Britons, who seem to have formed no combined plan of resistance, retired to the woods and marshes, and it was some time before the Romans could discover their retreat, and bring them to battle. At length, however, the Britons ventured to fight, not collectively, but in divisions, and Plautius defeated first Caractacus (who is named by Dio Cassius, our authority for these events, Cataracus), and then his brother Togodumnus. In pursuing these chiefs, the Roman commander had overrun the south of England as far as Oxfordshire and Gloucestershire, the country of the Dobuni, who were at this time under the dominion of the Catuellani, the hereditary tribe of Cassivellaunus, and probably of Cunobeline. The Dobuni submitted, and Plautius raised a fortress and left a garrison to hold them in subjection, and then pursued the sons of Cunobeline. Among the distinguished officers who served in Britain under Plautius were two future emperors, Vespasian, and his son Titus. In one of the obstinate engagements with the Britons, which occurred after the advance of the Romans from the country of the Dobuni, the life of the father was saved only by the bravery of his son. It was thus in our island, as it has been well observed, that the arms were trained, which were destined to be the instrument of God's vengeance against the stubborn people of Israel. The sons of Cunobeline, after having retreated before the Romans towards the west, seem to have doubled upon their pursuers, and to have sought refuge in the marshes which covered the lower part of Essex towards the mouth of the Thames. Here also they were pursued and attacked, and Togodumnus, one of the brothers, was slain in battle. The death of their chief seems to have provoked the Britons to a more obstinate resistance, and the Roman commander found himself obliged to act upon the defensive. He sent information of his position to the emperor, who hastened to command in person his legions in Britain. On the arrival of Claudius, they again crossed the Thames, defeated the Britons in battle, and took possession of Camulodunum, the royal seat of Cunobeline. The Britons now submitted, and the emperor hastened back to Rome to celebrate his triumph, leaving Aulus Plautius in command of the army. The emperor and his son were both honoured by the senate with the title of Britannicus, and a coin was subsequently struck to commemorate the conquest of the Britons.*

That conquest, however, was as yet very imperfect, and included only the south-eastern district of the island. But a foreign power, like that of Rome, established in a hostile manner in one district of Britain, could not long remain without excuses for attacking the others. The south-western division of the island, extending from Hampshire to the extremity of Cornwall, was held by two powerful tribes, called the Belgæ and the Damnonii or Dumnonii. Both appear to have been late settlers from the opposite continent, and to have been able to resist successfully the influence of Cunobeline. In retaliation for assistance, which they had probably given against the Romans in the war with Caractacus and Togodumnus, their country was now invaded by Vespasian with the second legion, and after an

* This coin, which is found in silver and gold, has a laureated head of Claudius on the obverse, with the inscription, TI . CLAVD . CAESAR . AVG . P . M . TR . P . VI . IMP . XI, which is to be read, *Tiberius Claudius Cæsar Augustus, pontifex maximus, Tribunitia potestate sextum, imperator undecimum*. On the reverse, a triumphal arch is surmounted by an equestrian statue between two trophies, with the inscription DE BRITANN, i.e. *de Britannis*, on the conquest of the Britons.

obstinate and apparently a long struggle, in which Vespasian fought nearly thirty battles and captured twenty of the British *oppida*, or fortified posts, these two tribes, with the adjacent island of Vectis (Wight), were reduced to submission.*

Previous to the year 50, Aulus Plautius was recalled, and he seems to have left the Roman legions engaged in war with the Britons. It was now the tribes of the interior who had taken up arms against the invaders, and were making inroads upon the tribes who had submitted to them, considering their submission as a just cause for attacking and plundering them. They had chosen for this attack the moment when the Roman army in Britain was without a commander-in-chief, and when the immediate approach of winter promised them a sufficient period of impunity to enable them to secure their booty. In the midst of this confusion, a new governor or *propraetor* of Britain arrived from Rome. His name was Ostorius Scapula, a good soldier, and a man of eminent abilities. He had no sooner landed than he collected such troops as were at hand, and, falling upon the Britons unexpectedly, defeated them with great slaughter, and drove them out of the Roman territory. He then proceeded to inclose and protect the latter with a line of forts from the Avon to the Severn,† from which it appears that the whole country within these rivers, from the farthest coast of Norfolk to the Land's-End, and thence to the extreme point of Kent, had at this time, voluntarily or by compulsion, submitted to the power of Rome.

Among those who had submitted voluntarily was the extensive and powerful tribe of the Iceni, who occupied the modern counties of Suffolk, Norfolk, Cambridge, and Huntingdon. The Iceni were jealous of the attempt of the Romans to establish their power by these forts, and, confident in their own strength, which had not yet been tried with the Romans, they

---

* Our knowledge of this war is taken chiefly from Suetonius, who says of Vespasian, 'Inde in Britanniam translatus, tricies cum hoste conflixit, duas validissimas gentes, superque xx. oppida, et insulam Vectem Britanniae proximam, in deditionem redegit.' From the mention of the island of Vectis, and other circumstances, there seems little reason to doubt that the *duae gentes* were the Belgae and the Damnonii, although it is not so clear whether the thirty (or, according to Eutropius, thirty-two) battles did not include four or five battles Vespasian is known to have fought in the previous war.

† 'Cinctosque castris Antonam et Sabrinam fluvios cohibere parat.'— *Tacitus.* The Antona is usually considered to be the Nen, but it seems more probable that it here signifies the Avon. I understand that some editions or MSS. read *Aufona*.

DEFEAT OF THE BRIGANTES.

put themselves at the head of a confederacy, with some of the neighbouring tribes, and when Ostorius marched against them, they prepared for battle in a place which they had inclosed with ramparts of earth, with a narrow entrance to hinder the approach of cavalry.* But this was of little avail against the discipline of their opponents, and Ostorius, with only a few cohorts of auxiliaries, attacked them in their entrenchments, made a breach for the entrance of his cavalry, and defeated them with great slaughter. The Iceni now returned to their obedience, and other tribes, which had before hesitated, submitted.

Beyond the boundary which Ostorius had formed by his line of forts, the interior of the island was inhabited by tribes who were fiercer and less civilized than the southern nations. The chief of these was the great tribe of the Brigantes, extending through the mountainous and wooded districts from the borders of Lincolnshire, through Yorkshire, Lancashire, Westmoreland, Cumberland, and Northumberland. The lesser tribes, such as the Cornavii and Coritavi, which were intermediate between the tribes subject to the Romans and the Brigantes, probably acknowledged the superiority of the latter. The Brigantes seem to have been so much discouraged by the defeat of the Iceni, that they sought the alliance of, or rather bought their peace with, the Romans. Ostorius, relieved from the hostilities of the various tribes just mentioned, carried his army into Shropshire and North Wales, and had proceeded as far as the tribe of the Cangii on the shores of the Irish Sea, when he was recalled by a revolt of the Brigantes, which was apparently partial and easily subdued. The only formidable enemy now in arms on the borders of the Roman possessions was the tribe of the Silures, which had rallied under Caractacus, the defeated son of Cunobeline, who, after various turns of fortune, had been elected the chief of this tribe, and entered into a confederacy with the Ordovices of North Wales.

After the defeat of the Brigantes, Ostorius gave his attention to the interior arrangement of the province committed to his charge. He made Camulodunum, which was raised to the rank of a *colonia*, the head-quarters of the Roman power, and established there a numerous body of veterans, among whom the conquered lands were distributed. The city was adorned with public buildings, and more especially with a temple dedicated

* 'Locum pugnæ delegere, septum agresti aggere, et aditu angusto ne pervius equiti foret.'—*Tacitus, Annal.*, lib. xii. c. 31.

to Claudius, and was increased in size and importance. Having settled these things to his satisfaction, Ostorius marched against Caractacus. That chief, leaving the more open country of the Silures to be overrun by the enemy, had withdrawn into the wilder country of the Ordovices, where he chose a strong position, difficult of access even without the assistance of artificial defences. On the more accessible parts of the high hills he threw up a kind of rampart of stone, while below and in front was a river difficult to ford.* Here the British chief awaited the attack of his enemies, or, perhaps, amused himself with the belief that his stronghold was too formidable to be attempted, for he had with him his family, consisting of a wife and daughter. The Britons, thus posted, and excited by the example and exhortations of their leader, presented a formidable opposition to the Roman legionaries, protected as they were by the river which ran before them, and the steep declivity which was in their way. 'But the soldiers,' to use the words of Tacitus, 'were clamorous for the attack, crying out that their valour would overcome all opposition, and the inferior officers seconding the same wish, to give additional courage to the men. Then Caractacus flew over the ground to see which were strong and weak points, which access he had on the eager to inspire with hope, others to arouse to arms. When they saw on the one hand the ramparts thrown up, on the other the river before them, and there were sent down their several chiefs for showers of darts, he was soon reached by missiles irregular as a storm, and scorching beneath, on less certain ground, where they got loose from the ranks, they came onward, but not till their shields were up in a close body, and when the Romans advanced to the attack of the stockade or rallied themselves in heavier squadrons, the wild and disorderly mass of barbarians gave way, destitute of defensive armour to protect them from the swords and spears of the legionaries, and armed scarcely, for an attack, by the formidable weapons of a foreign foe. Here the wife they turned upon the latter, the auxiliaries destroyed them with their sabres and javelins.'*

This victory was a decisive one. The wife and daughter of Caractacus fell into the hands of the conquerors, and two brothers who had shared his fortunes submitted. Caractacus himself escaped from the battle, and fled to the tribe of the Brigantes, from whose queen, Cartismandua, he sought protection; but this princess, anxious to remain in friendship with the Romans, threw him into chains and delivered him to his enemies. The dignified appearance of Caractacus and his family at the court of Rome, as related by the historian Tacitus, is the theme of every schoolboy. The loss of their leader did not discourage the Silures, who, trusting to their woods, continued to carry on a fierce warfare against the Romans, cutting off their stragglers, and in more than one instance nearly overwhelming the legions which were left to erect fortresses in their country. 'After this,' says Tacitus, 'there was incessant fighting, generally of a predatory character; sometimes the armies would meet in the woods, at other times in the midst of marshes, according as chance or their own headlong valour directed: many an engagement took place by accident, while others were the result of stratagem and military manœuvre; many an expedition was undertaken to revenge some previous defeat, while others had plunder for their object; and they were sometimes undertaken by order of the generals, and at other times without their knowledge. The Silures were the most obstinate in their resistance, and their obstinacy was increased by the threat of the Roman commander, that he would root the very name of the Silures out of Britain, as had been done with the Sigambri, who had been transported to Gaul. These words enraged the Silures, who assailed and cut off two cohorts of the auxiliaries, and stirred up the other tribes to revolt by giving them a large share of their booty, and thus exciting their love of plunder. In the midst of these disorders, Ostorius, overcome by the troubles with which he was surrounded, departed this life; and the Britons rejoiced at his death, not merely as if they had gained a battle, but rather as if the war was entirely at an end.'

An old officer, Avitus Didius Gallus, was appointed to succeed Ostorius as proprætor, and hastened to Britain to take

* 'Et si auxiliaribus resisterent, gladiis ac pilis legionariorum, si hae verterent, spathis et hastis auxiliarium sternobantur.'

the command. Before he arrived, a Roman legion had been defeated by the Silures, but he immediately marched against them, and gave them in their turn a severe defeat. Then, unequal to the arduous character of this war, Didius left it to be conducted by his subordinate officers, and relapsed into the inactivity which was more in accordance with his advanced age. It was probably in this war that the second legion, which had had Vespasian for its commander, was established at Isca (Caerleon, on the Usk).

At the time of the arrival of Didius in Britain, a civil war arose among the Brigantes, which threatened to add to the embarrassments of the Romans. I have already mentioned that this powerful tribe was now governed by a queen, named Cartismandua, who proved a woman of high spirit and some abilities. Her conduct with regard to Caractacus had naturally drawn upon her the hatred of those who were most hostile to the Romans, and this included many of her own subjects. She had married one of her chiefs, named Venusius, who, as far as we can gather from the brief account of Tacitus, quarrelled with his wife because she would not surrender to him the supreme power over her tribe, and he then placed himself at the head of a party in the state who cried out against the indignity of men living under the rule of a woman. Cartismandua, whose party appears, at first, to have been the strongest, claimed the protection of the Romans, and her husband, who seems to have been driven from among the Brigantes, endeavoured to make himself popular among the other tribes, by now placing himself at the head of the party who were in arms against the invaders. It was this man who, commanding the Silures and their allies, had defeated the Roman legion commanded by Manlius Valens before the arrival of the new proprætor Didius. After this success, Venusius, collecting his allies, and joined by the party of the Brigantes who were opposed to the Roman influence, proceeded to make war on his wife Cartismandua, who had crushed the first attempt against her government, and captured and put to death a brother and other relatives of Venusius. A Roman army was immediately sent to assist the queen of the Brigantes, and in a well-contested battle overcame the Britons who were in arms against her. About the same time another Roman legion, commanded by Cæsius Nasica, obtained a decisive victory over an army of Britons.

Thus the administration of Didius had not been entirely without credit, when, towards the end of the year 58, he was replaced by Veranius, who made one or two successful expeditions against the Silures; but he died before he had been a year in Britain, at a moment when the greatest expectations were formed from his military talents. He was immediately succeeded by Caius Suetonius Paullinus, one of the most warlike and skilful of the imperial generals. The Roman arms had experienced a reverse (*gravis clades*) before the arrival of Suetonius, and he found the districts from the Silures to the Brigantes in great disorder.

It seems that in Britain, as in Gaul, as foreign intercourse and consequent civilisation advanced, the head seat of the old Druidical religion was removed more and more into the remoter districts, until in the latter country it established itself on the Armorican coast and in the Channel Islands, and in the former it retreated into the distant island of Mona (Anglesea), equally arrested in its further advances by the waves of the ocean. We gather from the Roman historians that it was the Druids of Mona who excited the Ordovices and the Silures and their other allies to obstinate resistance, and it was in that island that were collected together the bravest and bitterest enemies of the foreign invaders, ever ready to issue forth and incite their countrymen to insurrection. Suetonius Paullinus soon discovered the influence which Mona exercised against him, and he determined to reduce it to obedience to Rome. For this purpose he marched his forces to the coast of Caernarvonshire, and having caused a number of flat-bottomed vessels to be constructed, he placed the foot soldiers in them, and ordered the cavalry to try to ford the strait which divided the island from the mainland; or, if they found this impossible, to go in the boats and tow their horses after them. When they approached the island, an unusual scene presented itself to their view. 'The shore of the island was lined with the hostile army, in which were women dressed in dark and dismal garments, with their hair streaming to the wind, bearing torches in their hands, and running like furies up and down the ranks. Around stood the Druids, with hands spread to heaven, and uttering dreadful prayers and imprecations. The novelty of the sight struck our soldiers with dismay, so that they stood as if petrified, a mark for the enemy's javelins. At length, animated by the exhortations of their general, and encouraging one another not to fear an army of women and fanatics, they rushed upon the enemy, bore down all before them, and involved them in their own fires. The troops of the enemy were completely defeated, a garrison placed in the island, and the groves which had been the consecrated scenes of the most barbarous superstitions, were levelled with the ground. It had been their practice to sacrifice on the altars prisoners taken in war, and to divine the pleasure of their gods by inspecting human entrails.' Suetonius was called off from this expedition by the most alarming revolt of the Britons in the Roman province that had hitherto occurred.

The Romans were seldom conciliatory or generous towards the provinces they had conquered, and the empire was now ruled by Nero, under whom those provinces were delivered to the worst of tyranny, by governors whose only principle of action was to grind the unfortunate people under their charge in order to contribute to the avarice and luxury of Rome. The more distant the province, the more cruelly was it oppressed, and Tacitus, in the account he gives us of the consultations among the tributary chiefs in Britain on their wrongs, affords a sufficient view of the manner in which this island was treated. 'They reflected,' he says, 'on the miseries attendant on servitude, and when they came to compare their several injuries, they were heightened tenfold by putting them together. It was clear that passive submission would but encourage their oppressors to proceed to still greater lengths. Instead of one king, as formerly, they had now two, the lieutenant and his procurator; the former exercising his tyranny over their persons, the latter over their goods. Whether their governors were at harmony together or at variance, it was alike fatal to their unhappy subjects; the one oppressed them by his troops and his centurions, the other by his insolence and extortion. Nothing was now safe from their avarice, or from their licentiousness. In battle it was the bravest or strongest man who carried off the spoil; but here the meanest-spirited and most contemptible of men entered and pillaged their houses, carried away their children, and made them enlist in the Roman armies as if they were ready to die for anything but their country. If the Britons would but consider their own numbers, they would find that the Roman troops who were among them were but a paltry and inconsiderable force. . . . Their country, with their wives and parents, should be so many motives for them to support a war, to which their enemies were urged only by avarice and luxury, and the armies of Rome would no doubt retire as Cæsar had done, if the Britons would but imitate the bravery of their ancestors, and not be discouraged by the issue of one or two battles.'

It was usual, during the earlier period of the Roman conquest, to leave the British chiefs in nominal command of their tribes, with more or less power or wealth, according to their tried obedience and devotion to their imperial masters. In Cogidunus or Cogidubnus, a chief of the Regni of Sussex, we have an instance of a British prince who was so faithful to the Romans, that he was allowed to enjoy his dignity and title of *rex*, or king, from the reign of Claudius to that of Trajan, and his name appeared down to the latest period of Roman rule on an inscription as one of those who embellished the city of Regnum (Chichester) with public buildings.* Others, who, although they acknowledged the supremacy of the Romans, had not shown the same submissive spirit, were treated more oppressively. The Iceni, as we have seen, were kept in obedience only by fear, and their chief, or king (as he was called), Prasutagus, who had hoarded up immense wealth, dying in the reign of Nero, when the licence of the imperial officers in the provinces was at its height, attempted to secure protection for his family by leaving one half of his riches to the emperor, and the other half to his two daughters. But he was no sooner dead, than the Roman officers took possession of his kingdom, and treated it as a conquered province. His queen, Boadicea, a woman of high spirit, resisted or expostulated, which only provoked the haughty Romans to act with greater brutality. The queen was publicly scourged; her two daughters were

* In the earlier part of the last century, as some workmen were digging a cellar in a house at the corner of St Martin's-lane and North-street, in Chichester, they came to the massive walls of a building, near which lay, with the inscribed face downwards, a mutilated stone with the following inscription:—

. EPTVNO . ET . MINERVAE
TEMPLVM
. . O . SALVTE . DO . . . DIVINAE
AVCTORITA . . . CLAVD.
. . . GIDVBNI . R . L . . . VG . . . IN . BRIT.
. . . GIVM . FABROR . E . . QVI . IN . EO
. . . D . S . D . DONANTE . AREAM
. . . ENTE . PVDENTINI . FIL.

which has been read thus: 'Neptuno et Minervae templum pro salute domus divinae ex auctoritate Tiberii Claudii Cogidubni regis legati augusti in Britannia collegium fabrorum et qui in eo a sacris sunt de suo dedicaverunt donante aream Pudente Pudentini filio.' This inscription refers, no doubt, to the same British prince mentioned by Tacitus as receiving favours from Claudius, and who appears by it to have taken the name of the emperor in addition to his own. 'Quaedam civitates Cogiduno regi erant donatae; is ad nostram usque memoriam fidissimus remansit, vetere ac jam pridem recepta populi Romani consuetudine ut haberet instrumenta servitutis et reges.'—*Taciti Agric.*, c. 14.

violated; and other members of the royal family, or relatives of the deceased chief, were thrown into prison, and even sold as slaves. It is not to be wondered at if the Iceni rose in arms to avenge their wrongs, and the Trinobantes of Essex immediately joined in the revolt. The latter seem to have been goaded into rebellion by the insolence of their Roman masters in Camulodunum. According to Tacitus, 'they looked upon the temple which the Romans had built and dedicated to Claudius, as a kind of citadel to hold them in perpetual bondage, and the priests who celebrated religious worship in it as so many harpies who lived upon the substance of the natives. It would be no difficult task, they thought, to destroy the Roman colony, for it had no fortifications to protect it, an omission into which the Romans were led by paying more attention to the gratification of their luxury than to provide for their public safety.'

Before the insurrection broke out, the Romans appear to have been alarmed by unequivocal indications of an approaching storm, and we are told that there were not wanting prodigies to warn them of their danger. The account which Tacitus gives of these is curious, as throwing some light on the condition of the town and country. 'At Camulodunum,' he tells us, 'the statue of Nero fell to the ground, and turned its back where the face had been, as if it fled before the enemy. Women were seen as if mad, singing wild songs, in which they foretold the destruction of the colony [perhaps they were native women, aware of the conspiracy, and employed to create alarm]. Strange noises were heard in the house of assembly, and loud howlings in the theatre. In the estuary of the Thames there was an appearance like that of a sunken town. The sea assumed the colour of blood, and human forms appeared to be left on the shore by the ebbing tide. All these things were of a nature to encourage the Britons, whilst they overwhelmed the veterans with terror.' The inhabitants of Camulodunum, in their alarm, applied for assistance to the procurator Catus Decianus, who commanded in the absence of Suetonius, but who appears to have slighted the warning. 'He sent them only two hundred men, very imperfectly armed, and to these were added a small body of soldiers belonging to the town. The temple of Claudius was taken possession of by these troops, as a citadel, but their measures of defence were thwarted by those around them who were in the secret of the conspiracy; so that they had neither dug a fosse nor cast up an earthen rampart for protection, and the precaution, usual in such cases, of sending away the old men and the women, and retaining only the young and active, had been entirely neglected. They were, indeed, taken by surprise in time of profound peace, and found themselves suddenly surrounded by the barbarians. Everything but the temple was plundered and burnt at the first attack, and the temple itself, in which the soldiers had taken refuge, was captured after a siege of two days.'

The success of the attack on Camulodunum gave courage and force to the insurgents. It appears that the ninth legion, commanded by its lieutenant, Petilius Cerealis, had its stationary camp within the territory of the Trinobantes. Cerealis hurried to the relief of Camulodunum, but he arrived too late, and, rashly engaging the insurgents, he was entirely defeated, his infantry, comprising the great mass of the legion, was utterly destroyed, and the cavalry, with Cerealis himself, fled to their camp and shut themselves up in their entrenchments. The alarm of the Romans was now so great, that the procurator Catus, fearing to expose himself to the resentment of the natives whom his own avarice had excited to revolt, deserted his post and fled into Gaul.

Suetonius, engaged in the reduction of the distant island of Mona, heard of these alarming disorders, and hastened back. As he approached towards the head seat of the Roman power in Britain, he found the whole country in arms and in possession of the insurgents. Nevertheless, 'he marched through the midst of the enemy to Londinium (London), which was not yet honoured with the name of a colony, but considerable from the resort of merchants, and from its trade. Here, hesitating whether he should make that town the seat of war, he considered how weak the garrison was, and warned by the check which Petilius had incurred by his rashness, he determined to preserve the whole by sacrificing one town. Nor did the tears and lamentations of the people imploring his assistance prevent him from giving the signal for marching, though he received into his army all who chose to follow him. But all those whom the weakness of sex, or the infirmities of age, or attachment to the place, induced to stay behind, fell into the hands of the enemy. The same calamity befell the municipal town of Verulamium ; for the barbarians, neglecting the fortified stations (*castella*) and garrisons, plundered the richer and more defenceless places, their principal object being booty. Seventy thousand citizens and allies are said to have perished in these places; for they made no prisoners to sell or exchange them, according to the usual practice in war, but thought of nothing but slaughter, hanging, burning, and crucifying, as if to retaliate for former sufferings, and eager to quench their thirst for vengeance.'

The Roman commander had now collected about ten thousand regular troops, consisting of the fourteenth legion with the vexillarii of the twentieth, and the auxiliaries from the nearest military posts, and he determined to give battle to the numerous but tumultuous hordes who followed the standard of Boadicea. 'He made choice of a spot defended by defiles, and closed in the rear by a forest, as the safest position to receive an enemy who would make their attack in front, while the open plain before him relieved him from all fear of ambuscades. The legionaries were drawn up in many deep ranks, the light-armed troops disposed around in companies, and the flanks covered with the cavalry. The British forces bounded about (*exsultabant*) in companies and troops, an innumerable multitude, and with so much confidence that they brought their women to be witnesses of their victory, and placed them in waggons on the outer circuit of the plain. Boadicea, who rode with her daughters in a chariot, as she came to the several clans, with whom it was not unusual for a woman to command an army, told them that she considered herself not as the descendant of noble ancestors, possessed of sovereignty and great riches, but as one of the community, prepared to avenge the loss of liberty, the stripes inflicted upon her body, and the dishonour done to her daughters; for the lusts of the Romans were risen to such a height, that neither their persons, their age, nor their chastity was safe. The gods, however, she said, favoured their just revenge; the legion which had attempted an engagement was cut off; those who had escaped had concealed themselves within their fortresses (*castris*) or were preparing for flight. The Roman army now opposed to them would never stand the shouts and clamour of so many thousands, much less their shock and fury. If they considered the number of forces, or the causes of the war, they would resolve that day to conquer or die; this was the last resource for her, a woman; let the men, if they pleased, live and be slaves.'

This address of the British queen contains, at least, the sentiments that actuated the Britons in this revolt, as they were well known to the contemporary Roman historian, who has placed it in her mouth. Suetonius also addressed his troops, urging them not to fear the immense numbers of their enemies, or to be alarmed at the dreadful shouts with which they were accustomed to march into battle. The legion acted on the defensive, protected by its position, until the fury of the first attack was exhausted. It then formed in a wedge, and marched steadily on the Britons, while the auxiliaries made the same movement, and the cavalry, rushing down with their spears levelled, bore all before them. The Britons were soon routed with terrible slaughter, for the circle of waggons impeded their flight, and the Roman soldiers spared none, but massacred the women, and even the beasts. Eighty thousand Britons are said to have been slain on this fatal day, and then queen Boadicea, unwilling to survive the destruction of her country, put an end to her own life by taking poison.*

The Iceni were utterly crushed in this revolt. The numbers assembled in the last disastrous battle, and the fact of their being accompanied with their women, show that the tribes engaged in it had arisen *en masse*, and their country was now left without defenders, and probably almost without inhabitants. Their lands were overrun and plundered by the Roman troops, and all the other tribes whose inclinations were known to be hostile or wavering, were ravaged by fire and sword. The troops were augmented by the arrival of two thousand legionaries, eight cohorts of auxiliaries, and a thousand horse from Germany; and out of these, the ninth legion, which had suffered so much, was recruited. Although the war lingered on for a time, the defeat of this insurrection had fixed so firmly the Roman yoke, that we hear no more of serious revolts in the conquered provinces, although from time to time an outbreak among the oppressed natives furnished the excuse for destroying the families of their chiefs and reducing the natives to a more degrading state of slavery.

The reduction of the rebellion of the Iceni led, however, to at least a temporary change of policy towards the Britons, and even the Roman soldiers seem to have been satiated with the wholesale slaughter. Suetonius Paullinus appears to have been a harsh and rigorous ruler, and his disinclination to show any

---

* Our numismatists have ascribed to Boadicea certain British coins which bear the inscription BODVOC. I think too hastily; for the history of the British queen is that of a hurried insurrection, suppressed immediately, and scarcely affording time for a distinctive coinage. Previous to the rising, she had no authority or power, and the miserable woman who was subject to the lash at the pleasure of her Roman masters, is not likely to have possessed a mint. Boduoc may have been some one of the British chiefs whose existence has not been recorded by history.

lenity towards the conquered Britons is said to have been a subject of dispute between the general and the new procurator, Julius Classicianus, who had been sent as the successor of the fugitive Catus Decianus. Polycletus, an imperial agent, repaired to Britain to enquire into the state of the province, and it was probably his report that led soon after to the recall of Suetonius. He was succeeded by Petronius Turpilianus, a man who had just laid down the consulship, and whose only qualification mentioned by the historian, was a spirit of forbearance and lenity, which the commanders who had been accustomed to tyrannise over conquered nations looked upon with contempt. The mild administration of this proprætor, however, soothed the wounds with which this distant province was bleeding, and seems to have wiped away the last traces of the ferocious struggle which had taken place under his predecessor. A short time before the death of Nero, Petronius resigned his office and was succeeded by Trebellius Maximus, who governed the province with equal moderation and affability. While the rest of the empire was torn by civil commotion, the province of Britain enjoyed unusual tranquillity, and was disturbed only by a quarrel between the proprætor and Roscius Cœlius, the lieutenant of the twentieth legion. As the soldiers seem in general to have taken part with Cœlius, this feud ended in the flight of Trebellius, who went alone and without followers to join the standard of Vitellius, leaving Britain to be governed nominally by the lieutenants of the different legions, but really by Roscius Cœlius. Vitellius had already drawn from Britain a body of eight thousand troops, while Suetonius Paullinus had carried over the whole of the fourteenth legion to fight under the standard of Otho.

When Vitellius had rid himself of his competitors, and secured the purple, he sent to Britain, as proprætor, one of his immediate attendants, Vettius Bolanus, who carried back with him the fourteenth legion, which was in disfavour, because it had fought for one of the unsuccessful pretenders to the throne. Tacitus tells us that the government of Bolanus 'was too mild for so fierce a province; and that Agricola, who was still serving in Britain, checked the ardour of his own martial disposition, lest he should be suspected of disobedience or disaffection towards his commander-in-chief.' The insecurity of the province was increased by the number of troops which were now draughted off to join in the new struggle for the empire between Vitellius and Vespasian. It was at this moment that symptoms of insubordination again began to show themselves among the Britons. The insurrection began with the extensive tribe of the Brigantes, where the authority of Cartismandua appears to have been still supported by the Romans.* This imperious lady remained separated from her husband, and in contempt of him, she had taken to her bed his armour-bearer, Vellocatus, and deputed to him a part of her power. Many of her subjects were shocked by this scandalous proceeding, and Venusius soon raised a powerful party, and pursued the queen with so much vigour, that she was only rescued with difficulty by a body of Roman troops after several battles. The revolt of the Brigantes had become so general, that the Romans were obliged for a moment to leave them in a state of independence with Venusius at their head.

On the accession of Vespasian, various changes were made in the establishment in Britain. Petilius Cerealis, the commander of the ninth legion, who had incurred the signal disaster in the war against Boadicea, was sent to succeed Vettius Bolanus as proprætor, while an officer of great talents, both as a soldier and as a statesman, Julius Agricola, was appointed to the command of the twentieth legion, which had shown some unwillingness to acknowledge the new emperor. An affectionate friendship had long subsisted between Agricola and Cerealis, and they joined heartily in carrying on the war which had now broken out in Britain. But after several successful engagements with the Brigantes, by which a large portion of that tribe was reduced to obedience, Cerealis was recalled, and Julius Frontinus appointed in his place. Under this proprætor the Silures, who had hitherto remained independent in the fastnesses of the mountains, and had perhaps taken part with the Brigantes, were conquered. But the spirit of disaffection was now spreading widely, and when in the year 78, Julius Frontinus was recalled, the Ordovices of North Wales rose and destroyed a troop of cavalry which was stationed in their country, and various other tribes were preparing to rise in a general revolt.

At this moment the man of all others most capable of wrestling with the dangers which seemed on all sides to threaten

---

* From the manner in which Tacitus introduces the history of Cartismandua and her husband in the Histories and the Annals, it appears somewhat confused, and it has been usual to regard the two notices as relating to one event. I think, however, that they are distinct, and I have treated them so in this sketch.

the province, was appointed as a successor to Frontinus. It was towards the close of the summer of the year 78, when Julius Agricola returned from Rome to assume the government of Britain. In spite of the advanced period of the year, he immediately assembled the legions and a small number of the auxiliaries, and, marching into the mountains of the Ordovices, he caused nearly the whole tribe to be put to the sword. He then passed over to Mona (Anglesea), and reduced that island entirely under the Roman power. As the time of the year was now past for further military operations, and the slaughter of the Ordovices had struck terror through most of the other tribes, Agricola spent the winter in regulating and reforming the government of the province, and correcting the innumerable abuses which had crept into the administration. As the summer of the year 79 approached, the legions were again in motion, and by a mixture of rigour towards those who resisted, and extraordinary lenity towards those who submitted, he succeeded in establishing the Roman power throughout the island, almost to the borders of Scotland. In the midst of these successes, the emperor Vespasian died, and left the purple to his son Titus. Agricola, who was continued in the government of Britain, spent the remainder of the year in securing his conquests. He now, as Tacitus tells us, saw the necessity of weaning the fierce passions of the Britons from the unsettled state of war and tumult to which they had become habituated, and of leading them to adopt the pursuits of peace and the refinements of civilisation. He saw that this could only be effected by giving them a relish for the arts and a taste for elegant pleasure. To this he excited them by his conversations in private and by his public measures. He encouraged them to erect temples, forums, and houses. He caused the sons of the British chiefs to be instructed in the language and knowledge of their conquerors. Such measures produced rapid effects. The Britons soon began to adopt the Roman dress, and they exchanged the rude garb of their ancestors for the dignified toga. The manners of the Romans also gradually took root among them, and they gained a taste for erecting porticos and baths, and indulging in other luxuries.

In the spring of the year 80, Agricola placed himself again at the head of the army, and, proceeding to invade and reduce the lowlands of Scotland, extended the Roman territory as far as the estuary of the river Taus (the Tay). When this campaign was over, the Roman troops were employed under the eye of their leader in erecting fortresses over the newly-acquired territory, and the sites were chosen with so much judgment that it was a common remark that no *castellum* built by Agricola was ever taken by the enemy, while they were placed near enough together to communicate easily with each other. Agricola's fourth summer (A.D. 81) was employed in the erection of a chain of forts between the two estuaries known to the Romans by the name of Clota and Bodotria (the Clyde and Forth), as a check upon the incursions of the northern highlanders; and in the following spring he brought his fleet into the Solway Firth, and carried his troops over to the country where it approached nearest to Ireland, which also he secured with fortresses and troops. The exact locality of these operations has been a matter of some dispute, but the opinion which seems to carry most weight places it in the country known in more modern times by the name of Galloway. It was understood that the Roman general already projected an invasion of Ireland. One of its petty princes, driven into exile by a domestic sedition, had repaired to Agricola to ask for assistance from the Romans, and Agricola was ready to seize the occasion of carrying over a Roman legion, had his intention not been drawn away by other events.

Early in the year 83, which was Agricola's sixth campaign, the Roman general marched with his army into the country beyond the line of fortresses erected two years before, to reduce the northern tribes, who appear to have harassed his borders by their inroads. Having assembled his fleet in the Firth of Forth, he ordered it to accompany the march of his army, which proceeded through the districts bordering on the eastern coast. The Caledonian tribes harassed the Roman legions on their march; and when they had reached a position supposed to be a little to the south of the Ochil mountains, the ninth legion, which was in advance and obliged to encamp in an unfavourable position, was so vigorously attacked that, had it not been soon relieved by the arrival of the rest of the Roman forces, it might have experienced a disaster more serious even than that which fell upon it in its march to Camulodunum. The object of this campaign appears to have been to take possession of the districts of Fife and Kinross, preparatory to the entire reduction of the northern parts of the island in the following year. Accordingly in the summer of the year 84, having ordered his fleet to sail round Scotland and alarm the enemy by making descents on the coast, he advanced with the army, in which the southern

Britons now served as Roman auxiliaries, and reached the foot of the Grampian mountains, on the declivity of which he found thirty thousand of the bravest warriors of the north, under a celebrated chief named Galgacus, assembled to resist his further advance. As the Romans advanced to the attack, they suffered much from the arrows of the enemy, while the north Britons, who were armed with long pointless swords and small round shields, used them so skilfully that they parried off the Roman missiles. Agricola, observing the inequality of this mode of combating, chose three troops of Batavians and two of Tungrians, and ordered them to hurry forward and attack the Britons with their swords. These were short and pointed, and therefore much better calculated for close action than the long swords of their opponents. The attack was made with courage and success; the Britons, crowded together too closely in their ranks, were deprived of the free use of their arms to strike with their swords in their usual manner, while their faces and bodies were exposed to the deadly thrusts of their opponents, and they soon began to give way. The rest of the Roman troops had now come up, and the main body of the Caledonians, which had remained in their position on the hill, rushed down to the assistance of their companions, so that the battle became general. The discipline of the Romans, however, soon overcame the bravery of their opponents, and the north Britons were routed with terrible slaughter. About ten thousand are said to have been killed, and those who escaped fled with their families into the more remote and inaccessible parts of the country.

This last great battle of Agricola is believed to have been fought on the moor of Ardoch, in Perthshire. It made the Romans masters of the whole island. Agricola left his army to winter in the district of the Horestii, and returned to his seat of government in the south. His fleet made the circuit of North Britain, and, while they took a survey of its coasts and obtained information relating to the interior, they filled the inhabitants with terror and alarm. They took possession of the Orkney Islands. The merits of Agricola were, however, too bright for the worthless ruler who then sat on the imperial throne; and this distinguished propraetor, with an empty triumph, was deprived of his command in Britain, to experience at home the ingratitude of Domitian. He left the province of Britain in perfect tranquillity; and, though history has told us nothing of the events of the next few years, it seems probable that the Roman troops in Britain, finding no employ-

AGRICOLA IN IRELAND.

ment at home, passed over to Ireland, and reduced that island to nominal subjection. The poet Juvenal, who is said to have written his satire in A.D. 96, just twelve years after Agricola's last campaign, speaks of Ireland as one of the most recent acquisitions of the Roman arms—

> 'Arma quidem ultra
> Litora Juvernæ promovimus, et modo captas
> Orcadas, ac minima contentos nocte Britannos.'

Britain was now entirely subjected to the power of imperial Rome. Its people had irrecoverably lost their independence, and they soon lost their nationality, when their new rulers began to divide the province of Britain into departments. The very nations, many of whom had so bravely fought for their freedom, lost their names, and gradually merged into Roman subjects, or rather Roman slaves. A little more than thirty years after the recall of Agricola, the celebrated geographer, Claudius Ptolemæus, published his survey of the world as then known, in which he has given us a very exact survey of the coasts of Britain and Ireland, with an enumeration of the native tribes. From this account, compared with the allusions of other writers, it appears that the south-eastern part of the island, or the district now occupied by the county of Kent, was occupied by the Cantii, a large and influential tribe, which, in Cæsar's time, was divided among four chiefs or kings. To the west, the Regni held the modern counties of Sussex and Surrey, from the sea-coast to the Thames. Still farther west, the Belgæ occupied the country from the southern coast to the Bristol Channel, including nearly the whole of Hampshire, Wiltshire, and Somersetshire. The whole of the extensive district extending from the Belgæ to the extreme western point of the island, then called Antivestæum or Bolerium (now the Land's End), including Devonshire and Cornwall, was occupied by the Dumnonii, or Damnonii. On the coast, between the Dumnonii and the Belgæ, the smaller tribe of the Durotriges held the modern county of Dorset. On the other side of the Thames, extending northwards to the Stour, and including the greater part of Middlesex, as well as Essex, lay the Trinobantes. To the north of the Stour dwelt the Iceni, extending over the counties of Suffolk, Norfolk, Cambridge, and Huntingdon. The Coritavi possessed the present counties of Northampton, Leicester, Rutland, Derby, Nottingham, and Lincoln; and the south-eastern part of Yorkshire was held by the Parisi. Between the tribes last enumerated, in the counties of Buckingham, Bedford, and

Hertford, lay the tribe called by Ptolemy the Catyeuchlani (Κατυευχλανοί), and by others Catuvellani. Another name apparently for this tribe, or for a division of it, was the Cassii. West of these were the Attrebates, in Berkshire; and still further west were the Dobuni, in the counties of Oxford and Gloucester. All these tribes are supposed to have been later settlers than the tribes of the interior, those nearer the coast being always, of course, the more recent colonies, and it is far from improbable that some of them were of German origin.

The interior of the island northward was occupied by the Brigantes, who held the extensive districts, difficult of approach on account of their mountains and woods, extending from the Humber and the Mersey to the present borders of Scotland. This extensive tribe appears to have included several smaller ones. Two of these are called by Richard of Cirencester, the Voluntii and the Sestuntii, the former in the west of Lancashire, the latter in Westmoreland and Cumberland. The Jugantes and the Cangi of Tacitus, on the borders of the Irish Sea, are also understood to have belonged to, or been dependent upon, this tribe. The Brigantes are believed to have been the original inhabitants of the island, who had been driven northward by successive invasions and settlements, and they appear to have been the least civilised tribe of South Britain; their wild independence was encouraged and protected by the nature of the country they inhabited. Wales also was inhabited by a primitive population. The northern counties, Flint, Denbigh, Montgomery, Merioneth, and Caernarvon, with the island of Anglesea (then, as we have said before, called Mona), was the territory of the Ordovices. The south-eastern counties of Cardigan, Caermarthen, and Pembroke, were held by the Demetæ. The still more celebrated tribe of the Silures inhabited the modern counties of Hereford, Radnor, Brecknock, Monmouth, and Glamorgan. Between these and the Brigantes lay the Cornabii, or Carnabii, who occupied the present counties of Warwick, Worcester, Stafford, Salop, and Chester, and perhaps the adjoining part of Flintshire.

The wilder parts of the island of Britain, to the north of the Brigantes, were inhabited by a great number of smaller tribes, some of whom seem to have been raised in the scale of civilisation little above savages. Of these we have the names of no less than twenty-one. Bordering on the Brigantes, were the Otadeni, inhabiting the coast from the Tyne to the Firth of Forth, including a large portion of Northumberland, with the modern counties of Berwick and East-Lothian, and part of Roxburghshire. Next to them were the Gadeni, occupying the western part of Northumberland, the small part of Cumberland north of the Irthing, the western part of Roxburghshire, the whole of the county of Selkirk, with Tweedale, a great part of Mid-Lothian, and nearly all West-Lothian. The Selgovæ inhabited Annandale, Nithsdale, and Eskdale, in Dumfriesshire, with the east of Galloway. The Novantes inhabited the remainder of Galloway. The Damnii, a larger tribe, held the country from the chain of hills separating Galloway from Carrick, northward to the river Ern. These tribes lay to the south of the Forth and Clyde. Beyond the narrow boundary formed by these rivers lay, first, the Horestii, who occupied the modern counties of Clackmannan, Kinross, and Fife, with the eastern part of Strathern, and the country to the west of the Tay. The Venricones occupied a part of Perthshire, the whole of Angus, and a large part of Kincardineshire. The northern part of the Mearns, and the greater part of Aberdeenshire, were inhabited by the Taixali. The Vacomagi possessed the country forming the modern shires of Banff, Elgin, and Nairn, with the east part of Inverness and Bræmar, in Aberdeenshire. The Albani held the districts of Braidalban and Athol, with parts of Lochaber and Upper Lorn. The ferocious tribe of the Attacotti inhabited part of Argyleshire, and the greater part of Dumbartonshire. The wild forest country of the interior, known as the *Caledonia Sylva* (or forest of Celyddon), extending from the ridge of mountains between Inverness and Perth northward to the forest of Balnagowan, including the middle parts of Inverness and Ross, was held by the Caledonii, which appears to have been at this time the most important and powerful of all the tribes north of the Brigantes. The eastern part of Ross was inhabited by the Cantæ. On the south-eastern coast of Sutherland were the Logi. Beyond them, the Carnabii occupied the greater part of Caithness, leaving only the north-west corner, which, with a part of Sutherlandshire, belonged to the Catini. The interior of Sutherlandshire was peopled by the Mertæ; while the north and west coasts, and a small part of the western coast of Ross, were inhabited by the Carnonacæ. A tribe named the Creones dwelt on the west coast of Ross; the Cerones held the western coast of Inverness and part of Argyleshire; and the neck of land, now known by the name of Cantyre, was the seat of the Epidii. We have no information on the ethnological character of these tribes; some of them are sup-

... from Scandinavia and the opposite coast of ... no doubt originated in migrations from the ... again probably came from Ireland.

... known to the Romans by the names of Hibernia ... appears to have been tolerably well known in the ... Ptolemy, who gives us a description of its coasts, and ... the tribes and towns both in the maritime districts ... in the interior. On the northern coast dwelt the Veniconii, in the northern county of Donegal, and the Robogdii, in Londonderry and Antrim. Adjoining to the Veniconii, westward, were the Ronali or Erpeditani, and next to them the Magnatæ, all in Donegal. Farther south were the Auteri, in Sligo; the Gangani, in Mayo; and the Velibori, or Ellebri, in the district between Galway and the Shannon. The south-west part of the island, with a great portion of the interior, was inhabited by the Iverni, who gave name not only to the great river, but to the whole island, and who may, perhaps, be considered as the aboriginal inhabitants. The south-eastern promontory, now called Carnsore Point, was then known by the title of the Holy Promontory (ἱερὸν ἄκρον), to the north-west of which, in the modern counties of Waterford and Tipperary, Ptolemy places a tribe called the Usdiæ or Vodiæ, according to the variations of the manuscripts. In the modern county of Wexford dwelt the Brigantes; and northward from them were the Coriondi, in Wicklow; the Menapii, in Dublin; the Cauci, on the banks of the Boyne; the Blanii, or Eblani, on the bay of Dundalk; the Voluntii, in Down; and the Darini, bordering on the Robogdii, in Antrim.

Three, at least, of the tribes who held the eastern coast of Ireland, the Brigantes, the Menapii, and the Voluntii, were, no doubt, colonies from the opposite shores of Britain. This circumstance gives additional force to the conjecture that the Brigantes, with their dependent tribe, the Voluntii, are to be considered as the remains of the earlier Celtic population of the latter island. Driven inward by the later settlers, whether Celtic or Teutonic, they were obliged also to seek new settlements in the neighbouring island.*

It is evident that these various tribes, not only governed by different chiefs, but belonging to different races, must have differed also in their manners and in their comparative civilis-

* It also gives rise to a supposition that the original Celtic language of Britain is represented rather by the modern Irish than by the Welsh, which, for several other reasons, is more than probable.

ation, and that we should be wrong in applying to them all the various notices on this subject found in ancient writers, and much more so in transferring to the inhabitants of Britain, without reserve, the description which the old geographers and historians have left us of the people of Gaul. Most of the descriptions found in subsequent writers are little more than a repetition of the scanty information given by Cæsar, who was himself acquainted only with the south-eastern part of the island.

We should probably form the best appreciation of the condition of our Celtic forefathers before their conquest by the Romans, if we compared them with the septs or clans in Ireland and the highlands of Scotland in the twelfth and thirteenth centuries. Each chief exercised the same independent and unrestrained authority over his clan, and the disunion of the whole was probably increased by difference of language and race. There seems to be no reason for assuming that the different tribes were accustomed to unite under one head (or, as he has been termed, Pendragon) in cases of emergency. On the contrary, we observe, as far as their history is known, that they never acted together, unless when their union was caused by conquest, or by the alliance of one or two neighbouring and, perhaps, kindred tribes.* The statement that they went naked, and that they painted their bodies, can only have been true of some of the more barbarous tribes. We have no very distinct information on the costume of the Britons, except that we know from the earlier Roman writers that they wore breeches (*braccæ*), like the Gauls and Germans. They are described as being in person taller than the average height of the Romans. The brief account of Tacitus confirms the views already stated, as to the difference of races which peopled the island. He imagined that the red hair and masculine forms of the Caledonians bespoke a German origin; that the Silures, by their complexions (*calorati vultus*), and curly hair, were a colony of the Iberi of Spain; and that the tribes who inhabited the coasts came from Gaul; and one of the arguments he adduces for believing that the maritime tribes were of Gallic origin, the similarity of language (*sermo haud multum diversus*), leads us to believe that the lauguage of these tribes was totally different from that of the

* Tacitus, speaking of the British tribes, says, 'Nec aliud adversus validissimas gentes pro nobis utilius, quam quod in commune non consulunt. Rarus duabus tribusve civitatibus ad propulsandum commune periculum conventus; ita, dum singuli pugnant, universi vincuntur.'— *Tacitus, Agric.*, c. 12.

Silures, or from that of the Caledonians, and of the tribes of the interior.

In one particular, we are justified in considering the description of the manners of the people of Gaul as applicable to those of Britain, I mean their religion. All the ancient writers agree that the Druidic system was the same in both countries. All that we really know of it is given by Cæsar, and may be best repeated in his own words. 'The Druids,' he says, 'act in all sacred matters; they attend to the sacrifices, which are offered either by the tribe in general, or by individuals, and answer all questions concerning their religion. They always have a large number of young men as pupils, who treat them with the greatest respect. For it is they who decide in all controversies, whether public or private, and they judge all causes, whether of murder, of a disputed inheritance, or of the boundaries of estates. They assign both rewards and punishments, and whoever refuses to abide by their sentence, whether he be in a public or private station, is forbidden to be present at the sacrifices to the gods. This is in fact their most severe mode of punishment, and those who have been thus excommunicated are held as impious and profane; all avoid them, no one will either meet them or speak to them, lest they should be injured by their contagion; every species of honour is withheld from them, and if they are plaintiffs in a lawsuit, justice is denied them. All the Druids are subject to one chief, who enjoys the greatest authority among them. Upon the death of the chief Druid, the next in dignity is appointed to succeed him; and if there are two whose merits are equal, the election is made by the votes of the whole body, though sometimes they dispute for pre-eminence with the sword. . . . The Druidic system is thought to have had its origin in Britain, from whence it was introduced into Gaul; and it is still customary for those who wish to study it more thoroughly, to pass over into Britain for that purpose. The Druids enjoy peculiar privileges; they are exempted from service in war, and from the payment of taxes; they have also many other immunities, which cause their order to become so numerous and influential, and young men are gladly placed with them by their parents and relations to learn their doctrines. In their schools the pupils are said to learn by heart a large number of verses, and in this way some of their scholars pass twenty years in completing their education; for it is unlawful to commit their doctrines to writing, though they are not ignorant of the art of writing; and for all other pur-

poses, both in their public and private reckonings, they make use of the Greek characters. It seems to me that they have two motives for this conduct : in the first place they are unwilling that their tenets should become known to the vulgar; and, secondly, they are afraid that their pupils will be less apt to cultivate their memories, if they trust to written characters, which often have the effect of checking diligent study. Among their most important tenets is that of the immortality of the soul, which they believe passes after death into other bodies; they hold this to be a great inducement to the practice of virtue, as the mind becomes relieved from the fear of death. Their other doctrines concern the motions of the heavenly bodies, the magnitude of the earth and the universe, the nature of things, and the power and attributes of the immortal gods.'
'All the Gallic nations,' Cæsar adds, 'are much given to superstition; for which reason, when they are seriously ill, or are in danger through their wars or other causes, they either offer up men as victims to the gods, or make a vow to sacrifice themselves. The ministers in these offerings are the Druids; and they hold that the wrath of the immortal gods can only be appeased, and man's life be redeemed, by offering up human sacrifice, and it is part of their national institutions to hold fixed solemnities for this purpose. Some of them make immense images of wicker-work, which they fill with men who are thus burned alive in offering to their deities. These victims are generally selected from among those who have been convicted of theft, robbery, or other crimes, in whose punishment they think the immortal gods take the greatest pleasure; but if there be a scarcity of such victims, they do not hesitate to sacrifice innocent men in their place.'

'Their principal deity,' continues Cæsar, 'is Mercury, in whose honour they have erected numerous statues; they hold him to be the inventor of all the arts, and the god who protects men on a journey, and leads them on their way; moreover, they ascribe to him the power of granting success and prosperity in affairs of gain and commerce. Next to Mercury come Apollo, Mars, Jupiter, and Minerva, to whom they ascribe attributes similar to those which are attributed to the same deities among other nations. Apollo is believed to heal diseases, Minerva to initiate mankind in the arts and sciences, Jupiter to be the king of heaven, and Mars to be the god of war. When the Gauls are about to fight a battle, they often make a vow to dedicate to Mars the spoils which they may take from their

If there be a superabundance of cattle taken in war, ... is offered up in sacrifice. The rest of the spoil is .... into one mass. In many of their tribes, large heaps of these things may be seen in their consecrated places; and it is a rare occurrence for any individual sacrilegiously to conceal part of the booty, or to turn it to his own use; the severest punishment, together with bodily torture, is inflicted on those who are guilty of such an offence. The Gauls boast that they sprung from father Dis (Pluto); and say that they derive their information from the Druids. This is the reason why they measure time by nights and not by days, and their birthdays, together with the commencement of their months and years, are so arranged, that the days are reckoned as parts of the preceding nights.'

Cæsar had an interest in collecting all the information he could relating to the Druids and their religion, but we are almost led to suspect that he obtained it from different races, German and Celtic, and that he mixed it together without due discrimination. The five deities which he gives to the Gauls seem to be Teutonic, the same whose names have been preserved in our modern days of the week. The great god of the Germans was Woden, who is always identified with the Roman Mercury; Jupiter was Thor; Mars was Tuisco; Minerva was, no doubt, Frigga; and Cæsar's Apollo was perhaps intended for Sæter, the god whose name has been preserved in our Saturday. It has always been the custom of the Germans to reckon time by nights—we still say *se'nnight, fortnight,* &c., for what the French call *huit jours, quinze jours,* but we know so little of the Celts, that we cannot venture to assert that they did not reckon time in the same way.

An edict of the emperor Claudius proscribed the Druidic caste, with its superstitions, and they quickly disappeared from Gaul. A curious passage of Tacitus, where he compares the tribes on the south and south-eastern coast of Britain with the Gauls on the Continent, and points out as a point of similarity, in which the other British tribes did not partake, the resemblance of their religious rites,* would lead us to imagine that Druidism prevailed only among those maritime people. As the

---

* 'Proximi Gallis, et similes sunt .... eorum sacra deprehendas, superstitionum persuasione.'—*Taciti Agric.,* c. 11. We must bear in mind that Druidism was abolished when Tacitus wrote, so he could only speak of the traces of it which remained among the people; yet we know by many instances how long such traces endure.

Romans advanced, their ban still fell upon the Druids, who made their last stand in Mona, and were destroyed there by the arms of Suetonius Paullinus. Subsequent writers only speak of them as a race who belonged to past ages, and they add nothing to our knowledge, at least nothing in which we can place any trust. It is Pliny who tells us of their respect for the mistletoe. 'The Druids,' he says, ' who are the magi of Gaul, esteem nothing more sacred than the mistletoe, and the tree on which it grows, if only it be an oak. Indeed they select groves of oaks, and use their leaves in all their sacred rites, so that their very name of Druids may seem to be derived from the Greek name for oak ($\delta\rho\tilde{\upsilon}\varsigma$). Everything which grows upon these trees is considered by them as sent from heaven, and a sign that the tree is chosen by the deity himself. But the mistletoe is very rare to find, and where it occurs is sought with great avidity; particularly on the sixth moon, which, among these nations, marks the beginnings of their months and years, and of a generation after thirty years, because it then has abundance of strength, though not yet half of its full size. They call it in their language by a name which signifies all-heal (*omnia sanantem*), and when they have made ready their sacrifices and banquets under the tree, they bring up two white bulls, whose horns are then bound for the first time. A priest clothed in a white robe ascends the tree, and with a golden pruning-knife lops off the bough, which is caught in a white towel. They then immolate the victims, praying that God may prosper the gift to all who shall partake of it; for they believe that by using it as a drink barren animals are rendered fruitful, and all kinds of poisons are deprived of their noxious power.' *

* Plinii Hist. Nat., lib. xvi. c 95.

CHAPTER III.

British Antiquities—Barrows—Cromlechs, and Sepulchral Chambers—Circles; Stonehenge—Other Monuments of Stone—Various descriptions of British Barrows—Their contents—Pottery—Instruments of Stone—Instruments of Metal—Other articles—Their value as illustrative of History—The British Coinage—Earthworks, and supposed sites of towns and villages.

SUCH is all we know from record of the history and condition of the inhabitants of Britain before it was finally reduced to a Roman province. We are able to add little to this knowledge from the discoveries of the antiquary, for the monuments of the British period are few, and uncertain, on account of the difficulty of appropriating them in a satisfactory manner. It has been the custom to consider all articles of rude make, which appeared not to be Roman, as belonging to a period antecedent to the Roman invasion; but later experience, and more careful investigation, have shown that this view was altogether erroneous. Much which used to be called British, is now known to be Saxon, and it is impossible to say how much of the rest belongs to the period of the Roman occupation, or to that which immediately followed it.

The only monuments to which people in a rude state of civilisation seem to have been anxious to give durability, were their graves, and to the contents of these we must look for any traces of the character and manners of those who built them. From the remotest ages it was customary to mark to future generations the last resting-place of the honoured dead, by raising mounds, more or less elevated according to circumstances connected with the locality, or according to the power and influence of the deceased. To these sepulchral mounds our Anglo-Saxon forefathers gave the names of low (*hlœw*), and barrow (*beorh, bearw*); of which the former is chiefly preserved in names of places, such as Bartlow, Houndslow, Ludlow, &c., while the latter has been generally used by English writers on archæology as the technical term for all ancient sepulchral mounds. Both are equivalent to the Latin *tumulus*. The form of the barrow was in its original state more or less conical, especially when it was of large dimensions, but ages of exposure to the elements and to other actions, which have swept so many of them entirely from the soil, have no doubt greatly modified the forms of those which are left, and, whatever may once have been the distinction of form, we can now only judge of the people to whom they belonged by their contents. Sir Richard Colt Hoare, an earnest and diligent antiquary, if not always a correct one, opened a great number of barrows in the south of England, and hastily undertook to classify them according to their outward forms, inventing a nomenclature which has been too blindly followed by antiquaries of later times.* He thus not only distinguished by their outward forms what were British barrows, but he subdivided the British barrows themselves. Yet his own errors show how little truth there was in this system, for he confounds British with Saxon, and sometimes either or both with what may have been Roman.

It is only by probability, greater or less, that we can attribute any of these barrows to the British period, for unfortunately we have no known and undoubted monuments of British manufacture with which to compare them, as is the case with the Roman and with other later periods. The very fact that great errors have been made, obliges us to proceed with the more caution in forming our judgment.

There is one class of barrows, and those usually large ones, which, when found in this island, antiquaries in general seem to agree in ascribing to the Britons—mounds which contain a rude chamber of rough stones, often of colossal dimensions. In the greater number of instances, the superincumbent mound has been removed, either for the sake of the earth, or in the belief, prevalent during the middle ages, that treasure was contained under it, and the massive chamber of rough stones alone has been left standing. Groups of large stones arranged in this manner have been found scattered over various parts of the

---

* The chief varieties in the classification alluded to, have received the names of conical barrows, bell barrows, bowl barrows, Druid barrows, broad barrows, twin barrows, long barrows, and pond barrows. No doubt barrows with the forms indicated by these names are found, but it is most probable that they frequently owe them to accidental circumstances, among which we must not omit the caprice of the makers.

British islands, as well as in other countries. Our antiquaries have applied to them the name of *cromlechs*, and have given to them every sort of absurd explanation, the most general of which was that which made them Druids' altars. But recent researches have left no room for doubt that they are all sepulchral chambers denuded of their mounds. In fact they have been found with their original coverings in the Channel Islands, in Brittany, in Ireland, and in England. One instance occurred about the year 1800, at Lanyon, in the parish of Maddern, or Madron, near Penzance in Cornwall, which has been more carefully recorded than other similar discoveries in England, and it furnishes us with an example of the motives which have led to the removal of the original mounds. The farmer to whom the ground belonged had often cast a longing eye to what appeared to be an immense heap of rich mould, and at length he resolved to clear it away and spread it over his field. As these large barrows are generally raised in localities where the soil is not very deep, the earth of which they are formed is the more attractive. When they had carried away about a hundred cart loads, the labourers came to a great stone, and not knowing what this might be, they removed the surrounding earth more carefully, and thus brought to light a large cromlech, formed, like many known examples, by three upright stones, making the three sides of the sepulchral chamber, covered with a massive cap-stone. Within were found a heap of broken urns and human bones, but it was evident that it had been disturbed at some former period, probably by treasure-seekers.

The word *cromlech* is said to be Celtic, and to have a meaning not differing much from that of the name *dolmen* given to them in France, which signifies a stone table.* Indeed, their appearance in an uncovered state readily suggests the idea of a table, and the peasantry in France often call them fairies' tables and devils' tables. These chambers are usually closed in only on three sides, and consist of four stones, three of which raised on their ends form the sides of a square, while the fourth serves as the covering. Such is the very remarkable cromlech on the hill between Maidstone and Rochester, in Kent, known by the name of Kits-Cotty House. In the annexed view of the cromlech of Chûn-Quoit, in the parish of Morvan, in the western part of Cornwall, only the lower corner of the stone forming the

---

* Some of our Celtic antiquaries, not satisfied with the name of 'cromlech,' had named them *kist-vaens*, or, as they interpret it, 'stone-chests.'

transverse side is seen. These monuments vary in size, though they are often very large. The covering stone of the cromlech

Cromlech of Chûn-Quoit in Cornwall.

of Chûn, just described, is calculated to weigh about twenty tons; the covering stone of one at Lanyon, in the parish of Madron, in Cornwall, weighs about fifteen tons; that of Kits-Cotty House, in Kent, has been estimated at ten tons and a half. Others are much smaller. Three upright stones, with a covering, constitute the cromlech in its simplest form. The stones are usually joined as close together as their shape will permit, for they seldom present any traces of having been squared with a tool; sometimes they are left with interstices between them, which give the chamber a still more rude appearance; and they are sometimes not arranged in a regular square. In some instances, as they now stand, the back stone has been carried away, and the cromlech consists only of three stones, two standing like the portals of a door, to support the transverse cap-stone or lintel; in others, where the cromlech has fallen, only two stones are left, one upright, and the other leaning upon it with one edge on the ground; and in many instances all that remains of the original cromlech is a single stone, standing upright or lying flat. We owe these forms doubtless to the dilapidations of time, and examples are known of the destruction of whole cromlechs to break up the stones for roads, or other purposes. But the old antiquaries had made different classes of all these imperfect monuments, and in France they gave them distinctive names. They termed the first *lichavens*, which is interpreted also as meaning *stone-tables*, but later French antiquaries have given them the Greek name of *triliths*, on account of the *three stones* of which they are composed; the second are called by the French antiquaries *demi-dolmens*; and the third class they have termed indiscriminately *ménhirs*, or *peulvans*, Celtic terms signifying *long stones*, or *stone pillars*.

This, as I have said, was the simplest form of the British sepulchral chamber, but it was sometimes much more complicated in its structure. In some instances it presents the form of a ponderous cap-stone, supported at its corners by four stones, and leaving the sides of the chamber more or less open. In other instances the chamber is made more complete, its sides being formed by a number of stones joined side by side, with one or more very large cap-stones above. Cromlechs thus constructed are found in different parts of England, and especially in the Channel Islands. Sometimes more than one cromlech is found under the same mound. On the hills between Gloucester and Cheltenham, a rather low, but very extensive oblong mound, overgrown with fir-trees, was a few years ago accidentally dug into at one end, and a small cromlech was brought to light. From the appearance of the mound, we are justified in supposing that one or more similar cromlechs still remain uncovered in the part which has not been touched. There is a remarkable monument of this kind at Plas Newydd, in the Isle of Anglesea; it consists of two cromlechs close together (the French antiquaries call it a double dolmen), one considerably larger than the other.* The cap-stone of the largest, which measures about twelve feet in length by ten in breadth, and from four and a half to three and a half feet in thickness, rests on five upright stones; it is said to have had originally seven supports. These two cromlechs were no doubt included in one mound.

A glance at the monument last described shows us how readily the idea would present itself of building-galleries, or a series of chambers, in these large sepulchral mounds, probably to serve as family tombs. Vast works of this kind are found

* It may be mentioned, as a sample of the absurdities which have been published on the subject of these monuments, that a writer of the earlier part of the present century, describing this monument, 'had no doubt' that the greater cromlech was appropriated to the sacrifice, and the lesser to the priest while he attended it!

in Brittany, as well as in Ireland. The chambered monument of New Grange, in Meath, in the latter country, is celebrated

Cromlech at Plas Newydd, Isle of Anglesea.

among Celtic antiquaries; it contains a chamber twenty feet high by thirty feet in circumference, approached by a narrow passage from the side of the mound, the entrance to which was closed by a large slab of stone. The researches of Mr Lukis among the Celtic sepulchres of the Channel Islands, show that these stone chambers had been there used by generation after generation through many ages. As far as antiquarian researches have yet been carried, extensive monuments of this kind are of rare occurrence in England. They are found, however, in Wiltshire. When denuded of their covering of earth, they have been more easily thrown down than the simple cromlech, or perhaps they have afforded greater temptation to those who were in want of stone for other purposes. The monument at Ashbury, in Berkshire, to which the Saxons attached the name of *Welandes Smiththan* (Weland's Smithy—Weland was the Saxon Vulcan), a name which has been corrupted to that of Wayland Smith's cave, appears to have been originally a gallery with chambers of this description. A very curious monument of the same kind, near Wellow, in Somersetshire, was opened by Sir Richard Colt Hoare, in the May of 1816, and an account of it published in the nineteenth vol-

... of the *Archæologia*. The barrow, composed of stones instead of earth, and of a very irregular form, stood on the side of a sloping field called Round Hill Tyning, at a place called Stoney Littleton, about three quarters of a mile west of Wellow church. The barrow was a hundred and seven feet long, fifty-four feet in its extreme width, and thirteen feet high in its most elevated part. When opened it was found to contain a long gallery with chambers on each side. The annexed cut represents a section of the barrow in the length of the gallery,

Barrow at Stoney Littleton, in Somerset.

and a plan. The entrance was on the north-west side, where a stone upwards of seven feet long, and three and a half wide, supported by two others, left a square aperture of about four feet high, which had been closed by another large stone. This entrance led to a long passage or avenue, extending in the direction from north-west to south-east forty-seven feet six inches, and varying in breadth. There were three transepts, or recesses, on each side. The side-walls were formed of thin laminæ of stone piled closely together without cement, and a rude kind of arched roof, made by stones so placed as to overlap each other. Where the large stones in the side walls did not join, the interstices were filled up with layers of small ones. This, like so many of the larger barrows, had been disturbed, and the deposits removed or scattered about. In one of the recesses, fragments of an earthen vessel with burnt bones were found; but in general the deposits had been taken out of the recesses and scattered over the avenue, which was strewed with fragments of bones, mostly unburnt. In one place, just before the second transept, a stone had been placed across the avenue, which closed the access to the further part, but with what object it is not easy to guess.

The mound or barrow, which, as we have stated, originally covered these cromlechs and stone structures, was generally formed of fine mould, and the value of the earth as soil has doubtless been the principal cause of their removal. Sometimes, however, the mound is composed of small loose stones, or of stones and earth mixed. That at Stoney Littleton, in Somersetshire, appears to have been peculiar in its construction, *built*, as it were, of small stones. The reason of the use of stones instead of earth may generally be traced to the natural character of the locality, as such barrows are found most frequently on spots were stone was much more easily obtained than earth. A few instances have occurred in Wiltshire, but they are seldom found in the interior or in the south of England, except in Cornwall, where they are not uncommon. They are common in Wales, and are found also in the north of England. In Scotland, where they are known by the name of *cairns*, they abound. The Welsh call them *carnydd*. In France they call the mounds of stones *galgals*.

The base of the larger sepulchral mounds, and very often of the smaller ones, was usually defined either by a shallow fosse, or by a circle of stones, and sometimes the two were combined. In some instances, especially in Cornwall, instead of the circle of stones, the base of the barrow was supported by a sort of low wall. These circles have often disappeared with the mound, as the stones of which they were composed were smaller and more portable than those which constituted the cromlech. But they as often remain encircling the cromlech. At Molfra, in Cornwall, on a bare hill with a commanding view of Mount's Bay, a fine cromlech is surrounded by a circular base of stonework, thirty-seven feet in diameter, and two feet high. A cromlech at Zennor, or Sennor, in Cornwall, is surrounded by a similar base. Our cut of the cromlech at Chûn shows the circle of stones round that monument. The circles of stones are frequently found with the cromlechs in various parts of England. They are also often found without any cromlech in the centre. One of these, called Dance Maine,

.... of St Burian, near the Land's End, is
.... accompanying sketch. This circle is about
.... diameter. There are several other good examples
in Cornwall, nearly of the same magnitude, such as the circle at
Boscawen-un, in the parish of Sancred, near the Land's End,

Circle called Dance Maine, near the Land's End, Cornwall.

about the same size as that of Dance Maine; one in the parish of Madron, seventy feet in diameter; and two adjoining circles in St Just, each between sixty and seventy feet in diameter. The last stands on an eminence commanding a view of the Scilly Islands. There is a similar circle on the summit of the lofty Pen-maen-mawr, in North Wales. There are remains of others at Salkeld, near Carlisle, at Rollrich, near Banbury in Oxfordshire, and in several other places in England. One, called Arbor-low, in the Peak of Derby, nearly one hundred and fifty feet in diameter, is surrounded by a deep intrenchment. Sometimes the stones forming the circle are nearly equal in size, while in other cases they are very irregular. The latter is especially the case in a circle near Winterburn in Dorsetshire. It does not necessarily follow that the mounds raised on all these circles contained each a cromlech—the interments may, in some cases, have been made without a chamber, as it has been found to be the case in some larger barrows.

Antiquaries observed these circles before they noticed how

often they accompanied cromlechs, or were aware that cromlechs are sepulchral monuments, and they gave them the name of *Druids' circles*, imagined that they were temples, or courts of justice, or places of assembly, and even built extravagant speculations on the number of stones which formed each circle. It is now quite certain that the majority of such circles were originally made to support or inclose sepulchral mounds, and even the circle at Arbor-low, which has been set down so positively as being the great Druidical temple of the Peak of Derby, would seem, by its name of *low*, to have had another object, and when that name was given, to have presented a different appearance. Yet we should be rash in asserting, with our scanty knowledge of the subject, that some few of the circles of stones still remaining on our own soil may not have been erected for other purposes, though it is difficult to make the distinction. The greater number of these circles are not larger than the basis of ordinary large barrows, and there are sepulchral mounds known, whose bases are equal to the largest; yet I am not aware that any barrow so large has yet been discovered in this country resting on such a circle of stones. Moreover, as we pursue these circles through the ascending scale of magnitude, we become still more embarrassed when we reach the gigantic monuments of Avebury and Stonehenge.

The extraordinary monument called Stonehenge, an Anglo-Saxon term meaning the hanging stones, is situated on a gentle knoll in the midst of a wide and barren tract, only distinguished from a plain by not very considerable elevations. It consisted originally of an outer circle of thirty upright stones, sustaining as many others placed horizontally, so as to form a continuous impost. These upright stones were about fourteen feet high above the ground, and seven feet broad, by three in thickness. They differ from other Celtic stone monuments in the circumstance that the stones have been hewn and squared with tools, and that each of the upright stones had two tenons or projections on the top, which fitted into mortices or hollows in the superincumbent slabs. Within this first circle, which was about a hundred feet in diameter, was another circle, eighty-three feet in diameter, containing about the same number of perpendicular stones, but much smaller, and without imposts. This again inclosed two elliptical arrangements of large and small stones, the former arranged in what the French archæologists term triliths, or groups of three stones, two upright ones and an impost, and the other formed by a series of small upright stones, three of which stood before each trilith. The triliths were from sixteen to twenty-one feet in height. In the central space, in front of the principal trilith, is a large flat stone, which those who look upon the whole as a primeval temple, call the altar. Such is the arrangement of this monument as nearly as we can judge from its present condition, which presents to the eye at first sight an apparently confused mass of upright and fallen stones, the appearance of which, as seen from the W.N.W., is exhibited in our engraving, taken from a sketch by Mr Fairholt. The form of the tenon on the uprights of the outer circle is shown on the leaning stone in front, somewhat more prominently than it is really seen, in order to make it more intelligible to the reader. This structure of stones occupies the centre of an area, inclosed by a circular intrenchment, consisting of a ditch and bank, three hundred feet in diameter. It was approached by a wide intrenched avenue from the north-east, which, at the distance of a few hundred feet, branched off in two ways, running north and east.

The ground around Stonehenge is covered with barrows, and was evidently the cemetery of a very extensive tribe, but nothing has yet been discovered to throw any light upon the object or date of the structure itself. The earliest existing legends relating to it describe it as a monument raised to the memory of the dead; a notion which may easily have arisen from the number of sepulchral monuments surrounding it.* The earliest writer who mentions it, Henry of Huntingdon,† looked upon it as involved in the same impenetrable mystery which still envelopes it, and which will probably never be cleared. From the arrangement of the stones, the most probable conjecture seems to be that which makes it a temple for some kind of worship; but the wild speculations to which this and other suppositions have given rise should be deprecated by

---

* Geoffrey of Monmouth, and the host of writers who translated and paraphrased his fabulous History of the Britons, pretended that these stones were brought from Ireland, and that they were raised to the memory of the British princes fabled to have been murdered by Hengist and his Saxons.

† In the list of the wonders of Britain, written in the earlier half of the twelfth century, and given by Henry of Huntingdon, Stonehenge is the second wonder. 'Apud Stanhenges lapides miræ magnitudinis in modum portarum elevati sunt, ut portæ portis superpositæ videantur, nec potest excogitare qua arte elevati sunt, vel qualiter constructi.'—'At Stanhenges stones of wonderful magnitude are raised in the manner of doors, so that they seem like doors placed over doors, nor can any one imagine by what art they were raised, or how constructed.'

Stonehenge, from the W.N.W.

all who are sincerely desirous of arriving at truth.* It has been observed with regard to the stones of which this monument is constructed, that the outer circles of large stones, as well as the inner triliths, are of the sandstone found plentifully in the neighbourhood, whereas the inner circle of small stones, as well as the small stones within the triliths, are of a different sort of stone, which appears to have been brought from Devonshire. This has led to a conjecture that Stonehenge was built at two different periods, but those who have adopted this opinion differ as to which was the earliest and which the latest part.

A series of circles more remarkable even than those of Stonehenge, is found at the village of Avebury, distant from Stonehenge about twenty miles. It consisted originally of an area, about fourteen hundred feet in diameter, inclosed by a deep ditch and bank, immediately within which was a first circle of a hundred stones. Within the area were two double circles, which have been designated as temples, one having three stones in the centre, and the other one only. The stones with which these various circles were composed, were no less massive than those at Stonehenge, varying from five to twenty feet in height. Two entrances were approached by two winding avenues, each consisting of a double row of upright stones, branching off to the extent of about a mile and a half to the west and south. These avenues of approach, from their form, have been a fertile subject of speculation, and have been imagined to have some connection with the worship of the serpent. At no great distance from the outer circle of Avebury is a fine cromlech with its attendant circle of stones. The remains at Avebury are much less known than those of Stonehenge; and they are not easily observed, on account of the extent of ground they cover, and its subdivision by hedges and other inclosures. The space inclosed by the earthen embankment contains a village, with various fields and buildings, over which the stones that remain are scattered in apparent confusion.

Stones which have been classed by our antiquaries under the indiscriminate title of Druidic, but which come under the head

* The young antiquary is particularly to be warned against such speculations as have recently been published in a book entitled 'The Druidical Temples of the County of Wilts,' by the Rev. E. Duke, as more calculated to throw ridicule upon science than to promote it. Very good accounts of these monuments are given by Mr Britton, in his articles on Stonehenge and Avebury in the 'Penny Cyclopædia.'

of none of the monuments already described, are found in groups, or singly scattered, over many parts of our island. Some of these appear to be natural formations, others have been set up at different periods for various purposes, and others are probably the remains of cromlechs and circles. Geologists and antiquaries seem now generally agreed that the rocking-stones are not works of art, but that they are the result of natural causes, and that they have been classed erroneously among Druidic remains. In the neighbourhood of Boroughbridge, in Yorkshire, there are masses of scattered rocks which in the same manner have been erroneously supposed to be Druidical. In some cases a few scattered stones are the remains of circles or avenues. Single stones belonging to a long avenue of this kind are still traced here and there in a line from the foot of the hill on which Kits-Cotty House stands, across the valley to the opposite chalk-hills, a distance of five miles. Celtic antiquaries have given to these single stones the names of *peulvan* (i. e. stone pillar), and *ménhir* (long stone). They have no doubt been erected at different periods, and for different purposes. Some, as I have just observed, are the last remains of cromlechs. Others are sepulchral monuments, often of the Roman or post-Roman period, which is proved sometimes by inscriptions. Several such inscribed stones have been found in Wales and Cornwall; and there is a celebrated one near Joinville, in France, with the inscription in Roman characters, VIROMARVS ISTATILI F (Viromarus the son of Istatilius). Two, found in the neighbourhood of Neath, in Glamorganshire (the Roman Nidum), have severally the inscriptions IMP. C. FLA. VAL. MAXIMINO INVICTO AUGUS [TO], and IMP. M. C. PIAVONIO VICTORINO AUGUSTO, and were perhaps boundary-stones or mile-stones. There is a rough uninscribed stone of this description, perhaps a boundary-stone, standing on the common at Harrowgate, in Yorkshire, concerning which the inhabitants can only tell you, that 'the oldest man that ever lived there knows nothing about it.' A single stone, or peulvan, in the department of the Haute-Marne in France, is said to bear a Latin inscription, stating that it marked the ancient limits of the Leuci. That such stones marked the sites of battles, or were memorials of celebrated events, is a mere assumption. Although the stones of the so-called Druidic monuments are in general rough and untouched with a tool, some instances are known, as in the extraordinary sepulture of Gavr'inis in the Morbihan (Brittany), and at New Grange, in Ireland, where they have been sculptured with rude ornaments. In some instances in England, one of the stones of a cromlech is pierced with a round hole, perhaps accidental, or the result of caprice.

Long after the people who raised them had passed away, and when their meaning, and the object for which they were erected, were alike forgotten, these monuments of stone continued to be regarded by the peasantry with reverence, which, combined with a certain degree of mysterious fear, degenerated into a sort of superstitious worship. In this feeling originated legends connected with them, and the popular names which are often found attached to them. Stonehenge was called the Giants' Dance (*chorea gigantum*), a name no doubt once connected with a legend which has been superseded by the story attached to it by Geoffrey of Monmouth. A circle in Cornwall, of which we have given a sketch on a former page, is called Dance Maine, or the dance of stones, and is said to be the representation of a party of young damsels who were turned into stones because they danced on the Sabbath Day. According to a somewhat similar legend, a party of soldiers, who came to destroy Long Compton, were changed into the Rollrich stones in Oxfordshire. The people of Brittany declare that the extraordinary multitude of stones arranged upright in lines at Carnac, was an army of pagans changed into stones by St Cornilly. As we have seen, the Saxons believed that a cromlech in Berkshire was a workshop of their mythic smith Weland. A cromlech on Marlborough Downs is called the Devil's Den. Legends like these, which are found in every part of our island, are generally good evidence of the great antiquity of the monuments to which they relate. In France, as in England, and indeed in most countries, they are usually connected in the popular belief with fairies or with demons—and in England often with Robin Hood. In France this latter personage is replaced by Gargantua, a name made generally celebrated by the extraordinary romance of Rabelais. A cromlech near the village of Toury, in Brittany, is called Gargantua's stone; a not uncommon name for the single stone or ménhir is *palet de Gargantua* (Gargantua's quoit). A very common name for cromlechs among the peasantry of France is fairies' tables, or devils' tables, and in one or two instances they have obtained the name of Cæsar's table; the covered alleys, or more complicated cromlechs, are similarly named fairies' grottos, or fairy rocks. The single stones are sometimes called fairies' or devils' seats. The prohibition to worship stones occurring so frequently in the earlier Christian ecclesiastical laws and ordinances, relates no doubt to these Druidical monuments, and was often the cause of their destruction. Traces of this worship still remain. In some instances people passed through the Druidical monuments for trial, or for purification, or as a mode of defensive charm. It is still a practice among the peasantry at Columbiers, in France, for young girls who want husbands, to climb upon the cromlech called the *Pierre levée*, place there a piece of money, and then jump down. At Guerande, with the same object, they depose in the crevices of a Celtic monument bits of rose-coloured wool tied with tinsel. The women of Croisic dance round a ménhir. It is the popular belief in Anjou, that the fairies, as they descended the mountains, spinning by the way, brought down the Druidical stones in their aprons, and placed them as they are now found.

In a great number of cases, the British cromlechs, like the barrows of other periods, are placed on lofty hills, commanding extensive views of the sea, if on the coast, or, when inland, of the surrounding country. It seems always to have been the desire of the chiefs to be buried in such commanding positions. A cromlech at Molfra, in Cornwall, is thus situated on a bare hill, which commands a wide range of view over Mount's Bay. The mound of some Celtic chief has once been raised on the elevated summit of Pen-maen-mawr, in Wales, of which the circle of stones that confined its base alone remains at the present day. It would be difficult to select in this respect a finer position than that occupied by Kits-Cotty House, in Kent, of which a slight sketch is given in the cut in the next page. This large cromlech stands on the summit of a lofty knoll, a little in advance of the chalk-hill which rises behind. Below, the Medway winds in its course from Maidstone to Rochester. Further on extends a wide valley, bounded on the north by another range of chalk-hills. Under these latter hills, at the spot indicated in the cut by three crows, lies the parish of Addington, in which are several circles, cromlechs, and other early sepulchral monuments; and from this spot, proceeding in a direct line eastward, large upright stones are found at intervals, which seem to have belonged to an avenue extending from the group of monuments at Addington to the foot of the hill on which Kits-Cotty House stands, a distance of not less than five miles. The hill behind Kits-Cotty House is also covered with sepulchral monuments, consisting of smaller cromlechs and circles, either thrown down or partly buried; and there are several remarkable cromlechs and circles in the fields below; all seeming to indicate that this valley was the burial-place of a British tribe. Another class of monuments are found on the hill above Kits-Cotty House.

Kits-Cotty House, in Kent, from the hill above.

Large stones, resembling the ménhirs, are found lying flat on the ground, and, on excavating, it is discovered that they are placed over round pits cut in the chalk, and filled up with flints. None of these have yet been carefully investigated, but, on the opposite hills, and in other parts in the neighbourhood, are found similar pits open, communicating with chambers cut in the chalk, regarding the purpose of which many conjectures have been hazarded, but it is not improbable that they were sepulchral.

Very few of the cromlechs and stone chambers in Britain had been uncovered from their mounds of earth in recent times, under proper examination. This deficiency has been compensated, in some measure, by the extensive and careful researches among the cromlechs of the Channel Islands, by Mr Lukis,[*] although there would, no doubt, be found a marked difference between their contents, which belonged to Gaul, and those of the British monuments of a similar character. But there is another numerous class of barrows, which are generally

---

[*] Mr Lukis's different accounts of his researches in the Channel Islands will be found in the first volume of the 'Archæological Journal,' pp. 142, 222; and in the 'Journal of the Archæological Association,' vol. i. pp. 25, 305, 311; vol. iii. pp. 4, 269, 342; vol. iv. p. 323.

considered to be British, but which do not contain the sepulchral chamber or cromlech. Numerous examples of this class of barrows have been opened in Wiltshire, Dorsetshire, and Derbyshire, and a few in other parts.* These are the only barrows in this country which have furnished us, to any extent, with articles which, from a chain of indirect evidence, are believed to be British. These barrows differ very much in form and size. The interment is sometimes placed on the level of the ground, and sometimes in a shallow grave dug below the surface, with variations in the manner of burial which can only have arisen from individual caprice. The body is sometimes found to have been buried entire, while, perhaps, in a majority of cases, it had been burnt, and the ashes deposited in rude urns. When the body was interred without cremation or burning, it was sometimes stretched at full length, and at others doubled up and laid on one side, or was sometimes placed in a sitting position. The urns containing the burnt bones are sometimes found in their natural position, and sometimes inverted, with the mouth downwards. When upwards, the urn is often covered with a flat stone. There is no evidence to support the conjectures of some writers, that these different modes of burial belong to different dates; it seems more probable that they were fashions adopted by different families, or by subdivisions of tribes or septs, but it would be a vain speculation to attempt to give a decided opinion on such questions, with the little we know of the manners and history of the ancient inhabitants of this island. It is certain, however, that all these different modes of interment are often found in the same barrow, for some of the barrows seem to have been family graves, and it is rare to find only one interment, while the larger barrows contain usually a considerable number of urns and bodies. In many cases these are distinguishable into primary and secondary interments, and so on, and in opening these barrows the excavator is never sure in what part of the mound he will find a deposit. A very large

* Numerous barrows in Wiltshire were opened by Mr W. Cunnington and Sir Richard Colt Hoare, the latter of whom has given copious descriptions of them in his 'Ancient Wiltshire;' those of Derbyshire have been largely examined by Mr Thomas Bateman, and described in a very useful volume, the 'Vestiges of the Antiquities of Derbyshire.' Some of the British barrows in eastern Yorkshire have been opened by Lord Londesborough; many of those of Dorsetshire were opened by the late Mr Sydenham, by Mr Warne, Mr C. Hall, and other local antiquaries, whose reports of their discoveries are found scattered over volumes of the 'Archæologia,' and of the 'Journal of the Archæological Association.'.

barrow near Dorchester, was found to consist of a low primary barrow, on which subsequently a second interment had been placed, and then a new mound raised over it. Sometimes the different interments are arranged in regular order. In the Deverill barrow, between Whitechurch and Milbourne St Andrew, in Dorsetshire, opened in 1825, and described in a little volume by W. Augustus Miles, the urns were found arranged in a circle under protecting stones. Throughout these early barrows we find much irregularity, and evidently a good deal of caprice in the mode of burial.

Some few years ago I had the direction of the opening of a large tumulus at St Weonard's in Herefordshire. This was a large barrow, its diameter at the base being, as near as I could roughly measure and calculate it, about a hundred and thirty feet, and its elevation from the ground somewhat more than twenty. The summit forms a circular platform, about seventy-six feet in diameter, levelled in such a manner that my first impression was that the tumulus had been truncated. The edge of this platform is planted with large fir and other trees, among which is a decayed yew tree, of great antiquity, and a tall poplar stood exactly in the centre. It appears that, until a recent period, the platform on this mound was the usual scene of village-fêtes, and that it was the spot especially chosen for morris-dancing, a custom very prevalent in Herefordshire, and that the poplar tree in the middle was used as the village maypole. Placed on a bold isolated eminence in the middle of the village, the height of the mound gives to its summit a wonderfully extensive prospect around. In the popular belief these mounds were generally looked upon as sepulchral, and this at St Weonard's was believed by some to have been the grave of the hermit so named, from whom the neighbouring church had taken its name, and by others that of some great chieftain. The appearance of this tumulus at the time it was excavated is shown in the accompanying cut. The men began their work on the south-eastern side, with a cutting from eight to nine feet wide, in a direct line towards the north-west.

I have described the process of opening this fine tumulus in the first volume of my Essays on Archæological Subjects,* from which I extract the following. 'At about six feet above the level of the base of the tumulus there was an evident difference

---

* 'Essays on Archæological Subjects and on various questions connected with the History of Art, Science, and Literature, in the Middle Ages,' vol. i. p. 62.

in the character of the soil, and the appearances were strongly in favour of the belief that this was the original surface of the

Sepulchral Tumulus at St Weonard's, Herefordshire.

ground, which must in that case have been very uneven. Acting on this belief, we took this as the level of our cutting, which was exactly fourteen feet deep from the top of the mound. On a Thursday afternoon, when the workmen had arrived within about fifteen feet from the centre of the mound, they came upon what appeared to be the base of a heap of large flat stones (the sandstone of the spot, which breaks up into this form), rudely built up one over the other, and so completely free of earth within that we could thrust our arms in between them. My first impression was that we had come upon a cairn, and I thought it advisable to clear away the earth from above, before removing the stones. This operation occupied the whole of the day on Friday. We found that, instead of being the base of a large cairn, the stones formed a small mound, and then sunk again; but we found also a layer of these large stones along the level of our cutting, until near the centre they began to rise again, and evidently reached a somewhat greater elevation than before. It was now thought advisable to carry the cutting to a little distance beyond the centre, and the poplar tree was sacrificed. It was not till Saturday night that this operation was nearly completed, leaving uncovered a great part of the heap of stones in the centre, which presented the appearance of the exterior of a rude vault. On Monday, the 16th [of April], the stones in the centre were cleared away, and within them appeared a mass of much finer mould than the rest of the mould. This mould also was cleared away to the level of the cutting; but as yet no indications of a sepulchral interment presented themselves, although the workmen were still of opinion that they were on the original hard surface of the ground. But of the accuracy of this opinion I now became very doubtful, and on the following morning I directed the men to sink a pit on the spot which had been covered by the vault of stones. They had not proceeded far before they came to a mass of ashes, mixed with pieces of charcoal and fragments of burnt human bones, which was found to be about a foot and a half thick, and was apparently about nine or ten feet in diameter. A piece of thigh bone, part of the bone of the pelvis, and a fragment of the shoulder-blade, were picked up here; and it appeared evident that the whole of the ashes of the funeral pile had been placed on the ground at this spot, and that a small mound of fine earth had been raised over them, upon which had been built a rude roof or vault of large rough stones. No traces of urns, or of any other manufactured article, were met with. Having been thus successful in discovering the central deposit, our attention was now turned to the first mound of stones, and it was determined to clear those away and dig below our level there also; and the result was the discovery of another interment of ashes, also mixed with human bones in a half-burnt state. This last operation was performed on the morning of Wednesday, the 18th of April; after which the excavations were discontinued.

'The accompanying diagram, giving a section of the mound in the direction of our cutting (which is shown in the shaded part), will give the best notion of the position of the two deposits

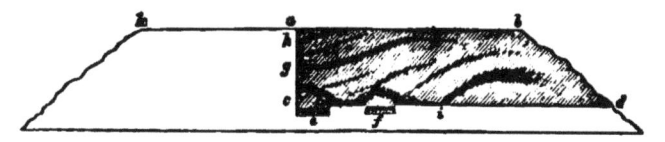

Section of the Tumulus at St Weonard's.

at *e* and *f*, which represent the two pits dug through the ashes, (represented by the black lines), to a small depth below. One o. the most interesting circumstances connected with the cutting itself was that of the regular discolorations visible on the surface, arising, of course, from the employment of different kinds of material, and displaying in a most remarkable manner the mode in which the mound was raised. These are carefully figured on the accompanying section. As I have already stated, the mass of the mound consists of a uniform light-coloured sand; but from the point (*i*) near where we first fell in with the stones, a narrow arched stripe occurs of a much darker mould, as represented in the cut. Beyond this, two or three other bands of a similar description, but thinner, and of a lighter-coloured soil, and, therefore, less strongly marked, follow each other until, at *g*, we come upon a narrow band of small stones, also represented in the cut, and at *h*, near the summit of the mound, there is another bed of similar stones. It is evident, therefore, that when the small mounds roofed with stones had been raised over the deposits of ashes, a circular embankment was next formed round the whole, and from this embankment the workmen filled up the interior inwards towards the centre. When they began filling in they appear to have fallen in with some darker mould, which has formed the band at *i*, and this dark band probably defines very nearly the outlines of the first embankment. The lighter-shaded bands show the successive fillings-in towards the centre, until at last the workmen made use of a quantity of stones and rubble, taken perhaps from the quarry which furnished the large stones of the interior vaults. This bed of stones forms a kind of basin in the middle of the mound. They went on filling again with the sand till the work was nearly finished, when they returned to the stony material again, which appears at *h*. The length of our cutting from *c* to *d* was, as near as I could measure it with accuracy, 46 feet 6 inches, and that of the surface from *a* to *b*, was 64 feet 5 inches; as I have stated before, the height of this cutting was 14 feet. The distance from *a* to *k* was 29 feet 7 inches, making therefore the diameter of the platform on the top of the mound, in the direction of our cutting, exactly 76 feet. This I found to be rather the longest diameter, for the circle had not been quite a perfect one, though very nearly so.'

The excavation of this fine barrow left no doubt of its sepulchral character, but no remains were found to show definitely the people to whom it belonged, or the period at which it was erected. It belongs to that class of monuments which are evidently not more modern than the Roman period, and, having no decidedly Roman character, have been set down as British. Perhaps the truth is that it belongs to the perhaps earlier Roman period, but that the persons to whom it belonged were natives of the soil who sought to be buried in the Roman manner. The old road from Monmouth to Hereford, which runs by it, was perhaps a Roman road from *Blestium* to *Magna*.

To judge by the barrows hitherto opened, it was not the custom of the Britons to inter with their dead many articles of value. By much the greater number of barrows, whether large or small, are found to contain nothing but urns and burnt bones. In some cases we find a few implements of stone or bronze, and, in much rarer instances, beads and fragments apparently of other personal ornaments occur. As these articles furnish the only evidence of the age of the barrow, and as they admit of easy classification, they deserve particular attention. The pottery, as being of more universal occurrence, demands our first consideration. It is in general, though not always, very rudely made, not baked, but merely dried in the sun. Its forms are peculiar, and have none of the elegance of the Roman urns. They are ornamented more or less with parallel lines, zigzags, crosses, dots, and other marks, which appear usually to have been made by the hand, with some instrument like a stick sharpened to a point, though they are sometimes more elaborately and skilfully worked. Many, however, have no ornament at all, which are usually those containing burnt bones.

A few examples are here given of the more ordinary forms of what are believed, and apparently with good reason, to be British urns. The most remarkable, and in general the most carefully ornamented, class of British earthen vessels is that of which specimens are here given, marked 1, 2, 3, 4. They vary much in size, and in general have nothing in them. Some have called them incense cups, while others have believed them to be drinking cups. No. 1 was found by Sir Richard Colt Hoare, at the side of a skeleton in a barrow near Stonehenge; the original is about nine inches and a half high. No. 4, found by Mr Cunnington, also in a barrow in Wiltshire, was about the same height, and six inches and a half in diameter over the brim, holding about two quarts. This was a red ware, not bright like the Roman pottery called Samian ware; and Mr Cunnington found, at the same time, a much smaller vessel, of the same form, but of a darker-coloured pottery. Nos. 2 and 3 were found by Mr Bateman: the first in a barrow called Green Lowe, on Alsop Moor, in Derbyshire, with a skeleton; and the other in a large barrow at Castern, near Wetton, in Staffordshire, also with a skeleton. In the latter instance, Mr Bateman says, that the vase had internally an incrustation, as though it had contained some liquid when deposited in the grave. Urns of this description, which are baked, and not sun-dried, are found more frequently in the south of England than elsewhere.

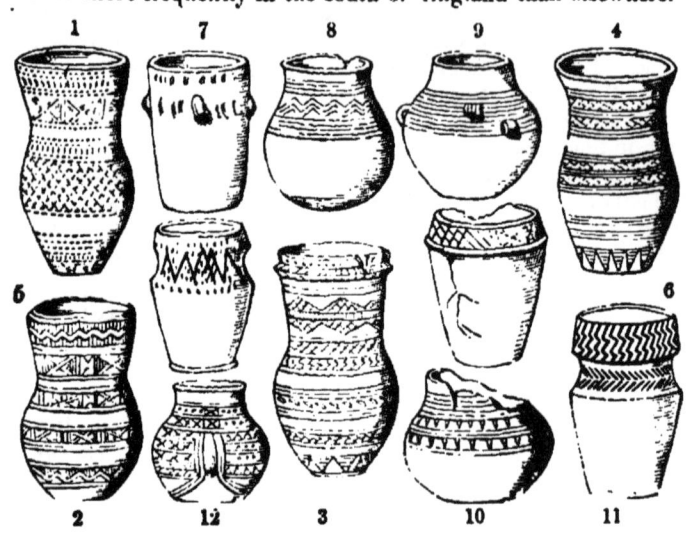

British Pottery.

One found by Sir Richard Colt Hoare, in a barrow at Stonehenge, was not above three inches high. These cups are usually found with skeletons. The urns, Nos. 5 and 6, are from barrows in the neighbourhood of Dorchester, opened by Mr Sydenham, and described in the thirtieth volume of the Archæologia. The first was seven inches and a half, the other nine inches in height, and both had contained burnt bones. Urns of the form No. 6, are frequently found in an inverted position. Nos. 7, 8, 9, and 10, were found with a great many others, more or less similar in form, in the Deverill barrow. The loops found in Nos. 7 and 9 occur not unfrequently in these British urns, but it is uncertain if they were intended for fixing cords for suspension, or if they were merely ornamental. An urn closely resembling No. 7, and found in a cromlech in the Channel Islands, has been engraved by Mr Lukis. The other three, and especially No. 10, bear a rather striking resemblance in form to a class of burial urns, which recent researches have proved to be Saxon, although they were formerly considered British. Specimens of these will be given further on; but one, taken from an Anglo-Saxon cemetery near Derby, is given here, No. 12, for the sake of comparison. The Anglo-Saxon urns are generally harder baked than the British; they are distinguished by some peculiarities in the form, and on closer examination the ornament will be seen to be of a different character, and made in a different manner. No. 11, in our cut, is an urn containing burnt bones, taken from a barrow in Cornwall. Similar urns are found in Wiltshire, Dorsetshire, and other parts, especially in Yorkshire.

The foregoing are the more usual forms of supposed British pottery, and will serve to give a general notion of its character. Many other varieties, and some much more rude in form and construction, occur, but they will generally be recognized by the similarity of ornament to those given here.

As I have already observed, the other articles found in the British barrows are not much diversified, and are of rare occurrence. They consist chiefly of implements of stone and implements of bronze. Those made of the former materials are usually the heads of axes or hammers, chisels, and arrow-heads.

Implements made of stone are found abundantly in all parts of the British Islands, and we might add, all over the world; and nothing seems more natural, not only in a very rude state of society, but also in much more civilized times, when communication between different parts of the country was slow, and metal was not always to be had, than to form rough tools or weapons, especially for the chase, of hard stones. Stones of a siliceous character, which were chipped into the required forms without much difficulty, were used most generally for this purpose. But other kinds of stone were also used.* Our cut in the next page represents a few of the more usual types of the implements of stone found in this country, chiefly taken from originals preserved in the museum of the Society of Antiquaries. Nos. 1 and 2 are different samples of axe-heads, the first, which is elaborately cut, found by Mr Bateman in a barrow in Derbyshire, the other from the bed of the Severn at Ribbesford in Worcestershire; 3 and 4 appear to have been used as chisels,

* Mr Lukis (Journal of the Br. Arch. Ass., vol. iii. p. 127) gives the following list of the substances from which stone weapons in his possession, chiefly found in the Channel Islands, are made: serpentine, greenstone, granular greenstone, indurated claystone, trap greenstone, claystone, quartz, syenite, schistus, yellow hornstone or chert, granular porphyry, siliceous schist, serpentine or jade.

96 THE BRITONS. [CHAP. III.

and are very sharp at the broad end. No. 8 is a spear-head
9 is an instrument apparently intended for stabbing or boring;
7 is a chisel of a different form from the others; and 10 is a
piece of flint notched at the edge, so as to serve as a saw.
Several of these stone saws have been found in different parts

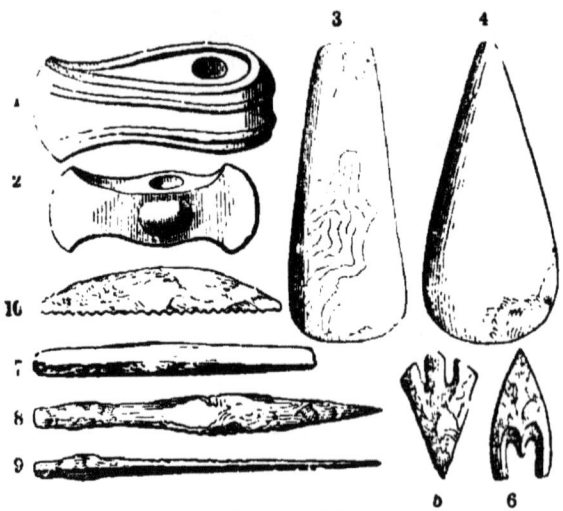

Implements of Stone.

of England. Nos. 5 and 6 are arrow-heads, taken by Sir
Richard Colt Hoare from barrows in Wiltshire, where, as well
as in Derbyshire, they are frequently found. A very large and
remarkable collection of stone implements, found chiefly in the
more easterly districts of Yorkshire, has been made by Mr
Edward Tindall, of Bridlington.

Stone knives are mentioned in the Old Testament (Joshua
v. 2), in a way which shows that implements of this material
may have been employed at times for special purposes. It has
been assumed rather hastily that where we find these implements of stone, the people to whom they belonged were not
acquainted with the art of working metals. That stone and
metal were in use for such implements at the same time is quite
evident from the manner in which they occur together. In the
tumuli in Wiltshire, the stone arrow-heads are usually found
with bronze daggers. In Derbyshire stone implements are found
not only with bronze, but with iron. Thus, in a barrow opened

at Minninglowe by Mr Bateman, an upper deposit of two skeletons was accompanied with an urn, a flint arrow-head, a small piece of iron, and part of a horse's bit; and lower down, in the same barrow, an earlier interment, in a stone cist or cromlech, was accompanied with an iron knife or dagger in a sheath of the same metal. Another interment in the same barrow was accompanied with an ornamented urn of the same description as the four first figures in the preceding group of British pottery, a small brass pin, and an arrow-head of grey flint. In a small barrow at Middleton-by-Yolgrave, a flint arrow-head was found with one of the small bronze chisels or axes, which will be described further on. In a barrow called Carder-lowe, along with a great number of implements of flint, were found a bronze dagger and an iron knife; there had been several interments, no doubt at different periods, but the bronze dagger was found in a lower, and therefore older, deposit than one which contained nothing but flint implements. A large barrow opened by Mr Bateman in 1846, was supported at the base by a regular circle of large stones, and had in the interior a cromlech. Within the latter was found a skeleton, which was accompanied with 'a brass dagger of the usual type, measuring six inches and a quarter in length, and in the highest preservation; it has the appearance of having been silvered, and still retains a brilliant polish. . . . near it were two instruments of flint, and two more were found during the progress of the examination of the tumulus.' A barrow with a cromlech cist opened by the same gentleman in 1847, contained a skeleton, with a flint spear-head and a bronze pin or bodkin, which had been inserted in a wooden handle.

The stone chisels or axes are less frequently found in tumuli, than in accidental localities where there is nothing to fix their date or to indicate the people to whom they belonged. They are sometimes met with in a very rough condition, and sometimes more or less finished, and in one or two instances, bundles of finished and rough stone implements have been found, as though they belonged to the stores of a manufacturer. This is most frequently the case with the arrow-heads. In other instances, especially in Scotland, bundles of flint chippings, or, as they have been termed, flint flakes, have been found, which appear to have been struck off from a solid mass, and, as these generally occur in districts where flint is not found naturally, we are justified in regarding them as importations of the rough article, merely formed to the size required by the manufacturer. In examining these implements in the different stages of their manufacture, as thus presented to us, we become convinced that not only must implements of metal have been used in making them, but that some machine like a lathe must have been used in boring and finishing them. Besides the fact just stated of their having been deposited in the same interments with instruments of metal, insulated facts have occurred corroborating the conclusions which we should naturally draw from this circumstance. In France some of the stone implements are said to have been found with handles of bone, but we are assured of a circumstance still more interesting, that at old Toulouse one of these stone implements was found, in the place of its original deposit, surrounded with *a circle of iron* that had evidently fixed it to its handle.* Instances might be adduced of the continuation of the use of implements of stone down to a much more recent date. According to the recital of William of Poitiers, some of the Anglo-Saxons fought with weapons of stone at the battle of Hastings : † and they are said to have been employed by the Scots as late as the wars of Wallace.

The older implements of metal found in this island are generally of bronze. I here give a group of the more usual forms of those attributed generally to the British period, all, except No. 8, taken from specimens in the museum of the Society of Antiquaries. No. 1 is the usual form of the bronze axe-head or chisel, to which the name of celt has been given, not because it was conceived to be characteristic of the Celtic race, but because our earlier antiquaries supposed it to be the instrument to which the Romans gave the name of *celtis* (a chisel).‡ It has a socket for receiving the handle. Nos. 2

---

* See a paper in the *Mémoires de la Société Archéologique du Midi de la France*, tom. i. p. 78.

† Jactant cuspides ac diversorum generum tela, sævissimas quasque secures, et lignis imposita saxa. p. 201, ap. Duchesne. These stones, fixed on pieces of wood, were perhaps used for striking, as with clubs.

‡ The earliest dissertation on these instruments I know, is one by the well-known antiquary, Thomas Hearne, to whom the historian Thoresby communicated some examples in his possession, found in Yorkshire. Hearne wrote a long and learned epistle to Thoresby, in the December of 1709, which he printed as an appendix to the first volume of his edition of Leland's Itinerary, under the title of 'A Discourse concerning some Antiquities found in Yorkshire,' and in which he stated his opinion that these instruments were the Roman *celtes* or chisels. This opinion seems to have been generally acquiesced in by Hearne's contemporaries, and this particular tool obtained the name of a *celtis* or *celt*. Subsequent writers, ascribing these instruments to the Britons, have retained the name, forgetting its

CHAP. III.]   BRONZE IMPLEMENTS.   99

and 3, the latter found in the Isle of Thanet, and lately in the museum of my friend Mr Crofton Croker, are also common

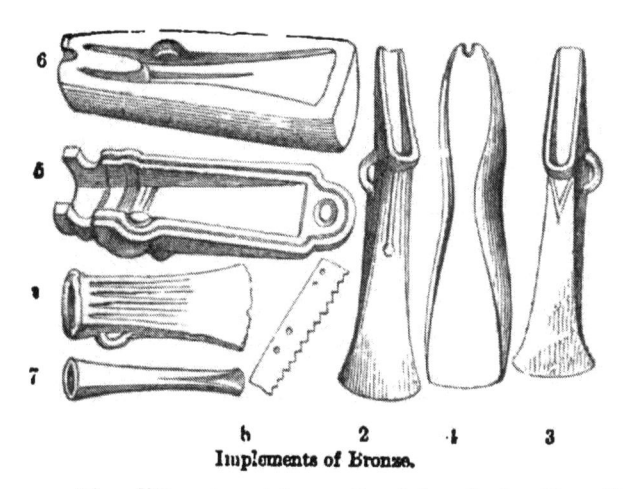

Implements of Bronze.

forms, with a different contrivance for fixing the handle. No. 4 is another variety, exhibiting a much rarer form. There can be no doubt that these were tools in very common use by workmen in England at some period, for they are found very frequently, though very rarely in sepulchral interments, all over the island; and rather numerous instances have occurred of the discovery of considerable quantities of them, whole or broken, under circumstances which can leave no doubt of their having been the stock in trade of some maker of such instruments. They are found in great abundance in the county of Norfolk: and they generally occur along with chisels of different forms, and sometimes with spear-heads and daggers. In a meadow at Stibbard, in the county of Norfolk, no less than seventy of the so-called celts, and ten spear-heads of bronze, were found in a single lot. In 1845, a quantity of such instruments, including the chisels or axe-heads of the usual forms, with punches, gouges, and other similar instruments, as well as several pieces of unused metal, one of which appeared to have been the resi-

origin, and have applied it indiscriminately, not only to other implements of bronze, but even to the analogous instruments of stone. It is not good as a technical term, because it is mistaken too generally as implying that things to which it is applied are Celtic, and it would therefore be better to lay it aside.

duum left in the melting-pot, were found at a village near Attleborough, in the same county. A similar discovery of bronze chisels, gouges, &c., with portions of a bronze sword, was made at Sittingbourne, in Kent; and another occurred some years ago in Shropshire, at the foot of the Wrekin. More recently, at Westow, about twelve miles from York, a collection of sixty similar instruments, presenting the same varieties, with the addition of a piece of dagger or sword, and a similar piece of bronze, which appeared to be the residuum from melting, were found in an earthen jar or vase. A very similar hoard was found in the parish of Lanant, in Cornwall, in the year 1802; and Leland has recorded the discovery of a similar hoard in the parish of St Hilary, in the same county, in the time of Henry VIII.* A parcel of the so-called celts, spear-heads, and fragments of swords, of bronze, were found by Mr Lukis in the Isle of Alderney, under similar circumstances.

No. 7, in our cut, represents a bronze chisel, from a specimen in the museum of the Society of Antiquaries, and will serve to give a general idea of the forms of these instruments, as found with the 'celts.' We are convinced at once that all these instruments have been cast in moulds, and accordingly several examples of these moulds have been found, both in England and other countries. I have given examples, Nos. 5 and 6, from casts in the museum of the Society of Antiquaries, of two such moulds, found in Normandy; they represent the two varieties of which we have examples in the cut, Nos. 1, 2, and 3. No. 8, in our cut, is a fragment of a bronze saw.

I have stated that antiquarian writers have been in the habit of calling these bronze tools British, but I am inclined to believe that Hearne was nearer the truth when he pronounced them to be Roman. The localities in which they have been usually found, especially when they have occurred in any quantities, have generally been Roman sites. One of the moulds engraved above, is said to have been found by the side of a Roman road, and the other at a place well known for its Roman antiquities. The discovery at Sittingbourne, in Kent,

* 'There was found of late yeres syns, spere heddes, axis for warre, and swerdes, of coper, wrappid up in lynin scant perishid, near the mount in St Hilaries paroch in the tynne works.'—Leland's Itin., ed. Hearne, vol. iii. p. 7. The discoveries alluded to in the text will be found more fully described in the 'Archæologia,' vol. xv. p. 118; in the 'Journal of the British Archæological Association,' vols. i. pp. 51, 69, and ii. pp. 9. 58; and in Mr Roach Smith's *Collectanea Antiqua*, vol. i. pp. 101, 106.

was made also near a Roman road, in the immediate vicinity of an extensive Saxon cemetery, and perhaps further researches will lay open Roman remains. The general shape and character of these instruments seem to be much more like Roman than anything we know of Celtic make; and I believe they are found in Italy. The question here raised is, however, one of considerable obscurity, until further discoveries, and a more

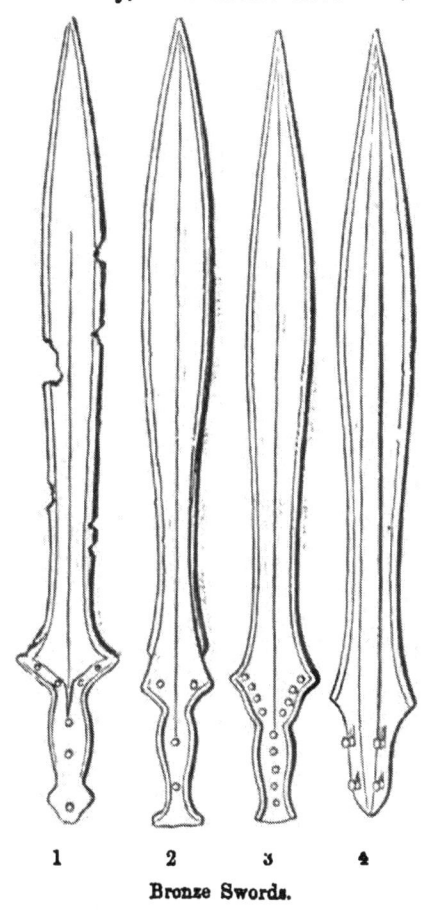

1   2   3   4
Bronze Swords.

careful observation of the circumstances under which they are found, shall enable us to clear it away.

The fragments of swords found in one or two instances with these parcels of bronze instruments, were apparently placed there as old metal. They belong to a class which have usually been considered as Celtic by English antiquaries, but which I have always regarded as unmistakably Roman. They are found in England and Scotland, in Ireland, in Denmark (less frequently), in Germany, in France, and, I believe, in Italy. Four specimens are given in the preceding cut. The first is preserved in the museum of the Society of Antiquaries of England, but it is uncertain where it was found. The second was found at Arthur's Seat near Edinburgh, and is now preserved in the museum of the Society of Antiquaries of Scotland. The third was found in the bed of the Thames, near Vauxhall, and the fourth at Twerton, near Bath. The two last are engraved in the Journal of the Archæological Association. They are short, usually from sixteen to eighteen inches in length, and were evidently used for thrusting rather than for cutting.

These swords, in whatever country we find them, are so uniform in shape, that we can hardly doubt their being all the workmanship of one people. They do not answer the ancient descriptions of the swords used by the Celts and Germans, who, from the time when Marius encountered the Cimbrians and Teutons, to the great battle in which Agricola defeated the Britons under Galgacus, are described as using long pointless swords.* Indeed, I believe, all people in a rude state, whose soldiers are not highly disciplined, are more apt to use swords for striking than thrusting. We know that the Romans had an advantage over their British foes in close combat, from the circumstance, that they used their short and pointed swords in thrusting, while the Britons were unable to use with the same effect their long pointless ones. The swords of the form figured above have, I think, been generally found on or near Roman sites. Many are taken up from the Thames, where such multitudes of Roman Antiquities are found, but no other swords that can be accounted Roman. The question, however, seems to be set at rest by discoveries in France. One of these swords was found at Heilly, in the department of the Somme, with other articles, among which were four

---

* Besides the mention of these long swords in the accounts of the battles mentioned in the text, Dion Cassius, lib. xxxviii. c. 49, in his account of Cæsar's battle with Ariovistus, in Gaul, mentions the large long swords of the barbarians.

brass coins of Caracalla; and another was found in another locality along with skeletons and coins, some of which belonged to the emperor Maxentius, so that they could not have been deposited there before the beginning of the fourth century after Christ.* It may be added, that in the museum of the Louvre, in Paris, there is one of these bronze leaf-shaped swords (as they are usually termed), with its sheath, the latter undoubtedly Roman; and I am informed that there is another similar sword and sheath in the Musée de l'Artillerie, also in Paris.

It is well known that in some countries the use of copper and bronze for weapons and other instruments preceded that of iron. Copper weapons are supposed to have preceded those of bronze. The alloy of tin in the latter metal gave it a hardness and a brittleness not possessed by the pure copper, and the ancients are said, though on late and doubtful authority, to have employed a method of tempering it as we do steel. The weapons of the Homeric age were of these materials, which appear to have been regarded almost with a superstitious veneration by the Romans. In the treaty between Porsena and the Roman people, about four hundred years before the Christian era, it was expressly stipulated that the Romans should not use iron except for implements of agriculture.† It was not till three hundred years later—that is, after the second Punic war—that the Romans began to use iron in the fabrication of arms; and it is a very remarkable circumstance, that in the battle in which the Gauls were defeated by the consul Æmilius, when the Romans used swords of bronze, those of the Gauls, as we are told by Polybius, were long, and so badly tempered, that they bent when the Gallic warriors struck a hard blow against the Roman armour. It would appear, from their being tempered, that they were made of iron.‡

Among the most curious of the instruments of bronze found in this country, are the daggers or knives, which are not unfrequently found in the barrows supposed to be British, and were no doubt peculiar to the people who were buried in them.

* These are described in the fifth volume of the *Mémoires* of the Institute of France, class of *Littérature et Beaux Arts*, pp. 193 and 501. I give the reference from the work of M. Mauduit, mentioned below.

† In fœdere quod repulsis regibus populo Romano dedit Porsena, nominativè comprehensum invenimus, ne ferro nisi in agricultura uterentur.—*Plinii Hist. Nat.* lib. xxxiv. c. 14.

‡ Much information on the early use of bronze will be found in the *Découvertes dans la Troade*, by M. Mauduit, Paris, 1840.

The usual forms of these instruments will be best understood by the accompanying cut. They are found frequently without

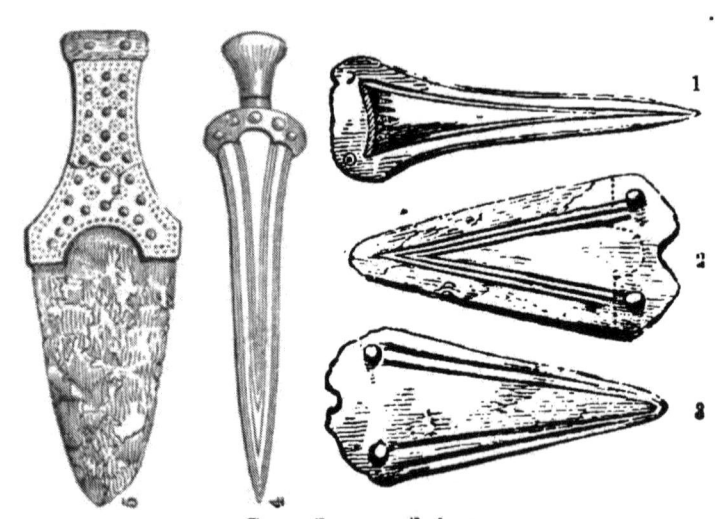

Bronze daggers or knives.

handles, but with the rivets which fixed them, and the blade generally bears marks of having been placed in a shank of wood. The handle appears to have been generally of the same material, and has only been preserved where, in particular instances, it has been made of ivory or bone. The blades are from six to ten inches long; sometimes they are much smaller. At first, until one was found with a handle, they were supposed to be spear-heads. In a barrow at Normanton, in Wiltshire, Sir Richard Colt Hoare found the handle of one of these daggers, of wood, richly ornamented with zig-zags and lines, resembling those found on the pottery, formed by innumerable diminutive points or pins of gold driven into the wood. It is in the barrows of Wiltshire and Dorset that these bronze daggers are found most abundantly. A few have been met with in Derbyshire, and they occur more rarely in Scotland; they are, however, not uncommon in Ireland; they are also found in Gaul. The figure No. 2, in the group above, represents one of these dagger or knife blades of the more usual form, which was found in a barrow called Dowe-lowe, near Church-Sterndale, in Derbyshire, opened by Mr Bateman: it accompanied a skeleton. No. 5, is a dagger of the same form, with a handle, found by Sir Richard Colt Hoare in a barrow at Brigmilson in Wiltshire, accompanying an urn with ashes; and No. 3 is a blade of exactly the same form, found in Ireland, and formerly in the possession of my friend the late Mr Crofton Croker. No. 1 is a somewhat similar bronze blade, found at Pitcaithly, in Perthshire; while the other, No. 4, with the same shaped blade, but with its handle of ivory, came from a barrow near Blandford, in Dorsetshire. This latter is in a perfect state of preservation; it was found with two bronze spear-heads, lying beside an urn with burnt bones.

There are very few other articles found under circumstances which could lead us to ascribe them to the Celtic population of our island. Bronze spear-heads, often with loops at the side, are found under the same circumstances as the swords, and no doubt belonged to the same people. A few personal ornaments, chiefly beads, with now and then a piece of bone or metal, are found in some of the barrows of Derbyshire, Wiltshire, and Dorset. Several discoveries have also been made of circular shields, generally of bronze, and of rather small dimensions, which have been considered to be British, though the justice of this appropriation is doubtful. Traces of a metal covering for the breast, very thin, and therefore more for ornament than protection, have also been found with skeletons, apparently of this early date. The most remarkable discovery of this kind was made in the October of 1833, at Mold, in Flintshire. A mound, composed of pebbles and stones, had long stood at the corner of a field, and it was then cleared away for agricultural purposes. It was found to contain interments of urns and burnt bones, and also, in another part of the mound, a skeleton, round the breast of which was a corset of thin gold, embossed with an ornamentation resembling nail heads and lines. This interesting article is now in the British Museum. This barrow was called by the Welsh peasantry *bryn-yr-ellyllon*, or the hill of fairies or goblins; and it was believed to be haunted. But the most curious circumstance connected with it was the declaration, made before it was opened, of a woman of the neighbourhood, that, as she was going home late one night and had to pass by it, she saw moving over the barrow, a spectre '*clothed in a coat of gold*, which shone like the sun.'

It is the business of the antiquary, by comparing and discriminating the objects of each period, to make them throw new light on the manners and condition of the people to whom they belong, and also to endeavour to trace, by their peculiarities, the movements of the different tribes, and the positions they occupied. Unfortunately, the antiquities of the British period have as yet proved but of little use in either of these points of view. The solitary dagger, with the few fragments of pottery, and two or three beads or pins, can give us no satisfactory notion of the dress or riches of the person who wore them. If, as Cæsar says was the practice among the Gauls, the Britons buried with their dead all the articles of value they possessed, they must indeed have been poor. But it is hardly probable that the contents of the graves, as we now find them, are any fair measure of the wealth of those who were buried in them. We can feel no doubt, after a comparison of their contents, that the cromlechs and the other barrows of which we have been speaking, belong to the same people, and that they are of about the same date. They occur in large groups. The Kits-Cotty House group belongs to Kent; there was another group in the valley of the White Horse, in Berkshire; another lay in Oxfordshire; a larger group lay in Dorsetshire; then came the vast group about Stonehenge; and finally, a tolerably numerous one in Cornwall. The only large group of the interior is that of Derbyshire. There is a group towards the south-east of Yorkshire, and they are scattered over Wales, and in the Isle of Anglesea. This distribution would certainly lead us to imagine that the barrows and other monuments of this island, which we are accustomed to attribute to the Druids, belong, not to the earlier Celtic population, but to the later settlers. If this be the case, we might perhaps go further, and assume that the British population of the earlier mining districts, Cornwall, Wales, and Derbyshire, was also composed of later settlers, who knew how to work the metals, of which the earlier aboriginal tribes were perhaps ignorant. But these are obscure questions, which we are, from want of accurate knowledge, unable to solve; and it must not be forgotten that the cromlechs are numerous in Ireland.

The next question that presents itself, with relation to these monuments, is their date, which I am inclined to believe less remote than is usually imagined. It has often been a fault among antiquaries to be too eager in fixing great antiquity on everything about which they are uncertain. The comparison of these barrows with one another, while it shows that some of them had served apparently for family sepulchres during a length of time, would lead us to think that they may in general be placed within no very wide limits. In times like these of which we are now treating, individuals possessed but a small quantity of personal property; the communication between one place and another was slow and uncertain; and while one man, by accident or through his superior wealth and power, had weapons and other implements of bronze or iron, or even of silver and gold, his neighbour might be obliged to remain content with a chisel or axe of stone, or, if a hunter, he might be satisfied with a few flint-headed arrows to his bow. In the same way, one man might be rich or ostentatious enough to depose in the grave elegant vessels of superior manufacture, while another at the same time would use only the rude urn of clay and gravel baked hastily in the sun. Nothing indeed is more unsafe than the rule that mere rudeness of construction is a proof of antiquity. One or two circumstances have been discovered that are certainly rather startling. In Belgium, on the borders of the Ardennes, a cromlech with a Roman interment in it has been recently found in the middle of a Roman cemetery.* A discovery of a somewhat similar kind was made by Mr Bateman, in his researches among the barrows of Derbyshire, which he describes as follows: 'In a plantation on the summit of Minninglowe Hill,' he says, 'are two tumuli of large size, one being nearly fifteen feet high from the level of the ground. In the centre, and in four places in the area of the circle, are large cists, or, as they now appear, from the soil being removed from them, large cromlechs, exactly of the same construction as that well-known Druidical structure, Kits-Cotty House. They are formed of the large limestones of the country, and have all had covers of the same, only two of which now remain in their places. . . . . The soil in the interior of the cists of the large barrow was removed down to the surface of the rock on the 5th of July, 1843, when it was found that all the interments had been before removed, with the exception of one, which was a skeleton, laid at full length on the outside of the cist, unaccompanied by any weapon or ornaments. In the cell near which this body lay, were found fragments of five

---

* 'Le seul tombeau qui, dans ce cimetière Romain, méritait ce nom, consistait en cinq énormes pierres en quartiers de roches. Trois de ces pierres formaient un triangle dont les deux autres étaient la base et le couvercle. Dans ce tombeau, ainsi que près des assiettes mortuaires, j'ai trouvé des ferrements et des clous, qui indiqueraient que ces restes de Romains auraient été enfermés dans une sorte de cercueil en bois, dont il ne reste plus trace.'—*Bulletin de la Société Historique et Archéologique de Soissons*, tom. iii. p. 187.

urns, some animal bones, and six third brass Roman coins, namely, one of Claudius Gothicus, two of Constantine the Great, two of Constantine Junior, and one of Valentinian. An attempt to penetrate the substance of the mound was then made, which, from want of time, proved ineffectual. A few human teeth, and a third brass coin of Constantine, were the only relics found in this part of the excavation.' Sir Richard Colt Hoare also found Roman coins in one of the supposed British barrows in Wiltshire.

These facts might perhaps be considered to be accidental; but it is very remarkable that the only excavation within the area of Stonehenge of which we possess any account, brought to light Roman remains. We are informed by Aubrey that the Duke of Buckingham, in 1620, 'did cause the middle of Stonehenge to be digged, and this under digging was the cause of the falling downe or recumbencie of the great stone there.' He tells us that in the course of this 'digging' they found 'a great many horns of stags and oxen, charcoal, batter-dashes (?), heads of arrows, some pieces of armour eaten out with rust, and rotten bones.' An inscribed tablet of tin is pretended to have been found at Stonehenge, in the reign of Henry VIII.; and, according to Inigo Jones, the cover of a *thuribulum*, or incense-cup, was found within the area at a later period. 'In more modern times,' adds Sir Richard Colt Hoare, whose description is more to be depended upon, 'we have found, on digging, several fragments of Roman as well as of coarse British pottery, parts of the head and horns of deer and other animals, and a large barbed arrow-head of iron. Dr Stukeley says that he dug close to the altar, and at the depth of one foot came to solid chalk. Mr Cunnington also dug about the same place to the depth of nearly six feet, and found that chalk had been moved to that depth; and, at the depth of three feet, he found some Roman pottery, and, at the depth of six feet, some pieces of sarsen stones, three fragments of coarse half-baked pottery, and some charred wood. . . . In digging into the ditch that surrounds the area, Mr Cunnington found similar remnants of antiquity; and in the waggon tracks, near Stonehenge, you frequently meet with chippings of the stones of which the temple was constructed. Soon after the fall of the great trilithon in 1797, Mr Cunnington dug out some of the earth that had fallen into the excavation, and found a fragment of fine black Roman pottery, and since that another piece in the same spot; but I have no idea that this pottery ever lay beneath the stones, but probably in the earth adjoining the trilithon, and, after the downfall of the latter, it fell with the mouldering earth into the excavation.'

Although some of the remains of antiquity which are from time to time dug up in our island may belong to an age more remote, the most probable view of the case seems to be, that the mass of our British antiquities belong to the age immediately preceding the arrival of the Romans, and to the period which followed.

The date of one class of British antiquities, the coins, are more easily fixed, and they will, perhaps, eventually throw some light on one period of British history. These coins have been found in considerable quantities in most parts of England, often in hoards, and they are remarkable for the large proportion in gold and silver. Many of them have inscriptions, always in Roman characters, which, as far as we can judge from discoveries hitherto made, express the names of the chiefs for whom they were minted. In form they resemble the Greek coinage, being thicker in proportion to their size than Roman coins, and usually slightly convex on one side and concave on the other. Some of these British coins show a considerable degree of artistic skill, and bear distinct representations of human heads, animals, and other figures, while a still greater number are extremely rude, and some of them bear confused marks and attempts at devices which appear totally inexplicable. These, like everything that is mysterious, have furnished ground for many theories, founded on the supposition that they had some connection with the mythology or history of the British tribes. But a more careful study and comparison has shown us that the British, like the Gallic coinage, consisted merely of imitations of Greek and, subsequently, of Roman coins. It appears that when the chiefs began to mint money, they adorned it with mere copies of the figures on foreign coins brought as models by their coiners, and that, while their relations with Rome induced them to adopt Roman inscriptions, they chose in preference the forms and pictorial devices of the money of Greece, selecting especially those of the Macedonian kings. The first minters were probably brought over from Gaul, and they made tolerably good copies of the originals, as we find to be the case in many of the coins of Cunobeline. Subsequently these copies served again as models to British and very unskilful artists, and in their hands they gradually degenerated into forms which can only be understood when we place them beside the more perfect copies from which they were imitated. Sometimes we only trace the British imitation of the Greek coin through an intermediate Gallic copy. To explain better this gradual degeneration, and furnish at the same time an example of one of the ruder types of the British coins, we give a cut representing three gold coins, in their obverses and reverses. The uppermost is a gold stater of Philip of Macedon. The

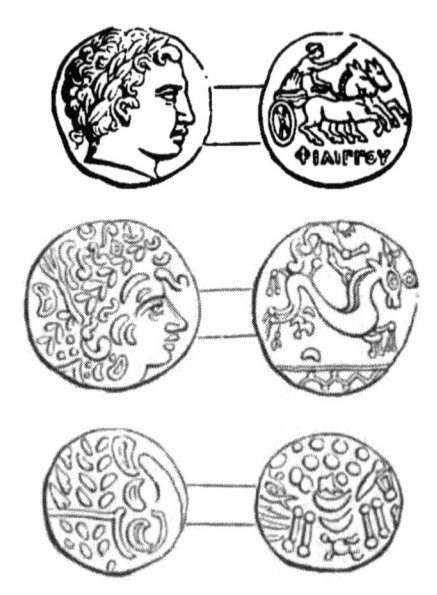

Greek and British Coins.

second is a gold coin of one of the Gaulish chiefs, in which the head of the king is copied in a very rude manner, with the wreath round the head; but the charioteer and horses are given in a manner much more rude, though still distinguishable. The name of Philip has been transformed into a rude ornament. The lowermost coin is a rude British copy of the same type—one of a hoard of British gold coins found in Whaddon Chace. Until compared with the two previous coins, we cannot even guess at what the coiners intended to represent; but on laying the three coins thus side by side, we trace distinctly on the obverse the wreath and ears of the head of Philip of Macedon, while it is equally evident that the reverse was intended as a copy of the charioteer. In this, as in many cases of the British coinage, the die was cut clumsily and much larger than the piece of metal which was to receive the impression. Hence the coin only represents a part of the subject, and as the metal sometimes fell on one side of the field, and sometimes on another, we have often to compare several examples of a British coin before we get the design complete; and the accidental discovery of one which contains a portion of the design not previously found often explains what was before unintelligible. Our next cut represents another palpable copy

Greek and British Coins.

of a Greek coin. The large figure is the obverse of a silver tetradrachm of Alexander the Great, in which that monarch is represented under the character of Hercules, with the head and mane of the lion's skin over his head, and the claws tied in a knot under his neck and chin. The smaller coin beside it is a silver coin of a British chief, whose name is represented by the Roman letters EPAT. Mr Beale Poste has, I think, mistaken part of what was intended to represent the lion's claws for a Greek K, and he proposes to read the inscription in Greek characters, KEPAT (*kerat*), which he interprets as referring to Caractacus. But, in general, the British coins seem rather to have been struck by chiefs who were friendly or submissive to the Romans, than by those who were warring against them. The eagle on the reverse of the coin just described was probably also copied from a Greek or Roman model. Among the Roman coins copied by the Britons is one of Augustus, with a figure of Victory seated on the reverse. Future examinations and discoveries will, no doubt, lead to the identification of them all. A figure of an animal, on some British brass coins found in Kent, is evidently the rude copy of an elephant, from one of the consular coins. The charioteer of the coin of Philip, copied more or less rudely, is rather a common reverse of the British coins. Many of the figures, still unintelligible, will probably be explained by future discoveries. One of the reverses of the coins of Tasciovanus, which has been described as 'an unknown ornament,' seems to have been intended for the prow of a Roman galley.

The knowledge of British coins is as yet in its infancy, and comparatively little has been done towards classifying them in a satisfactory manner. From the process of degeneration shown above, and other circumstances, it appears that the ruder coins are often to be considered, in point of date, as the latest, and not as the earliest. The best in point of workmanship, and the most numerous, are those of Tasciovanus and Cunobeline: of the latter nearly fifty varieties are already known. Of the names inscribed on these coins, the varieties are not numerous, and it seems most probable that they all represent chiefs. The greater number are, unfortunately, without inscriptions, and, therefore, it is impossible from the coins themselves to determine the tribes or chiefs to whom they belonged. By careful observations of the places where they were discovered, certain types have been found to be peculiar to certain districts, and it is not unreasonable to suppose that they belonged to the British tribes there located. But we must wait till further discoveries throw light on this subject. It is impossible to say how long the British coinage remained in circulation; but it has been found mixed with Roman money, though I believe the latter was of the consular period or of the earlier emperors.

Among the monuments of a remote period which it is most difficult to class, are the earthworks and entrenchments which are found in considerable numbers in every part of our island. In some parts there is scarcely a hill-top which is not crowned with a circle of ditches and embankments, and in some cases they are of colossal magnitude. These have been ascribed, too indiscriminately and too hastily, to the British period, and have been called British camps and British towns. In some cases, it will be found, on examination, that these entrenchments were merely intended to inclose a barrow or a cemetery. Some of them were, probably, medieval. They may, in some instances, have inclosed a primitive town or village: and we know that the early Anglo-Saxon mansion was a mere structure of wood inclosed by an earthen entrenchment. It has been also rather too hastily assumed that the Romans never, under any circumstances, departed from the rectangular system of castrametation, which is not justified by a careful examination of facts.

Nevertheless, if there is a difficulty in fixing the date of what are usually called British camps, there is one very interesting class of earthworks which, doubtless, belong to an early period, and which are scattered over many parts of our island. They are generally found at some distance from the Roman towns, but they are usually not far from Roman roads. These are groups of shallow pits, or rather of bowl-shaped excavations, on the surface of the ground. These curious works have been observed with most care by Sir Richard Colt Hoare, in Wiltshire, who calls them British villages; but they occur in Leicestershire, Derbyshire, Yorkshire, and probably in most other parts of the country, where the traces of them have not been obliterated by cultivation; but some of the most perfect specimens are met with on the Wiltshire downs. Two such traces of settlements are found on Knook Down, near Heytesbury, which seem to have been protected by an ancient fortress, now called Knook Castle. Sir Richard Colt Hoare states that 'the site of these villages is decidedly marked by great cavities and irregularities of ground, and by a black soil. Where the moles were more abundant, numerous coins were constantly thrown up by them, as well as fragments of pottery of different species. On digging in these excavations, we find the coarse British pottery, and almost every species of what has been called Roman pottery; also *fibulæ*, and rings of brass worn as *armillæ* or bracelets; flat-headed iron nails, hinges of doors, locks and keys, and a variety of Roman coins, of which the small brass of the lower empire are the most numerous, and particularly those of the Constantine family. Of the larger and first brass, we have coins of Vespasian, Nerva, Antoninus, Trajan, Julia Mammæa, and Postumus; of the denarii, we have Caligula, the elder Faustina, Julia Mammæa, the elder Philip, Gallienus, and Gratianus : the small brass are too numerous to particularize, but some of the smallest are remarkable, having only a radiated head (often very rude), and one or two Roman letters, which, perhaps, may have been struck during the latest struggles between the Britons and Saxons. In digging within these British villages, we have but rarely discovered any signs of building with stone or flint; but we have several times found very thin stones laid as floors to a room. The fire-places were small excavations in the ground, in which we have frequently found a large flat hearthstone; and in two parts of this extensive village we have discovered hypocausts similar to those in the Roman villa at Pitmead, near Warminster. These are regular works of masonry, made in the form of a cross, and covered with large flat stones, well cemented by mortar. We have also, during our investigations of this spot, repeatedly found pieces of painted stucco, and of brick flues; also pit-coal, and some fragments of glass, or crystal, rings, beads, &c. In one of the banks raised for the old habitations, we discovered a skeleton with its head laid towards the north; at its feet was a fine black celt [of stone], and at the distance of a few feet was a bead. In this, as well as in the generality of other British villages, the attentive eye may easily trace out the lines of houses, and the streets, or rather hollow ways conducting to them; these are particularly visible in the upper village on these downs, as well as the entrance to it. The whole adjoining country is also strongly marked by the intersection of slight banks along the sides of the hills, which point to us the limits of ancient British cultivation, and in many instances the smallness of them will show the contracted scale on which agriculture was at that time carried on.'

Several groups of similar works are described by the same writer in different parts of his great work on ancient Wiltshire. Of these not the least remarkable is the very extensive group called the Pen Pits, near Stourton, the character of which appears somewhat doubtful. Another group, of a more definite character, runs along the brow of a slight eminence in the neighbourhood of Wily, known by the popular name of Stockton Works. 'Stockton Works,' says Sir Richard Colt Hoare, 'appear to have been originally surrounded by a ditch, and a single rampart of earth, of which a considerable part towards the east still remains; but the western boundary, and many of the interior works, have been much defaced by a great waggon track, which for many ages has passed through the works. The original entrance was on the eastern side, near the head of a steep valley; but many other adits, of a more modern date, have been made for the accommodation of waggons frequenting the wood. At one point there is also an entrance to an inner work, where we see numerous excavations, &c., and near the centre is a singular little work of a pentagonal form; and beyond it the irregularities and cavities continue deep and numerous for a considerable distance to the westward. These works cover the space of sixty-two acres, and extended, probably, much further towards

the west, and into the wood on the south, but they are so defaced in many places, and in others so very doubtful, that what now remains can only be considered as a very imperfect specimen of the original works. We have dug in various places within the area, and found both large and small Roman coins, pieces of brass, iron nails, fragments of millstones, brick flues, tiles, and both British and Roman pottery; also the neck of a glass bottle, of a sea-green colour; in short, all the vestiges of a numerous population.' The writer from whom we are quoting adds:—
'A series of coins, from the first Claudius to Theodosius, mark also their continued residence on this spot for a long period; they are so numerous and common, that the labourers employed to dig flints throw them up and leave them amongst the stones: twice, on visiting these works, I found coins in this situation.'

There can be little doubt that the excavations described by Sir Richard Colt Hoare are the floors of dwellings, the superstructure of which consisted of perishable materials; and we should be justified in considering them as the remains of the villages occupied by the pastoral and agricultural population during the Roman occupation of the island. What he calls British pottery was no doubt the commoner and rougher description of Roman ware; and the coins, which he could not appropriate, seem to have been the small rude coins, or possibly the later imitations of the Roman money, known to antiquaries by the name of *minimi*. This may be remarked as a very curious circumstance, because, though it has nothing to do with the antiquities of the British period, it seems to show, that in some parts of the island, even in the country villages, the peasantry were not driven from their habitations. In other parts of the country, we have not always the same certain indications of the people who inhabited the settlements indicated by their excavations, as were found in Wiltshire, and in some places perhaps they only mark the sites of villages of a much later date, destroyed amid the turbulence of the middle ages.*

---

* A careful antiquary makes the following remarks, in the *Leicester Chronicle*, on the 'Deserted Villages' of Leicestershire:—'On the north-eastern side of the county of Leicester may be found, apart from human habitations, sites of ancient villages, of which not a fragment is now visible above-ground. One of these lies near Ingarsby, a second near Cold Newton, and a third near Humberstone. An ordinary passer-by would not notice these curious sites, and the peasant may daily pass over their broken surfaces without experiencing any emotion of curiosity or interest; but it is not so with the intelligent man and the reader of history. In their

We find the habitations of the early inhabitants of these islands under circumstances which seem to denote a still lower scale of civilisation. These are the caves on the sea-coast, such as Kent's Hole, near Torquay, in Devonshire, and other caves on that and the Cornish coast, which interest the geologist as well as the antiquary. The cave just mentioned was explored by a local geologist, who has given the following account of the appearances which presented themselves when it was first examined:—'The floor of the entrance, except that it had the appearance of being broken up, offered nothing remarkable to detain us. We shall have occasion to return to it presently. Not so the lateral branch by which it communicates with the body of the cavern on the left. Under a ledge on the left was found the usual sprinkling of modern bones, and, in the mould beneath, which had acquired the consistence of hard clay, were fragments of pottery, calcined bones, charcoal, and ashes; in the midst of all were dispersed arrow-heads of flint and chert. The ashes furnishes a large proportion of the mould. In the same heap were discovered round slabs of roofing slate, of a plate-like form, some crushed, others entire. The pottery is of the rudest description, made of coarse gritty earth, not turned on a lathe, and sun baked; on its external margin it bears zigzag indentations, not unlike those represented on the urns found by Sir Richard Colt Hoare in the barrows of Wiltshire. These fragments, there seems no reason for doubting, are the remains of cinerary urns, which once contained the substances scattered around, and to which the slates served for covers. At a short distance, nearer the entrance, were found, in a continuation of the same mould, articles of bone of three sorts; some of an inch long, and pointed at one end, or arrow-

minds these spots excite inquiry and reflection. They know that the face of the country has witnessed many a "bloody broil," and that populous hamlets have been razed to the ground in the times of civil war or feudal contest. One of the sites well calculated to elicit observation lies, as we have hinted, near to Humberstone. About two miles to the north-east of it, midway between Barkby and Scraptoft, may be found a field presenting numerous irregularities of surface, which is known as the "Town field." On paying a visit to this a few days ago, we were struck with the evidence it afforded of former occupancy, and of having been covered with buildings and fortified works. It slopes in a northerly direction, a brook running along the lower ground. On the upper part may be traced very clearly three sides of an encampment or enclosure, defended by a mound and trench. In the part bordering on the brook, but higher up in the field, traces of the existence of buildings are obvious. There can be little doubt this is the site of the town of Hamilton, which is marked in maps as being in this quarter.'

heads; others about three inches long, rounded, slender, and likewise pointed. Conjecture was long busy as to their destination. They were thought by some to be bodkins, by others for confining the hair, like those ornaments used by the women in Italy; lastly, they were supposed, with more probability, to be a species of pin for fastening in front the skin which served savages for garments. The third article does not seem so easy to explain; it is of a different shape, quite flat, broad at one end, pointed at the other; the broad part retains the truncated form of a comb, the teeth of which were broken off near their root; whether it was used for a comb, or for making nets for fishing, is not clear. There was only this solitary example found, and two of the former, but several of the first, with a quantity of bone chips. All three bore marks of polish. Nearer the mouth we collected a good number of shells of the mussel, limpet, and oyster, with a palate of the scarus. This, as well as the nacre of oysters, which was thickly disseminated through the mould, served, as they do at the present day among the savages, most probably for ornament. The shell-fish may have furnished bait for fishing. The presence of these rude articles renders it probable that they were collected here by the ancient aborigines, who divided their time between the chase and fishing in the adjacent sea. Close to the opposite wall, in the same passage, buried in black mould, I found a stone hatchet, or celt, of sienite, the only one found in the cavern. Another of the same material, but of a different shape, I found shortly after, not far from the cavern, near Anstis Cove, which labourers engaged in making the new cut had just thrown up with the mould. As we advanced towards the second mouth, on the same level, were found, though sparingly, pieces of pottery. The most remarkable product of this gallery were round pieces of blue slate, about an inch and a half in diameter, and a quarter thick. In the same quarter were likewise found several round pieces of sandstone grit, about the form and size of a dollar, but thicker and rounder at the edge, and in the centre pierced with a hole, by means of which they seem to have been strung together like beads. Clusters of small pipes or icicles of spar, such as depended from the roof at our first visit, we saw collected here in heaps, buried in the mud. Similar collections we had occasion to observe accompanied by charcoal, throughout the entire range of the cavern, sometimes in pits excavated in the stalagmite. Copper ore, with these various articles in the same stuff, was picked up; a lump much oxydised, which the late Mr Phillips analysed, was found to be pure virgin ore.

'Having taken a general survey of the surface of the floor, we returned to the point from which we set out, viz., the common passage, for the purpose of piercing into the materials below the mould. Here, in sinking a foot into the soil (for of stalagmite there remained only the broken edges adhering to the sides of the passage, and which appeared to be repeated at intervals), we came upon flints in all forms, confusedly disseminated through the earth, and intermixed with fossil and human bones, the whole slightly agglutinated together by calcareous matter derived from the roof. My collection possesses an example of this aggregation in a mass, consisting of pebbles, clay, and bone, in the midst of which is imbedded a fine blade of flint, all united together by sparry cement. The flints were in all conditions, from the rounded pebble as it came out of the chalk, to the instruments fabricated from them, as arrow and spear-heads, and hatchets. Some of the flint blocks were chipped only on one side, such as had probably furnished the axes; others on several faces, presenting planes corresponding exactly to the long blades found by their side, and from which they had been evidently sliced off; other pebbles still more angular and chipped at all points, were no doubt those which yielded the small arrow-heads. These abounded in by far the greatest number. Small irregular splinters, not referable to any of the above divisions, and which seem to have been struck off in the operation of detaching the latter, not unlike the small chips in a sculptor's shop, were thickly scattered throughout the stuff, indicating that this spot was the workshop where the savage prepared his weapons of the chase. . . . With the exception of a boar-spear (of iron) and a blade of the same metal not far from it, very much rusted, all the articles in the mould or in the disturbed soil consisted of flint, chert, sienite, and bone.' *

These caves, like the remains of the villages already described, were probably inhabited in the time of the Roman rule, but by that portion of the population who lived by fishing. We need only look to the condition of the fishers and wreckers on the wilder parts of the Cornish coast not a hundred years ago, to form a notion of what must have been the savage mode of life of a similar class in the same localities long after the Roman

* 'Cavern Researches; or, Discoveries of Organic Remains, and of British and Roman Reliques, in the Caves of Kent's Hole, Anstis Cove, &c.' By the Rev. J. MacEnery.

occupation. Caves of a very similar character have been discovered more recently in King's Scar, near Settle, in Yorkshire,* in which the remains are mostly Roman, and they were here mixed with coins, some of which were Roman, while the greater proportion belonged to that class of rude copies of Roman coins, struck when the island was losing its dependence on Rome. The fisher population is thus traced in these rude habitations, uninterrupted in their vocation, and probably unchanged in their condition and manners, through the revolutions of empires.

* A description of these singular caves, with a number of engravings, will be found in Mr Roach Smith's 'Collectanea Antiqua,' vol. i. p. 59.

CHAPTER IV.

Britain at the beginning of the Second Century—Towns enumerated by Ptolemy—Hadrian—The Wall—Lollius Urbicus; the Wall of Antoninus—Rebellion of the Soldiery in Britain—Albinus contends for the Purple—Campaigns of Severus, who dies at Eburacum (*York*)—The Caledonians—Carausius usurps the Purple—Allectus—Britain restored to the Empire by Constantius—Constantine the Great—Revolt of Magnentius—The Picts and Scots.

BEFORE the end of the first century, Britain was reduced to a Roman province; it began to receive an influx of population from foreign lands, and there appears to have been a frequent and general intercourse between this island and Rome. Its exports, and even its peculiarities, were already well known in Italy. The oysters of Rutupiæ (*Richborough*) were favourites at the table of the rich—

———— Rutupinove edita fundo
Ostrea,

and the whales which were seen in the British seas were proverbial for their magnitude—

Quanto delphinis balæna Britannica major.

The same poet, Juvenal, tells us that the learning and eloquence of Greece and Rome had established themselves in the far west—

Nunc totus Graias nostrasque habet orbis Athenas;
Gallia causidicos docuit facunda Britannos;
De conducendo loquitur jam rhetore Thule.

A boast of his contemporary, Martial, leaves no doubt of the rapid progress which civilisation had made in this land after the Roman legions had taken possession of it—

Dicitur et nostros cantare Britannia versus.

Indeed, various circumstances in subsequent history show that whatever was new at Rome was quickly communicated to this distant province of the empire.

The Roman troops had now, indeed, been long engaged in building towns and in making roads ; and under their influence the face of the country was undergoing a rapid and extraordinary change. We have seen that, after some of the British chiefs entered into relations with the Romans, a town or two were built, such as Verulamium and Camulodunum, in imitation, probably, of those on the Continent, and differing entirely from what had been called towns in the time of Cæsar. We have no means of ascertaining how many such towns were built, and it is by an assumption without authority that writers have been accustomed to say that this or that Roman town was built on the site of a previous town of the Britons. But under the influence of Roman manners and refinements, cities and towns soon rose up on all sides, and were joined together by an immense system of military and other roads. The first indication of these towns on any considerable extent is found in the pages of Ptolemy, who has merely enumerated those which were then of most account. We find that when he wrote (about A.D. 120), Rutupiæ was already the principal port of Kent, and the usual point of debarkation for visitors from the Continent. Not very far from it was another principal town of Kent, called Darvernum ($\Delta\alpha\rho o\nu\acute{\epsilon}\rho\nu o\nu$), no doubt a corruption of Durovernum (*Canterbury*). Londinium, which Ptolemy places in Cantium, was already, in the time of Tacitus, known as a great trading town. Within the district of the Regni of Surrey was Noviomagus, which seems to have stood in the neighbourhood of Bromley, on the borders of Kent. In the ancient district of the Belgæ were three important towns, Venta (*Winchester*), Aquæ Calidæ (*Bath*), and Ischalis (*Ilchester*). The small district of the Durotriges, in Dorset, possessed but one town which Ptolemy thought worthy of notice, and of that his copyists seem to have corrupted the name ; for it is probable that what he calls Dunium, was the same place called by later writers Durnovaria (*Dorchester*). Further west, in the territory of the Dumnonii, four towns are enumerated, one of which, Isca, is known to have occupied the site of the present Exeter, but the other three, Voliba, Uzela or Uxela, and Tamare, are less certain, though they are supposed to have stood respectively, the first on the river Fowey, the second in the neighbourhood of Bridgewater, and the third on the Tamar. The two districts to the north of the Belgæ, those of the Attrebates and the

Dobuni, had each an important city, the first called Caleva (*Silchester*), the other, Corinium (*Cirencester*).

North of the Thames were the towns of Camulodunum (*Colchester*), in Essex, and another, Venta (*Caistor*), in the country of the Iceni, in Norfolk. More westward lay Verulamium (*St Albans*), and, to the north of this town, another called Salinæ (Σαλῆναι), the site of which is supposed to be Salndy, or Sandy, near Biggleswade, in Bedfordshire. In the country of the Coritavi were Lindum (*Lincoln*), and Ragæ, or, according to the more correct reading, Ratæ (*Leicester*). In the small coast district to the north of the Humber, which had been the territory of the Parisii, there was a town called by Ptolemy, Petuaria, the site of which is not certain. Some of the most important Roman towns in the island were now scattered over the once wild haunts of the fierce Brigantes. First of these was Eburacum (*York*), the head-quarters of the sixth legion. The others were Isurium (*Aldborough*), Caturactonium (*Catteric*), Olicana (*Ilkley*), all in Yorkshire; Galagum or Galacum, an uncertain site, but supposed to be near Kendal, in Westmoreland; Epiacum (*Lanchester*), in Durham, Vinnovium (*Binchester*), in the same county, Rigodunum, believed to be the place subsequently called Coccium, in Lancashire, and Camunlodunum, or, as later writers call it, Cambodunum (*Slack*), in Yorkshire. Deva, the garrison of the twentieth legion, occupied the site of the present city of Chester. Below it stood Viroconium or Uriconium (*Wroxeter*), in Shropshire; Brannogenium (supposed to be near *Leintwardine*), on the northern borders of Herefordshire; and, more westwardly, Mediolanium, a town on the banks of the Tanad, in North Wales. Far down in the western part of Wales, in a part of Cardiganshire still rich in antiquities, was a town named Luentinum (*Llanio*); further south was Maridunum (*Caermarthen*); and eastward again, in the borders of the Silures, was Bullæum, supposed to be the same town which is mentioned at a later period under the name of Burrium (*Usk*). By confounding two names, Ptolemy has omitted the Silurian Isca (*Caerleon*), which was the head-quarters of the second legion.

Since the campaigns of Agricola, the conquerors had covered the lowlands of Scotland, as far as the borders of the great Caledonian forest, with an extraordinary number of towns and stations on the sites of most of which the spade still brings to light traces of Roman civilisation. Ptolemy enumerates no less than twenty towns (πόλεις) to the north of the Brigantes, the names of which were Lucopibia (*Whithern*), and Retigonium

(*Stranraer*), in the district of the Novantæ, on the extreme coasts of Galloway; Carbantorigum (*Kircudbright*), Uxelum, Corda, and Trimontium, the three last of uncertain site, but believed to have ranged across the district north of the head of Solway Firth, as they were in the district of the Selgovæ. The first two have been supposed by some to be represented by entrenchments found at Raeburnfoot, in Eskdale, and Birrenswork Hill, in Annandale. The Roman Trimontium is supposed to be Eildon, in Lauderdale. The Roman towns in the extensive district of the Damnii, who occupied the larger portion of the lowlands, were Colania (*Carstairs*), Vanduara (*Paisley*), Coria (*uncertain*), Alauna (*Kier*), Lindum (*Ardoch*), and Victoria (*Dealgin Ross*). In the district of the Otadeni were built Curia (*Currie*), and Bremenium (*Rochester*); in that of the Vacomagi,, bordering on the district of the Caledonians, Banatia (*Bonness*), Tamia (*Braemar Castle*), Pteroton Castrum (*Burghhead*), and Tuesis, a town on the Spey, perhaps at Cromdale; in that of the Venicontes, Orrea (*Bertha* at the head of the Tay); and among the Texali, Devana (*Old Aberdeen*).

The strength which was thus permanently established in the north shows us to what a state of dependence the Romans had now reduced all the southern parts of the island. Further evidence of this is seen in the distribution of the Roman legions, which had now been placed in the permanent quarters which they held until nearly the moment of their final withdrawal. The fourteenth legion, the one which had crushed the insurrection of Boadicea, had been drawn from Britain by Vitellius in the year 70, and had never returned. Several of the others had left at a still earlier period. Four only remained—the second, sixth, ninth, and twentieth. Of these, the second was posted at Isca (*Carleon*), and the twentieth at Deva (*Chester*), whence they held in restraint the mountaineers of Wales, and of Cumberland and Westmoreland, the retreat of such of the Brigantes as still retained their wild independence, and protected the country from the Irish pirates, who landed usually in the Severn and the Dee. The sixth legion was established at York, from whence it could be marched quickly into Scotland. After the last campaign of Agricola, the ninth legion suddenly disappears, and is no more heard of in history; but as we find it commemorated in inscriptions found at York, it is supposed to have been combined with, or incorporated into, the sixth. The north of England and the lowlands of Scotland were thickly covered with posts of auxiliaries; and we trace other bodies of auxiliaries scattered in the towns of the south, but not in such numbers as to lead us to believe that they were placed there as a curb on the population.

The Roman writers have, unfortunately, left us very few notices of the internal affairs of our island after it was reduced to a province; and for many years subsequent to the departure of Agricola, Britain is hardly noticed. We are, probably, to suppose from this, that it remained without any serious disturbances, and that the progress of Romanising and civilising went on without interruption. We do not even know who succeeded Agricola in the propraetorship, and we only learn incidentally that the governor of this province, towards the end of the reign of Domitian, was an officer named Sallustius Lucullus, whom that tyrant caused to be put to death for having allowed a new-formed spear he had invented to be called, after his own name, Lucullian. But the frequent weakness of the central power, and the various struggles for the empire, gradually enfeebled the imperial power in the distant provinces, and threw them into disorder. This was especially the case in Britain. During the reduction and conquest of the lowland tribes, the fierce Caledonians had risen into so much importance, that their name began not only to be used for the collective tribes to the north of the Brigantes, but it was adopted very often as a common term for the Britons in general—that is, for all those who had not acknowledged themselves Roman subjects. They probably carried on the same plan of warfare which was continued by their descendants to a comparatively recent period. Rushing unexpectedly from their strongholds in the mountains and forests, they swept over the open country, plundering, slaughtering, and burning, and disappeared with their booty before a sufficient force could be brought together to encounter them. In such warfare, wild tribes, who used to move about rapidly, with no permanent residences or possessions, had great advantages over a rich and civilized country, which it required a steady government and active and skilful commanders to protect. These seem to have been wanting during that period which preceded the accession of Hadrian, and it is probable that the successes of the Caledonians had encouraged some other British tribes to revolt. The emperor Hadrian visited Britain in person in the year 120, and he is said to have found many things that required reformation. We have no account of his proceedings, but it appears that he restored the island to order, and that he drove back the Caledonians into their fastnesses. We are justified in believing that he marched in person into the northern wilds, from the satirical verses of a contemporary poet,* and we learn from direct testimony that he caused that formidable barrier to be built across the island from the Solway to the Tyne, of which we still trace the stupendous remains; a massive wall, nearly seventy miles in extent, extending over plain and mountain, from Bowness on the Solway Firth to the now celebrated locality of Wall's End on the Tyne, accompanied on its southern side by an earthen vallum and a deep ditch, and fortified with a formidable series of twenty-three stationary towns, with intermediate mile-castles and watch-towers. It has been the custom to consider the wall only as the structure raised by Hadrian, while the earthen vallum or rampart was ascribed to Severus; but I entirely agree with Mr Collingwood Bruce, who has recently published a most interesting volume on 'The Roman Wall,' that both are parts of one work, erected by the former emperor.

This immense work seems to have been part of a system of circumvallation adopted by the emperor Hadrian, for it appears that remains of similar walls are found on the distant frontiers in Germany. I suspect it has been rather hastily supposed that it implies that this emperor relinquished the territory between it and the more northerly line of forts erected by Agricola; for the towns and forts to the north of the wall seem still to have been kept up, and to have been continued till the decline of the empire. Perhaps it was intended to protect the richer and more highly cultivated country to the south of the 'lower isthmus' from the sudden and destructive inroads to which it had previously been exposed. We know from the history of the border, at a later period, how far, without a barrier of this kind, the ravages of the Scots might be carried, and what damage might be effected before a sufficient force could be gathered on any particular point to drive them back.

* The historian Spartianus has preserved the epigram written on Hadrian by the poet Florus, as well as the emperor's reply. The first was contained in the three lines:

> Ego nolo Cæsar esse,
> Ambulare per Britannos,
> Scythicas pati pruinas.

To which the emperor replied as follows:—

> Ego nolo Florus esse,
> Ambulare per tabernas,
> Latitare per popinas,
> Calices pati rotundos.

The expedition of Hadrian seems to have been followed by a period of profound tranquillity,* and we learn from the historian Xiphilinus, that, about twelve years afterwards, the proprætor, or, as he was then called, the legate of Britain, named Julius Severus, was able to carry away some of his best officers and troops to assist in the war against the revolted Jews. The name of another proprætor under Hadrian, perhaps the successor of Julius Severus, Priscus Licinius, has been found in inscriptions, but nothing further is known of him.

Hadrian was succeeded, in the year 138, by the emperor Antoninus Pius. His proprætor in Britain, Lollius Urbicus, was a man of energy and talent, which he was soon called to exercise in withstanding a new irruption of the northern barbarians. We learn, quite incidentally, of an insurrection to the south of Hadrian's wall, at this period.† The remains of the Brigantes seem to have preserved a precarious independence, perhaps in the rugged country extending from the wilds of Lancashire over the lake district, in the same manner as wild Irish clans occupied the Wicklow mountains for ages after the surrounding plains had acknowledged the domination of the Anglo-Normans, and these probably imitated the northern Caledonians in making occasional predatory outbreaks. On the present occasion these had attacked a small tribe living under Roman subjection, called the Genuni, to which they had perhaps been encouraged by the invasion of the Caledonians beyond the wall. The Brigantes were quickly overwhelmed, and we are told that the greater part of the tribe was destroyed. The Roman arms were equally successful against the Caledonians, who were driven into their mountains, and Lollius Urbicus caused a new barrier to be raised for their restraint. We have seen how, when Agricola had reduced the lowland districts to subjection, he erected a line of forts across what has been termed the upper isthmus, from the Forth to the Clyde. Lollius Urbicus raised, on the same site, a new line of forts, and joined them together by an immense continuous rampart, of earth and turf, which from the name of the emperor under

---

* The expedition of Hadrian to Britain was commemorated by several coins in large and middle brass, which are interesting, because some of them give on the reverse a figure seated with a spear and shield, which, as it is surrounded by the word BRITTANNIA, is supposed to have been intended for a personification of Britain. These coins, especially the large brass, are rare.

† This insurrection and destruction of the Brigantes is mentioned by Pausanias, Arcad. lib. viii. cap. 43.

whom it was built, is usually called the wall of Antoninus. It is now called popularly Graham's Dike, and along its course are frequently found inscribed tablets commemorating the portion built by the different troops and cohorts of the Roman army.* We learn from these inscriptions that, besides the numerous bodies of foreign auxiliaries which were permanently stationed in the north, the three legions in Britain, the second, the sixth, and the twentieth, were all drawn from their quarters to take part in the campaign of Lollius Urbicus. His successes threw splendour on the reign of Antoninus, and coins were struck bearing on the reverse a figure of Victory surrounded by the letters of the word BRITANNIA.

In spite of the energetic measures of Urbicus, the Caledonians soon reappeared in arms, and the circumstance that they seem almost always to have risen on the death of the emperor, shows that the barbarians must have had intelligence among their enemies. They calculated, no doubt, that, amid the hesitating inactivity which naturally followed such an event, they might make an extensive raid with less danger of interruption. The Roman province was thus invaded on the accession of Marcus Aurelius, in 161, but the invaders were checked by a new proprætor, Aufidius Victorinus. An invasion of a still more formidable character followed the accession of Commodus; a Roman commander, who attempted to arrest their progress, was killed, and his army cut to pieces; and the emperor was obliged to send an officer who was remarkable for his extraordinary perseverance and capability of sustaining the hardships of war, named Ulpius Marcellus, to support the authority of Rome in this distant province. From this man the Caledonians met with terrible reverses, and the island was again restored to peace. Ulpius Marcellus was, however, soon recalled, for, in the eyes of a tyrant like Commodus, merit itself was a crime. His departure was followed by a mutiny among the troops in Britain, arising from dissatisfaction at the proceedings of the imperial favourite Perennis, who displaced the men of senatorial rank from the commands which they had always held, and

---

* The following, from a richly sculptured stone found at West Kilpatrick, is the usual formula of these inscriptions:

IMP. C. T. AE. HADRIANO ANTONINO AUG. PIO P.P. VEX. LEG. XX. V. V. P. P. P. $\overline{IIII}$ CDXI.

To the emperor Cæsar Titus Ælius Hadrianus Antoninus Augustus Pius, the father of his country. A vexillation of the twentieth legion, (surnamed) the valiant and victorious, executed four thousand four hundred and eleven paces.

appointed in their stead younger men taken from the equestrian order. The officers in Britain met and consulted, and they finally sent an armed deputation of fifteen hundred men to lay their grievances at the foot of the throne. When they arrived at the gates of Rome, Commodus went out to meet them, and, aware that there was discontent among his other troops, and that it might be dangerous to provoke them, he abandoned his minister to his accusers, and they put him to death. Still the troops in Britain remained unsatisfied, and the mutiny continued, on which Publius Helvius Pertinax, a commander of great military talent, was sent to appease them; but instead of returning to their obedience, they disclaimed the authority of Commodus, and invited their new commander to be their emperor. This he prudently declined, and he succeeded in restoring order in the province, though not without considerable personal risk, for, in opposing himself to the fury of one of the mutinous legions, he was struck down, and left for dead.

At length Pertinax obtained his recall, and was succeeded in the proprætorship by Decimus Clodius Albinus. This governor soon made himself popular in his government, especially among the troops, and he seems even to have retained the favour of the emperor Commodus, who conferred upon him the title of Cæsar. At length an unfortunate accident had nearly proved his ruin. It was reported that Commodus was dead, and this rumour quickly reaching Britain, Albinus assembled his troops, and addressed them on the event. He used some expressions in his speech which, being repeated before the emperor, gave so much displeasure, that an order was immediately despatched for the recall of the proprætor, and a creature of Commodus, named Junius Severus, was appointed to succeed him. But the murder of Commodus, before the order could be carried into execution, saved Albinus for a more glorious, if not for a happier fate.

The imperial throne was now occupied for a moment by the same Pertinax who had preceded Albinus in the government of Britain. He was raised to the purple by the prætorian guards, who, three months afterwards, rebelled and cut off his head, and then offered the empire for sale. The disgraceful purchase was made by a rich but worthless merchant, named Didius Julianus. Three commanders, in different parts of the empire, stepped forward at this moment to resist the tyranny of the prætorian soldiery, and expel the emperor of their choice; these were, Severus in Pannodia, Pescennius Niger in Syria, and Albinus in Britain. Severus, with his characteristic activity, was the first in the field, and, marching upon Rome, put to death the usurper, degraded the prætorian guards from their privileges, and assumed the purple. Severus was a man possessing extraordinary talents for empire, indefatigable in pursuing the object of his ambition, unscrupulous in attaining the object of it, and merciless towards those who stood in his way. He had gained possession of the empire, but he had still two competitors in the field, against whose united forces he would perhaps have been unable to struggle. It was his policy therefore to separate his rivals, and while he prepared to march against Niger, he pacified Albinus with professions of the warmest friendship, conferred upon him the title of Cæsar, and, making him nominally his associate in the empire, caused money to be coined in his name, and statues to be erected in his honour. Albinus thus gained over, Severus proceeded to the east to encounter Pescennius Niger.

This occurred in the year 193. Niger was defeated in battle near Antioch, and slain, and after a protracted struggle, Severus returned victorious to Rome in 196, and prepared to rid himself of his other rival Albinus. The governor of Britain was a formidable antagonist; he also was a man of great military talents; he was popular in his province as well as in Gaul, and he was closely allied by blood and friendship with some of the greatest and oldest families in Rome. He was ambitious, too, and, though his vanity had been flattered by the honours showered on him by Severus, he seems to have let it be known that he was not yet satisfied, and that he aimed at securing for himself the imperial dignity. We are told that, during the absence of Severus in the east, Albinus had been invited to Rome to assume the purple, and that it was the knowledge of these intrigues which determined the emperor Severus to destroy him. This was not, however, an easy task. It is evident that the Roman province of Britain had become at this time extremely populous and rich. Multitudes of auxiliary troops had been gradually transplanted into it, and had no doubt taken with them or been followed by colonies of their countrymen. Merchants, tradesmen, artisans, even probably artists, and men of letters, had sought their fortune where the increase of commerce and civilisation opened a field for their exertions. The strength of the native Britons had been drawn off to serve in foreign countries;* and that part of the original population which re-

* It was the constant policy of the Romans to draught off the rising

mained at home had probably been greatly diminished in numbers, and reduced to the condition of serfs. In fact, from this time forward, when the Roman writers speak of the Britons who existed in the island as a people, they include under that name only the Caledonian tribes of the north. Britain was thus looked upon as one of the most powerful and important provinces of the empire; and its proprætor, surrounded by troops devoted to his person, with a population which seems to have been always ambitious of an independent emperor of its own, might easily set the court of Rome at defiance. Severus, therefore, aware of all these circumstances, determined to destroy his opponent by treachery, and he wrote him a letter in terms of the most affectionate friendship, which was entrusted to messengers in whom he could confide for the execution of his secret orders. These were, that they should endeavour to obtain a private interview with Albinus, and if they succeeded they were instantly to slay him; if they were not admitted to a private interview, they were to insinuate themselves among his cooks and with the servants who waited at his table, and by bribing them, convey a deadly poison, which the emperor had given them for that purpose, into his food. It happened that Albinus and his officers were well aware of the treacherous character of Severus, and that they were on their guard. His messengers had no sooner arrived in Britain, than they were seized, and so strictly examined, that they made a full confession. They were at once ordered for execution, and Albinus, conscious that now his only chance of safety was immediate action, caused himself to be proclaimed emperor, and declared war against Severus. He marched into Gaul, and took possession of the city of Lyons, near which was fought the decisive

population of the conquered provinces, and send them to occupy stations; and, in fact, to form colonies in other countries. It was, indeed, the most effectual manner of destroying the nationality of the people they had subjected to their power; for, feeling no natural sympathy with the land in which they were settled, and regarded only as Roman soldiers, they gradually came to consider themselves as a part of Rome. We find, mentioned in old writers and in inscriptions, numerous *alæ* and cohorts of Britons in various parts of the Roman empire. According to the Notitia, the fourth ala of Britons was stationed in Egypt. The twenty-sixth cohort of Britons occurs in Armenia. A body of the 'Invincible Younger Britons' were stationed in Spain, and one of the 'Elder Britons' in Illyricum. The 'Younger British Slingers' *exculcatores* are found among the Palatine auxiliaries. Other bodies of Britons are found in Gaul, Italy, and other countries. Britons of the tribe of the Horesti (in Scotland) have been traced by Mr Roach Smith on the banks of the Rhine. See his 'Collectanea Antiqua,' vol. ii. p. 134.

BATTLE OF LYONS.

battle which secured the empire to Severus, and put an end to the ambitious projects of Albinus by his death. The power of the province of Britain was exhibited in the numerous and excellent army which its governor led into the field. The ancient historian from whom we obtain the most detailed account of these events, Xiphilinus, estimates his force at a hundred and fifty thousand men, part of whom probably were Gauls; and, if we suppose this to be exaggerated, it is certain that his soldiers were sufficiently numerous and brave, to leave the event long doubtful in a contest with the military force of the empire under the command of the emperor himself.

The great battle of Lyons was fought on the 19th of February, 197. It appears probable that the victor immediately appointed to the government of Britain one of his commanders who had served in the campaign against Albinus, named Virius Lupus, who perhaps led back the shattered remains of the British legions. At all events, we find this officer established there as proprætor very soon afterwards. At this period some great change was taking place in the population of North Britain, which we have a difficulty in explaining, though it is supposed to have arisen from a large immigration of foreign tribes, perhaps from the north of Europe. The slight notices of events in Britain given by the Roman writers throw no light upon the subject, further than showing us that the Caledonian tribes had suddenly become much more numerous and formidable, and that apparently a new tribe under the name of Mæatæ had established themselves immediately to the north of the barrier of Antoninus. Dion Cassius, the historian of these events, informs us that 'the two greatest tribes among the Britons are the Caledonii and the Mæatæ, for even the names of all the other tribes have in a manner merged in these two. The Mæatæ dwell close to the wall which divides the island into two parts, and the Caledonii live beyond them. Each of these people inhabit wild mountains, where there is no water, and desert plains and marshes, where they live without walls or cities; neither do they practise husbandry, but live by pasturage, or the chace, and on berries which grow in the woods; for they never taste fish, although their lakes and rivers furnish an inexhaustible supply.* They live in tents, naked and barefooted, having their wives in

---

* It is a curious circumstance, that the apparently superstitious aversion to the eating of fish was preserved in Scotland to a very recent period; and I am not sure if it does not still to some degree exist in the Highlands.

common, and they rear all the children which are born to them. The government of these tribes is democratic, and they delight above all things in pillage. They fight from chariots, which are drawn by small swift horses; they fight also on foot, run with great speed, and are most resolute when compelled to stand. Their arms consist of a shield and a short spear, which has a brazen knob at the extremity of the shaft, that when shaken it may terrify the enemy by its noise. They use daggers also. They are capable of enduring hunger, thirst, and hardships of every description; for they will plunge into the marshes, and remain there several days, with only their heads above the water. When they are in the woods they subsist on bark and roots; and they prepare for all emergencies a certain kind of food, of which if they eat only so much as the size of a bean, they neither hunger nor thirst.'

Such were the northern tribes, as report, probably applying the description of those who were in the lowest state of civilisation to the whole, pictured them at Rome. We have before had occasion to observe that the Caledonians appear to have had quick intelligence of the condition of the southern province, and they seem, according to the same policy which led their descendants at a much more recent period to select the moment when the Edwards and Henries were absent in their French wars, to make their most formidable inroads into England, to have chosen the moment of the insurrection of Albinus, and of the troubles and weakness which followed, to invade the Roman province. The history of these invasions is extremely obscure. It appears to have been the Mæatæ who conducted them, and the sudden turbulence of this people, their strength and their position, certainly give force to the opinion that they were a new colony from Scandinavia or from the north of Germany. Virius Lupus was at length induced to adopt the dangerous expedient of purchasing peace with the Mæatæ, who received the money, and then, entering into an alliance with the Caledonians, renewed their hostilities. The propraetor gave them more gold, and they remained quiet during two years, and then in conjunction with their allies recommenced their predatory excursions with more ferocity than ever. At length, in the year 208, Virius Lupus was so much embarrassed by the attacks of these northern enemies, that he sent an urgent message to the emperor Severus, praying for a considerable reinforcement of troops, and representing the advantage which would arise from the presence of the emperor himself.

SEVERUS IN BRITAIN.

Severus had found little happiness in the gratification of his ambition; the severity of his rule on one hand, and the weak indulgence he displayed towards his own family, had raised him troubles both abroad, where he was annoyed by frequent insurrections, and in his own household, where his domestic hours were embittered by the undutiful and even cruel conduct of his sons Caracalla and Geta. He was not unwilling, therefore, to change his domestic torments even for the hardships of a campaign in the inclement north, although age, now advancing upon him, was rendered more burthensome by the attacks of a cruel disease. When the letter of Virius Lupus arrived, announcing that the Roman province was overrun by the northern plunderers, the sound of war seemed to stir up the spirit of the old veteran, as if he had suddenly recovered his youthful energies. He instantly assembled his army and placed himself at its head, and, ordering his sons to accompany him, he made a forced march through Gaul, stopping nowhere, although the painful disease of his joints, with which he was habitually afflicted, was at this time so severe, that he was obliged to be carried on a litter. He thus reached the shores of Britain in an incredibly short space of time. It was late in the year 208, yet, without a moment's delay, he drew together the armies from different parts, and, with those he had brought with him, concentrated a vast force, and marched at once to meet the enemy. The latter were astonished at the rapidity of his movements, and quickly ceasing their hostilities, they sent envoys, who met him perhaps at Eburacum (*York*), begging for peace, and offering to make amends for their previous offences. But Severus had come too far to be so easily satisfied, and he was resolved to deprive them of the power of further hostility. He detained their ambassadors for some time, and then sent them away without any answer to their demands.

The emperor established his court at Eburacum, the second city of the island, and the station of the sixth legion. He there made extensive preparations for the war, and at the beginning of the year 209 he put his forces in motion. He found it necessary to separate his two sons, who not only treated their father with insolent disrespect, but quarrelled with each other. Geta was left to command the southern province, assisted by a council of the oldest and most experienced of the emperor's friends, while Caracalla accompanied him into the wilds of Caledonia. They had no sooner passed the boundary formed by the Forth and Clyde, and the wall of Antoninus (τὰ προβεβλημένα ῥεύματά τε καὶ χώματα τῆς ῾Ρωμαίων ἀρχῆς), than they were involved in daily skirmishes with the barbarians, who only showed themselves in small bodies, and manifested a resolution to avoid a general engagement. The Romans had to undergo extraordinary hardships, for as they drove the enemy before them they were obliged to force their way through thick forests and immense morasses, with a climate to the asperity of which they were unaccustomed. But everything seemed to yield to the stern will of their extraordinary leader, who, in the midst of the most incredible difficulties and hardships, caused bridges and roads to be thrown over the marshy places, actually filling some of them up, so as to give his troops a solid footing; while he cut down forests, and made roads over the mountains. In the course of these labours the Roman soldiers frequently fell into ambuscades of the natives, who exposed sheep and oxen a little way out of the line of their march, and then fell upon them suddenly when they went to carry away the booty. So certain were they that all stragglers would be killed without mercy, and probably subjected to horrible indignities, that whenever a soldier was rendered unable to keep up with the march of his comrades, we are told that they put him to death, rather than let him fall alive into the hands of their enemies. We are assured by the old writers, that the Romans lost not less than fifty thousand men in this invasion. Yet neither marsh nor forest, rain nor storm, of which there seems to have been no lack, averted the inflexible will of the aged emperor, who, sometimes on horseback, but more frequently stretched on his litter, which he was not able to leave for days together, continued to advance until he reached the extreme northern coast of Britain. He there observed the parallax of the sun, and the comparative length of the days and nights, and he ascertained beyond a doubt that Britain was an island. Severus was now willing to treat with the Caledonians, against whom his operations had often been hindered and embarrassed by the unfilial behaviour of Caracalla. At times when the old man was unable to leave his bed, he tried to persuade his son to take the command of the troops, and march against the barbarians. But Caracalla only occupied himself in corrupting the soldiers, in order that, in case of his father's death, he might use them against his brother Geta, and obtain the empire entirely for himself. He was even impatient of the lingering duration of his father's life, and is said to have attempted to bribe his physicians and servants to hasten his death. When he found the old king's attendants too faithful to listen to his proposals, he resolved to slay him himself. One day Severus, having had the soles of his feet punctured, had thus obtained so much relief from his complaint, that he was enabled to ride on horseback. He left the camp with his son and a detachment of his forces, to receive a surrender of arms from the Caledonians and to confer with them on terms of peace. The emperor rode forward towards the enemy, with his son behind him, and the troops following in the rear. At this moment Caracalla suddenly checked his horse, and, drawing his sword, prepared to stab his father in the back; but the troops, who saw the treacherous movement, set up a shout, which made the emperor turn round, and thus saved his life. Severus had seen the drawn sword, but, without appearing to take any further notice, he proceeded in his negotiation with the Caledonians. When this was concluded, he retired to his tent, and sending for his son, reproached him with his murderous intentions in the presence of two of his confidential friends, Papinian, the celebrated lawyer, and Castor. Provoked at the conduct of his children, Severus hastened the treaty with the Caledonians, and it was agreed that they should give up a considerable portion of their territory to the Romans, on condition that he should retire with his army into the Roman province. He accordingly returned to York, it is supposed towards the end of the year 209. It has been popularly supposed that the following year was employed in the construction of that immense line of fortification which recent examinations and a careful consideration of ancient testimonies have left little doubt was the sole work of the emperor Hadrian. It is not, indeed, probable that, after having added to the Roman territory towards the north, a man like Severus would raise a barrier on the limits to which the Roman power had been confined, when almost at its lowest ebb.*

It is possible, however, that Severus may have repaired the wall, and it seems that, during his stay at Eburacum, he not unfrequently visited its towns and garrisons. We are told that on one of these visits to the wall, he was returning to the nearest station (*mansio*), when he was accosted by an 'Ethiopian' soldier, celebrated among his comrades for his wit,† who bore

---

* We owe the account of the Caledonian campaigns of Severus chiefly to the historian Herodian, who wrote about thirty years after they took place. Some particulars are added by a later writer, Xiphilinus.

† Æthiops quidam e numero militari, claræ inter scurras famæ, et celebratorum semper jocorum.—*Ælius Spartianus, de Vit. Sever.* c. 22.

a crown of cypress, and who, when the emperor seemed offended by what he looked upon as an ill omen, addressed him in a tone of vulgar adulation, 'You have been everything, and conquered everything; now then be a god.' * Other fatal omens accompanied the emperor's progress, one of which occurred at Eburacum, when on his return thither he went to offer sacrifice in the temple of Bellona. While he was there, confiding in the solemn promises of the northern barbarians to preserve the peace, news suddenly arrived that the Mæatæ had again united with the Caledonians, and that they had recommenced their predatory inroads. The emperor was furious at the faithlessness of the barbarians, and raising himself up, to order his officers to prepare for a new campaign, he addressed them in the words of Homer—

———Τῶν μή τις ὑπεκφύγοι αἰπὺν ὄλεθρον
Χεῖράς θ' ὑμετέρας· μηδ' ὅντινα γαστέρι μήτηρ
Κοῦρον ἐόντα φέροι, μηδ' ὃς φύγοι αἰπὺν ὄλεθρον.

which is translated by Cowper—

Die the race!
May none escape us! Neither he who flies,
Nor even the infant in the mother's womb
Unconscious.

But Severus was sinking rapidly under his bodily infirmities, and he was at this moment suffering under so severe an attack of his disease, that he was unable to walk or ride. The troops, murmuring at his absence, and agitated by the intrigues of his worthless son, saluted Caracalla with the imperial title of Augustus. When this was told to Severus, all the energies of the warrior were roused, and, causing himself to be placed on the tribunal, he commanded the new emperor, Caracalla, with all who had joined in the act of insubordination, whether tribunes, centurions, or private soldiers, to appear before him. Then suddenly addressing them, he said, 'Soldiers, it is not the feet, but the head, which discharges the duties of a general;' and in the same breath he gave the order to march against the enemy. But the old man's effort was fatal to him. He relapsed into a state of helpless weakness, was carried back to his palace, and died in Eburacum, or York, on the 4th of February,

* We have not much difficulty in fixing the scene of this anecdote. A detachment of Moors was, as we learn from the 'Notitia Imperii,' stationed at Aballaba (*Watch-cross?*), which was no doubt the town where the emperor on this occasion sought a lodging.

211. By his will, his two sons, Caracalla and Geta, were to share between them his enormous treasures and the Roman empire.

Caracalla, eager to secure the grand object of his ambition, and to possess alone his father's empire and his treasures, seems to have kept the real state of the health of Severus from the knowledge of his mother and brother until his death. He then caused most of the officers of his father's household to be put to death, and tried to corrupt the army; but they remained faithful, and insisted on acknowledging the two brothers as equal, according to their father's will. Failing in his attempt upon the soldiery, Caracalla made a hurried peace with the barbarians, and, pretending to acquiesce in the will of Severus, he hastened to the south to join his brother and mother. The body of the late emperor was consumed on a funeral pile at York, and the ashes having been placed in an urn of alabaster, they carried it with them to Rome.

Such were the events which have given a classic celebrity to the city of York. A long period passed over, and many emperors sat on the throne, before Britain is again mentioned in the ancient historians. The government seems to have been carried on with a silent tranquillity, which leaves us to suppose that the island prospered, and that it was visited by no great dangers or troubles to excite attention at Rome. In fact, the next great events that we shall have to contemplate are not overwhelming attacks of the barbarians, but revolts of the island against the imperial government. Two or three inscriptions found in different parts of England refer distinctly to this period, and as they belong principally to dedications and restorations of buildings, they seem to confirm the supposition that the island remained in peace. One of these, raised by the troop of Asturians stationed at Cilurnum on the Wall (*Chesters*), relates to the rebuilding of a temple, and shows us not only that in 221, under the reign of Heliogabalus, Marius Valerianus was proprætor of Britain, but that the troops and people in this distant province took so much interest in the revolutions at Rome, that no sooner had Heliogabalus been deposed and assassinated, than his name was erased from the inscription, in this remote and comparatively obscure town. Another inscription, found in Cumberland, shows that the proprætor of the emperor Gordian, in the year 243, was Nonnius Philippus.

Amid the disorder and anarchy of the reign of Gallienus (260 to 268), a number of usurpers arose in different parts of the rulers, who were popularly called the thirty tyrants, of whom Lollianus, Victorinus Postumus, the two Tetrici, and Marius, are believed on good grounds to have assumed the sovereignty in Britain. Perhaps some of these rose up as rivals at the same time, and from the monuments bearing the name of Tetricus, found at Bittern, near Southampton, we are perhaps justified in supposing that the head-quarters of that commander lay at the station of Clausentum and along the neighbouring coasts. We have no information of the state of Britain at this time, but it must have been profoundly agitated by these conflicting claimants to empire. Yet, though so ready to rise in support of their own leaders, the troops in Britain seem to have turned a deaf ear to all solicitations from without. When an officer in the Roman army, named Bonosus, born in Spain, but descended of a family in Britain, proclaimed himself emperor, in the reign of Aurelian, and appealed for support to the western provinces, he found no sympathy among the British troops. Another usurper, whose name has not been recorded, had taken advantage of his appointment to the government of the island by the emperor Probus to assume the purple. The frequency of such usurpations within the island seem to show a desire among the inhabitants to erect themselves into an independent sovereignty. We are told that a favourite courtier of Probus, named Victorinus Maurusius, had recommended this usurper to the propraetorship, and that, when reproached on this account by the emperor, Victorinus demanded permission to visit Britain. When he arrived there, he hastened to the propraetor, and sought his protection as a victim who had narrowly escaped from the tyranny of the emperor. The new sovereign of Britain received him with the greatest kindness, and in return was murdered in the night by his guest. Victorinus returned to Rome to give the emperor this convincing proof of his 'loyalty.' Probus was succeeded in the empire by Carus, and he was followed by Diocletian, who began his reign in the year 284, and who soon associated with himself in the empire the joint emperor Maximian. Their reign, as far as regards Britain, was rendered remarkable chiefly by the successful usurpation of Carausius.

About this time another great change was taking place among the independent tribes in the north, the particulars of which are lost in the obscurity of history. It is supposed that the Dalreadic colony, under a leader whom tradition in the time of Bede named Reuda, now passed over from Ireland into the wilds of Lorn and Kintire, and laid the foundation of that people who ultimately gave to the whole of North Britain the name of Scotland. It is certain that, after the period of which we are now speaking, we lose sight of the old name of Caledonians, and even of the more recent one of Mæatæ, and in their place appear those of Picts and Scots, with a tribe which was apparently of older date, and which now gained notoriety for its savage ferocity, the Attacotti. At the same time the eastern and south-eastern coasts of Britain began to be infested with the predatory incursions of the Saxon seafarers from the mouth of the Elbe. To oppose these it was found necessary not only to erect a series of fortresses along the coast, but to establish and keep up a strong fleet in the channel, which had its places of rendezvous at Gessoriacum (*Boulogne*), and in the ports on the coasts of Kent, Sussex, and Hampshire.* Among the officers of this fleet who distinguished themselves most against the enemy, was a Menapian of low birth, probably of the Batavian tribe of the Menapii, named Carausius, whose talents soon caused him to be singled out from his fellow-soldiers, and he was eventually appointed to the command of the whole fleet. His ambition seems now to have been fixed on a higher aim, and he appears to have formed leagues and alliances, the object of which could hardly be misunderstood. He showed his military and naval skill in his frequent victories over the German pirates; but information was carried to the emperors that the plunder which he recaptured from the barbarians was seldom restored to those from whom it had been first taken, and it was even intimated, that instead of preventing the attacks of the enemy, he always contrived to let them first load themselves with plunder, and then attacked them and deprived them of their prey. By these or other means Carausius collected enormous wealth, which also was reported to Maximian, who sent orders to put the commander of the British fleet to death. Carausius was soon informed of the emperor's intentions, and became aware that he had only one chance of safety. He seems to have been extremely popular among the soldiery both on land and in the fleet; his great wealth gave him the means of attaching the mercenary to his fortunes; and, making use of both these advantages, he entered into an alliance with the Franks, on whose borders he seems to have been born,

---

* The British fleet is mentioned in an inscription found at Lymne, the *Portus Lemanis*, one of the Roman ports on the southern coast; it is the dedication of an altar, probably to Neptune, by Aufidius Pantera, præfect of the British fleet .... IV ... ARAM .... AVFIDIV PANTERA PRAEFECT CLAS: BRIT.

and with other German tribes, seized the great naval station of Gessoriacum, and proclaimed himself one of the emperors of Rome. Embarrassing revolts in other parts of the empire encouraged him in his design.

Having thus proclaimed himself the equal and colleague of Dioclesian and Maximian, the talents of Carausius enabled him to retain his usurped sovereignty during a period of seven years. History has left us no account of the manner in which his government was carried on, but he was evidently a man of very extraordinary abilities, for it is said that, during this period, he not only set the power of Rome at defiance, but that he protected his subjects from the Saxons, and that he compelled the barbarians of the north to keep within the limits of their woods and marshes. One of the most extraordinary characteristics of the short reign of Carausius is the number and variety of his coinage. Upwards of three hundred different types are known, and there can be little doubt that there are many others yet unknown. These authentic monuments throw some light on his character and history, and we have every reason to hope, that, in the hands of a skilful antiquary, they will some day be rendered still more available.* Of the great variety of reverses found on these coins, many, no doubt, refer to historical events. One of these, with the legend EXPECTATE VENI, is supposed to have been struck on his arrival in Britain, after having assumed the imperial title at Gessoriacum; the figure beneath the inscription represents the genius of Britain, with a trident in her hand, welcoming the new emperor. A number of coins having such inscriptions as ADVENTVS CARAVSI, ADVENTVS AVGVSTI, &c., with others inscribed VICTORIA AVGVSTI, and VIRTVS AVGVSTI, seem to have been struck on his return from successful expeditions against his enemies. One, with a figure of a trophy between two captives, and the inscription VICTORIA GER, perhaps commemorated some exploit on the coast of Germany. His care to conciliate the troops is shown not only in coins with the inscriptions CONCORDIA MILITVM and FIDES MILITVM, but in others struck in honour of each particular legion. The second legion, with its badge the capricorn, and the twentieth, with its badge the boar, are thus commemorated, as well as

---

* The antiquary Stukeley published a 'Medallic History of Carausius,' which, although it displays too much of that writer's hasty speculations and conclusions, shows us with how much advantage the coins might be made to illustrate the history. My friend Mr Roach Smith has announced a work on the coins of Carausius and Allectus, which we may be sure will be a valuable addition to the early history of this island.

several legions or parts of legions stationed in Gaul, which no doubt took part with the usurper. Other inscriptions, such as VBERTAS AVG, AEQVITAS AVG, FORTVNA AVG, FELICITAS AVG, HILARITAS AVG, LAETITIA AVG, PAX AVG, PROVIDENTIA AVG, RESTITVT SAECVLI, SAECVLI FELICITAS, TEMPORVM FELICITAS, no doubt were intended to proclaim the prosperity and happiness of the province under the rule of Carausius. When embarrassments in other parts of the empire obliged Maximian to leave him for a while to the enjoyment of his assumed dignity, and even, it is said, to agree to a treaty of friendship with him, Carausius proclaimed himself an associate in the empire by coins with inscriptions such as CARAVSIVS ET FRATRES SVI (round the three heads of Carausius, Dioclesian, and Maximian), PAX AVGGG, SALVS AVGGG, PIETAS AVGGG, &c., the three G's indicating the three emperors. But the most curious of all the coins of Carausius yet discovered, is one which was formerly in the possession of my friend, Mr Roach Smith, and which, contrary to the universal practice of the earlier Roman coinage, gives the emperor's head with a front face, instead of a profile. From this circumstance, and from its superior execution, Mr Smith is inclined to believe that it was struck expressly as a

correct portrait of this remarkable man, and as thus it forms one of the most interesting records of our history, it is here given from his 'Collectanea Antiqua,' where it was first published. This unique coin is in small brass, in an excellent state of preservation, and was found at Wroxeter, in Shropshire, the site of the Roman town of Uriconium.*

We have said that Carausius held the supreme power in Britain during nearly seven years (from 287 to 293). In 292, the two emperors, Maximian and Dioclesian, strengthened their government by the appointment of two Cæsars, Constantius and

---

* This coin is now, with Mr Roach Smith's collection of antiquities from Roman London, in the British Museum.

Galerius; and Constantius, to whose lot the provinces of the west fell, prepared immediately to reduce the island chieftain. We have the account of the events that followed chiefly from imperial panegyrists, who conceal all the circumstances advantageous to the usurper, but their outline is no doubt correct. Constantius having collected a very powerful army, made a rapid march to Gessoriacum, and laid siege unexpectedly to the grand naval station of Carausius. Then, as now, this port could only be entered at full tide, and Constantius took advantage of the ebb to block it up entirely with an embankment of piles and stones. Before this, however, had been effected, Carausius, who was in Gessoriacum at the time of the arrival of Constantius, took to his ships and sailed away to Britain.

Gessoriacum soon surrendered to the imperial arms, but Constantius found a greater obstacle to his immediate success in the want of ships. Four years passed away in the construction of a fleet, in the course of which Carausius himself had ceased to live. The empty bauble of empire had excited the ambition of Allectus, an officer whom Carausius had placed at the head of his fleet, and who basely and treacherously murdered his master. Allectus immediately seized the imperial authority, and, without the abilities of Carausius, attempted to follow in his course. During three years, while Constantius remained inactive, or only occupied in reducing to obedience the Franks and other allies of the usurper, Allectus was allowed to remain undisturbed. His coins include some which are different from those of his predecessor, and, considering the duration of his reign, they are almost as numerous. At length, in the year 296, Constantius had completed his vast preparations for invasion, and he is said to have been the first to set sail. His principal force, under the command of the præfect Asclepiodotus, which had assembled in the mouth of the Seine, immediately followed, and directing their course towards the western coast of Britain, were enabled by a thick fog to elude the fleet of Allectus, which was stationed off the Isle of Wight. It was afterwards said in praise of Asclepiodotus, that he ventured out to sea on a stormy day, with a side wind (which was then considered bold seamanship), and that when he landed on the British coast, he burnt his galleys, that his troops might find their only safety in victory.

Meanwhile Allectus, who expected that the imperial forces would cross over directly into Kent, had taken up a position in the neighbourhood of London. He no sooner received intelligence of the landing of Asclepiodotus, than he hurried hastily to meet him, carrying with him only a part of his troops, and those chiefly his Frankish auxiliaries. The consequence was that he was defeated in his first engagement with his enemies, and he was himself slain in the battle. As much of his army as escaped fled to London, plundered that rich city, and prepared to sail with the spoils to the continent. But they were so closely pursued by the imperial army, that the greater part of them are said to have been slain in the streets of the capital. According to the panegyrists, the population of Britain hailed the day of the arrival of Constantius as that of their redemption from an oppressive and cruel tyranny. The imperial commander took up his residence in York, from which we may perhaps assume that he had been called to the north to repress the turbulence of the Picts and Scots. But all we know of his proceedings is the simple fact, that he had been in Britain nine years when, in the year 305, the resignation of Dioclesian and Maximian left the Roman empire to Galerius and Constantius.

Constantius, who is usually known by the name of Constantius Chlorus, was the father of Constantine the Great; but the story that his wife Helena was of British origin appears to be a mere fable. At the time of his father's accession to the empire of the West, Constantine was serving in the army under Galerius, in Nicomedia, and it is supposed that Galerius, who would willingly have been without a partner in the empire, intended to keep him as a hostage for his father. But Constantine made his escape, and travelling with extreme rapidity, reached Gessoriacum in safety, and finding his father there, passed with him into Britain, where he assisted in the government, and soon ingratiated himself with the troops and with the people. They proceeded immediately to the north, to direct an expedition against the barbarians, but Constantius was already struck with disease, and, after this expedition, on the 25th of July, 306, he died at York. The soldiers immediately saluted his son Constantine as their emperor, and Galerius was induced to yield to their wishes. Constantine remained resident in our island, though his acts are not recorded, until, six years afterwards, he was called away to enter upon the contest which ended in making him sole ruler of the Roman world.

Britain now enjoyed a continued calm of more than thirty years. The emperor Constans paid a visit to Britain in 347, but we know not for what purpose; though it is probable that the British legions had begun again to show an inclination to throw off their dependence on Rome. Three years after his return from Britain, Constans fell a sacrifice to the ambition and treason of Magnentius, one of his officers, a Briton by birth. The troops in Britain probably supported the cause of Magnentius, and, after that usurper's defeat and death, in 353, the province suffered severely from the anger of the conqueror. The historian Ammianus Marcellinus tells us that a Spanish notary, named Paulus, who had gained by his cunning and astuteness the surname of Catena (the chain), was sent to Britain to institute proceedings against those who had espoused the cause of Magnentius. Paulus made use of the powers which had been given him by the emperor in so cruel and oppressive a manner, that he became an object of general detestation; and when the civil ruler of the island, whose name was Martin, interfered in favour of his victims, he attempted to involve him, and many of his officers, under the same accusations. Ammianus tells us how Martin tried to save himself and his friends by slaying the imperial accuser, but failing in the attempt, he immediately killed himself with his own sword. 'Paulus returned to court steeped in British blood, and dragging with him a multitude of wretched victims loaded with chains, whose looks depicted the hopelessness of their destiny. Some of these suffered horrible tortures at the hands of the executioners; while others were proscribed and exiled, and others had their heads struck from their bodies on the scaffold.'

The visitation of Paulus Catena was followed by one of a different kind, but no less disastrous to the inhabitants of the province. The Picts and Scots joined together, and began to carry their ravages far into the south. Britain had, no doubt, been robbed of much of its military force in the recent struggles for empire, and it had been further weakened by the severities of Paulus; its troops, therefore, were insufficient for its defence, and they were obliged to send over into Gaul to ask assistance of Julian, to whom Constantius had entrusted the defence of that province against the incursions of the Germans. Julian sent to Britain his *magister armorum*, or camp marshal, Lupicinus, a brave and experienced officer, who took with him some light auxiliary troops, with a few companies of the Heruli, Mæsians, and Batavians, and hastened over from Gessoriacum to Rutupiæ, and thence to London. We have no further account of his expedition, but he probably retaliated severely on the northern invaders, for the island seems to have had again a long period of undisturbed tranquillity.

CHAPTER V.

A Journey through Roman Britain—Londinium—Great Road from Londinium to Segontium—Verulamium; Uriconium, &c.—Direct Northern Road from Londinium; Durobrivæ, Lindum, Danum, Eburacum, Isurium—Passage of the two Walls—Stations on the Wall—Branch to Luguballium and Blatum Bulgium—Eastern Road; Camulodunum, Camboricum—From Londinium to Calleva—Branch to Corinium and Glevum; Isca, and Maridunum—From Glevum by Magna to Deva, and thence through Coccium to the North—Cross Roads—Salinæ and other towns—The Western Road, from Calleva to Sorbiodunum, Durnovaria, and Isca Dumnoniorum—Aquæ Solis—The *trajectus* to Wales, and the Sarn Helen—The Road on the Southern Coast; Venta Belgarum, Clausentum, Portus Magnus, Regnum, Anderida, Portus Lemanis.

At the period we have now reached, the face of the island was strangely altered from that which it presented when visited by Cæsar. Well inhabited and well cultivated, it was divided like a network by innumerable roads, many of them wide and all of excellent construction, which formed a communication between a multitude of flourishing cities and towns. Several principal lines of roads carried the traveller into and across the island in different directions.*

---

* Two imperfect itineraries, giving us the names and distances from each other of the towns and stations on the principal military roads, have been preserved. The first is contained in the great *Itinerarium* of the Roman empire, which goes under the name of Antoninus, and is believed to have been compiled about A.D. 320. The other is contained in the work of Richard of Cirencester, and is supposed to have been copied by a monk of the fourteenth century, from an older itinerary or map. They differ a little from each other, and, though our faith in Richard's Itinerary is not strong, it is certain nearly all the roads he gives which are not in Antoninus have been ascertained to exist. Traces of many Roman roads are found all over the country, not mentioned in these itineraries, and names of a great number of towns found neither in Antoninus nor in Richard, are given by an anonymous geographer of Ravenna, who wrote about the middle of the seventh century; but as he has placed them in no regular order, it is very difficult now to identify their sites.

The stranger who embarked at Gessoriacum, on the coast of Gaul, was carried, guided at night by the light from the lofty pharos of Dubræ (*Dover*), into the port of Rutupiæ, celebrated for its oysters, which was the usual place of landing from the Continent. The citadel of Rutupiæ stood on an elevation commanding the beach, and its massive walls still remain at Richborough, about three-quarters of a mile to the north-east of the modern town of Sandwich. From the masses of white marble that have been scattered about, it is evident that this citadel was adorned with handsome buildings. The town lay behind the citadel, spread over a gentle declivity, while at the top of the hill to the north are still seen the remains of its amphitheatre. Rutupiæ stood on the edge of the isle of Thanet, separated from the rest of Cantium by a creek which ran through to the mouth of the Thames, where its entrance was defended by another town and citadel, named Regulbium, now Reculver, of which a portion of the walls still remains. Another Roman port seems to have occupied the site of the modern harbour of Ramsgate.*

From Rutupiæ the traveller crossed over the water—the place whence the Rutupine oysters were taken, and where, in digging, the remains of the oyster-beds are still found—to the site of the present town of Sandwich, and here he entered the high road, which led directly over the downs, by the present village of Ash, to a large town called Durovernum, which occupied probably the whole site of the modern city of Canterbury. Part of the Roman walls were standing a century ago, and tesselated pavements and other antiquities discovered there at different times, show its importance. It was the point from which several roads branched, communicating with the towns on the coast, Regulbium, Rutupiæ, Dubræ, and the Portus Lemanis. The road leading to the interior of the island left Durovernum on the north-east, and proceeded over the high grounds of the forest of Blee, by a town named Durolevum, the probable site of which seems to be Davington, but which was apparently one of those unimportant stations that have left scarcely a trace behind, to a more important town named Durobrivæ, on the site of the present city of Rochester, situated on a river then called the Madus, now the Medway. The road then proceeded across towards the

---

* On the antiquities of Rutupiæ and Regulbium, the reader should consult the excellent work by Mr Roach Smith, 'The Antiquities of Richborough, Reculver, and Lymne,' in which they have been investigated with remarkable skill and care. It is itself almost a manual of Roman antiquities.

banks of the Thames, where the traveller arrived at a town named Vagniacæ, the situation of which is also somewhat doubtful, though it is generally believed to have stood in the neighbourhood of Southfleet. Traces of Roman settlements are found thickly scattered along the line of this road, and between it and the Thames. From Vagniacæ the road proceeded by Dartford, over Shooter's Hill, across Blackheath, and to a town in the territory of the ancient tribe of the Regni, called Noviomagus, which is supposed to have stood on the side of Holwood Hill, in the parish of Bromley. Fifteen Roman miles to the north brought the traveller again to the banks of the Thames, at the foot of the bridge by which he entered the great commercial town of Londinium.

Roman London was built on the elevated ground on both sides of a stream, known in after time by the name of Wallbrook, which ran into the Thames not far from Southwark Bridge, and extending westward to the edge of a hill overlooking another stream, called in later times Holbourne, and on the east almost to the Tower. Its walls were identical with those which enclosed the mediæval city of London. At this time it seems to have had two principal lines of streets, one running from the bridge northward in the line of Bishopsgate-street, the other branching from it, and running along or near the line of the modern Watling-street, till it left the city by Ludgate. At the western end of this street the principal temples and public buildings seem to have stood, crowning the hill, and occupying the side which sloped down to the river. The northern and north-eastern parts of the town were occupied with extensive and—to judge by the remains which have been brought to light—magnificent mansions. Londinium had increased much in extent since it had been founded by the Romans. It has been supposed by a recent writer that the first town was confined to the hill on the east of Wallbrook.*
Mr Roach Smith discovered, in excavations on the site of the Royal Exchange, pits which had been receptacles of the rubbish from the shops and houses of Roman London at an earlier period of its existence, and which had been afterwards filled up and built over. At the period to which our last chapter has brought us, the city had extended to the other side of the

---

* This notion on the earliest form of Londinium was published in an essay on the original site of Roman London, by Mr Arthur Taylor, in the thirty-third volume of the 'Archæologia.'

Thames, and the borough of Southwark stands upon ground which covers the floors of Roman houses and the pavings of Roman streets.*

Two principal roads led out of Londinium on the north side of the Thames; one apparently in the direction of Bishopsgate, the other westward, through Ludgate, across Holbourne, and in the direction of Fleet-street and the Strand. Without Newgate, on each side of this road, the principal sepulchral monuments of the citizens of Londinium appear to have stood. It was the grand route to the west of Britain; but somewhere near the present site of Knightsbridge another large road branched off northward, and proceeded in a direct line along the modern Kilburn road, until the traveller arrived at a town named Sulloniacæ, the traces of which are now found on an elevation called Brockley Hill, a little south of Elstree, on the borders of Hertfordshire. Hence the road continued its direct course, through a rich and varied country, to the grand municipal city of Verulamium, the extensive walls of which are still traced in the neighbourhood of St Albans. Verulamium was the fashionable town of the south-east, and possessed, what probably few towns in Britain did, a theatre.

From Verulamium the road proceeded through the same rich country, nearly straight, to a town named Durocobrivæ, which must have stood at or in the immediate vicinity of the modern town of Dunstable, which is marked as an ancient station by the number of tumuli and intrenchments in the neighbourhood. It was apparently the great market of these agricultural districts, over which the goddess Diana presided, as it was known also by the name of Forum Dianæ. On leaving this place the traveller continued his route across the beautiful country to the south of Woburn till he entered a more open valley, where he reached the town of Magiovintum, supposed to have stood at the place where the road crossed the river Ousel, in the immediate vicinity of Fenny Stratford. The road then again

---

* Numerous particulars relating to Roman London will be found in papers by Mr Roach Smith, scattered through the volumes of the 'Archæologia,' of the Society of Antiquaries, and other archæological works. See also a paper on this subject in my 'Archæological Album.' Whenever excavations are made within the limits of the city of London, the workmen come to the Roman floors at a depth of from twelve to eighteen or twenty feet under the present level. Since the first edition of this volume was published, Mr Roach Smith has given to the public his valuable work on the early antiquities of the capital of Britain, entitled 'Antiquities of Roman London.'

mounted higher ground, passing over the site of Stoney Stratford, and so on to Lactodorum, a town occupying the site of the modern Towcester. The road then turned slightly north to Weedon, at which point a cross road turned off leading to what some have considered two towns, Isannavaria and Bennaventa, which have been placed at Burnt Walls and Burrow Hill, ancient sites near Daventry, though others have imagined this to be one town under two different names. The main road continued its course from Weedon in a straight line across an open country to the neighbourhood of the modern town of Lilburne, where it crossed the river Avon at Dove Bridge. Here stood a town called Tripontium, which must have possessed something remarkable in its bridge or bridges across the river. Tumuli and earthworks, scattered over the country around, again mark it as a place of some importance. The country now became more uneven, and the road proceeded till it reached the top of a hill within the borders of Leicestershire, where stood the town of Benonæ, the site of which is now occupied by High Cross. The next town at which the traveller arrived was Manduessedum, occupying the slope of a hill over the river Anker, and surrounded by high grounds. The site of this town is now called Manceter (in the county of Warwick), and the square intrenchments of the ancient station are still seen, while the hills to the south are covered with tumuli. After leaving Manduessedum, the traveller passed through a continuation of rich agricultural district, open to the north, but rising into a fine hilly country to the south, the road generally taking the higher grounds, until it reached the town of Eteocetam. The last traces of its buildings have long disappeared, but the tradition of them appears to be preserved in the modern name of the site, Wall, in Staffordshire. The road turned hence westward, proceeding direct through Stretton, till it crossed the little river Penk, where stood the town of Pennocrucium. The road now went through a more wooded and hilly country, until the traveller arrived at Uxaconium, apparently but a small unimportant town, which has been placed by some at Red Hill, a little to the north-east of Shiffnall, in Shropshire, and by others at Oaken-gates, near Wembridge. It proceeded thence, turning slightly south, to the important town of Viroconium or Uriconium, the remains of which are found at the modern village of Wroxeter. Important excavations have been, during the last few years, made on this site, which have thrown considerable light on the early history of our island. Uriconium

... ... Roman cities in Britain. It was sur-
... ... and foss, the remains of which may be traced
... ... upwards of three miles in extent, and inclose
... ... that of Roman London. The town
... ... and strong position, at the foot of the
... ... Shropshire hill of the Wrekin, which, perhaps, gave
... ..., and on the bank of the river Severn, just
... ... by the Tamar. It was evidently of con-
... ... importance, and well inhabited; it had a forum of
... ..., and it possessed a theatre of considerable size
... ... of the town, as well as an amphitheatre outside.*
... ... branch of the great road crossed the Severn, and
... ... in a north-westwardly direction to Rutunium, a
Roman town, the site of which is generally placed at Rowton,
in Shropshire, after which it entered Wales, passing under the
... end of the Breidden mountain, to a town called
Mediolanum, situated where the road crossed the river Tanad.
The traveller then pursued his way among the wild mountains
of North Wales, till he approached the majestic heights of
Mons Heriri (*Snowdon*), and halted at a station of that name,
the intrenchments of which are still observed at a place named
... them Tomen-y-mur, in the valley of Maentwrog. Thence
the road led down to the coast, where the traveller entered
Segontium, one of the most important Roman towns in Wales,
the walls of which are still visible at Caer Seiont, near Caernarvon, on the coast of the Irish Sea.

If the stranger were not bound for the midland districts, he
might leave Londinium by the gate known in later times by the
name of Bishopsgate, and pursue the great road to the north.
His way at first ran through woods and corn districts, and the
traveller passed over considerable distances without meeting
with towns or stations. His first halting-place was a small
station named—we are not certain why—Ad Fines, the site of
which is supposed to have been at Broughing, in Hertfordshire,
at the confluence of two streams, the Rib and the Quin.
Thence the road proceeded in a direct line to Durolipons, the
site of which is fixed without doubt at Godmanchester, on the
river Ouse. The traveller had now entered upon the low, flat

* I have published an account of these excavations, and of the discoveries made in the course of them, in a rather large volume entitled 'Uriconium; a Historical Account of the Ancient Roman City, and of the Excavations made upon its site at Wroxeter, in Shropshire, forming a sketch of the Condition and History of the Welsh Border during the Roman Period. By Thomas Wright, M.A., F.S.A. 8vo. London, 1872.'

country on the borders of the fens, to avoid which the road turned a little west, and then continuing its dreary course to the north reached a district covered with potteries, in the midst of which he entered a rich and elegant town named Durobrivæ, situated on one of the sluggish rivers of this district, which in modern times is called the Nen, and the site of the Roman town is now occupied by an obscure village called Castor.* Hence the road continued nearly north, with a slight curve, to another town of some importance, named Causennæ, or, according to other authorities, Isinæ, situated on slightly elevated ground. There can be no doubt that this town occupied the site of the modern Ancaster, which has been celebrated for its Roman antiquities since the time of Leland.† Another stage brought the traveller to Lindum, a noble city, both for the elegance of its buildings, and its position on a lofty isolated hill, commanding extensive views on every side over the flat country around. Its modern representative is easily recognized in the city of Lincoln.

The traveller who is not willing to follow the dreary road we have been describing, might take another route, which, though less direct, lay through a more beautiful country, in which the towns were more numerous and interesting. He left Londinium by its western gate, and, proceeding along the road already described, he passed through Sulloniacæ, Verulamium, Durocobrivæ, Magiovintum, Lactodorum, and Tripontium, to Venonæ. There, instead of continuing his route to Manduessedum, he took another great road which turned off to the north-east, and proceeded direct to Ratæ, one of the largest and most important of the midland cities, adorned with rich mansions

---

* The very interesting antiquities of this Roman town were explored by the late Mr E. Tyrrell Artis, of Castor, who published them in a series of expensive plates, but which were not accompanied with a text.

† Leland, in his Itinerary, vol. i. pp. 28, 29, has left us the following note on the antiquities discovered at Ancaster in his time:—'In tymes past it hath bene a celebrate toune, but not waullid, as far as I could perceive. The building of it lay in lenghth by south and north. In the south ende of it be often tymes founde in ploughing great square stones of old buildinges and Romayne coynes of brasse and sylver. In the west ende of it, where now meadowes be, ar founde yn diching great vaultes. . . . An old man of Ancaster told me that by Ureby, or Roseby, a ploughman toke up a stone, and found another stone under it, wherein was a square hole having Romaine quoin in it. He told me also that a ploughman toke up in the feldes of Harleston a 2 miles from Granteham a stone, under the which was a potte of brasse, and an helmet of gold, sette with stones in it, the which was presentid to Catarine princes dowager. There were bedes of silver in the potte, and writings corruptid.'

and temples, and other public buildings.* Its site is now occupied by the town of Leicester. Thence, keeping to the eastward of the great forest of Charnwood, the road proceeded over a rich country to Verometum—a town supposed to have stood in the immediate neighbourhood of Willoughby, on the borders of Nottinghamshire. A few miles more brought the traveller to a town on the river Trent, named Margidunum, supposed to have stood at or near Bridgeford, and next he reached a station on the same river, called, no doubt from its bridge over the river, Ad Pontem, believed to have stood near the modern village of Farndon. The next halting-place was Crococolana, a town supposed to have stood at Brough, in Lincolnshire, from which another stage took him to Lindum.†

Here he again took the north road from Londinium, and soon after leaving Lindum he turned off westwardly, and, after a short stage, repassing the river Trent, halted at the town of Segelocum, or Agelocum, on the site of the modern town of Littleborough. Thence, still keeping a little westward, the road brought him, after a somewhat longer stage, to the more important station of Danum, a site now known by the somewhat celebrated name of Doncaster. From Danum the road turned north, and after a shorter stage, reached Legiolium, supposed to have occupied the site of the modern village of Castleford, at the confluence of the Ayr and the Calder, and proceeded thence to the town of Calcaria, which probably received its name from its lime-works, and is now represented by Tadcaster, the last station before reaching Eburacum, the second, if not the first, city in Britain.

There was another road from Lindum to Eburacum. It proceeded in a direct line from the former place to a town or station on the Humber (*Abus*), called—no doubt from the great river near which it stood—Ad Abum, supposed to have been at Winterton. The traveller arrived here in two stages, stopping only at a half-way station, the only name of which that has come

---

* The importance and beauty of Ratæ are evinced by the numerous fine tesselated pavements that have been found there. Some of its public buildings appear to have been standing in the time of Geoffrey of Monmouth, who speaks of a subterranean temple of Janus: 'In quodam subterraneo quod sub Sora fluvio intra Legecestriam fieri præceperat. Erat autem subterraneum illud conditum in honorem bifrontis Jani.'—*Galf. Mon. Hist. Brit.*, lib. ii. c. 14.

† The Roman towns between Ratæ and Lindum have been less almost than any others examined by modern antiquaries, and their sites are only fixed by conjecture.

down to us is one taken from its position, In Medio. From Ad Abum the traveller crossed the Humber in a boat, and landed at another town, called, from the river on which it stood, Ad Petuariam, supposed to have occupied the site of Brough, on the Humber, where interesting Roman antiquities have been found. From Brough the road seems to have proceeded to Eburacum without any intermediate station, a distance estimated in the ancient Itinerary at forty-six Roman miles, so that it perhaps went by a circuitous route, joining some one of the roads from Eburacum to the coast.

Eburacum, or Eboracum* (as its name was differently spelt), occupied the banks of a navigable river called the Urus (now the Ouse). Within its walls, which were of considerable extent, stood the imperial palace, and no doubt other magnificent edifices, and both within and without were temples to most of the Roman gods, as well as to the eastern deities, Serapis and Mithras. Outside the walls, the city was surrounded with extensive and well-built suburbs.†

Many roads branched off from Eburacum in different directions. Several of these ran towards the coast, and communicated no doubt with trading ports. Of these the principal was a military road, leading by two towns, named Derventio and Delgovitia, to an apparently important town on the coast called Prætorium. Various positions have been fixed for these towns, chiefly on the assumption that Prætorium stood at Flamborough Head. There are extensive remains of an important Roman station at Old Malton, on the river Derwent, and as we know that there was a Derventio in the interior of the island on a river called the Derwent, it is not improbable that the station at Old Malton may have been Derventio. But the Roman antiquities of East Yorkshire have as yet been very imperfectly explored.

The great north road which we have been pursuing, after leaving Eburacum, turned westward, in the direction of the Ouse, until at the end of a comparatively short stage, the tra-

---

* *Eburacum* is the spelling given in the Itinerary of Antoninus, in Ptolemy, and in the geographer of Ravenna, while an inscription formerly found at York, but not preserved, as well as the Roman historians who mention this place, call it *Eboracum*. The weight of authority, however, seems to be turned in favour of the former, by an inscription more recently discovered, and certainly reading EBVR.

† An excellent volume on the Roman antiquities of York was published by the Rev. C. Wellbeloved, of that city, under the title of ' Eburacum, or York under the Romans,' which is recommended earnestly to the student of the history and antiquities of the Romans in Britain.

veller arrived at another large and well-built town, Isurium, the walls of which are still traced at Aldborough, and within them the excavator meets continually with the tesselated floors of the Roman houses.* A longer stage carried the traveller to Cataracto, or Cataractonium, the ancient name of which has been preserved by the village of Catteric, on the river Swale, and a few miles further the road crossed the river Tisa (*the Tees*), it is supposed at Piercebridge, near Darlington, where there was also a station. The traveller had now entered the modern county of Durham, and the road pursued its course nearly north, through a rich and interesting country, to Vinovium, a town of some extent, of which there are considerable remains in the modern hamlet of Binchester, near Bishop Auckland. The next town on this road was Epiacum, which occupied a lofty brow on a tongue of land formed by the junction of two small streams on the west side of the modern village of Lanchester, where abundant remains of the Roman town have been found. It appears by inscriptions found on this site, that this town had its basilica or court-house, and its public baths and arsenal, and other important buildings. The road now turned westwardly again till it reached Vindomora, which is supposed to be the station traceable at Ebchester, on the borders of Northumberland.† A few miles further he came to the town of Corstopitum, the modern site of which is called Corchester, near Corbridge on the Tyne, and before he reached it, a bridge, of which the remains are still to be traced, carried the traveller over the river Tina. He was now only about two miles from the great wall erected by the emperor Hadrian, which the road passed at an opening a little to the west of the station of Hunnum. On the other side of the wall the road separated into two branches, one of which turned off towards the coast, while the other proceeded to the town of Habitancum (now Risingham), situated on a pleasant stream, in a small valley, sheltered by surrounding hills. An inscription found in this place commemorates the rebuilding, in the reign of Caracalla, of the gate and of the

---

* A series of very carefully executed plates of the tesselated pavements of Isurium were published by Mr H. Ecroyd Smith, who has since published a quarto volume, illustrated with numerous engravings, on the Antiquities of Aldborough.

† Some doubt has been thrown on the appropriation of these two last sites, though it does not appear to be well founded. No other sites answer so well to Epiacum and Vindomora, and we can find no other names for what, by the remains still visible, were evidently towns of considerable importance

walls, which had become ruinous by age: the remains, which after so many centuries still present themselves, show that they were rebuilt well. A very little further stood the town of Bremenium, which an inscription identifies with the modern village of High Rochester. Here also a bridge passed over the river. The traveller then pursued his way by longer stages by Trimontium, which has been fixed at Eildon, and Curia, placed by some at Currie, and by others at Borthwick Castle, to the eastern end of the vallum of Antoninus, and passing it, if he were bound to the far north, he proceeded to the towns of Alauna, Lindum, Victoria, and Orrea.

In the course of the great road from Eburacum to the north, it had several smaller offsets or branches. One of these led apparently from Vinovium to the important town of Pons Ælii, or Newcastle, and another to the stations which commanded the mouth of the Tyne, at Jarrow and South Shields. A larger branch turned off a little beyond Cataracto, and carried the traveller westward to the town of Lavatræ, which, there seems little reason for doubt, occupied the site of the present town of Bowes. A few miles further he reached Verteræ, which is supposed to have stood on the site of the town of Brough in Westmoreland, where many Roman antiquities have been found at different times.* He was now on the confines of the mountainous district which had formed the stronghold of the Brigantes; to the south rose the heights of Stanemoor, while to the west were seen the still nobler mountains of the lake district, which he approached nearer as he reached the next town of Brovonacæ, supposed to have stood at the modern village of Kirby-Thore, where Roman antiquities are found, and Brocavium, which its position and the numerous antiquities found there seem to identify with Brougham.† Another stage and the traveller arrived at the important city of Luguballium, or Luguvallium, with its temples and palaces, and other public

* In the time of Leland, Brough seems to have been proverbial for the antiquities continually found there. He says:—'Borow, now a vyllage, set in Lunesdale a vi. myles beneth the footo of Dentdale, hath beene by likelyhod sum notable town. The ploughmenne find there yn ering *lapides quadratos*, and many other straung thinges; and this place is much spoken of the inhabitants there.'—*Itinerary*, vol. vii. p. 48.

† 'At Burgham is an old castel that the commune people ther sayeth doth synke. Abowt this Burgham plowghmen fynd in the feldes many square stones, tokens of old buildinges. The castel is set in a stronge place by reasons of ryvers enclosing the cuntery therabowt.'—*Leland's Itinerary*, vol. vii. p. 49.

edifices. There can be no doubt that the modern city of Carlisle stands upon its ruins.* From Luguballium the road again passed the wall of Hadrian, proceeding by the Castra Exploratorum, which is identified with the modern Netherby, where numerous antiquities have been found, Blatum Bulgium, which is placed at Middleby, and Uxelum, which is supposed to have stood at Castleover, and so on to Colania, the modern Lanark, and Vanduaria, or Paisley, where it passed the western extremity of the great barrier of Antoninus, and ended at the remote town of Theodosia, or Dumbarton.†

The traveller in Britain has thus, by two different roads, passed the wall of Hadrian, and the more northern earthen vallum of Antoninus. The first of these monuments must have attracted his attention by its extraordinary character, and he would be tempted to cross the island by the great road which accompanied its course. As he approached it from Eburacum he entered a populous region, which marked the great commercial importance of the stations on the Tyne. Strong posts commanded the entrance to the river both on the south and on the north. One of these stood at Tynemouth, where, as we learn from a mutilated inscription still preserved, the usurper Maximinus, then an officer in the sixth legion, erected some public buildings, which included a basilica, as well as a temple, which seem to have occupied the site of the famous abbey of after ages. A few miles up the bank of the river brought the

---

* There is a curious passage in Bede's Life of St Cuthbert (chap. 27), where the saint is described as visiting the city of Lugubalia, and as being taken by the citizens to see the Roman walls, and the wonderful fountain which had been built there by the Romans. 'Venit ad Lugubaliam civitatem (quæ a populis Anglorum corrupte Luel vocatur). . . . Postera autem die deducentibus eum civibus ut videret mœnia civitatis, fontemque in ea miro quondam Romanorum opere exstructum.' This was in the seventh century. Leland, at the beginning of the sixteenth century, speaks of the numerous antiquities found at Carlisle in his time (*Itin.*, vol. vii. p. 54). 'In diggying to make new building yn the towne often tymes hath bene, and now a late, fownd diverse fundations of the old cité, as pavimentes of streates, old arches of dores, coyne, stones squared, paynted pottes, mony hid yn pottes so hold and muldid that when it was stronly towchid yt went almost to mowlder; as yn M . . . glalbyls howse yn digging for the squaryng . . . . his gardin and orchard, the which ston . . . eth much sowth. The hole site of the towne is sore chaungid. For wher as the stretes where and great edifices now be vacant and garden plottes. In the feldes abowt Cairluel yn plowghing hath be found diverse cornelines and other stonys well entayled for seales, and in other places of Cumbarland in plowinge hath be fownd brickes conteyninge the prints of antique workes.'—Page 54.

† The Roman antiquities of Scotland have been collected in a volume, entitled 'Caledonia Romana,' by Robert Stuart. Edinburgh, 1845.

traveller to the town or station of Segedunum. Here the wall of Hadrian began, and from this circumstance the spot has received in modern times the name, now so widely celebrated, of Wallsend. The wall was a massive work of masonry, varying from six to nearly ten feet in thickness, and from eighteen to nineteen feet high. On the north it was accompanied by a foss thirty-six feet wide, and fifteen feet deep. To the south was another lesser foss, with a triple entrenchment of earth and stones. At no great distance apart, along the line of the wall, were stations or towns, each consisting of a citadel, strongly walled, with streets and habitations within, and often extensive suburbs without. Between these towns stood smaller fortresses, which, from the circumstance of their occurring at the distance of one Roman mile from each other, have been termed milecastles; and between each of these again were four small subsidiary buildings, which for distinction have been termed watchtowers.

The wall, as we have just stated, began on the east at Segedunum. It there advanced to the south into the river Tyne, as far as the low-water mark, while it pursued its course westwardly to a town of great extent and commercial importance, named, from its bridge across the river Tyne built by Hadrian, Pons Ælii, which occupied the site of the present town of Newcastle. Little more than two miles from this place brought the traveller to Condercum, a town beautifully situated on an elevated knoll, which commands views of the valley of the Tyne to the southwest, and northwardly of the distant and lofty Cheviots. The houses and walls of the ancient town may still be traced in the unevenness of the sod which covers them, at a spot which is now called Benwell. Thence the wall proceeded over hill and vale, for the country was here much varied, to the next town, which appears to have been of less importance, and was called Vindobala; its site is now called Rutchester. The next town which presented itself to the traveller was named Hunnum, apparently a handsome and well-inhabited place, the deserted site of which may now be distinctly traced at Halton-Chesters. He now crossed the great road which passed the wall in its way from York, and, pursuing the course of the wall, crossed the northern Tyne by a bridge, of which the piers still remain, and entered the large town of Cilurnum, the extensive ruins of which, well described as a British Pompeii, are visible near the modern hamlets of Chesters. This station also had its temples and public buildings, which, to judge from the broken statues and fragments of

architectural decoration which are found there, must have been
distinguished by their beauty. The next town, Procolitia, distant only a short stage, is traced at the spot now called Carrawburgh. Another stage, about the same length, brought the
traveller to the fine town of Borcovicus, perhaps, after Pons Ælii,
the largest on the wall, the very extensive remains of which are
found at a place now named Housesteads. He was now among
the hills, surrounded with magnificent scenery, and might contemplate in the distance the rugged mountains which sheltered
the northern enemies of Rome. A little to the west of Borcovicus, he left the wall to proceed a short distance south, to the
town of Vindolana, the site of which is now marked distinctly
by the remains of walls and houses at Chesterholm. He then
regained the wall, and arrived at Æsica, the walls of which are
still seen at Great Chesters. The wall now again ran its course
through the mountains, in some places rising up or descending
precipitous heights, which struck the traveller with astonishment
and even with terror. The ground was unfit for towns, and the
next he came to, Magna, was built a little to the south of the
wall, on the ground below, at a place now called Carvoran, on
a little river, and by the side of a high road which ran southward to the town of Aliona, which is believed to have stood at
Whitley Castle, about two miles to the north of Alston, and
northward into the country between the two walls. Hence,
following the valley, the traveller came soon to Amboglanna, a
larger town, of which there are very extensive remains at Birdoswald, in a rich valley on the river Irthing. Further on, a
little south of the wall, stood Petriana, at a place now called
Cambeck Fort, and a short distance south-east of this, on a road
which led from Magna direct to Luguballium, thus avoiding
the circuit here made by the wall, was another station, named
Bremetenracum, the intrenched area of which is supposed to be
still traced in the park at Brampton. The next town on the
wall was Aballaba, supposed to have stood at Watch-cross, though
its site is not quite certain. The traveller, in following the
course of the wall, now passed successively the towns of Congavata, near which the wall joined the city of Luguballium,
Axelodunum, Gabrosentæ, and Tunnocelum, where it ended
on the coast of the estuary of Ituna (*the Solway Frith*). The
last-mentioned town is supposed to have occupied the site of
Bowness; the others are doubtful, but they have been placed by
conjecture at Burgh-upon-Sands and Drumburgh. A road from
Luguballium led through a series of towns which were evidently

connected with the wall as a system of defence against the incursions of the northern barbarians and their allies from Hibernia. This road proceeded from Luguballium to Olenacum, which is supposed to have been the strong station now seen at Old Carlisle; Virosidum, supposed to be identical with the Roman remains at Maryport and the adjacent village of Ellenborough, on the coast of Cumberland; and Glanovanta, the site of which is more doubtful.*

The stranger who was desirous of visiting the eastern districts of Britain, the old territory of the Trinobantes and the Iceni, might have proceeded from the south to Lindum by a more circuitous route. Leaving the great northern road soon after it quitted Londinium, he proceeded by a road which took an easterly direction, till he reached a town named Durolitum, or Durositum, which is believed to have stood near Romford in Essex. The next town he came to was called Cæsaromagus, and is generally identified with the modern Chelmsford. Canonium, which followed, is usually placed in the vicinity of Kelvedon, on the river Pant. From thence the traveller approached the grand city of Camulodunum, or, as it is called in the Itinerary, Camalodunum, the capital of the British princes after they had submitted to the Romans, and the first Roman city in the island which was honoured with the rank of *colonia*. History speaks of its temples and public buildings; and if, at any early period of its history, it was exposed to attack without walls of defence, that want was so well supplied at a subsequent period, that the ponderous masonry of its walls has endured to the present day, and ought never to have allowed anybody to hesitate in placing the site of this ancient city at Colchester.† A few

* No district in England is so interesting for its antiquities as that of the wall of Hadrian. It has been made the subject of an excellent and most instructive volume, by the Rev. J. Collingwood Bruce, of Newcastle-upon-Tyne, under the title of 'The Roman Wall: a historical, topographical, and descriptive Account of the Barrier of the Lower Isthmus, extending from the Tyne to the Solway, deduced from numerous personal Surveys.' The Wall district shows us in a remarkable manner the effect of modern cultivation in destroying ancient monuments. From Newcastle to the ancient Amboglanna (*Birdoswald*), which extends over a wild and insecure country, the stations and posts are easily identified, and buildings of all kinds lie in masses of ruins, which are only slightly covered by the accumulation of earth. To the west of Amboglanna, the country has been more highly cultivated, and the plough has so completely obliterated the trace of Roman works, that we can only guess at the sites of ancient towns, and the positions of all the western stations of the wall are very doubtful.

† The only good account of the Roman antiquities of Colchester will be found in a paper by Mr Roach Smith, in the 'Journal of the Archæological Association,' vol. ii. p. 29.

miles to the north of Camulodunum, the road crossed the river Sturius (*Stour*), where there was a station called Ad Ansam, supposed to have stood on the site of the present village of Stratford. The traveller then proceeded by longer stages to the towns of Combretonium and Sitomagus, which are conjectured to have stood at Burgh, near Woodbridge, and at Dunwich, on the coast. The course of this road is, however, at present very uncertain, and we only know that it ended at the eastern Venta, or Venta of the Iceni, which, there seems no reason to doubt, stood at Caistor, near Norwich. From Venta the Itinerary brings us, without any intermediate station, to Camboricum, which occupied the site of the modern town of Cambridge. Another road from Colchester led by Villa Faustini, the position of which seems to be exceedingly doubtful, to Iciani, a town which has been conjectured, perhaps only from a fancied resemblance of name, to have occupied the site of the modern Icklingham, and in that case the road seems there to have joined the other road from Venta to Camboricum. There was also a direct road from Camulodunum to Camboricum, of which the Itineraries give no account. Camboricum was without doubt a very important town, which commanded the southern fens. It had three forts or citadels, the principal of which occupied the district called the Castle-end, in the modern town of Cambridge, and appears to have had a bridge over the Cam or Granta: of the others, one stood below the town, at Chesterton, and the other above it, at Granchester.* Numerous roads branched off from this town. One of these proceeded to Durolipons (*Godmanchester*), where it joined the great north road, and proceeded by it to Lindum. Another ran north into the Fens, towards Ely and Lynn. Others proceeded to Venta of the Iceni and to Camulodunum. Another proceeded southward to London, having stations at Chesterford and perhaps at other places in its course. Lastly, a continuation of the road from Venta ran in a south-westerly direction towards the fashionable districts of Gloucestershire and Somerset. Bede calls the representative of Camboricum, in his time, 'a little deserted city,' and tells us how, when the nuns of Ely wanted a coffin for their saintly abbess, Etheldreda, they found a beautiful sculptured sarcophagus of white marble outside the city walls of the Roman town.†

---

* A very valuable essay on the Roman antiquities of Cambridge, and on the Roman roads branching from it, by a well-known and distinguished antiquary, Mr C. C. Babington, was published by the Cambridge Antiquarian Society, 8vo. 1853.

† ' Venerunt ad civitatulam quandam desolatam, non procul inde sitam,

WESTERN TOWNS—GLEVUM.

If the traveller, when he entered Britain, desired to visit the western parts of the island, he left Londinium by its western gateway, and proceeded along the great road, leading through the present towns of Brentford and Hounslow to Staines, where it crossed the Thames over the bridge, from which the Roman town at this place took the name of Pontes. Having here passed the river, the traveller came to a town named Bibracte, the position of which is not known, and then continued his way through a rich and varied country to the great town of Calleva, the walls of which, as they still remain at Silchester, on the northern border of Hampshire, enclose an area three miles in circuit. Thence he proceeded over hilly grounds and heaths to a town named Spinæ, the name of which seems to be preserved in the modern village of Speen, in Berkshire. The road then carried him over a more level and open country, after a long stage, to Corinium, a town filled with magnificent houses and public buildings, which occupied the site of the modern Cirencester. Some of the richest and most elegant mosaic pavements in this island, dug up here, show its ancient splendour.* Another stage conducted the traveller over the hills to the large colonial city of Glevum, now represented by Gloucester.

Glevum was a town of great importance, as standing not only on the Severn, near the place where it opened out into the Bristol Channel, but also as being close to the great Roman iron district of the Forest of Dean. A road passed the Severn, and ran north-westward over the hilly country on the east of the forest to the town of Ariconium, the great station of the iron manufactures of this district, a fine position, commanding an extensive prospect over the surrounding country. Its site is now called Weston, at a short distance to the south-east of Ross. The road proceeded hence across the beautiful country on the banks of the Wye, among hills covered with cinders and iron furnaces, to the town of Blestium, which antiquaries agree in placing at Monmouth, on a bend of the river. Thence the old road, continuing nearly in the same direction, carried the traveller to Burrium, another considerable town, the remains

quæ lingua Anglorum Grantacestir vocatur; et mox invenerunt juxta muros civitatis locellum de marmore albo pulcherrime factum, operculo quoque similis lapidis aptissime tectum.'—*Bedæ Hist. Eccl.*, lib. iv. c. 19.

* See the recently published work on the Roman antiquities of Cirencester, by Messrs Buckman and Newmarch, entitled 'Illustrations of the Remains of Roman Art, in Cirencester, the site of Ancient Corinium.'

of which have been found at Usk. This beautiful country, and all the southern coast of Wales, were well inhabited. After a short stage the traveller arrived at the grand city of Isca, the head-quarters of the second legion, remarkable for its theatre, its temples, and its palaces.* It stood on the river Usk, in a deep bottom, surrounded by lofty hills. Part of its massive walls still remain at Caerleon. The road proceeded hence to a station on the banks of the river Tibia (*the Taaf*), which it crossed, and continued its course to the town of Bovium, which is supposed to have stood at Ewenny, and to that of Nidum, the name of which appears to be preserved in that of Neath. A shorter stage than the two last brought the traveller to the town of Leucarum, the name of which is again preserved in the village of Llychwr, on the borders of the counties of Glamorgan and Caermarthen. Another stage conducted him to the more important town of Maridunum, finely situated on a beautiful river. Its site is occupied by the modern town of Caermarthen.† Twenty Roman miles further west was a station, which was probably of too little importance to have a name of its own, as it is simply designated in the Itinerary as Ad Vigesimum, which we may translate 'at the twentieth milestone.' Its site is supposed to be the spot now called Castle Flemish. The traveller next arrived at the town of Menapia, represented by the modern city of St David's, on the point of the pro-

---

* A large portion of the buildings of Isca seem to have been standing in the latter part of the twelfth century, when Giraldus wrote. He speaks of splendid palaces, a gigantic tower, public baths, a theatre, temples, subterranean buildings, aquæducts, or sewers, and he remarks the ingenious method of warming the houses by means of hypocausts; 'Erat autem hæc urbs antiqua et autentica, et a Romanis olim coctilibus muris egregie constructa. Videas hic multa pristinæ nobilitatis adhuc vestigia; palatia immensa aureis olim tectorum fastigiis Romanos fastus imitantia, eo quod a Romanis principibus primo constructa et ædificiis egregiis illustrata fuissent; turrim giganteam; thermas insignes; templorum reliquias; et loca theatralia muris egregiis partim adhuc extantibus, omnia clausa. Reperies ubique, tam intra murorum ambitum quam extra, ædificia subterranea, aquarum ductus, hypogeosque meatus. Et quod inter alia notabile censui, stuphas undique videas miro artificio consertas, lateralibus quibusdam et præangustis spiraculi viis occulte calorem exhalantibus.'—*Girald. Camb., Itiner. Cambriæ*, lib. i. c. 5. Recent discoveries of considerable interest, made on the site of Isca, have been described by Mr John Edward Lee, of Caerleon, in a quarto volume, entitled 'Delineations of Roman Antiquities found at Caerleon,' and in a supplementary volume, entitled 'Description of a Roman Building and other Remains lately discovered at Caerleon.'

† The Roman walls of Maridunum were partly standing in the time of Giraldus Cambrensis, who says: 'Est igitur hæc urbs antiqua coctilibus muris partim adhuc extantibus egregie clausa.—*Itin. Camb.*, lib. i. c. 10.

montory called by Ptolemy Octopitarum Promontorium. This was one of the ports from which ships passed over into Ireland.

From Burrium, a branch road turned off to the north-east, and carried the traveller towards the mountains of the interior of Wales, until he reached, at the foot of lofty hills, a town of no great magnitude, named Gobannium, which is supposed to have occupied the site of the present town of Abergavenny. Thence, returning eastwardly, he entered a fine open country surrounded with hills, in the centre of which was a town of much larger dimensions, which probably, from that circumstance, was called Magna. Its site is still to be found at Kenchester, near Hereford, where its tesselated floors are found in digging. The traveller here joined the direct road which had proceeded from Ariconium, through the rich country now forming the county of Hereford, to Magna, and thence it continued its course northwardly to Bravinium, a Roman town, supposed to have stood on the banks of the Teme, near the village of Leintwardine. The road proceeded thence to Uriconium, or Wroxeter, on the Severn,* and so continued its course northwardly. But the traveller might at Uriconium take the north-eastern road, which has been followed before, to Rutunium, the modern Rowton, or Ruyton, from whence another branch road carried him first to a town named Bovium, and, at a later period, Banchorium, which later name seems to be preserved in that of the modern village of Bangor on the border of Flintshire, and thence to the great city of Deva, the station of the twentieth legion, the interesting remains of whose labours are still found at Chester, on the Dee.

Deva, as may be supposed from its importance, both in a military and in a commercial point of view, was the centre of an extensive system of roads. One of these proceeding westwardly, carried the traveller first to Varæ, which stood at the modern Bodfari, the pass through the range of mountains which bound the Vale of Clwyd, and then to Conovium, a town, of which the remains are found at Caer-hûn in the vale of the Conway, at the northern foot of the mountain range of Snowdon. Another stage carried him to Segontium. If the traveller had taken the western road from Deva, at the end of the first stage, he would have reached the town of Condate, supposed to be Kinderton in Cheshire. Here he joined the northern road from Uriconium, and proceeded by it to Man-

* See before, p. 150.

cunium, now Manchester, and to the important town of Coccium, the site of which is found at Ribchester, celebrated for its Roman antiquities.* The next town on this road was near the sea, and was called, no doubt from the river on which it stood, Ad Alaunam. Its site is now occupied by Lancaster. Roads from this town and from Coccium met at Bremetonacæ, which has been placed at Overborough in Lancashire. Thence, in one direction, the road continued straight to Bronovacæ, and so forwards to Luguballium. The other road turned into the lake district, and proceeded first to the town of Galacum, supposed to have stood at or near Kendal, then to Alonæ, which has been identified with Ambleside, at the head of Windermere, thence to Galava, which is supposed to have occupied the site of the modern town of Keswick, and so on to Glanoventa and the coast towns at the entrance of the Solway.

From Coccium a road led eastwardly to the coast, where a port-town named Portus Sistuntiorum is supposed to have occupied the site of the town of Freckleton in Lancashire. Eastwardly from Coccium this road passed over a ridge of hills on the borders of Yorkshire, where, in one of the passes, was a station named from them Ad Alpes Penninos, to a town apparently of some importance called Olicana, now Ilkley in Yorkshire, from whence there was a road direct to Isurium, and another by Calcaria to Eburacum. Another road from Olicana led the traveller back to Mancunium, which also was the centre of several roads. One of these led eastward to Cambodunum, which seems to be rightly placed at Slack in Yorkshire, whence branch roads proceeded to Calcaria and to Danum. We will return, however, by the southern road to Condate, whence the road proceeded by another Mediolanum, which is placed at Chesterton in Staffordshire, to Eteocetum, or Wall, on the north-western road. Hence a road proceeded south, through an intermediate station, of which the name is lost, to the town of Salinæ, remarkable then for its salt-works and its salt-baths.†

* An altar found at Ribchester, and now preserved in St John's College, Cambridge, which has only recently been correctly read, seems to identify Ribchester with Bremetonacæ, in which case the Roman topography of this district requires a new investigation and arrangement.

† In a very curious Latin tract on the marvels of Britain, attached in manuscript to the pretended history of Nennius, and as old, no doubt, as the earlier part of the twelfth century, we have an account of a warm bath at Wich, or Droitwich, the walls of which were built of tiles and stones, and in which the bather always found the water of the temperature he wished : ' Tertium miraculum : stagnum calidum quod est in regione

Its site has still the same celebrity, and is called Droitwich. Ptolemy, at a much earlier period of the Roman rule, mentions a town called Salinæ, which he seems to place in the south of Lincolnshire; but this may possibly be an error of his copyists. The Salinæ of which we are speaking was a place of importance, on account of its salt trade, and several Roman roads are still traced from it; one of these led eastwardly, by another town called Alauna, now Alcester, on the river Alne in Warwickshire, crossing the river Avon at Stratford-upon-Avon. Another road led southerly, from Salinæ to a town of which the name is lost in the ancient Itinerary, but which we can hardly doubt occupied the site of the modern city of Worcester. This last place stood on the verge of the iron district, and seems to have been distinguished by its forges, as Alauna was by its smiths.* The road next crossed the Avon at a station named, from the river, Ad Antonam, and so continued its course to Glevum. The station on the Avon was the first stage in proceeding from Glevum to Alauna, and so to Benonæ and Ratæ, and to Lindum. The road by Salinæ and Eteocetum was also continued northerly, to a town called—also, no doubt, from a river—Ad Trivonam, supposed to have stood at Bury, in the parish of Bramston in Staffordshire. Thence the road proceeded to Derventio, which occupied the site of the hamlet of

Huich, et muro ambitur ex latere et lapide facto, et in eo vadunt homines per omne tempus ad lavandum, et unicuique sicut placuerit illi lavachrum sic fiat sibi secundum voluntatem suam; si voluerit lavachrum frigidum, erit, si calidum, calidum erit.'

* A very curious legend relating to the destruction of this town, is given in the life of St Egwin, the founder of Evesham, in Capgrave's 'Nova Legenda Angliæ.' The inhabitants, we are told, were an arrogant race, given to every kind of luxury. 'Erat namque juxta Eovesham ad octomilliaria castrum Alnecester, regale tunc mansum, cujus loci habitatores quanto rerum opulentia et temporalium abundantia affluebant tanto magis gulæ et luxuriæ dediti, studentes avaritiæ et cupiditati misericordia Dei se indignos efficiebant.'—They were principally workers in iron, and when the saint came to preach to them, in contempt of his doctrine they beat upon their anvils with a great noise.—'Et cum castrum illud veluti nemoribus undique consitum conflandi ferrum locus esset aptissimus, et fabris et ferri exclusoribus maxime repleretur, gens incredula incudes ferreis malleis tanto strepitu continue percutiebat, ut beati viri sermo non audiretur et a castro recedere cogitaretur.'—Upon this, he addressed his prayers to Heaven,—'contra artem fabrilem castri illius dominum imprecatus est.'—And the town was immediately destroyed. 'Et ecce subito castrum ipsum terra absorbuit, ita quod novo super veteri qualitercumque reædificato usque in hodiernum diem in constructione novarum domorum in fundamentis antiqua ædificia reperiuntur. Nunquam enim postea in loco illo aliquis artem fabrilem recte exercuit, nec aliquis eam exercere volens ibi vigere potuit.'

Little Chester on the Derwent. The road now entered the great mining district of the mountains of the Peak, and conducted the traveller to the town of Lutudarum, now Chesterfield, where the metals were brought to be transported to the south or the north. The road continued its course thence through the town of Morbium, supposed by some to have occupied the site of the modern Templeborough in Yorkshire, to Legiolium, and so on to the city of Eburacum. Morbium was on the western coast, a *Notitia* station. It is identified in Moresby by an inscription recording the Cataphracteridæ located there.*

The central districts of Roman Britain appear to have been traversed in every direction by cross roads. The traveller, in his return to the south, when he reached Eteocetum, might turn by the great road south-eastward towards Londinium, till he reached Tripontium, whence he turned off, by Benaventa and Isannavaria, south-westward to the town of Brinavæ, which is believed to have stood at a place called Black Ground, near Chipping Norton, where considerable remains are found. The country he now entered was thickly populated, and seems to have been covered with small towns and elegant villas. Two of the former stood near together at Bicester and Alcester, in Oxfordshire. The latter is considered to be the Roman Ælia Castra, the next station on this road, which proceeded thence over Ottmoor to Dorocina, which is identified with Dorchester in Oxfordshire. Six Roman miles hence the road passed the Thames to a station which, if we could suppose the number in the old Itinerary was wrong, might be the post on Sinodun Hill, which has been celebrated for its antiquities ever since the days of Leland,† otherwise we must either place it at or near Wallingford. The Itinerary of Richard of Cirencester calls it Tamesis. Hence the road proceeded direct to Calleva, but the Itinerary mentions no intermediate station.

The traveller from the metropolis passed through this city on

---

* Horseby is in error in placing all these towns and stations in close sequence. There seems to have been a station at Templeborough, but the name is not known.

† 'From Walingford to Sinodune a mile and a half. This place is wonderful dikid about, and stondith on a hille in Barkshir, hanging over the Tamise. It is yn by estimation half a mile. And withyn it hath beene sum toune, or, as the communne voice sayith, a castelle in the Britannes tyme, defacid by lyklihod by the Danes. At this tyme it berith very plentifullye both barley and whete, and *numismata Romanorum* be ther found yn ploughyng. About this Sinodune beginnith the fruteful vale of Whitehorse.'—*Leland's Itin.*, vol. ii. p. 14.

his way to the western extremities of the island. From Calleva he had a choice of two routes; one led him to the southern Venta, or, as it was called, from the tribe in whose district it stood, Venta Belgarum, an important town, represented by the modern city of Winchester. Hence the same road proceeded to the post of Clausentum, now Bittern, on the Southampton Water, from whence he might sail over to the Isle of Vectis, or Wight. Between Venta and Clausentum was a small town or station called Ad Lapidem.* Another road proceeded westward from Venta to the town of Brigis, or Brige, supposed to have stood at or near Broughton, in Hampshire, and soon after leaving this place the traveller approached the commanding fortifications of Sorbiodunum, surrounding the summit of a bold hill in the midst of a valley, and now called Old Sarum. The other road from Calleva ran direct by a town called Vindomis, supposed to have stood near Finkley beyond Whitchurch and St Mary Bourne, over the eastern part of Salisbury Plain to Sorbiodunum. The main road, leaving Sorbiodunum, proceeded to a town called Vindogladia, the traces of which are believed to be visible on the Dorsetshire Downs, near the Gussages, in the neighbourhood of Blandford. The next town of importance was Durnovaria, now Dorchester, but there appears to have been an intermediate station, the name of which is lost. The road now passed nearer the coast, and, after a long stage, in which there were probably some intermediate stations the names of which are not known, reached the town of Moridunum, placed by some at Honiton and by others at Seaton, and then pursued its course to the western Isca, called, from the British tribe which inhabited the district, Isca Dumnoniorum, a rich and important city on the borders of the mining districts. Its representative is the modern Exeter, remarkable for the number of Roman antiquities which have been from time to time dug up in it. The road next made a bend southward to avoid the wilds of Dartmoor, crossed the river Durius (*the Dart*), where there was a station, and there appear to have been others

---

* This place, which no doubt received its name from some remarkable monumental stone which was standing in the time of the Anglo-Saxons, was still known by its Roman name in the time of Bede, who tells us how the two young brothers of Oswald, king of Wight, were carried thither to be concealed from their enemies—perhaps among the ruins of the ancient town: 'Ubi cum delati essent in locum qui vocatur Ad Lapidem, occulendos se a facie regis victoris credidissent.'—*Bed. Hist. Ecc.*, lib. iv. c. 16. The memory of the monument that gave name to the Roman station, seems to be preserved in its present name of Stoneham.

where the road crossed the rivers Tamara (*the Tamar*), Voluba (*the Fowey*), and Cenia (*the Fal*), on its way to the extremity of Cornwall. This was a wild country, and perhaps thinly inhabited.

The extensive and rich district between Sorbiodunum and Glevum was covered in every direction with extensive and magnificent villas, marking it out as the most fashionable part of the island. In its centre stood a city remarkable for its splendid edifices, its temples, its buildings for public amusement, and still more so for its medicinal baths. For this latter reason it was called Aquæ Solis, the Waters of the Sun, and for the same cause its representative in modern times has received the name of Bath. Remains of the Roman bathing-houses have been discovered in the course of modern excavations. Among its temples was a magnificent one dedicated to Minerva, who is supposed to have been the patron goddess of the place.* From inscriptions found at different periods, it appears that military commanders, high municipal officers, and other persons of rank, frequented this city for the benefit of its waters, and, perhaps, to mix in its fashionable society.

As might be expected, Aquæ Solis was the centre of many roads, which communicated with every part of the island. One road went northwardly to Corinium (*Cirencester*), whence the traveller might proceed across the island to Lindum (*Lincoln*), or he might go to Glevum (*Gloucester*) and to the towns on the Severn, or he might turn eastward towards London. The road from Corinium to Aquæ Solis continued its course southwardly from the latter place to another bathing town called Ad Aquas, and now known by the somewhat similar name of Wells. Here the road separated into two branches, one of which proceeded to a town called, from the river on which it stood, Ad Uxellam, now Bridgewater, and thence to Isca (*Exeter*); the other led by a town of some importance named Ischalis, now Ilchester, to Moridunum on the southern coast. The traveller, who would proceed direct from Londinium to Aquæ Solis, followed the western road till he reached the town of Spinæ (*Speen*), where

* The temple of Minerva, at Bath, is mentioned by Geoffrey of Monmouth (*Hist. Brit.*, lib. ii. c. 10), and it was, perhaps, standing in his time. The ruins of it were found in the course of excavations for the foundations of a new Pump Room, at the close of the last century. A magnificent volume on the Roman antiquities of Bath, was published by Samuel Lysons, and forms a part of his *Reliquiæ Romano-Britannicæ*. Leland (*Itin.*, vol. ii. p. 34) describes a considerable number of Roman sculptures then (in the time of Henry VIII.) built up in the town-walls of Bath.

he turned off by a branch road which led him by the towns of Cunetio, the site of which has been traced, by Roman antiquities found there, at Folly Farm, near Marlborough, and Verlucio, which, for similar reasons, has been fixed at Highfield, in Sandy Lane, near Heddington, to Aquæ Solis. From Aquæ the same road was continued to a station on the Avon called Ad Abonam, or Abona, which seems to be correctly placed at Bitton, and thence to another post on the banks of the Avon, where it enters the Bristol Channel, thence called Ad Sabrinam, and believed to have stood at Sea-Mills, a short distance from Bristol. Hence was the *trajectus*, or passage, across the estuary, and the traveller landed on the opposite coast at a station called Ad Trajectum, supposed to have stood on a spot now called Severn-Side. He now entered upon the great road through Wales, called still by the Welsh the Sarn Helen, or road of Helen, from a notion that a Roman empress of that name caused it to be made. A short stage brought him to a strongly fortified town, name Venta, and often, to distinguish it from other towns of the same name in the island, Venta Silurum. Its walls are still seen at Caerwent. If he liked he might proceed hence to Isca (*Caerleon*), and so along the southern road, which is called by some old writers the Via Julia, to Menapia; but his direct road lay by Burrium (*Usk*), and Gobannium (*Abergavenny*), whence the Sarn Helen is distinctly traced across the mountains to the Luentinum of Ptolemy, which, from its remains that have been discovered at Llanio, in Cardiganshire, seems to have been an important post, and thence in a direction parallel to the western coast up to Conovium and Segontium.

One road only remains to be noticed. When the traveller was at Clausentum, on the Southampton river, he might have returned eastward along the coast. The first stage on this road carried him to Portus Magnus, the extensive and massive walls of which are still standing at Porchester. The next stage brought him to Regnum, a large town, represented by the modern Chichester. Where the road passed the river Avon was a station, probably a mere posting place, called, from its distance from Regnum, Ad Decimum, but of which no traces are left to mark its site. The road then carried him to the important port of Anderida, which there can hardly be a doubt is Pevensey, a place remarkable for its imposing remains of Roman builddings.* A road went hence across the weald to Novioma-

---

* Considerable excavations were made in the Roman area at Pevensey,

gus and Londinium, having a station in the midst of the forest, which from it was called Silva Anderida. The coast road, after leaving Anderida, proceeded to a post, or station, on the Lymne river, named Ad Lemanum, and then running across the land to avoid the low marshes on the coast, about ten miles further it reached the Portus Lemanis, at the place now called from it Lymne, where so many interesting discoveries have recently been made.* The road next passed behind Folkestone, where, though not mentioned in the Itinerary, there was probably a small town, perhaps the elevated entrenchments now called popularly Cæsar's Camp, which contained a lighthouse or pharos. At the next station, Dubræ, now Dover, the pharos itself, within somewhat similar entrenchments, is still standing. The road now conducted the traveller to Rutupiæ, whence, having thus traversed the whole island, and viewed the excellence of its roads, its flourishing towns, the highly-cultivated plains of the interior, its forests and mountains rich in mineral productions and game, he might embark and return to Gaul.

in 1852, under the direction of Mr Roach Smith, and have been described in his 'Report on Excavations made upon the site of the Roman Castrum at Pevensey, in Sussex, in 1852,' 4to, 1858.

* The account of the recent excavations on this interesting site is given in Mr Roach Smith's 'Antiquities of Richborough, Reculver, and Lymne,' and in a separate volume by the same well-known antiquary, entitled a 'Report on Excavations made on the site of the Roman castrum at Lymne in Kent, in 1850,' 4to, 1852.

CHAPTER VI.

A Roman Town in Britain—Its Walls, Towers, and Gates—Materials and Modes of Construction—The Houses—Their Plan and Arrangement—The Tesselated Pavements and Frescoed Walls—Method of Warming the Houses; the Hypocausts—The Baths—Windows and Roofs—Distribution of the Houses in Streets—Public Buildings; Temples, Basilicæ, Theatres, Amphitheatres—The Suburbs and Burial-places—Sanitary Arrangements; Sewers, Rubbish-pits.—The Language of Britain.

WE have seen in the preceding chapter how thickly Roman Britain was studded with towns, even if we only reckon those marked in the official Itineraries, which have perhaps come down to us themselves in an imperfect form. When we look, on one hand, at the description of Britain in the anonymous cosmography of the seventh century, where many names occur that are not mentioned elsewhere; and when we consider, on the other hand, the numerous sites of Roman towns or stations that may still be traced in different parts of the island, which are not mentioned in the Itineraries, we are still more struck with the picture of Roman Britain as it thus presents itself to us. The English reader of the nineteenth century will naturally be curious to have some notion of the appearance of these towns, and of their comparative magnitude and comforts; and fortunately, although much remains to be done by the antiquary in this respect, accidental discoveries have furnished us with considerable materials for gratifying his wish.

We have no means of ascertaining the periods at which, or the circumstances under which, the Roman towns in Britain were built. The Roman Camulodunum we know was founded by a body of disbanded veterans, and the other towns seem to have been built in the same manner by bodies of troops, Romans or auxiliaries, as they advanced in the occupation of the island. We learn from the earlier historians, that, though the troops had here and there fortified stations—*castra* or *castella*—the towns were not surrounded with walls. Such was the case with Camulodunum, Londinium, and Verulamium. But subsequently—we cannot fix the period, though it was no doubt at the time when the towns rose into political importance—they were all surrounded with walls, and these walls, which were so massive in character that in some instances they have outlived sixteen centuries, must have formed so prominent an object in the outward appearance of the town, that they will naturally first attract our attention.

The more usual form of the enclosure, following that of the Roman camp, was a parallelogram more or less elongated, but in some cases, especially in large towns, such as Calleva (*Silchester*), Magna (*Kenchester*), Uriconium (*Wroxeter*), and perhaps Durovernum (*Canterbury*), the walls inclosed an area of a very irregular form. When the town stood on the coast, or on the banks of a large river, there were usually walls only on three sides, the side to the sea or river being open. From their ruinous condition in modern times, we are imperfectly acquainted with the altitude of the walls of the Roman towns in Britain. The walls of Rutupiæ (*Richborough*), where most perfect, are nearly thirty feet high, but this was perhaps an unusual elevation. The walls of Gariannonum (*Burgh in Suffolk*), where they appear to be of nearly their original height, have an elevation of only fourteen feet. The great wall of Hadrian was not above eighteen or nineteen feet high. The highest part of the wall at Lymne is about twenty-three feet. At Lymne, the walls are about fourteen feet thick; those at Richborough are at the bottom between eleven and twelve feet thick, and diminish slightly towards the top; while those at Burgh, in Suffolk, are not more than nine feet in thickness

The walls were supported at the corners, and at certain distances along their face, by towers, either square or round. At Richborough, there were round towers at the corners, and two square towers at each side wall. The round towers have been here so entirely destroyed that their existence was only ascertained by excavations. The cut on the next page represents the lower part of the tower at the south-west angle, as thus brought to light, with a part of the adjacent wall. It will be seen that the angle of the wall was built first, and that the tower, which, as far as it remains, is a solid mass of masonry, was added afterwards. The square towers along the face of the wall seem to have been attached much in the same way; they projected only about eight feet from the wall, and were solid to the height

CHAP. VI.] TOWERS AND GATEWAYS. 173

of eight feet from the foundation, after which they were hollow in the centre and they were built into the main wall at the

Wall and Tower at Richborough (Rutupiæ).

top. This was probably the case with the round towers also. At Burgh Castle the towers are all round, and they are singular in their construction. From the foundation to about one half their elevation, that is, to the height of about seven feet, they are entirely detached from the wall, but at that height they become enlarged in diameter, so as to join to the wall. They consist of solid masonry, with the exception of a hole in the centre of the upper surface, two feet deep, and as many wide, the object of which is by no means evident. The towers at Lymne appear to have been quite solid. The most perfect of them is represented in the cut on the next page. It remains about ten feet in height, and seems, like those at Richborough, to have been built separate from the wall; the other towers at Lymne have been segments of circles, joined to the wall. In other instances we find no round towers, but only square buttresses; at Aldborough and York these seem to have been small hollow towers. At Caerwent the wall is supported by a series of pentagonal towers or buttresses, perfectly solid, and built up against the wall, and not into it, though they may have been attached at the top. At York, the large multangular tower which occupied one corner of the walls is still standing.

Each fortress or town had generally one principal entrance gate, which, for its importance, was usually called the decuman gate (*porta decumana*). Sufficient remains of the principal

Tower at Lymne (*Portus Lemanis*).

gateway have been preserved in very few instances in Britain to enable us to understand its form, probably because it was often composed, more or less, of larger stones, which offered a temptation to mediæval builders. At Lymne, the great entrance gateway stood about the middle of the eastern wall. It consisted of two semicircular solid towers, with the gate probably in a curtain between them. It was raised upon a solid platform of immense stones, and, when recently uncovered, the stones which formed the pavement bore distinct impressions, worn by the wheels of the carriages which had passed over them. Our engraving represents the ruins of this gateway as they appeared after the earth which covered them had been dug away. The lower part of the tower on the left was well preserved, and the stones of the lower course of the other were in their place when first opened, but they were soon cleared away or covered, and the tower is only represented by a small mound of shapeless masonry. The stones, partly displaced, which formed the platform, are seen in front; the stones of the gateway were thrown in confusion in a deep hollow behind. Some of them appeared by their mouldings to have formed the

Ruins of the Gate at Lymne (*Portus Lemanis*).

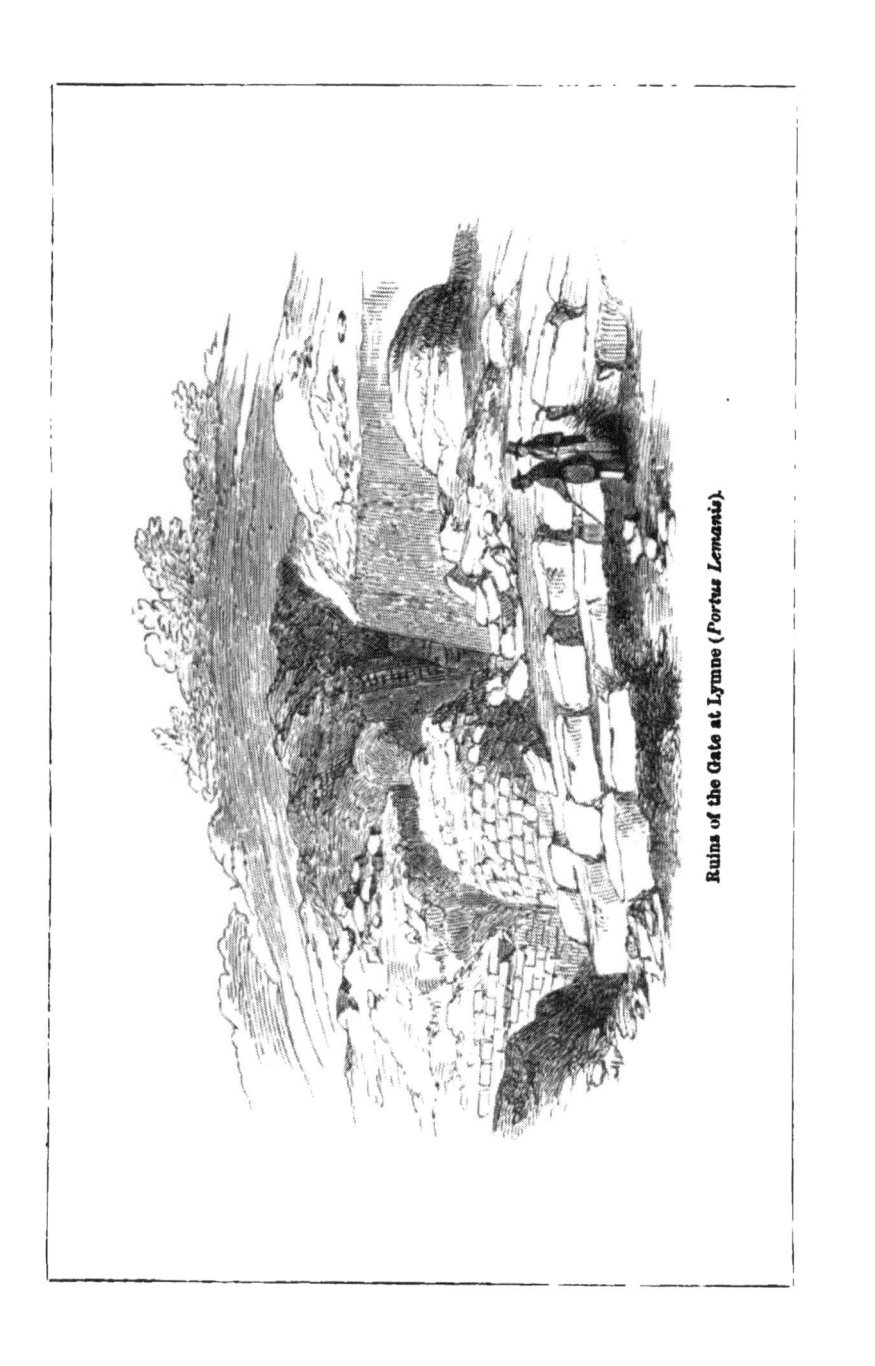

lintels; one seemed to be the base of a column, and in others were found holes still containing masses of lead which had fixed the ironwork of the hinges of the gate. On the left is seen the wall as it joined up to the gateway tower. The most singular circumstance in the structure of this gateway was the manner in which the semicircular towers joined the wall. The latter was cut off vertically at right angles, and the corner of the tower joined the corner of the wall, so that the inner flat surface of the tower was in a line with the outer surface of the wall. Thus the tower and the wall did not support each other, and if there was nothing else to strengthen them, an enemy might have broken his way through the point of junction with the greatest ease. This, however, is probably to be explained by supposing that the gate itself was an edifice built of large blocks of stone, and forming the continuation of the wall, and that the two towers were only facings or supports to it.

The decuman gate at Richborough was in the middle of the western wall, and excavations have shown that it also stood on a platform of large stones. The wall adjoining to it has been much damaged and broken, but it appears to have been cut through by a small opening in its whole height, in which opening a gateway was' built of larger stones. There are no traces of its having had towers as at Lymne. At Pevensey (*Anderida*), the principal gateway stood at one corner of the angular area, and had side towers, as at Lymne. The foundations of the buildings of this gateway have been laid open in the course of recent excavations. The most perfect example of a Roman gateway now existing in this country is that called the Portway gate, at Lincoln, which is represented in our cut on the next page. It will be seen at once that this differs essentially from those we have been describing, and in fact it is not the decuman or principal gate of the Roman city of Lindum, but one of the subordinate entrances. The two actual entrances, one for carriages and the other for foot passengers, are well preserved, and the wall, running off inwardly at right angles between them, appears to have formed part of the portal buildings, containing guard-rooms and other offices. At Colchester, Mr Roach Smith discovered very interesting remains of the buildings attached to one of the gates of Camulodunum. It was the gate on the west side of the town, and consisted of a chief entrance for horses and carriages, and a subordinate archway, apparently on each side, for foot passengers. It was protected by advanced bastions. The chief entrance was not quite twelve feet wide. The subordinate archway on the right hand on entering is preserved in comparatively a perfect state, the upper part of it entirely composed of long tiles. By the

Roman Gate at Lincoln (*Lindum*).

side of it is a room in the form of a quadrant, twenty-six feet in length by fourteen in width, entered by a large arched doorway, and which, there can be little doubt, was a guard-room. At Borcovicus (*Housesteads*), on the wall of Hadrian, the gateways, especially that on the western side, remain in a state in which we can easily understand their details. This western gateway had two portals or passages, with a square guard-room on each side. Its outer face was level with the wall of the station, and each portal led through a passage which extended the depth of the two guard-rooms, which were entered by doors from the passage. At Colchester, the entrance to the guard-room was not from the passage, but from the interior wall. 'This gateway,' says Mr Collingwood Bruce, speaking of the entrance to Borcovicus, 'as well as the others which have been explored, is, in every sense of the word, double. Two walls must be passed before the station can be entered; each is provided with two portals, and each portal has been closed with two-leaved gates. The southern entrance of the outside wall has alone, as yet, been entirely cleared of the masonry which closed it. The jambs and pillars are formed of massive stones of rustic masonry. The doors, if we may judge from the fragments of corroded iron which have been lately picked up, were of wood, strengthened with iron plates and studs; they moved, as is apparent from the pivot-holes, upon pivots of iron. In the centre of each portal stands a strong upright stone, against which the gates have shut. Some of the large projecting stones of the exterior wall are worn as if by the sharpening of knives upon them; this has probably been done by the occupants of the suburban buildings after the closing of the gateway. The guard-chambers on each side are in a state of choice preservation, one of the walls standing fourteen courses high. Were a roof put on them, the antiquary might here stand guard, as the Tungrians did of old, and, for a while, forget that the world is sixteen centuries older than it was when these chambers were reared.'

Besides these larger gateways, there were posterns and smaller gateways, more or less numerous, according to the extent of the walls. At Richborough there is a well-preserved postern gate, of a peculiar construction, in the middle of the north-eastern wall. The gate is covered by an advanced wall, which outwardly has the appearance of a large square tower. The entrance is on one side, and runs first by the side of the main wall and between it and the advanced wall, and then turns at a right angle through the main wall into the inclosure. It appears to have been open to the top, without any covering. At Lymne there appear to have been several small portals, and some of what were outwardly semicircular towers had small chambers below.

From the dilapidated state in which the walls of the Roman stations in this country now present themselves, we cannot form a perfect idea of their appearance when entire. The walls of Chester, and probably those of other places, were crowned with an ornamental coping, above which perhaps rose battlements. There is an illuminated MS. of the Psalter in the British Museum (MS. Harl., No. 603), which appears to belong to the latter end of the Anglo-Saxon period, and in which we find several pictures of walled towns, no doubt either copied from much more ancient drawings of such objects, or representing the walls as they were still seen. In either case, though they are often defective in regard to perspective, and the artist, by a conventional mode of treating his subject which was common in the middle ages, represents the buildings of the interior only by a temple or public edifice, these pictures no doubt give us a tolerably accurate notion of the appearance which the walls of a Roman town must have presented. Our engraving represents a part of one of these pictures, in which the mode of representing the sun (Apollo) is peculiarly classical. The serpentine figure in the interior is intended to represent water running in two streams from a pond or reservoir. The supporting towers, with the exception of those of the gateway, are here square, and they all appear to be, like those in our Roman remains, solid up to a certain height. The diminishing of the gateway towers, as they rise, is also to be remarked. The principal gateway at Lymne must, when entire, have borne a close resemblance to the one in this picture. Another similar gateway is shown in

Sketch of an ancient Town-wall, from MS. Harl. No. 603.

the smaller cut annexed, taken from the same manuscript. The supporting towers are here round, still solid at the bottom, and terminating at the top in the same manner as those of the gateway. The opening at the bottom of the tower to the right is probably intended to represent a postern entrance, rather than a low window.

The masonry of Roman buildings in this country is universally good, and the materials well chosen and well prepared. The town walls generally consist of two parallel facings of stones and tiles, the interior filled up with a mass of mortar mixed with rubble and other materials. The stone for building may be generally traced to neighbouring quarries; but if none good enough is found in the neighbourhood, it was often brought from a considerable distance. Some of the stone used for building at Richborough is supposed to have been brought over from

Part of the Walls of a Town, from MS. Harl. No. 603.

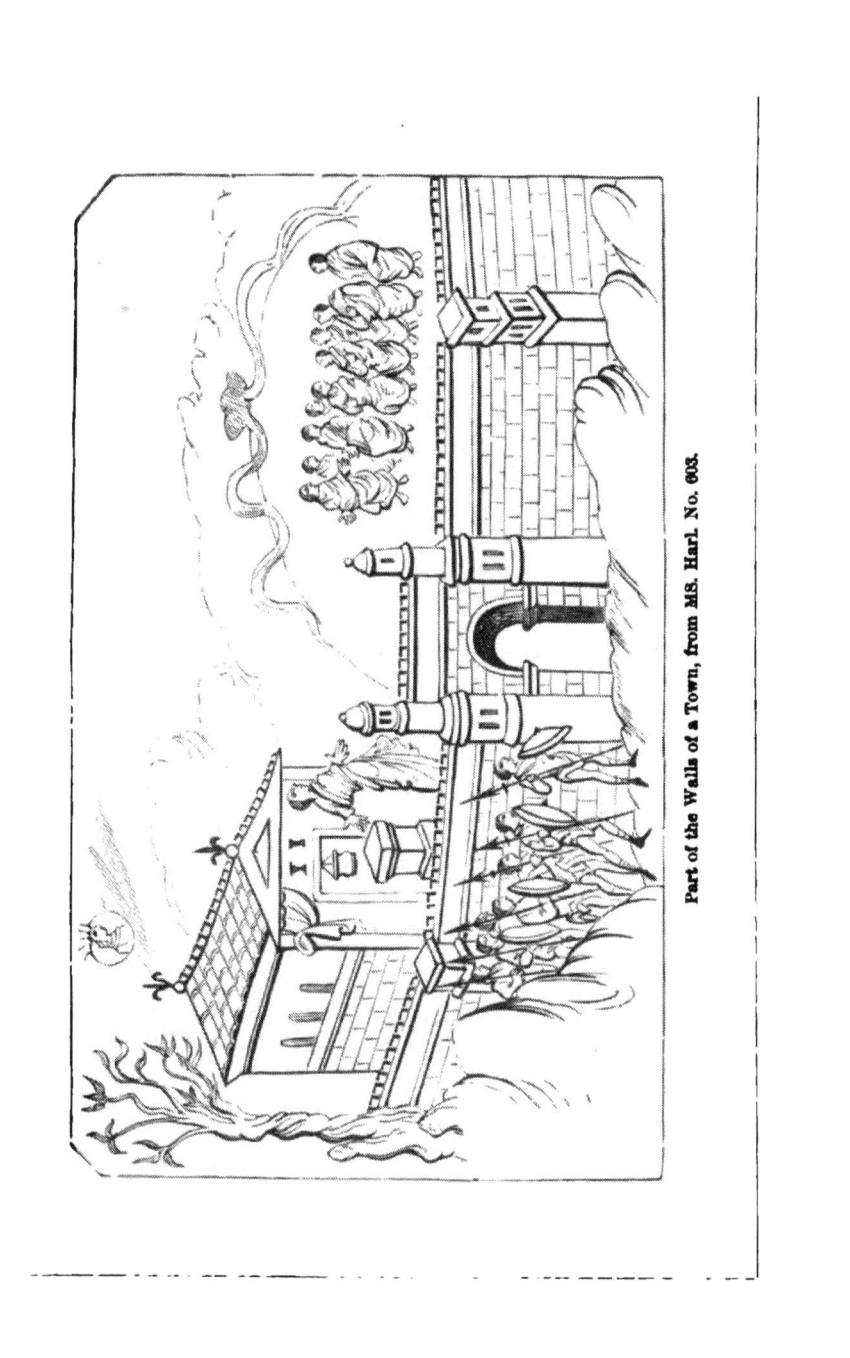

Gaul. The careful and exact manner in which even the small facing stones of the walls are squared, shows them to be the work of excellent masons. In general, these facing stones are slightly wedge-shaped, the smaller end being placed towards the interior of the wall, which seems to have been intended to give them a better hold on the mortar. In Hadrian's Wall, the facing stones, which taper towards the inner extremity considerably, are remarkably long in comparison to the size of the face which presents itself outwardly; the latter being usually eight or nine inches by ten or eleven, while the length inwardly is as much as twenty inches. This was no doubt designed for strength. The part of the stone exposed to the weather was cut across what masons call the bait, to hinder its scaling off by the lines of stratification. The facings of the stones in Hadrian's Wall are sometimes roughly tooled, or, as it is technically termed, scabbed with the pick; and in some parts of the line this tooling takes a definite form. Sometimes the pattern thus formed consists of upright, or nearly upright, lines; at other

Facings of Stones, Hadrian's Wall.

times the stone is scored with waved lines, or with small squares, and with other designs. Of the three examples here given, the one in the middle, which is usually termed diamond-broaching, is the most common. The masons' marks are often found on the stones in Roman buildings, and resemble most closely those of the masons of the middle ages. Sometimes they consist of a letter, perhaps the initial of the mason's name; but they are more usually crosses, triangles, and other geometrical figures. The cut in the next page represents four of the more common masons' marks on the Wall of Hadrian.

One of the most remarkable characteristics of Roman building was the extensive use of bricks, or, perhaps more properly speaking, tiles; for the latter word, as we now understand it, expresses more accurately the form of the Roman building tiles. They are always flat, generally from half an inch to an inch, or even two inches, in thickness, and the smaller tiles are generally

Masons' Marks, Hadrian's Wall.

about seven inches square. But others are found considerably larger, and these are often much longer than broad. The old writers, such as Pliny and Vitruvius, give exact directions for the making of tiles, and in those found in England the clay has evidently been prepared and tempered with great care; they are most commonly of a dark red colour, but in others the colour is much brighter, and tiles of the two colours are mixed together in a regular arrangement, no doubt for the purpose of ornament. Our cut on the next page represents a group of the different sorts of tiles most commonly used in Roman buildings in Britain. In front are three ordinary building tiles, of different shapes and dimensions; one, taken from the remains of a house found at Dover (*Dubræ*), has four holes, which had been used in some way or other to fix it in its place. The two standing behind are flue tiles, for the passage of air or water. These are always scored, in patterns of great variety, apparently for the purpose of being fixed more tenaciously by the mortar. Many of them, for purposes which will be explained hereafter, have square holes at the sides. The tile lying flat on the left has its edges turned, or, as it is technically termed, flanged, and was used principally for roofing, though we find these flanged tiles employed sometimes for forming the body of drains, and they are not unfrequently met with in the bonding courses of walls, probably when the builders fell short of the regular building tiles.* The other is a ridge tile.

* An example of this will be found in the cut on p. 174, from Lymne, where there is a row of flanged tiles in the walls adjacent to the tower.

The ordinary building-tiles often bear inscriptions indicating the troops or officials, by whom, or under whose directions, the

Roman Tiles.

buildings were erected. This is especially the case with the different legions. Thus at Chester (*Deva*) the tiles bear the name and title of the twentieth legion, LEG. XX. V. V. (*legio xx. valens victrix*); at Caerleon (*Isca*) and the stations thereabouts, and in South Wales, we find tiles with the inscription LEG. II. AVG. (*legio ii. Augusta*); and at York (*Eburacum*) the inscriptions on the tiles are LEG. VI. VICT. (*legio vi. victrix*), and LEG. IX. HISP. (*legio ix. Hispanica*). At Lymne and Dover, on the Kentish coast, the usual inscription on the tiles is CL. BR., which is supposed to mean *classiarii Britannici*, the marines of the British fleet. The inscriptions on tiles found in London are more difficult of interpretation. They read PRB. LON, or PPBR. LON, or as it occurs in one case, P. PR. BR. This latter form of the inscription occurs on a flanged tile, found in excavations in the city, which is represented in the annexed cut. The most probable interpretation is that which explains it as *proprætor Britanniæ Londinii*, the Proprætor of Britain at Londinium. This inscription has thus a peculiar interest, as

Flanged Tile from London.

showing that Roman London was the seat of government of the province.

The tiles were probably made in the neighbourhood of the buildings in which they were used, and the brick-yards seem to have been unenclosed, for we find on the surfaces of many of them the indentations not only of the feet of men, but of a considerable variety of animals which have passed over them before they were baked. On bricks found at Wroxeter (*Uriconium*), we find the footsteps of several kinds of dogs, of sheep, of goats, and of pigs. The tile to the right in the annexed cut, which was found at Wroxeter, has the prints of the feet of a dog; the other, from an extensive Roman villa, at Linley Hall, near Bishop's Castle, in Shropshire, presents the impressions of the two shoes of a man who has stood upon it. They are remarkable for their numerous and large nails. The tiles found at Wroxeter also present impressions of the feet of a cow, and of those of apparently a colt.

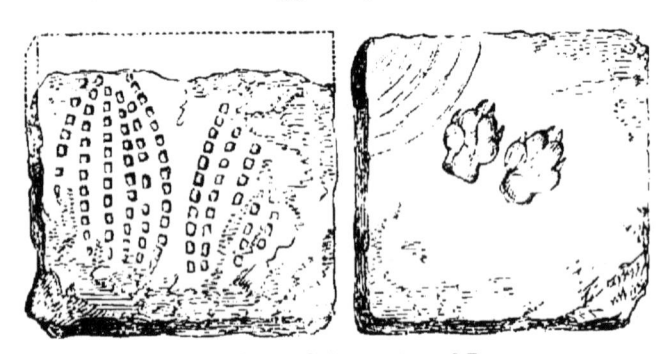

Roman Tiles with Impressions of Feet.

As stated before, the Romans chose good stones for their buildings, and squared them and fitted them together with great care, and even where the facings of their walls have been exposed to the air so many centuries, if not injured by the hands of man, they preserve a remarkable freshness of appearance. But wherever they have been buried by the accumulation of soil, when the earth is removed the masonry appears as fresh as if it had been the work of yesterday. Such was the case with the town walls at Lymne, as well as the lower parts of the walls at Richborough as shown in our cut on p. 178. On the walls of Cilurnum, on Hadrian's Wall, as on those of

Pevensey, the marks of the trowel on the mortar are still distinctly visible, and our cut annexed shows the regular appearance of the masonry at another station on the wall, Borcovicus, as it appeared when uncovered.

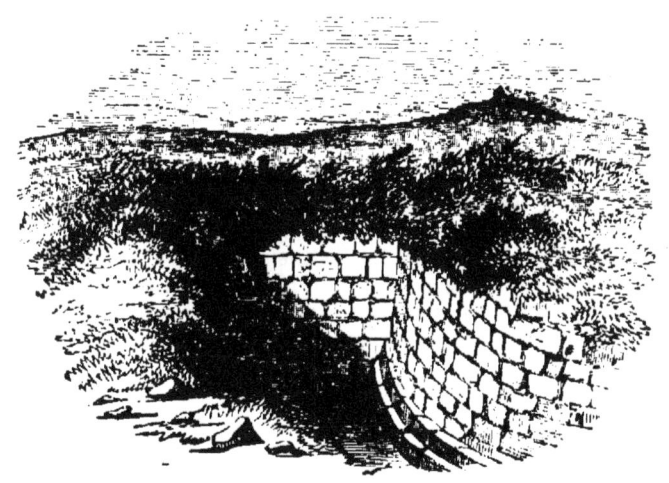

Wall at Housesteads in Northumberland (*Borcovicus*).

This latter is a very good example of Roman masonry. The walls, even in houses, had generally one or two set-off courses of stone at the bottom. There were two, as we here see, in the walls of Borcovicus, and this seems to have been generally the case on the line of Hadrian's Wall. In some instances the second course was bevelled off into a moulding. At Richborough, as shown in our cut on page 173, there was one footing course bevelled off in this manner. In the Wall of Hadrian, as we are informed by Mr Bruce, the foundation had been prepared by the removal of the natural soil to the width of about nine feet. This excavation was at most from fifteen to eighteen inches deep. On the outer and inner margins of the ground thus bared, two rows of flags, of from two to four inches in thickness, and eighteen to twenty in breadth, were generally laid without mortar. On these lay the first course of facing-stones, which were usually the largest stones used in the structure. In higher courses the facing-stones are uniformly of freestone, but on the ground course a whin-stone is occasionally introduced. The flag-stones of the foundation usually project from one to five inches beyond the first course of facing-stones, and these again usually stand about an inch or two beyond the second course, after which the wall is carried straight up. The foundation of the walls at Richborough is formed of two rows of boulders, laid upon, or a very little below, the surface of the natural soil, which is a compact pit-sand. At Burgh Castle, in Suffolk, the ancient Gariannonum, the massive walls were simply built upon the plain ground. The chalk and lime of the original soil was covered with earth hard beaten down; upon this were laid planks of oak nearly two inches thick, and upon them a bed of coarse mortar, on which the first stones of the superstructure were placed. Some years ago, one of the round towers, undermined by a channel cut by continual floods of rain, was overthrown, and thus the nature of the foundation was shown, the form and even the grain of the oaken planks being impressed on the mortar. At Wroxeter (*Uriconium*), in the buildings of the town, the walls have very deep foundations in the ground.

The Roman bricks, or tiles, were not used in construction as we use them now, to form the mass of the wall, but they were built in as bonding courses, or used for turning arches, and for various other purposes of ornament or strength. The bonding courses of bricks are peculiarly characteristic of Roman masonry in this country, as well as on the continent. They are shown, as seen at Richborough and Lymne, in our cuts on pages 173 and 174. In both these localities, the courses consist of two rows of tiles; at Burgh, in Suffolk, there are three rows of tiles in each course; and at Colchester there are three and four rows of tiles in a course. Sometimes they are still more numerous. In the multangular tower at York there are five rows in a course; and the walls of a building in Lower Thames Street, London, discovered in 1848, were constructed entirely of tiles set in mortar, without any courses of stones. At Richborough the first bonding course of tiles commences at three feet four inches from the surface of the ground at its present level, and about five feet from the bottom of the wall; and they are repeated upwards at distances varying from three feet three inches to four feet three inches. The distances between the bonding courses vary in other places, and they appear not to have been regulated by any fixed rule. In some rare instances the rows of tiles went through the whole thickness of the wall, but generally they only run one tile deep. They are almost always multiplied at the angles and turnings of walls. At Richborough, in the angles, there are generally two short courses between each of the regular courses. In some instances, more especially in houses and public buildings, the angles of the walls are composed entirely of tiles. Arches are generally formed of tiles placed in a position radiating from the centre. In some instances, large arches and vaults are composed entirely of immense masses of tiles placed in this manner, as in the fragment called the Jury Wall, at Leicester, and in the arched gateway already mentioned at Colchester.

The system just described was the one generally followed in Roman buildings in this country, though there are exceptions. In the walls of several Roman towns, as at Reculver (*Regulbium*), Silchester (*Calleva*), Kenchester (*Magna*), Caerwent (*Venta Silurum*), Chester (*Deva*), and in Hadrian's Wall, and all the stations adjacent to it, tiles are not used. It is not possible, with our present knowledge, to assign any reason for this deviation from the general practice. At Silchester there are bonding courses of single rows of large flat stones. At Caerwent, where the walls are faced with limestone, there are four bonding courses of red sandstone, which when fresh would look like tiles. Similar variations are found in regard to the stone-masonry. The walls at Chester were formed of large squared stones, and must have had a very noble appearance. The walls of Burgh Castle and Silchester, and those of Richborough, in the interior, were faced with flints. At Silchester, the flints were placed in what is popularly called herring-bone work. The small remains of walls at Kenchester also exhibit herring-bone work. Variations like this arose no doubt from fashion or caprice which prevailed in particular districts, or was adopted by certain masons. The herring-bone masonry is often found in Roman buildings; and was seen in its perfection in the numerous houses brought to light by the excavations of Mr Artis at Castor (*Durobrivæ*).

The mortar employed by the Romans possesses several peculiarities; and we learn from the directions of Vitruvius, that the composition of it was attended to with great care. It strikes the ordinary observer by its extreme strength and durability; he will break with much greater ease the stones with which the wall is faced than the mortar which holds them together. As we find it in Britain, the Roman mortar is generally composed of lime, pounded tiles, sand, and gravel, more or less coarse, and even small pebble stones. These ingredients vary in their quantities, but usually the lime and pounded tiles predominate, which is the cause of its extreme hardness. Occasionally, as at Silchester, Caerwent, and Kenchester, the pounded tiles are omitted, and in common buildings, mortar of an inferior description is used, composed merely of sand and lime. At Richborough, the mortar used in the interior of the wall is composed of lime, sand, and pebbles, or sea-beach; but the facing-stones throughout are cemented with a much finer mortar, in which pounded tile is introduced.*

The mode in which the wall was constructed seems to have been as follows. The facing-stones were first built up to a certain height, and set in mortar of a finer and better description. Then fresh liquid mortar was poured in in large quantities in the space between, heaps of rubble or stones were cast in with it, and the whole soon hardened into a solid mass. In some instances, the stones of the interior of the wall are placed in layers, and are arranged with considerable precision. The

* 'The tenacity of the mortar which was used forms an important element in the strength of the whole fabric. That which is in use now is generally spoiled, from a variety of circumstances. The prevailing practice is, first of all to slack the lime by pouring a quantity of water upon it when lying in a heap; in most cases this does not sufficiently pulverize it; it is then mixed with any earth bearing the least resemblance to sand, and the two are worked together very imperfectly with a shovel. The mortar thus made often stands and hardens, so as to require to be once and again mixed with water, and worked up before it is used. It thus becomes quite impoverished; and after all, for the convenience of the mason, it is employed in so dry a state, that the stone soon takes all the moisture from it, and it becomes little better than powder. The gigantic railway operations of recent times have driven men out of the beaten track, and compelled them afresh to discover the Roman method of preparing mortar. On the authority of engineers well acquainted with the Roman Wall, I am enabled to state, that the mortar of that structure is precisely similar to the grout and concrete of the railway mason of the present day. Specimens of the ancient and modern grout are before me, and there cannot be a doubt as to the identity of their preparation. The following is the mode in which the railway engineer prepares his mortar. The lime, in the state in which it comes from the kiln, is first ground to powder, and is then mixed with sand and gravel, and chippings of stone. The purposes for which the mortar is required, indicate the coarseness and quantity of the intermingling gravel. When wanted as concrete, to form, independently of other materials, the foundation of some heavy structure, stony fragments of larger size are mingled with the lime than when the mortar is to be used to cement chiselled stones, or even than when wanted to constitute, with rubble, the interior of a wall. The mixture of pounded lime and gravel, when made, is not mingled with water until the moment of application to the work for which it is required, but it is then intimately united with an abundant quantity of it. When used as concrete, the mass will, in three hours, have solidity sufficient to bear the weight of a man, and in about three days it will have acquired a rock-like firmness.'—*Bruce's 'Roman Wall*,' p. 86.

interior of the walls at Lymne is composed chiefly of the hard stone of the neighbourhood, which has been thrown into the mortar in rough pieces as quarried. In the Wall of Hadrian, whin-stones, as the material most abundant in the district, were 'puddled in' amongst the mortar to fill up the interior of the wall. When this had been done, more courses of facing-stones were built up, and then the interior was filled in in the same manner, and when the whole was finished it formed a solid, compact mass. In the walls at Richborough, and at other places, we trace a number of small holes on the face of the walls, which were probably made to support scaffolding. In some cases, where the walls, as in the buildings at Wroxeter (*Uriconium*), were not more than three feet thick, these holes go right through.

In some parts of the Roman walls in Britain we observe irregularities, which seem to have arisen from the accidental deficiency of particular kinds of materials. In the pharos at Dover, when the masons ran short of the large tiles which are so plentifully employed in its construction, they hewed pieces of the Folkestone rock into the form of tiles, and used them instead. In other instances, we find roof or other tiles used instead of building tiles. An instance has been already noticed, and will be seen in our engraving of the tower at Lymne, on p. 174, where, at the bottom of the wall, on the left, tiles with turned or flanged edges are used along with the plain flat tiles.

Having thus examined the walls, with their towers and gates, let us pass through the latter, and survey the interior. A town consisted then, as now, of its private and its public buildings, the former of which would naturally vary much in form and magnitude, according to the caprice as well as the quality of those for whom they were built. The discovery of the buried city of Pompeii first threw any considerable light on the domestic arrangement of Roman houses, yet difference of climate, and many other causes, existed in this island which should make us cautious in applying to Roman houses in Britain the rules which we know were observed in Italy. The only instance with which we are acquainted of a small separate house in a Roman town in this country, is one recently discovered at Lymne, in Kent, a plan of which is here given. This house, which stood north and south (the semicircular projection looking due south), was about fifty feet (east and west), and thirty feet in the transverse direction, exclusive of the semicircular part and the eastern recess. The walls evidently remain only to the level of what was originally the floors, and we have no indica-

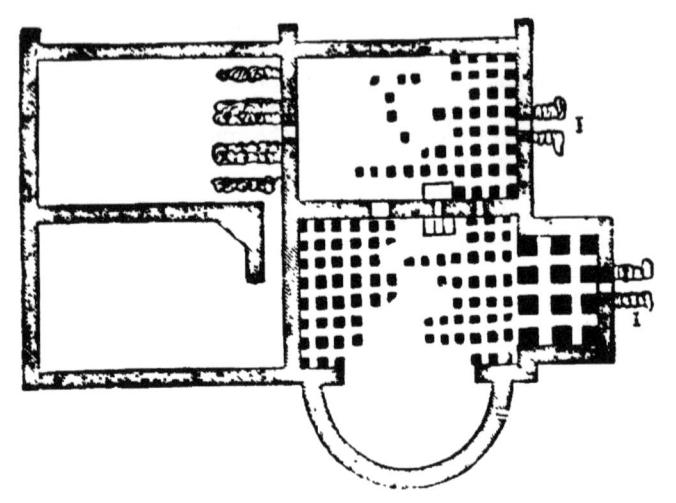

Plan of a house at Lymne (*Portus Lemanis*).

tion of the position of doors or windows; but, from an examination of the motion that must have been given to the ruins by the ancient landslip which reduced them to their present condition,* it is probable that this house stood on the south side of the street at the entrance of the principal gateway, and therefore that the entrance-door of the house stood at its northern wall, which was supported by buttresses. The arrangement of this house was very simple, for it seems that it consisted of four rooms of about the same dimensions. We have no means of ascertaining whether it had any upper story, but there seems little doubt that it was a detached house. The accompanying engraving of Roman foundations laid open at Aldborough in Yorkshire, clearly represents a long row of

* At some period long after the Roman town at Lymne had been ruined and deserted, an extensive landslip took place on the site, which is easily explained by geologists, the consequence of which was that a great part of the walls has been overthrown, and much of the interior appears to have been entirely defaced and destroyed. The house of which the plan is given above had suffered less than most of the other buildings, and although the walls were in part dislocated, it was easy to restore them in the plan

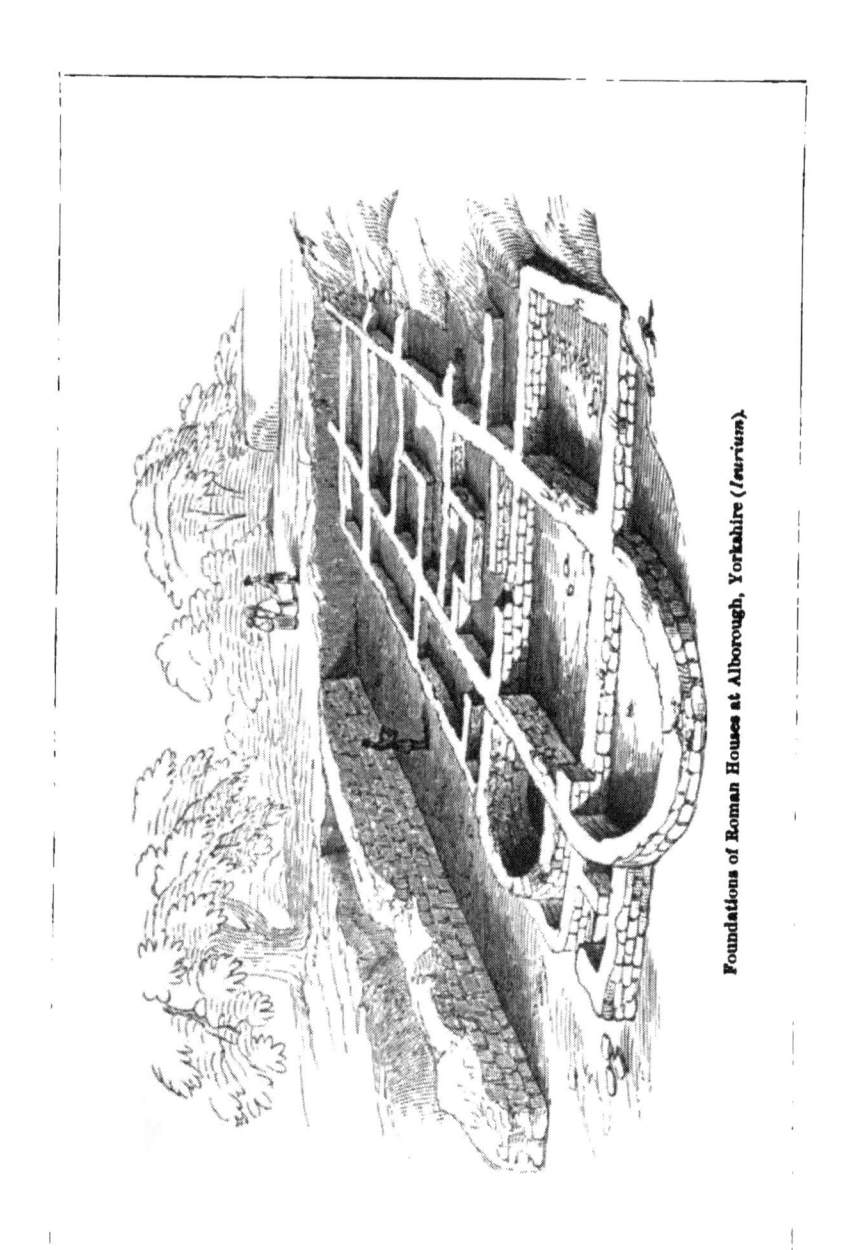

Foundations of Roman Houses at Alborough, Yorkshire (*Isurium*).

houses, though they are by no means easily explained. The corner to the left appears to have been a little shop, and the other rooms in a line with it may perhaps have served the same purpose.

It has been questioned whether the Roman houses in this country were built of stone and brick up to the roof, or whether they were only raised a little above the floor, to support a superstructure of wood. It is a remarkable circumstance that, in most of the numerous villas which at different times have been discovered and examined, the walls are found remaining about as high, or very little higher, than the floors, and that they do not terminate in a broken line as though the walls had been thrown down, but in a regular level through the whole building. We must, however, take into consideration, on the other hand, the circumstance that the upper walls would, in the middle ages, be gradually carried away for materials down to the then level of the ground : and instances have occurred, especially in the larger country villas, where the walls remain at a greater elevation in some parts than in others, and in which they have evidently been broken away. Walls of timber, too, would hardly have supported such heavy roofs as those formed of flags, and we might expect to find more distinct indications of them. Perhaps the safest conclusion to which we can come is, that in houses of people of wealth and importance the walls were of masonry, while in the more ordinary houses the masonry of the walls may have risen only two or three feet above ground, and sometimes not so much, to support a superstructure of timber. In exposed districts, and more especially in the north, houses of stone were no doubt more common. Mr Roach Smith discovered a Roman house in the neighbourhood of Hadrian's Wall, the walls of which, built of stone, are still standing to an elevation above the doors and windows, the openings of which remain.*

Generally, however, the only parts of a Roman house which remain perfect are the floors and substructure, which, therefore, will naturally first attract our attention. We invariably find that in a certain number of the rooms of a Roman house in Britain the floors were supported, not on the solid ground, but upon a number of short thick columns, arranged in regular

---

* An engraving of this house is given in Mr Roach Smith's *Collectanea Antiqua*, vol. ii. p. 188.

rows, with narrow passages between them. These formed what were called the hypocaust (from a Greek word signifying literally *fire* or *heat underneath*); it was the Roman method of warming a house. These pillars were generally formed of piles of square tiles; sometimes, as in a building found at Inverness in Scotland, described in Stuart's 'Caledonia Romana,' in one found at Wroxeter (*Uriconium*), and described in the ninth volume of the 'Archæologia,' and in other instances, the columns supporting the floor were of stone, or stone columns mixed alternately or irregularly with brick pillars. Along with these supporting pillars were rows of flue tiles, chiefly against the walls, and flue tiles of various forms were laid against the walls above, so as to distribute the hot air over the building. These flue tiles have square holes on one side to admit hot air or smoke, from the fires of the hypocaust. Sometimes, but this is of rarer occurrence, instead of these pillars, the floor was supported on parallel walls of masonry, with passages in which the fires were made, and through which the heat was conducted. The fire was made under the arch in the outer wall below the level of the ground, and appears to have been approached from without by the servants who had the care of the fires, in the same manner that we now approach the stoves of hot-houses. Similar arches in the foundations of the walls communicated between the hypocaust of one room and that of another. In our plan, just given, of the house at Lymne, the two rooms on the right had hypocausts with pillars of square bricks, the lower parts of most of which were found when the covering of earth was first cleared away. At I and I were the passages, built in rougher masonry than the walls, which led to the fire-places under the two arches indicated in the walls. Three other arches, through the wall which divided these two apartments, all neatly turned with the large flat tiles, formed the communication between the hypocausts. Another similar arch in the western wall of the more northerly of these two rooms communicated with the parallel walls of rough masonry which formed a hypocaust under a part of the room marked B. The small recessed room at the south-east corner, supported by much thicker columns of bricks than those of the other hypocaust, may perhaps have served as the kitchen, or cooking room. The arrangement of the hypocaust will perhaps be better understood by the annexed cut of one of these structures found in a Roman house at Cirencester, which we give because it presents several peculiarities. One of the supports here is a stone pillar, another stands upon a stone base. Between the last row of pillars and

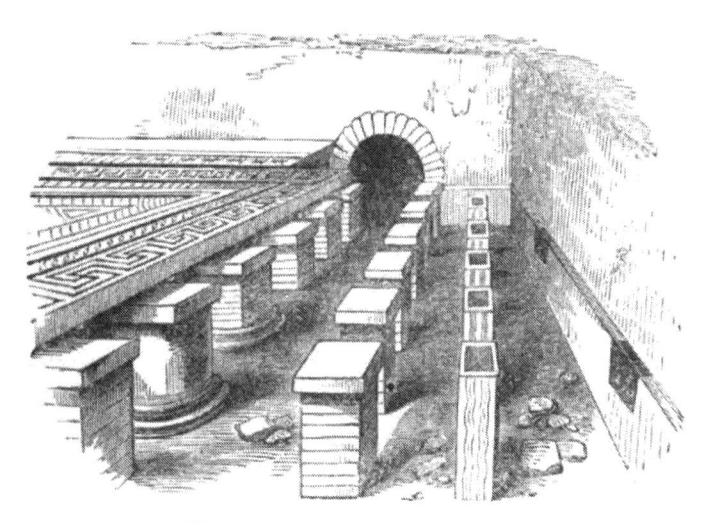

Hypocaust at Cirencester (*Corinium*).

the side-wall, is a row of upright flue-tiles, and in the wall itself are two apertures, intended no doubt to convey the hot air into the upper part of the building. In this instance the hypocaust only extended under one half of the room, the pavement of the other half resting upon a prepared solid foundation.* The room marked B, in the plan of the house at Lymne, seems to have had a similar arrangement in this respect. The more we

---

* We should avoid giving refined and unnecessary explanations where very simple ones are sufficient. In Messrs Buckman and Newmarch's work on the Roman remains at Cirencester, from which our cut of the hypocaust is taken, the circumstance of the hypocaust extending under one half only of the floor, is explained by considering that 'the two parts of the room were intended for use at different seasons of the year, and that it was the *triclinium* of the house; that portion over the hypocaust being the *triclinium hybernum*, and the other end the *triclinium æstivum* for use in warm weather.' It seems to me very easy to understand how a room may be perfectly well warmed by a hypocaust on one side only, but I do not perceive how this arrangement would make one half of the room warm and the other half cold, which I presume is the meaning of this explanation. If there were in summer no fire in the hypocaust, it would be quite as cool over it as on the other side of the room; and if there were a fire in it, no part of the room could be cool.

examine the remains of Roman buildings in Britain, the more we are struck with the care and ingenuity displayed in providing for internal warmth, as well as for other comforts. In many instances, the subterranean hypocausts are elaborately arranged. The excavations in the large villa at Woodchester, in Gloucestershire, at the latter end of the last century, brought to light a hypocaust which is represented in an engraving in our next chapter. It consisted of parallel walls, pierced with an elaborate system of flues, formed of ridge tiles placed two and two together, so as to form pipes. Rows of flanged tiles were placed along the sides of the walls, thus making hollows through which the hot air was distributed equally over the whole interior surface of the walls of the apartment.

In laying the floors, a layer of large flat tiles was first placed on the columns of the hypocaust. Flanged tiles were not unfrequently used for this purpose, with the flanged edges sometimes turned upwards and sometimes downwards, perhaps according to the caprice of the builder. Sometimes there were two layers of tiles, and in some cases, where tiles were probably not at hand, thin flag-stones were used instead. Upon these was laid a mass of fine mortar or concrete, generally about six inches thick, in the surface of which the pavement was set. This pavement was variously constructed according to the richness and elegance of the house, and to the purposes for which the apartment was designed. In rich houses the principal floors were beautifully ornamented with figured pavements, composed of very small cubes or tesseræ of different colours. In less expensive houses, the ornament was plainer, and formed of much larger tesseræ. Ordinary floors were usually paved with tesseræ of brick, which we should perhaps rather call small tiles, one or two inches square. In a few instances a mere floor of flag-stones has been found laid regularly over the mass of concrete.

It is quite impossible, in the condition in which the foundations of the Roman houses are found, even to offer a probable conjecture on the use or objects of the several rooms which we are enabled to trace by them. We can have little doubt that the principal rooms warmed by hypocausts were those in which the masters of the house were accustomed to assemble together, or receive visitors. In the larger country villas it has been observed that the rooms with hypocausts lie often on the southern part of the building, and it has therefore been assumed that they were the winter apartments, while the summer apartments were placed with a more northern aspect, and were without hypocausts; but this observation does not hold good in all cases. There is one peculiarity which is observed almost invariably in Roman houses in Britain; one room has always a semicircular recess or alcove, and in some, but rarer, instances, more than one room possesses this adjunct. It is not omitted even in the little house at Lymne, of which we have given a plan. There is, generally, as in the example just cited, at each side where it joins the room, an advancing piece of wall or pier, as though a curtain, or something of that kind, had been drawn across to separate the recess from the room. In a suburban villa, which was partially excavated in Leicester (*Ratæ*), a short pillar was found lying upon the tesselated pavement of the semicircular recess, which seemed to have served as an altar, or to have supported a small statue, and it has been conjectured that this recess served as the sacrarium, or place of domestic worship, where the image of the patron god of the family was placed. A Roman house of any extent generally presents to view such a numerous assemblage of crowded and very small rooms, that we are led to believe that some of the transverse walls have only been raised to a slight elevation above the floor, and that they served for seats or other purposes in the middle or at one side of the room. In one or two instances low projections have been observed in the interior of the wall of a room, which have every appearance of having been intended for stone seats. Drains and gutters are often found in and under the floors, for carrying off water, and these are sometimes ingeniously, and even elaborately, constructed; generally of tiles; pieces of leaden pipe have also been found, formed by turning a thin plate of lead rounded into the form of a cylinder.

Many writers have concluded hastily, that every house with a hypocaust was a public bath; but it required very little observation and comparison to expose this error. In some instances, but more especially in country villas, we find baths belonging to the house, generally in a room which seems to have been set aside for them. Two such baths were observed in the villa excavated at Hartlip, in East Kent. One of these, which is represented in the cut annexed, was of very small dimensions, being only three feet six inches in length by three feet one inch in width, and about two feet deep. At the bottom, on one side, was a seat six inches and a half wide. A moulding of plaster ran round the floor and up the angles, and the interior was originally covered entirely with stucco, painted

THE ROMANS.

Bath in a Villa at Hartlip, Kent.

of a pink or red colour, as appeared by portions of it still remaining. From the size of this bath, it must have been

Second Bath in the Villa at Hartlip.

intended for partial immersion and ablution; in fact, after the use of the hot vapour bath, which was usually in an adjacent room. Adjoining was another bath, represented in our second cut, of larger dimensions than the former. It was six feet two inches in length, by fourteen in width,

The Process of Fresco-Painting, from a Monument at Sens, in France.

PAINTINGS OF THE WALLS.

but it was only fourteen inches deep. Both baths were perhaps deeper when the building was perfect. This bath also had a seat extending the whole length of one side, but it was composed of hollow flue-tiles, placed lengthways, and coated over with a thick layer of cement; the sides, as in the former, had been stuccoed and painted, and a similar moulding ran round the bottom. Both had leaden pipes still remaining, which conducted the water from the baths through the external wall of the house. There was no pipe or channel of any kind for conducting water to either of these baths, so that either hot or cold water must have been brought when wanted in buckets or other vessels. A room adjoining was probably open to the baths; a recess in the wall of this room is supposed by Mr Roach Smith to have held a cistern for warm water.

Internally, the walls of the apartments were invariably covered with a thick coating of plaster, or stucco, composed of lime, sand, and small stones, so tempered as to harden into a very solid and firm mass. The surface of this was made perfectly smooth, and upon it was laid a very thin coating of fine calcareous cement. On this, while moist, the various designs were painted, and the whole became so durable, that on the broken fragments we pick up among the ruins of the houses and villas in this country, the colours often look as bright and fresh as if they had but just been laid on. The accompanying engraving, from Mr Roach Smith's valuable work on Roman London, represents the process of painting the walls in fresco as sculptured on the sepulchral monument of a Roman painter, found at Sens in France (*Senonæ*). 'The subject,' Mr Smith says, 'represents the decoration of a corridor in fresco painting. A low scaffold is constructed, partly on tressels, and partly resting upon the basement of the corridor. Upon this scaffold are the painter and his plasterer. The latter is on the right side of the relief, and is exhibited in the act of laying on the thin finishing coat of plaster (*intonaco*) for the painter, who is following him. He has his *float* in his left hand, and is passing it over the wall, while his right hand is thrust downward into a pail of water, most likely to reach a brush to sprinkle the rough coat or ground so as to render it sufficiently moist to receive the *intonaco*, or thin cement of lime, which, in general, would not be thicker than a crown piece. The painter is following the plasterer, to lay on his colours while the plaster is still wet. He appears as if resting one foot upon a stool, which, perhaps, has also a tablet of mixed colours upon it.

Behind him is a cylindrical box, in which, it may be imagined, he has his rolls of paper or parchment with designs of the work he is engaged upon. There is a short ladder to mount the scaffold, by the side of which is a stool, with a tablet of colour upon it; and close by this the painter's assistant is mixing tints; and his action is energetic, no doubt to indicate haste. This is quite in accord with the modern practice of fresco-painting, which requires every department to be conducted with rapidity as well as with skill. The assistant must always have the tints ready mixed, and in sufficient quantity for the work. Under the arch of the corridor, at the left side of the relief, is the director or master-designer. He is seated with an open book or tablet before him, and appears to be studying or reviewing the design.'* Some of the fragments found among the ruins of Roman houses in Britain belong to walls painted of a uniform colour; others are striped, or made to represent arabesques and other patterns. Some fragments in the museum of Mr Roach Smith (now in the British Museum), taken from the site of a large building near Crosby Hall, in London, exhibit a sort of decorated trellis-work on a red ground, in the divisions of which are stars, or flowers, in yellow, white, and dark blue colours, with a man carrying a staff and what appears to be a basket; the whole pattern, man and all, being repeated over the face of the wall, and enclosed in a dark border, upon which is a stripe of white. The cut in the next page represents a fragment of this design, drawn on a scale of one-third the actual size. Other fragments are painted in imitation of coloured marbles. A considerable variety of rather elegant patterns were found in the ruins of a Roman villa at Chesterford, in Essex, among which were some representing portions of the human figure. The most remarkable of the latter was the foot of a female, as large as life, with drapery flowing round it. In one of the larger rooms of the villa at Combe-End, in Gloucestershire, the lower part of the wall remained covered with the fresco painting, on which were a row of feet, also as large as life, which had belonged to the figures in some grand historical painting that had once adorned the walls of this apartment. In one of the rooms of a building at Wroxeter (*Uriconium*), the walls were tesselated, the tessellæ being half-an-inch by three-fifths in dimension, and of alternate colours, so as to produce the effect of chequer work.

* Illustrations of Roman London, by Charles Roach Smith, p. 61.

Where we find the openings of doors, they are in general narrow, and they appear to have been square-headed, like the

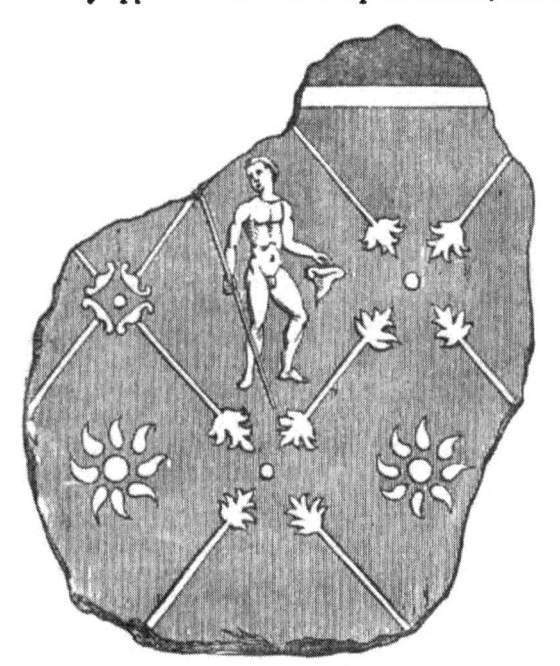

Roman Wall-Painting, from London.

ordinary doors of the present day. Among the stations on Hadrian's Wall, where the materials of the buildings have not been so extensively cleared away, ornamental heads of doors and windows in stone have been found, and some of them are engraved in Mr Bruce's 'Roman Wall.' We seldom open Roman houses of any extent without finding abundant fragments of window-glass, so that there can be no doubt that the Roman windows were glazed. Some fragments of very thin window-glass were picked up under the walls of the houses within the Roman town of Lymne, where the walls had no doubt been pierced with windows above. At Wroxeter, on the contrary, the Roman window-glass hitherto found is very thick, some slightly exceeding the eighth of an inch. We have little information on the nature of the ceilings and roofs of the Roman houses in Britain. Supporting columns, and fragments of ornament and plaster, found in some of the villas, seem to show that the more important apartments were sometimes vaulted; but it is probable that the ceiling was more usually flat. In the midland and southern parts of Britain, the houses appear to have been most commonly roofed with tiles, consisting of parallel courses of flanged tiles, with the flanges turned upwards, and the joints covered with ridge tiles. This arrangement will be best understood by the accompanying cut. In other cases, especially in the northern parts of England, the houses were roofed with slates. In the stations on the wall, thin slabs of free-stone slate, with nail-holes in them, as well as the nails themselves, are found on the ground. Sometimes the roofing was formed of flags of stone, shaped into hexagons, as at fig. *b* in our next cut, with half-flags (*a*) for the top. These overlapped one another, so as to form a pattern of lozenges, as

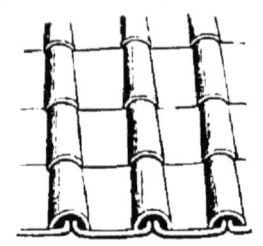

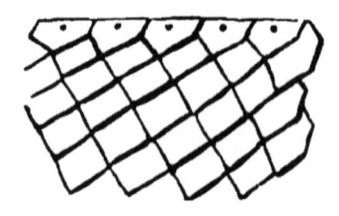

Arrangement of Roof Tiles.

Arrangement of Roof Flags.

represented in the cut, the ridge being no doubt covered with a row of ridge-tiles. This kind of roof seems to have been common at Wroxeter (*Uriconium*), where the fallen flags are found scattered about in great abundance, with the iron nails which held them to the woodwork still remaining. These flags, at Wroxeter, are formed of the micaceous laminated sandstone found on the edge of the North Staffordshire and Shropshire coal-field, and must have given the houses a very glittering appearance in the sunshine. At Maryport, in Cumberland, when some parts of the interior of the station were excavated, it was found that the houses had been roofed with Scotch slates, which, with the pegs that fastened them, lay scattered about in the streets. In the Roman villas in the south, we often find the roofing tiles scattered over the floors of the rooms in the same manner.

We have few opportunities of examining the internal arrangements of a Roman town, and until the uncovering of Pompeii, our knowledge on this subject was very limited. Where a modern town stands on the site of an ancient town, which is the case with most of the more important Roman cities in Britain, it is of course impossible to excavate; and where such is not the case, there have usually been so many difficulties to contend with in obtaining permission to dig, and raising the necessary funds, that very little progress has yet been made. Yet there are many localities in this island, where the site of an ancient city of great extent lies merely covered with earth, and that not very deep, and in which excavations would, no doubt, lead to very interesting results. Among the more remarkable of these, we may enumerate Silchester (*Calleva*), Old Verulam (*Verulamium*), Aldborough (*Isurium*), Ribchester (supposed to be *Coccium*), Caerwent (*Venta,*) Wroxeter * (*Uriconium*), Kenchester (*Magna*), and some others. Some of the towns on Hadrian's Wall, though not so large or magnificent as these great cities, appear, from the comparative neglect in which their ruins were left, to promise perhaps more than some of the larger sites. It has been often assumed by some that the streets of the Roman towns in Britain were arranged with great regularity, and by others that they were in general identical with the streets of the modern towns that occupy their sites; but both seem equally erroneous. At Wroxeter (*Uriconium*), as far as the excavations have been carried, the streets appear to have run at right angles to one another, and to have been tolerably wide. They are paved with small cobble-stones, like the streets of our mediæval towns. A variety of excavations, however, in the city of London have proved that the principal streets, such as Cheapside, Cornhill, &c., are in almost every instance traversed by masses of Roman houses underneath. We have learnt from the discoveries at Pompeii, that Roman streets were arranged irregularly, and they were there in general narrow. Perhaps even in Roman London there were only two or three lines of streets through which any kind of carriage could pass, and

---

* It need hardly be remarked that very important excavations have now been made at this place under the direction of the author of the present volume; and a volume has been published under the title of 'Uriconium: a Historical Account of the Ancient Roman City, and of the Excavations made upon its site at Wroxeter, in Shropshire;' by Thomas Wright. London, 1872.

the rest were only narrow alleys. A small part of the Roman town of Cilurnum, at Chesters in Northumberland, has been

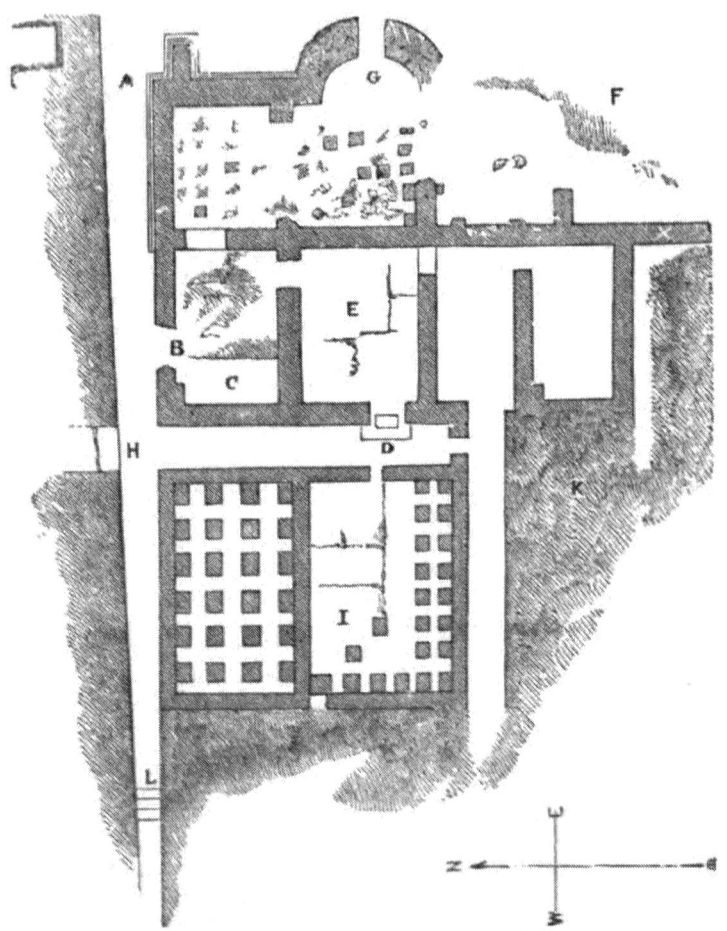

Plan of Houses at Chesters in Northumberland (*Cilurnum*).

uncovered, and presents us with a curious example of these small alleys and houses. A plan of it is given in the cut on the present page. Eight apartments are here represented, which belonged to at least two, if not to three, houses. Descending a few steps at L, we enter a street or alley, three feet wide at one extremity, and four at the other.

At H, another street runs off at right angles, which is about four feet wide. At D, an entrance door, approached by steps, leads into the room E, which, as well as the other rooms with which it communicates, is paved with thin flag-stones, and has a hypocaust underneath. There is one of the semi-circular recesses at G, which has an aperture through the wall, perhaps one of the fire-places of the hypocausts, though Mr Bruce tells us that the furnace, which warmed the suite of apartments, stood near F, at the south-eastern extremity of the building. When these hypocausts were first opened, the soot in the flues was found as fresh as if it had been produced by fires lighted the day before. In the room to the north of that we first entered, at C, was found a bath, in good preservation, covered with stucco, which was painted red. Near it, at B, the exterior wall of the house had been broken in, and among the rubbish was found the statue of a river god. The pavements had been damaged by the falling in of the roof. The steps at D were much worn by the tread of feet, and stones had been inserted in place of others which had been worn out, which also were partially worn; hence Mr Bruce thinks that this was a public building of some kind. Outside the circular recess, A, there seemed to have been a larger open space than the street first mentioned. A door nearly opposite that at D led into the house I, of which two apartments were uncovered, both having similar floors and hypocausts. The street H D appears to communicate by a narrow passage with another transverse street, but the ground beyond has not been cleared away. The rooms of the house I are in dimension each about twenty-four feet by seventeen; that at E about nineteen feet by fifteen. The walls of the latter house had been covered internally with a stucco painted dark red.

At Maryport, in Cumberland, where excavations were made in 1766, the streets were found to be paved, like those at Cilurnum, with large flag-stones, which we are told 'were much worn by use, particularly the steps into a vaulted room, supposed to have been a temple.' The foundations at Aldborough, represented in our plate, at p. 193, seem evidently to have belonged to a row of houses, apparently with shops in front; but the artist has, by an oversight, represented them as parallel to the town wall, whereas in reality they are at an angle to it. They have not been excavated to any extent backwards; but there are reasons for supposing that in the more important towns, the great dwelling-houses stood, as at Pompeii, back from the street, and that each was inclosed outwardly with small houses and shops. At Durobrivæ (*Castor*), as far as we can judge from Mr Artis's plan, the houses were scattered about in no regular order.

The numerous pieces of sculptured stone which are found about the ruins in the remains of Roman towns, show that the houses did not want in architectural ornament. Capitals and shafts of columns, cornices, mouldings, and other fragments, are frequently met with; but as these materials were in after times much more useful, and more easily carried away, than the masonry on the walls, it seldom happens that there is a sufficient quantity left to enable us to form a notion of the manner in which the building was adorned. It is remarkable, also, that these architectural fragments, although often very elegant, are seldom of pure style; instead of plain or simply fluted columns, we often have them covered with scales, or leaves, or other designs, as if the models had been brought from Egypt or India; and the bases and capitals are sometimes profusely ornamented. The same circumstance of the utility of the materials caused the public buildings to disappear sooner than the dwelling-houses, and there are few cases in which they have been distinctly traced out in modern times. Lysons discovered so many architectural fragments of the Temple of Minerva at Aquæ Solis (*Bath*), that he was enabled to make a restoration of the building; and considerable remains are said to have been found, and perhaps still exist under-ground, of the temple of the same goddess at Coccium (*Ribchester*). No doubt, every town had its temples, of greater and less magnificence, which were filled with the votive altars that are discovered so numerously in some parts of the country. A few inscriptions have been found recording the building or repairing of such edifices. At Regnum (*Chichester*), a temple was dedicated to Neptune and Minerva.*
At Condercum, on Hadrian's Wall (*Benwell*), an officer stationed there 'rebuilt from the ground' a temple dedicated to the Deæ Matres, and to the genius who presided over his troops.†
At Cilurnum (*Chesters*), a temple which was dilapidated through age, was rebuilt in the year 221, during the reign of Heliogabalus.‡ At Petriana (*Cambeck Fort*), a temple to the

---

* See the commemorative inscription in our note on p. 51.
† MATRIBVS .... TEMPLVM A SOLO RESTITVIT.—*Bruce's* 'Wall,' p. 140.
‡ TEMPLVM VETVSTATE CONLAPSVM RESTITVERVNT.—*Bruce*, p. 186.

deities 'of all nations,' which had through age fallen into decay, was similarly restored.*

Such slabs were generally placed against the walls of the building they commemorated, and it was not always thought necessary to describe in them the nature of the building itself, so that they are now often useless for identification. Yet in some instances public buildings are commemorated by name. Thus an inscription found at Habitancum (*Risingham*), commemorates the restoration of the gate and walls.† We learn also, from such inscriptions, that at Epiacum (*Lanchester*), the public baths and basilica (or court-house) were built from the foundations in the reign of Gordian; ‡ that some other buildings (the name is partly obliterated), with a basilica and temple, were built on the site of the modern Tynemouth; § that public baths and a basilica were rebuilt at Coccium (*Ribchester*); || that the public baths at Lavatræ (*Bowes*) had been burnt down, and rebuilt and dedicated to the goddess Fortune (they were probably joined with a temple), under the propraetor Virrius Lupus; ¶ and that, at the Roman town which occupied the site of Netherby in Cumberland, a basilica for riding, which appears to have taken some time in building, was completed under Severus Alexander (A.D. 221—235).** As well as its basilica and public baths, Epiacum (*Lanchester*) had an arsenal and a building for the commanding officer, or governor's lodgings.††

It appears from these inscriptions that every town of any importance had a basilica, or court-house, and public baths, and that these were usually placed together, and joined often with a temple. In several of our ancient Roman towns, as at Leicester, and, formerly, at Kenchester, masses of masonry within the town, which it has not been easy to account for, may have formed part of these combined buildings. Remains

---

* . . . OMNIVM GENTIVM TEMPLVM OLIM VETVSTATE CONLABSVM.—*Horsley*.

† PORTAM CVM MVRIS VETVSTATE DILAPSIS.—*Bruce*, p. 331.

‡ BALNEVM CVM BASILICA A SOLO INSTRVXIT.—*Lysons*.

§ . . . . GYRVM CVM BASI ET TEMPLVM FECIT.—*Bruce*, p. 319, so read by Mr Bruce; Horsley read it CVBVM; but on examining this altar, which is in the collection of the Society of Antiquarians, with Mr Roach Smith, I agree with him that the true reading seems to be CYPVM (for *cippum*) CVM BASI ET, &c. The stone is much worn in the upper part.

|| BALINEVM REFECT . . . ASILICAM VETVSTATE CONLABSAM SOLO RESTITVTAM.—*Whitaker*.

¶ BALINEVM VI IGNIS EXVSTVM.—*Horsley*.

** BASILICAM EQVESTREM EXERCITATORIAM IAMPRIDEM A SOLO COEPTAM AEDIFICAVIT CONSVMMAVITQVE.—*Lysons*.

†† PRINCIPIA ET ARMAMENTARIA CONLAPSA RESTITVIT.—*Lysons*.

of public baths have been found in excavations in some of the Roman towns in Britain, as, for instance, at Silchester. The basilica and public baths of Uriconium (*Wroxeter*) have been uncovered; the former was 226 feet long, and the baths covered a square of about 200 feet. Of other public buildings we know little. Giraldus Cambrensis speaks vaguely of buildings for theatrical purposes at Caerleon, but perhaps he only meant the amphitheatre. A theatre of considerable extent, and elaborate construction, has been brought to light at Verulamium (near St Albans).* A theatre has also been found at Wroxeter. The Romans were everywhere passionately addicted to gladiatorial exhibitions, and almost every station had its amphitheatre. We need only mention those at Richborough, Colchester, Silchester, Dorchester, Cirencester, Wroxeter, and Caerleon. The amphitheatre at Richborough has been recently excavated, and it was then found that it was not, as had been supposed, a mere raised circle of earth, but that it had been surrounded with walls, and had doubtless seats and passages of masonry. The same was probably the case with the other amphitheatres just referred to. At Aldborough there are remains of a stadium, and perhaps also at Leicester.

The walls of the Roman towns in Britain varied much in extent. Those of Silchester, which are three miles in circuit, inclose an area of about a hundred and twenty acres; the walls of Wroxeter are upwards of three miles in circuit; those of Kenchester inclosed about twenty-one acres; the walls of Colchester included a hundred and eight acres; while the walls of Lymne inclose only twelve acres, and those of Richborough not more than four. It is evident that, in cases like the latter, we must consider the fortress as a mere citadel, and suppose that the town stood around. In the other instances, the wall surrounded the town. In many cases, however, the population became gradually too large to be contained within the inclosure, and then suburbs were built outside. Most of the stations along Hadrian's wall appear to have consisted of an inner town and an outer town. There are reasons for believing that the walls of Roman London were erected at a later date, when that city had reached its full extent, and hence we cannot trace that it had any suburbs on the northern side of the Thames; but it had apparently a large one on the southern

* An account of this discovery was published in a pamphlet entitled 'A Description of the Roman Theatre of Verulam,' by Mr R. Grove Lowe, of St Albans, under whose care the excavations were carried on.

bank. Eburacum had been probably fortified earlier, and it had increased more rapidly, and accordingly we find that it had extensive suburbs at each of its gates. That on the side towards Calcaria (*Tadcaster*) extended, as we are informed by Mr Wellbeloved, as much as a mile along the road, and the one on the road to Isurium (*Aldborough*) was nearly as long. Extensive suburbs have also been traced round Caerleon, and it is the tradition of the place, that the ancient city filled a circuit of nine miles. Considerable suburban buildings have, in like manner, been discovered at Leicester.

The suburbs were probably not built so closely as the town itself, but consisted often of detached villas. They were also the site of the cemeteries, and the tombs generally stood along each side of the road. The principal sepulchral monuments of the Roman citizens of London appear to have stood outside Ludgate, where inscribed stones have been found; but we know also that there was a large cemetery at the outside of Bishopsgate. At York, the burial-places were without all the gates, but the road leading to Calcaria has been called emphatically, on account of the great number of interments found along it, the Street of the Tombs.

Before we quit the Roman towns, we must notice one of their important features, the sanitary precautions. We have seen how careful the inhabitants were to keep themselves warm and dry, and they seem not to have neglected cleanliness. Traces of pipes and drains are found in their houses, which were no doubt intended to carry off superfluous water and filth. We have no means of ascertaining how the streets were drained, but we seldom carry on excavations long on the sites of Roman towns without meeting with large and extensive sewers. At Wroxeter one of the streets has a gutter running down the sides, well formed of hewn stones, and something like those still found in old towns like Salisbury. A large drain of this description was found outside the town at Hunnum, on the Wall (*Halton-Chesters*). 'My informant,' Mr Bruce tells us, 'crept along it for about one hundred yards; the bottom of it was filled with hardened mud, imbedded in which were found a lamp and many bone pins, such as those with which the Romans fastened their woollen garments.' The Roman sewers at Lincoln are still in good preservation, and are constructed of excellent masonry. They are covered with large flags of stone. A smaller transverse drain brought down the waters from each house. The accompanying cut, representing a part of the interior of one of these sewers, with the mouths of two transverse drains, is taken from a sketch by Mr Roach Smith,

Interior of a Sewer at Lincoln (*Lindum*).

who walked up it about a hundred yards. Mr Smith tells me that the sewers of the city of Treves (the Roman Treviri), still in use, bear a close resemblance to those of Lincoln, and they are probably of Roman origin.

As far as we can judge by existing remains, water was not conducted into the Roman houses. It was probably brought by aqueducts or watercourses to a fountain or conduit in the town, whence the inhabitants fetched it in buckets. We learn from Bede, how St Cuthbert was shown the extraordinary Roman fountain at Carlisle, which, no doubt, had supplied the citizens of Luguballium with water. Giraldus Cambrensis speaks of watercourses at Caerleon, but, as his words are somewhat vague, these may perhaps have been merely sewers. But on the line of Hadrian's Wall, we still see the curious watercourse which supplied the Roman town of Æsica (*Great Chesters*), and which was worked through a tortuous course of six miles. In a similar manner, an aqueduct (or rather two aqueducts), of considerable extent and labour, was constructed to bring the water from a distant stream to Epiacum (*Lanchester*); they delivered their water into a reservoir outside the walls, near the south-west corner of the station, and there, no doubt, the inhabitants went to take it for their domestic purposes

One circumstance remains to be noticed with regard to the economy of the Roman towns. We have as yet discovered no arrangements about the Roman houses for personal easement, but close at the outside of Roman towns are found numbers of deep and very narrow round wells, which, no doubt, are the remains of conveniences for this purpose. The discovery of such wells is the sure sign of the proximity of a Roman station. They are numerous at Richborough and at Winchester, and have indeed been observed in many other places, and they are rich mines for the antiquary, from the great number of miscellaneous articles they contain. In fact, they appear to have been common depositories for refuse of every description, such as animals' bones, broken pottery, and a variety of other articles which have been dropped in by chance, or thrown in intentionally, and they have hence been very properly termed rubbish holes. The earth taken from the bottom of those at Richborough, on being examined by an experienced chemist, was pronounced to be the remains of stercoraceous matter. These pits are formed so carefully, and are some of them so small in diameter, and at the same time so deep, that we might almost suppose that they had been made with a large cheese-scoop. Perhaps they were originally covered with some light structure. Some antiquaries, from finding broken urns in them, have imagined that these pits were sepulchral, but they have probably been misled by erroneous impressions of accidental circumstances connected with them.*

There is one other question of great interest and importance connected with the towns of Roman Britain,—the origin and formation of our language.

It is remarkable how generally in the earlier ages of peoples, fable usurps the place of history. And even long after the memory of the past has assumed a form which we look upon as history, it still continues to be little more than legend and romance. It is one of the great results of the deeper and more comprehensive studies of the present day, to dispel by degrees the dark clouds of error thus formed, and drag from behind them the truth which has been so long hidden.

* See a paper in the 'Archæologia,' vol. xxxii., on such pits, found at Ewell, by Dr Diamond, and another, in vol. xxxiv., on a similar pit found at Stone, Bucks, by Mr Akerman. In the latter it is stated, erroneously, that sepulchral deposits were found in the wells at Richborough; they were carefully examined by good antiquaries as they were cut away by the railway excavators, and most certainly there was nothing sepulchral about them; they had literally been receptacles of filth and refuse.

There is, perhaps, no part of history which has been more
affected by the causes alluded to than that of the Roman and
British period of our island, and yet it is one in which we
ought to take the greatest interest. Our old histories represent
the Romans as finding the isle of Britain occupied by an aboriginal population of Celtic races, formed into tribes under a
number of great chieftains, whom with much trouble they reduced to subjection, in which subjection they remained during
the Roman period, and then, when the Romans departed from
the island, they recovered their old position of British chieftains, and retained it, till they fell before the Saxon invaders.
Various researches and discoveries, but especially a more comprehensive study of the written records of history, and a more
extensive examination of the remaining monuments of the Roman age of our island, have shown us that most of our common
notions of our condition during that period are very erroneous.
I will endeavour to put this in a more correct light.

The Romans appear to have had an especial regard for the
Western provinces of the Empire, and the natural consequence
was that those provinces soon became far more entirely Romanised than the provinces of the East. This, indeed, was more
easy in the one case than in the other; for the Eastern Empire
was founded upon bygone civilisations which far exceeded that
of Rome itself, whereas the population of the Western Empire
consisted chiefly of only half-civilised tribes, which hardly had
one common system of action, and which, therefore, were more
easily acted upon. The province of Gaul was especially Roman,
both politically, and in the extent of its Roman civilisation.

This province of Gaul had already been completely formed
under the rule of the emperor Augustus. It was then, as we
have just seen, covered with towns and cities connected with
each other by admirable roads. The cities were, in every respect, Roman cities, filled with noble buildings, and other objects, displaying the perfection of Roman art. The population
was dressed in the Roman costume, and their manners were
entirely Roman. The only language talked through the province, with the exception of two remote districts the conditions
of which are explained by other causes, was Latin. This was
the case in all the Roman provinces of the West, and was insisted upon, at all events in theory, in the East also. The
emperor Claudius, who was himself a native of Lugdunum
(*Lyons*), the capital of Gaul, is said to have been especially
firm in insisting upon the use of the Latin language. We are

informed by the historian Dio Cassius, that a Roman citizen from Lycia, having been sent by his province on a deputation to the emperor, and not being able to reply to his questions in Latin, was immediately deprived of his rights of citizenship. 'No man,' said Claudius, 'can be a citizen of Rome who is ignorant of the language of Rome!' Claudius is understood to have introduced the common use of the Latin language into Britain.

Not only did the Latin language become that of the towns in the provinces, and no doubt that of the people also, but art and literature sprang up and to some degree flourished among them. One or two well-known Latin writers of the later Roman period came from the provinces. I need hardly say that the almost classic poet Ausonius was a native of Burdigala (*Bordeaux*). And, in fact, all the writing we can trace in Gaul during the Roman or post-Roman period, was undoubtedly in the Latin tongue. It continued, indeed, long after the overthrow of the Roman empire in the West to be the vernacular language of the people of Gaul, and it was by the Gauls themselves called Roman—in fact, they then considered themselves Romans—and so firmly was it identified with them, that even the conquests of the Franks, whose language of course was Teutonic, not unlike our Anglo-Saxon, did nothing towards unseating it. We have a curious record of this condition of the Latin language in Gaul so late as the middle of the 9th century; when, at a great meeting at Strasbourg, in the March of the year 842, Charles le Chauve, king of France, and his brother Louis, the king of Germany, made mutually a solemn oath for their two peoples, Louis made his oath in German, while Charles made his in Latin, or, as they call it, *Romana lingua*, and Charles's Roman is still pure Latin in words, though it has undergone a certain amount of degradation in form. After the 11th century, this language, still under the name of *Romane*, begins to come out largely in literature; it still preserves the remains of Latinity in form. This, in the abundance of literary monuments of the ages which follow, goes on softening down, until the memory of Romanism itself is lost, and then it is called French.

Thus was formed gradually the French language of the present day from the Roman or Latin language as talked in Gaul. There is mixed with it, in its modern form, a German element, derived from the Franks, but no Gallic (Celtic) element that I am aware of. In this same manner have been formed the

modern languages of all the Roman provinces of the Western
Empire, and they all betray their origin. The Latin, or Roman,
language as talked in the Southern Peninsula produced the
Italian, that of Aquitania produced the Provençal, and that of
Hispania the Spanish. All these languages were known in the
middle ages to those who spoke them by the name of *Romane*
tongues. It is a name which plays an interesting part in the
mediæval literary history of Western Europe. There is only
one exception to what I have just been describing, and that is
found in the instance of the province of Britain. It is a very
interesting and important question, which is worthy of our consideration.

When the Romans came to Britain, they found the island
occupied by a number of independent tribes, under different
chieftains, the greater part of which appear to have been of
Celtic race, talking a Celtic tongue, but to judge from the
accounts they have left, there were some tribes of a different
origin. Such, for instance, were the Belgæ, who no doubt had
passed over from Gaul, and spoke the language of the Belgæ
there. To the latter they applied the term *Wælisc* or *Wælsc*.
In the German of the middle ages, the French language
was always spoken of as *Wælsch*, and it is the name used
to signify Italian in the German of the present day. In
fact the principal foreigners to them were the provincials
of the Roman provinces, whom they always found speaking
Latin. So, when our Anglo-Saxon forefathers came to
Britain, they called the Roman population they found here
Wælsc, or Welsh, no doubt on account of the language
they spoke. Thus all circumstances combine to show that
Latin was the language spoken in the Roman province of
Britain. I have a strong suspicion, from different circumstances I have remarked, that the towns in our island
continued, in contradistinction from the country, to use the
Latin tongue long after the empire of Rome had disappeared,
and after the country had become Saxon, and they settled in
our south-western counties, Hampshire, Wiltshire, and Somersetshire. The Belgæ, no doubt, talked Latin, and it was
equally the language of their colonists in Britain; and there,
as in other parts of the island, Latin was no doubt the language
talked in the Roman provinces and towns. We have evidence
of this in the fact that in exploring the Roman remains here,
whether in town or country, when we meet with inscriptions,
they are invariably expressed in Latin. Even in Wales, where

Roman inscriptions are tolerably abundant, I have never heard of one which was Romano-Celtic. And, in fact, the existence of anything of this kind is so rare, that I think we may consider it doubtful if we have now any authentic sample left of the language which the Britons talked when the Romans came to our island. It was no doubt a Celtic dialect, but it seems to be only preserved to us in the formation of the names of places which are older than the Anglo-Saxon, chiefly of mountains and rivers, and we are rather led to believe that it closely resembled the languages of Ireland and Scotland. I confess that I am much inclined myself to the opinion that the Welsh language has a different origin, which may perhaps be accounted for as follows: It seems to be commonly acknowledged, that the Welsh is the same dialect of Celtic as the Breton tongue of Armorica, and several stories are told in connection with the Peninsular War of the earlier part of the present century, of the ease with which the Welsh soldiers in our army understood and conversed with the Bretons our allies. There can be little doubt that, during the period at which the Saxon settlement of our island took place, the Bretons of France were great adventurers on the sea. At a very early period, but rather later than this, they were the principal visitors to Newfoundland; and I think it more than probable that in the time of which we are speaking they sent expeditions to the coasts of Britain in the same manner as the Angles and Saxons, and as it was in a manner the part of the island which looked to them, just as the others regarded at this time the various peoples of the northern race. Thus the Bretons formed their establishment in Cornwall and Wales, and the Welshmen, to whom the Anglo-Saxons gave a name which signified strangers, and the Cornish, who speak the same dialect, began soon to consider themselves as the original inhabitants of Britain, and have been so considered ever since. This belief was strengthened by the circumstance that the settlers had brought with them from Brittany their national legends, which seem to have formed the mass of the early British poetry in Geoffrey of Monmouth and that class of writers. Thus I myself feel very strongly the belief that the Welshmen of the present day are not the descendants of the ancient inhabitants of our island, but a later Celtic colony from Armorica, and this explains how they became so familiar with the Bretons of the maritime districts of the north-west of France.

On a fair consideration of all these facts, I am led to the

belief that the language spoken throughout the isles of Britain was Latin, and that if the Angles and Saxons had never come, we should have been now a people talking a Neo-Latin tongue, closely resembling French. The Irish or Gaelic has perhaps the best claim to be considered as representing the language of the Ancient Britons.

CHAPTER VII.

The Country—Roman Roads, and their Construction—Milliaria: the Roman Mile—Bridges—Roman Villas; Woodchester, Bignor, &c.—Tesselated pavements, and the Subjects represented on them—Rustic Villages—Agriculture and Farming—Country Life; the Chase—British Dogs.

WITH the imperfect view which we have thus been able to obtain of a Roman town in Britain, we see enough of comfort and elegance to convince us that the island was then inhabited by a population which had reached a high degree of civilisation and refinement. Of this we shall find still more remarkable traces when we leave the town and proceed into the country. The first objects that would there attract attention were the roads, which were constructed with such extraordinary skill that even now many of the best roads in England are laid upon the ancient Roman foundation.

Vitruvius has given exact directions for making a road. They began, it appears, by making two parallel furrows, the intended width of the road, and then removed all the loose earth between them till they came to the hard solid ground, and they filled up this excavation with fine earth hard beaten in. This first layer was called the *pavimentum*. Upon it was laid the first bed of the road, consisting of small squared stones, nicely ranged on the ground, which was sometimes left dry, but often a large quantity of fresh mortar was poured into it. This layer was termed *statumen*. The next was called *rudus* or *ruderatio*, and consisted of a mass of small stones, broken to pieces and mixed with lime, in the proportion of one part of broken stones to two of lime. The third layer, or bed, which was termed *nucleus*, was formed of a mixture of lime, chalk, pounded or broken tiles, or earth, beaten together, or of gravel or sand and lime mixed with clay. Upon this was laid the surface or pavement of the road, which was called technically *summum dorsum*, or *summa crusta*. It was composed sometimes of stones set like the paving stones in our streets, and sometimes of flag-stones cut square or polygonally, and also, probably oftener, of a firm bed of gravel and lime. The roads were thus raised higher than the surrounding grounds, and on this account the mass was termed *agger*.

The result of the above process would be a Roman road of the most perfect description; but we must not suppose that in any part of the empire these directions were always strictly adhered to. On the contrary, there are few Roman roads existing which do not in some way or other vary from them; some are entirely without the *nucleus*, in others there was no *statumen*. Nevertheless, there is always found a sufficiently close resemblance between the structure of the old Roman roads as they exist, and the directions given above. They are often found in our island in an extraordinary degree of perfection; where they have been used to the present time as highroads, they are naturally worn down, and it is only at rare intervals that we can find any characteristic to identify them, except it be the extraordinary straightness of the course; but where the course of the road has been changed at a subsequent period, and especially where it runs along an uncultivated heath, the ancient Roman road often presents itself to our view in an imposing embankment for several miles together. When they came upon higher ground, the Romans were not in the habit of entrenching, but they often raised the embankment higher even than in the plain, probably as a measure of precaution. Thus, on the summit of the Gogmagog hills, near Cambridge, the embankment of the Roman road is very lofty and remarkably perfect. They seem seldom to have turned out of their course to avoid a hill, and, in some instances, we find the Roman road proceeding direct up an acclivity which we should not encounter at the present day. A Roman road runs over the top of one of the mountains of Westmoreland, almost two thousand feet above the level of the sea, which is named from it, High Street.

The roads here described are of course to be looked upon as the grand military roads of the empire, those along which the lines of the Itineraries are traced, and which formed the direct communication between the towns in this island which have been enumerated in a former chapter. But there were numerous other roads in all parts of the island, such as the Romans termed *viæ vicinales*, branch roads, *privatæ*, private roads, *agrariæ*, country roads, *deviæ*, by-roads. These were constructed with much less labour than the others, yet they were still sufficiently good and durable to have left distinct traces down to the present time. They were sometimes paved with flag-stones, as is the case with one over the hills near Monmouth, where the stones are fitted together with care, though they are of all shapes and sizes. This, as it has been already observed, was probably a common way of paving the streets of towns. The Roman road leading direct from Lymne to Canterbury, seems, by old accounts, to have been paved in this manner, and it is still, no doubt from that circumstance, called Stone Street. The stones themselves, in the course of ages, have been carried away for various purposes of utility. Other larger roads, which seem to have traversed nearly the whole island, and which were not constructed in the same laborious manner as the military roads, were probably intended for commercial purposes, such as those which branch from the salt districts of Droitwich, and from the mining districts. Antiquaries seem often to have been so misled by their dissimilitude to the great Roman military roads, as to imagine many of these to have been British. It is not very probable that the older inhabitants of the island, such as Cæsar found them, divided into separate and hostile tribes, which seem often to have changed their boundaries, as they were pressed forwards by other colonies, should have been great road-makers.

We know that the Roman roads were constructed and regulated at an enormous expense, and we learn, from ancient writers, that the office of *curator viarum* was one which implied considerable honour. Nearer the centre of the empire, if not in the distant provinces, there were from place to place *mutationes*, or places where post-horses might be taken, which were termed *agminales*, and which were conducted by *veredarii*, or postilions. The keepers of these stations were called *statores*. It was by means of these posts that Constantine, the son of Constantius Chlorus, made his rapid and celebrated progress from the east to join his father in Britain, and as they appear to have been continued to the coast of Gaul, it is probable that they were also established in this island. There were also found by the road-side *diversoria, cauponæ,* or *tabernæ diversoriæ,* places of entertainment for man and horse, which were kept by *diversores* and *caupones*. Further, at stated intervals, stood *mansiones*, the keepers of which, named *mancipes*, stopped the passengers to examine their *diplomata*, or passports.

Through all the immense systems of great roads which thus

run over the whole Roman empire, the distances were marked out with the greatest care, and at the end of each *mille passus*, or Roman mile, was erected a milliary column or milestone, (*milliarium*), with an inscription, indicating the distance from the next town. These milestones usually consisted of a large plain cylinder of stone, raised on a base; and the inscription stated the name of the emperor under whose reign it was erected, so that they were probably often changed, in order to honour a new emperor's name. After the Romans had departed from the island, these monuments were gradually taken for the material, and only a few of them have been preserved, which is to be lamented, as they would have thrown great light on the Roman topography of Britain. The only perfect example known at present in this country is one preserved in the local museum at Leicester, and its inscription, which is as follows, states that it was set up under the emperor Hadrian, at the distance of two miles from Ratæ.

    IMP CAESAR
  DIV TRAIAN PARTH F DIV
   TRAIAN HADRIAN AVG
  PONT IV COS III A RATIS
     II.

It is a perfect cylinder, three feet six inches in height, and five feet seven inches in circumference, and was dug up, in 1771, by the side of the ancient Roman road, called the Foss-way, about two miles to the north of Leicester, thus identifying the Roman name of that town. There is another with an inscription nearly perfect, at Caton, near Lancaster, also erected under Hadrian. These milestones have been found more numerously in Gaul, and one of them, discovered near the town of Vic-sur-Aisne, has the following inscription, stating that it was raised in the fourteenth year of the reign of Caracalla, or A.D. 212, at the distance of seven leagues from Soissons.

    IMP CAES
   M AVRELIO AN
   TONINO PIO
   AVG BRITANNI
   CO MAX TRIB
  POT XIIII IMP II
   COS III PPPRO
   COS AB AVG
   SVESS LEVG
    VII.

It will be seen by this last inscription, that in ancient Gaul, as in modern France, they reckoned by leagues, and not, as in Britain, by miles. If we had but two consecutive milliaria remaining in their places, we should be able at once to solve the much-debated question of the length of the Roman miles in Britain; but, unfortunately, no such discovery has yet been made. We know that the mile consisted of a thousand *passus*, or *paces*, which, according to D'Anville, was equivalent to 756 French toises, or 4834·28 English feet. The English mile is 5280 feet. We gain, however, not much in knowing the exact measure of the Roman mile, because we cannot place trust in the numbers given in the Itineraries. The Roman numerals were easily altered by careless copyists, and they are found to be so often wrong in the texts of the Itineraries as they now exist, that we can place no confidence in them, at all events as far as regards Britain, and the only safe method of applying them to the actual sites is first to find the traces of the stations, and then compare them with the Itinerary.

One of the most remarkable characteristics of the Roman roads is the extraordinary straightness of their course. The great military roads may often be traced for many miles without a single deviation from the direct line. When there is a deviation, if between two stations, it was for some very important reason, and may generally be explained by the circumstances of the locality. As we have before remarked, hills, even when of considerable elevation, presented no obstacle to the course of the road. The Roman engineers even drained or filled up marshes, when they stood in their way, if there were any advantage to be gained by passing across them. We have many proofs that the rivers in this country were passed by an extensive system of bridges—it is probable, indeed, that a military road seldom passed a river without one. Some of the more important Roman bridges remained till a recent period, forming the foundation of the modern structures which replaced them. Such was the case little more than twenty years ago at London, and when the old bridge over the Tyne at Newcastle was taken down in 1771, the piers were found to be Roman masonry. The foundation was laid upon piles of fine black oak, which were in a state of perfect preservation. The remains of three bridges are found along the line of the Wall. When the old Teign-bridge in Devonshire, by which the Roman road crossed the Teign in its way to Totness and Plymouth, was taken down in 1815, the Roman work beneath was found in a remarkable state of preservation. It is the opinion of Mr Bruce and of other antiquaries that the bridge at Newcastle, as well as the others in the Wall district, had no arches, but that a horizontal roadway of timber was laid on the piers. 'The foundations of the piers of three Roman bridges in the region of the Wall,' Mr Bruce tells us, 'still remain; one across the Tyne at Corstopitum, one across the North Tyne at Cilurnum, and another across the Rede-water at Habitancum; an examination of these has induced me to believe that they, at least, had no arches. The piers are of a size and strength sufficient to withstand the thrust of the waters without the aid of an arch; and in one at least of these cases, the requisite spring of the arch would have raised the road to an inconvenient height. An experienced mason, who examined carefully the ruins of the bridge at Habitancum, told me that he observed that all the stones which encumbered the spot were square, none of them having the shape of stones used in building arches. It is certain that in the mediæval period the Newcastle bridge had a road of timber.' We cannot doubt, nevertheless, that many Roman bridges had arches. Mr Roach Smith has pointed out a very fine semicircular arched bridge over the little river Cock, near its entrance into the Wharfe, about half-a-mile below Tadcaster, on the Roman road leading southward from that town (the ancient Calcaria), which he considered as Roman. The masonry of this bridge is massive, and remarkably well preserved, and the stones are carefully squared and sharply cut, and on some of them the mason's mark, an R, is distinctly visible. The roadway was very narrow. The Saxons seem to have preserved carefully the bridges they found in existence, though they probably built few themselves; and I am inclined to believe that most of the bridges in this country at the time of the Norman conquest were Roman. The preservation of these ancient bridges was considered of so much importance, that the charge of them was often thrown upon the hundred, or on the county. Thus, at Cambridge, the county was bound to see that the bridge was kept in repair, and certain lands were allotted for the expense of the repairs; and I have very little doubt that the bridge which in the thirteenth century was in such a ruinous condition, that people's carts used to fall over into the river, was the ancient bridge of the Roman town of Camboricum.* It was probably from a broken Roman bridge,

* Dicunt quod reparatio et refectio magni pontis Cantebrigiæ pertinent ad comitatum Cantebrigiæ, et quidam de comitatu prædicto tenent terras

the remains of which seem to have been visible in the time of Leland, that the town of Pontefract, in Yorkshire (*pons fractus*) derived its name.

The objects, however, which must have struck the traveller most forcibly as he passed along the road between one town and another, were the numerous country villas or mansions, many of them magnificent palaces, covering as much ground as a whole town. Modern discoveries have shown us how marvellously the country was covered, especially in some of the southern and midland districts, with these great rural residences, which will be better understood by the reader, if we describe the relative positions of two or three known groups. Perhaps the largest and most magnificent Roman villa yet discovered in England is that at Woodchester, in Gloucestershire. Woodchester is situated in a beautiful valley in the high grounds bordering on the vale of Gloucester, on the bank of a stream which runs down thence into the plain to join the Severn, and at about four miles from the Roman road from Corinium (*Cirencester*) to the *trajectus Augusti* (*Aust Passage*) across the Channel. It was about twelve miles from the town just mentioned, and the same distance from Glevum (*Gloucester*). If we left Corinium by the ancient road just mentioned, we should first have seen on a hill to the right, between this road and the road to Glevum, a villa of some extent, the remains of which have been discovered at Daglingworth, about three miles to the north-west of Cirencester. Close to the road on the left, under a hill about five miles from Corinium, was a Roman station, or building, at a place now called Trewsbury. About two miles further, on the right-hand side of the road, stood another handsome villa, which has been excavated to some extent at Hocberry, in the parish of Rodmarton. Two miles more brought us to a villa on the opposite side of the road, and, like the last, close to it, which has been discovered in the parish of Cherington. About six miles further, on the same side of the road, extensive buildings have been found at a place called Kingscot, which belonged either to a villa or to a station. About halfway between the two last places, a by-way probably led to the

---

geldabiles qui debent pontem reficere quando pons indiget reparatione et refectione. Dicunt etiam quod pons prædictus debilis est, fractus, et dissolutus, ita quod carectæ magnatuum et aliorum ibidem transitum facientes cadunt in aqua, ita quod tam homines quam equi emergunt ad magnum periculum et dampnum ibidem transientium.—*Hundred Rolls* vol. ii. p. 392.

villa at Woodchester, among the hills to the right. Eight or nine miles from Kingscot, at a place called Croom-hall, remains of another villa, or mansion, have been found, close to the left-hand side of the road, where it passes over an eminence. A few miles carried the traveller hence to the shores of the Bristol Channel. If we had taken the road from Corinium to Glevum, we should first have seen the villa at Daglingworth, on the hill to the left, and then, on the right hand, and near the road, about seven miles from Corinium, we should have seen a fine villa which has been discovered at Combe-end. On the other side of the road, in a fine valley among the hills, about half-way between the road and Woodchester, was another rich villa, the remains of which have been discovered at a place called Brown's Hill. In the vale of Gloucester, at the foot of the hills, about four miles to the west of Woodchester, stood another handsome villa, or perhaps a small town, at Frocester. All these places are within a very small circuit, and have been discovered accidentally, so that there may be others within the same compass.

Let us now turn to Somersetshire, and take as a centre the ancient town of Somerton, situated on a Roman road leading from Ilchester in the direction of Glastonbury. If we follow this road towards Ilchester, two miles from Somerton, two extensive Roman villas have been traced in the parish of Kingsdon, one near the Roman road, the other a little to the east, on the bank of a small stream called the Cary. Further east, on the other side of the stream, a third villa has been found at Lytes Cary. These three villas are included in a distance of about a mile. In the parish of Hurcot, joining Somerton to the east, two villas have also been found, one near Somerton, the other about three-quarters of a mile to the north-east. Barely half a mile to the south-east of the latter is another extensive Roman villa at Charlton Mackrel; and in the opposite direction, somewhat more than half a mile from the Hurcot villa, is another at Copley. To the east of this, in the parish of Littleton, close to the Roman road just mentioned, a group of several Roman villas has been found. Proceeding along the road northwardly, at about four miles from Somerton, we arrive at Butleigh Bottom, where a Roman villa of considerable extent has been traced. Villas are found in equal abundance within two or three miles to the west of Somerton, among which the most extensive is that at Pitney, covering an acre and a half of ground, and containing a very remarkable pavement. It may be remarked that the walls of the villas in this district abound in herring-bone work. We might give similar examples of the profusion with which the Roman villas were scattered over the country in Hampshire and Oxfordshire. In the latter county, two noble villas stood within a mile of each other, in the parishes of Stonesfield and North Leigh, near the Roman road now called the Akeman Street. The splendid Roman villa at Bignor, in Sussex, at the foot of the hills to the north of Arundel, close by the Roman road from Regnum (*Chichester*) to London, has a situation something like that of Woodchester. Over the hills, between two and three miles to the north-west of Bignor, a villa has been traced near the church at Duncton. To the north-east, by the side of the Roman road to London, at about two miles distant from Bignor, traces of Roman occupation are found, and about three miles further, in the parish of Pulborough, there has been a Roman station. Rather more than six miles to the south of Bignor, the discovery of a Roman sepulchre at Avisford seems to indicate the vicinity of another villa; about six miles eastwardly from this place a villa has been found in the parish of Angmering: and another villa has been found on the coast of Bognor, about seven miles to the southward of Avisford.*

While we are thus speaking in general terms of villas scattered over the country so thickly, few will imagine what an immense pile of building a Roman villa usually was. I will, therefore, proceed to describe one of the largest in this country, that of Woodchester, which was opened partly under the superintendence of Mr Lysons during the years from 1793 to 1796. Nothing could be finer than the site which the Roman proprietor had here chosen for his residence. A square level platform, with a little narrow gorge on the north, down which a small stream ran into the larger stream that washed the foot of its eastern declivity, was backed by a hill which sheltered it from the damp winds of the west.

---

* The villas of Woodchester and Bignor formed the subject of very splendid publications by Lysons. An account of the Pitney villa and pavement was published by Sir Richard Colt Hoare, in a thin 8vo volume, printed in 1832. A description of the North Leigh and Stonesfield villas was printed in 1836, by Mr Henry Hakewill, in a similar form. The great collection by Lysons contains, in addition to Woodchester and Bignor, accounts of villas at Littlecote in Wiltshire, Frampton in Dorset, Withington in Gloucestershire, Horkstow in Lincolnshire, and some others, all illustrated with magnificent plates of pavements, &c. Accounts of other villas will be found in the various volumes of the Archæologia of the Society of Antiquaries.

230   THE ROMANS.   [CHAP. VII.

It was also sheltered from the east winds by a hill which rose on the opposite side of the stream. The main valley

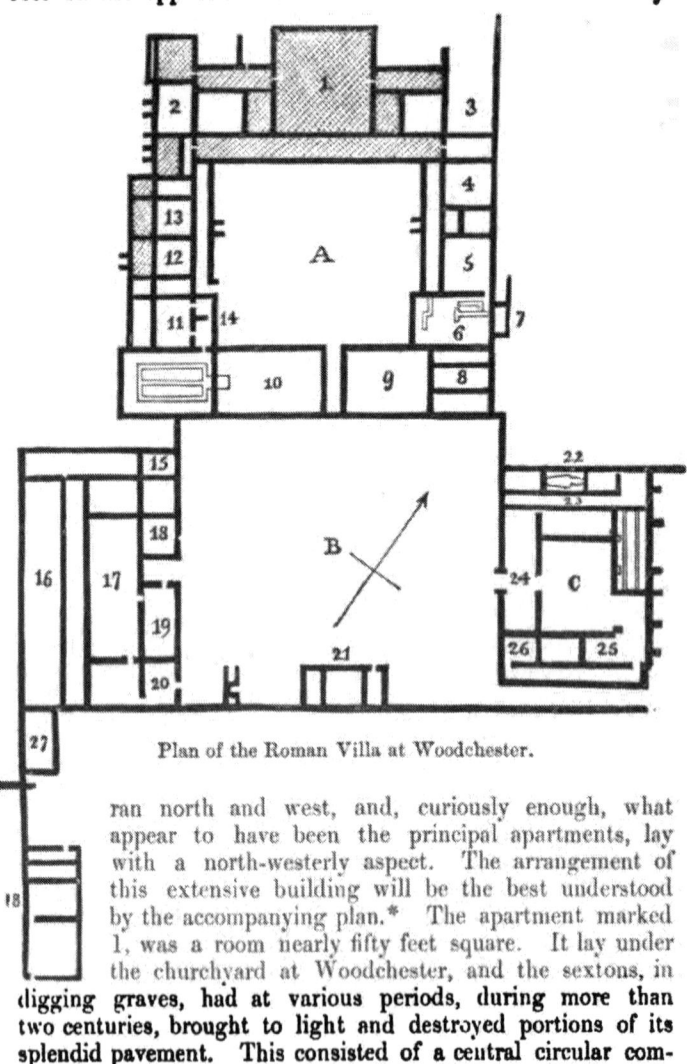

Plan of the Roman Villa at Woodchester.

ran north and west, and, curiously enough, what appear to have been the principal apartments, lay with a north-westerly aspect. The arrangement of this extensive building will be the best understood by the accompanying plan.* The apartment marked 1, was a room nearly fifty feet square. It lay under the churchyard at Woodchester, and the sextons, in digging graves, had at various periods, during more than two centuries, brought to light and destroyed portions of its splendid pavement. This consisted of a central circular com-

* The rooms in which mosaic pavements were found, are shaded in the plan.

partment of about twenty-five feet in diameter, consisting of an outer border formed of a Vitruvian scroll, edged on each side by a guilloche, and enriched with foliage proceeding from a mask of Pan, having a beard of leaves. Immediately within this border was a wide circular band containing representations of twelve different animals, on a white ground, with trees and flowers between them. Within this circle was a smaller band, separated from it by a guilloche and a border of acorns, and containing representations of birds on a white ground. Among them was a figure of a fox. On the southern side was a figure of Orpheus playing on the lyre. This band was bounded internally by a twisted guilloche, and within was a central hexagon about ten feet in diameter. This centre had been entirely destroyed long before the time of the opening of the villa by Lysons, but some old drawings, made on former partial openings, show that the field was covered with figures of fish and sea monsters. I am inclined to think that it was a little lower than the rest of the pavement, and formed the floor of a shallow reservoir for water. The circular compartment I have been describing was inclosed in a square frame, consisting of twenty-four compartments, enriched with a great variety of guilloches, scrolls, frets, and other ornaments, edged on the inside with a braided guilloche, on the outside with a labyrinth fret, between a single fret and a braided guilloche. In the four angular spaces between the great border of this gorgeous pavement and the great circular compartment were the remains of female figures, two of which appear to have occupied each space; they had evidently been naiads. At the four inner corners of the square were found sufficient indications that they had once been occupied by columns, which had no doubt supported the roof, which was probably vaulted. It was found that the pavement was supported by a hypocaust, or system of flues, intended to warm the room.

On each side of this large apartment was found a passage, twenty-nine feet four inches long by seven feet and a half wide, the entrance into which was by a door three feet wide. The floor of these passages was paved with coarse mosaic work, ornamented with a double labyrinth fret of a dark bluish-grey on a white ground, surrounded by a plain red stripe. Curiously enough, at the extremity of the eastern of these passages, part of another pavement was discovered laid over it, a foot above its level, formed of much coarser materials than the original one, and very ill executed; the design being merely stripes of white, blue, and red, very irregularly put together. It had evidently been an alteration made at a late period.

To the southward of these two passages, were, on each side of the great apartment, two rooms, of which that nearest to the great apartment on each side had a mosaic pavement, of the same degree of coarseness as the passages, but of a simple and elegant design, consisting of a mat of three colours, dark grey, red, and white, surrounded by a double red border.

These were the first discoveries made, and they led to a more extensive investigation. On the south of the great apartment a gallery was discovered, a hundred and fourteen feet in length, by ten in width, except where it passed the wall of the great pavement, where it was only nine feet wide. The mosaic was of the same degree of coarseness as that of the other passages, but it was ornamented with a great variety of patterns, consisting chiefly of labyrinths, mats, and stars, for the most part in a good taste, forming square compartments, with a single twisted guilloche and two plain red stripes running round the whole of them. Those parts of the wall of this gallery which remained on the south side were two feet thick, and beyond it towards the south was a hard terrace floor. As the pavement of the gallery was destroyed at the centre, and no foundations of the wall remained there, it was impossible to ascertain if there had been any entrance from this gallery immediately into the room of the great pavement.

Excavations were now commenced at the end of the southern gallery running from the large apartment, and the room to the north of that marked No. 2 was found. This apartment, which had been a square of twenty-two feet ten inches, appeared also to have been new floored, for on excavating to the depth of three feet, the workmen came to a floor of very hard cement or terrace, on removing some of which a small fragment of mosaic pavement was discovered, six inches below the level of that floor. The whole of the terrace floor was then removed, not without much difficulty, on account of the extreme hardness of the cement. Under it were found four fragments of a mosaic pavement, which had been partly broken up. They were in a very good style, and the design had consisted of five octagonal compartments, containing figures on a white ground, surrounded by a double labyrinth fret; immediately within which, on the north side, was a scroll of flowers, with a vase in the centre. In the remains of the compartments, at the north-west and south-east corners, were fragments of Bacchanalian figures.

The octagonal compartment at the south-west corner was entire, and contained figures of two boys holding up a basket of fruit and leaves, with the inscription BONVM EVENTVM under them, in large capital letters. The compartment at the north-east corner had been nearly destroyed, but the letters BIINJI C . . . remained, evidently for BHNH COLITE, the Greek H being used for the Latin E, of which there are other examples. The inscription, when entire, would thus be, *Bonum Eventum bene colite*, a recommendation to worship well Bonus Eventus, one of the twelve deities who presided over the affairs of husbandry.* The walls of this room were two feet thick, formed of stone, roughly hewn, and remained to the height of about three feet on every side. Fragments of stucco, painted in fresco, lay scattered about. On the west side the wall was double, with a space of six inches between, to secure the room against humidity. Another system of flues for warming was found under this room, the passages being about four feet deep.

The room adjoining, No. 2, had no tesselated pavement, but the same hypocaust of flues extended under it, and outside the wall was the fire-place communicating with them. The aperture under the wall, where the fire seemed to have been placed, was formed by bricks, one foot five inches long, one foot wide, and two inches thick; it was one foot eleven inches wide at the bottom, and six inches at the top, where a sort of arch was formed by the edges of the bricks gradually advancing beyond each other. This fire-place had walls one foot eight inches thick on each side; they were four feet two inches apart, and projected outwards four feet from the wall. A considerable quantity of skulls and bones of animals, chiefly sheep, were found near the fire-place.

To the south of the room marked 2, was another apartment, twenty feet long, by twelve feet eight inches wide, which contained a mosaic pavement, of a tasteful design. It consisted of a circular compartment, between two oblong ones, united together by a single twisted guilloche, with a border formed by a labyrinth fret, between which and the wall was a considerable space filled up with plain red tesseræ, rather more than an inch

---

* So we are informed by Varro, de Re Rustica, lib. i. There was a temple of Bonus Eventus at Rome, and Pliny mentions statues of this deity, which represented him holding a patera in the right hand, and an ear of corn and a poppy in the left. He is represented in the same shape on the reverse of a coin of Titus; and the reverse of one of Geta has a female figure holding a dish of fruits in her right hand, and ears of corn in her left, with the inscription BONI EVENTVS.

square. The circular compartment was nearly destroyed, but it had probably contained a figure. This floor was also supported by a hypocaust, and it had a fire-place outside the wall, near which was found a coin of Magnentius.

Two rooms were subsequently opened, between the room No. 2, and the large room No. 1, and the one adjoining to the latter had a tesselated pavement, consisting of two square compartments, filled with labyrinths, and united together by a braided guilloche, on the outside of which were two narrow red stripes. The parts of the building next explored were the large rooms, numbered 9 and 10, and the room to the left of the latter. One of them was thirty-eight feet square; another was thirty-eight feet by forty-six; and the third was thirty-eight feet by fifty-one. The walls remained in several places, to the height of four feet from the foundation. Those on the north side were two feet two inches thick, and were in some places lined with brickwork; the south walls were one foot ten inches thick. These walls were in several places plastered on the outside, and painted of a dull red colour. Many fragments of the stucco which had covered the walls internally, and had been painted in fresco, with various colours, were found among the rubbish. Some of them were painted with large capital letters, which had formed parts of inscriptions. These rooms appeared to have had tesselated pavements, which had been broken up; and several slices of marble of different sorts, but chiefly foreign, were also found. These had, perhaps, been employed to encrust the walls, a practice which we know prevailed among the Romans. Some of these pieces of marble were not more than a quarter of an inch thick. Parts of two stone columns, and fragments of statuary, were subsequently found in the room No. 10, and in the room adjoining it to the left; on digging trenches across, several inner walls, two feet four inches wide, were discovered running in the directions indicated by the light outlines in our plan. These walls were covered with large flat stones on the top, which did not rise higher than the foundations of the other walls, so that it is probable that they supported a floor, and that their object was to prevent humidity in the apartment above. Among the ruins of this room were found quantities of tesseræ, many fragments of the figured Samian ware, and of glass vessels, and portions of two statues in Samian marble, which seemed to have belonged to figures of Diana Lucifera and Meleager. At the east end of the room, No. 9, great part of an arch was discovered, about three feet below the surface of the earth, which was doubtless connected with the substructure of the floors.

From the autumn of 1795 to the summer of 1796, the excavations were carried on more to the south, and the great court, B, was traced, with the various apartments round it. On the west side was a mass of buildings, containing twelve rooms, which had been entered from the court by a vestibule, between the rooms marked 18 and 19. In this vestibule a fragment of a beautiful group, in white marble, of Cupid and Psyche, was found, which had evidently been copied from the same model as a well-known group of sculpture in the Museum Florentinum. The walls in this part of the building were of stone, with bonding courses of brick; and among the ruins were found thin slabs of stone, of an irregular hexagonal form, which, no doubt, belonged to the roof. Pieces of stags' horns, several of them sawed off at the ends, were also found here; and several human bones were met with in the buildings on the north and west sides of the great court. Many coins, chiefly in small brass, were found here and in various parts of the building.

A wall extended along the whole length of the south side of the great court, B, near the centre of which were discovered the foundation walls of three rooms, or perhaps of a gateway, with a door on each side (No. 21). Here, as in many other parts of the building, the walls were destroyed down to the foundation, so that it was impossible to ascertain the width of more than one of the doorways, which was four feet wide. Fragments of large columns were found here, which showed that there had been an imposing display of architectural ornament. A little to the west of these foundations, and attached to the long southern wall, were the remains of a singular building, consisting of two parallel walls, three feet distant from each other, connected by two transverse walls, having an opening between them. At the bottom of this opening there was a considerable quantity of coal ashes, and, at the west end, at the height of fifteen inches from the bottom, was a small flue through the wall. This building is described as presenting very much the appearance of having held a boiler.

Considerable remains of buildings were also discovered on the eastern side of this great court. A gallery first presented itself, marked 24 in our plan, and measuring sixty-five feet eight inches in length, by ten feet four inches wide. The entrance from the court was eight feet eight inches wide. Another opening in the east wall, immediately opposite and nearly of the same dimensions, led into what appears to have been a court, C, surrounded with apartments. In one of these rooms, to the east of the court, there were two parallel narrow walls (fifteen inches wide), running the whole length of the room, and square projections from the west wall. As these walls rose no higher than the foundation part of the other walls, they probably supported a pavement. At the north end of this room was found the leg of a statue, of white marble, and not far from it was a foundation of square stones, which appeared to have been intended as a pedestal. The outward wall on the east side of this range of building was entire to the height of from four to five feet. It was three feet thick, and built of stones roughly hewn, with six projections on the outside, which were evidently buttresses. We may, therefore, suppose that this was the exterior of the whole building on this side.

At the north end of the range of rooms of which we are now speaking, at No. 22, were found the remains of what Lysons considered to be a *laconicum*, or sweating-room. At the depth of five feet below the surface of the ground the excavators met with a very hard cement floor, eight feet ten inches wide, and nine feet ten inches long. On removing this floor, which was eight inches thick, a layer of bricks was discovered under it, which proved to be the covering of flues that ran under the floor. The flues were two feet two inches in depth, and one of them was longitudinal, and four transverse. The longitudinal flue was one foot nine inches wide at the bottom, and seven inches at the top. The transverse flues were six inches wide at the top, and one foot six inches at the bottom. They were built partly of unhewn stone, and partly of brick, forming rude kind of arches. The intermediate space between the transverse flues was filled up with ridge tiles formed into funnels, and placed between layers of brick and stone; while the interstices, which were much wider than is usual in walling, were filled with a reddish clay. The funnels were on an average eighteen inches long, and four and a-half in diameter, some formed by only one of the curved tiles. A row of perpendicular funnels extended along the north and south walls, and seemed to have been carried up to the top of the building. This elaborate hypocaust is shown, as it appeared when opened, in our accompanying plate, which is a view taken from the south-west corner, and exhibits a

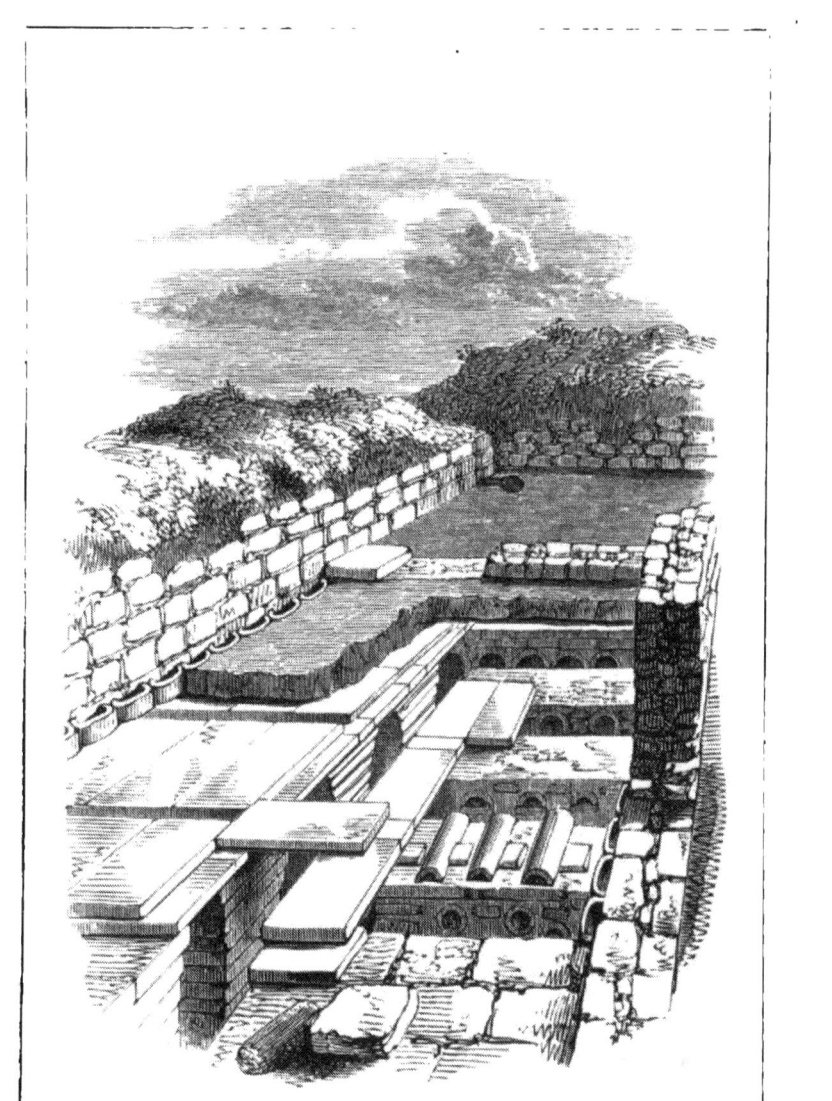

Hypocaust in the Roman Villa at Woodchester.

fragment of the cement floor, as well as the floor of another room on the east. The latter has no flues or hypocaust underneath, but at the north-east corner was a sort of basin hollowed in the floor, from which a leaden pipe passed through the wall. From the opposite corner of this room was a passage, with a floor of cement, rising towards the west, to more than three feet above the level of the other part. The upper part of it is destroyed, but at the south-east corner of the great court is a passage, which appears to have been one of the entrances to it.

From excavations made in different parts, it appeared that the great court, B, had been laid with a coarse sort of terrace pavement. Further excavations outside the southern wall of the great court, brought to light a continuation of the western wall, with an apartment in the corner, No. 27, and further on a range of rooms, at 28. The excavations were next carried on from the north-east corner of the great court, B, along the eastern side of the court, A, which led to the discovery of a new series of apartments, Nos. 3 to 8, with traces of pavements and hypocausts. These and the corresponding rooms on the west side were carefully examined. In the room, No. 11, were found eight square stone pillars, two feet nine inches and three-quarters high, which seemed to have been the supports of a hypocaust. On each side of the court was a gallery, sixty-two feet five inches long, and eight feet five inches wide, each of which had possessed handsome mosaic pavements, and which joined up to the great gallery on the north side of the court. These galleries had had flues under them, and on the outside of the walls of each, within the court, were short parallel walls, that appeared to have been the fire-places to hypocausts. In some of the rooms on the west side, remains of very handsome mosaic pavements were discovered. The floors on the east side of the court appeared to have been much more thoroughly destroyed than on the west. The walls of the apartment, No. 3, were continued northwardly, but could not be traced except at intervals, as they ran under the churchyard and the church; and it was evident that the whole mass of buildings had extended much further in that direction. Perhaps there was another court. A transverse wall below the room, No. 27, appeared also to lead to other buildings, so that in spite of the immense extent of the building thus uncovered, it appears that it was by no means the whole villa.

Our cut on page 237 gives a plan of as much of this extensive building as has been explored, and will furnish us with a general notion of its arrangements. It covers an area of five hundred and fifty feet by above three hundred feet. The approach was by a level platform from the south, with outbuildings on the left, if not also on the right. Here the visitor approached apparently a long dead wall, with the grand portal in the centre. On passing through the entrance gateway, he found himself in an immense court, about a hundred and fifty feet square, with masses of buildings on each side. In front of him was another gateway, which led him into a second court, ninety feet square, surrounded on three sides by a gallery, or, as the ancients called it, *cryptoporticus*, which was, no doubt, either closed in, or capable of being closed in, as the hypocausts under it show that it was intended to be warmed. Opposite the gate by which the visitor entered, was probably another portal that led him through the northern cryptoporticus into the grand hall, No. 1, which was decorated with every kind of ornamentation, and perhaps with a fountain or basin of water in the middle. It is possible that beyond this there was another small court, surrounded by buildings, the foundations of which lie under the churchyard and church. A simple glance at the plan is sufficient to show us that it is useless to attempt to give any explanation of the mass of rooms which surround these different courts. It seems reasonable to suppose that the more elegant and private apartments were those built round the inner court, A. The apartments round the little side court, C, were perhaps, as Lysons supposed, baths and rooms for purposes connected with them. Perhaps those on the other side of the court were rooms for recreation and conversing, and they seem to have been adorned with sculptures, and perhaps with pictures, ornamental pottery, and plants.*

The only common feature in the Roman villas in Britain seems to have been the large courts round which the buildings were grouped: and it is in this alone that they bear any close

---

* The Roman villas no doubt long remained, as imposing ruins, after the departure of the Romans. The earth gradually accumulated, till, at a much later period, the upper parts of the walls were cleared away for the materials, leaving the substructure underneath. The pavements have suffered most from being accidentally discovered, from time to time, by the ignorant peasantry, who broke them up, imagining that treasures were concealed under them. Perhaps the Caledonian or Saxon invaders often destroyed the pavements for the same cause. The early Saxons imagined that all statues and busts were implements of magic, and that the dangerous spell could only be broken by breaking them. Hence, we seldom find more than fragments of statues.

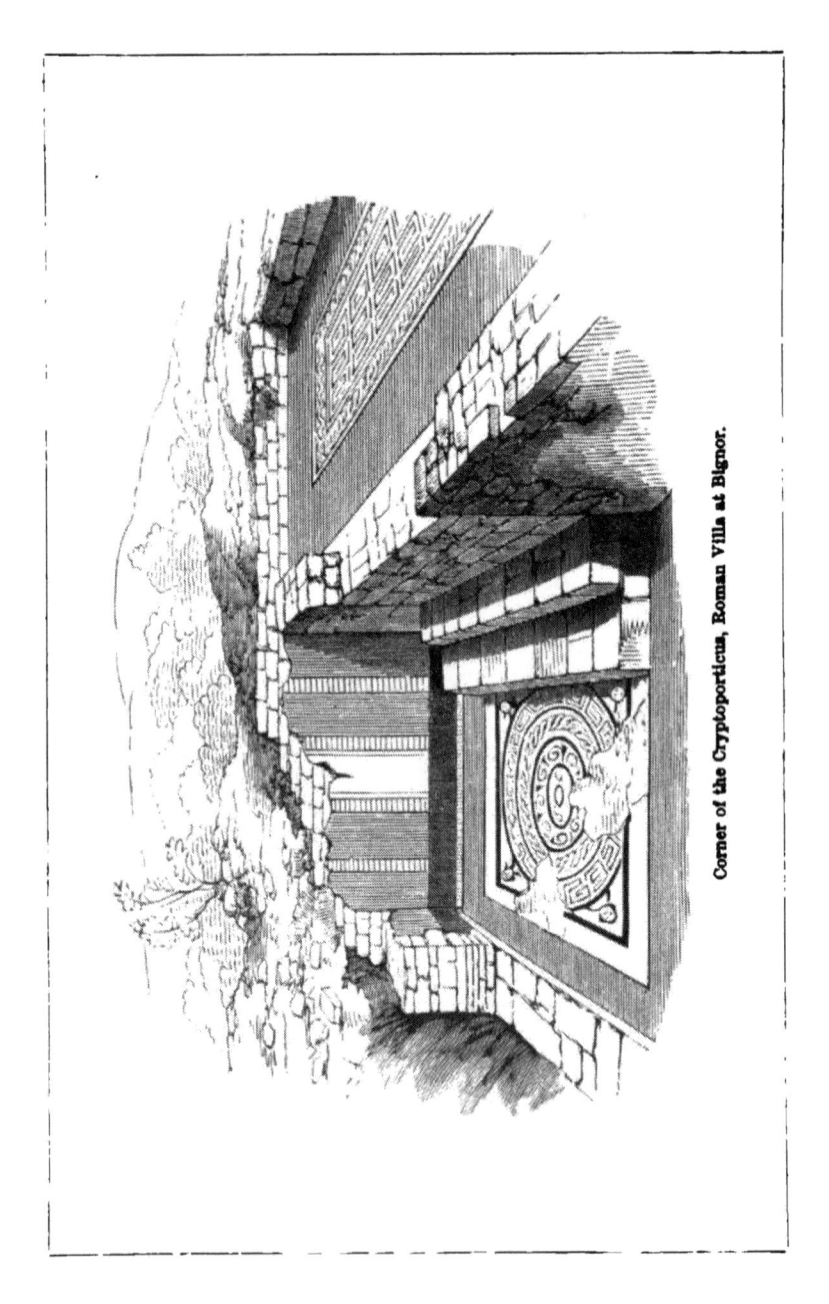

Corner of the Cryptoporticus, Roman Villa at Bignor.

resemblance to the directions given by Vitruvius.* In the villa at Bignor there were also two courts, larger even than those at Woodchester, but they lay with a different aspect, running north-west and south-east, instead of nearly north and south. The inner court at Bignor was surrounded by a more perfect and extensive cryptoporticus than that at Woodchester. The court itself was a parallelogram, not quite perfect, as the northern side was a little longer than the side opposite. The southern cryptoporticus measured a hundred and thirty-seven feet nine inches in length, and eight feet in width. The western cryptoporticus, extending across the width of the court, was ninety-six feet long, by ten wide. The great outer court appeared not to have had buildings round it, although traces of buildings were found towards the middle of the area. There appears to have been a large entrance gate from the outside of the building into the inner court on its southern side. The baths, which were more extensive and more clearly defined than at Woodchester, were attached to the inner court, near its south-eastern corner. The cryptoporticus of the villa at Bignor had had tesselated pavements; the level of the floor on the northern side was more elevated than the others, and at the northern corner, where this northern cryptoporticus joined the western one, there was a small square room, with a very elegant pavement, through which, by means of steps, people passed from one into the other. The accompanying plate represents this room as it appeared when first discovered. The painted stucco remained fresh on the wall. The end of the floor of the northern cryptoporticus is seen to the right. It is singular that under the middle of the court at Bignor, foundations of old walls were found, which appeared to have belonged to a previous villa that had been rebuilt on a different plan. At North Leigh, in Oxfordshire, the stone materials of a former building had been made use of, for the stones of an arch which were found in one of the larger rooms, had been made out of fragments of columns, and the mouldings of bases and capitals still remained on the back. The inner quadrangle only of this villa has been explored, if it ever consisted of more than one. There was a large entrance gateway with several rooms adjoining on the south-eastern side, and the apartments round the other three

---

* Lysons attempted to trace out the design of the villa at Woodchester, by applying the rules given by Vitruvius, but I think without much success, although that villa is more regular in its plan than most of the others. To most of them the rules of Vitruvius seem quite inapplicable.

sides are very numerous. The quadrangle is not an exact square; the dimensions of its four sides being, north-east, a hundred and sixty-seven feet; south-east, a hundred and eighty-six feet; south-west, a hundred and fifty-three feet; and north-west, two hundred and thirteen feet.

Many of the Roman villas hitherto discovered in this country appear to have been of nearly equal extent with those described above, and we derive an extraordinary notion of the condition of the island at this period from the number of these extensive and evidently magnificent buildings which have been discovered. As these discoveries have generally been the result of accident, there can be no doubt that we are only acquainted with a small number of the villas which were scattered over the soil of Britain. The number already discovered amounts probably to not less than a hundred. Some of the most magnificent lay in the south-west. In Gloucestershire, besides the great villa at Woodchester, and the extensive group which has already been mentioned as scattered over the country around it, large villas have been discovered at Lidney Park, Great Witcombe, Rodmarton, Combe-end, Withington, Bisley, and Stancombe Park, near Dursley. No less extensive villas have been found in Somersetshire, at Combe St Nicholas, East Coker, and Wellow; in Wiltshire, at Bromham, Littlecote Park, Pitmead near Warminster, and Rudge near Froxfield; in Dorset, at Frampton, Lenthy Green near Sherborne, and Halstock; in Hampshire, at Bramdean, Crondall, West Dean, and Thruxton; in Sussex, at Bignor, and in other places; at Basildon, in Berkshire; in Oxfordshire, among many other places, at North Leigh, Stonesfield, Great Lew, and Wigginton; in Northamptonshire, at Cottersbook, Welden, Burrow Hill, Harpole, &c.; in Nottinghamshire, at Mansfield Woodhouse. Kent and Essex appear to have been covered with extensive villas, but they seem to have been generally less magnificent than those in the west, and no fine tesselated pavements have yet been found in them. In the former of these two counties they lay thickly scattered along the road from Canterbury to London, and on the banks of the Medway towards Maidstone, as well as on the southern coast. Among the principal villas found in Essex are those at West Mersey, discovered long ago, and those explored more recently in the north-west of the county, at Icklington, Chesterford, and Hadstock. Lincolnshire appears to have been a rich and important district, and large villas with magnificent pavements have been found at Horkstow, Winterton, Roxby near the Humber, Haseby, Storton, Scampton, and Grantham. It must be borne in mind that Lincolnshire is comparatively unexplored, and so are most of the northern and midland counties. Yorkshire must have contained many fine country mansions of this kind, yet I am only aware of the discovery of one, at Hovingham, in the North Riding. Some years ago, remains of a Roman villa were found at Buxton, in Derbyshire, which seems even at that early period to have been visited for its mineral waters; and several have been found on the Welsh border in Shropshire and Herefordshire, as well as in North and South Wales.

Many of the villas which have been opened present unequivocal traces of having been plundered and injured by the violence of invaders, and sometimes they bear traces of having been burnt. Here and there human bones have been found, and while many of these may be accounted for by subsequent interment, yet in some cases there can hardly be a doubt of their having belonged to persons who were slain when the building was attacked. In 1833, some excavations at Silchester brought to light Roman baths, in a good state of preservation, having, like the baths discovered in the villas, leaden pipes to carry off the water. In one of these pipes were found two hundred Roman coins in brass, and in the bath lay a human skeleton, which, with a slight stretch of the imagination, may be supposed to have been that of an inhabitant of Calleva, who had sought refuge there when the city was invaded by the enemy, in the hope of saving his little treasure by concealing it where no one would think of seeking for it. Perhaps, if we carefully noted the articles of domestic use which are dug up in the excavations, we might at least form probable conjectures on the purposes of the rooms in which they were found. The number of such articles found at Woodchester was much less than might be expected from the space excavated; they consisted chiefly of several knives and choppers, a weight, a key, some fibulæ and buckles, and several hair-pins, and other small personal ornaments of this kind; two spears, and parts of weapons, with a considerable quantity of pottery, and a certain number of coins. The latter are always found scattered about. We are often tantalised by finding mere fragments of what might have given us the most important information relating to the occupiers of these villas. Such are the fragments of inscriptions on the walls found at Woodchester. Inscribed stones were found within the quadrangle of the villa at Pitney, but they also proved mere fragments, one of them having the words:—

> PATER
> PATRI
> SANC

The other, which appears to have been a sepulchral inscription, and to commemorate probably some member of the household who had been buried in the court, had the imperfect inscription:—

> VIXI SIN
> TRIGINTA
> QVÆ CAPI
> NONO A

The most interesting portion of the villas, as they now remain, is, however, the tesselated pavements. These are beautiful as works of art, and interesting for the subjects they represent; and they must have been the result of immense labour and great skill. These tesselated pavements were not confined to the country villas, but were used in the better mansions in the towns, and examples have been found in London, Cirencester, Gloucester, Caerleon, Caerwent, Kenchester, Leicester, York, Aldborough, Lincoln, Colchester, Canterbury, Dorchester, &c. Some of those found in London, Circencester, and Leicester,* are of very superior execution. As I have stated before, these pavements are formed with a number of small tesseræ, or cubes, set into a fine cement, and arranged in patterns or subjects, somewhat in the manner of Berlin wool patterns; but in the pavements the cubes are of different sizes, which enabled the artist to give far more freedom to his lines and effect to his picture. The cubes were made of different substances, in order to produce various shades of colour; some being of stone, others of terra-cotta, and others again of glass. Professor Buckman, in his description of the beautiful pavements found in Cirencester, has given us an excellent analysis of the materials of which they are composed. Six of the colours employed there are natural substances, and show us how skilfully the Roman artist turned to account the materials furnished by the neighbourhood.

* Part of an extremely fine Roman tesselated pavement has been uncovered in the cellar of a grocer in Leicester, who has kept it open, and shows it to visitors at a shilling each. It is well worth visiting. The principal pavements at Bignor, in Sussex, have also been kept open, and they are protected by buildings erected over them.

F →

D → ⅙ SCALE

- SECTION -
- INCH SCALE -

Tessellated Pavements at Wroxeter, No. 1.

White was produced by small cubes of chalk, which, on account of its softness, was used very sparingly, and only where it was necessary to produce very high relief. The hard, fine-grained free-stone from the quarries round Cirencester furnished a cream colour, and, when it had been exposed to a certain degree of heat, it served for a grey. Yellow was furnished by the oolite of the gravel drift of the district. The old red sandstone, from Herefordshire, was used to produce a chocolate colour; and slate-colour was furnished from the lime-stone bands of the lower lias in the vale of Gloucester. Three colours, light red, dark red, and black, were produced by terra-cotta; and one, a transparent ruby, by glass. Other materials are used in different parts of the country, the coloured glass being always the rarest. 'When the tesseræ were all set, and the cement hardened, the finish appears to have been given by polishing over the surface of the whole, which not only gave a perfectly smooth surface to the floor, but increased the brilliance of the effect; the cream-coloured and grey stones, from their hardness, took a fine polish, whilst we may conceive that the reds, being made of terra-cotta, would remain opaque, and this very contrast tended to heighten the effect, which was perhaps the reason why substances capable of high polish were not chosen in all instances.'

When the tesselated floor had no hypocaust under it, it was usually laid on a very substantial foundation. Mr George Maw, of Benthall Hall, near Broseley, who carefully examined the fragments of tesselated pavements recently discovered at Wroxeter, in the corridor of the large building supposed to be the basilica of Uriconium, has given me the following account of its structure, with the drawings, from which the illustrations in our two plates are engraved:—'As one of the numerous evidences of the great interest the Romans entertained for this tesselated work, the care and expense they went to in the preparation of the foundations may be noticed. At Wroxeter they consist of four distinct strata of materials, forming together a bed between two and three feet in thickness. On the native ground they first placed a layer of large lumps of sandstone, rather irregularly disposed, and above eighteen inches thick ($e\ e$ in the section in our first plate), the uneven surface of which was made tolerably smooth by a bed of soft concrete or mortar ($d\ d$), exactly like that now used in ordinary building. In breaking up the foundations, its surface, pressed in between the broken stones, looks, after an existence of fifteen hundred years, as fresh as the day on which it was prepared. On this bed of mortar was placed the stratum (*c c*) on which the tesseræ were laid, about two and a half inches thick, exceedingly hard and evidently composed of a mixture of roughly-pulverised burnt clay and lime, prepared with more care than the others, being of a very uniform thickness, and having its upper and under surfaces perfectly level. On this hard and even stratum the tesseræ (*a a*) were bedded in a layer of white and very hard cement (*b b*), not more than half an inch thick. The patterns of these Wroxeter pavements are all of a very simple description, and not comparable either in design or execution to many existing specimens. They are mostly very simple arrangements of geometrical forms, surrounded by fret borders or plain bands, consisting for the most part of but two materials, viz., a cream-coloured compact limestone or marble, and a bluish-black limestone. It is probable that both these materials have been brought from a distance, or perhaps imported, as they occur nowhere in the neighbourhood. The light stone is identical with that of a similar colour composing the Roman mosaics found on the continent and the mediæval mosaics of Italy, where it is called *palombino*. The dark stone appears to have been sparingly used, as though it were difficult to procure. In the plain dark margins next the walls it is replaced by a much coarser stone of a dark green colour (travertine), obtained, I believe, at the foot of the Wrekin, close at hand. Fragments of this stone also occur interspersed here and there in the body of the pavements, probably used to repair them. In addition to these three materials, bits of red earthenware are introduced in a guilloche border surrounding one of the panels.'

In the subjects represented on these pavements, we observe a considerable variety; though, as far as the discoveries go, two or three subjects seem to have been more popular than the others. It is not impossible that the subjects thus chosen may have had some reference to the purpose for which the room was designed. One of the most popular subjects hitherto observed, is that of Bacchus seated on a tiger or leopard, which perhaps indicates a love of conviviality among the people to whom these extensive residences belonged. This subject, which usually forms the centre of a pavement, was found in the fine pavement discovered in Leadenhall-street, in London; in the pavement at Thruxton; and in others at Stonesfield and Frampton. Another very popular central subject was Orpheus playing on the lyre, which seems to have been a favourite, because it gave the opportunity of picturing birds and beasts in the field of the pavement.

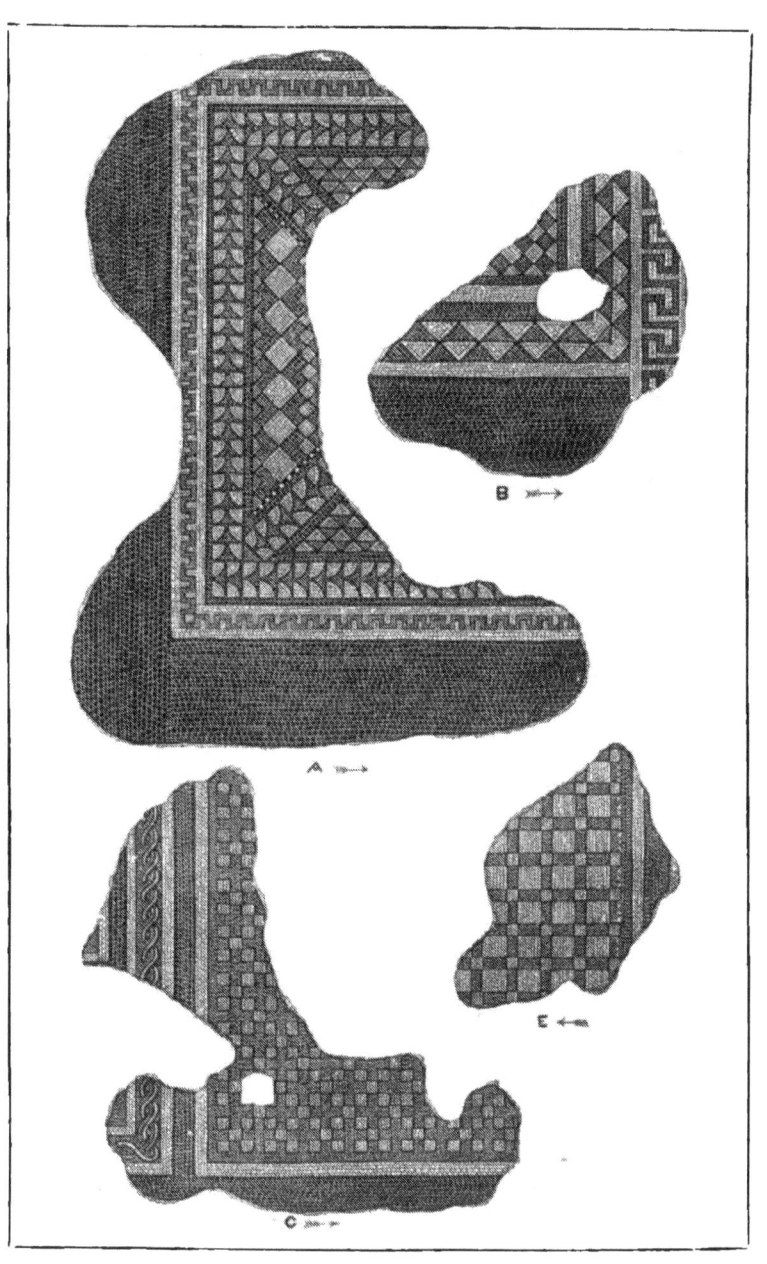

Tessellated Pavements at Wroxeter, No. 2.

This subject has been found in pavements at Woodchester, Horkstow, Winterton, and Littlecote. A field covered with fishes and sea monsters is also not an uncommon subject, and has been found at Witcombe, Cirencester, Withington, and Bromham in Wiltshire. The four seasons formed another favourite subject, which has been found at Thruxton, Littlecote, and Cirencester; in the latter place, the seasons are represented by heads in medallions, in a circle alternating with four other medallions, of which two are destroyed, but the two which remain contain respectively Bacchus on the tiger, and Actæon. At Littlecote, the seasons are represented by female figures riding on different animals in a circle round the figure of Orpheus. The Gorgon's head forms a centre piece in pavements found at Bignor and Bramdean; an Amazon encountering a tiger, at Frampton; Actæon, at Cirencester; Mercury, at Dorchester; and Hercules and Antæus, at Bramdean. A fine pavement at Horkstow was divided into compartments, each containing a group of mythological and emblematical figures; along the side were represented chariot races, enlivened by accidents, one carriage being overthrown by the wheel going off, and another with the horse fallen down. The pavement at East Coker represented hunting scenes, and, on a fragment preserved from destruction, were seen the attendants carrying home the slaughtered deer. On one of the pavements at Bignor there is a border of winged Cupids, or Genii, in the characters of gladiators, in armour, with shields, swords, and tridents. The large pavement at Frampton was also divided into compartments containing mythological subjects, such as Bacchus, Neptune, Diana hunting, &c. On the sides of a compartment containing a large bearded head of Neptune, was an inscription, intended evidently for verse, and relating to the picture; on one side are the lines,—

NEPTVNI VERTEX REGMEN
SORTITI MOBILE VENTIS

On the other,--

SCVLTVM CVI CERVLEA EST
DELFINIS CINCTA DVOBVS

Under a compartment, which was nearly destroyed, was the fragment of another inscription,—

. . . . NVS PERFICIS VILVM
. . . . . GNARE CVPIDO.*

* Lysons supplies it: '*facinus perficis ullum . . . ignare cupido.*' The

A pavement at Thruxton bore an inscription, which seems to have commemorated the person for whom the villa was built; but unfortunately only a portion of it remains perfect, which is distinctly read as follows:—QVINTVS NATALIVS NATALINVS ET BODENI. Of the line at the other side of the pavement (the continuation of the inscription), fragments only of two letters were found, apparently a V and an O, and some antiquaries have rather hastily concluded that these must have belonged to the word voto, and propose to read the whole *Quintus Natalius Natalinus et Bodeni fecerunt ex voto*, i.e., Quintus Natalius Natalinus and the Bodeni have made this in fulfilment of a vow. But there are strong reasons against such an interpretation: it is not probable that this is a votive offering; the Bodeni seem to be an invention of the interpreter, and a comparison of the space with the number of letters in the first half of the inscription and the position of the fragments, will show that there must have been more letters in the lost part than are here supplied, and that the last *o* of the supposed *voto* was not the end of the inscription. We should perhaps have found a letter or two at the beginning of the second line, which would have completed the name of the wife of Quintus Natalius Natalinus.*

It must be observed that, when we compare the different pavements representing the same subject, we do not find them copied after the same model, or treated in the same manner. It is also curious that the subjects most frequently repeated were the same on the continent as in Britain. The central Orpheus, with his circle of animals, has been found in a pavement at St Colombe, in France, and in one at or near Friburg, in Switzerland; the Gorgon's head has also been found in pavements in France; and a pavement of fishes and sea monsters was found at Pau. Perhaps the artists who made the pavements, carried about with them a professional list of subjects which they offered for choice, if their employer had not a subject of his own to propose.

It is impossible to discover, from the appearance of these villas, to what class of the community they usually belonged, but we can hardly doubt that their owners were men of wealth,

meaning these inscriptions were intended to convey, is more evident than the construction of the words.

* The interpretation alluded to was proposed by the late Dr Ingram, of Oxford, and has been recently published under the sanction of the Archæological Institute of Great Britain, in the proceedings of the Salisbury meeting of 1849.

who sought here that splendid country retirement to which we know the Roman gentry were much attached. When we consider the great number of rooms which were grouped round the different courts, we must be convinced that the lord of the mansion had a numerous household, troops of slaves, and menials, and clients; and it is not improbable that some of the buildings, more distant from the domestic apartments of the family, were separate dwellings, tenanted by his farmers, and even by their labourers. But the peasantry in general, no doubt, lived in huts, slightly constructed, and of perishable materials, either separately, or grouped together in villages. These villages are apparently the settlements, the nature of which has been described in a former chapter, and which have been commonly called British villages. The coins and other remains found in them, show that they belonged to the Roman period, but it is highly probable that the peasantry who inhabited them were chiefly of the old British race.

We know very little of the state of agriculture in this island under the Romans, though, as it was celebrated for its fertility, it was probably extensively and highly cultivated. When Cæsar visited the island, he remarked chiefly the large herds of cattle, which are the principal wealth of uncivilised peoples, but under the Romans it appears to have been celebrated for the production of corn. The emperor Julian, in one of his orations, states that when he commanded in Gaul, about the year 360, agriculture had been so entirely interrupted in the countries bordering on the Rhine, by the ravages of war, that the population was in danger of perishing by famine. In this emergency, Julian caused six hundred corn-ships to be built on the Rhine, with timber from the forest of the Ardennes, and these made several voyages to the coast of Britain, and, returning up the Rhine laden with British corn, distributed it among the towns and fortresses on that river, and he thus obtained a sufficient supply to prevent the threatened calamity. Gibbon has supposed that each of Julian's corn-ships carried at least seventy tons, which I am told is a very low estimate. But taking this, and reckoning wheat at sixty pounds a bushel, the six hundred vessels would have carried at each voyage a hundred and ninety-six thousand quarters, which would not be a very large export. But as we are ignorant of the number of voyages they made, and the estimate of tonnage is perhaps too small, we are justified in supposing that the export was large enough to prove that this country was very extensively, and, perhaps, for the age, very well cultivated. In many parts of Britain we find distinct marks of former cultivation on land which is now common, and has certainly lain fallow for ages, and it is not impossible that it may have been the work of the Roman ploughshare. A curious legend has been told in some parts to explain these appearances of ancient cultivation; it is pretended that when, in the time of king John, the country lay under an interdict, the pope's ban fell expressly on all cultivated land, and that the superstitious peasantry, imagining that the lands which were not cultivated when the bull was written were excepted from its effects, left their cultivated lands, and ploughed the wastes and commons as long as the interdict lasted. The suggestion made above is at least as probable an explanation as the legend. Mr Bruce observed similar traces of cultivation on the waste lands in Northumberland, and he is probably right in attributing them to the Romans. 'A little to the south of Borcovicus,' he says, 'and stretching westward, the ground has been thrown up in long terraced lines, a mode of cultivation much practised in Italy and the East. Similar terraces, more feebly developed, appear at Bradley; I have seen them very distinctly marked on the banks of the Rede-water, at old Carlisle, and in other places.' It is probable that Julian's corn-ships came for their cargoes to the Tyne or the Humber.

Bronze of a Roman Ploughman.

To judge by the accompanying cut, the plough used in Roman Britain was rather of a primitive construction. It represents a Roman bronze, said to have been found at Piersebridge in Yorkshire, and now in the collection of Lord Londesborough.

The figure of the ploughman gives us probably a correct picture of the costume of the Romano-British peasant. Fruit-trees were also cultivated with care, and the Romans are said to have introduced, among others, the cherry. We may probably add the vine.

One of the chief occupations of country life among the higher classes was the chase, to which the Romans were much attached. If we cast our eyes over the map of Roman Britain, we perceive considerable tracts of land which the great roads avoided, and in which there were apparently no towns. These were forest districts, represented by the mediæval forests of Charnwood, Sherwood, and others, which abounded in beasts of the chase. Some of the more extensive forests were inhabited by wild boars, and even by wolves. The chase of the boar appears to have been a favourite pursuit in Britain. An altar was found at Durham, dedicated to the god Silvanus, by the prefect of an *ala* of soldiers, who had slain an extraordinary fine boar, which had set all the hunters before him at defiance.[*] At Birdoswald in Northumberland (*Amboglanna*), was found a small altar dedicated also to Silvanus by the hunters of Banna.[†] The Roman pottery, made in Britain, was frequently ornamented with hunting scenes, in which the stag or the hare is generally the victim, and it gives us pictures of the dogs for which Britain was famous.[‡] These are at times represented with something of the character of the modern bull-dog or mastiff, while others have the more delicate form of the greyhound and stag-hound. Skulls of dogs found at Wroxeter have been pronounced to be those of mastiffs and greyhounds. The classic writers contain not unfrequent allusions to the dogs of Britain. Claudian, enumerating those peculiar to different countries, speaks of the British breed as capable of overcoming bulls:—

'Magnaque taurorum fracturæ colla Britannæ.'

---

[*] SILVANO INVICTO SACRUM C TETIVS VETVRIVS MICIANVS PRÆF ALAE SEBOSIANAE OB APRVM EXIMIAE FORMAE CAPTVM QVEM MVLTI ANTECESSORES EIVS PRAEDARI NON POTVERVNT V. S. L. P. This inscription is given in Camden.

[†] Banna was a town or station not mentioned in the *Notitia Imperii*, or in the Itineraries, but it is found in the list of Roman towns in Britain given in the Ravenna Cosmography, which places it between Æsica and Uxellodunum. An ornamental bronze cup was found in a rubbish pit at Rudge in Wiltshire, more than a century ago, having the names of five of these towns in an inscription round the rim—ABALLAVA VXELLODVM G AMBOGLAN S BANNA . A . MAIS. It seems to have been made for a club or society of persons belonging to these towns, perhaps hunters.

[‡] Figures of these dogs will be given in the next chapter.

The more delicately-shaped dog, often found on the Romano-British pottery, appears to be the one named by the Romans *vertragus*, which was also derived from this island. Martial says,—

'Non sibi, sed domino, venatur vertragus acer,
 Illesum leporem qui tibi dente feret.'

And Nemesian speaks of the export of British hounds for the purpose of hunting :—

'Sed non Spartanos tantum, tantumve molossos
 Pascendum catulos; divisa Britannia mittit
 Veloces, nostrique orbis venatibus aptos.'

CHAPTER VIII.

Manufactures of the Romans in Britain—Pottery—The Upchurch Ware—Dymchurch—The Potteries at Durobrivæ—The Samian Ware—Romano-Salopian Wares—Other Varieties—Terra-cottas—Roman Glass—Kimmeridge Coal Manufacture—Mineral Coal—Metals—The Roman Iron Works in Britain; Sussex, the Forest of Dean, &c.—Tin and Lead—Other Metals—Bronze—The Arts; Sculpture—Medicine; the Oculists' Stamps—Trades; a Goldsmith's Sign.

WITH a considerable population, great riches, as evinced by its numerous splendid villas, and an advanced state of civilisation, manufactures and trade must doubtless have been carried on in Britain to a very considerable extent. Many of these were naturally of a description which left few traces behind them, but of the existence of others we have proofs of a more substantial kind, and as they form a rather important class of our antiquities, they deserve especial attention. We begin with that of which the remains are most numerous, the pottery.

Any one who has sailed up the Medway, will have observed that the left bank of the river, a little above Sheerness, consists of low flat ground, cut by the water into innumerable little creeks, and at high water almost buried by the sea. This is called the Halstow and the Upchurch marshes. In the time of the Romans the channel of the river appears to have been here much narrower, and the 'marshes' had not been encroached upon by the sea as they are now. If we go up the little creeks in the Upchurch marshes at low water, and observe the sides of the banks, we shall soon discover, at the depth of about three feet, more or less, a stratum, often a foot thick, of broken pottery. This is especially observable in what is called Otterham creek, and also in Lower Halstow creek, where it may be traced continuously in the banks, and may be brought up by handfuls from the clay in the bed of the creek. This immense layer of broken pottery, mixed with plenty of vessels in a perfect, or nearly perfect, state, has been traced at intervals through an extent of six or seven miles in length, and two or three in breadth, and there cannot be the least doubt that it is the refuse of very extensive potteries, which existed probably during nearly the whole period of the Roman occupation of Britain, and which not only supplied the whole island with a particular class of earthenware, but which perhaps also furnished an export trade; for we find urns and other vessels precisely similar to the Upchurch ware in considerable quantity among the Roman pottery dug up in the neighbourhood of Boulogne. The clay which constitutes the soil in the Upchurch marshes is very tenacious, of a dark colour, and of fine quality, well calculated for the manufacture of pottery.

The prevailing colour of the Upchurch pottery, which is of a fine and hard texture, is a blue-black, which was produced by baking it in the smoke of vegetable substances. A sufficient number of perfect examples have been found, to show that the variety of forms was almost infinite; but a few of the more remarkable are given in the lower group on the accompanying plate. The patterns with which it is ornamented, though generally of a simple character, are also extremely diversified. Some are ornamented with bands of half-circles, made with compasses, and from these half-circles lines are in many instances drawn to the bottoms of the vessels with some instrument like a notched piece of wood. Some are ornamented with wavy intersections and zigzag lines; while on others, the ornament is formed by raised points, encircling the vessels in bands, or grouped into circles, squares, and diamond patterns. The crossed-lined pattern of the large urn in the back-ground of our group, is a very common one. Mr Roach Smith has found tracings of buildings in the neighbourhood of the marshes, which perhaps mark the habitations of the potters. It is evident from the extent of the bed of pottery, that a great number of workmen must have been employed here; and, as might be expected, we scarcely excavate a Roman site in any part of the island without finding samples of the Upchurch ware.

There can, indeed, be no doubt that the Upchurch marshes furnished a great proportion of the commoner pottery used in Roman Britain. A few years ago, as Mr James Elliott of Dymchurch, the engineer of the Dymchurch marshes, was carrying on excavations connected with the works of the sea-wall there, where the clay differs not much from that at Upchurch,

Roman Pottery from Castor (*Durobivæ*).

Roman Pottery from the Upchurch Marshes.

P. 263. Castor, Northamptonshire (*Durobrivæ*).

P. 264. Roman Pottery-kiln, at Sibson.

be found traces of extensive potteries on that part of the southern Kentish coast. The examination of the ground was not carried out sufficiently to decide on the character of the ware manufactured there, but the fragments seemed to be rather those of amphoræ, and such-like vessels, than the sort of pottery made at Upchurch.

The site of the potteries which produced another prevailing sort of Romano-British pottery, was discovered by the late Mr Artis, at Castor, on the eastern boundaries of Northamptonshire, the site of the Roman town of Durobrivæ. These potteries extended thence westward, along the country bordering on the Nen, to the neighbourhood of Wansford. The Durobrivian pottery was of a superior quality, and adorned with more elegance than that made in the Upchurch marshes. Some examples of this ware are given in the upper group on our plate. It also is usually of a bluish or slate colour, but the ornaments, which are in relief, and added with the hand after the vessel had been made and burned, are sometimes white. They consist often of elegant scrolls, like those in our engraving, and of a variety of other patterns. Among these, scenes of stag and hare hunting are very common, and they are executed with a freedom of touch which shows much artistic skill in the workmen. The annexed cut represents on a diminished scale one of

Hunting Subject, from Durobrivian pottery.

these hunting scenes, in which we have a picture of a British stag-hound. In some rare instances, figures of men are introduced, urging on the dogs, or spearing the stag or boar: and the costume of these figures indicates a rather late period of the Roman sway in Britain. In the pictures of hare-hunting scenes the dog has much the same form as that here represented, but in some fragments, of which our second cut is an example, we see a dog of a stronger and fiercer description, which, perhaps, if we had the whole pattern, would be found to be engaged in hunting the boar. Other favourite representations on this pottery were dolphins and other fishes. Indented vases, usually of a dark copper colour, like that in the middle of our group, are also characteristic of the potteries of Durobrivæ: in examples found at Chesterfield, in Essex, these indentations are filled with figures of the principal deities, in white. Similar pottery appears to have been manufactured in Flanders; and the large urn in the back-ground of our group was found at Bredene, in the department of the Lis.

British Dog.

The Roman potteries at Castor have a peculiar interest from the circumstance that Mr Artis's researches were there rewarded by the discovery of the potters' kilns, and that he was thus enabled to investigate the process of the manufacture. This we shall be best able to describe in his own words, giving in the accompanying engraving a sketch of one of the kilns, as it appeared when uncovered. One of these kilns, discovered in 1844 at Sibson, near Wansford, Mr Artis described as follows:—'This kiln,' he says, 'had been used for firing the common blue or slate-coloured pottery, and had been built on part of the site of one of the same kind, and within a yard and a half of one that had been constructed for firing pottery of a different description. The older exhausted kiln, which occupied part of the site of that under consideration, presented the appearance of very early work; the bricks had evidently been modelled with the hand, and not moulded, and the workmanship was altogether inferior to that of the others, which were also in a very mutilated state; but the character of the work, the bricks, the mouths of the furnaces, and the oval pedestals which supported the floors of the kilns, were still apparent. The floors had been broken up some time previous to the site being abandoned, and the area had then been used as a receptacle for the accumulated rubbish of other kilns.

'During an examination of the pigments used by the Roman potters of this place,' Mr Artis continues, 'I was led to the conclusion that the blue and slate-coloured vessels met with here in such abundance, were coloured by suffocating the fire of the kiln, at the time when its contents had acquired a degree of heat sufficient to insure uniformity of colour. I had so firmly made up my mind upon the process of manufacturing and firing this peculiar kind of earthenware, that, for some time previous

Roman Potter's Kiln at Castor (*Durbriva*).

to the recent discovery, I had denominated the kilns in which it had been fired, *smother kilns*. The mode of manufacturing the bricks of which these kilns are made, is worthy of notice. The clay was previously mixed with about one-third of rye in the chaff, which, being consumed by the fire, left cavities in the room of the grains. This might have been intended to modify expansion and contraction, as well as to assist the gradual distribution of the colouring vapour. The mouth of the furnace and top of the kiln were no doubt stopped; thus we find every part of the kiln, from the inside wall to the earth on the outside, and every part of the clay wrappers of the dome, penetrated with the colouring exhalation. As further proof that the colour of the ware was imparted by firing, I collected the clays of the neighbourhood, including specimens from the immediate vicinity of the smother-kilns. In colour, some of these clays resembled the ware after firing, and some were darker. I submitted them to a process similar to that I have described. The clays, dug near the kilns, whitened in firing, probably from being bituminous. I also put some fragments of the blue pottery into the kiln; they came out precisely of the same colour as the clay fired with them, which had been taken from the site of the kilns. The experiment proved to me that the colour could not be attributed to any metallic oxide, either existing in the clay, or applied externally; and this conclusion is confirmed by the appearance of the clay wrappers of the dome of the kiln. It should be remarked, that this colour is so volatile, that it is expelled by a second firing in an open kiln.

'I have now traced these potteries to an extent of upwards of twenty miles.[*] They are principally confined to the gravel beds on the banks of the Nen and its tributary streams; the clay used at some of them appears to have been collected at some little distance from the works. The kilns are all constructed on the same principle. A circular hole was dug, from three to four feet deep, and four in diameter, and walled round to the height of two feet. A furnace, one-third of the diameter of the kiln in length, communicated with the side. In the centre of the circle so formed was an oval pedestal, the height of the sides, with the end pointing to the furnace mouth. Upon this pedestal and side wall the floor of the kiln rests. It is formed of perforated angular bricks, meeting at one point in the

---

[*] Mr Artis, in another report, estimates the number of hands who must have been employed at once in the Durobrivian potteries, at not less than two thousand.

centre. The furnace is arched with bricks moulded for the purpose. The sides of the kiln are constructed with curved bricks, set edgeways, in a thick slip (or liquid) of the same material, to the height of two feet.* I now proceed to describe the process of packing the kiln, and securing uniform heat in firing the ware, which was the same in the two different kinds of kilns. They were first carefully loose-packed with the articles to be fired, up to the height of the side walls. The circumference of the bulk was then gradually diminished, and finished in the shape of a dome. As this arrangement progressed, an attendant seems to have followed the packer, and thinly covered a layer of pots with coarse hay or grass. He then took some thin clay, the size of his hand, and laid it flat on the grass upon the vessels; he then placed more grass on the edge of the clay just laid on, and then more clay, and so on until he had completed the circle. By this time the packer would have raised another tier of pots, the plasterer following as before, hanging the grass over the top edge of the last layer of plasters, until he had reached the top, in which a small aperture was left, and the clay nipt round the edge; another coating would be laid on as before described. Gravel or loam was then thrown up against the side wall where the clay wrappers were commenced, probably to secure the bricks and the clay coating. The kiln was then fired with wood.† In consequence of the care taken to place grass between the edges of the wrappers, they could be unpacked in the same sized pieces as when laid on in a plastic state, and thus the danger in breaking the coat to obtain the contents of the kiln could be obviated.

'In the course of my excavations, I discovered a curiously-constructed furnace, of which I have never before or since met with an example. Over it had been placed two circular earthen fire vessels (or cauldrons); that next above the furnace was a third less than the other, which would hold about eight gallons. The fire passed partly under both of them, the smoke escaping by a smoothly-plastered flue, from seven to eight inches wide. The vessels were suspended by the rims fitting into a circular groove or rabbet, formed for the purpose. The composition of

* See the kiln represented in the accompanying engraving, in which the two labourers are standing on the original level of the ground, while the single man, with the spade, stands on a level with the bottom of the pit in which the kiln was built.

† In the furnace of a kiln discovered by Mr Artis in 1822, there was a layer of wood ashes from four to five inches thick. This kiln, which was in a very perfect state, was covered in again undisturbed.

the vessels was that of a clay tempered with penny-earth. They contained some perfect vessels and many fragments. It is probable they had covers, and I am inclined to think were used for glazing peculiar kinds of the immense quantities of ornamented ware made in this district. Its contiguity to one of the workshops in which the glaze (oxide of iron) and some other pigments were found, confirms this opinion.'

Mr Artis then proceeds to explain the process by which the Durobrivian pottery was ornamented. 'The vessel, after being thrown upon the wheel, would be allowed to become somewhat firm, but only sufficiently so for the purpose of the lathe. In the indented ware, the indenting would have to be performed with the vessel in as pliable a state as it could be taken from the lathe. A thick slip of the same body would then be procured, and the ornamenter would proceed by dipping the thumb, or a round mounted instrument, into the slip. The vessels, on which are displayed a variety of hunting subjects, representations of fishes, scrolls, and human figures, were all glazed after the figures were laid on; where, however, the decorations are white, the vessels were glazed before the ornaments were added. Ornamenting with figures of animals was effected by means of sharp and blunt skewer instruments, and a slip of suitable consistency. These instruments seem to have been of two kinds: one thick enough to carry sufficient slip for the nose, neck, body, and front thigh; the other of a more delicate kind, for a thinner slip for the tongue, lower jaws, eye, fore and hind legs, and tail. There seems to have been no retouching after the slip trailed from the instrument. Field sports seem to have been favourite subjects with our Romano-British artists. The representations of deer and hare hunts are good and spirited; the courage and energy of the hounds, and the distress of the hunted animals, are given with great skill and fidelity, especially when the simple and off-hand process, by which they must have been executed, is taken into consideration.'

The two descriptions of pottery just described were undoubtedly made in England; the Upchurch ware is found more or less in almost all Roman sites, but that manufactured at Durobrivæ is by no means so common. We now come to a third description of pottery, which is found in great quantities in Britain, though we have every reason for believing that it was not made in this island. It is that which is usually termed Samian ware; and, if it be not the pure Samian pottery of antiquity, it appears to have been an inferior description of the same class of ware. The Samian ware was of great repute among the ancients, and is frequently alluded to by Roman writers as that most used at table. It appears certain that it was of a red colour, and the terms applied to it in the classic authors answer to the specimens which are found in such great abundance in England.* It is frequently mentioned by Plautus as the ordinary ware used at table, as well as for sacred purposes. Pliny speaks of it as being in common use for the festive board; and he gives the names of several places famous for their pottery, among which Aretium, in Italy, holds the first place. Sarrentum, Asta, and Pollentia, in Italy, Saguntum in Spain, and Pergamus in Asia Minor, were, as we learn from this writer, celebrated for the manufacture of cups. Tralleis in Lydia, and Mutina in Italy, were also eminent for manufactures of earthenware. The manufactures of these different places were exported to distant countries.† Isidore of Seville, at the end of the sixth century (he died in 610), speaks of the red pottery made at Aretium (the modern Arezzo) which he calls Aretine vases, and also of Samian ware, with an expression of doubt as to the exact locality which produced the latter; so that it was probably made under that name in different parts of Roman Europe. Modern researches at Arezzo, in Italy, have not only brought to light a considerable quantity of the Aretine ware, but also the remains of the kilns in which it was baked; and a scholar of that place, A. Fabroni, has published a book on the subject, under the title of *Storia degli antichi Vasi fittili Aretini*. The specimens given in his engravings bear a general resemblance to the Samian ware found in Britain, and there are some points in which the one seems to be imitated from the other, yet there are also some very strongly marked circumstances in which they differ. The names of the potters are different, and they are marked in a different form and position

---

* Among a large and very curious collection of Græco-Roman terracottas from Lycia, are some fragments of red ware, closely resembling what we call Samian ware, with the potter's name, in Greek, similarly impressed. These are now in the possession of Mr Mayer of Liverpool. Perhaps they are samples of pure Samian ware.

† The words of Pliny (*Hist. Nat.*, lib. xxxv. c. 12) are as follows: 'Major quoque pars hominum terrenis utitur vasis. Samia etiamnum in esculentis laudantur. Retinet hanc nobilitatem et Aretium in Italia; et calicum tantum Surrentum, Asta, Pollentia; in Hispania, Saguntum; in Asia, Pergamum. Habent et Tralleis opera sua, et Mutina in Italia; quoniam et sic gentes nobilitantur. Hæc quoque per maria terrasque ultro citroque portantur, insignibus rotæ officinis Erythris.'

Group of Samian Ware found in England.

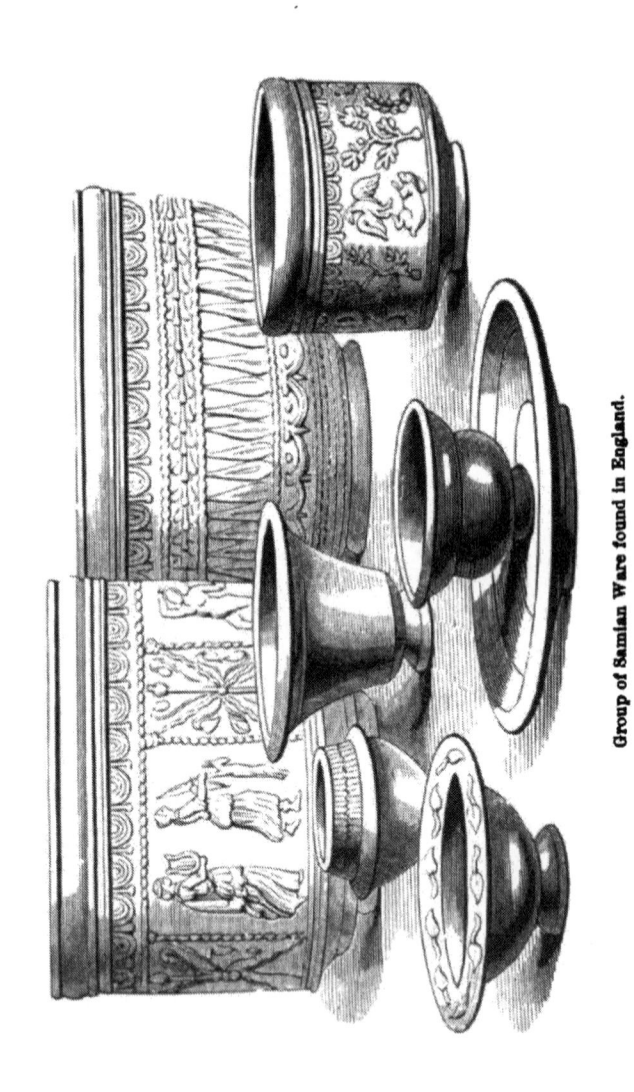

on the vessels; the red of the Aretine ware is of a deeper shade, the figures are in a superior style of art, and they seem to be of an earlier date.

The common Samian ware is of an extremely delicate texture, having somewhat the appearance of fine red sealing-wax. The vessels composed of it are of all sizes and shapes, sometimes strong, but more frequently thin, and consequently very fragile; and it is only under favourable circumstances that we find them unbroken. The frailty of the pure Samian ware appears, in classical times, to have been proverbial; when, in Plautus, a person is desired to knock gently, he exclaims, in surprise, 'You seem to fear that the door is made of Samian ware.'

M. Placide pulta. *P.* Metuis, credo, ne fores Samiæ sient.—
Menæchm., 1. 98.

And, on another occasion, the brittleness of Samian ware is directly mentioned—

Vide, quæso, ne quis tractet illam indiligens—
Scis tu, ut confringi vas cito Samium solet.—*Bacch.*, 1. 166.

It is by no means unusual to find bowls and pateræ of the ware of which we are speaking, that have been broken by their possessors in former times, and subsequently mended, generally by means of leaden, but sometimes of bronze, rivets. This shows the value which must generally have been set upon it.

The question whether this so-called Samian ware was ever manufactured in Britain has given rise to some discussion among antiquaries. In the mouth of the Thames, a short distance from the Kentish coast between Reculver and Margate, is a spot known popularly by the name of the Pan Rock, and Pudding-pan Sand, because, almost from time immemorial, the fishermen in dragging there have been accustomed to bring up pieces of ancient pottery, and not unfrequently entire vessels. These are chiefly of the fine red or Samian ware. It was at first supposed that these marked the site of an extensive manufacture of this ware; but other writers suggested as a more probable explanation that some Roman ships laden with it, perhaps from the potteries on the Rhine, had been wrecked in this place, and the notion that it was the site of a pottery seems to be abandoned. More recently, fragments of this ware having been picked up about the Upchurch marshes, I believe in one or two spots rather plentifully, it has been supposed that it might have been manufactured there, and by experiment it appeared that the clay of the locality was capable of being made into similar ware. But the evidence that such ware was manufactured there appears to be quite insufficient; and the opinion generally received among antiquaries, after all the discussion which has taken place, seems to be, that the Samian ware was not made in England, but that it was imported from the continent.

The accompanying engraving represents a group of vessels of Samian ware found in England; but it is far from giving

Subjects from Samian ware.

any notion of the great variety of forms, or the still greater diversity of ornament, which they present. Many of the smaller vessels are quite plain, or are merely adorned with the ivy-leaf, a very favourite ornament on this kind of ware. The characteristic moulding is the festoon and tassel, to which the somewhat inappropriate term of egg-and-tongue border has been given. The subjects represented on the more ornamental vessels are extremely varied. Many of them are groups taken from the ancient mythology, such as the labours of Hercules, the amours of Jupiter, Diana surprised by Actæon, and Actæon attacked by his dogs, Apollo and Daphne, and figures of Venus and other personages of ancient fable. Many of the figures and groups were evidently copied from some of the well-known masterpieces of ancient art; thus we have Jupiter and Leda, an evident imitation of a celebrated sculpture at Rome, and the figures of the Farnese Hercules, the Apollo Belvidere, and the Venus de Medici, are often repeated. Some represent genii, Cupids riding upon marine animals, tritons, griffins, and other imaginary beings: others again represent domestic scenes, hunting subjects, gladiatorial combats, groups of musicians and dancers, and subjects of a still more miscellaneous description. In the preceding cut are given three samples of the more common subjects—combats of gladiators—the war between the pygmies and the cranes—and a dancing scene. Another series of designs comprises scrolls of foliage, fruits, and flowers, arranged in different manners, and always with great elegance. A multitude of the Samian vases found in this country, as well as other articles, such as lamps, bronzes, and even knife-handles, represent licentious scenes of the most infamous description. Drinking vessels of this class are alluded to by Pliny;* and their comparative frequency in Britain, shows how deeply not only the manners but the vices of Rome had been planted in this distant province.

A great proportion of the vessels in this ware have the name of the potter stamped in a label, usually at the bottom, in the inside, but sometimes, especially on the embossed bowls, on the outside. The manner in which the label is stamped across the centre of the vessel is shown in the accompanying cut, from a specimen found at Wroxeter (*Uriconium*). In this instance the reading of the name is somewhat obscure, from the doubtful character of the two letters in the middle, which may either be ligatured letters, each standing for DE, or merely capricious forms of the D. In the former case it might be read TEDEDEI. It is probable, however, that there is only one ligature, and that we must read the name TEDDI. The name is given in the nominative with F for *fecit*, or in the genitive, with O, or OF, or M, for *officina* or *manu:* thus SABINVS F. *Sabinus fecit* (Sabinus made it), AMICI M., *Amici manu* (by the hand of Amicus), OF. FELIC, *officina Felicis* (from the workshop of Felix). The name was often put merely in the genitive singular, without the addition of OF, or M, as in

---

* 'In poculis libidines cœlare juvit ac per obscænitates bibere.'—*Plin. Hist. Nat.*, lib. xxxiii., prœm. 'Vasa adulteriis cœlata.'—*Ib.*, lib. xiv. c. 22.

the example in the foregoing cut. These names, of which long lists have been made, are many of them Gaulish and German, and they seem to point to the countries from whence this class of pottery was derived. In fact, potteries of the ware we term Samian have been found in France, particularly on the banks of the Rhine, as at Brusche (Bas-Rhin), Luxembourg, Saverne (near Strasburg), and especially at Rheinzabern, in Bavaria. In these places not only have the potters' kilns been found, but the moulds, and the implements for stamping borders and names. The annexed cut represents

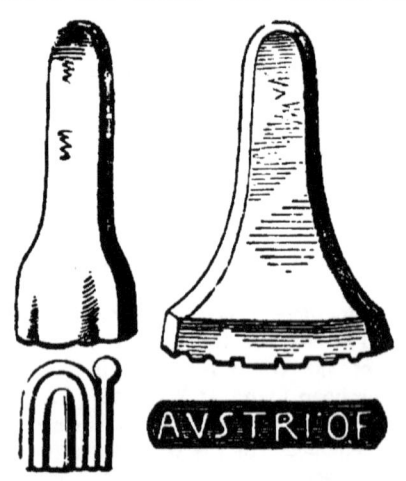

Potters' Stamps from Gaul.

two such stamps, from potteries discovered at Lezoux in Auvergne. One has been used for stamping the pattern so commonly found serving as a sort of frieze round the vessel; the other the stamp of the potter's name, AUSTRI . OF, and as this name occurs on the Samian ware found in England, it furnishes at least one proof of importation. Some of the moulds from Rheinzabern are now preserved in the national museum in Paris. These are earthenware bowls, with the figures impressed on the inner surface, so that the vessel when formed of soft clay, being placed in the mould and pressed in it, took the figures in relief, and when dry had shrunk sufficiently to be taken out. Sometimes the moulds were made in more than one piece, like our moulds for plaster-of-Paris casts, but this was only when the subjects were in higher relief. The impressions in the moulds seem to have been made by a great number of small stamps, each containing a single ornament, or a single figure or group, and these were varied continually in making the moulds. It is thus that we see the same figure often repeated on different examples of the pottery with totally different accompaniments. This also explains why the figures on the pottery are so seldom sharp and fresh; in the course of making the impressions in the moulds and casting from them the impression had become imperfect, and the figures look often like impressions in sealing-wax rubbed or bruised. The clay seems to have received its redness from some substance mixed up with it, which is supposed to have been oxides of iron and lead. The kilns found in France appear to have borne a general resemblance to those discovered by Mr Artis. A few examples of this red ware, which are now chiefly in the collection of Mr Roach Smith, have been found in England, exhibiting a much higher degree of artistic excellence, the figures of which are in higher relief than the others, and have not been made with the pottery, but moulded separately and then attached to the surface of the vessel. This class of pottery is very rare. The ware found in these foreign potteries is identical with that which our antiquaries have agreed to call Samian ware in England, it evidently came from the same moulds, and the potters' names are the same, so that we have little room for doubting that it was imported into this country. I believe, however, that Mr Artis discovered in the Durobrivian potteries traces of an unsuccessful attempt to imitate the foreign red ware, and such imitations of the Samian ware have been found among the pottery at Wroxeter.

On this last-mentioned site, the Roman city of Uriconium, a considerable quantity of different sorts of pottery have been found, no doubt of local manufacture, as they are evidently made from the clays of the Severn valley, apparently from the neighbourhood of Broseley. Two sorts, especially, are found in considerable abundance, the one white, the other of a rather light red colour. The white ware, which is made of what is commonly called Broseley clay, and is rather coarse in texture, consists chiefly of rather handsomely-shaped jugs, of different sizes, the general form of which is represented by the example given in the accompanying cut; of mortaria, differing somewhat in form from the mortaria found on Roman sites in other parts of England, and of which a fragment of one is also given in our cut; and of bowls of different shapes and sizes, which are often painted with stripes of red and yellow. The red Romano-

Romano-Salopian Ware.—White.   Romano-Salopian Ware.—Red.

Salopian ware is also made from one of the clays of the valley of the Severn, but is of finer texture, and consists principally of jugs not dissimilar to those in the white ware, except in a very different form of mouth, one of the simplest examples of which is represented in our cut, and of bowl-shaped vessels pierced with a multitude of small holes, which have no doubt served the purpose of colanders.

Among the examples of pottery found in exploring Roman sites, are many others which are totally dissimilar to the ware made in the great potteries at Upchurch and Castor, and which were probably derived from other potteries in Britain, the sites of which have not yet been ascertained. Traces of potteries have been noticed, I believe, in Lincolnshire and in several other parts of England, but they have not yet been explored. Some of the examples alluded to are very peculiar in character, and of very rare occurrence. The two fragments represented in the cut on the next page were found at Richborough; but I understand that similar ware has been found in one of the Roman stations in Wales. They are of a red colour, and are stamped with the ornament which, in the first example, is evidently a rude copy of the festoon and tassel pattern of the Samian ware. The lower one is curious for its resemblance to the ornamentation of the Frankish pottery, which we shall

CHAP. VIII.]   OTHER KINDS OF POTTERY.   279

describe further on. Our next cut represents an urn found at York; it is of a dusky grey colour, with a very singular ornament in relief, which may be described as a frill pattern, and which is far from inelegant. Two or three samples of this pot-

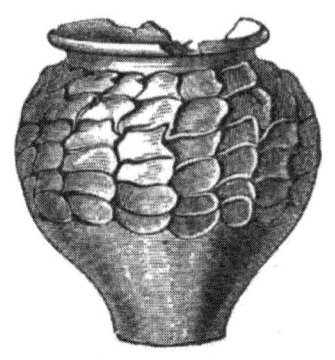

Pottery from Richborough.

Urn from York.

tery may be seen in the York museum, but it appears to have been found nowhere else, and came probably from some manufactory in Yorkshire or Lincolnshire.

Other potteries produced vessels of a different character, intended for other purposes than those of which we have been speaking. Among the most important of these were the amphoræ, or wine vessels. They are of large dimensions, and strongly made, usually of a reddish yellow colour. There are two distinct forms of amphoræ. Some are long and slender, and very elegantly shaped. The two examples on next page, one of which has lost its neck and handles, were dug up at Mount Bures, near Colchester. The other form of amphoræ is much more spherical in shape, and is therefore more capacious. These are shorter in the neck than the others. Both sorts were pointed at the bottom, for the purpose, it is said, of fixing them in the earth; one of our examples, however, has a knob. Numerous fragments of broken amphoræ are generally found in the rubbish-pits, mentioned in a former chapter; and they occur so abundantly elsewhere, that we can hardly doubt their being made in the potteries in **Britain.**

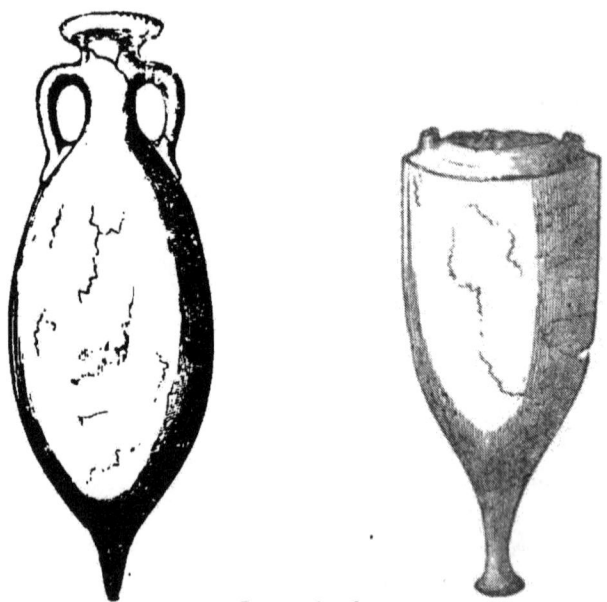

Roman Amphoræ.

Another class of domestic earthenware utensils have been termed *mortaria*, because it is supposed that they were used for pounding vegetables and other soft articles for the kitchen with a pestle. They are usually made of yellow, drab, or fawn-coloured clay, and the surface of the interior is often studded with small siliceous stones, broken quartz, and scoria of iron, no doubt to counteract attrition. The one here represented is in the possession of Mr Roach Smith, and was found in London. It is made of clay, kneaded with a mixture of about one-third of tile, broken small, and it is

A Mortarium.

studded with small white siliceous stones. Other examples are shallower, but the general form is the same. The names of the potters are often marked on the amphoræ and mortaria, much

CHAP. VIII.] RICHBOROUGH TERRA-COTTAS. 281

in the same way as on the Samian ware. It appears from the researches of Mr Artis, that mortaria were made in the Durobrivian potteries.

Before we leave the subject of pottery, we must not overlook one class of vessels, which, though of very rare occurrence in this country, are of peculiar interest. They are probably of foreign manufacture. They are urns, or jugs, ornamented at the mouth with heads, usually of females. The two examples

Heads of Roman Jars from Richborough (*Rutupiæ*).

given in our cut were found at Richborough. Each is four inches and a half across, so that they have belonged to large vessels. They are of brown clay. It has been observed that they are evidently the prototypes of a class of earthenware vessels which were popular in the middle ages. The rubbish-pits of Richborough also furnished the museum of Mr Rolfe of Sandwich with some broken terra-cotta statuettes, a class of Roman antiquities which are now extremely rare. The Richborough terra-cottas were by no means of a low style of execution, as works of art, but they were unfortunately all fragments. A portion of a figure of Venus, represented in our cut, was perhaps the best; in its present state it is four inches high. These statuettes were probably imported from Gaul. A manufactory of such articles was discovered a few years ago near the village of Heiligenberg, about three miles from Mutzig, on the Rhine.

Terra-Cotta from Richborough.

Whenever we open Roman sites, we are astonished at the quantities of pottery which lie scattered about, and we feel convinced that this article must have formed a large proportion of the furniture of a Roman house. It was used, indeed, for a much greater variety of purposes than at the present day, and we find many proofs that earthenware vases were continually employed as the receptacles of money and of a variety of little articles, which we should lay up in chests and boxes, or in baskets, bags, caskets, or work-boxes.

There was another manufacture in which the Romans attained to great excellence, that of glass, and we are struck not only with the extraordinary beauty, but with the endless variety of the samples that are continually found on Roman sites. All our readers will be familiar with the old story of the accidental discovery of glass-making by the merchants who lit their fires upon the sands of the river Belus on the coast of Syria. Pliny gives a brief account of the manufacture of glass in his time, from which we gather that the great glass furnaces were generally established on the sea-coast, where a fine sand was found adapted to the purpose. In these manufactories the glass was made in lumps, in which form it was distributed to the workshops of the workers in glass, who melted the lumps as they wanted them, and it was then coloured and formed into bottles, vessels, and other articles, sometimes by blowing, at other times by grinding on a wheel or lathe, and at others by embossing or casting in a mould.* Pliny goes on to tell us that the working of glass was carried to such a perfection in Rome that the emperor Tiberius put a stop to it, lest the precious metals should be thrown into discredit. Sidon was the site of the great glass-works of antiquity, but the most celebrated establishment of the Romans was that situated on the coast between Cumæ and Lucrinum. In the time of Pliny, glass manufactories had been established on the coasts of Spain and Gaul.†

I have always believed, from the quantity of Roman glass that is found in this island, that we should some day trace the existence of Roman glass manufactories in Britain, and it is naturally to the coast that we must look for them. But I was not aware that anything of the sort had yet been observed, until I was informed by my friend, Augustus Guest, Esq., LL.D., of a very curious discovery he had made on the

* Continuis fornacibus ut æs liquatur, massæque fiunt colore pingui nigricantes. Ex massis rursus funditur in officinis, tingiturque, et aliud flatu figuratur, aliud torno teritur, aliud argenti modo cœlatur.—*Plin. Hist. Nat.*, lib. xxxvi c. 26.

† Jam vero et per Gallias Hispaniasque simili modo arenæ temperantur.

coast at Brighton, the sand of which I am told is extremely well calculated for the manufacture of this article. Dr Guest told me that in 1848, as he was searching along the shore for specimens of agates, he picked up, on that portion of it extending from opposite Kemptown towards Rotting or Rotten Dean, several pieces of what, in consequence of the attrition to which it had been subjected, appeared, on placing them before a strong light, to be coloured pebbles; but on taking them to an intelligent lapidary in the town, he at once recognised them as pieces of glass, of which, after a heavy sea, he occasionally found considerable quantities. He produced several large pieces, the colours of which were amethyst, amber, emerald green, and deep maroon, the latter colour being the rarest. The lapidary was accustomed to cut and polish small sections of the glass, and to apply them to ornamental purposes, as brooches, &c. The largest piece shown to Dr Guest was about double the size of a man's fist; it was of an amber colour, and much encrusted by marine insects. A large portion of the cliff on this spot has evidently given way under the action of the sea, which has here encroached considerably on the land, and it is not improbable that one of the slips common in the chalk formation has at some distant period carried away with it the remains of one of the Romano-British glass manufactories. The fragments cast upon the shore are no doubt parts of the lumps (*massæ*) of the material which were sent away hence to the glass-workers in the greater towns through the island. Pliny seems to intimate that the mass of glass thus sent out was colourless, and that it was coloured by the glass-workers, but it seems here to have been made in coloured masses, to be still more ready for use.

From the brittle character of the material, glass vessels are found in a perfect state much more seldom than pottery;

Roman Glass Vessels.

indeed, perfect specimens are rarely found, except in sepulchral interments, where they have been intentionally protected. The shapes and uses of vessels of glass were evidently very numerous, and one or two only of the forms more worthy of notice are given in the accompanying cut. The two vessels to the left are those usually found, with calcined bones, in Roman sepulchres. They are generally of green glass. The three smaller ones to the right are also frequently found in sepulchres, and are usually termed lachrymatories, from the somewhat romantic notion that they were filled with the tears of the mourners; the received opinion among antiquaries at the present day, is that they contained the unguents and aromatics which it was usual to depose with the dead. The jug in the middle exhibits one of the simpler forms of the embossed ornaments on the moulded glass. Some of these are elaborate and beautiful, and would present difficulties even to the modern glass-makers. This is said to be especially the case with a class of round cups or bowls, which are by no means uncommon in green, blue, and mixed colours, and which are ornamented with projecting pillars. This pillar-moulding was considered to be one of the great inventions in modern glass-making, and it was not supposed among glass-workers that it was a mere revival of an ornament common among the Romans. The cups alluded to are nearly all of the same form, and would be described now as sugar-basins, though they were probably

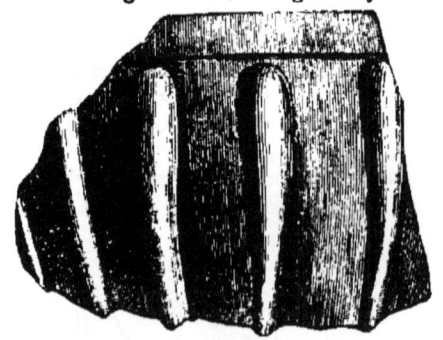

Part of a Roman Glass Bowl or Cup.

drinking cups. The annexed cut represents a fragment of one of these cups, given by Mr Roach Smith from the excavations at Richborough; it is here engraved the full size of the original.

In some instances the embossed ornaments were much more elaborate, and, as on the ornamental pottery, it extended to

CHAP. VIII.] EMBOSSED AND FIGURED GLASS. 285

figures and to inscriptions. This figured glass ware is, however, rare, and was no doubt precious. Mr Roach Smith has published in his 'Collectanea' a fragment of a very remarkable cup in green glass, found in the Roman villa at Hartlip in

Roman embossed Glass Cup, from Hartlip, Kent

Kent. It is here given, from his book, about half the actual size, the thin lines indicating the form of the vessel when entire. The subjects represented upon it are chariot racing and gladiatorial combats, with the names of the charioteers and combatants. The figures are in the original somewhat indistinct, and the letters so faint, that it is questionable if they are all given correctly. Mr Smith possessed, in his museum, two similar fragments, found in London, one of which is identical with the Hartlip fragment in its design, and appears to be from the same mould; the other is from a vessel of a different shape, and has a quadriga in bas-relief. We have before had occasion to observe how popular gladiatorial subjects and the games of the circus were among the Roman inhabitants of this island, and how often we find them represented on the pottery as well as on the glass. In the Hartlip glass the charioteer has just reached the goal, which is marked by three conical columns of wood raised upon a base. This was the usual form of the *metæ*, and it is said to have been assumed as the imitation of the form of a cypress tree:—

'Metasque imitata cupressus,'

says Ovid (Metamorph. lib. x. L 106). The names here given to the charioteers and combatants are probably mere conventional appellations. A series of gladiatorial subjects are sculptured on one of the tombs of Pompeii, with names attached to them in a similar manner, although in this instance they appear to have been the real names of the individuals represented. The charioteer is here driving the biga; in the other example of embossed glass in the possession of Mr Roach Smith, he rides, as we have stated, the quadriga. It no doubt formed part of a scene from the circus. Embossed glass vessels of this description are of the utmost rarity, and I am not aware of the existence of any other examples in this country.

Drinking-cups, with inscriptions, are found not unfrequently. It was a trait of Roman sentiment, both on the continent and in Britain, to accompany familiar or domestic occupations with invocations of happiness or good fortune upon those who took part in them, and this seems to have been especially the case in their convivial entertainments. Cups have been found with such inscriptions as BIBE FELICITER (drink with good luck!), or BIBE VT VIVAS (drink that you may live!), or again, VIVAS BIBERE (may you live to drink!). An analogous drinking formula was preserved in the middle ages, in the Anglo-Saxon *wæs hæl* ('be thou in health!). Mr Roach Smith, in his 'Collectanea,' has given samples of cups in red pottery with inscriptions in white letters, such as AVE (hail!), VIVAS (may you live!), BIBE (drink), IMPLE (fill). In excavations on the site of the Roman villa at Ickleton, in Essex, Lord Braybrooke found a fragment of a drinking-cup of fine earthenware, with an inscription, inscribed with a stilus, or some sharp instrument, of which there remained the letters CAMICIBIBVN, no doubt part of the words *ex hoc amici bibunt* (out of this cup friends drink). Among fragments picked up in a Roman, and subsequent Saxon, cemetery, near Holme Pierrepoint, in Nottinghamshire, was part of a small cup of thin yellow glass, with a portion of a raised inscription (of which the word SEMPER only remained), above the figure of a bird. The figures in this and most similar articles are rather rude, but there are specimens in which the execution shows not only a high feeling of art, but also an extraordinary skill in manipulation on the part of the workman. The cut annexed represents the base of a handle to a vase, of fine blue glass, representing the head of a female, in very high relief. It was dug up in Leadenhall-street, in London, and is now in the collection of Lord Londesborough. Mr Roach Smith possessed a similar fragment in green glass, but of still finer execution, also found in London.

The skill of the Roman glass-workers, in the manipulation of their art, is shown still more remarkably in the manner in which they fused into each other pieces of glass of different colours, so as to form the most elegant and tasteful patterns. This art was displayed especially in the manufacture of glass beads, which are found in considerable quantities on Roman sites in this country. They present so many varieties in form and colour, that it would be impossible here to give any description that could include them all; yet there are a certain number of types which occur more frequently than others, and I will give a few of these which have sometimes been misappropriated. The large bead to the left in the accompanying group is one of common occurrence, and it and some other Roman beads of different forms have been fancifully and very erroneously termed druids' beads. They are sometimes found of a large size, twice or even thrice the size of the one in

Embossed Glass.

Roman Glass Beads.

our cut. The most common forms of Roman glass beads are slight variations of the upper figure to the right, which are executed in glass of different colours, though most commonly blue, sometimes very light, at others of a deep shade, and sometimes of a material that has been only imperfectly vitrified. The other bead, in which a serpentine ornament is infused into the glass, was found among the ruins of Cilurnum in Northumberland. In many of these beads of compound colours, the shades are exquisitely blended together. Our second cut represents a bead and a button, both of glass, found at Richborough. The bead is of blue glass, with white enamel; the body

Roman Glass Bead and Button.

of the button is dark blue, with the central dot red, and the other four light blue. Mr Smith informs us that a considerable number of such buttons, but chiefly in plain white and blue glass, have been found with sepulchral remains on the site of a Roman burial-ground near Boulogne.

Extensive traces of the manufacture of personal ornaments from another material have been discovered in Britain. This material was what the Romans seem to have designated by the name of *gagates*, or jet, and which is now popularly called in the different localities where it is found, Kennel coal and Kimmeridge coal. In our own time Kennel coal has been extensively used in the manufacture of ornamental vases, turned on the lathe, and other such articles. The articles in jet of the Romans in Britain were also made on the lathe, and consisted chiefly of rings, armlets, beads, buttons, and similar ornaments, and, as I have just said, the traces of the manufactories in one district have been discovered. In the wildest and least frequented part of the isle of Purbeck, on the coast of Dorset, are two small secluded valleys, opening to the sea into what are termed the Kimmeridge and Worthbarrow bays, and divided by an intervening ridge of considerable elevation. The soil of these valleys, laid out from time immemorial in uninclosed pastures, has never been disturbed by the ploughshare, and when for any accidental purpose it is dug, at a few inches under the surface are found great numbers of small, round, and flat pieces of a mineral substance, found in extensive beds on this part of the coast, and known by the name of Kimmeridge coal. It is a bituminous shale, which burns freely, with a white ash and slaty residue, diffusing a disagreeable bituminous odour, in this respect answering to Pliny's description of the *gagates*. The round pieces found in such abundance in these localities are generally from a quarter to half an inch thick, and from an inch and a quarter to two inches and a half in diameter, with bevelled and moulded edges, and having on one side two, three, or four round holes, and on the other side a small pivot hole. In a few instances these round holes are absent, and the pieces are wholly perforated with a single central square hole.

A single glance at these articles is sufficient to convince any one acquainted with the use of the lathe, that they are simply the refuse pieces of the turner, the nuclei of rings and other articles formed by his art. The round holes were evidently made to attach the piece of material on the point of the chuck; and the square one was for fixing it on a small square mandril-head; circumstances, it has been observed, which prove that the people who made these articles were well accustomed to the use of the lathe, not in its primitive rude form, but as an improved and, in some degree, perfected instrument. Much irregularity is observable in the number of the holes. The greater number hitherto found have two holes; while pieces with four holes are rare, and generally of a small size. Fragments of the raw material are frequently found mixed with these round pieces. Some of these show the marks of cutting tools, as if prepared for the lathe, whilst the shale, being fresh from the quarry, was comparatively soft. Others exhibit lines, angles, circles, and other figures, drawn with mathematical accuracy, the central point, in which one leg of the compasses was inserted, being often visible. Pieces of rings of the same material, and sometimes a perfect ring, are also found scattered about; so that we cannot have the least doubt that here existed once an extensive manufactory of this material. Fragments of Roman pottery, mixed here and there with these remains, fix the date to which they belong. Yet, with all these facts before them, our antiquaries of the old school have remained blind to their real character, and it was gravely conjectured, and even asserted, that these refuse pieces from the Roman lathe had been manufactured to serve the purposes of money by Phœnician traders, who came in the remote ages of the world to trade with the primeval Celts.*

---

* The real character of these remains was, I believe, first pointed out by the late Mr Sydenham, a gentleman known to antiquaries by his contribu-

Articles of this material seem to have had a peculiar value from the circumstance that it was supposed, as we are told by Pliny, to possess the virtue of driving away serpents. Probably future discoveries will bring to light similar manufactories in other parts of the island, and it is not unlikely that they continued to exist through the earlier Anglo-Saxon period. Bede describes the *gagates* as being in his time an important production of Britain, and he speaks of its quality, when burnt, of driving away serpents, and tells us how, when warmed with rubbing, it has the same attractive quality as amber.* In interments, chiefly of the Roman period, and on Roman sites, rings, and other articles, of the Kimmeridge and Kennel coal have been found.

The Romans were more attentive to the utility of the mineral productions of our island than we are accustomed to suppose. There cannot be a doubt that they knew the use of mineral coals, and that they employed them, but they only obtained them where the coal-bed was near the surface, and the coal was probably burnt chiefly in the district where it was found. Mineral coal has been supposed to be referred to by Solinus, when he tells us that Minerva was the patron of the warm springs in Britain, alluding apparently to Bath, and that the fire that burnt on her altars did not fall into white ashes, but as the fire wasted away it turned into stony globules.† A more unequivocal proof of the use of this fuel is, however, furnished by the fact that the cinders of mineral coal have been not unfrequently found in the fire-places of Roman houses and villas in different parts of the island. It is found abundantly among the fire-places of the hypocausts of the buildings of Roman Uriconium, at Wroxeter. Mr Bruce assures us that in nearly all the stations on the line of the wall of Hadrian, 'the ashes of mineral fuel have been found; in some, a store

---

tions to the Archæologia on Dorsetshire barrows. The notion of their being made by Phœnician merchants, to represent money, and of t eir being used also in the religious worship of the natives of Britain, was set forth, among others, by Mr Miles, in an appendix to the account of the Deverill barrow.

* Gignit et lapidem gagatem plurimum optimumque; est autem nigrogemmeus et ardens igni admotus; incensus serpentes fugat, attritu calefactus applicita detinet æque ut succinum.—*Bede, Hist. Eccl.* lib. i, c. 1. It must be stated that Bede's account is taken almost literally from Solinus.

† Quibus fontibus præsul est Minervæ numen, in cujus æde perpetui ignes nunquam canescunt in favillas, sed ubi ignis tabuit, vertit in globos saxeos.—*Solini Polyhist.*, c. 22.

of unconsumed coal has been met with, which, though intended to give warmth to the primeval occupants of the isthmus, has been burnt in the grates of the modern English. In several places the source whence the mineral was procured can be pointed out; but the most extensive workings that I have heard of are in the neighbourhood of Grindon Lough, near Sewingshields. Not long ago a shaft was sunk, with the view of procuring the coal which was supposed to be below the surface; the projector soon found that, though coal had been there, it was all removed. The ancient workings stretched beneath the bed of the lake.'

The metals of Britain formed, we know, the great proportion of its exports, under the Roman occupation. They consisted chiefly of iron, lead, tin, and copper. Round pigs of the last-mentioned metal, belonging to the Roman period, have been found in Wales, whence, and from Cornwall, the Romans derived their chief supply. One of these, still preserved at Mostyn Hall, in the county of Flint, bears the inscription SOCIO ROMAE, which has not been satisfactorily explained. Iron was obtained by the Romans in vast quantities from various parts of the island, though the principal Roman iron-works were in the wooded district of the country of the Silures, now called the Forest of Dean, and in the extensive forest of Anderida, forming the modern weald of Sussex and Kent. Traces of the Roman occupation are found abundantly in both these districts. In various places in Sussex, as in the parishes of Maresfield, Sedlescombe, and Westfield, immense masses of ancient iron scoriæ, or slag, are found. At Oaklands, in Sedlescombe, there is a mass of very considerable extent, which, on being cut into for materials for road-making, was ascertained to be not less than twenty feet deep. The period to which they belong is proved, by the frequent discovery of Roman coins and pottery intermixed with the cinders. At Maresfield, especially, the fragments of Roman pottery and other articles are so abundant, that, as we are informed by Mr M. A. Lower, of Lewes, who first laid these facts before the public, when one of these cinder-beds was removed, scarcely a barrow-load of cinders could be examined without exhibiting several fragments. The material for the Roman furnaces was the clay ironstone, from the beds between the chalk and oolite of this district, which is found in nodular concretions, consisting often of an outer shell of iron ore, with a nucleus of sand. These are found near the surface of the ground, and the Romans dug small pits from which they extracted these nodules, and carried them to the furnaces, which stood in the immediate vicinity. These pits are still found in considerable groups, covered almost always with a thick wood, and the discovery of pottery, &c., leaves us no room to doubt that they are Roman works. Large as the Sussex works seem to have been, those in the Forest of Dean, and more especially along the banks of the Wye, appear to have been much more extensive. Here the ground for miles rests upon one immense continuous bed of iron cinders, the antiquity of which is proved by the occasional discovery of Roman coins and other remains, with unmistakeable traces of Roman settlements. The ore is here of a much richer description, and lies in veins at no great depth under the ground. The Romans sank a large pit until they came to the vein of metal, which they then followed in its course, and thus excavated caverns and chambers under-ground, extending often to some hundred feet. In the neighbourhood of Coleford these ancient excavations are called Scowles—a term of which the derivation is not very evident. They are often looked upon with a superstitious feeling, and have received names from it. Thus, in a hill on the banks of the Wye, called the Great Doward, is an extensive Roman iron mine, popularly called 'King Arthur's Hall,' at the bottom of which tradition says a chest of treasure is concealed. In this district the river Wye formed a convenient medium of transport, and either the pure ore, or the iron in its first rough state, was carried up the Severn as high at least as the present city of Worcester, where large beds of iron scoriæ with Roman remains have been discovered. We have already quoted a tradition which describes the Roman Alauna (*Alcester*, in Warwickshire) as a town of iron-workers. Traces of Roman iron-works are met with in various other parts of Britain. Large beds of cinders, or, as they are technically termed, slag, mixed with Roman remains, have been found in Northumberland and, I understand, in Yorkshire.

The process of smelting among the Romans appears to have been simple and imperfect. The fuel used was charcoal, pieces of which are often found impressed in the cinders. It is supposed that layers of iron ore, broken up, and charcoal, mixed with lime-stone as a flux, were piled together, and inclosed in a wall and covering of clay, with holes at the bottom for letting in the draught, and allowing the melted metal to run out. For this purpose they were usually placed on sloping ground.

Rude bellows were perhaps used, worked by different contrivances.* In Sussex, and in the Forest of Dean, they appear to have been worked by means of water, at least in some of the streams in those districts remains of ancient tanks are found, which are supposed to have been made to collect the water for that purpose. Mr Bruce, in his account of the 'Roman Wall,' has pointed out a very curious contrivance for producing a blast in the furnaces of the extensive Roman iron-works in the neighbourhood of Epiacum (*Lanchester*). A part of the valley, rendered barren by the heaps of slightly covered cinders, had never been cultivated till very recent times. 'During the operation of bringing this common into cultivation,' Mr Bruce says, 'the method adopted by the Romans of producing the blast necessary to smelt the metal was made apparent. Two tunnels had been formed in the side of a hill; they were wide at one extremity, but tapered off to a narrow bore at the other, where they met in a point. The mouths of the channels opened towards the west, from which quarter a prevalent wind blows in this valley, and sometimes with great violence. The blast received by them would, when the wind was high, be poured with considerable force and effect upon the smelting furnaces at the extremity of the tunnels.'

Any one who takes one of these ancient cinders in his hand, will be at once convinced by its weight how imperfect had been the process of smelting, and how much metal still remains in

---

* This primitive mode of smelting is still in use among some peoples unacquainted with the improvements of civilized nations. We are told by the early Spanish writers, that the Peruvians built their furnaces for smelting silver on eminences where the air was freest; they were perforated on all sides with holes, through which the air was driven when the wind blew, which was the only time when the work could be carried on, and under each hole was made a projection of the stonework, on which was laid burning coals to heat the air before it entered the furnace.

The smelting furnaces for iron in the Himmaleh mountains of Central Asia are described as follows :—A chimney is built of clay, about four feet and a half high, by fifteen to eighteen inches in diameter, upon a stage of stonework, over a fire-place. In an opening below the stage there is a hole, through which the metal when melted flows, and this is stopped with clay or earth, easily removed with an iron poker. The fire is blown with two pair of bellows, each made of a goat's skin, and worked by a woman or boy. The iron ore was mixed with pounded charcoal, and thrown into the chimney. A somewhat similar tower of clay was made for smelting by an African people, visited by Mungo Park, but they trusted partly to the wind for a blast, and placed the iron ore, after it had been broken into pieces of the size of a hen's egg, in alternate layers with charcoal. See further on this subject, Scrivener's 'Comprehensive History of the Iron Trade.'

it. During the seventeenth and eighteenth centuries the Roman iron scoriæ in the Forest of Dean and in Worcestershire, were re-smelted on a very extensive scale; and it is said that, being gathered with so little trouble, they were actually found more profitable than fresh ore which had to be dug from a considerable depth in the ground. Besides the marks of charcoal still visible on some of the cinders, examples occur which show the effects of the irregular heat produced by this fuel. One, which I picked up among a vast heap of cinders at Sedlescombe, in Sussex, proved by coins found in it to be Roman, exhibits a curious appearance of a compact mass with veins and drusy cavities with crystalline iron; in this instance an imperfect steel or carburet of iron has been the result of the excessive heat produced by the wood fuel.

Among the other principal metallic productions of our island, worked by the Romans, were lead and tin, called by the Romans, *plumbum nigrum* and *plumbum album*. The latter we know was, under its Greek name of *cassiteros*, the chief and most valuable production of the Brittanic Isles at a very remote period, and procured for them the name of the Cassiterides, or Tin Islands. We are told by ancient writers that lead was found so plentifully, and so near the surface of the ground, that it was found necessary in the earlier period of the Roman occupation to make a law limiting the quantity to be taken each year.* The tin districts were, as at present, Cornwall and Wales, and I believe that Roman mines have been traced, and that blocks of Roman tin have been found, though they are of extreme rarity. This, however, is not the case with lead; for

Roman Pig of Lead, from Hampshire.

the traces of Roman lead mines are very numerous, and pigs of lead, with the official stamps of the Roman miners, are by no means of uncommon occurrence. This stamp usually consisted

* In Britannia summo terræ corio adeo largo, ut lex ultro dicatur, ne plus certo modo fiat.—*Plin. Hist. Nat.*, lib. xxxv. c. 17.

CHAP. VIII.]   THE LEAD MANUFACTURE.   295

of an inscription giving the name of the emperor under whose reign the lead had been produced from the furnace. The foregoing cut represents one of these pigs of lead, found in 1783, on the verge of Broughton brook, near Stockbridge, in Hampshire. It will serve to give a general idea of the form and character of these articles, and it has a certain historical interest from the circumstance that it was made the year before the insurrection of Boadicea. The main inscription is, NERONIS AVG. EX KIAN IIII COS BRIT. On one side are the letters HVL PMCOS; on the other, EX ARGENT and CAPASCAS, with the numeral XXX.* Other examples found at different times have presented the following inscriptions:—

1. TI CLAVDIVS CAESAR AVG P M TRIB P VIII IMP XVI DE BRITAN
2. IMP DOMIT AVG GER DE CEANG
3. CAESARI . . . . . . VADOM
4. IMP CAES DOMITIAN AVG COS VII BRIG
5. IMP VESP VII T IMP V COS DE CEANG
6. TI CL TR LVT BR EX ARG
7. IMP CAES HADRIANI AVG MET LVT
8. IMP HADRIANI AVG
9. IMP DVOR AVG ANTONINI ET VERI ARMENIACORVM
10. L ARVCONI VERECVND METAL LVTVD
11. C IVL PROTI BRIT LVT EX ARG

The greater number of these inscriptions, it will be seen at once, commemorate the emperor in whose reign each was made. The two last, no doubt, give us the names of private individuals, either governors of the province, or persons appointed to superintend the mines of Britain. Some of the words of these inscriptions have provoked rather long disquisitions, yet they are capable of a simple explanation. LVT is supposed to be an abbreviation of *lutum*, washed, in reference to the process through which the metal (MET) had passed; and the EX ARG, or EX ARGENT, is explained by a passage of Pliny, who informs us that lead was found under two different forms, either in veins by itself, or mixed with silver.† The latter had to go through a more com-

---
* Mr Roach Smith observes on this inscription:—'As Nero never assumed the title of Britannicus, and as the numerals precede the cos, I suspect the inscription should be read—

(Plumbum *or* Metallum) Neronis Aug. cos. iiii., Ex. Kian. Brit.

The P.M. Cos may belong to the above, and the rest be the name of some superintendent.'

† Plumbi nigri origo duplex est: aut enim sua provenit vena, nec quicquam aliud ex se parit; aut cum argento nascitur, mistisque venis conditur.—*Plin. Hist. Nat.*, lib. xxxiv. c. 16.

plicated process of extraction, which is referred to by the words of the inscription, *lutum ex argento*, and which it seems the Romano-British metallurgist considered it necessary to specify. The examples on which the words BRIG and DE CEANG occur, were found chiefly in Cheshire and Yorkshire, and these words are supposed to signify that they came from the tribe of the Ceangi, or Cangi, and the Brigantes. The words EX KIAN on the pig of lead represented in our cut, are supposed to refer to the same tribe of the Ceangi, by an earlier mode of spelling the name. It had no doubt been left in Hampshire on its way to the coast for exportation.

It is indeed difficult in many cases to form any opinion relating to these relics from the place where they were found. Three of them were found near Matlock, in Derbyshire, no doubt in the neighbourhood of the mines from which they were taken. They have been found also in Shropshire, near the site of ancient lead mines. The inscriptions are curious, as belonging mostly to the earlier emperors, and showing that the metallic riches of Britain were among its first resources turned to account by the Roman conquerors.*

The wording of some of the above inscriptions is sufficient evidence that the Romans obtained silver from the mines in Britain, and the island province appears also to have furnished gold, though probably in very small quantities. Gold has been traced in the quartz formation near Lampeter, in Wales, in the immediate neighbourhood of a Roman settlement, where enormous mounds of broken and pounded quartz remain as memorials of the Roman gold diggers. A still more curious memorial, perhaps, of the British silver mines was discovered in the latter part of the last century, among remains of very old masonry cleared away in digging the foundations of the then new office for the Board of Ordnance, in the Tower of London. It had apparently been a square ingot of silver, about three-eighths of an inch thick, but it had subsequently been beaten at each end with a hammer, till the whole had assumed the form of a double wedge. From its weight, when found, there could be little doubt of its having been originally a Roman pound of silver.

---

* For further information on these pigs of lead and on the Roman mining operations in this island in general, the reader is referred to very excellent papers by Professor Phillips and Mr Albert Way, in a recent volume of the 'Archæological Journal,' and by Mr James Yates, in the eighth volume of the 'Proceedings of the Somersetshire Archæological and Natural History Society.'

In the middle, on one side, within a simple square label, was the inscription:—

EX OFII
HONORI

in which the last letters of each line had been partly effaced, probably by a blow of the hammer. It seems doubtful if the Honorius here commemorated was an officer of the Roman mint in Britain, or the emperor of that name; though the probability seems to be turned in favour of the latter by the discovery close by it of three gold coins, one of which was of the emperor Honorius, while the two others belonged to his partner in the empire, Arcadius.* In this case, it would belong to the closing period of the Roman rule in Britain.

The metal most in favour among the Romans for the manufacture of useful and ornamental articles, appears to have been bronze. It would extend beyond our limits, and be of no real practical utility, to give a description of the almost endless variety of articles of bronze belonging to the Roman period, which have been found in this country, some of very rude workmanship, and others showing a very high state of art. It is not possible to say how many of the articles were made in Britain, and how many were imported, but there can, I think, be little doubt that such articles were manufactured here in considerable quantities. As the rough, unformed glass was distributed from the manufactory to the small glass-workers, so the bronze was probably sold in lumps to small manufacturers, who, either with the hand, or more frequently by melting it into moulds, formed statuettes, vessels of various kinds, ornaments, tools, and toys, under which latter head I suspect we ought to place a large number of the small, rude figures of animals, &c., in bronze, which are frequently found on Roman sites. I believe that the fragments of old bronze with chisels and other implements of the same metal, already described (p. 98), as found in different parts of England, belonged to the Roman workers in bronze. Smelting pots, with remains of molten bronze, and lumps of the same metal, and even entire foundries, with moulds and the articles cast in them, have been found in different parts of Germany, as at Demmin, in Mecklenburgh; Gross Jena, in Thuringen; Braunfels, in Hessen; and at Zurich, in Switzerland; and, I believe, in France; and if I am not mistaken,

* This ingot of silver and the three coins are engraved in the fifth volume of the 'Archæologia' of the Society of Antiquaries.

they will be found to have been all discovered in localities occupied by the Romans.

That Roman art did flourish to a certain degree in Britain, we have proofs in the various traces of ornamental decoration in the houses, in articles of bronze and other material, and in the remains of statuary. Some few fragments of wall-paintings that have been rescued from the general destruction of the frescoes of the Roman houses, are artistically executed; and, although many of the sepulchral and other sculptures found in our island are of a rude character, others are quite the contrary. It is probable that most of the finer pieces of sculpture in marble, found in the Roman villas and elsewhere, were executed abroad; but other similar remains of great beauty have been found sculptured in materials which were undoubtedly obtained in the island, and generally near the spot where they seem to have been erected. Such were the statues, which exhibit a very high degree of art, found by Mr Artis in 1844, 1845, and 1846, near Sibson, in Bedfordshire, and at a place between Wansford and King's Cliff, in the same county, known as Bedford Purlieus, which were formed of the oolite of the district, popularly known as Barnack rag. They are now preserved in the collection of the Duke of Bedford, and include large portions of figures of Hercules, Apollo, and Minerva Custos. At Birrens, in Scotland, was found a dedicatory inscription, by Julius Cerealis Censorinus, who is described as the image-maker (*sigillarius*), or fabricator of the statues of the gods, to the college of *ligniferi*; and the mutilated trunk of a colossal statue of Mercury, found at the same spot, was supposed to be a relic of his works.

Of the other professions of the Romans in Britain, we find, from their very nature, fewer traces among existing remains, though one or two of them are commemorated in inscriptions. Thus, a votive statue to the goddess Brigantia, found at Birrens in Scotland, was dedicated, if not made, by Amandus the architect. A monumental stone, found at Housesteads in Northumberland, commemorates a young medical practitioner, Anicius Ingenuus, physician in ordinary to the first cohort of the Tungrians.*

There is, however, a class of monuments relating to the Roman medical profession and their practice in Britain, which are so curious, that they require a more minute description and

* D M ANICIO INGENVO MEDICO ORDI COH PRIMAE TVNGR VIX AN XXV.

explanation. These are the stamps used for impressing the names of the makers and the purposes of certain medicinal preparations.

Numerous examples of these medicine stamps have been found in Germany, France, and Italy, as well as in Britain; and in the former countries they have been the subject of several learned treatises.* They are usually made of a greenish schist, or steatite, and consist of a small thin square block, generally with an inscription on each of the four edges. In a few instances the stone is of an oblong form, and has only two inscribed sides. The inscriptions are inverse and retrograde, and they were evidently intended as stamps; but when first noticed, they were a great puzzle to the antiquary. The example given in our cut, which was found a few years ago at Kenchester in Herefordshire (*Magna*), belongs to the former of these two classes. The inscription usually expresses the name of the

Roman Medicine Stamp from Kenchester (*Magna*.)

maker of the medicine, that of the medicine itself, and the disease for which it was intended as a specific. From the places in which they are found, the name appears to be generally that of a medical practitioner in one of the principal towns, who composed the medicines, and, perhaps, sold them in packages to the minor practitioners or dealers in the smaller towns and in the country, in the manner that patent medicines used to be sold in England. It is somewhat remarkable, that in all the examples yet found, amounting in number to at least sixty, the diseases are uniformly those of the eyes, and hence they are

---

* Two French writers especially have written at length on this subject: M. Sichel, in a tract entitled *Cinq Cachets inédits de Médecins-Oculistes Romains* (Paris, 1845), and M. Duchalais, *Observations sur les Cachets des Médecins-Oculistes anciens, à-propos de cinq Pierres sigillaires inédites* (Paris, 1846). Still more recently an interesting paper on the Roman medicine stamps found in Britain has been contributed to the 'Monthly Journal of Medical Science,' by Professor Simpson, of Edinburgh, but a part only of which has, as far as I can learn, been yet printed.

supposed to have been only used by physicians who treated that very numerous class of diseases, and some writers have spoken of them by the name of oculists' stamps.*

Any one who will turn to the index to an ordinary edition of Pliny's Natural History, will see at one glance how much attention the Romans gave to diseases of the eyes, which appear to have been extraordinarily prevalent, not only in Italy, but throughout the western provinces. This is probably to be attributed to some circumstance connected with the diet or way of living of the ancients. The Greek medical writers enumerate more than two hundred diseases of the eyes, for which an immense number of different ointments, or *collyria*, were invented. The reader will remember the lines of Horace—

> 'Hic oculis ego nigra meis collyria lippus
> Illinere.'

These collyria were composed of a great number of ingredients, and were many of them celebrated among all physicians by their particular names. These were sometimes taken from those of the original inventors, as the collyrium of Dionysius, and the collyrium of Sergius. A more numerous class received their names from the characteristic of the mixture or from some particular ingredient. Thus we have the collyrium *chloron*, named from its green colour; the *cirrhon*, from its yellow tint; the *evodes* (εὐώδες), from its pleasant smell; the *cnicetum* (ἀνίκητον, invincible), because pretended to be superior to all the others; the *crocodes*, made of crocus or saffron; the *nardinum*, containing spikenard; the *diasmyrnes*, containing myrrh; the *diarrhodon*, containing roses; and so on. The example given above, which was found at Kenchester, had belonged to a physician named apparently Titus Vindacius Ariovistus, who, to judge from his name, appears to have been of German race. On the upper surface is the word SENIOR, the first three letters of which are repeated on the lower surface, and it has been suggested that it was probably the name of a subsequent possessor. The four inscriptions of the sides, which are in double lines, are—

(1) T. VINDAC. ARIO
VISTIANICET

---

* *Medici ocularii* and *medici ophthalmici* are mentioned by the Roman medical writers in a manner to make us believe that this formed a special branch of the practice.

(2) T. VINDACIAR
    OVISTI . NARD

(3) . . VINDAC . ARI
    OVISTICHLORON

(4) T . VINDACARIO
    VISTI . . .

The name of the collyrium, indicated in the last, has been lost by a fracture of the stone. The other three were the *anicetum*, the *nardinum*, and the *chloron*, well known collyria, all mentioned above. Another of these stamps, found at Cirencester in 1818, is now in the possession of P. B. Purnell, Esq., of Stanscombe Park, Gloucestershire. It is an oblong piece of hone-stone, or whet-slate, with two sides inscribed, which commemorate a physician named Minervalis. They are—

(1) MINERVALISDIALER
    ANVMADIMPETLIPEXOV

(2) MINERVALISMELINV
    ADOMNEMDOLOREM

The dialebanum was composed with the plant ledanum or ladanum found in Crete, and it is here directed to be used with egg (*ex ovo*) on the first attack of lippitudo—*ad impetum lippitudinis*. The second was a well-known collyrium, which is mentioned by the old medical writers under the same name of *melinum*, but the origin of the name seems very doubtful. Another medicine stamp was found at Bath in 1781. A fourth was dug up at Gloucester (not, as some writers have stated by mistake, at Colchester), at the beginning of the last century, and was published by Chishull. It bore the name of the physician, Quintus Julius Murranius, and had two inscriptions—

(1) QIVLIMVRRANIMELI
    NVMADCLARITATEM

(2) QIVLMVRRANISTACTV
    MOPOBALSAMATADCAL

The first of these was another *melinum*, which was to be efficacious for producing clearness of vision—*ad claritatem*. The second was an opobalsamic *stactum*, or liquid (from στάζω), intended as a remedy for dimness of sight—*ad caliginem*. In 1808, a medicine stamp of an unusual form was found at Wroxeter in Shropshire (*Uriconium*); it was a round, instead of quadrangular, stone, with the inscription on the face, as in a seal. It is now preserved in the Museum of Wroxeter anti-

Oculist's Stamp, from Wroxeter (*Uriconium*).

quities in Shrewsbury, and the inscription is easily read as follows—

<pre>
TIBCLM
DIALIBA
AD'OM
NE Δ VIT
O EX O
</pre>

Intimating that it was the *dialibanum* of Tiberius Claudius the physician (*medicus*), for all diseases of the eyes (*ad omne vitium oculorum*), and was to be applied, like the *dialebanum* of Minervalis, *ex ovo*, with egg.

It is curious that we have thus a series of these medicine stamps belonging to the great Roman towns in the west, Corinium, Aquæ Solis, Glevum, Magna, and Uriconium. None have yet been found, as far as we have any distinct information, in the Roman towns of the eastern and northern parts of the island, but there are two, or at least fragments of two, preserved in the British Museum, which are stated to have been found in this country, although the exact locality is not known. One of these is a flat quadrilateral stone, and commemorates a physician named Sextus Julius Sedatus. It is inscribed only on three sides; which is also the case with at least one of the foreign examples. The inscriptions are—

<pre>
(1) SEXIVLSEDATI
    CROCODPACCIAN
(2) SEXIVLSEDATICRO
    CODFSDIALEPIDOS
(3) ... IVLSEDATICMO
    ... ESADDIATHES
</pre>

These collyria were all of the class already mentioned as taking its name *crocodes* from one of its ingredients, the crocus or saffron. The first was distinguished by the name *Paccianum*, from its inventor, Paccius, a celebrated ancient oculist, several of whose medicines, as well as this identical *crocodes Paccianum*, are mentioned by Galen. The *crocodes dialepidos*, the second on our stamp, is also mentioned by the ancient medical writers, and derived its name from the circumstance that it contained the scales (λεπίδες) of burnt copper, or the black peroxide of that metal. The second stamp in the British Museum, which is evidently a mere fragment, bears the letters—

COLLYR·P·CLOC

They are probably to be read *collyrium post caliginem oculorum*, a collyrium to be used after an attack of dimness of the eyes. The Museum of the Society of Antiquaries of Scotland, at Edinburgh, contains one of the oblong medicine stamps, which was found at Tranent in East Lothian, near Inveresk, the site of an extensive Roman town. It had belonged to an oculist named Lucius Vallatinus. The two inscriptions are—

(1) LVALLATINIEVODESADCI
    CATRICESETASPRITVDIN

(2) LVALLATINIAPALOCRO
    CODESADDIATHESIS

The first was the collyrium named *evodes*, and was a remedy against cicatrices of the eyes and granulations of the eyelids. The second was some modification of the usual character of the *crocodes* (*apalocrocodes*), which has been interpreted 'a mild crocodes,' used as a general remedy against affections of the eyes—*ad diatheses*.* The person who cut the inscription has made an error in the termination of the last word.

It has been supposed by writers on the subject of these stamps, that the various preparations were hardened with gum or some viscid substance, and kept in a solid state to be liquefied with fluids when required for use; the stamps being impressed just before the medicines attained the last stage of solidification

---

* An account of this stamp was first communicated by Mr Daniel Wilson (afterwards Dr Wilson), Secretary of the Society of Antiquaries of Scotland, to the 'Journal of the Archæological Association,' vol. v. p. 351, where an editorial note has been added, to state that 'diathesis can only imply a particular state of the body *disposing* to any disease, and not mean the disease itself.' This is the use of the word in modern medicine, but the ancient physicians used it in the sense of an affection or disease.

The Cirencester stamp is said to have been found in a Roman urn, but no further particulars of the discovery have been preserved. It is a curious circumstance that Caylus (vol. vii. p. 261) has given the rim of an earthen vessel marked by one of these medicine stamps, which might be supposed to indicate that the mark was intended to be placed on the vessel containing the medicine, and not on the medicine itself. But this may have arisen from some accident which we cannot now explain, and the circumstances under which the stamps are generally found seem to contradict such an inference.

Of Roman trades, in this island, we have fewer indications even than of professions. What appears to have been the workshop of an enameller, or perhaps of a fabricator of ornamental objects in metal of various kinds, has already been opened in the excavations at Wroxeter on the site of Uriconium. It is probable that the Roman tradesman was seldom commemorated in a sepulchral inscription. Mr Roach Smith found in a very ancient rubbish pit, deep under the site of the Royal Exchange, in the city of London, the refuse of the shops of Roman shoemakers, weavers, and workers in other such handicrafts. I owe to the pencil of the same zealous and skilful antiquary the sketch of a monument of a still more remarkable character—the sign of a Roman goldsmith, found amid the ruins of a town at Old Malton in Yorkshire, which probably represents the Roman Derventio. It is a large stone, which has

Goldsmith's Sign, from Old Malton (*Derventio ?*).

apparently been let into a wall, and bears on one face, within a label, an inscription which seems to commemorate the shop of a goldsmith named Servulus. The inscription is as follows—not very correct in its Latinity :—

>   FELICITERSIT
>   GENIO LOCI
>   SERVULE VTERE
>   FELIXTABERN
>   AM AVREFI
>   CINAM

I have had occasion more than once to allude to the practice of the Romans of invocating good fortune on every occasion.* The sign of an artisan here begins with an invocation to the presiding genius or spirit of the locality,—a propitiation to the divinity of the spot on which he settled, that his undertakings there might prosper,—and next comes the wish that the owner of the shop may have good fortune in his profession. Mr Wellbeloved has published the fragment of the commencement of an inscribed stone, found at York, and containing the words—

>   GENIO LOCI
>   FELICITER

which he believed to be part of a votive tablet. But on comparing it with the complete inscription found at Old Malton, I am inclined to think that this also may have formed part of a tradesman's sign.

* These invocations were used in private houses, as well as in shops, and are sometimes joined with the name of the possessor. Thus, a mutilated Roman tesselated pavement found at Salzburg, in Germany, presented the following fragment of an inscription (the name of the person is lost) :—

>   . . . . . . HIC HABITAT
>   NIHIL INTRET MALI

i. e. (———) *dwells here—may nothing evil enter.* This supports our interpretation of the inscription on the Thruxton pavement.

CHAPTER IX.

Ethnological Character of the Roman Population of Britain.—Countries from which it was derived—The Auxiliary Troops—Names and Birthplaces of Individuals—Traces of Languages; Inscribed Pottery; the Roundels found at Colchester—Debased Latinity—Remains of the British Population.

WHEN we contemplate these numerous towns and cities, so many buildings and public works of all descriptions, manufactures, and monuments of art and science, our inquiries naturally return to the people from whom they came, and we ask who were the Romans in Britain? It is a question much more complicated in its various bearings than it would appear at the first thought to those who have not previously studied the subject.

When Rome first established colonies, they were composed purely of Roman citizens, usually of veterans or soldiers, who, having completed their time, were no longer compelled to serve, except in defending the town and territory which was given to them. The land of this territory was distributed among them. Such was the foundation of Camulodunum (*Colchester*), as we learn incidentally from the narrative of Tacitus. As their conquests extended, the Roman legions, which still consisted of Italian soldiers, were accompanied with numerous bodies of auxiliaries, or troops raised from the different countries which had been successively subdued. It was a policy henceforth pursued with great steadiness by the Roman conquerors to transplant, under the name of auxiliaries, colonies from one nation to another, and they thus not only made a gradual amalgamation of the different peoples who composed the empire, but they established effective defences without exhausting the central force.* Gradually, however, while destroying the nationalities of other peoples, Rome lost its own nationality in

---

* Cicero, in more passages than one, speaks of the Roman *coloniæ* as the defences of the empire, *propugnacula imperii*.

the mass. Men from those very nations upon whom ancient Rome had trampled as barbarians, were made commanders in its armies, nobles in its senate, and emperors on its throne. The Roman legions were now recruited indiscriminately, and we shall have to point out officers of the legions in Britain, who were natives of countries far distant from Italy.

Even with our present imperfect information, we can trace the parcelling out of Britain among colonies of almost every people who had been subdued by the Roman arms, and it must have presented a strange assemblage of races.* The *Notitia Imperii*, composed under Theodosius the younger, and therefore at the close of the Roman domination in Britain, gives us a rather long list of the auxiliary nations who held the towns and stations along the south-eastern and eastern coasts and in the north, the parts then exposed to invasion by the Saxons and the Picts. Thus we learn from that valuable record, that Othona (supposed to be the lost town of Ythancester, on the coast of Essex), was occupied by a body of Fortensians, who came from the town of Fortia in Asiatic Sarmatia. Dubræ (*Dover*) was held by Tungricanians, supposed to be only another form or an error of the scribe for Tungrians. At the Portus Lemanis (*Lymne*) there were Gauls from Tornacum (*Tournay*). The Abulci, a Spanish people, held Anderida (*Pevensey*). At Regulbium (*Reculver*) was the first cohort of Vetasians, or Betasians, from Belgic Gaul. On the coasts of Suffolk and Norfolk, we find Stablesians, perhaps a tribe from Germany, at Garriannonum (*Burgh Castle*), and Dalmatians at Branodunum (*Brancaster*). There were Dalmatians, again, at Præsidium (*Broughton*, in Lincolnshire); Crispians, from a town named Crispiana in Pannonia, at Danum (*Doncaster*); a people called Barcarii Tigrienses, perhaps from Africa, at Arbeia (*Moresby ?*); and Nervians, from Belgium, at Dictis (*Ambleside ?*). Returning eastward again, we find Solenses, from Cilicia, at Maglone (supposed by Horsley to be *Gretabridge*); and Pacensians from Lusitania or Portugal, at Magæ (*Piercebridge*). Along the line of Hadrian's Wall, the inhabitants of the different towns were still more varied in their races. Segedunum (*Wallsend*) was occupied by Lingones from Belgium; Pons Ælii (*Newcastle*) by a people called Cornovii; Condercum

---

* I here use the word *colony*, not in its Roman legal sense, but to signify any town or settlement formed in one country by a body of people from another.

(*Benwell*) by Asturians from Spain; Vindobala (*Rutchester*) by Frixagi; Hunnum (*Halton Chesters*) by a tribe whose name has not been preserved; Cilurnum (*Chesters*) by another body of Spanish Asturians; Procolitia (*Carrawburgh*) by Batavians; Borcovicus (*Housesteads*) by Tungrians; Vindolana (*Chesterholm*) by Gauls; Æsica (*Great Chesters*) by another colony of Asturians; Magna (*Carvoran*) by Dalmatians; Amboglanna (*Birdoswald*) by Dacians; Petriana (*Cambeck-fort*) by Tungrians; Aballaba (*Watch-cross?*) by Moors; Congavata (*Stanwicks*) by Lingones; Axelodunum (*Burgh-on-the-Sands*) by Spaniards; Gabrosentis (*Drumburgh*) by Thracians. There were Morini from Gaul at Glannibanta (a town of uncertain site); Nervians at Alionis (*Whitley Castle*) and at Virosidum (*Ellenborough*).

These are the different races established in Britain mentioned in the Notitia, because, by their position and the circumstances of the time, they were obliged to be on active duty. We must not, however, imagine that they were bodies of troops in temporary quarters which could be changed at pleasure, for inscriptions on altars and tombstones, found on many of these sites, show us that they had remained in the same place from a very early period of the Roman occupation of the island, and some monumental stones are stated to have been set up by the heir or heirs of the deceased (*hæres, hæredes*), which seems sufficient to prove that they were possessors of the land. No doubt the colonists of these towns were accompanied or followed by relations and friends, and as evidently they were recruited from their own countries, they must have gone on increasing and strengthening themselves. They were all, however, obedient to Roman laws and institutions, used the Latin tongue, and had indeed become entirely Romanised, as we shall see more and more fully in subsequent chapters.

Many others of the races, who thus colonised towns in Britain, are now unknown, though a few from time to time are recovered by the discovery of inscribed stones. In different places in Cumberland there appear to have been Gauls, Dacians, and Lingonians. A people called the Carvetii are found at Old Penrith. Spaniards, Dalmatians, and Betasians, were established at, or in the neighbourhood of, Ellenborough. At Brougham, there were Germans. In Scotland, inscriptions mention the Tungrians in several places; Gauls at Cramond and at Castlehill on the Wall of Antoninus; Spaniards at Ardoch; Thracians; Hamii from the Elbe, at Barhill fort on Antoninus's Wall; Nervians, Germans, and Cugerni, a people of Belgic Gaul, between the Ubii and the Batavi. The Roman town at Risingham, Habitancum, was held by the Vagiones, a people from the banks of the Rhine. The Varduli, from the foot of the Pyrenees in Spain, were established at Bremenium (*Rochester*), and they are mentioned also in an inscription found at Epiacum (*Lanchester*). An inscription found at Bowes, in Yorkshire, proves that that site, the Roman Lavatræ, was held by Thracians. In Lancashire, Coccium (*Ribchester*) was a settlement of Sarmatians, while Mancunium (*Manchester*) was a colony of Frisians, called, in the inscriptions, *Frisingi, Frisones,* and *Frisavi.* The latter seem to have found some difficulty in expressing the name of their country in the language of their conquerors. If we descend towards the south, Cirencester appears to have been occupied by Thracians. The rarity of inscriptions in the midland and southern towns renders it at present impossible to identify the races from which they severally drew the nucleus of their population.

We see still more how people from all parts of the world came to intermingle in our island, when we compare their names as they occur in inscriptions. Thus, in one of the inscriptions found at Cirencester, Dannicus, who belonged to the cavalry stationed there, was a citizen of Rauricum, in Switzerland. Sextus Valerius Genialis, the subject of another monument at Cirencester, who belonged to the Thracian cavalry, was a Frisian. Titus Domitius Heron, prefect of the second cohort of Gauls at Old Penrith in Cumberland, came from Nicomedia of Bithynia in Asia Minor. Æmilius Crispinus, prefect of the ala Augusta at Old Carlisle, was a native of Tusdrus, in Africa (*natus in provincia Africa de Tusdro*). Publius Ælius, also prefect of the ala Augusta at Old Carlisle, was a native of Mursa, in Lower Pannonia (*de Mursa ex Pannonia inferiore*). Marcus Censorius, prefect of the cohort of Spaniards at Ellenborough, was of Nîmes, in Gaul (*ex provincia Narbonensi domo Nemausensis*). Lucius Duccius, an officer buried at York, was of Vienna, in Gaul. Flavius Longus, a tribune of the twentieth legion at Chester, was a native of Samosata, in Syria, the birth-place of Lucian. An individual mentioned in an inscription at Lincoln, named Nominius Sacer, the son of Bruscus, was of the tribe of the Senones, in Gaul (*civis Senonii*). Caius Valerius, standard-bearer of the second legion at Caerleon, was a native of Lugdunum, in Gaul (*Lyons*). Julius Vitalis, the *fabriciensis* of the twentieth legion, commemorated in the celebrated inscription found near Bath, was a

Belgian (*natione Belga*). Caius Murrius, of the second legion, also buried at Bath, was a native of Fosum Julii in Gaul (*Frejus*). Caius Cornelius Peregrinus, the tribune of a cohort at Maryport, in Cumberland, was a native of Mauritania (*ex provincia Mauritaniæ Cæsariensis domo Se* . . . . the name of the town is broken off). Cornelius Victor, a soldier of the Gauls of Vindolana at Chesterholm, was a citizen of Pannonia (*civis Pannoniæ*). Although the barbarians frequently assumed a Roman name, yet in the inscriptions found in Britain we often meet with names which betray their provincial origin. Such are Blescius Diovicus, probably the name of a Gaul, found in an inscription at Risingham; Titus Oisedio, at Cambeck-fort; Menius Dada, at Carvoran; Audagus, at Brougham; Iminius Honius Tertullus, a Gaul, at Cramond, in Scotland; Marcus Decius Voconticus, also in Scotland; and Fabius Bera, in the same country. Hermagora, commemorated in an inscription at Riechester, and a worshipper of Astarte named Pulcher, at Corbridge, were no doubt Greeks.

When we contemplate the facility with which the Romans moulded the nations they had conquered to their own government and manners, we feel inclined to doubt the existence among the ancients of those deeply implanted sentiments of nationality which are observed in modern times. The moment a new country was subdued, its inhabitants seem to have rivalled each other in their eagerness to become Romanised, and to have soon relinquished the manners, the worship, and even the language, which they had received from their forefathers. Yet it was hardly possible that here and there some sentiment of attachment for the land of nativity and its recollections should not outlive the change, some confession of the influence of old superstition, some remains of reverence for the gods of their ancient land, or some remembrance of friends, or places, or language. We have seen how often the original country of the deceased was commemorated on his tombstone. Perhaps, if we examine closely the names of Romano-British towns, and could compare them extensively with those of the countries from which their founders came, we should find, as in British America at the present day, that they also were more or less commemorative of the land they had left.* Instances

---

* It has often struck me that we ought to look for the derivation of the names of the Roman towns in Britain rather from the countries from which the settlers came, than from the *presumed* language of the original Celtic population. Thus we know that Aballaba in the North was a colony of

have also been met with among the Roman remains found in Britain of inscriptions rudely scratched on cups and bowls, and other articles, in languages of which we are now ignorant. Some of these were in the possession of Mr Roach Smith, and have been pronounced by an oriental scholar, I think somewhat hastily, to be Arabic. Perhaps we should look rather for the language in which they are written, to Spain or Africa. I believe these inscriptions have been found chiefly in London and at Exeter. At Colchester, a very curious class of antiquities has been found, the use of which is not very apparent. These are thin roundels of reddish earthenware, on the surface of which inscriptions—usually names or numerals—and figures of animals, &c., have been scratched. It has been conjectured that these may have been tickets of admission to the theatre or amphitheatre. One of them has a roughly drawn Egyptian cartouche, with a name in hieroglyphics, a proof that there was at least one Egyptian resident at Camulodunum. Others appear to be Hebrew.

It is also to be noticed, as illustrating the variety of race which here passed under the name of Romans, that the inscriptions not unfrequently contain errors in spelling and in Latinity, which seem to show that they were composed by persons whose mother tongue was not Latin. In an inscription at Caerleon an adjective in the feminine gender is joined with a masculine name. In an inscription found in Cumberland we have *domu* instead of *domo*. We find still more frequently such errors as *numeni* for *numini*, *aginte* for *agente*, and the like, which show the Latin tongue spoken by a people whose pronunciation was organically different from that of the Romans. Thus we trace, at this early period, one of the causes which led to the formation of the neo-Latin dialects of the middle ages.

Among this variety of races, we are led naturally to inquire, what had become of the original Britons? What portion of the population of the island did they form? Unfortunately we are entirely wanting in the materials for solving so interesting a question. It appears that British troops served as auxiliaries in the Roman army in Britain during the wars of Agricola; and we know that they afterwards served thus in various parts of the Roman empire, though it seems contrary to the Roman policy to have employed them thus in their native land.

Moors, and certainly the name sounds Moorish. Some of the names of Roman towns in Britain are identical with towns on the continent, from which the settlers may have been brought.

Horsley gives a fragment of a votive tablet found at Castlecary in Scotland, on which was traced the word BRITTON; and another was found at Ebchester in Durham, dedicated to the goddess Minerva by Julius Gneneius, who is styled ACTVARIVS COHORTIS IIII. BR, but the last letter appears to have been doubtful. Inscriptions are said also to have been found in the north conveying the words CIVITAS DOMNI, CIVITAS DVMNON, CIVITATE CATUVELLAVNORVM, and CIVITAT BRICIC, signifying that the British tribes thus indicated were employed in the erection of Hadrian's Wall. This would show that at that period they were still allowed a certain degree of political existence. But this no doubt was soon taken from them, and the few glimpses we have of the earlier period of their history would seem to show that they were gradually reduced to the lowest degree of dependence. In the towns of the legions or of the auxiliaries they would not be allowed to enjoy any rights, and it is probable that in the latter part of the Roman period the British blood in the south was found chiefly in the peasantry. The name of Britons was then applied almost exclusively to the independent tribes of Caledonia.

CHAPTER X.

Religious Worship of the Romans in Britain—Roman chief Deities: Jupiter, Mars, Apollo, Minerva, Ceres, &c.—The eight Deities—Lesser Deities; Silvanus, Æsculapius—Grecian and Eastern Deities; the Tyrian Hercules, Mithras, Serapis—The Nymphs and Genii, Fortune, and Deified Personifications—Deities of the Auxiliary Races: the Deæ Matres, Viteres or Vitris, Belatucadrus, Cocidius, Mogontis, &c.—Did Christianity prevail or exist in Roman Britain?

No characteristics of races are more permanent than their religious belief and superstitions, and we may expect in these, if in anything, to perceive some traces of the original peoples who formed the Roman state of Britain through the outward covering of Roman forms. Our expectations in this respect will not be entirely disappointed, for amid the immense numbers of altars found in this island dedicated to the gods of Rome, we find some dedicated to deities whose names are new to us, and who, there can be little doubt, belonged to the distant province to which the auxiliary owed his birth. We know how tolerant in this respect the Roman mythology ever showed itself, and though, as a matter of course, those who served under its banners were bound to show reverence to Rome's gods, they were not restricted from offering homage to those who had been worshipped by their own forefathers.

We have already stated that almost every town, or station, had its temple, or more usually, its temples, dedicated to different deities. Of these, as far as discoveries have yet gone, few traces now remain. The materials of which they were built were too valuable in subsequent ages to remain untouched, and the stones were cleared away, and their sculptures and inscriptions defaced, by mediæval builders. Immense quantities of altars shared the same fate, and the great number of these monuments which still exist, shows beyond a doubt how very numerous they must have been. In the wild country along the line of Hadrian's Wall, where they have escaped destruction in greater numbers than elsewhere, it was a practice among the peasantry, even within the memory of man, to chip away the sculptures and inscriptions wherever they found them, because they associated them in their minds with notions of magic and witchcraft. The altars to the different deities—especially to the lesser objects of worship—seem to have been placed within the temples of the superior gods in the same manner that the saints had their chapels and shrines in the Romish churches; and they were perhaps also placed in the open air, by the forum, or on the roadside, or in the cemeteries, like the Romish crosses.

The Roman altar consisted usually of a rectangular block of stone, with an inscription in front. On each side were carved ornaments, usually representing the instruments of sacrifice, the *præfericulum*, or pitcher, which contained the wine for the offering; the *patera*, a dish with a handle, used for throwing a portion of the wine upon the altar; the *securis*, or axe, with which the animal was slain; and the *culter*, or knife, used in cutting it up; with a figure of the whole or part of the victim, usually the head of an ox. Sometimes other figures were introduced, emblematical of the deity to whom the altar was dedicated, or relating perhaps in some cases to the dedicator. The back of the altar is usually rough, which shows that it was intended to be placed against a wall. The upper part was the most elaborately ornamented, and in the middle of the upper surface a basin-shaped cavity was sunk in the stone, called the *focus* (or hearth), which received the portion of the victim that was offered up in sacrifice, and burnt in the fire kindled in the *focus*. The inscription set forth first the deity to whom the altar was dedicated, next the name and condition of the dedicator, and often concluded with stating the cause of dedication. This was usually a vow.

This description will be best understood by comparison with the annexed cut, which represents a Roman altar dedicated to Jupiter, found at Tynemouth, in Northumberland, and now preserved in the museum of the Society of Antiquaries of London. It was dedicated by the prefect of the fourth cohort of Lingones, which, we are informed by the Notitia, was stationed at Segedunum, usually placed at Wallsend, of which Tynemouth is, probably, the site of an advanced outpost; or, perhaps, it may have been carried from the ruins of Segedunum,

WORSHIP OF JUPITER.

as materials for the foundations of the celebrated monastery at the mouth of the Tyne. On one side, which is concealed in the perspective view, but given in the side sketch, are seen the

Altar to Jupiter, found at Tynemouth.

præfericulum, the *securis,* or axe, and the *culter,* or knife, with the usual ox's head. On the other side is the *patera,* supported by two serpents, which had no doubt a symbolical signification. The inscription commences with the ordinary initials of dedication to the chief deity of the mythology of Rome, I. O. M., and must be read as follows:—

I[OVI] O[PTIMO] M[AXIMO]	To Jupiter the best and greatest,
AEL[IVS] RVFVS	Ælius Rufus
PRÆF[ECTVS] COH[ORTIS]	the prefect of cohort the
IIII LINGO	fourth of the Lingo-
NVM	nes.

Numerous inscriptions to Jupiter have been found in Britain, which show that all the various races brought together in this island joined in worshipping the chief deity of Rome. We have just seen that he was reverenced by the Lingones at Wallsend. An altar found at Birdoswald (*Amboglanna*), was dedicated to Jupiter by the Dacians; another, found at Cambeck-fort (*Petriana*), was dedicated to the same deity by the Tungrians; and a third, found at Maryport, by the Spaniards. Other altars dedicated to Jupiter have been found at Auchindayy, in Scotland; at Old Carlisle (*Olenacum*); at Chesterholm (*Vindolana*), dedicated by Gauls; at Housesteads (*Borcovicus*), by the Tungrians; at Ellenborough (*Virosidum*), by Spaniards; at Plumpton Wall (*uncertain*), by Gauls; at Netherby (*Castra exploratorum*); at Lanercost and Bewcastle (*uncertain*), all by Dacians; at Lanchester (*Epiacum*); at Chester (*Deva*), by the twentieth legion; at Caerleon (*Isca*), by the second legion; and at York by the sixth legion. Many others might be added to the list. In some of these altars the deity is distinguished by peculiar appellations, or is joined with others. Three altars have been found in Britain dedicated to Jupiter Dolichenus. One of these was found in the middle of the seventeenth century in the neighbourhood of Caerleon, at a place named St Julians, and was read as follows:—

IOVI.O.M. DOLICHV	To Jupiter the best and greatest,
I. ON.° AEMILIANVS	the Dolichene, Æmilianus
CALPVRNIVS	Calpurnius
RVFILIANVS . . . EC	Rufilianus (*dedicates this*) by
AVGVSTORVM	the emperors'
MONITV	direction.

There appears to have been a peculiar aptness in the epithet as used in this locality, which was on the edge of the great iron district. Reinesius has printed an inscription found at Rome which describes this title as bearing reference to a place where iron was produced:—

IOVI OPTIMO MAXIMO DOLYCHENO
VBI FERRVM NASCITVR C SEMPRO
NIVS RECTVS CENT VII FRVMENTARIVS
D D

'The Doliche,' Mr Roach Smith observes,* 'which gives the name of Dolichenus to Jupiter, was most probably the town of that name in Macedonia, a country which, Strabo says, abounded in iron; and to this Doliche, the words in the last inscription, *ubi ferrum nascitur*, where iron is produced, seem more applicable, than to Dolichenes, a city of Commagene,

* In the first number of his Collectanea, where he has published some other inscriptions to Jupiter Dolichenus.

in Asia, whence, according to Stephanus, this name was derived.' Two other altars dedicated to Jupiter Dolichenus are published by Horsley, one found in the neighbourhood of Newcastle, in the midst of the coal district, where remains of ancient coal-mines have been found, the other at Risingham (*Habitancum*).

Early in the seventeenth century, an altar was found at Chester dedicated to Jupiter under the name or epithet of Tanarus :—

I. O. M. TANARO	To Jupiter, best and greatest, Tanarus,
T. ELVPIVS GALER	Titus Elupius Præsens of the tribe Galeria,
PRAESENS GVNTIA	of Guntia (a town in Vindelicia),
PRI. LEG. XX VV	prefect of the twentieth legion, styled *valens victrix*,
COMMODO ET	Commodus and
LATERANO	Lateranus
COS	being consuls,
V. S. L. M.	performed his vow willingly and dutifully.

The date of this inscription is fixed, by the names of the consuls, in the year 154. It is curious for several reasons. Tanarus is supposed, and apparently with good reason, to be the Teutonic Thunar, the Scandinavian Thor, whose name is preserved in our Thursday, and who is always identified with the classic Jupiter. It thus shows the influence of Teutonic feelings in England at a very early period.

Jupiter is often combined in these inscriptions with other deities or objects of worship. An altar found at Chesterholm in Northumberland (*Vindolana*), is dedicated by Quintus Petronius, prefect of the Gauls established there, *Jovi optimo maximo cæterisque diis immortalibus et genio prætorii*—to Jupiter, best and greatest, and to the rest of the immortal gods, and to the genius of the prætorium. A centurion of the second legion dedicated an altar, found at Auchindavy in Scotland, to Jupiter and Victoria victrix—Victory the vanquisher. An altar found at York bore the following inscription :—

I. O. M.	To Jupiter best and greatest,
DIS. DEABVSQVE	and to the gods and goddesses
HOSPITALIBVS . PE	who preside over the household,
NATIBVSQ . OBCON	and to the penates, for the
SERVATAM . SALVTEM	preservation of the health
SVAM . SVORVMQ	of himself and his family,
P . AEL . MARCIAN	Publius Ælius Marcianus,
VS . PRAEF . COH	prefect of a cohort,
ARAM . SAC . P . NC . D.	dedicated and consecrated this altar.

Even the emperor himself was thus associated with the deity. At Housesteads, on the Wall of Hadrian (*Borcovicus*), an altar has been found with the inscription—

I. O. M.	To Jupiter the best and greatest,
ET NVMINIBVS	and the deities
AVG COH I TV	of Augustus, the first cohort
NGRORVM	of the Tungrians,
MIL CVI PRAEE	a military one, commanded
ST Q VERIVS	by Quintus Verius
SVPERSTIS	Superstis,
PRAEFECTVS	its prefect.

'The emperor himself,' as Mr Bruce observes, 'is probably intended by this phrase, not the gods whom the emperor worshipped. The use of the noun in the plural number, *numina*, is not opposed to this view. Horsley remarks that *numina* is frequently, in classical writers, applied to a particular deity; thus we have *numina Dianæ* in Horace, and *numina Phœbi* in Virgil. The emperors, we know, were frequently worshipped as gods. The Mantuan bard, addressing Augustus, has no doubt of his divinity, though he knows not what region to assign to his especial care:—

> . . . . urbesne invisere Cæsar,
> Terrarumque velis curam ; . . . .
> An deus immensi venias maris, ac tua nautæ
> Numina sola colant.'

Other altars have been found in Britain dedicated to Jupiter *et numinibus Augusti*, or *Augustorum*.

Perhaps, after Jupiter, the deity most extensively worshipped in Roman Britain was Mars, which is easily explained by the military character of the mass of the settlers. Mars, like Jupiter, is often coupled with other divinities, and distinguished by various epithets. At Benwell (*Condercum*), an altar was found dedicated to Mars, the conqueror and avenger—*deo Marti victori vindici*. An altar was dedicated by the Bætassi at Ellenborough to the military Mars,—*Marti militari*—which we should imagine to be an unnecessary epithet. One found at Lanchester (*Epiacum*), was dedicated *Marti Augusti*, to Mars of Augustus. An altar found at Ribchester (*Coccium*), was dedicated *deo Marti et Victoriæ dominorum Augustorum*—to the god Mars and Victory of the emperors. Another altar found at the same place was dedicated *Marti pacifero*—to

Mars the peace-bearer. Among several altars dedicated by a Roman officer named Cocceius Firmus, and found at Auchindavy, in Scotland, was one with the following inscription:—

MARTI	To Mars,
MINERVAE	to Minerva,
CAMPESTRI	to the deities of the fields,
BVS HERO ...	to Hero,
EPONA	to Epona,
VICTORIAE	to Victory,
M COCCEI	Marcus Cocceius
FIRMVS	Firmus,
C LEG II AVG	centurion of the second legion called Augusta.

A singular epithet is given to Mars on an altar found at Haddon Hall, in Derbyshire, with the following inscription:—

DEO	To the god
MARTI	Mars
BRACIACAE	Braciaca,
OSITTIVS	Osittius
CAECILIAN	Cæcilianus,
PRAEFECT	prefect
COH I AQVITANI	of the first cohort of the Aquitani,
V . S	in performance of a vow.

Horsley supposes that Braciaca is the name of a place. Other epithets, or synonyms, applied to Mars, will be mentioned further on. Altars dedicated to this god have also been found at Lanchester, Castlesteads, Lancaster, and other places.

Dedications to Apollo, in his simple classical character, are of rarer occurrence. One found on the line of Hadrian's Wall bears the following inscription:—

DEO APOL	To the god Apollo
INI ET O. N	and all the deities,
SINIS EXPL	the left wing of exploratores (or guides),
CVI PR SVLP	under the command of Sulpicius,
VOTVM S	in discharge of a vow,
L. L. M.	most willingly and dutifully (*dedicates this*).

An altar found at Ribchester (*Coccium*), dedicated to this deity, is more curious, though somewhat more obscure. It was first described by Camden, and the inscription very incorrectly copied, and it was afterwards supposed to be lost, till Dr Whitaker discovered it in 1815 at Salisbury Hall; it is now preserved in St John's College, Cambridge. The inscription runs thus:

DEO SANCTO	To the holy god
APOLLONI APONC	Apollo Aponus,
OB SALVTEM DN	for the health of our lord (the emperor),
AL EQ SARM	the wing of Sarmatian horse
BREMETNN	of Bremetenracum,
SVB DIANIO	under Dianius
ANTONINO	Antoninus,
C LEG VI V	centurion of the sixth legion, called
IC DOMV	the conquering, his native town
ELIBER	was Eliber.

The god is said to have received his appellation of Aponus from the Fontes Aponi, warm springs near Padua, at a place still called Poni, which were celebrated for their medicinal qualities. At Inveresk, in Scotland, an altar had been found dedicated to Apollo Grannus; and at Auchindavy there was one dedicated conjointly to Apollo and Diana. An altar and the dedication of a temple to Diana, have been found at Caerleon (*Isca*).

Altars to the female deities of Rome are not numerous among those hitherto found in Britain. I am not aware of any instance of a dedication to Venus, but I believe there is one to Juno. Minerva occurs on several occasions. Under the title of Suliminerva she had a magnificent temple at Bath (*Aquæ Solis*), the inscription on which was restored by Lysons. There was a temple to Minerva at Ribchester (*Coccium*), the dedication of which was commemorated in an inscription found there in 1811.* Minerva is joined with Neptune in the celebrated inscription relating to the dedication of a temple at Chichester (*Regnum*). A small altar found at Rochester in Northumberland (*Bremenium*), was dedicated to Minerva in the following simple inscription:—

DEAE MI	To the goddess
NERVE IVL	Minerva, Julius
CARANTVS	Carantus
S. C.	dedicated this.

Minerva is joined with Mars in an inscription already mentioned as found at Auchindavy, in Scotland. At Kirk Haugh,

---

* DEAE MINERVAE PRO SALVTE IMP ALEXANDRI AVG ET IVLI MAMMEAE MATRIS DN ET CASTR SVOR ET VAL CRESCENTIS FULVIANI LEG VIVS PP PR PR T FLORIDVS NATALIS LEG PRAEP N ET REGINAE TEMPLVM A SOLO EX RESPONSV RESTITVIT ET DEDICAVIT.

in Northumberland, an altar was discovered, dedicated *deæ Minervæ et Herculi victori*—to the goddess Minerva, and to Hercules the conqueror. But perhaps the most curious inscription found in this country, is a slab discovered in 1816 at Carvoran (*Magna*), containing an inscription relating to the goddess Ceres, consisting of a sort of mystical declaration of the creed of a Roman tribune composed in iambic verse. The annexed cut, taken from Mr Bruce's work on the Roman Wall,

Inscription to Ceres, found at Carvoran (*Magna*).

represents this slab and its inscription, which, arranged properly in lines, is as follows:—

        Imminet leoni virgo cælesti situ
        Spicifera, justi inventrix, urbium conditrix,
        Ex quis muneribus nosse contigit deos.
        Ergo eadem mater divum, pax, virtus, Ceres;
        Dea Syria; lance vitam et jura pensitans.
        In cælo visum Syria sidus edidit
        Libyæ colendum, inde cuncti didicimus;
        Ita intellexit, numine inductus tuo,
        Marcus Cæcilius Donatinus, militans
        Tribunus in præfecto dono principis.

It has been thus translated by Mr Bruce:—

> The Virgin in her celestial seat overhangs the Lion,
> Producer of corn, inventress of right, foundress of cities,
> By which functions it has been our good fortune to know the deities.
> Therefore the same Virgin is the mother of the gods, *is* peace, *is* virtue, *is* Ceres;
> *Is* the Syrian Goddess, poising life and laws in a balance.
> The constellation beheld in the sky hath Syria sent forth
> To Libya to be worshipped, thence have all of us learnt it;
> Thus hath understood, overspread by thy protecting influence,
> Marcus Cæcilius Donatinus, a warfaring
> Tribune in *the office of* prefect, by the bounty of the emperor.

'Cæcilius,' as Mr Bruce observes, 'probably prepared this exposition of his faith on being admitted into the mysteries of Ceres.' An altar dedicated to the goddess under one of the titles here mentioned—DEAE SVRIAE—was found at Little Chesters, in Northumberland; it was raised by an officer of one of the auxiliary cohorts, named Aulus Licinius Clemens, in the proprætorship of Calpurnius Agricola, that is, between the years 162 and 180.

Mercury is often figured among Roman remains found in this island, and an altar was found at Birrens, in Scotland, dedicated to this deity by Julius Cerealis Censorinus, image-maker of the college of the ligniferi, which appear to have been a religious order attached to the worship of the gods, and the occupation of Cerealis was to make their statues:—

DEO MERCV	To the god Mercury,
RIO IVL CER	Julius Cerealis
CENS SIGILL	Censorinus, image-maker
COL LIGN CVLT	of the college of ligniferi, his worshippers,
EIVS D S D	gave it at his own cost,
V. S. L. M.	in performance of a vow willingly and dutifully

Mercury appears to have been the favourite deity of this college, for they also dedicated a statue of Mercury to the god and to the emperor—*numini Augusti deo Mercurio.*

We have already seen how the principal deities were often combined together, or with others. One of these combinations, which was very popular, consisted of the deities who presided over the days of the week—the *signa* or planets—combined with another to make up the number eight. They were Sol, or Apollo, who presided over Sunday (*dies solis*); the moon, or Diana, for Monday; Mars, for Tuesday; Mercury, for Wednesday; Jupiter, for Thursday; Venus, for Friday; and Saturn, for Saturday. They are thus enumerated in an 'eclogue,' or epigram, of Ausonius —

> Primum supremumque diem radiatus habet Sol;
> Proxima fraternæ succedit Lunæ coronæ;
> Tertius assequitur Titania lumina Mavors;
> Mercurius quarti sibi vindicat astra diei;
> Inlustrant quintam Jovis aurea sidera zonam;
> Sexta salutigerum sequitur Venus alma parentem;
> Cuncta supergrediens Saturni septima lux est;
> Octavum instaurat revolubilis orbita Solem.

In most of the Roman monuments the week commences with Saturn (Saturday), and not, as in Ausonius, with Sol (Sunday). A fragment of an octagonal monument in stone, sculptured with the eight deities, which long lay neglected in a blacksmith's shop at Chesterford, in Essex, and is now in the British Museum, contains four of these figures, namely Mars, Mercury, Jupiter, and Venus. It is a curious circumstance that at the same station, Chesterford, portions of two of the indented earthenware vessels made in the Durobrivian potteries have been found, which had the eight deities figured in eight indentations. In the volume of the 'Magna Britannia' of Lysons for Cumberland, are engravings of sculptures, in rather superior workmanship, of deities found at Plumpton Wall, which appear also to have belonged to the eight deities. They are represented in the tesselated pavement of what has been called the Medusa room, in the Roman villa at Bramdean, in Hampshire. Mr Roach Smith possesses a very curious bronze forceps, found in the bed of the Thames, the purpose of which is by no means evident; but representations of these planetary deities in busts are arranged on the two parallel shanks. They commence at the bottom of the left shank with Saturn, and conclude at the bottom of the opposite side with the bust of a female divinity, supposed to be Ceres, which completes the number eight. It is from this number that the French still call the week *huit jours*, and the Germans *acht tage*. We have ourselves preserved the reckoning of our Saxon forefathers, and instead of calling the week *huit jours*, and the two weeks *quinze jours*, with the French, we call them *sennight* (seven nights), and *fortnight* (fourteen nights). Mr Roach Smith, who has given some remarks on these deities in the second volume of his 'Collectanea,' informs us that there is, 'in the Museum at Mayence, a votive altar, found at Castel, on the opposite side of the Rhine, which belongs to the same class of mythic representations as those on the Bramdean pavement and on the forceps. This monument is about three feet and a half high, and is divided into two parts, the lower of which is quadrilateral; the upper, of smaller dimensions, octagonal. On the former are sculptured the full-length figures of Mercury, Hercules, Minerva, and Juno; the latter contains busts of Saturn, Sol, Luna, Mars, Mercury, Jupiter, and Venus; the eighth compartment is inscribed IN H D D, *in honorem domus divinæ*. Over the left shoulder of Saturn is a sickle in form of our modern bill-hook; Sol wears a radiated crown; Luna, a crescent; Mars is helmeted, and carries a shield; the head of Mercury is winged; the bust of Jupiter has been injured, and his emblems are not clearly to be recognised; Venus carries a mirror. Other museums in Germany, I am informed, contain sculptures of the planets similarly arranged. Montfaucon has published an engraving of the seven busts, in a boat, or more probably a half-moon, in bronze.' In the Bramdean pavement, where they are similarly represented in busts, Saturn, as the first, has been destroyed with a portion of the pavement; Sol is represented with the radiated crown, and with his usual attribute, a whip; Luna has the crescent; Mars is distinguished by his helmet and spear; Mercury has a winged cap, and the caduceus in his hand; Jupiter, a sceptre in the form of a trident; and Venus, a mirror. The eighth head has been destroyed by the same fracture which has erased the figure of Saturn. This eighth figure seems to have been chosen almost at pleasure.

The minor deities and heroes of Roman mythology also have their place among the Roman altars found in Britain. Silvanus, the god of forests and of hunting, was an object of general reverence. We have already (p. 257) given an inscription dedicating an altar to Silvanus, in consequence of the slaughter of an enormous boar. An altar found at Birdoswald (*Amboglanna*) bears the following inscription:—

DEO SANCTO	To the holy God
SILVANO VE	Silvanus,
NATORES	The hunters of
BANNE SS	Banna have consecrated this.

At Moresby, in Cumberland, an altar was found dedicated to the God Silvanus (DEO SILVANO), by the second cohort of Lingones. Another, dedicated to the same deity, was found at Netherby, and another at Newcastle-upon-Tyne. An altar found in the north of England was dedicated *Silvano Pantheo*. In Scotland, a mutilated altar dedicated to Silvanus was found at Castlecary; and one found at Eidon bore the following inscription:—

DEO SILVA	To the god Silvanus,
NO PRO SA	for the health (or welfare)
LVTE SVA ET	of himself and
SVORVM CAR	his family,
RIVS DOMITI	Carrius Domitianus,
ANVS ɔ LEG XX	centurion of the twentieth legion
VV VS LL M	the valiant and victorious, performs his vow most willingly and dutifully.

Altars were dedicated to other gods for health and welfare. An altar to Æsculapius found at Lanchester, in Durham, bears a Greek inscription, stating that it was dedicated to the god by a tribune named Titus Flavius Titianus, for the recovery of his health (ὑπὲρ σωτηρίας). Altars dedicated to Hercules are not very uncommon. They have been found on the line of Hadrian's Wall and in Scotland. An altar was dedicated by the Vangiones at Habitancum (*Risingham*) to Hercules, as the unconquered god—*deo invicto Herculi*. Another altar found in the north was dedicated to Hercules and the deity of Augustus—*Herculi et numini Aug.* An altar found at Polmont in Scotland, was dedicated by a soldier in a troop of Tungrian cavalry to Hercules Magusanus, an epithet which the deity derived from Magusa, a town of Ethiopia, from whence, perhaps, the dedicator came. At Corbridge an altar was dedicated by a Grecian priestess to the Tyrian Hercules, with the brief inscription:—

ΗΡΑΚΛΕΙ	To Hercules
ΤΙΡΡΙΩ	the Tyrian,
ΔΙΟΔΩΡΑ	Diodora
ΑΡΧΙΕΡΕΙΑ	the high-priestess.

Several of the Syrian and Oriental deities shared with those of Rome the devotion of the inhabitants of Britain. At Corbridge (*Corstopitum*), where there appears to have been a Græco-Syriac population, an altar has been found dedicated to the Phœnician Astarte, the Ashtaroth of Scripture, with an inscription which forms a line in Greek hexameter verse.

ΑΣΤΑΡΤΗΣ	Of Astarte
ΒΩΜΟΝ Μ	the altar me
ΕΣΟΡΑΣ	you see,
ΠΟΥΛΧΕΡ Μ	Pulcher me
ΑΝΕΘΗΚΕΝ	dedicated.

The curious figured plate of silver found at Corbridge in 1734, and known as the Corbridge lanx, had no doubt some connection with the mysterious worship which these inscriptions show to have existed there under the Romans. It contained figures of Diana, Minerva, Juno, Vesta, and Apollo, with other objects, the meaning of which is obscure

Another eastern superstition, the Mithraism of Persia, had planted itself deeply in this island. The worship of Mithras was established at Rome under Trajan, and it afterwards spread through the western provinces of the empire. An altar found at Housesteads in Northumberland (*Borcovicus*) was erected in the year 252, when Gallus and Volusianus were consuls. It bears the following inscription, in which the title of Jupiter (I. O. M., or *Jovi optimo maximo*), is usurped:—

D. O. M.	To the god best and greatest,
INVICTO MIT	the invincible Mith-
RAE SAECVLARI	ras, lord of ages,
PVBL PROCVLI	Publius Proculi-
NVS ⊃ PRO SE	nus, centurion, for himself
ET PROCVLO FIL	and his son Proculus,
SVO V S L M	performs his vow willingly and dutifully,
DD NN GALLO ET	our lords Gallus and
VOLVSINO COS	Volusianus being consuls.

This altar was found in a Mithraic cave. We know that a cave, or, at least, a dark and generally subterranean room representing a cave, was properly the scene of the worship of this deity, which continued long established in the western empire. We are told that as late as the year 378, Gracchus, prefect of Rome, destroyed the cave of Mithras in that imperial capital. Porphyry tells us that Mithras was worshipped in a cave, because this was the image and symbol of the world, and that it was dark, because the essence of the virtues is obscure. The mysticism of the Mithraic worship entered deeply into the doctrines of the Neo-Platonists, to whose school Porphyry belonged. 'The cave at Housesteads,' says Mr Bruce, 'was situated in the valley to the south of the station. It was discovered in 1822 by the tenant of the farm in which it stood, who fixed upon the spot as one likely to yield him the material which he required for building a stone fence hard by. The building was square; its sides faced the cardinal points; it had been originally, as was usually the case in a Mithraic temple, permeated by a small stream. Hodgson, who saw it as soon as it was laid bare, says, "The cave itself seems to have been a low contemptible hovel, dug out of a hill-side, lined with dry walls, and covered with earth or straw." Though the building has been entirely removed, a small hollow is left which marks the spot where it stood. All the sculptured stones have happily been placed in the custody of the Society of Antiquaries of Newcastle-upon-Tyne.'

The largest of these sculptures appeared to have been broken to pieces, and part of it carried away; it has been one of those remarkable bas-reliefs of which so many examples have been found on the sites of the Mithraic worship in the Roman provinces. The god was usually represented as a youth wearing the Phrygian bonnet and costume, and kneeling on a prostrate bull, which he is sacrificing. Among the numerous figures and emblems attendant on this group, the most conspicuous are a personage carrying an uplifted torch, representing the sun in the vernal equinox, and another with an extinguished and reserved torch, representing the sun on its approach to the winter solstice. These two figures are otherwise explained as the guides and guardians of souls into and out of life; the one with the inverted torch denoting the descent of the souls to earth; the other, with the torch erect, their return to heaven. One of these figures, nearly entire, was found among the fragments in the cave at Housesteads. The remaining portions of this monument had, no doubt, been carried away and broken up at a remote period—perhaps for the sake of the material—by the ignorant peasantry of the neighbourhood. Another sculptured stone, found in the same place, represented a figure of Mithras, holding a sword in his right hand, and a rather indefined spiral object in his left, in the centre of an egg-shaped tablet, on which were sculptured the signs of the zodiac. Other altars, besides the one of which the inscription is given above, were found in this cave. One bore an equally interesting inscription, which was easily read as follows:—

DEO	To the god
SOLI INVI	the sun, the in-
CTO MITRÆ	vincible Mithras,
SAECVLARI	the lord of ages,
LITORIVS	Litorius
PACATIANVS	Pacatianus,
B F. COS. PRO	a consular beneficiary, for
SE ET SVIS. V. S	himself and family, fulfils his vow
L. M.	willingly and dutifully.

An inscription found at Riechester in Northumberland commemorates the dedication of a temple, *deo invicto soli socio sacrum*, by Lucius Cæcilius Optatus, a tribune of the first cohort of the Varduli. Another smaller altar found in this cave, from that circumstance, identifies Mithras with the sun; it bears the simple inscription,—

SOLI	To the Sun,
HIERON	Hieronymus,
V. L. M.	performs his vow willingly and dutifully.

It is to be regretted that even bare walls, which marked the site in this island of those dark and fearful mysteries, which were said to have been stained with human blood, and which are represented as having been a principal cause of the murder of the imperial tyrant, Heliogabalus, should have been wantonly destroyed. It was a national monument of no little value. The important town of Borcovicus, where these remains were found, was held by a cohort of Tungrians. At Chesters (*Cilurnum*), another town on the line of the wall, held by Asturians from Spain, a sculptured slab of stone was found, which is supposed also to refer to the worship of Mithras.* Hodgson has hazarded the following description and explanation of it:—' The sculpture is in two compartments: that on the left seems to contain a lion, statant, raising the head of a naked and dead man; that on the right, a figure of Mithras seated on a bench, and having a flag in one hand, a wand [or sceptre] in the other, and on its head the Persian tiara (?). I would hazard a conjecture that the whole relates to the Mithraic rites, called Leontica; for the lion, in the zodiac of the ancient heathens, stood for Mithras, or the sun, which threw its greatest heat upon the earth during its course through the constellation Leo.'

Monuments of the Mithraic worship are said to have been found in Cambeck-fort in Cumberland; and a portion of a sculptured entablature of Mithras and the bull was found early in the last century at Chester. But the most perfect of these monuments yet seen in Britain was one found at York, and still preserved in the vestibule of the museum of that city. An engraving of it is given in Mr Wellbeloved's 'Eburacum.' It represents Mithras stabbing the bull, with all the usual attend-

* Engravings of these altars and sculptures will be found in Bruce's 'Roman Wall.' On the monuments of the worship of Mithras, see Von Hammer's 'Mithriaca,' and especially the French work of M. Lajard on this subject.

ant figures. It is supposed that the spot where this very interesting monument was discovered was the site also of a Mithraic cave, where the rites of the Persian deity were performed by the ancient citizens of Eburacum.

At York also has been found a monument commemorative of one of the deities of ancient Egypt. It is a large slab, with an inscription dedicating a temple to Serapis, in the following words :—

DEO . SANCTO	To the holy God
SERAPI	Serapis,
TEMPLVM . ASO	this temple from the
LO . FECIT	ground made
CL . HIERONY	Claudius Hierony-
MIANVS . LEG	mianus, legate
LEG . VI . VIC	of the sixth legion, *called* the victorious.

It is not necessary here to speak of the prominent place held by the god Serapis among the objects of worship in imperial Rome, and we are not surprised to find that a temple was dedicated to him in almost the first city in Roman Britain. If we had a few more of the altars and other religious monuments which have been destroyed, or are yet buried under the sod, we should, no doubt, trace his worship in other parts of Britain. An altar dedicated IOVI SERAPI (to Jupiter Serapis) has been found at Appleby, in Cumberland.

There was another class of Roman deities which were, no doubt, better understood by the Teutonic, and probably by the Gallic races, because they bore a closer affinity to that popular class of mythic beings which are represented by our elves and fairies—the nymphs and genii. These are commemorated in numerous altars found in this island. The nymphs presided over groves and meadows, and especially over fountains. Close by a spring of clear water overlooking the ancient station of Habitancum (*Risingham*), was found an altar dedicated to the nymphs of the spot in the following hexameter couplet :—

Somnio præmonitus miles hanc ponere jussit
Aram quæ Fabio nupta est nymphis venerandis.

The writer was evidently more anxious to preserve the measure of his verse than to make himself intelligible, and the sense intended to be conveyed is far from clear. Mr Bruce has offered two explanations. 'Taking *nupta est* to signify dedicated, a peculiar use of the word, suggested perhaps by its etymological relationship with the one which it governs, *nymphis*, the inscription will read—"A soldier, warned in a dream, directed the erection of this altar which is dedicated by Fabius to the nymphs to whom worship is due." The other method of rendering it is the following:—"A soldier, warned in a dream, directed her (*eam* supplied) who is married to Fabius, to erect this altar to the nymphs to whom worship is due." According to either interpretation the altar was erected to the sylphs of the fountain in consequence of a dream.' An altar found near Chester (*Deva*), to the east of the town, on a spot abounding in springs, bore the inscription:—

NYMPHIS	To the nymphs
ET	and
PONTIBVS	fountains,
LEG XX	the twentieth legion,
V V	the valiant and victorious.

It reminds us of the poet's description of Æneas, who, when he had reached an unknown land,

Nymphasque et adhuc ignota precatur
Flumina.

The nymphs and kindred deities were, in fact, regarded by the Romans with extreme reverence, not less than that shown by the Germans to their popular deities, which has not been entirely eradicated from the minds of the peasantry even at the present day. Another altar dedicated to the nymphs was found at Nether Croy, in Scotland; and at Rutchester (*Vindobala*), one was dedicated to a kindred class of deities, the gods of the mountains. The gods of the fields have also their altars, and in one, found at Castle Hill, on the wall of Antoninus, they are identified with Britain.—

CAMPES	To the field deities
TRIBVS ET	and the deities
BRITANNI	of Britain,
Q PISENTIVS	Quintus Pisentius
IVSTVS PREF	Justus, prefect
COH IIII GAL	of the fourth cohort of Gauls,
V S LL M	performs his vow most willingly and dutifully.

Even the roads had their deities; an altar preserved in a mutilated state at Tretire, in Herefordshire, on the borders of the great Roman iron district, was dedicated, apparently, to the god who presided over cross roads, *deo trivii;* and a more perfect altar, found at Gretabridge, in Yorkshire, had the following inscription:—

DEO QUI VIAS	To the god who ways
ET SEMITAS COM	and paths has de-
MENTVS EST T IR	vised, Titus Ir-
DAS S C F V LL M	das performed a holy vow most willingly and dutifully.
Q VARIVS VITA	Quintus Varius Vita-
LIS ET E COS ARAM	lis, beneficiary of the consul,
SACRAM RESTI	the holy
TVIT	altar restored,
APRONIANO ET BRA	Apronianus and Bra-
DVA COS	dua being consuls.

The altar erected by Titus Irdas having become dilapidated, Quintus Varius Vitalis appears to have caused another to be made in its place; he may have been a relative of the first dedicator. Apronianus and Bradua were consuls in the year 191. An altar has been found in the neighbourhood of Hadrian's Wall dedicated to the gods who preside over cultivation, *dis cultoribus.*

The genii were a somewhat different description of divinities, having each a peculiar object entrusted to his care. We have seen how, even when a man opened a shop or established a trade, he began by propitiating the genius of the place on which he settled. When Æneas arrived at the mouth of the Tiber, he invocated *genium loci.* An altar found at Chester was dedicated to the genius of the place for the health of the two emperors (probably Diocletian and Maximian); and the same genius occurs in more than one other instance on Roman altars found in Britain. One of these, found in the camp at Maryport, in Cumberland, and remarkable for its elaborate ornamentation, is represented in the annexed cut. The inscription must be read as follows:—

GENIO LOCI	To the genius of the place,
FORTVNAE REDVCI	to fortune, who had brought him back
ROMAE AETERNAE	to eternal Rome,
ET FATO BONO·	and to propitious fate,
G CORNELIVS	Gaius Cornelius-
PEREGRINVS	Peregrinus,
TRIB COHOR	tribune of a cohort,
EX PROVINCIA	from the province of
MAVR CAESA	Mauritania Caesariensis,
DOMO SE	native of Se ....

The last line of the inscription, probably containing the
usual formula, V S L L M (*votum solvens libentissime merito*), has

Roman Altar found at Maryport.

been entirely erased, and we have only two letters left of the
name of the town from which Peregrinus came; perhaps it was
on the river Serbes.* 'Peregrinus,' observes Mr Bruce, 'addresses first the deity of the place over which his arms had
triumphed; lest the local god should not smile benignantly, he

* The last remaining letters of the inscription have usually been explained *domos e(versos)*, and supposed to refer to some buildings which the
tribune Peregrinus had restored, but the interpretation given above is the
only one authorised by a comparison of other similar inscriptions.

resorts to Fortune, who had conducted him safely to the land of his adoption. If this deity should fail him, he thinks to find a refuge in the genius of the eternal city; but, driven from this resource, there is nothing for it but to trust to fate or chance.'

Besides the genii which presided over each particular locality, there was a genius of each province of the empire, and a genius of imperial Rome itself. At Auchindavy, in Scotland, were found several altars, dedicated to different deities by a centurion of the second legion, named Marcus Cocceius Firmus. On one of these was the inscription:—

GENIO	To the genius
TERRAE	of the land
BRITA	of
NNICAE	Britain,
M COCCEI	Marcus Cocceius
FIRMVS	Firmus,
O LEG II AVG	centurion of the second legion, the Augustan

The pedestal of a statue, which probably represented a figure of Britannia, was dug up at York in the middle of the last century, with the inscription:—

BRITANNIAE	To sacred
SANCTAE,	Britain,
P . NICOMEDES	Publius Nicomedes,
AVGG . N . N	of our two emperors
LIBERTVS	the freedman.

The two emperors were no doubt Severus and Caracalla.

At Whitby Castle, in Northumberland, an altar was dedicated by the Nervii to the genius of Rome, *genio Romæ*. At Maryport, in Cumberland, was found another inscription, ROMAE AETERNAE ET FORTUNAE REDVCI. One at Riechester was dedicated, *deæ Romæ*, to the goddess Roma. A tablet was found at Stanwicks, in the same county, with an inscription which has been interpreted as follows:—

LEG. VI.	The sixth legion,
VIC. P.F.	the victorious, pious, and faithful,
G. P. R.F.	to the genius of the Roman people made (or erected) this

There were genii who presided even over palaces and public

offices. The fine altar represented in our cut, was found at Chesterholm (*Vindolana*); it is ornamented with figures of the

Roman Altar found at Chesterholm (*Vindolana*).

usual instruments of sacrifice, and with another object, which is not so easily explained, and it may be observed that the focus, or hollow at the top, was reddened by the action of the sacrificial fire. The inscription is:—

GENIO	To the genius
PRAETORI	of the prætorium
SACRVM PI	sacred, Pi-
TVANIVS SE	tuanius Se-
CVNDVS PRAE	cundus præ-
FECTVS CHO IIII	fect of the fourth cohort
GALLOR	of Gauls.

An altar was found at Lanchester (*Epiacum*), dedicated to the same genius by a tribune of the Lingones:—

GENIO PRAETORI	To the genius of the prætorium,
CL EPAPHRODITVS	Claudius Epaphroditus
CLAVDIANVS	Claudianus,
TRIBVNVS CHO	tribune of the second cohort
.. I LING V L P M	of Lingones, placed his vow
	willingly and dutifully.

An altar was found at Caerleon (*Isca Silurum*), dedicated to the genius of the second legion; and one found in North Britain was dedicated to the genius of the first wing of Spaniards, *genio alæ i. Hispanorum*. Thus each prætorium, or quarters, and each troop, had its presiding genius. An altar recently discovered at Chester has the still more curious inscription:—

GENIO	To the genius
AVERNI	of Avernus,
IVL QVIN	Julius Quin-
TILIANVS	tilianus.

which shows that even the presiding genius of the infernal regions had his worshippers in Roman Britain.

The *numen*, or divinity, of the emperors, was also an object of worship, and occurs rather frequently on altars. We have already referred to examples in which the imperial *numina* were combined with other deities. At Chester, an altar was found dedicated *numini Augusti*, to the deity of Augustus. The dedication, *numinibus Augusti*, is common on altars found in different places in Northumberland. One found at Risingham was dedicated by the fourth cohort of Gauls, *numinibus Augustorum*, which is supposed by Horsley to refer to Severus and Caracalla, and by others to Caracalla and Geta. An altar, found also at Risingham, which will be given further on, is dedicated, *numini domini nostri Augusti*, to the divinity of our lord the Augustus. Another, found in Cumberland, has, *numini imperatoris Alexandri Augusti*, to the divinity of the emperor Alexander the Augustus, referring to Alexander Severus, who held the empire from 222 to 235. In an inscription found at Hexham, in 1726, the emperor, supposed to be Commodus, is spoken of as, *præsentissimum numen dei*.

Numerous altars have been found dedicated to Fortune, who seems to have been a popular deity among the towns of Roman Britain. We have one on the line of the wall of Antoninus, in Scotland, dedicated conjointly by detachments of the second and sixth legions. An altar, dedicated to the same goddess by a centurion of the sixth legion, occurs at Chesterholm (*Vindolana*), in Northumberland. A lady, whose father belonged to the second legion, dedicated an altar to Fortune, at the headquarters of the sixth legion at Eburacum (*York*). This monument, which may still be seen in the York museum, has the inscription:—

DEAE	To the goddess
FORTVNAE	Fortune,
SOSIA	Sosia
IVNCINA	Juncina,
F ANTONI	daughter of Antonius
ISAVRICI	Isauricus,
LEG AVG	of the Augustan legion.

An altar at Netherby was dedicated by the Spaniards, *deæ sanctæ Fortunæ*, to the sacred goddess Fortune. On an altar at Whelp Castle, in Westmoreland, she is reverenced as *Fortuna servatrix*. One at Manchester was dedicated, *Fortunæ conservatrici*; and on several altars the goddess is worshipped as *Fortuna redux*. An altar at Chester was dedicated conjointly to Fortuna redux, Æsculapius, and Salus. One found at Chesterholm (*Vindolana*), was dedicated, *fortunæ populi Romani*, to the fortune of the Roman people. But the most interesting of all the inscriptions to this goddess is one found at Bowes in Yorkshire (*Lavatræ*), which was raised by the celebrated pro-prætor, or governor of Britain, Virius Lupus:—

DEAE FORTVNAE	To the goddess Fortune,
VIRIVS LVPVS	Virius Lupus,
LEG AVG PR PR	legate of Augustus, proprætor,
BALINEVM VI	the bath, by force
IGNIS EXVST	of fire burnt,
VM COH I THR	of the first cohort of the
ACVM REST	Thracians, restored,
ITVIT CVRAN	under the care
TE VAL FRON	of Valerius Fronto,
TONE PRAEF	præfect
EQ ALAE VETTO	of the wing of horse of Vettones.

Victory was no less favourite a deity with the Romans in Britain than Fortune. A large sculptured figure of this goddess has been found at Housesteads in Northumberland (*Borcovicus*). An altar at Rough Castle in Scotland was dedicated to Victory by the Nervii. Another, at Ribchester in Lancashire (*Coccium*), was dedicated to Mars and Victory. A sculptured figure of Victory at Cambeck-fort in Cumberland bore the inscription VICTORIAE AVG, to victory of Augustus; and the same words occur in the dedicatory inscription of an altar found at Hexham. At Benwell (*Condercum*), an inscribed slab, probably belonging to a temple, was found with the following dedicatory inscription, in a label supported on each side by a winged figure :—

VICTORIAE	To Victory
... GG NN PR	of our two Augusti (*this*) made
N S SENECIO	the nephew of Socius Senecio
N COS FELIX	the consul, Felix,
ALAE I ASTO	of the first wing of the Asturians
... M PRAE	præfect.

At Castlesteads, in Cumberland, was found an altar dedicated DISCIPVLINAE AVG, to the discipline of the Augustus. This is an inscription which is found on several of the Roman imperial coins. Virtues or moral principles were deified in the same manner. We have seen before (p. 233) the god Bonus Eventus commemorated in the tesselated pavement of a Roman villa; at Binchester in Durham a mutilated altar was found with an imperfect inscription, to Mars and Bonus Eventus, by a tribune of the first cohort of Cartovians (?) :—

. . . . . .	. . . . . .
TRIB COHOR I	tribune of the first cohort
CARTOV	of Cartov
MARTI VICTORI	to Mars the victor,
GENIO LOCI	to the genius of the place,
ET BONO	and to good
EVENTVI	event.

An altar at Caerleon was dedicated to Fortune and Bonus Eventus. An inscription was found at Elsdon in Northumberland, near the Watling Street, which Horsley reads as follows :—

BONO GENERIS	To the good of the
HVMAN IMPE	human race,
RANTE CALPVR	by order of Calpur-
NIO AGRICOLA	nius Agricola,
AVG PR PR POSVIT	the proprætor of Augustus (*this*) placed
AC DEDICAVIT	and dedicated,
C A ACILIVS	Caius Aulus Acilius.

Calpurnius Agricola was proprætor of Britain under Antoninus, and the inscription was probably the dedication of the temple, but I am not aware of any other instance in which the good of the human race was deified. Not less singular is an inscribed altar found at Risingham (*Habitancum*) to a goddess who is supposed to be the personification of the tertian ague :—

DEAE TER	To the goddess
TIANAE SA	Tertian
CRVM AEL	sacred, Ælius
TIMOTHEA P	Timothea placed it,
V S LL M	performing a vow most willingly and dutifully.

At Carvoran a small altar was found, dedicated DEAE EPONAE—to the goddess Epona, who presided over mules and stables; the favourite deity of the gay jockey in Juvenal (*Sat.* viii. 155),—

> Interea dum lanatas torvumque juvencum
> More Numæ cædit Jovis ante altaria, jurat
> Solam Eponam et facies olida ad præsepia pictas.

Some of the dedicators, not content with invoking one deity, endeavoured to include them all under one invocation. Thus a præfect of the Dalmatian cohort at Ellenborough, dedicated an altar collectively to the gods and goddesses, *diis deabusque*. Another altar found at Chesters (*Cilurnum*), was dedicated to Apollo 'and all the deities,' *deo Apollini et omnibus numinibus*. There has been found also in the neighbourhood of Hadrian's wall an altar inscribed, *deabus omnibus*, to all the goddesses.

We now come to a class of divinities which have a peculiar interest in connection with the early history of our island, the deities of the auxiliary races who formed so important an element of its population. Among these we must place, first, a class of deities commonly known by the title of the *deæ matres*. Altars and inscriptions to these deities are very numerous in Belgic Gaul and Germany, and more especially along the banks of the Rhine, where they are often called *matronæ* instead of *matres*, and they seem to have belonged to the Teutonic race. Not more than one altar to these deities has, I believe, been found in Italy, and we do not trace them in the classic writers. When the *deæ matres* are figured on the altars or other monuments, they are always represented as three females, seated, with baskets or bowls of fruit on their knees, which were probably emblematical of the plenty which they were believed to distribute to mankind. In the accompanying representation of the upper part of an altar preserved in the museum at Cologne, the group of the three goddesses has suffered less injury than is usually the case with such monuments.

We are fortunately enabled in this instance to identify the

people to whom these deities belonged, for it is an interesting fact that the reverence for the three goddesses who presided over the woods and fields, pre-arranged the fates of individuals,

The Deæ Matres, from the altar at Cologne.

and dispensed the blessings of Providence to mankind, may be traced down to a comparatively late period both in Germany and England. Among the slight and contemptuous notices of Germanic paganism by the Christian writers of the earlier ages after the conversion of the Teutonic tribes, we find allusions to the conjoined images of three deities, but not sufficiently explicit to allow us to identify them completely with those which remain on the Roman altars. When, in the sixth century, Columbanus and St Gall arrived at Bregenz (*Brigantium*), in Switzerland, they found that the people there paid adoration to *three images* placed together against the wall of their temple.* Probably this was a monument of the *deæ matres* in their original country. But it is among the popular

---

* *Tres ergo imagines æreas et deauratas superstitiosa gentilitas ibi colebat.*—Anon. *Vit. S. Gal.*—Repererunt autem in templo *tres imagines* æreas deauratas parieti affixas, quas populus .... adorabat.—*Walafrid Strabo, Vit. S. Gal.*

superstitions that we shall find the most distinct allusion to the three personages, who are looked upon often as three wood-nymphs, and who are characterized by the same appellations, of *dominæ, matronæ, dames, bonnes dames,* &c., which we find on the Roman monuments.*

They are sometimes regarded as the three Fates—the *Norni* of the north, the *wælcyrian* of the Anglo-Saxons (the weird sisters, transformed in Shakespeare into three witches), disposing of the fates of individuals, and dealing out life and death. But they are also found distributing rewards and punishments, giving wealth and prosperity, and conferring fruitfulness. They are the three fairies, who are often introduced in the fairy legends of a later period, with these same characteristics. In a story of the Italian Pentamerone, *tre fate* (three fairies) are described as residing at the bottom of a rocky dell, and as conferring gifts upon children who went down into it. In the collection of superstitions condemned by Burchard, bishop of Worms, who died in 1024, we are told that the German women of his time had the custom, at certain times of the year, of spreading tables in their houses with meat and drink, and laying *three knives,* that if the *three sisters* should come (whom Burchard interprets as being equivalent to the Roman Parcæ), they might partake of their hospitality.† These were the later fairy women who visited people's houses by night, and whose benevolence was thus conciliated. In the older legends, the fairies are most commonly three in number. In later German tales, we have sometimes three females occupied in spinning, described as hateful old women; sometimes they are old women, but not engaged in this occupation; in another story, they are two young women sitting spinning, and a third, the wicked one, bound below. In one instance, on a Roman altar, the middle figure seems to be bound. Instances of most of these will be found in the *Kinder-Märchen,* and in the *Deutsche Sagen,* of the Grimms. It may be observed that the Norni and the wælcyrian were represented sitting and spinning. When Fridlaf went to

---

* It was a feeling of dread in the popular superstition of the middle ages not to call such beings by their particular names; and the same sentiment exists still in Ireland, and even in some remote parts of England, where the peasantry dare not call the elves and fairies by any other name than the respectful title of *the good people, the ladies,* &c.

† Fecisti ut quædam mulieres in quibusdam temporibus anni facere solent, ut in domo sua mensam præparares et tuos cibos et potum cum tribus cultellis supra mensam poneres, ut si venissent tres illæ sorores. quas antiqua posteritas et antiqua stultitia Parcas nominavit, ibi reficerentur.

consult the oracle of the fates, he saw, within the temple, *three seats*, occupied by *three nymphs*,* each of whom conferred a gift upon his son Olaf, two of them giving good gifts and the third an evil one.

At the beginning of the eighth century, according to a pious legend, a Worcestershire swine-herd, forcing his way through the dense thickets of the forests which then covered that part of the island, in search of a stray swine, came suddenly to a fair open lawn, in the midst of which he saw *three* beautiful maidens, clad in heavenly garments, and singing sweetly, one being superior to the others; (we have here the distinction constantly observed in the traditionary legends between two of the goddesses and the third;) he told his story to the bishop, Egwin, who accompanied him to the spot, and was also favoured with the vision. Egwin *decided* at once that it was the Virgin Mary, accompanied by two angels; and he built on the spot a monastery, which was afterwards famous by the name of Evesham.† The vision is represented on the old abbey seal. In all probability the site of Evesham had been a spot dedicated by the unconverted Saxons to the worship of the three goddesses, and Egwin had seized the popular legend to consecrate it for a Christian establishment.

A Latin poet of Winchester, the monk Wolstan, who lived in the middle of the tenth century, has left us a singular story relating to the three nymphs who presided over that district, and whom, differing in this from Egwin, but agreeing with the generality of ecclesiastical writers when they handled the popular superstitions, he has blackened both in person and character. A citizen of Winchester one day went out to visit his farm, and returning somewhat late towards his home, near the little stream which passes by the city, he was stopped by two dark women in a state of nudity—

---

* Mos erat antiquis super futuris liberorum eventibus Parcarum oracula consultare. Quo ritu Fridlevus Olavi filii fortunam exploraturus, nuncupatis solenniter votis, deorum ædes precabundus accedit, ubi introspecto sacello *ternas sedes totidem nymphis* occupari cognoscit. Quarum prima indulgentioris animi liberalem puero formam, uberemque humani favoris copiam erogabat. Eidem secunda beneficii loco liberalitatis excellentiam condonavit. Tertia vero protervioris ingenii invidentiorisque studii fœmina sororum indulgentiorem aspernata consensum, ideoque earum donis officere cupiens, futuris pueri moribus parsimoniæ crimen affixit.—*Saxo Grammaticus*, lib. vi. p. 102.

† MS. Cotton, Nero E. I. fol. 26, v°, where the story is told by bishop Egwin himself.

> Nam prope præfatum solus dum pergeret amnem,
> Haud procul aspiciens furias videt ecce gemellas
> Ante suam faciem, nullo velamine tectas,
> Sed piceas totas obsceno et corpore nudas,
> Crinibus horrendas furvis et vultibus atras,
> Armatas gelido serpentinoque veneno.
> Quæ super extremam prædicti fluminis undam
> Ceu geminæ externis furium *sedere* sorores.
> Quæ mox ut coram sese properanter euntem
> Conspexere virum, surgunt, et cominus illi
> Occurrunt, et eum pariter hac voce salutant:
> 'Frater amande, veni; nostras adtende loquelas;
> Huc celer appropia, volumus quia pauca loquendo
> Verba referre tibi: tu stans ea protinus audi.'
> *Wolstani Mirac. S. Swithuni*, MS. Reg.
> 15 C. vii. fol. 74, v°.

The man, instead of paying due respect to the ladies by listening to them, ran away in a fright, and they pursued him, threatening vengeance for the disregard which he had shown to their commands—

> Cur, insane, fugis? quo, jam moriture, recurris?
> Non nos incolumis, miser, evasisse valebis,
> Sed *nobis spretis* horrenda pericla subibis.

He now gave himself up for lost, and his terror was increased when a third female, who had lain concealed on the hill, stopped his way.—It is not improbable that these nymphs haunted the deserted fortress of the pagans of old, and the barrow-covered downs which still overlook this ancient city, from which their worship had then been banished by the influence of the gospel.

> Tertia progreditur veniens *a vertice collis*,
> Terribilis vultu proceraque corpore vasto,
> Usa tamen niveo pictoque decenter amictu,
> Dissimilisque habitu vultuque prioribus extans.
> Hæc etenim latuit post collem fraude reperta,
> Propter iter per quod cupiit transire viator
> Quatinus hunc caperet, furvis si intactus abiret.

In her angry mood, the third nymph struck the inobedient mortal senseless to the ground, and then they disappeared in the waters of the river—

> Nec mora, cum furiis linquens abscessit in amnis
> Gurgite, præcipiti saliens ac præpete saltu.

The man gradually recovered his senses, but he found himself a cripple, and with difficulty crawled to the eastern gate of the city, which was not far distant.

Another Anglo-Latin poet, but who lived in the latter half of the twelfth century, Nigellus Wireker, has preserved in his *Speculum Stultorum*, a tale which furnishes a still more remarkable illustration of the character of the three goddesses when they had become mere personages of mediæval popular fable. Nigellus still compares them with the Latin *Parcæ*. The three sisters, he says, went out into the world to relieve men from their troubles and misfortunes—*

> Ibant *tres* hominum curas relevare *sorores*,
> Quas nos *fatales* dicimus esse *deas*.
> Unus erat cultus tribus his eademque voluntas,
> Naturæ vitiis ferre salutis opem ;
> Et quod avara minus dederat, vel prodiga multum,
> His emendandis plurima cura fuit.

As they went along, they found, under a shady bank, a beautiful maiden, of a noble family, and rich in the goods of the world, yet, in spite of all these advantages, she was weeping and lamenting. Two of the sisters proposed to relieve her of her grief, but the third opposed their desires, and gave them a short lecture on the ill uses some people make of prosperity.

> ' Venimus, ut nostis, nos tres invisere mundum,
> Ut ferremus opem, sed quibus esset opus.
> Non opus est isti, quia quam natura beavit
> In quantum potuit, et quibus ausa fuit,
> Cui genus et speciem formæ tribuit specialem,
> Debet id et nobis et satis esse sibi.
> Forsitan auxilium si præstaremus eidem,
> Posset de facili deteriora pati.'

They left the weeping damsel, and proceeded to a shady wood, where lay another maiden on a couch : she, like the former, was beautiful and intellectual, and, as it appears, like her, also rich ; but she was lame of her lower extremities, and, unable to walk, she had been brought thither to enjoy the green shade. She courteously addressed the three nymphs, and showed them the way to the most beautiful part of the wood, where a pleasant fountain gave rise to a clear stream. The two sisters now proposed to relieve the damsel of her infirmity, but the third again

---

* The extracts from this poem, taken from an old printed edition, are compared with a copy in MS. Harl., No. 2422.

interposed, on the ground that the lady enjoyed advantages sufficient to overbalance this one inconvenience under which she laboured, and which were granted to few of those who are made perfect in their limbs. The nymphs again passed on, and, towards evening, were proceeding towards a town, where, not far outside the gates, they saw a rustic girl, who, unacquainted with the delicacies of more cultivated life, performed an act in public which shocked the two nymphs who had shown so much compassion on the former occasions. The third nymph drew the others back.

> Erubuere duæ, visum vultumque tegentes,
>   Vestibus objectis, arripuere fugam.
> Tertia subsistens, revocansque duas fugientes,
>   'Ut quid,' ait, ' fugitis?' siste, quæso, gradum.'

She shows them that they have here really an occasion of bettering the condition of one who enjoyed none of the advantages of fortune, and they determine to give her all sorts of riches, and to make her the lady of the town.

> ' Quodque nequit fieri, naturam degenerare
>   Nolumus, injustas non decet esse *deas*.
> Res et opes adjici possunt, extraque liniri
>   Naturæ salva proprietate sua.
> Nos igitur *quibus est super his collata potestas*,
>   Demus abundanti munera magna manu,
> Divitias et opes, census, fundos, et honores,
>   Prædia, montana, pascua, prata, greges;
> Urbis et istius dominam statuamus eandem,
>   Ut nihil in nostro munere desit ei.'

It may be observed that, from the Pœnitentiale of Baldwin bishop of Exeter, the contemporary of Nigellus Wireker, who composed this work for the use of his own diocese, it would appear then to have been the common practice in England, to lay the table with *three* knives (at night, of course) to conciliate these three personages, that they might confer good gifts on children born in the house.*

In a fabliau of the thirteenth century, of so indelicate a character that we cannot even mention its title, the three goddesses appear in the character of three beautiful fairies bathing

---

* Qui mensam præparavit, *cum tribus cultellis* in famulatum personarum, ut ibi nascentibus bona prædestinent.—*Liber Pœnitent. Baldw Iscani Episc.* MS. Cotton. Faustina A. viii. fol. 32, r°.

in a fountain, and are still endowed with the same quality of conferring benefits. There was a beautiful shady fountain in the midst of a fair meadow.

> En la fontaine se baignoient
> *Trois puceles* preuz et senées,
> Qui de biauté sembloient fées;
> Lor robes à tout lor chemises
> Orent desor un arbre mises.

A knight passing that way, very ungallantly seizes upon their dresses; but softened by their urgent entreaties, he restores them. In return for this courtesy, each of them confer a gift upon him: the gift of the first was that he should be received into favour wherever he went; that of the second was, that he should always be successful in his suits to the ladies; and the third, who here again appears as giving something totally contrary in character to that of her two companions, conferred a gift which cannot easily be named. In a manuscript in the British Museum (MS. Harl. No. 2253), there is a different version of this fabliau, which seems to be the one current in England at the beginning of the fourteenth century; in it the scene of the nymphs bathing is thus described:—

> Ce fust en esté quant la flour
> Verdist e dount bon odour,
> E les oylsels sunt chauntanz,
> E dement solas graunz.
> Come il ererent en une pleyne,
> Qe ert delées une fonteyne,
> Si virent un petit russhel,
> Auke petit, més molt bele;
> Yleque virent *treis damoiseles*,
> Sages, cortoises, e tresbeles,
> Qu'en la russhele se bagnerent,
> Se desdurent e solacerent.

Roman monuments commemorative of the *deæ matres* are by no means uncommon in Britain. The lower portion, much damaged, of a large sculpture of the deæ matres was found in digging to the Roman level in Hart-street, in the City of London, and a good and correct engraving of it is given in Mr Roach Smith's 'Collectanea Antiqua.' It is now in the Guildhall. Monuments of the three goddesses have been met with at Ancaster and at Lincoln. An altar dedicated to them has been found at York; and more northwardly, especially in the Wall districts, where the Teutonic race predominated, they are very common. At Binchester, in Durham (*Vinovium*), an altar was found dedicated DEAB MATRIB Q L O, which has been interpreted *deabus matribus quæ locum occupant*, to the deæ matres who occupy the place. This was in accordance with the popular belief of the Germans, that every place had its presiding

Altar found at Risingham (*Habitancum*).

mothers. An altar found at Risingham, and represented in the annexed cut, is dedicated to the transmarine mothers, by one who preferred the presiding deities of his native land:—

MATRIBV	To the mothers
S TRAMA	transmarine,
RINIS IVL	Julius Victor
VICTOR . V . S . L . M	performs a vow willingly and dutifully.

The cone, which is introduced on this altar, is generally considered to have been an aphrodisiac emblem, and the ornaments round it seem to indicate rather a late date—they resemble those on some of the late Roman pottery.

An altar found at Brougham, in Westmoreland, was dedicated to the transmarine mothers by a vexillation of Germans, which is a further indication of the country to which these deities belong:—

DEABVS MATRIBVS	To the goddess mothers
TRAMAR VEX GERMA	transmarine, the vexillation of
NORVM PRO SALVTE	Germans, for the safety
RP V S L M	of the state, perform a vow willingly and dutifully.

A broken tablet found near Old Penrith, in Cumberland, was inscribed by a vexillation, of which the name of the country is lost, to the transmarine mothers, in conjunction with the emperor, Alexander Severus, and his mother, Mammæa:—

> DEABVS MATRIBVS TRAMARINIS
> ET N IMP ALEXANDRI AVG ET IVL MAM
> MEAE MATR AVG N ET CASTRORVM TO
> TI .... DOMVI DIVINAE AE
> .... LATIO ....

An altar found at York, with a somewhat difficult inscription, has been interpreted as dedicated, *matribus Africis, Italicis, Gallicis*, to the mothers of Africa, Italy, and Gaul; but this interpretation is rather doubtful. Another inscription found in England goes still further; it is a dedication, *matribus omnium gentium*, to the mothers of all nations. An altar found at Stanwicks, in Cumberland, was dedicated to the domestic mothers, *matribus domesticis*. Another, found at Cramond, in Scotland, was dedicated by the first cohort of Tungrians to the mothers of Alaterva and of the fields, *matribus Alatervis et matribus campestribus*. A slab found at Benwell (*Condercum*) commemorates the erection of a temple to the mothers of the fields—*matribus campestribus*—by the prefect of the first wing of Asturians from Spain. Curiously enough, an altar found at the same place, and which had, perhaps, been placed in the temple, was dedicated to the three deities under the title of *lamiæ*, denoting their noxious qualities, LAMIIS TRIBVS. Other altars, dedicated *diis Matribus*, have been found at Ribchester, South Shields, &c.; and one at Binchester, with the inscription MATRIBVS SACRVM. Broken sculptures of the deæ matres have been found at Netherby, and at other places in the north.

Mr Roach Smith has given examples from Germany, of dedications *matronis Afliabus* (the one engraved in our cut on p. 339), *Mahlinehis, Hamavehis, Rumanchabus, matribus Treveris*, and a great many others, which are evidently named from places; and he remarks that 'it will be observed, that while in Germany the adjective always represents the locality, in those found in England it is merely a general epithet, as though the divinities addressed were those of strangers to the country.'

The worship of the German or other colonists, as far as it was derived from their native countries, seems to have been generally directed to those popular deities which were not known to them by distinctive names. The names of the gods appear to have been regarded as too sacred to be entrusted to every tongue. Hence, in almost all cases where we can trace the origin of the names of such deities on altars in Roman Britain, they are found to be derived from the names of places, from whence probably the dedicators derived their origin. There are, however, one or two exceptions of names of foreign deities, which, from their frequent recurrence, must have belonged to a national mythology. Thus, in the north of England, several altars have been found dedicated to a god whose name appears to have been Veteres, Vetires, or Vetiris. At Netherby, in Cumberland, which appears to have been occupied by Dacians, two altars have been found, one dedicated DEO VETIRI SANCTO, the other DEO MOGONTI VITIRES. At Lanchester, in the county of Durham, a small altar bore the simple inscription DEO VIT. Another found at Ebchester, in the same county, on one side of which was the figure of a boar, and on the other that of a toad, had the following inscription:—

DEO	To the god
VITIRI	Vitires
MAXIMV	Maximus
S V S	performs a vow.

Two altars of the same deity had been found at Benwell (*Condercum*), in both of which he is distinguished by the

Roman Altar found at Benwell (*Condercum*).

epithet *sanctus*, or holy; on the first, which is represented in the accompanying cut, the inscription is merely DEO VETRI SANCT, to the holy god Vetris. This altar has the usual figures of the implements of sacrifice. The other has the figure of a hog, with the inscription VITIRB V S, which is either *vitirbus*, or *vitirb votum solvit*. The station at Benwell was occupied by Asturians. An altar at Thirlwall Castle, also on Hadrian's wall, was dedicated DEO SANCTO VETERI. Three altars to this god have been found at Carvoran (*Magna*), which was occupied by Dalmatians. The inscription on one was:—

DEO	To the god
VITIRI	Vitires
MENI	Menius
DADA	Dada
V S L M	fulfilled a vow willingly and dutifully.

A second had an inscription, of which the commencement was DEO VITIRINE . . . , the two last letters of which may be the commencement of another word, though, I think, there has also been found an altar dedicated DEO VETERINO. The third of the Carvoran altars bore the inscription:—

DIRUS	To the rustic gods
VITIRIBVS	Vitires,
DECCIVS	Deccius
V . S . L . M	performs a vow willingly and dutifully.

I translate it according to a suggestion which has been made that the first line should be read, *diis rusticis*. On some other altars the name is in the plural, *veteribus*, and *veterubus*. As the altars were dedicated apparently by people of widely different countries, they give us no assistance in appropriating this deity. The word has been supposed to be identical with Vithris, one of the names of the northern Odin, the Woden of the Germans.

Another deity, whose altars are found chiefly in Cumberland, where they are numerous, was named Belatucadrus; by which name, without any epithet, a small altar found at Ellenborough was dedicated by Julius Civilis. Several other altars dedicated to this deity have been found at Netherby, Castlesteads, Burgh-on-the-Sands, Bankshead, and other places. In some instances, as in an altar found at Drumburgh, the deity is addressed by the epithet, DEO SANCTO BELATVCADRO. In some altars he is identified with Mars, as on one found at Plumpton

Wall, dedicated DEO MARTI BELATVCADRI ET NVMINIB AUGG. Several attempts have been made to derive the name from Hebrew, Welsh, or Irish, and it has been hastily taken for granted that this god was identical with the Phœnician Baal. Altars to Belatucadrus have been found at Kirby Thore, at Whelpcastle, and at Brougham, in Westmoreland. The one at Brougham was dedicated by a man named Andagus, which sounds like a Teutonic name.

In Cumberland also are found rather frequently altars dedicated to a god named Cocideus or Cocidius. Four were found at Bankshead and Howgill. One at Netherby—dedicated DEO SANCTO COCIDIO—gives him the same epithet which has been before applied to Vetires and Belatucadrus. He is also identified with Mars in an inscription at Lancaster, DEO SANCTO MARTI COCIDIO, as well as in another found at Old Wall, in Cumberland. The latter was dedicated by a soldier of the first cohort of Dacians. Of the two found at Bankshead, one was dedicated by a soldier of the second legion, the other by one of the sixth. An altar was found at Bewcastle dedicated SANCTO COCIDEO TAVRVNC. It is probable that somewhere in the neighbourhood of Bankshead or Howgill there has been a temple dedicated to this god, important enough to give its name to a small town. The anonymous geographer of Ravenna mentions a town in this part of the country which in the ordinary printed text is called Fanocedi, but one of the manuscripts gives Fanococidi, which is no doubt the correct reading. The place was called Fanum Cocidi, from the temple of the deity. An altar to Cocidius at Netherby was dedicated by a tribune of the first cohort of Nervians.

Another deity, whose altars are found chiefly in Cumberland, is called, in the dative case, Mogonti; perhaps the nominative was Mogontis. An altar at Netherby, mentioned above, seems to identify him with Vetires. The inscription at Old Penrith, DEO MOGTI, is perhaps only an abbreviation of the name. The name DEO MOVNTI, found on an altar at Plumpton Wall, is probably only another form. At Risingham, in Northumberland (*Habitancum*), an altar was found with the inscription:—

MOGONT CAD	To Mongontis Cad . . .
ET . N . D . N . AVG	and the deity of our lord the Augustus,
M . G . SECVNDINVS	Marcus Gaius Secundinus,
BF . COS . HABITA	a beneficiary of the consul, at
NCI PRIMA STA	the first station of Habitancum,
PRO SE ET SVIS POS	placed it for himself and his family.

Another altar in the same place was dedicated DEO MOVNO CAD. Horsley supposes that *Cad* refers to the Caledonian tribe of the Gadeni, which I think is at least very doubtful. It appears that a cohort of Vangiones from Belgic Gaul was established here.

A considerable number of names of gods are found only once, and were, there can be little doubt, taken from the names of places. Thus an altar discovered recently at York was dedicated to a god named Arciaconus, probably from the town of Arciaca, in Gaul:*—

DEO	To the god
ARCIACON	Arciaconus,
ET N . AVG SI	and to the divinity of the Augustus,
MAT VITALIS	Simatius Vitalis
ORD V . S. M	.... performs a vow dutifully.

A goddess Ancasta is mentioned on an altar found at Bittern, in Hampshire, (*Clausentum*):—

DEAE	To the goddess
ANCA	Ancas-
STAE G	ta,
EMINV	Geminus
S MANTI	Mantius
V S L M	performs a vow willingly and dutifully.

At Birrens, in Scotland, is a dedication to a goddess Brigantia, with a winged figure of the deity, holding a spear in her right hand, and a globe in the left. It was supposed that this was the deity of the country of the Brigantes, but I am not aware that this country was ever called Brigantia, and it is not probable that the conqueror would worship the deity of a vanquished tribe. I feel more inclined to suppose the name was taken from Brigantium, in Switzerland, a town which occupied the site of the modern Bregentz. An altar found at Chester was dedicated DEAE NVMPHAE BRIG, which in this case would be 'to the nymph goddess of Brigantium.'

An altar dedicated DEO CEAIIO, to a deity named Ceajius, was found at Drumburgh, in Cumberland. One found at

---

* It has been remarked that in other provinces of the empire we find deities characterised by similar appellations. Thus we have among the inscribed altars found in the country on the Rhine, one dedicated 'Deae Bibracte,' a name perhaps taken from the town of Bibracte, in Roman Britain.

Gretabridge, in Yorkshire, was dedicated DEAE NYMPHAE ELAVNAE, to the nymph goddess of Elauna. An altar found at Plumpton Wall, in Cumberland, gave us the name of a god called Gadunus. One found at Thirlwall, on the wall of Hadrian, was dedicated to a *dea Hammia*, who is supposed by Hodgson to have been named from Hamah, on the Orontes. Perhaps, however, this goddess may have been named from the Hamii, a tribe from the banks of the Elbe, who are found stationed in this part of Britain. A goddess named Harimella —DEAE HARIMELLAE—is mentioned in an inscription found at Birrens, in Scotland. An inscription, DEO HERCVLENTI, occurs at Ribchester; and one to a goddess called Jalona is said to have been found at the same place. An altar at Armthwaite, in Cumberland, presented the following inscription to a god Maponus, dedicated by Germans :—

DEO	To the god
MAPONO	Maponus,
ET N AVG	and to the divinity of the Augustus,
DVRIO	Durio
ET RAMI	and Rami
ET TRVPO	and Trupo
ET LVRIO	and Lario,
GERMA	Germans,
NI V S L M	performed a vow willingly and dutifully.

Another altar inscribed to this deity was found at Hexham. An altar found at Elsdon, in Northumberland, is dedicated to a god Matunus—DEO MATVNO. A goddess named on an altar found at Birrens, in Scotland, *dea Ricagm* . . ., is shown by the inscription to have belonged to the *Beda pagus*, in Germany. Mr Roach Smith, who first pointed out this fact, has also suggested that a title given to Neptune in an inscription on an altar found in the north of England, *Neptuno Sarabo sino*, may be explained as referring to the Saravus, now the Sarr, a tributary of the Moselle, commemorated in the lines of Ausonius :—

> Tuque per obliqui fauces vexate Saravi,
> Qua bis terna fremunt scopulosis ostia pilis.

A *dea Setlocenia* is mentioned in an altar found at Ellenborough, in Cumberland. At Ilkey, in Yorkshire (*Olicana*), was found an altar dedicated to Verbeia—VERBEIAE SACRVM. Lastly, a goddess called Viradesthi appears on the altar at Birrens, dedicated by a Tungrian soldier:—

DEAE VIRADES	To the goddess Viradesthi
THI PAGVS CON	Pagus Condustris,
DVSTRIS MILI	a soldier in
IN COH II. TUN	the second cohort of Tungrians,
GR SVB SIVO	under Sivus
AVSPICE PR	Auspex,
AEFE	the præfect.

Such is a general view of the character of the religious monuments of the Roman period found in Britain. It cannot but excite our astonishment that among such an immense number of altars and inscriptions of temples, and with so many hundreds of Roman sepulchres and graves as have been opened in this country, we find not a single trace of the religion of the Gospel. We must bear in mind, moreover, that a large proportion of these monuments belonged to a late period of the Roman occupation; in many of the inscriptions relating to temples, the building is said to have been rebuilt, after having fallen into ruin through its antiquity—*vetustate collapsum*; and the examination of more than one of the more magnificent villas has proved that they were erected on the site of an older villa, which had probably been taken down for the same reason. We seem driven by these circumstances to the unavoidable conclusion that Christianity was not established in Roman Britain, although it is a conclusion totally at variance with the preconceived notions into which we have been led by the ecclesiastical historians.

The accounts of the supposed establishment of Christianity in our island at this early period may be divided into three classes. First, we have a few allusions to Britain in the earlier Christian writers, which must evidently be taken as little better than flourishes of rhetoric. Britain was the western extremity of the known world, and when the zealous preacher wished to impress on his hearers or readers the widely extended success of the gospel, he would tell them that it extended from India to Britain, without considering much whether he was literally correct in saying that there were Christians in either of these two extremes. We must probably consider in this light certain passages in Tertullian, Origen, Jerome, and others. In the second class we must place the statements of certain ecclesiastical writers who lived at no great length of time after the Roman period. In the year 314, the emperor Constantine called the first ecclesiastical council, at Arles, to settle a dispute among the African bishops; a list of the clergy who attended has been preserved, and is printed in the Collections of Councils, but I am not aware that it reposes upon any good authority; in it are said to have come from Britain, Eborius, bishop of Eburacum (York); Restitutus, bishop of London; Adelfius, bishop of *Colonia Londinensium;* Sacerdos the priest; and Arminius the deacon. I confess that the list looks to me extremely suspicious, much like the invention of a later period. In the year 360, under the emperor Constantius, a council was called at Ariminum (*Rimini*), in Italy, on account of the Arian controversy, and it is said to have been attended by four hundred bishops. The prelates assembled on this occasion were to be supported at the public expense, but we are told by the ecclesiastical historian, Sulpicius Severus, who wrote about forty years afterwards, 'that this seemed unbecoming to the bishops of Aquitaine, Gaul, and Britain, and they chose rather to live at their own charge, than at the public expense. Three only from Britain, on account of their poverty, made use of the public provision; for, though the other bishops offered to make a subscription for them, they thought it more becoming to be indebted to the public purse, than to be a burthen upon individuals.' If this account be true, and three bishops really went from Britain, they were perhaps only missionaries, whose converts were too few and too poor to be able to support them.*

A third class of authorities is much less valuable, and far more extravagant. When the popes began to claim a sovereign power, they were anxious to make it appear that the whole of the western empire had been converted at an early period, and had been dependent on the Roman see. For this purpose, legendary stories were invented which will not bear criticism. Such were the stories of Joseph of Arimathea and St Paul, who were each said to have planted Christianity in Britain not long after the death of Christ. It need hardly be stated that there is no authority for either of these legends. According to a legend existing in the time of Bede, Lucius, king of the Britons, in the year 156, wrote to the pope Eleutherius,

---

* It seems to me that the three names of British bishops pretended to have been at the council of Arles, had been made to answer to the three bishops mentioned by Sulpicius Severus. I think it has not been yet satisfactorily ascertained when the name *Britanni* was first applied to the people of the country now called Bretagne.

'beseeching him to issue a mandate that he might be made a Christian; and afterwards he obtained the object of his pious petition, and the Britons preserved immaculate and sound, in peace and tranquillity, the faith which they had received, until the reign of the emperor Diocletian.' There are anachronisms in this story which have furnished matter for much discussion; but the whole is quite as inconsistent with history, and with what we know of the state of the island, as with chronology. The story of king Lucius can be regarded as nothing more than a Romish fable. The pretended persecution in Britain under Diocletian is a kind of sequel to the history of king Lucius. A persecution of the Christians is not likely to have taken place under the orders of the tolerant Constantius, who was governor of Britain when the persecution of Diocletian commenced, and who became emperor two years later, and in another year left his title to his son Constantine. The outline of the legend of St Alban was probably an invention of the sixth century, at the latter end of which his name is mentioned by the poet Fortunatus, who enumerates him among the blessed martyrs,—

Albanum egregium fœcunda Britannia profert.

In the 'Biographia Britannica Literaria' (Anglo-Saxon period), I have pointed out, I think, substantial reasons for doubting the authenticity of the work attributed to Gildas, on which chiefly our notions of the establishment of Christianity in Roman Britain are founded; and the more I examine this book, the more I am convinced of the correctness of the views I there stated. If the authority of such writers be worth anything, we must take it for granted that at least after the age of Constantine, Roman Britain was a Christian country; that it was filled with churches, clergy, and bishops, and, in fact, that paganism had been abolished throughout the land. We should imagine that the invaders, under whom the Roman power fell, found nothing but Christian altars to overthrow, and temples of Christ to demolish. It is hardly necessary to point out how utterly at variance such a statement is with the result of antiquarian researches. I have stated that not a trace of Christianity is found among the innumerable religious and sepulchral monuments of the Roman period found in Britain.* One

---

* In considering questions of this kind we should avoid, as much as possible, conjectures and suppositions, and accept nothing but absolute facts. Writers have at times taken for granted that certain modes of interments, or forms of ornament, indicated the sepulchres of followers of

solitary memorial of the religion of Christ has, however, been found, and that under very remarkable circumstances. On the principal tesselated pavement in the Roman villa at Frampton in Dorsetshire, the Christian monogram (the X and P) is found in the midst of figures and emblems, all of which are purely Pagan. Lysons, who published an engraving of this pavement, attempted to explain this singular anomaly, by supposing that the monogram of Christ had been added at a later period by a Christian, who had become possessed of the old Pagan house. But there seems to have been no appearance in the work of the pavement that it had been a subsequent insertion, and it must be agreed that a Christian of this period was not likely to be so tolerant of heathenism, as to place a Christian emblem among pictures and even inscriptions relating to that profane mythology on which he was taught to look with horror, and which he could not for a moment understand. I am inclined to think it more probable that the beautiful Roman villa at Frampton had belonged to some wealthy proprietor who possessed a taste for literature and philosophy, and with a tolerant spirit which led him to seek to surround himself with the memorials of all systems, he had adopted among the rest that which he might learn from some of the imperial coins to be the emblem of Christ. Jesus, in his eyes, might stand on the same footing as Socrates or Pythagoras.

We can understand, without difficulty, when we consider that this distant province was, from its insular position, far more independent of the central influence of the empire than other parts, why the new faith was slow in penetrating to it, and was not readily adopted. No doubt, among the recruits who were sent to the Roman troops, and the strangers who visited the island as merchants, or settlers, there must have been individuals who had embraced the truths of the Gospel. But we must bear in mind also, that the population of Britain, during the later period of the Roman power, seems to have been recruited more and more from the Pagan tribes of Germany and the North.

the gospel. Thus some have supposed that burial of the body without cremation was an evidence of Christianity, which certainly is not the case. Others have insisted that the presence of a wreath, or palm-branch, among the ornaments of sepulchral inscription, is a proof that it stood over the body of a Christian. Before, however, we can take this for granted, we must be satisfied that such an ornament could not be employed on a Pagan monument.

CHAPTER XI.

Modes of Sepulture in Roman Britain—Cremation and Urn-Burial—Modes of Interment—Burial of the Body entire—Sarcophagi—Coffins of Baked Clay, Lead, and Wood—Barrows—Sepulchral Chambers—Inscriptions, and their Sentiments—Various Articles deposited with the Dead—Fulgor Divom.

THE burial customs of a people are closely allied to its religious belief; but the settlers in Roman Britain appear to have adopted exclusively the Roman forms of sepulture. We learn from the ancient writers that it was the earlier practice of the Romans to bury the body of their dead entire, and that it was not till the time of the dictator Sylla that the custom of burning the dead was established. From this time either usage continued to be adopted, at the will of the individual, or of the family of the deceased; but in the second century of the Christian era the older practice is said to have become again more fashionable than that of cremation, and from this time it gradually superseded it. We find that both modes of burial were used indiscriminately in Roman Britain, and it is probable that the different peoples who composed the Roman population adopted that practice which was most agreeable to their own prejudices. The practice of burning the dead and burying the ashes in urns seems, however, to have predominated.

The earliest code of the Roman laws, that of the Twelve Tables, prohibited the burial or burning of the dead within the city, and it was only in rare instances that this prohibition was evaded or transgressed. The same law was acted upon in the towns of the provinces. A sepulchral interment, consisting of a skeleton laid in a tomb of Roman tiles, was found a few years ago in Green Street, in the very heart of the city of London; it formed an exception to the general rule in Roman Britain, where, as in Italy, the cemetery was always placed outside the town, usually by the side of the roads which led from the principal gates. In the country we generally find the burial-places in the immediate neighbourhood of the villa or of the hamlet.

When a Roman had breathed his last, his body was laid out and washed, and a small coin was placed in his mouth, which it was supposed he would require to pay his passage in Charon's boat. If the corpse was to be burnt, it was carried on the day of the funeral in solemn procession to the funeral pile, which was raised in a place set apart for the purpose, called the *ustrinum*. The pile, called *rogus*, or *pyra*, was built of the most inflammable wood, differing in size according to the rank or wealth of the individual; and when the body had been placed upon it, the whole was ignited by the relations of the deceased. Perfumes and spirituous liquids were often poured over it; and objects of different kinds, which had belonged to the individual when alive, were thrown into the flames. When the whole was consumed, and the fire extinguished, wine was scattered over the ashes, after which the nearest relatives gathered what remained of the bones and the cinders of the dead, and placed them in an urn, in which they were committed to the grave. The site of the *ustrinum* has been traced, or supposed to be traced, in the neighbourhood of several towns in Roman Britain. A Roman cemetery, found at Litlington, near Royston, is described in the twenty-sixth volume of the 'Archæologia;' it formed a square of nearly four hundred feet, and the wall or boundary was distinctly traced. At two of the corners, where there was no trace of interments, the original level of the ground was covered with a great quantity of ashes, which, no doubt, in each place, marked the site of the *ustrinum*, or place set apart for burning the dead. I believe the site of the *ustrinum* has also been discovered outside the walls of the Roman town of Isurium, at Aldborough, in Yorkshire. We are told by Herodian that, on the death of Severus at Eburacum, his sons caused his body to be burnt, and placed the ashes with aromatics in an urn of alabaster, which they carried with them to Rome. Persons of rank were burnt with greater ceremonies than were observed on ordinary occasions, and on a spot chosen for the purpose (*bustum*) instead of the ordinary *ustrinum*. A large barrow, about twenty feet high, and about two hundred feet in circumference, stands on the side of a hill in the parish of Snodland in Kent. In 1844, a trench was cut through the middle of the mound, and it was discovered that it stood on a level and smooth floor cut in the side of the hill, and covered with a thin layer of wood-ashes. All doubt that these were the remains of an immense funeral pile were set at rest by the circumstance, that numbers of very long nails were scattered about among the ashes. As far as the excavations were carried, there were no traces of a sepulchral deposit; so that, perhaps, this was the scene of the last ceremonial of a Roman of distinguished family, whose ashes had been gathered into an urn and carried to Italy, to be deposited in the tomb of his kindred, while the mound was raised as a memorial over the spot where he had been burnt.

Sepulchral Urn and Leaden Case from Wroxeter.

The cinerary urns found in the cemeteries in Britain are generally plain, large (often holding as much as two gallons), of a hard dark-coloured pottery, and of the form represented in the two large vessels in the back-ground of the cut on the next page. The other figures in the same cut are some of the varieties of urns which have been found containing bones and ashes. The cut here given in the margin represents a singularly formed sepulchral urn, with a leaden case in which it was closed; it was found in the cemetery of Uriconium (*Wroxeter*), and is now preserved in the Museum at Shrewsbury. In some instances, where the regular sepulchral urn perhaps could not be obtained, vessels which were made for domestic purposes have been used as sepulchral urns. Sometimes the ashes are deposited in glass jars, which are usually of the forms represented in the first two figures of our group on p. 283. Among the ashes we often find the coin, the offering to Charon; and sometimes fragments of different articles which have been burnt with the body. One of the small unguent bottles, usually but erroneously called lachrymatories, is often found within the urn.

Sometimes the cinerary urn, with its contents, was placed

merely in a hole in the ground, and covered with a tile or flat stone. We cannot tell in such cases what sort of memorial,

Roman Sepulchral Urns.

if any, was placed above-ground, as everything of this kind has been long cleared away. Perhaps each was covered with a small mound of earth. But when we open a regular Roman cemetery, we usually find the cinerary urn surrounded by a group of vessels of different descriptions, which perhaps held wine, aromatics, and other such articles. Among these are often elegant cups and pateræ of the red Samian ware. In the cemetery of the Kentish Durobrivæ (*Rochester*), the groups consisted generally of three or four vessels; at Litlington they varied in number from three to five. They have been found similarly grouped in other places. In many cases traces of the decayed material seem to prove that each group of urns had been enclosed in a chest of wood, but they were usually covered above with a large tile or flat stone. The chest, or grave, was itself often formed of tiles or stones, instead of wood; a tile was laid flat for the floor, one long tile formed each side of the chest, and a shorter one the end, and another large tile formed the cover. Such sepulchral chests are frequently found on the site of the Roman cemeteries at Colchester. In one, opened a few years ago, which was fifteen inches long

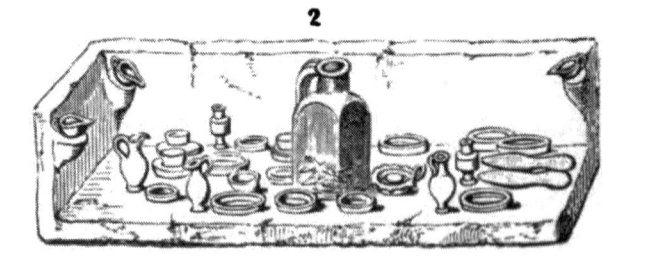

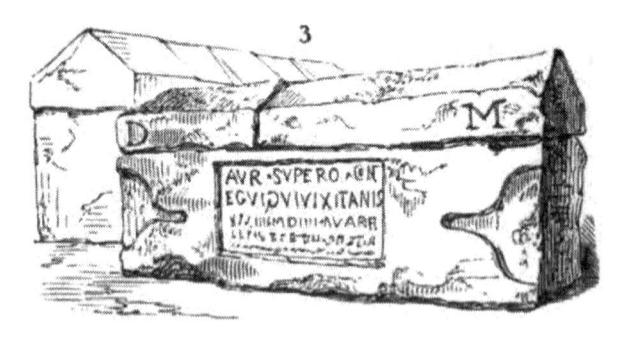

Roman Tombs.

and twelve wide, an urn was found in the middle, lying on its side, containing bones, and beside it were three small vessels, which had probably been used for ointments, balsams, and other funeral offerings. Another similar chest of tiles, in the same locality, contained two earthenware *ampullæ*, or bottles, an urn with burnt bones, and a lamp; the space between the vessels was filled with a sandy earth. The largest group of sepulchral vessels found in this cemetery consisted of fifteen, comprising two large and two small earthen bottles, six pateræ, three small urn-shaped pots, a terra cotta lamp, a lachrymatory, and the fragments of a large urn, no doubt the one which had contained the bones or ashes. A group of twelve vessels comprised an urn with calcined bones, one large ampulla and three small ones, two pateræ of Samian ware, an earthen lamp, three small urn-shaped pots, and a bottle of blue glass with a long straight handle. We are told that, from the scorched appearance of some of the vessels, it appeared that both of these last-mentioned deposits had been placed on the live embers of the fire of the funeral piles of the persons at whose obsequies they had been used. The practice of enclosing or covering the sepulchral deposits with tiles appears to have been so general, that the word *tegula*, a tile, was often used to signify a tomb. The reader will at once call to mind the lines of Ovid:—

> Est honor et tumulis; animas placate paternas,
> Parvaque in extinctas munera ferte pyras.
> Parva petunt manes; pietas pro divite grata est
> Munere; non avidos Styx habet ima deos.
> *Tegula* projectis satis est velata coronis,
> Et sparsæ fruges, parcaque mica salis.

It appears from these lines that it was the custom for the relatives to place on the tile, which covered the sepulchral deposit, garlands, fruits, and salt.

At York, graves have been found made of tiles, in a very peculiar arrangement, which is represented in the upper figure in the accompanying plate, taken from one which is still preserved in its original form in the museum of that city. It was found in the February of 1833, at the distance of about a mile from York, on the north-west side of the Roman road from York (*Eburacum*) to Tadcaster (*Calcaria*). It was formed of ten roof-tiles, each one foot seven inches long, one foot three inches and a half broad, and an inch and a quarter in thickness. Four of these tiles were placed on each side, and one at each end, with a row of ridge-tiles on the top. Each tile bore the impress, LEG VI VI (*legio sexta victrix*, the sixth legion victorious). No urn or vessel of any kind was found under these tiles; but there was a layer of the remains of a funeral pile, consisting of charcoal and bones, about six inches thick, mixed with iron nails. Such was not the case with another similar tomb, dug up at a short distance without the city walls, in 1768. It was formed in the same manner, of three tiles on each side, covered where they joined each other by ridge-tiles, and with ridge-tiles on the top. Within had been deposited several urns, containing ashes and earth, standing on a flat-tiled pavement. One of them was nearly entire, but the others were more or less broken. A coin of Vespasian and another of Domitian were picked up near the tomb. On each tile was the inscription LEG IX HISP (*legio nona Hispanica*, the ninth legion, the Spanish). Tombs exactly similar to these have been found at Strasbourg on the Rhine (*Argentoratum*), erected over soldiers of the eighth legion, which was stationed there. One of them is represented in an engraving in the tenth volume of the 'Histoire de l'Académie des Inscriptions.' Each tile in the Strasbourg tomb was stamped with the words LEG VIII AVG (*legio octava Augusta*, the eighth legion, the Augustan).

Sepulchral chests made of stone are much more rare in Roman burial-places than those formed of tiles. One of the most remarkable was that found at Avisford in Sussex, in 1817, which is represented in the middle figure (No. 2) in our plate. Avisford is in the immediate neighbourhood of the Roman road leading from Regnum to the station called in the Itinerary, Ad Decimum. It appears to have been a chest formed out of a solid stone, and covered with a flat slab or lid. In the middle was a large square vase of fine green glass, like those already alluded to, containing calcined bones. Around it were arranged on the floor of the chest, three elegantly-shaped earthen vases with handles, several pateræ, a pair of sandals studded with numerous little hexagonal brass nails fancifully arranged, three lamps placed on supporting projections of the stone, an oval dish and handle escalloped round the edge, containing a transparent agate of the form and size of a pigeon's egg, and a small double-handled glass bottle placed in one of the pateræ. Lamps are frequently found in Roman sepulchres, and popular superstition has given rise to stories which represent them as being discovered still burning in ancient sepulchral vaults. This notion is so absurd, that we cannot but wonder how it ever gained credit: but they were probably burning when placed in the grave. Among other inscriptions relating to this custom, Gruter has published the following, which, it will be seen, was intended to form three lines in verse:—

HAVE · SEPTIMIA	Adieu, Septimia;
SIT · TIBI · TERRA · LEVIS	May the earth lie light upon you!
QVISQVE · HVIC · TVMVLO	Whoever on this tomb
POSVIT · ARDENTE · LVCERNAM	has placed a lamp burning,
ILLIVS · CINERES	may his ashes
AVREA · TERRA · TEGAT	a golden soil cover!

Instances occur of more singular contrivances for producing the sepulchral chest, or tomb. In a Roman cemetery at Cirencester was found a stone which had been cut into the shape of a short cylindrical column; this had been sawn through the middle, and in the centre of the lower half a cell was cut to contain the urn, which was enclosed by joining the two parts of the column together. This probably had stood aboveground. Several instances have been met with in which an amphora has been used for a tomb; the upper part, or neck, having been sawn or broken off, the cinerary urn, with the other vessels and articles usually deposited with the urns, were placed inside; and the neck was then rejoined to the body of the amphora, and the whole buried in the ground. An instance of this mode of interment was found at Colchester in 1844. The upper part of a large globular amphora, of a pale red colour, had been sawn off, and replaced after the different articles were deposited inside. These articles were a cinerary urn, with a lid, represented in front of our group of sepulchral urns on p. 360, filled with calcined bones, a lachrymatory of pale green glass, a small earthen lamp, and another lamp of a finer clay, a number of iron nails, and a coin of second brass with the head of Faustina Junior. One or two instances have occurred in which, instead of the calcined bones or ashes being placed in an urn, the sepulchral chest was partly filled with a loose heap of ashes. One of the tombs at York described above furnishes an example of this practice. An instance of one of the small rectangular cists of tiles, thus filled with ashes, has occurred, I think, at Colchester. We may perhaps explain this, by supposing that, in consequence of some accident, the ashes of the deceased had been so mixed with those of the funeral pile, that it was not possible to separate them, and that therefore the relations had gathered all the ashes near where the body must have lain, and thrown them into the tomb.

When the body was buried entire, it was interred in several

different manners. The skeleton, as now found, appears often as though it had been merely committed to the earth; but as it is in most instances accompanied with a quantity of large iron nails, it is probable that in all these cases the body was placed in a chest or coffin of wood. In some places, and especially at York, massive chests, or sarcophagi, of stone, have been found, which appear from their forms and inscriptions to have stood above-ground. The accompanying cut represents a sarcophagus found at London, and somewhat remarkable

Sarcophagus found in London.

for its ornaments. In the centre of the front side is a sunken medallion containing a youthful bust, no doubt intended as a portrait of the person interred in it. The back was quite plain, as though it had stood against a wall or other building. It contained a skeleton. Several fine examples of these sarcophagi may be seen in the museum of the Philosophical Society at York; and examples are given, from the plates to Mr Wellbeloved's 'Eburacum,' in the third or lower group in our plate at p. 362. Such sarcophagi have been frequently found at York, and they present a very peculiar mode of sepulture. After the body had been laid, apparently in full dress (those hitherto discovered have generally contained the remains of ladies), on its back at the bottom of the sarcophagus, liquid lime was poured in until the body was covered. This, becoming hard, has preserved, to a certain degree, an impression of the form of the body, of which the skeleton is often found entire. Of one of these sarcophagi, which was found by the side of the road from Heslington to Grimston, and is now in the York museum, Mr Wellbeloved gives the following description:—'On removing the lid, the coffin appeared to be about half filled with lime, excepting the place in which the head had lain. The lime having been very carefully taken out, the lower surface presented a distinct impression of a human body, over which, with the exception of the face, the lime had been poured in a liquid state: the body having been first covered with a cloth, the texture of which is still clearly to be seen in the impression on the lime. The feet had been crossed, and covered with shoes or sandals, having nails in the soles; the marks of which on the lime were distinctly visible, and several of the nails themselves were found in the coffin, in a very corroded state. A very small portion of the bones remained; sufficient, however, to indicate that they were those of a female, and, according to the opinion of a very eminent surgeon, that she had been buried in a state of pregnancy. All the teeth, except one, were found, with the enamel undecayed. Just above the left shoulder a small portion of a gold ring appeared, and the lime surrounding it having been carefully scraped away, the remnants of a lady's ornaments were brought to light, consisting of fragments of large jet rings, two earrings of fine gold, two bracelets, several brass or copper rings, one of which resembled a cog-wheel, about two inches in diameter, three finger-rings, one of them of jet, of a modern pattern, and two necklaces. One of the necklaces was formed of glass beads, yellow and green; the other of small beads of coral, intermixed with smaller beads of blue glass, strung, in both cases, on very slender twisted silver wire.' In a coffin of this description more recently found at York, and also deposited in the museum, the lime bears the impression of a female with a small child laid in her lap, and the colour, a rich purple, as well as the texture of the cloth which covered her, is distinctly visible in the impression. One of these coffins, found at York, had contained the body of a large man, whose skull was cloven as though by the blow of an axe or sword. The lids of these stone sarcophagi were often fastened to the lower part, or chest, with iron cramps.

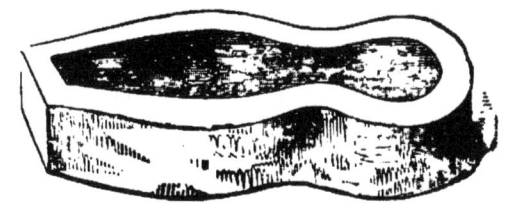

Clay Coffin found at Aldborough (*Isurium*).

Sarcophagi, for the reception of the body when not burnt,

were sometimes made of baked clay, either in one piece with a lid, or in several pieces, so formed as to fit together. Several examples of such clay coffins have been found at York, and at the neighbouring town of Aldborough; in the latter place they are found somewhat resembling violin-cases in form. The accompanying example of these clay coffins from Aldborough is shaped like the sole of a shoe.

A description of coffin found more frequently in this country was formed of lead. Many examples of these leaden coffins have been met with in the Roman cemeteries at Colchester, York, London, and elsewhere. When these coffins are ornamented, the ornaments consist almost always of scallop shells and bead-mouldings, sometimes interspersed with small circles. The annexed cut represents one of these coffins dug up, a few

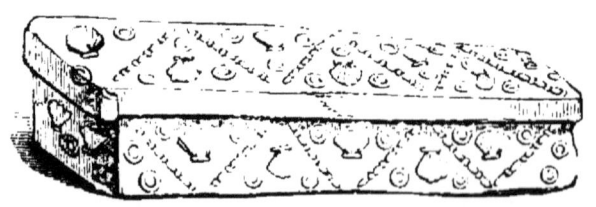

Leaden Coffin from Colchester (*Camulodunum*).

years ago, in a Roman cemetery near Colchester. It was four feet three inches in length, fifteen inches wide at the head, and eleven at the feet, and nine and a half inches deep exclusive of the lid. It was formed of a sheet of lead cast in a mould, and bent upwards on each side, with square pieces, soldered at the top and bottom, to form the ends. The lid was formed by being notched at the head and feet, and then bent down at the edges and soldered, to lap over the coffin. The entire exterior was tastefully ornamented with scallop shells, rings, or circles, and a beaded pattern. All that is known of its contents is that, like the stone coffins found at York, it was partly filled with lime. The coffin itself is now in the private museum of Mr Bateman, of Yolgrave, in Derbyshire; another leaden coffin, found at Colchester about the same time, was sold for old lead, and melted down; but from a sketch which was taken of it before it was destroyed, it appears to have been still more elaborately ornamented, chiefly with the same scallop shells, rings, and bead moulding. Morant records the discovery of a similar leaden coffin at Colchester, in the March of the year

1750. It contained what was called a quantity of dust, perhaps lime, but very little of the bones remained. 'There lay near the head two bracelets of jet, one plain, the other scalloped, and a very small and slender one of brass wrought, and four bodkins (? hair-pins) of jet. The coffin was cast, or wrought, all over with lozenges, in each of which was an escallop shell. Near it was found an urn, holding about a pint, in which were two coins of large brass, one of Antoninus Pius, and the other of Alexander Severus.'

Several Roman leaden coffins have been found at different times on the sites of the cemeteries of Roman London. One, dug up in Mansell-street, Whitechapel, in 1843, had contained the body of a child, and resembled in construction and ornament the one engraved above. In the immediate vicinity, and on the same level, were found skeletons, urns with burnt bones, and various articles, such as are usually found in Roman cemeteries. In a leaden coffin dug up at Stratford-le-Bow, in 1844, the remains of a skeleton were found embedded in lime. In Weever's 'Funeral Monuments,' published in 1631, we are informed that, 'within the parish of Stepney in Middlesex, in Ratcliffe-field, where they take ballast for ships, about some fourteen or fifteen years ago, there was found two monuments, the one of stone, wherein was the bones of a man, the other a chest of lead, the upper part being garnished with scallop shells, and a crolister border. At the head of the coffin and the foot, there were two jars, of a three-feet length, standing, and on the sides a number of bottles of glistening red earth, some painted, and many great vials of glass, some six, some eight square, having a whitish liquor within them. Within the chest was the body of a woman, as the chirurgeons judged by the skull. On either side of her there were two sceptres of ivory, eighteen inches long, and on her breast a little figure of Cupid, neatly cut in white stone. And amongst the bones two painted pieces of jet, with round heads in form of nails, three inches long. It seemeth (saith Sir Robert Cotton, from whom I had this relation) these bodies were buried about the years of our Lord 239; besides there were found divers coins of Pupienus, Gordian, and the emperors of that time; and thus one may conjecture by her ornaments, that this last body should be some prince's or proprietor's wife here in Britaine in the time of the Roman government.' It need hardly be remarked that, to the modern antiquary, Sir Robert Cotton's conjectures seem very ridiculous. Stepney is known to be the site of one of the cemeteries of Roman London. A similar coffin was found towards the close of the last century in a Roman burial-place in Battersea-fields; it was ornamented with scallop shells and cord moulding, and contained a skeleton embedded in lime. Another, found in 1811, in the Kent-road, near the Asylum for the Deaf and Dumb, is engraved in the 'Archæologia.' It was bordered and divided into five compartments by the band and fillet ornament. In the uppermost compartment were two figures of Minerva, counterparts of each other; the three intermediate compartments were diagonally crossed by the same ornament, and the lowest compartment contained two scallop shells. The remains of a skeleton were found also in this coffin.

The leaden coffins found at York are supposed, by Mr Wellbeloved, to have been encased in wood. Wooden coffins appear to have been extensively used in Roman cemeteries in this country. They are traced by the marks of decayed wood, and more especially by the presence of large long nails which had been used to attach the planks of the coffin together. These nails are found in great quantities in the Roman cemeteries at Colchester, and elsewhere on similar sites. In a cemetery in Bourne Park, near Canterbury, several skeletons were found, lying near each other, and accompanied with such nails, from six to nine inches long. Four or six nails are said to have been found with each skeleton, near the shoulders, hands, and feet, which are the positions into which they would naturally have fallen from the coffin as it decayed. From the nature of the ground, here, as in many other places under similar circumstances, after such a great length of time, the decay of the wood had been so complete, that no further trace of it was perceived; and it was rather hastily supposed that the presence of these nails proved that the skeletons were the remains of crucified martyrs.

Wooden coffins of another fashion are found in this country, chiefly towards the north, and they seem to have been peculiar to the part of our island represented in modern times by East Yorkshire. These are rudely constructed out of the trunks of large trees. In the year 1834 a large tumulus on the cliffs near the village of Gristhorpe, some six miles from Scarborough, was opened, and was found to contain what was at first taken for a mere rough log of wood; but, on further examination, it proved to be a wooden coffin formed of the rough trunk of an old oak tree, the external bark of which was still in good preservation. It had been roughly hewn at the extremities, split, and then hollowed internally to receive the body. My cut will give the best idea of the appearance of this primitive coffin, which was much damaged in its removal from the tumulus. The trunk of the tree had been split tolerably equally for the

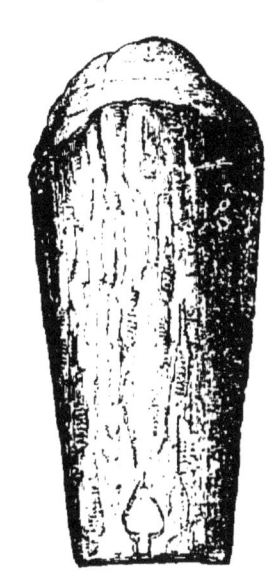

Wooden Coffin found at Gristhorpe.

coffin and its cover were of nearly the same dimensions. The only attempt at ornament was what was taken for a rude figure of the human face cut in the bark at one end of the lid, which appeared to have been held to the coffin only by the uneven fracture of the wood corresponding on each part. At the bottom of the coffin, near the centre, a hole, three inches long and one wide, had been cut through the wood, apparently for the purpose of carrying off the aqueous matter arising from the decomposition of the body. This coffin was about seven feet long by three broad. When first opened it was nearly full of water; but on this being cleared away, a perfect and well-preserved skeleton presented itself, which was laid on its right side, with its head to the south. The body, the skeleton of which measured six feet two inches, having been too long for the hollow of the coffin, which was only five feet four inches long, the legs had been necessarily doubled up. Several small articles were found in this coffin with the skeleton, which are represented in the following cut. These were three pieces

.... (figs 1, 2, and 6); a well-executed ornament, ... a large stud or button, apparently of horn, which

Articles found in the Gristhorpe Coffin.

had every appearance of having been formed by the lathe (fig. 6); a pin of the same material, which lay on the breast, and had apparently been employed to secure a skin, in which the body had evidently been enveloped (fig. 7); an article of wood, also formed like a pin, but having what would be its point rounded and flattened on one side to about half its length (fig. 8); fragments of an ornamental ring of similar material to the stud, and supposed, from its large size, to have been used for fastening some part of the dress (fig. 3); the remains of a small basket of wicker-work, the bottom of which had been formed of bark, and a flat bronze dagger or knife (fig. 5). None of these articles give us much assistance in fixing the age of this curious interment, except the dagger, and that is not very certain. Chipped flints are found very frequently in Roman interments, both in this country and on the continent; and I have also found them in Saxon graves; but the dagger belongs to a type of which several examples have been found in the Wiltshire barrows, as well as in similar interments in other parts of England, which, from all the circumstances connected with them, we should be led to ascribe to a remote date, probably to the earlier period of the Roman occupation of our island. A quantity of vegetable substance was also found in the coffin, which was rather hastily conjectured to be the remains of mistletoe. The coffin, after being deposited in its grave, had been covered over with large oaken branches. It may be added that, above this, the tumulus was formed first of a layer of clay, followed by a layer of loose stones, another layer of clay, and a second layer of loose stones, and the whole was finally covered with soil, which had doubtless collected upon this tumulus during the long period since it was raised. This coffin was placed in the Museum at Scarborough. I was subsequently informed that a somewhat similar coffin had been found at Beverley Parks, near Beverley, in digging a drain there in 1848. It is represented in the accompanying cut. A slab, which had been cut or split from the rest, formed a lid; but it had been fastened to the chest by means of four oaken thrindles, or pegs, about the size of the spokes of a common

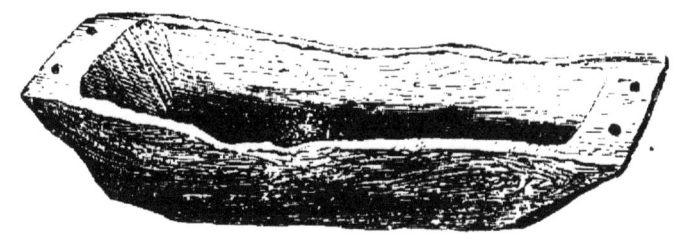

Wooden Coffin found at Beverley.

ladder, and the ends of the coffin had been bevelled off, so as to leave less of the substance of the wood where the holes for the pegs were drilled through. This coffin was nearly eight feet and a half long externally, and seven feet and a half internally; and it was four feet two inches in width. Some fragments of human bones were found in it, but not calcined. The next coffin of this description, which is represented in our cut, was found in a barrow on an elevated spot on the bank of

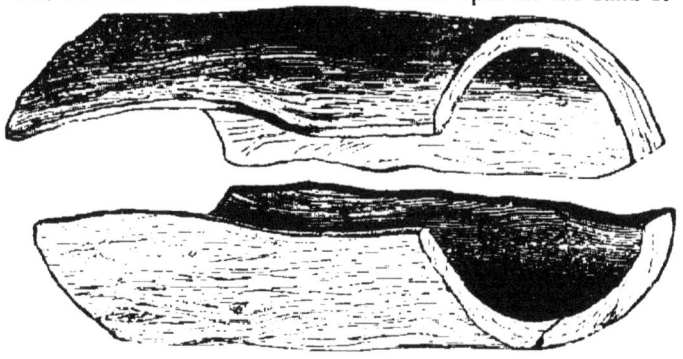

Wooden Coffin found near Great Driffield.

a stream in the neighbourhood of Great Driffield, near a place called Sunderlandwick. Two large and thick branches of trees had here, as at Gristhorpe, been placed over the coffin before the mound was filled in. The coffin, in this instance, was, like the others, hollowed from the solid trunk of an oak tree, but it differed from them in having no ends; and, though it came in two pieces when taken out of the earth (or rather in three, for the lid broke in two), it was supposed by those who found it that it had been originally one entire piece, a sort of large wooden tube, or pipe, formed by hollowing through the heart of the timber. This coffin was about six feet in length and four in breadth, the disproportion in breadth being accounted for by the circumstance that it was intended to contain three bodies, two of which were laid with their heads turned one way, and the other turned in the contrary direction. The coffin, in consequence of the ends being unprotected, was filled with clay and sand, which had become mixed with the human remains, and the bones were in so fragile a condition through decay that they fell to pieces when disturbed, and admitted of no careful examination. A quantity of ashes lay mixed with the surrounding soil, which are described as still retaining a smell of burning. The coffin in this instance lay east and west. From the remains that were found, it would seem that these coffins belonged to a date not later than the close of the Roman period.

I repeat these observations on the wooden coffins found in East Yorkshire from my Essays on Archæological Subjects, published in the year 1861.* At that time the local board of health at Selby was carrying on excavations for sewerage, &c. in that town, which brought to light numerous ancient remains. While cutting through a piece of ground called the Church Hill, which was understood to be the site of the ancient parish church, destroyed when the old abbey church was made parochial, the workmen met with no less than fourteen of these wooden coffins, all made, like those I have been describing, out of the solid trunks of oak trees, which had been separated into two pieces in order to form a chest and lid, and had been scooped out to form a receptacle for the corpse. I was informed that these coffins were found near the surface of the ground, some of them at a depth of not more than eighteen inches, lying parallel to each other, in a direction nearly east

* See my Essays on Archæological Subjects, London, 1861, vol. i. p. 36 to p. 47.

and west. The annexed cut represents one of these coffins, the only one which had been examined with much care. It contained what was pronounced to be the body of a full-grown

Wooden Coffin found at Selby.

female. This coffin was six feet ten inches long; another, which lay near it, measured nearly eight feet. All the other similar coffins were found to contain the remains of human skeletons. It may be remarked that in this Selby coffin the upper part, or lid, was hollowed out in a corresponding manner to the lower part. The two parts of the same coffin were, in all the wooden coffins found at Selby, fastened together by oval wooden pegs driven down into the side, as in the Beverley coffin. When first discovered, the wood of the upper part was decayed and broken away, so as to expose the face of the skeleton, as here shown.

Although the wooden coffins found at Selby contained no articles by which their age was determined, we can have no doubt that they belonged to Christian interments, and that they were laid in regular juxtaposition in a churchyard. There are, however, circumstances connected with the barrows in the maritime district of Yorkshire to the south of Scarborough which would lead us to believe that most of them belong to the later Roman period, in which case we may more easily understand how a particular form of coffin then in use may have continued in use during the subsequent Anglo-Saxon period. I am not aware of the discovery of coffins of the same description in other parts of the island; and they seem to show, which would indeed be a curious fact, that a peculiar burial practice had continued to exist in the district of Eastern Yorkshire from a period dating as far back as the commencement of the Roman occupation of our island to probably a late Anglo-Saxon period.

In some cases, the sepulchral chest was expanded into a

spacious chamber. One found at York, in the time of Thoresby, is described by that antiquary as large enough to contain two or three corpses; it was carefully paved with bricks eight inches square and two inches thick, and covered with bricks two feet square. When discovered, it was found to be empty. Another sepulchral chamber, larger than this, was found, as Mr Wellbeloved informs us, 'by some workmen in the year 1807, when digging for the foundation of a house, near the Mount, without Micklegate-bar. It is a small room or vault, about four feet below the present surface, eight feet in length, five feet in breadth, and six feet in height; the roof being arched and formed of Roman tiles, each of about one foot square, and two and a half inches in thickness. In this vault was found a sarcophagus, of a single grit-stone, covered with a blue flag-stone, containing a skeleton, in remarkable preservation; arising, probably, from its being immersed in water, which had filtered through the earth; the head elevated by being placed on a step. At the north end of the vault there was an aperture, too small to have admitted the sarcophagus, and carelessly closed by large stones. On each side of the skull a small glass vessel, usually called a lachrymatory, was found, one of them perfect, the other broken. The sarcophagus was without an inscription. The other sides of the vault were not seen, except that through which the workmen broke, and by which visitors are now admitted to view this interesting sepulchral antiquity.' Perhaps, if the whole were uncovered, an inscription would be found on the outside of the building. A large sepulchral chamber of rather a different description, and containing a variety of amphoræ, pateræ, and other articles, was found in 1849, at Mount Bures, near Colchester.

Sepulchral chambers, like that found at York, no doubt stood above-ground, forming conspicuous objects by the side of the highway. We find in Britain very few traces of sepulchral buildings of this kind, because where they existed they were no doubt cleared away during the middle ages for their materials.

In some cases, particularly at a distance from large towns, the sepulchral chamber was inclosed in a mound of earth, or barrow. The mound of earth was a form of monument which belonged to an early age, and was perhaps adopted in the case of Romans who died in the provinces, as more durable than the sepulchre of stone—

Ergo instauramus Polydoro funus, et ingens
Aggeritur tumulo tellus.—*Virg. Æn.*, iii. 62.

ROMAN BARROWS.

The most remarkable Roman tumuli, or barrows, in Britain, are the group called the Bartlow hills, in the parish of Ashdon, on the northern border of Essex. They were opened a few years ago, and the different modes in which the internal tombs were constructed seemed to show that they were not all erected at the same time. In form they are all conical. The height of the largest is forty-five feet, and its diameter a hundred and forty-seven. Six others, which complete the group, are of somewhat smaller dimensions. When the largest barrow was opened, it was found that the sepulchral chamber in the centre had been constructed of wood; it contained a large glass vessel resembling the second figure in our group on p. 283; a bronze patera, with a reeded handle terminating in a ram's head; a bronze dish; a lamp, also of bronze; a beautiful bronze enamelled urn with handle; a folding stool or seat; and a pair of strigils. A large amphora, filled with earth, ashes, and fragments of bones, was placed outside this wooden chest. In the centre of one of the smaller Bartlow barrows was found a closed vault, built of brick, six feet three inches long, two feet three inches and a half wide, and about three feet high, standing north and south on a bed of chalk, about a foot below the natural surface. The covering was formed of flat tiles overlapping each other. When these were removed, the tomb was found to contain a large glass vessel, which is the first figure in our group just alluded to, and which contained bones and ashes; a small glass vessel of the same form, containing a dark-coloured fluid; and a vessel of wood, formed like a pail, with a handle at the side.

In these barrows the body had undergone the process of cremation, but in a very remarkable one, called Eastlow hill, at Rougham in Suffolk, opened by Professor Henslow, in the year 1844, the body of the deceased had been buried entire. The tomb in this case was a miniature Roman house, of strong masonry, with a roof peaked and tiled on the outside. It was built upon a platform, fifteen feet square, formed of a concrete of large flints and very hard mortar mixed with sand. The length of the tomb, or house, on the exterior, was twelve feet, and its width six feet and a half. The thickness of the walls was two feet, and their height at the sides the same; the height of the roof, from the ground to the ridge, was five feet. The interior was found to be a cylindrical vault. In the middle of the floor stood a leaden chest or coffin, six feet nine inches long, one foot five inches broad, and one foot four inches deep. It had been formed of a sheet or sheets of lead, by turning up the sides and ends, after cutting out the piece at the corners. The edges were soldered on the inside. The lid was a loose sheet of lead, turned in at the edges in the same way. Within this chest lay the skeleton, which was in a tolerably good state of preservation. The leaden chest appeared to have been enclosed in wood-work, for a great many nails, from two to twelve inches long, were found lying by its side, among a mass of decayed wood. A Roman coin was found within the leaden tomb— Professor Henslow seems to say in the mouth of the skeleton— the obolus to propitiate Charon. A little chamber at one end, outside the vault, appeared to have contained glass and other vessels, which were broken to pieces. This large tumulus was one of a group of four; the others had been opened in the previous year, and had presented the usual appearance of urns, &c., which characterise Roman sepulture.

The tomb at Eastlow lay north-east and south-west. That in the Bartlow hill stood north and south. The most common position of the skeletons in Roman cemeteries is east and west, the feet usually towards the east, but this is by no means always the case.

The Roman sepulchral inscriptions, found in this country, possess much interest. They are generally met with in the cemeteries near towns, and consist usually of a slab of stone, which appears to have been fixed in the ground like our common churchyard gravestones. At York, the inscriptions are found on the sides of some of the large stone sarcophagi. Some of the slabs appear by their form to have been placed against a larger sepulchre of masonry. The inscription is often surmounted by a sculptured figure, intended sometimes to represent the individual commemorated by it. The usual inscriptions are dedicated at the beginning to the gods of the shades, perhaps meaning to the shades of the departed, *diis manibus*, which is most frequently expressed merely by the two letters D.M.* The name of the deceased is then stated, with his age, and, if a soldier, the number of years he had served. This is usually followed by the name of the person who has raised the tomb. The age is often stated with great precision, as in the following simple memorial found on a sepulchral slab at Ellenborough in Cumberland :—

D M	To the gods of the shades.
IVL MARITIM	Julia Maritima
A VIX AN	lived twelve years,
XII. M. III D. XXII	three months, twenty-two days.

* At Carrawburgh, in Northumberland (*Procolitia*), was found an altar

CHAP. XI.] SEPULCHRAL INSCRIPTIONS. 379

Another common form of inscription, omitting sometimes the D. M. at the beginning, closed with the words, *hic situs est*, is placed, or laid, here. We may quote as an instance of this formula a rather well-known tombstone found, a few years ago, at Cirencester, and represented in the annexed cut. The

Tomb from Cirencester (*Corinium*).

figure above is one often met with on the monuments of soldiers in the Roman cavalry. The inscription must be read,—

RVFVS · SITA · EQVES · CHO VI
TRACVM · ANN · XL STIP XXII
HEREDES · EXS · TEST · F. CVRAVE
H S E

It may be translated, 'Rufus Sita, a horseman of the sixth

dedicated to the *dei manes*, with the inscription D. M. D. TRANQVILA SEVERA PRO SE ET SVIS V. S. L. M.

2 A

cohort of Thracians, aged forty years, served twenty-two years. His heirs, in accordance with his will, have caused this monument to be erected. He is laid here.' In a monument found at Caerleon, the formula is varied as follows:—

D M IVL IVLIANVS	To the gods of the shades, Julius Julianus,
MIL LEG II AVG STIP	a soldier of the second legion, the Augustan, served
XVIII ANNOR XL	eighteen years, aged forty,
HIC SITVS EST	is laid here,
CVRA AGENTE	by the care
AMANDA	of Amanda
CONIVGE	his wife.

A sepulchral monument, found at Ellenborough in Cumberland, begins with the words HIC EXSEGERE FATA, here have undergone their fates. We see in these inscriptions how cautiously a direct allusion to death is avoided. We have an exception to this remark in an inscription found of late years at Caerleon, in which one of the persons commemorated is said to have died in a war in Germany.

D M	To the gods of the shades.
TADA · VALLAVNIVS VIXIT	Tadia Vallaunius, who lived
ANN · LXV · ET TADIVS · EXVPERTVS	sixty-five years, and Tadius Exupertus,
FILIVS · VIXIT · ANN · XXXVII · DEFVN	her son, who lived thirty-seven years, and
TVS · EXPEDITIONE GERMANICA	died in the German expedition.
TADIA · EXVPERATA · FILIA	Tadia Exuperata, a daughter
MATRI · ET · FRATRI · PIISSIMA	to her mother and brother most attached,
SECVS TVMVLVM	near the tomb
PATRIS POSVIT	of her father placed this.

In another inscribed slab, found at Caerleon, the tomb is called a *monumentum*, and another phrase is used,—

D · M	To the gods of the shades.
IVLIA · VENERI	Julia Veneria,
A · AN · XXXIII	aged thirty-three years.
I · ALESAN · CON	Alexander, her husband
PIENTISSIMA	most attached,
ET · I · BELICIANVS	and Julius Belicianus,
F · MONIME	her son, this monument
F · C	caused to be made.

In a sepulchral inscription, given by Camden as found at Silchester, the tomb is dedicated *to the memory* of the deceased,—

MEMORIAE	To the memory
FL · VICTORI	of Flavia Victorina,

NAB · T · TAM	Titus Tamphilus
VICTOR	Victor,
CONIVNX	her husband,
POSVIT	placed this.

In some instances, as in an inscription at York, and another found at London, *memoria* is used for *monumentum*, and the phrase *memoriam posuit* is adopted in the sense of 'raised a monument.' An inscription found at Ribchester, in Lancashire, which has been often quoted, commenced with the words *his terris tegitur Aelia Matrona*, with this earth is covered Ælia Matrona. It was the custom among the Romans for men of family or wealth to build up their own sepulchres before they died, which was usually expressed in the inscription by the letters V. F. (*vivus fecit*), V. F. C. (*vivus faciendum curavit*), or V. S. P. (*vivus sibi posuit*). Inscriptions of this kind were placed on monuments of a more ostentatious character, which were raised by the road-side, near large towns. An inscription was found at York, commemorating one of the magistrates of the city, which, from the form of the stone, must have been built in the wall of a large sepulchre. The inscription has been given as follows:—

M VEREC DIOGENES IIIIIIVIR COL
EBOR IBIDEMQ MORT CIVES BITVRIX
CVBVS HAEC SIBI VIVVS FECIT

which may be translated, 'Marcus Verecundus Diogenes, sevir of the colonia of Eburacum, and who died there, a citizen of Biturix Cubus, caused these to be made for him during his lifetime.' Biturix Cubus, it appears, referred to the district of Avaricum in Gaul (*Bourges*), as the native country of Marcus Verecundus Diogenes.

Many of the Roman sepulchral inscriptions found in this country display feelings of the tenderest and most affectionate description. They are addressed to the deceased by near relatives, who apply to them loving epithets. Sometimes they are addressed from parents to a child. Thus a large sarcophagus found at York was made to receive the body of an infant, whose father was a soldier in the sixth legion. The inscription is—

D · M · SIMPLICIAE · FLORENTINE
ANIME INNOCENTISSIME
QVE · VIXIT · MENSES · DECEM
FELICIVS · SIMPLEX · PATER · FECIT
LEG · VI · V

'To the gods of the shades. To Simplicia Florentina, a most innocent thing, who lived ten months, her father, of the sixth legion, the victorious, made this.' A monument in the form of an altar was found at Chesters, in Northumberland (*Cilurnum*), with the inscription,—

D M S	Sacred to the gods of the shades.
FABIE HONOR	To Fabia Honorata,
ATE FABIVS HON	Fabius Honoratius,
ORATIVS TRIBVN	tribune
COH I VANGION	of the first cohort of Vangiones,
ET AVRELIA EGLI	and Aurelia Egliciane,
IANE FECER	made this
VNT FILIE D	to their daughter
VLCISSIME	most sweet.

A stone slab found at Bath, and which seems also to have been placed on a building, bore the following inscription:—

D M	To the gods of the shades.
SVCC · PETRONIAE VIX	To Succia Petronia, who lived
ANN · III · M · IIII · D · IX · V PETRO	three years, four months, nine days, Valerius
NIVLVS · ET TVICTIA SABINA	Petroniulus and Tuictia Sabina,
FIL · KAR · FEO	to their dearest daughter, made this.

Several other such inscriptions to children, chiefly to little girls, have been met with in this country, as well as others from children to their parents. A stone found at Great Chesters, in Northumberland, presented, under the rude sculpture of a female figure, the short and simple inscription,—

DIS M	To the gods of the shades.
PERVICAE FILIA F	To Pervica, her daughter made this.

On another, found at the same place, was an inscription from a sister to her brother,—

D M	To the gods of the shades.
AEL · MERCV	To Ælius Mercurialis,
RIALI CORNICVL	a trumpeter,
VACIA · SOROR	his sister Vacia
FECIT	made this.

A wife is often found raising the monument to her husband. The following inscription was found on a sepulchral slab at Stanwicks, in Cumberland:—

DIS MANIBV	To the gods of the shades
S MARCI TROIANI	Of Marcus Trojanus
AVOVSTINII TVM FA	Augustinius the tomb
CIENDVM CVRAVI	erected
T · AEL · AMMIL LVSIMA	Ælia Ammilla Lusima,
CONIVX KARISS	his most dear wife.

An inscription found on the line of the wall in Northumberland, also addressed by a wife to her deceased husband, a native of Pannonia, furnishes us with an undoubtedly Teutonic name; the inscription is imperfect:—

D · M	To the gods of the shades.
DAGVALD · MI	Dagvald, a soldier
PAN · VIXIT · A . . .	of Pannonia, lived years . . . .
. . . PVSINNA	. . . Pusinna, his wife,
XTITVL	placed this monument.

This last line is not very distinct in the original, but it appears to be part of *conjux titulum posuit*. Several examples have been found of affectionate addresses from a father to a wife and several children. A sepulchral monument at Old Penrith, given by Camden, bore the inscription:—

D M	To the gods of the shades.
AICETVOS MATER	Aicetuos, the mother,
VIXIT A XXXXV	lived forty-five years,
ET LATTIO FIL · VIX	and Lattio, the daughter, lived
A XII · LIMISIVS	twelve years. Limisius,
CONIV ET FILIAE	to a wife and daughter
PIENTISSIMIS	most affectionate,
POSVIT	placed this.

In an inscription on a broken stone, found in the Roman cemetery at Bulmore, near Caerleon, a deceased lady is apostrophised by her husband and three sons:—

D M	To the gods of the shades.
CAESORIA CORO	Caesoria Coroca,
CA V A XLVIII REM · ·	who lived forty-eight years.
S CONIVX · · · · S ET	Remus, her loving husband, and
MVNAT · · · LEST	Munatius, and Lestinus,
NVS E · · · · EONTI	and Leontius,
VS FECERVNT	her sons,
FILI EIVS	made this.

A slab found at Carvoran in Northumberland (*Magna*), bears the following affectionate inscription:—

D M	To the gods of the shades.
AVRE FAIAE	To Aurelia Faia,
D SALONAS	a native of Salona,
AVR MARCVS	Aurelius Marcus,
O OBSEQ CON	a centurion, out of affection
IVG · SANCTIS	for his most holy wife,
SIMAE QVAE VI	who lived
XIT ANNIS XXXIII	thirty-three years
SINE VLLA MACVLA	without any stain.

Gruter has recorded a Roman sepulchral inscription, by one Marcus Aurelius Paullus, *conjugi incomparabili, cum qua vixit annis xxvii, sine ulla querela*—to his incomparable wife, with whom he had lived twenty-seven years, without any dispute.

When there was no near relation left, the tomb was erected by the heirs to the property of the deceased, generally, it would appear, by direction of the will. Many of the sepulchral monuments in Britain were thus raised by the heirs. The following inscription, found at Ardoch, in Scotland, will serve for an example of the ordinary formula used under such circumstances:—

DIS MANIBVS	To the gods of the shades.
AMMONIVS DA	Ammonius Damionis,
MIONIS Ɔ COH	centurion of cohort
I HISPANORVM	the first of the Spaniards,
STIPENDIORVM	having served
XXVII HEREDES	twenty-seven years. His heirs
F C	caused this to be made.

In an inscription found at Ellenborough, in Cumberland, the sons of the deceased acted under the name of his heirs,*—

D M	To the gods of the shades
MORI REGIS	Of Morus Rex
FILII HEREDES	the sons, his heirs,
EIVS SVBSTITVE	substituted this.
RVNT VIX A LXX	He lived seventy years.

We have several instances of the desire among members of the same family to be buried beside each other. A soldier slain in Germany was brought to Isca (*Caerleon*) to be interred beside his father. A broken inscription in one of the stations along the wall of Hadrian commemorates a native of Galatia, whose father having, as it appears, died in Britain, the son, who died in his native country, wished on his death-bed to be carried into Britain to be laid in his father's grave.

.... IL SER	.... son of Servius,
QVI NANAT	who, born
GALATIA DEC	in Galatia,

---

* Horsley observes on this inscription, 'It was customary with the ancients to erect sepulchral monuments for themselves and families, while they were living; which might possibly be the case here, with respect to this Morus Rex. But the monument he built might have fallen to decay, or by some accident have been demolished, before his death, and his sons, upon his decease, have rebuilt it. The word *substituerunt* seems to intimate something like this, which signifies the putting of some person or thing in the room of another which was there before. So we say *substituere judicem*; and by the Roman law the usufructuary was obliged *substituere pecora*, or *arbores*, in the room of such as died. It would be very difficult to put any other meaning upon *substituerunt* in this inscription; for, to take it in the sense of *constituerunt*, is perhaps without example.'

RVIT GALA . . .	died in Galatia;
XIT ANN	he lived . . . . years;
MORITV	on his death-bed
DESIDER	he desired
RIS INT	in his father's tomb to be buried.*

It has been remarked that, to judge from the ages set forth in these sepulchral inscriptions, the Romans in Britain generally died young. The average age seems to be not much more than thirty. We find, however, one or two instances of longevity. A decurion, or municipal magistrate, of the city of Glevum (*Gloucester*), was buried at the fashionable watering-place of Aquæ Solis (*Bath*), who died at the age of eighty-six. Length of years had perhaps increased his attachment to life, and he went thither to seek new vigour from the medicinal waters of the place. From the form of the stone we may suppose that it was placed on the wall of a tomb of some magnitude. The following is all that remains of the inscription:—

DEC COLONIAE GLEV	Decurion of the colonia of Glevum;
VIXIT AN · LXXXVI	he lived eighty-six years.

One instance has occurred of an age still more patriarchal. In a cemetery at Bulmore, near Caerleon (*Isca*), one or two monuments connected with the same family were found. On one was the inscription:—

IVL · VALENS · VET	Julius Valens, a veteran
LEG · II · AVG · VIXIT	of the second legion, the Augustan, lived
ANNIS · C · IVL	a hundred years. Julia
SECVNDINA · CONIVNX	Secundina, his wife,
ET IVL MARTINVS · FILIVS	and Julius Martinus, his son,
F · C	caused this to be made.

Close by this stone, another was found with an inscription recording the death of the wife of this aged veteran, and raised by their son. The inscription furnishes us with another formula, *dis manibus et memoriæ*, of which we have an example in Gruter, found on the continent. It is interesting to find this identity of expression and sentiment in different parts of the Roman world. The inscription on the Caerleon monument runs as follows:—

* The translation of this inscription is made after the ingenious restoration of Mr Roach Smith, who (Collectanea, ii. p. 202) explains it, I believe correctly, as follows:— . . . *fi*LIus SERvii QVI NATus GALATIA DECuRVIT GALATIA *vi*XIT ANNOS . . . MORITVrus DESIDERavit patRIS IN Tumulo sepeliri. In the second line, NANAT appears to be an error of the stone-cutter for NAT.

D M ET	To the gods of the shades, and
MEMORIAE	to memory.
IVLIAE . SECVNDI	To Julia Secundina,
NAE . MATRI . PI	a most affectionate mother,
ISSIMAE . VIXIT . AN	who lived years
NIS . LXXV . C . IVL	seventy-five, Caius Julius
MARTINVS . FIL	Martinus, her son,
F . C	caused this to be made.

Few inscriptions have yet been found referring to persons of any rank in society, or to officials, except officers in the army though we have seen inscriptions commemorative of a decurion of Glevum and a sevir of Eburacum.

A lingering sentiment of attachment to the living caused the Romans to select for the sites of their tombs spots by the side of the high-roads. The inscription on the grave of a Roman named Lollius, quoted from Gruter, said that he was 'buried by the road-side, that they who pass by may say, Farewell, Lollius.' It was from this circumstance that the inscription is not unfrequently addressed to the way-faring traveller, with such phrases as *siste, viator* (stop, traveller); *aspice, viator* (look, traveller); or *cave, viator* (beware, traveller). They were, nevertheless, anxious to protect the last dwellings of the dead from neglect or disrespect, and warnings to those who might be inclined to offer indignities to the tombs are not unfrequently incorporated in the monumental inscription. It seems to have been considered necessary to tell people that they should not throw dirt or rubbish against the tombs, or treat them otherwise in an unseemly manner.* In Italy, it is sometimes expressly forbidden by the inscription to raise a funeral pile against a tomb—*ad hoc monumentum ustrinum applicare non licet.* Sometimes a notice was given that punishment awaited the intruder who should bury any other body in a sepulchre already occupied. Warnings of this kind belonged more properly, perhaps, to family sepulchres. A broken stone found at Watercrook, in Westmoreland, contained an inscription of which a few letters at the end of each line were wanting, and the last line was not distinctly legible—it appears, by the form of the stone, to have been placed against the wall of a large tomb:—

```
P . AEL . P . F SERG . BASS . . . . .
Q D LEG . XX VV . VIX . AN . . . . .
```

---

* Horsley gives an inscription in which a still greater profanation is spoken of—C . CAECILIVS . C . ET . O. L. FLORVS . VIXIT . ANNOS . XVI . ET MENSIBVS . VII . QVI . HIC . MIXERIT . AVT . CACARIT . HABEAT . DEOS . SVPEROS . ET . INFEROS . IRATOS.

```
ET . P . RIVATVS LIBE . ET . HERO . . . . .
M . LEG . VI . VIC . FEC . SI Q . . . . . .
SEPVLC . ALIVM MORT . . . . .
ERIT . INFER . F . D . D . N . N . . . . .
. . . . . . . . . . . . . . . . . . . . .
```

As filled up and explained by Horsley, it may be translated: 'Publius Ælius Bassus, the son of Publius, of the tribe Sergia, quæstor designatus of the twentieth legion, the valiant and victorious, who lived . . . . years, ... and Publius Rivatus, his freedman, and Hero . . . . a soldier of the sixth legion, the victorious, caused this to be made. If any one shall intrude another corpse into this sepulchre, he shall pay as a fine into the treasury of our lords.' . . . . . .

A superstition, deeply imprinted in the minds of the people, taught that articles of various kinds burnt or interred with the deceased would add to the comfort of the departed spirit in the world of shades. The dead were, therefore, clothed in their full dress, with their jewellery and personal ornaments, and they carried with them the coin or coins to pay their passage. They were often furnished with wine or provisions. The occupant of the tomb at Avisford, in Sussex, carried with him or her a pair of sandals nailed with bronze instead of iron. A mirror was found in a Roman grave at Colchester. In the sepulchral chest, in one of the Bartlow hills, a folding stool and strigils were found. Fictile vases and vessels of glass seem, in many instances, to have been interred as useful for domestic purposes. Amphoræ were added probably for a similar reason. Sometimes we meet even with culinary utensils. In one instance, an iron tripod, for placing over a fire, was found with a chain and pot-hooks in the middle. Almost the only articles not found in Roman graves are arms, and I am not aware that in any example yet known in Britain, a Roman was buried with his warlike weapons. It must also be remarked that Roman graves, rich in such articles as are mentioned above, are not very common.

Branches and garlands of box and palm, as well as of other trees or shrubs, appear to have been also deposited in the grave. Such objects were also sculptured on the grave-stones, and they were perhaps borrowed as emblems by the Christians from their heathen predecessors. It has been rather hastily supposed by one or two writers that the presence of such sculptures—garlands and branches of palm—proves that the tombstones on which they occur were raised over converts to the

faith of the gospel. Mr Gage (Rokewode), in his account of the opening of one of the Bartlow hills, published in the twenty-eighth volume of the Archæologia, has made the following remarks on the traces of vegetable substances found there:—
'In the observations made in 1832 upon the objects found in the brick *bustum*,' he says, 'some conjectures were offered on a dark incrustation seen upon the cinerary urn. A branch of yew, or other dark vegetable substance, was supposed to have been the origin of it. This receives confirmation from the actual finding, on the present occasion, of vegetable remains scattered in the tomb, and adhering to several of the objects. Leaves were found adhering to the bottom of the cinerary urn, from which it would appear that some had been thrown in before the urn was deposited; while round the handle of the lamp a wreath would seem to have been entwined. "These vegetable remains," remarks Mr Brown, F. R. S., who has had the kindness to examine them, "appear to consist of the epidermis of leaves and ultimate branches of box, the vascular part and parenchyma being in most cases entirely removed; I judge the leaves to belong to box (*buxus sempervirens*), from their insertion as indicated in the ramuli, from their outline, size, thickened margin, and arrangement and form of stomata, which in most cases, however, are removed, leaving round apertures of the form and size of the whole stoma." Professor Henslow informs the writer of this memoir, that a skeleton was lately found in or near Chesterford churchyard, together with a Roman vase, and that box-leaves lay loose in the soil near the skull and vase. Some of the leaves are in my possession, and they are similar to those found at Bartlow.' Mr Gage cites, in illustration of these discoveries, the beautiful epigram of Martial (i. 89), in which the box and the palm are connected with the last home of mortality.

> Alcime, quem raptum domino crescentibus annis
>   Labicana levi cespite velat humus,
> Accipe non Phario nutantia pondera saxo,
>   Quæ cineri vanus dat ruitura labor;
> Sed fragiles buxos et opacas palmitis umbras,
>   Quæque virent lacrymis roscida prata meis.
> Accipe, care puer, nostri monumenta laboris;
>   Hic tibi perpetuo tempore vivet honor.
> Cum mihi supremos Lachesis perneverit annos,
>   Non aliter cineres mando jacere meos.

It is, of course, to be supposed that the sepulchres which we have been describing belonged to the better orders of society.

The process of cremation was an expensive one, and it was probably this circumstance which gradually led to its abolition. People of the lower class of society were regarded contemptuously, and were thrown into trenches in the ground with little ceremony or respect. The public burial-grounds for the poor were called in Italy, *puticuli*, from *puteus*, a pit, on account of the unceremonious manner in which the dead were thrown into the shallow pits or trenches. The ground was not even looked upon as consecrated, and it was without difficulty turned to other purposes. A burial-ground of this kind, at the Esquiline gate of Rome, was given by Augustus to his favourite minister, Mæcenas, to be turned into a garden, and the change was celebrated by Horace:—

> Nunc licet Esquiliis habitare salubribus, atque
> Aggere in aprico spatiari ; quo modo tristes
> Albis informem spectabant ossibus humum.
> *Lib.* i., *Sat.* viii., *l.* 14.

We have not sufficient information to enable us to trace the gradual disappearance of the practice of cremation, but we are told by Macrobius,* who wrote at the beginning of the fifth century, that the custom of burning had been then so long discontinued, that it was only from books he could gather any information relating to it. Persons who had committed suicide were never allowed to be burnt, and the same prohibition extended to those who died in their infancy. Those who were struck dead by lightning were believed to have suffered under the special visitation of the gods, and they were interred as they died, and on the same spot, if it were not a place where it was unlawful to bury. On the continent, several Roman inscriptions have been found, commemorative of the effects of the 'lightning of the gods,' and perhaps marking the place where some unfortunate mortal has been thus launched into eternity. One at Florence bears the inscription FVLGVR DIVM ; a similar inscription found at Nîmes (*Nemausus*) has FVLGVR DIVOM ; another at Palermo (*Panormus*), FVLGVR CONDITVM ; and another at Oderzo on the Adriatic (*Opitergium*), DE CAELO TACTVM ET CONDITVM. We have here another interesting link between the manners of the Romans in Britain and in their native Italy. A little to the west of the ancient town of Hunnum (*Halton-Chesters*) on the wall of Hadrian, has been found

* 'Deinde, licet urendi corpora defunctorum usus nostro sæculo nullus sit, lectio tamen docet eo tempore quo igni dari honor mortuis habebatur,' &c.—*Macrob. Saturnal.*, lib. vii. c. 7.

a stone, represented in the annexed cut, with the identical inscription mentioned above, FVLGVR DIVOM. Perhaps one of the soldiers of the station here met his death from heaven.

Inscribed stone at Halton-Chesters (*Hunnum*).

CHAPTER XII.

Domestic Life among the Romans in Britain as Illustrated by their Remains—Dress and Personal Ornaments—the Toilette—the Household; Furniture and Utensils—Female Occupations—Cutlery—Styli—Scales—Ornamental Articles—Weapons, &c.

If the numerous articles belonging to the ordinary usages of life, which have been found on Roman sites in different parts of the country, were collected together and arranged, they would, no doubt, go far towards giving us a perfect picture of the manners of the population of Britain under the Romans. Unfortunately, in times back, great quantities have been lost, or destroyed after their discovery, and those which remain are scattered about, mostly in private hands, from the want of any really national museum in which to depose them. They uniformly give evidence to the fact that the civilization of Britain, during the whole of this period, was purely Roman, and that whatever races settled here under the banner of Rome, they accepted unreservedly its dress and manners as well as its language and laws.

The dress of the Romans appears not to have varied much in its general character until the later period of the empire. It was simple in its forms, and the principal distinction between the garments of classes and individuals consisted in the richness of the material and in the brilliance of the colours. The dress of the male sex continued to be composed of the tunic, worn next to the skin, and the toga, over it; though in later times it was not unusual to wear more than one tunic, and the pallium or mantle, a garment borrowed from the Greeks, was thrown over the toga, or rather substituted in its place. The tunic worn by men reached generally to the middle of the thighs, or not, at all events, below the knees. Females had a longer tunic reaching to the feet, and over it they wore the stola, reaching a little below the knees, instead of the toga, and over it the pallium, or mantle.* In the formation of these dresses there was not much 'tailoring;' they consisted of little more than pieces of cloth, linen, or silk, with fringes and borders, wrapped loosely round the body. Almost the only fastenings appear to have been fibulæ, or brooches, which, from the numbers that are continually found on all Roman sites, must have been used in great profusion. We scarcely ever meet with even the smallest collection of Roman antiquities, but a considerable proportion of it consists of fragments of fibulæ. The annexed cut represents the more usual forms of these articles, which

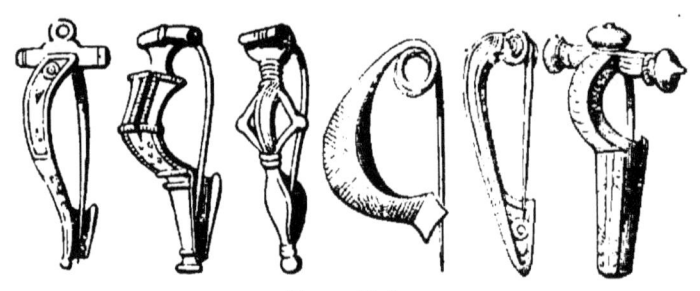

Roman fibulæ.

are sometimes more ornamental, but they always, with the exception of the circular brooches, follow these designs. The first on the left was found at Caerleon; the second, which is in my own possession, came from Boulogne; the third was found near Maidstone; the fourth, at Caerleon; the fifth, at Stroud in Kent; and the one to the extreme right, at Cirencester. The material is usually bronze, though Roman fibulæ in silver and gold have been found. A fibula of the form of the last to the right in our group, of a large size, and made of solid gold, was found at Odiham in Hampshire, in 1844. The round fibulæ appear, from figures in coins and pictures, to have been used for fastening the pallium over the shoulder. They are often more ornamental than the bow-shaped fibulæ, and are sometimes enamelled. Lysons has published an engraving of a beautiful circular fibula, in gold, with figures of griffons on one side, and bears on the other; it was found at Old Penrith, in Cumberland. Buttons are also found, sometimes elegantly

* For the forms of their articles of dress, the reader may refer to any of the general treatises on the history of costume, such as that by Mr Fairholt, which I would especially recommend.

ornamented, but the manner in which they were employed is not well known.

Bracelets (*armillæ*) for the wrists are also articles of common occurrence in bronze, silver, and gold. They consist generally of a simple narrow ring, seldom much ornamented, and often without any ornament at all. Roman rings, which are more frequently of gold, are so varied in form that it would not be possible to give any general description of them. They sometimes contain engraved stones, but these are more frequently found without their mounting. The frequency with which Roman engraved stones, or intaglios, are met with, show that they were very much in use in all parts of the empire. Roman ear-rings are usually in gold, though they sometimes occur in bronze; it would be as difficult to give a general description of them as of finger-rings. The beads of the Romans, which were mostly of glass, have already been described; they are found with various fittings and adjuncts, some of which were no doubt looked upon as amulets.

Among the articles of female ornament that occur in the greatest abundance are pins (*acus*), generally of bone or bronze, which were used for fastening the knot of the hair behind the head, and are represented as thus employed in ancient busts and statuettes. Those figured in the annexed cut are all of

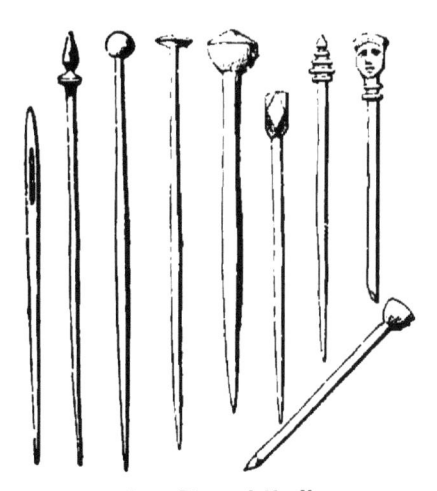

Bone Pins and Needle.

bone, and are represented half the size of the originals. They were in the museum of Mr Rolfe, of Sandwich, and are here taken from Mr Roach Smith's work on Richborough. Mr Smith's own museum presents a large and varied collection of such pins. They have sometimes large heads, and were elaborately ornamented, terminating, in some instances, in a bust, or in a figure. Some very curious Roman hair-pins, made of coloured glass, were found near Dorchester, in Dorsetshire, in 1850. Martial has left us a short epigram which illustrates the use of the hair-pin,—

Acus aurea.
Tenuia ne madidi violent bombycina crines;
Figat acus tortas sustineatque comas.
Epig. lib. xiv. 24.

An article of personal ornament, worn by men, the *torques*, *torquis*, or collar, must not be overlooked in speaking of the subject which now occupies our attention. The *torques* is said, by ancient writers, to have been originally used by the Persians in the east, and by the nations of northern and western Europe. Virgil describes it as worn by the Trojans, when they came to colonize Italy:—

Omnibus in morem tonsa coma pressa corona,
Cornea bina ferunt præfixo hastilia ferro;
Pars leves humero pharetras; it pectore summo
Flexilis obtorti per collum circulus auri.

It is first mentioned in Roman history in the year 360 B.C., when Manlius, having torn a torques of gold from the neck of a vanquished Gaul, placed it on his own, and received, from this circumstance, the name of Torquatus. From this time, in the wars with the Gauls, the example of Torquatus Manlius was often imitated, and the torques was adopted among the Romans as the reward of military merit. Torques are not unfrequently found in our island, and appear, in some instances, to be of British manufacture, though in others they are undoubtedly Roman. The Roman writers speak of them as worn by the Britons, and the queen of the Iceni, Boadicea, is described by Dion Cassius as having a torquis of gold round her neck. This was the metal of which they were usually made. They consisted of a long piece of gold, twisted or spiral, doubled back in the form of a short hook at each end, and then turned into the form of a circle. The usual form is represented in fig. 1 in the cut on the next page. The gold was sometimes worked with more elaborate ornament into twisted

CHAP. XII.] TORQUES AND ARMILLÆ. 395

cords, &c., and ended in serpents' heads, instead of plain hooks. An inscription found in France, and published by Montfaucon, mentions a torques dedicated to Æsculapius, which was made by twisting together two golden snakes. A very remarkable torques of fine gold was found in Needwood Forest, in Staffordshire, in 1848, where it had been turned up out of the earth by a fox. It was formed of eight plaited cords of gold, weighing together 1 lb. 1 oz. 7 dwts. and 10 grains. At Pattingham, also in Staffordshire, a golden torques was found in the year 1700, which weighed no less than 3 lbs. 2 oz. It is described as being 'curiously twisted and wreathed, with two hooks at each end, cut even, but not twisted.' Its value, probably, hindered it from being preserved. The torques found in Needwood Forest is now in the possession of her Majesty; and an engraving of it was given in the thirty-third

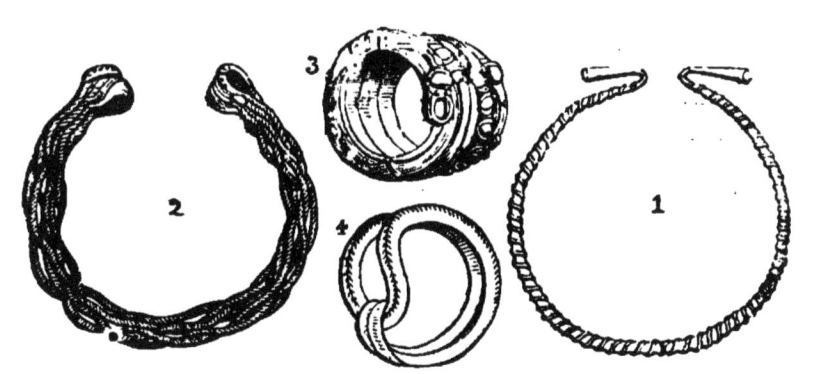

Torques and Armillæ.

volume of the 'Archæologia,' from which the one in our cut (2) is taken. The torques was sometimes bent into a spiral, instead of a circular, form, in which case it was intended for the arm, not the neck; it was in this case denominated *torquis brachialis*, and was usually of bronze. In some instances it is merely a piece of metal like that in fig. 1, twisted into a spiral form for the arm; but it is often much more massive. The elegant bronze armlet (fig. 3 in our cut), found on the coast of Murrayshire, in Scotland, weighed nearly two pounds and a half. Another description of bronze armlet, or bracelet, intended, like the one last mentioned, for the military, probably as a mark of honour, was formed of a triangular bar of bronze,

2 B

first doubled, with a lobe, and then twisted round into the form represented in fig. 4 in our cut. The example here given was found in Northumberland, on the line of Hadrian's Wall, and weighs about three-quarters of a pound.

The only part of the dress of the Romans in Britain which has come down to us entire, is the sandal or shoe (*caliga*). Many of these sandals, taken chiefly from the bed of the Thames opposite London, were in the possession of Mr Roach Smith. They are of leather, of various sizes, and the soles, formed usually of four layers of leather held together by nails clenched on the inside, are cut as in our modern right-and-left shoes. The layer of leather next to the sole of the foot is close sewn to the lower portions, and then forms an exterior ridge, from which, at the sides, rise strong loops for fastening the sandals over the instep with straps or fillets. In nearly all instances this ridge folds a little way over, and protects the extremities of the toes. Other examples, apparently intended for women and children, have reticulated work, also in leather, round the heels and sides, of various degrees of fineness, and more or less elegant in design. Three of these shoes, or sandals, are here given, from the collection of Mr. Roach Smith. The first of these has its upper-leather made in two pieces, and sewed at the toes and at the heel. In the

Sandal, seven inches long by three wide.

second, the upper-leather, which covered the foot up to the ankle, was sewed at the heel only, and appears to have been tied or laced up the front with a thong. The third example is constructed somewhat differently from the others in the upper part, as the latchets were intended to tie over the instep, and not fasten with a thong. In this case, the layers of the sole are preserved quite perfect, with the nails which held them together. In other examples, the heads of the nails are flat instead of pointed. The Roman sandals found in Britain have

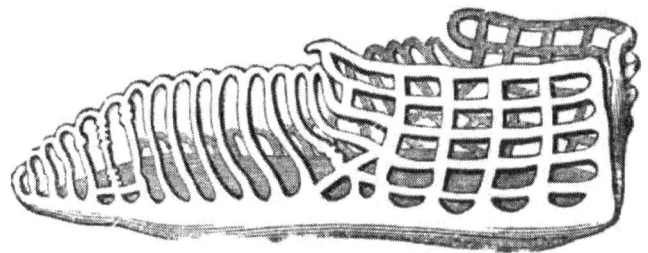

Sandal, ten inches long, by three and a half wide.

the soles almost always covered with nails, which are often very large and clumsy, though sometimes, as in those found in the tombs at York and Avisford, smaller and finer. In these nails

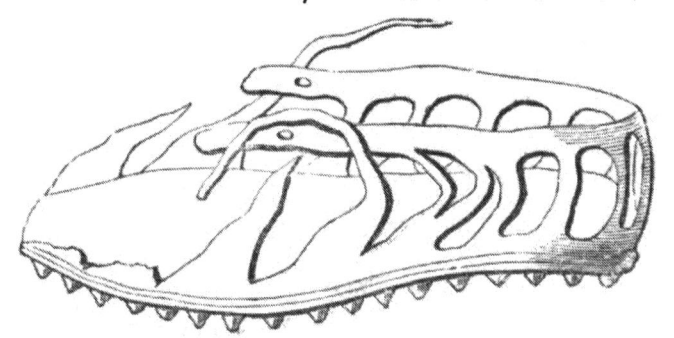

Sandal, nine inches long, by three wide.

we have another link between the manners of Roman Britain and those of Italy. Pliny, describing the scales of a peculiar fish, tells us that they resemble the nails of sandals;[*] and Juvenal, alluding to the profusion of nails with which the sole of the caliga was covered, says:—

> Dignum erit ergo
> Declamatoris mulino corde Vagelli,
> Qunm duo crura habeas, offendere tot caligas, tot
> Millia clavorum.—*Sat.* xvi., l. 22.

The sandals are here used to represent the soldiers who wore

---

[*] 'Squamis conspicui crebris atque peracutis, clavorum caligarum effigie.'—*Plin. Hist. Nat.* lib. ix. c. 18.

them, and we know that the caliga was the proper shoe of the military. The nailed soles from the tombs just alluded to belonged no doubt to the shoes of ladies; but the upper covering, whether of leather or other still more perishable material, is no longer remaining, and we cannot even guess at its form. The shoe (*calceus* or *calceamentum*), worn by the better classes of society, appears to have differed little in form from those made in modern times; they were of different colours, and of various materials. The ladies, and even men of fashion, appear to have worn them of linen, or silk, and sometimes ornamented with jewellery: the shoes of a female in a picture at Herculaneum are painted yellow.

Among the Roman antiquities found in this island, instruments of the toilette are by no means unfrequent. Among these was the mirror, or *speculum*, which consisted usually of a round plate of polished metal, set in a frame of the same shape, with a handle. For, when used, it was held up to the person using it by a servant. Several such mirrors of polished metal have been found in the cemeteries at Colchester; and one, found in an extensive Roman burial-place near Deverill-street, Southwark, is engraved in the twenty-sixth volume of the 'Archæologia.' They are usually small; those found at Colchester were between three and four inches in diameter. I am not aware that any other description of Roman mirror has been met with in this country; rare examples of square ones have been found in Italy, and we know that the Romans used mirrors of glass, and that they even placed large mirrors on their walls and ceilings.

The Roman comb (*pecten*) was usually toothed on both sides, and the common material in Italy was box-wood. This was so generally the case, that Martial, speaking ironically of the uselessness of such an instrument in the hands of a woman who was bald, adopts the name of the wood for the comb:—

> Quid faciet nullos hic inventura capillos,
> Multifido buxus quæ tibi dente datur?
> *Ep.*, lib. xiv. 25.

Bone and metal were also used. The museum of Mr Roach Smith contains fragments of Roman combs in wood and bone found in London. In one of the Roman rubbish pits at Chesterford in Essex, a comb of bronze, with a double row of teeth, was found. It is now in the museum of Lord Braybrooke. at Audley End, who also possesses a similarly shaped

Roman comb of iron, found on the site of the railway station at Chesterford. Small tweezers (*volsellæ*) are also frequently met with among the Roman remains in this country, and evidently formed a necessary part of the toilette of the ladies; their use, no doubt, was to pluck superfluous hairs from the body. Small articles in bronze have been dug up at Cirencester and elsewhere, which, from their form, appear to have been used for cleansing and dressing the nails.

We have very few remains that throw any light on the manner in which the houses of the Romans in Britain were furnished, and we can only assume, from the resemblance in other things, that the fashions of Italy, in this respect, also prevailed here. It has been already stated that the not unfrequent occurrence, in the remains of Roman houses, of walls which seem to run into apartments, and of projections at the lower parts of the walls internally, would induce us to suppose that these were intended to serve permanently as seats. Moveable furniture was generally made of perishable materials, and consisted of articles least likely to be left among the ruins of the houses when abandoned. The only article of this description that I can call to mind as having been found in Britain, was the metal frame of a folding seat found in one of the Bartlow hills. From the great number of keys of all sizes, which are found scattered about the floors of Roman houses when they are excavated, there must have been many chests, coffers, and caskets with locks, independently of the locks of the doors. Three rather common forms of keys are given in the annexed cut, taken from examples found in London. The

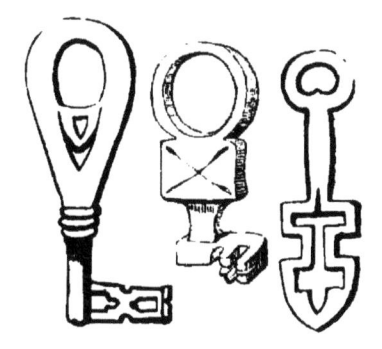

Roman Keys.

interment of small caskets of this kind in graves has been, in some instances, traced by the existence of decayed wood, and the presence among it of ornamental nails and fragments of metal. Several Roman locks, mostly of bronze, have been found in the cemeteries at Colchester, of which one of the most perfect is represented in the cut below. The plate of this lock was four inches broad by two and three-quarters deep, and it has evidently belonged to a chest. The key-hole was covered by a guard, as in modern locks of the same description. The forms of Roman keys are so extremely varied that it would be difficult to give any notion of them in a general description. They are most commonly, especially the smaller ones, of bronze. Many resemble closely the keys of the present day. Others present fanciful shapes, with a good deal of ornament. One form of key, of very frequent occurrence, evidently intended to be placed on the finger like a ring, is represented in our cut. The ring is at right-angles to the axle of the key, which is always very short. These keys are generally so small and delicate, that they can only have been used for locks of small caskets, which required the least possible force to turn them. The larger keys are often of iron, and they are sometimes found of a form resembling our modern latch-keys, and were no doubt used in the same manner. Two of these Roman latch-keys, found at Colchester, are represented in our cut; they are both

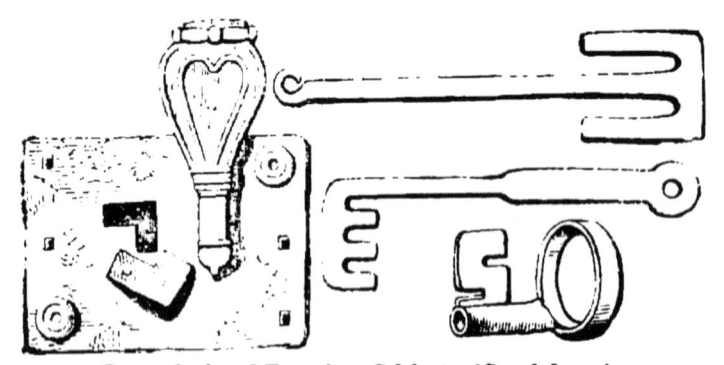

Roman Lock and Keys, from Colchester (*Camulodunum*).

of iron, the upper example eight inches long, and the other five inches and a half, so that they probably belonged to doors. Similar latch-keys were found in the Roman villa at Hartlip in Kent; and they have been met with elsewhere on Roman sites in this country. The padlock was also in use among the Romans, who termed it *sera pensilis*, a hanging lock; it was formed not like those at present in use, but somewhat like the cylindrical locks, which were in more general use some years ago, but are now becoming obsolete.

It has already been shown how the Roman houses were warmed by means of hypocausts, and no traces have yet been found of fire-places in the interior of the rooms. We know, however, that in the south, the Romans had portable fire-places, or braziers, of metal, which they could bring into the room when wanted, and which might be used equally for warming the guests, or for keeping warm the plates or viands; and we would fain believe that the exhortation of Horace,—

> Dissolve frigus, ligna super foco
> Large reponens,—

was as applicable in Britain, as in the land of the snow-clad Soracte. The appeals so frequently repeated in the Roman writers, that people should *amare focos*, love their fire-sides, and that they should *pugnare pro focis et aris*, fight for their hearths and altars, had doubtless some substantial foundation in the manners of the people. Mr Roach Smith has given an engraving in the second volume of his 'Collectanea' of a pair of andirons, or fire-dogs, of iron, discovered in 1839, in a sepulchral vault at Mount Bures, near Colchester. Each consisted of a frame, the two upright sides of which were crowned with heads of oxen, with a brass knob on the tip of each horn. Two very similar implements, also of iron, had been found near Shefford, in Bedfordshire, in 1832, and an engraving of them has also been given by Mr Roach Smith. Articles of the same character, but smaller, have been found at Pompeii, and in a tomb at Præstum. The Italian antiquaries seem to consider that they were used, not like the mediæval fire-dogs, to support the fuel, but that they were cooking utensils, intended to support iron bars to serve as a gridiron over the fire for cooking meat. The two fire-dogs found near Shefford terminated in stags' heads. The gentleman who found them, Mr Inskip of Shefford, has given the following account of the discovery, which seems to confirm the opinion of the antiquaries of Italy :—
'I employed two men,' he says, 'to dig on the spot, and we quickly found an iron fire-dog of simple construction, and doubtless used by the Romans for cooking. After this we met with a stout iron-bar, one end of which was curved somewhat

like a pump-sweep or handle, having a hole through it at the ends; for this I could at first assign no apparent use. I dug further, and found a second fire-dog, a duplicate of the former; they were both in a small degree mutilated, yet I was led to admire the grace and spirit with which all articles of Roman manufacture were executed. Their designs are still more striking; and, even in these homely utensils, the imitations of nature are of the boldest order; the graceful turn of the stag's neck, and the outline of the head, which form the ornamental part of each end, are singularly effective; and it is a matter of admiration, the simplicity of contrivance in these fire-dogs for cooking the greatest quantity of victuals at one and the same fire. To effect this, the bar before alluded to was laid longitudinally on one side of the stag's head; betwixt that and one of his horns, another bar lay parallel, on the opposite side; from both of which descended two rows of hooks, to supply the means of boiling or roasting, the curved ends of the bars having holes through each of them, into which might be thrust pivots of iron so contrived, that upon necessitous occasions, they would form four bars, and thus multiply the means of making the most of one fire. The end of each bar also turned up gracefully as a hook, from which might depend additional pots and kettles.' Mr Inskip's explanation may perhaps be altogether fanciful; but it is remarkable that an utensil undoubtedly intended for cooking was found at the same place. This was an iron tripod, consisting of three curved legs turning on a swivel at the top, under which was fixed a massive iron ring. Near it was found a chain and pot-hooks, which evidently belonged to the ring at the top of the tripod.

We have other examples of such tripods used by the Romans to support culinary vessels over the fire; but a great portion of their cooking appears to have been performed on stoves, and the few supposed culinary vessels that have been found in this country partake rather of the character of saucepans and frying-pans than of 'kettles. The vessels found in Britain most decidedly belonging to the Roman kitchen are the earthenware mortaria already described, and metal as well as earthenware strainers or colanders. The former were used for pounding or mincing meats and vegetables, and, from the profusion in which they are found, seem to show that the Romans in Britain were very partial to made dishes. The strainer (*colum*) was used in Italy for many purposes, the chief of which was that of cooling wine. This sort of strainers were called *cola nivaria*; they were formed like basins, and filled with snow or ice, and the wine was passed through them. Those found in this country consist generally of a rather deep bowl, perforated with small holes, and a long handle, and were evidently intended for taking cooked meats, &c., out of the boiler, without carrying the water with them—in fact, a ladle and strainer combined. Utensils of this kind were termed *trua* or *trulla*. They are found not unfrequently in this island. One was found at Chesterford, in Essex, in 1847, with the bowl partly filled with brass coins. One, exactly similar, even in pattern, and of the same material (bronze), was found some years ago at Whitfield, in Northumberland, along with three kettles or boilers, resembling campkettles, which were evidently intended to be placed over a fire. They are all now preserved in the museum at Newcastle-upon-Tyne. The kettles are also of bronze, but of extremely thin metal, so that they would readily feel the fire. They have been patched in several places. One of them has three feet to stand upon, which was a form of boiler invented to supersede the use of a simple pot placed over the fire upon a tripod.

A general description has already been given of the earthenware used for culinary and other domestic purposes; but it would be extremely difficult to point out the purposes for which each particular form of vessel was designed, though it is probable that most of them were intended for the table. The *mortarium*, as I have just stated, belonged peculiarly to the kitchen. The *amphora* was used to contain wine, and also olives, oil, or honey. The amphora contained these articles in large bulk, and occupied the place of our modern barrels; the liquids were served at table in the *ampulla*, or bottle, which was made of earthenware or glass, and was always distinguished by its narrow neck and swollen body. Hence the term ampulla was applied metaphorically to anything swollen, even to turgid language; for Horace talks of—

ampullas et sesquipedalia verba.

The other description of earthen vessel, which had the mouth not much less wide, or even wider, than the body, was designated by the general term of *olla*, pot or jar. The olla had sometimes a lid; it was used to hold solids rather than liquids, but it was often made large, to be placed on the fire for culinary purposes. Great quantities of vessels, answering all these descriptions, are found among the Roman remains in Britain. They are sometimes made of bronze, with very elegantly ornamented handles. Another article belonging to the Roman kitchen was the quern, or handmill, for grinding corn. It consisted of a couple of round stones, one forming a sort of socket to the other, and by turning the upper one round, the corn was pounded—a rude method of manufacturing meal. Corn appears to have been kept in the house in grain, and to have been thus ground by the hand whenever it was necessary to bake. These stone querns are found frequently on Roman sites in this country. In the back-yard of one of the houses of ancient Isurium (*Aldborough, in Yorkshire*), represented in our plate at p. 193, the querns were found in the situation in which they had been used.

Among other articles which belonged to the culinary department of the Roman house was the water-cock (*epistomium*). It is an article, as might be expected, of not very frequent occurrence; but Mr Roach Smith possesses, among his numerous relics of Roman London, an ornamental bronze water-cock, which issues from the mouth of a dog's head. It is rather a singular combination of names, that it was found in excavations in Philpot Lane, Fenchurch Street.

Before we leave the kitchen, we must speak of a class of remains intimately connected with its purposes. Attached to Roman villas and towns, we invariably find large heaps of the remains of provisions, consisting especially of the shells of fish and of the bones of animals. These organic remains are worthy of study in many points of view; they make us acquainted with the various classes of animal food consumed by the Romano-British population of our island: and they are particularly interesting to the naturalist, from the circumstance that they show the existence of some animals—such as the *bos longifrons* —which have now long been extinct. The proximity of Roman sites is almost always shown by the presence of immense quantities of oyster-shells, which show that there was a great consumption of oysters in Roman Britain; and the shells of cockles and mussels are also abundant. It has been supposed that the Romans fed snails as delicacies for the table, and it is a curious circumstance, that a large species of snail is often found still existing about Roman stations. In excavating on Roman sites, large quantities of shells of snails are not unfrequently found; at Lymne, in Kent, (*Portus Lemanus*), I have seen them dug up at the foundations of the walls, in masses almost as large as ordinary buckets, and completely embedded together. The snails may, however, have thus collected together in such places at a much more recent period than that with which their connexion with the ruins around would seem to identify them.

Among the animal remains found among relics of the Roman period in Colchester are horns of a short-horned ox, of the stag, and of a very large goat, as well as of the *bos longifrons*, just mentioned, a species of ox named from the length of its frontal bone, which is found by geologists among fossil remains, but which does not exist at present; bones of the ox. sheep, and goat; jaws, teeth, and tusks of wild hogs; and teeth and jaws of dogs, and apparently of wolves. The different forms of the horns discovered in different localities show that there must have been many varieties of oxen in Britain. The bones and horns of animals found with Roman remains in London include the *bos longifrons*, sheep, goats, deer, and swine. A deep pit attached to the Roman villa at Hartlip, in Kent, contained a large quantity of the bones of the sheep, hog, horse, and also of the *bos longifrons*. In a Roman villa at Dursley, near Gloucester, were found remains of the horse, stag, fox, wild boar, hares, rabbits, mice, wild ducks, chickens, goats, pigs, sheep, kids, lambs, rooks, and small birds, cats, polecats, and of a small kind of ox. The Rev. Mr Layton, of Sandwich, who watched the opening of the rubbish pits at Richborough, furnished Mr Roach Smith with the following account of the animal remains found there :—' The major part consists of the common bones of the ox, sheep, and roebuck--especially the first., I have seen one head also of the ox, with the frontal bone broken through, as if with a pole-axe, just as by a butcher of the present day. It may be noticed, too, that the oxen and sheep were small when compared with ours; and one is pleased with finding the account of Tacitus, in his "Germany," (*pecorum fecunda, sed plerumque improcera,*) so well illustrated by the dirt-pits of Richborough.' A great variety of animal bones are found at Wroxeter (*Uriconium*). Pieces of the horns of deer and other animals are found sawed off, no doubt for the purpose of manufacturing the different articles which were abundantly made of such materials. Boars' tusks are often found fitted up for ornaments, and sometimes apparently designed to be suspended on the person, or to the horse—perhaps tropies of the chase.

An article found very frequently on the sites of Roman buildings is the small bell (*tintinnabulum*), which was probably used to summon the slaves and attendants when their services were wanted. These bells are as frequently square as round, and are usually made of bronze. One, in the cabinet of Mr Roach Smith, is so well preserved, that it still produces a clear and sharp sound; it was found in the ruins of one of the houses of Roman London.

Another article of very frequent occurrence is the lamp (*lucerna*), made usually of terra-cotta. It has been already stated that lamps are frequently found in sepulchres. They were also used in lighting houses, apparently in considerable profusion, and it is evident that it would require a considerable number to illuminate a room effectively. In one corridor of the public baths of Pompeii, upwards of five hundred lamps were found; and in the course of excavating the different parts of the same building, more than a thousand were collected. The terra-cotta lamp is usually circular, from two inches and a half to three inches in diameter, with a projecting spout for the wick. A hole, or two holes, in the circular body, allowed the air to pass, and the spout was sometimes double or treble, to admit of two or three separate wicks. The annexed cut represents two examples of terra-cotta lamps, selected from several

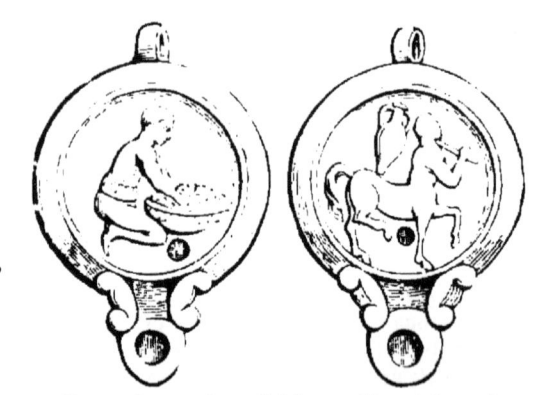

Roman Lamps, from Colchester (*Camulodunum*).

found at Colchester. The field, often plain, is, however, frequently ornamented with figures, which are no less varied and interesting than those on the red Samian pottery. Our two examples represent a centaur carrying an amphora of wine, and what appears to be a fuller at work. Others have theatrical masks, busts, mythological figures, gladiatorial subjects, domestic and sometimes licentious scenes, &c. Mr Roach Smith has several examples of a terra-cotta lamp, on which is the representation of a mill for grinding corn, turned by an ass, one of which is here given in a cut. Lamps made of metal, usually

Roman Lamp, from London.

bronze, are of rarer occurrence. One, in Mr Smith's museum, which was taken from the Thames, has been made from a bronze cup, of a very elegant pattern, by breaking in one side and adding a spout. An engraving of this curious relic is given in the Archæological Album. When used for domestic purposes, the lamp was placed on a little disc, raised on a shaft —a *candelabrum*. The York Museum contains two leaden stands with handles, evidently intended for carrying lamps about the house without the risk of dropping the oil. The metal lamps, which have frequently fanciful and grotesque forms, were often suspended by chains, or by a rod. One of these, with the rod which suspended it, was found in one of the Bartlow hills.

Among the articles of household furniture peculiar to the Romans, there is one class which deserves particular notice. These are the images of the household gods, the *penates* and *lares*, which answered in some respect to our mediæval fairies. They were supposed to watch over the prosperity of the house and its occupants, and visitors were in the habit of saluting them, for which purpose their images were placed in the house in conspicuous places. When Æneas had first experienced hospitality on the shores of Italy, he is represented as paying his respects to the household gods:—

Hesternumque larem, parvosque penates
Lætus adit.—*Virgil, Æn.* viii. 543.

They were called the little deities (*dii minuti*), and it was usual to propitiate them with offerings of the remnants of provisions, or other small articles, a custom to which Juvenal refers in the following lines :—

> O parvi nostrique lares, quos thure minuto,
> Aut farre, et tenui soleo exorare coronâ.—*Sat.* ix. 137.

In accepting such offerings they were supposed to exhibit a sort of goodfellowship towards the people of the house, and in this resembled the brownies and cluricaunes of modern times. They were supposed to show themselves at times in various forms, often of a grotesque description, and sometimes as animals, such as dogs, and even as serpents. A bronze figure of a lar, or household god, found at Herculaneum, represents him as a little old man sitting on the ground, with his knees up to his chin, a large head, ass's ears, a long beard, and a droll roguish face. There can be little doubt that many of the numerous bronze images of the Roman period found in this country were intended for such household gods. Others probably owed their existence to the same love of ornament which loads our chimney-pieces with figures in plaster or porcelain. Others, again, of the smaller bronze images, were probably mere toys—playthings for children. We must distinguish from all these the bronze statuettes of the Roman deities, which are also not unfrequent, and which were perhaps placed in some corner of the house set apart for private worship.

The traces of the domestic occupations of the female part of the household, found among Roman remains in Britain, are not very numerous. Much of their time was probably employed in spinning and weaving. In Mr Roach Smith's museum may be seen a number of small implements of wood, found in excavations in the city of London, which, from the circumstance that when brought to light the remains of wool were still attached to them, were no doubt used in the manufacture of cloth. Needles for sewing are of frequent occurrence. Several are in the collection of Mr Roach Smith. One, made of bone, and found at Richborough, is represented in our cut in p. 393. The Roman scissors (*forfex*) was usually of the form still common among clothiers; an example, found at Richborough, is represented in the accompanying cut. A more complete example, but differing somewhat in shape, is engraved in Mr Lee's 'Roman Antiquities of Caerleon.' Scissors of the same construction as those now in common use are also found, but

CHAP. XII.] SCISSORS AND KNIVES. 409

much less frequently. Our cut presents also some of the commoner forms of Roman knife-blades found in this country; they are all represented one-fourth of the real size. The knife

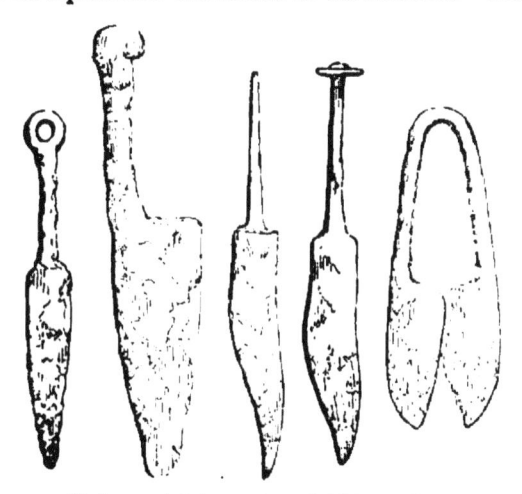

Knives and Scissors, from Richborough.

(*culter*) was generally straight on the cutting edge, and curved on the back. These probably have had handles of wood; but they are not unfrequently found with bone handles, well preserved. Several knives, with handles of bone, are in the museum of Mr Roach Smith; some of which have the ring at the end, like that in our example to the left in the cut, just escaping from the handle. This ring was no doubt intended for suspending the knife to the girdle. Juvenal, when describing the frugality of his country-house, speaks of bone handles to knives as a mark of poverty :—

> Adeo nulla uncia nobis
> Est eboris, nec tessellæ, nec calculus ex hac
> Materia ; quin ipsa manubria cultellorum
> Ossea.—*Sat.* xi. 131.

The handle (*capulus*) was often made of bronze, and very elegantly ornamented. It not unfrequently terminated in the head of an animal; in an example in the possession of Mr Roach Smith it is the head of a horse, while in two found at Caerleon and York it is that of a dog. Roman clasp-knives are by no means uncommon; and one shape of handle, representing a dog in close pursuit of a hare, seems to have been a great favourite, from the numerous examples which have been found in this country. The one given in the annexed cut was found

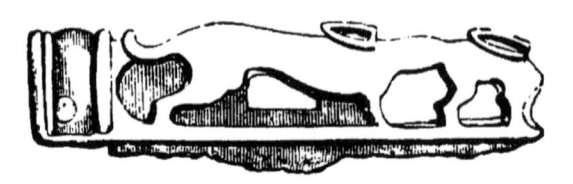

The Handle of a Clasp-knife.

at Hadstock, in Essex, and is now in the museum of the Lord Braybrooke, at Audley End; it has the remains of the steel blade shut into the handle. It is here represented the size of the original. Two, exactly similar, were found at Reculver, in Kent (*Regulbium*); and another at Kenchester, in Herefordshire (*Magna*). Mr Smith possesses what appears to be a Roman fork, and I believe that other examples of that instrument have been found. There is, also, in Mr Smith's collection, a steel for sharpening knives, taken from Roman London, exactly resembling those used by butchers at the present day, and still retaining the ring by which it was suspended to the girdle.

Spoons, of different shapes and sizes, are also of frequent occurrence. The one with the larger bowl (*cochlear*) has almost always a handle terminating in a point, and illustrates the epigrammatic description in Martial, who speaks of it as being applied to two purposes, for picking periwinkles or snails out of the shell (with the pointed end), or for eating eggs (with the bowl)—

> Sum cochleis habilis, sed nec minus utilis ovis,
> Numquid scis potius cur cochleare vocer?
> *Martial, Ep.* xvi. 121.

The bowl of the cochlear is more usually circular than oval. One found at Reculver was made of silver, but they are generally of bronze. The two examples of the diminutive spoon (*ligula*), given from Mr Rolfe's collection of Richborough antiquities, in the accompanying cut (figs. 1 and 3), are also of bronze. It is not easy to explain the exact purposes of these last-mentioned articles, but they have been supposed to be designed for taking ointments or prepared oils out of long-necked bottles.

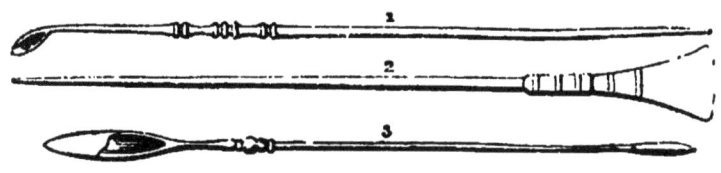

Ligulæ and a Stylus.

The article between the ligulæ in the last cut (fig. 2) is an example of the Roman *stylus*, used for writing on the waxed tablet (*tabula*). The tablet was composed of two or more thin pieces of wood, fastened at the back with wires, like a book. Wax was spread over the wood internally, and on this the person using it wrote with the pointed end of the stylus. The flat end was used for erasing what had been written, and smoothing the wax for writing again. Hence *vertere stylum*, to turn the stylus, for the purpose of erasing and correcting what had been ill or incorrectly written, became a proverbial expression:—

> Sæpe stylum vertas, iterum quæ digna legi sint
> Scripturus; neque te ut miratur turba labores,
> Contentus paucis lectoribus—

says the poet Horace (*lib.* i., *Sat.* x., 72). It is from the same usage that we derive the modern word *style*, applied primarily to the character of a man's writing, and thence to other characteristics. A painting, found in Herculaneum, represents a lady with a stylus, closely resembling the one in our cut, in her right hand, and the tablet in her left. The tablet and its styli was a very necessary article in the houses of educated people, for, among other purposes, it served for that of letter-writing. The letter was written upon the wax, the tablet was then closed and tied with a thread and sealed, and so dispatched to the person to whom it was addressed, who could rub it out, and write the answer on the same tablet, which was then returned to its original owner. Hence, when one of Plautus's characters wants to write a letter, he calls for a tablet, stylus, wax, and thread:—

> Effer cito stylum, ceram, et tabellas, et linum.
> *Bacchid.*, iv. 4, 64.

This accounts for the number of styli which are found in all

Roman sites in Britain. They are usually of bronze. As the tablet was made of more perishable materials, it is seldom found: but Mr Roach Smith possessed two leaves of these tablets, made of wood, found in London, from which however the wax has perished. One of them, which was an outside cover, is represented in the accompanying cut; the leaves had been threaded together by two holes running through one side, and the marks of the string or thong which tied it are distinctly visible. Other instruments, bearing some analogy to the stylus, are also frequently found on Roman sites, especially in London, which, from a comparison with the tools used at the present day by sculptors, appear to be modelling tools. Among instruments connected with the Roman arts in Britain, we must not overlook the compass

Leaf of a Tablet, from London.

(*circinus*). Two Roman compasses have been found at Cirencester, exactly representing those in use at the present day, and an engraving of one of them will be found in Buckman and Newmarch's work on ancient Corinium. Similar instruments have been found on other Roman sites.

The steelyard (*statera* or *trutina*) is also frequently met with among other Roman antiquities found in this island, and bears a perfect resemblance to those now in use. The two examples given in our cut on the next page were found at Richborough. A weight, found in the same place, is attached to one of them. The weights are always more or less ornamental; they often

Roman Steelyard Weights.

consist of highly-finished busts of emperors, or distinguished personages, deities, or fabulous heroes, or of figures of birds and animals. Three examples are given in the cut; the first, representing a dog's or wolf's head; the second, a female bust; and the third, a bust of Diana. On another example of the statera, found at Richborough, the yard is notched into fractional divisions, and is furnished with two hooks. In examples found at Pompeii, sometimes a hook, at others a scale, is suspended at the end of the yard.* Scales (*libra, bilanx*)

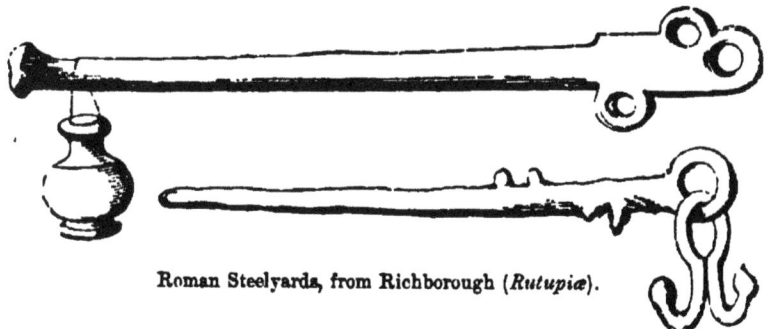

Roman Steelyards, from Richborough (*Rutupiæ*).

were also in use among the Romans from a very early period, and are often figured on coins and other works of art, but they are rarely met with in antiquarian excavations in this country.

Among other miscellaneous articles in use among the Romans in Britain, strigils are not unfrequently found, an additional proof how extensively the manners of Italy had been translated to our clime. The strigil was a curved instrument, generally of bronze or iron, with which the bather in the hot baths, after having been put into a profuse sweat, was scraped—somewhat in the manner that ostlers scrape a horse when he comes in hot. While this operation was performed, the patient sat upon a seat which was under the water—a seat of this kind is generally discovered in baths in Roman villas in Britain. Sometimes the bather performed the operation him-

* Vitruvius gives us the names for the different constituent parts of the Roman steelyard:—the scale (*lancula*), hanging from the head (*caput*), near which was the point of revolution (*centrum*), and the handle (*ansa*); on the other side of the centre from the scale was the beam (*scopus*), with the weight or equipoise (*æquipondium*), which was made to move along the points (*per puncta*) expressing the different weights.

It should be observed that in the upper figure in our cut, the steelyard is turned the wrong way up.

self, but if he was rich enough he had a slave for the purpose. Public baths were provided with strigils for the use of the bathers; but people of respectability had their own strigils at home, which their slaves carried after them when they went to bathe. Hence Persius,—

I, puer, et strigiles Crispini ad balnea defer.—*Sat.* v. 126.

This is sufficient to warn us against supposing that the discovery of strigils among the remains of buildings, is any proof that those buildings were baths. Two strigils of bronze were found in one of the Bartlow tumuli, which resemble the generality of those found in Italy, in having a hole in the handle through which the hand was passed in using them. One of the same material found at Reculver, in Kent, more than a century ago, and engraved in Mr Roach Smith's 'Antiquities of Richborough,' had a straight handle to grasp in the hand. This latter discovery furnishes a remarkable instance of the danger of forming hasty opinions on such objects, without the previous knowledge arising from careful comparison. An antiquary of the time, Aubrey, who examined the bronze strigil found at Reculver, immediately judged it to be one of the golden sickles with which the British Druids cut their mistletoe!* The strigil had, indeed, a sharp edge turned inward, which might lead a person ignorant of its real use to suppose that it was a cutting instrument. The operation of being scraped with it could not have been an agreeable one; and we are told that the emperor Augustus was subjected to considerable suffering by an over-violent application of the strigil. It was on this account customary to soften the edge by the application of oil.

We find fewer remains of Roman weapons and armour in Britain than almost any other article. As I have observed before, it is more than probable that the bronze swords which have been usually described as British, are purely Roman. The same may be said of the bronze spear-heads. A considerable number of spear-heads and arrow-heads of iron were found in the Roman camp on Hod Hill, in Dorsetshire. They are found also from time to time on other Roman sites. A few fragments of what is supposed to be Roman armour, formed both of scales and of rings, have also been found, and some remains of

---

* It is remarkable that the Roman bronze, under certain circumstances, especially when it has lain in the water where it was subjected to friction, bears an extraordinary resemblance to gold.

military standards. Very remarkable remains of one of the latter articles were found near Stoney Stratford at the beginning of the present century, and have been engraved and published by Samuel Lysons. Among the extensive Roman remains found in the camp at Hod Hill, already alluded to, were several spurs of iron, which resemble so closely the Norman prick-spurs, that they might be easily mistaken for them. I suspect that many of the prick-spurs which have been found on or near Roman sites, and hastily judged to be Norman, are, especially when made of bronze, Roman. As far, however, as comparison has yet been made, the Roman and the Saxon spurs are shorter in the *stimulus* than those of the Normans.

CHAPTER XIII.

The Roman Province—Its Divisions and Officers—the Military Force—Centurial and other inscriptions—Towns and their Municipal Constitution—the Coinage—Roman Coins relating to Britain—Spurious Coinage—Different methods of Hoarding Money.

THE importance of Roman Britain is shown by the circumstance that it was constituted a separate province of the empire. From the first, Britain was governed by a proprætor, who is stated, in inscriptions, to have been a *legatus Augusti*, or vicegerent of the emperor, from which we are to conclude that it was a province of the Cæsar, and not a province of the people. At the close of the Roman occupation, when the 'Notitia Imperii' was compiled, the governor of Britain was called a vicarius, and was honoured with the title of *vir spectabilis*. It is at this period only that we obtain any distinct information on the political divisions of the province and on its officers, and these had probably undergone considerable modifications. According to the 'Notitia,' the province of Britain was divided into five departments, called Britannia Prima, Britannia Secunda, Flavia Cæsariensis, Maxima Cæsariensis, and Valentia. The first of these consisted of the country to the south of the Thames and the Bristol Channel; Britannia Secunda answered to the modern Principality of Wales; Flavia comprised the middle portion of the island, from the Thames to the Humber and the Mersey; the country beyond this, extending twenty-five miles north of Hadrian's wall, formed the department of Maxima Cæsariensis; while the lowlands of Scotland were comprised under the title of Valentia. It is stated on the single and dubious authority of Richard of Cirencester, that the country to the north of the Wall of Antoninus was formed into a sixth department under the name of Vespasiana. After the time of Constantine, the first three were governed by presidents, while the two northern departments were placed under the jurisdiction of consulares. These officers were under the vicarius, who probably resided in Londinium, or London.

The vicarius of Britain was himself subject to the præfectus prætorio Galliarum, who resided first at Treviri (*Treves*), and afterwards at Arelatum (*Arles*). His official establishment consisted of a *princeps*, or chief officer; of two agents (*de scholu agentum in rebus*), chosen out of the *ducenarii*, or judges; a chief secretary (*cornicularius*);* two accountants or auditors (*numerarios duos*); a master of the prisons (*commentariensis*); a notary (*ab actis*); a secretary for despatches (*curam epistolarum*); an assistant (*adjutor*); under assistants (*subadjuvæ*); clerks for appeal (*exceptores*); serjeants, and other officers (*singulares, et reliquos officiales*).† For the revenues of the country, which were under the control of a superior officer in Gaul, entitled the *comes sacrarum largitionum*, there were a collector for the whole of Britain (*rationalis summarum Britanniarum*); an overseer of the Augustentian treasures in Britain (*præpositus thesaurorum Augustentium in Britannias*); procurators of the cynegia, or hunting establishment (*procuratores cyne iorum*); and another officer, entitled *procurator cynegii in Britannia Biennensis*. Under the count of the private affairs of the western division of the empire (*comes rerum privatarum*) was a collector of private affairs in Britain (*rationalis rei privatæ per Britannias*). The military affairs of the province also came at this time directly under the management of the government in Gaul, without the intermediation of the vicarius, or governor, of Britain. They were divided between three chief officers, the count of the Saxon shore (*comes litoris Saxonici*), the count of Britain (*comes Britanniarum*), and the duke of Britain (*dux Britanniarum*). The garrisons of nine fortresses along the coast from Portchester to Brancaster in Norfolk, were placed under the command of the first of these officers, who had an official establishment composed of a chief officer from the office, or court; of the general of foot in ordinary attendance (*principem ex officio magistri præsentalium a parte peditum*); two auditors (*numerarii*) and a

* In a sepulchral inscription found near Great Chesters in Northumberland, a cornicularius is commemorated, but whether he belonged to the departmental court, or not, is uncertain.—The inscription reads :—D . M . AEL . MERCVRIALI CORNICVL VACIA SOROR FECIT.

† In the interpretation of these various official titles I have chiefly followed Horsley; it is not easy to explain the exact duties of them all.

master of the prisons (*commentariensis*) from the same office; a secretary; an assistant, and under-assistant; a registrar (*regerendarius*): clerks of appeals, serjeants, and other officers. The count of Britain had an official establishment exactly similar, but apparently without any military command. The duke of Britain had under his command the sixth legion, which was at Eburacum (*York*), where, probably, the duke held his court, and all the garrisons in the north of Britain and along the Wall of Hadrian. His official establishment consisted of the same officers as the others.

This rather complicated system of officials, combined with the numerous secondary employés who must have been scattered over the island, shows us the regularity of administration which at this late period prevailed still in Roman Britain. We have no means of knowing the details of government, or the character or amount of the taxes which were raised from the island. The military force, as we have before stated, was fixed soon after its reduction to a province, at three legions, and it was now reduced to two, the second and the sixth. These were also, at the time of the composition of the 'Notitia' (the beginning of the fifth century), directly under the command of the imperial government in Gaul. The military force in Britain at this time has been estimated, from the information given in the 'Notitia,' at nineteen thousand two hundred infantry, and seventeen hundred cavalry.

This is the amount of the direct information we can at present obtain relating to the internal administration of the government in Britain and the amount of its military establishment. The Roman troops have fortunately left us abundant memorials of their presence in the numerous inscriptions commemorating their burial, their religious worship, or their labours. Both the legions and the auxiliary troops seem to have been constantly employed in works of public utility, and the share each legion, or cohort, or century took in them, is often indicated by their names and titles inscribed on tiles or stones. The latter are usually termed centurial stones, as they bear the name of the centuria, or troop, by which the building or other work, to which they were attached, was executed. This is often expressed in the simplest possible form. Thus, a centurial stone found near Cilurnum (*Chesters*), in Northumberland, is inscribed [*]—

[*] The words *centurio* and *centuria* are generally figured on the stones by a mark which is here represented by a c reversed, but in reality it is

COH V	The fifth cohort,
O CAECILI	The century of Caecilius
PROCOLI	Proculus.

Similar stones with such inscriptions as CENTVRIA PEREGRINI CENTVRIA ARRII, CENTVRIA HERENNIANI, COH VI O DELIVIANA, are found frequently along the line of Hadrian's Wall, and in Cumberland, and sometimes in other parts of the country. Sometimes, especially in the legionary inscriptions, there is more of ornament, the name being placed within a wreath or tablet, surrounded with the emblems of the legion and other

A Roman Legionary stone.

figures. One of these, found at Halton Chesters, in Northumberland (*Hunnum*), is represented in the accompanying cut, and is to be read thus,—

LEG	Legion
II	the second,
AVG	the Augustan,
F	made it.

An inscription of this kind, found at Whitley Castle, in Northumberland, speaks of the rebuilding, or making again, of some temple or other work :—

VEX . LEG	A vexillation of legion
XX VV	the twentieth, the valiant and victorious,
REFEC	remade it.

more like a >, though it was no doubt intended for a Ↄ. A cut is given a little further on which shows how oddly, at least at one period, the cutters of the Roman inscriptions joined letters together.

Sometimes the name of the officer who directed the work is added, as in the following inscription found at Risingham (*Habitancum*):—

COH . I . VANG	The first cohort of the Vangiones
FECIT CVRANTE	made it, under the direction of
IVL . PAVLLO TRID	Julius Paullus the tribune.

On a similar stone found at Rochester, in Northumberland (*Bremenium*), the name of the tribune only is given:—

P . AEL . ERAS	Publius Ælius
INVS TRIB	Erasinus, the tribune.

The soldiers frequently dedicated their work to the reigning emperor, or contrived to introduce his name into the inscription. Thus, along the line of the wall in Northumberland, inscriptions to Hadrian are very frequent, which leave no doubt on our mind that the great military works there were executed under that emperor. In the same manner the neighbourhood of the more northern wall presents us with numerous inscriptions commemorative of Antoninus. As an example of the inscriptions to Hadrian along the Northumberland wall, we may cite the following, found at Milking-gap:—

IMP CAES TRAIAN	Of the emperor Cæsar Trajanus
HADRIANI AVG	Hadrianus Augustus,
LEG II AVG	the second legion, the Augustan,
A PLATORIO NEPOTE LEG PR PR	Aulus Platorius Nepos being legate proprætor.

Similar inscriptions are found in other places in nearly the same words. The inscriptions along the Antonine wall are more precise, detailing the quantity of work performed in each case by those who set up the inscription, and are often very elaborately ornamented. They occur, moreover, in greater numbers. The following was found at West-Kilpatrick:—

IMP. C	To the emperor Cæsar
T. AE. HADRIA	Titus Ælius Hadrianus
NO. ANTONINO. AVG. PI. P. P.	Antoninus Augustus Pius, father of his country.
VEX	A vexillation
LEG XX	of the twentieth legion,
VV. FE	the valiant and victorious, made
PP IIII CDXI	four thousand four hundred and eleven paces.

In this instance the slab of stone is sculptured into the representation of a Corinthian portico; the emperor's name and titles are inscribed on the tympanum; the name of the legion is placed within a wreath or garland, held by a winged Victory between the supporting columns; while the number of paces is given at the foot, on each side of a boar, the ensign of that legion.

Inscriptions of the reigning emperors, or commemorative of them, are found in other places, where they have originally appeared on public buildings or other monuments. As we have before had occasion to observe, the emperors' names were always placed on the *milliaria*, or milestones. They are historically important, as showing us the interest which the people in this distant province took in all the changes and movements of the Roman empire. We find now and then an inscription to an emperor whose reign was so short and insignificant that we could hardly suppose the influence of his name would have been felt here. A fragment of an inscription to Numerianus, on which remained the words IMP C MAR AVR NVMERIANO, was found at Kenchester, in Herefordshire (*Magna*). Numerianus was the brother of Carinus, and reigned conjointly with him about two years (from 282 to 284). It is the only inscription yet found in Britain in which his name occurs. At Castor, in Northamptonshire (*Durobrivæ*), a cylindrical stone, apparently a milliarium, was found with an inscription to Florianus, the brother of the emperor Tacitus, who reigned not more than two or three months, in A. D. 276. It is imperfect, but appears to read as follows:—

IMP CAES	To the emperor Cæsar
M. ANNIO	Marcus Annius
FLORIANO	Florianus,
P. P. INVICTO	the pious and faithful, unconquered,
AVG.	the Augustus.
M. P. II	Two miles.

An inscription found at Ancaster (*Causennæ*), commemorates the emperor Constantine the Great (308—337):—

IMP C	To the emperor Cæsar
FL VAL	Flavius Valerius
CONSTANTINO	Constantinus,
P P INV	the pious and faithful, unconquered,
AVG	the Augustus.
DIVI	of the deified
CONSTANTI	Constantius,
PII AVG	the pious, the Augustus,
FILIO	the son.

A milestone found in Cumberland was dedicated to Flavius

Julius Crispus, a son of Constantine the Great, and therefore belonged to the earlier part of the fourth century. One found near Old Carlisle was dedicated to the emperor Marcus Julius Philippus, and is fixed by the mention of his consulship to the year 247. Another, found near the Roman road at Greta-bridge, in Yorkshire, was dedicated to the emperors Gallus and Volusianus, in the year 252.

At Bittern, in Hampshire (*Clausentum*), no less than six stones have been found with inscriptions to various emperors. Three of these are dedicated to Gordian the Younger, to Gallus and Volusianus, and to Aurelian. The other three are all dedicated to Tetricus, and are particularly interesting as being the only inscriptions yet found in Britain to any of the local usurpers, with the exception of one to Victorinus, found near Neath, in South Wales. It is remarkable that we have no such memorial now remaining of Carausius or Allectus, although they reigned during ten years, and their numerous coinage proves that they were not neglectful of commemorating themselves. The want of inscriptions with their names can only be explained by the great care which was probably taken to destroy or erase them, after the island was restored to its dependence on Rome. There are several instances among the inscriptions found in Britain of the erasure of the name of an emperor by

Inscription at Chesters (*Cilurnum*).

his successor or rival. An interesting inscription found at Hexham had contained the name of Severus and his two sons,

THE VALUE OF INSCRIPTIONS.

but that of Geta had been subsequently and carefully erased, no doubt after that prince had been murdered by his brother, Caracalla. An inscribed slab was discovered some years ago at Chesters, in Northumberland (*Cilurnum*), of which a representation is given in the accompanying cut, and on which also were clearly traced some intentional erasures. The inscription may be given, by comparing and supplying from similar contemporary inscriptions, as follows :—

```
IMP CAES Marc AVREL. . . .
AVG . . .    . . . . . . . . pont max
 . . . . . TRIB P COS . . PP DIVI Antonini fil
DIVI SEVER NEP . . . . . . . .
CÆSAR IMPER . . . . . . . . . duplares
ALAE II. ASTORVM templvm VETVSTAT conlapsum restitu-
ERVNT PER MARIVM VALERIAnum leg. avg. pr pr
INSTANTE SEPTIMIO NILO PRAE . . .
DEDICATVM III KAL NOVEM GRATO ET SELEUCO COSS.
```

which may be translated :—To the emperor Marcus Aurelius Augustus . . . . . . Pontifex Maximus, with the tribunitian power, fourth time consul, father of his country, son of divine Antoninus, grandson of divine Severus, to Cæsar our emperor . . . . . the duplares of the second wing of Asturians restored this temple, through age dilapidated, by command of Marius Valerianus, legate of the Augustus and proprætor, under the superintendence of Septimius Nilus the Præfect. It was dedicated on the third kalends of November (the 30th of October), Gratus and Seleucus being consuls.

Mr Bruce, from whose work on the Roman wall I take this inscription, makes the following illustrative remarks, which deserve to be impressed on the minds of all students of our early antiquities. 'Hutton,' he observes, 'who has done such good service to the wall, underrated the value of inscriptions. "When the antiquary," says he, "has laboured through a parcel of miserable letters, what is he the wiser?" Let this fractured and defaced stone answer the question. 1. This dedication was made by soldiers of the second wing of the Astures ;— we thus learn the name of the people who garrisoned the fort, and by a reference to the Notitia, ascertain with certainty that this was Cilurnum. 2. We acquire the fact that a temple, which through age had become dilapidated, was restored ;— learning thereby, not only the attention which the Romans paid to what they conceived to be religious duties, but their long occupation of this spot. It has been already observed, that some of the pillars of the hypocaust have been portions of a prior building;—the ruin and inscription thus corroborate each other. 3. The date of the dedication is given; the third of the kalends of November falls upon the thirtieth of October, and the year which Gratus and Seleucus were consuls corresponds to A. D. 221;—the data on which antiquaries found their conclusions are not always so vague as some imagine. 4. Even the erasures are instructive. By a reference to the date, we find that Heliogabalus was reigning at the time of the dedication of the temple; we find that what remain of the names and titles on the stone apply to him; he, consequently, is the emperor referred to. The year following he was slain by his own soldiers, his body dragged through the streets, and cast into the Tiber. The soldiers in Britain seem to have sympathised with their companions at Rome, and to have erased the name of the fallen emperor from the dedicatory slab. Human nature is the same in every age. How often have we, in modern times, seen a name cast out with loathing, which yesterday received the incense of a world's flattery!'*

This inscription also furnishes us with a name of a propraetor or governor of Roman Britain, who is not mentioned elsewhere. Other inscriptions have added to our list of propraetors, or confirmed the names of those who are mentioned in history. Thus:—

Aulus Plautius, the first propraetor, who came over under the emperor Claudius, is mentioned in an inscription found in Italy, and published by Gruter.

Licinius Priscus, who governed Britain under Hadrian, is commemorated in an inscription found at Bewcastle, in Cumberland, as well as on a monument found at Rome.

Lollius Urbicus, the celebrated propraetor of Antoninus Pius, is mentioned in an inscription found in Scotland.

Platorius Nepos is mentioned as propraetor under Hadrian in inscriptions found at more than one place along the line of the Northumbrian wall.

C. Valerius Pansa occurs as holding the same office under Trajan, in an inscription found at Novara, in Italy, published by Muratori.

Virius Lupus, the propraetor of the emperor Severus, occurs

---

* It may be observed that this inscription affords a remarkably good example of the combining of letters together, technically called *ligature*, so common in Roman inscriptions, especially of this age.

in an inscription found at Ilkey, in Yorkshire (*Olicana*), and in another found at Bowes (*Lavatræ*).

Claudius Xenophon, whose date is doubtful, is mentioned in an inscription found at Little Chesters, in Northumberland.

Marius Valerianus, under Heliogabalus, is mentioned in the inscription given above.

Mæcilius Fuscus, proprætor under Gordian, occurs in an inscription at Lanchester, in Durham.

Gnæus Lucilianus, proprætor under the same emperor, occurs in another inscription found at the same place.

Claudius Paulinus, proprætor, is mentioned in an inscription found near Caen, in Normandy, of the date of A. D. 240

Nonnius Philippus, proprætor also under Gordian, is mentioned in an inscription found at Old Penrith, in Cumberland, and in another at Old Carlisle, of the date 242.

As far as we can perceive, the military, civil, and fiscal departments of the administration of Britain were united, at first, in the office of the proprætor; but, as we have seen above, after Constantine had divided the empire into four governments, the different departments of administration in this island were each placed separately under the præfect of the west in Gaul. His vicar (*vicarius*) had the management of the civil government of the island. But there was another, and an independent jurisdiction, that of the towns, which it is of the utmost importance we should not overlook. The very doubtful treatise attributed to Richard of Cirencester, which, however, may possibly in this case offer us correct information, states that there were in Britain two municipal towns (*municipia*), Verulamium (*St Albans*), and Eburacum (*York*). The same authority enumerates nine *coloniæ*, Londinium (*London*), Camulodunum (*Colchester*), Rutupiæ (*Richborough*), Aquæ Solis (*Bath*), Isca (*Caerleon*), Deva (*Chester*), Glevum (*Gloucester*), Lindum (*Lincoln*), and Camboricum (*Cambridge*); ten cities under the Latin law (*civitates Latio jure donatæ*), Durnomagus, considered to be another name for Durobrivæ (*Castor*), Cataracto (*Catterick*), Cambodunum (*Slack*), Coccium (*Ribchester*), Luguballium (*Carlisle*), Ptoroton (*Burgh-head*), Victoria (*Dealgin Ross*), Theodosia (*Dumbarton*), Corinium (*Cirencester*), Sorbiodunum (*Old Sarum*); and twelve stipendiary towns, of less consequence,* Venta Silurum (*Caerwent*), Vonta Belgarum (*Winchester*), Venta Icenorum (*Caistor, near Norwich*), Segontium (*Caer Segont*), Mari-

* Deinde xii. stipendiariæ minorisque momenti.

dunum (*Caermarthen*), Ratæ (*Leicester*), Cantiopolis (*Canterbury*), Durinum (*Dorchester*), Isca (*Exeter*), Bremenium (*Rochester*), Vindonum (*in Hampshire*), and Durobrivæ (*Rochester*).

In earlier times the *coloniæ* were the cities out of Italy which possessed in the most perfect degree the rights of Roman citizens, but at a later period the *municipia* and *coloniæ* appear to have been nearly identical with each other. The Latian law was a modification of the municipal privileges and forms, which it is not necessary here to enter upon. The stipendiary towns are said to have been distinguished by the payment of their taxes in money, instead of giving a certain proportion of the produce of the soil. All these towns enjoyed the *civitas*, or rights of Roman citizens; they consisted of the town and a certain extent of land around it, and had a government of their own, republican in form, resembling the ancient constitution of Rome, and exempt from all control of the imperial officers. As soldiers, they were obliged only to defend their own town, and were not liable to serve elsewhere. They possessed, in fact, their own free constitution and officers, perhaps differing at times from one another; but, speaking generally, the Roman *municipium*, or town corporation, consisted of the people at large and the *curia* or governing body. The members of the *curia* were called *curiales, decuriones*, or senators; the rank was hereditary, the son of a *curialis* becoming a member of the *curia* by right of birth. Persons who were not of senatorial birth might, however, be elected into that body. The *curiales* received various emoluments, and possessed important privileges; they alone had the right of electing the magistrates and officers of the *municipium*. These officers were, first, two *duumviri*, or chief magistrates, who answered to the consuls at Rome, and whose authority extended over the *civitas*, or territory surrounding and depending upon the town. Sometimes the *municipium* had only one *duumvir*. The *duumviri* were chosen from among the *curiales*, no person not a member of the senatorial body being capable of election to that office. They were obliged to accept office, if elected; a *curialis* refusing to act as *duumvir*, or concealing himself to escape election, was punished by confiscation of his property. After the *duumviri*, a certain number of officers, termed *principales*, were elected out of the body of the *curia*, who were the administrators of the municipal affairs, and formed the permanent council of the *curia*. The *duumviri* were in general elected yearly; the *prin-*

cipales continued in office during fifteen years. Besides these, there were different inferior officers, equally elected by the *curia*. The whole body of the citizens—the *plebs*—elected an important officer, called the *defensor civitatis*, who was not to be a member of the *curia*, and whose duty it was to protect the populace against the senatorial body, when the latter acted unjustly or tyrannically; he was to the *municipium* what the tribune had been in Rome. There were also corporations or colleges of the different trades in the *municipia*, who chose their patrons among the senators or *curiales*.

At present we have unfortunately few inscriptions found in Britain which illustrate the municipal constitution of the towns under the Romans, probably because most of these which were thus constituted are now covered with modern towns, and the others have never been properly explored. The few which have been found leave no doubt that the Roman laws in this respect were firmly established here. We have already (p. 385) given an inscription commemorating a decurion of the *colonia* of Glevum (*Gloucester*), who died at Aquæ Solis (*Bath*). Another inscription (p. 381), mentions a sevir of the colonia of Eburacum (*York*). This word is generally understood as belonging to a military officer, but it must here refer to a municipal one. Several instances occur in which the *collegia* are mentioned in inscriptions in Britain. The *collegium ligniferorum* mentioned in inscriptions found at Castle Cary, in Scotland, has been conjectured to be of a religious character. A *collegium fabrorum* is mentioned in a celebrated inscription of an early date found at Chichester.* A still more celebrated inscription found near Bath, mentions a *collegium fabricensium*, a guild of smiths, or, as we should say now, smiths' company. This inscription relates to a member of this college who belonged to the twentieth legion, and is read as follows:—

IVLIVS VITA	Julius Vitalis,
LIS FABRICIES	smith of the
IS . LEG . XX . V . V .	twentieth legion, the valiant and victorious,
STIPENDIOR	who served nine years,
VM IX ANNOR XX	lived twenty-
IX. NATIONE BE	nine, by nation a Belgian,
LGA EX . COLLEGIO	by the college
FABRICE . ELATV	of the smiths carried to burial.
S . H S E	He is placed here.

* I have already given this inscription in a note to p. 51. It will be

Gruter has published an inscription, found on the site of the ancient Nomentum, in Italy, which commemorates an individual who held the office of *censitor* (or *censor*) of the citizens of Camulodunum (*Colchester*):—

CN . MUNATIVS . M . F . PAL AVRELIVS BASSVS	Cneius Munatius, Aurelius Bassus, son of Marcus, of the tribe Palatina,
. . . . PRÆF . COH . II ASTVRVM . CENSITOR . CIVIVM	. . . . præfect of the second cohort of the Asturians, censitor of the
ROMANORVM . COLONIAE . VIC- TRICENSIS	Roman citizens of the *colonia victrix* *
QVAE . EST . IN . BRITANNIA CAMOLODVNI	which is in Britannia at Camulodunum.

At first the rights of citizenship were given as a mark of honour and the reward of merit, chiefly to soldiers, for the Roman municipalities in the provinces were all originally military foundations; but subsequently they were granted more lavishly, and almost all the free population of the empire became eventually Roman citizens. In earlier times the grants of citizenship were duly registered at Rome, and copies of the grant, inscribed on plates of copper or bronze, appear to have been sent to the place where these new citizens resided. Several such plates have been discovered in Britain, as well as in other parts of the empire. One of these was dug up in the parish of Malpas, in Cheshire, in 1812; fragments of two others were found in a gravel-pit on Sydenham Common, in Kent, in 1806; and another was found at Stainington, in Yorkshire, in 1761. They are all decrees of the emperor Trajan, in favour of certain veterans serving in the troops in Britain, and conferring upon them the *civitas*, or rights of citizenship, and the consequent *connubium*, or civil rights belonging to legitimate marriage.† The inscription

understood that, in the inscription which follows, FABRICIESIS is merely contracted or mis-written for FABRICIENSIS.

* This epithet applied to the colonial town of Camulodunum, coincides with the account of Tacitus that it was placed under the auspices of Victory, whose temple served as a refuge to the inhabitants when attacked by the insurgent Britons.

† The Romans termed a discharge from military service, *missio;* and these inscribed plates, as honourable discharges, are called by antiquarians *tabulæ honestæ missionis*. Those found at Malpas and Sydenham were published by Samuel Lysons; the other is given in Gough's 'Camden,' edition of 1806.

TABULÆ HONESTÆ MISSIONIS.

found at Malpas, as the most perfect, may be given as an example of this important class of inscriptions:—

```
IMP . CAESAR . DIVI . NERVAE. F. NERVA . TRAIANVS
AVGVSTVS . GERMANICVS . DACICVS . PONTIFEX . MAX
IMVS . TRIBVNIC . POTESTAT VII IMP IIII COS . V . PP.
EQVITIBVS . ET . PEDITIBVS . QVI MILITANT . IN ALIS
QVATVOR . ET . COHORTIBVS . DECEM . ET . VNA . QVAE . AP
PELLANTVR . I . THRACVM . ET . I . PANNONIORVM . TAM
PIANA . ET . II . GALLORVM SEBOSIANA . ET . I . HISPA
NORVM VETTONVM . C . R . ET . I . HISPANORVM . ET . I
VALCIONVM . MILLIARIA . ET . I . ALPINORVM . ET . I
MORINORVM . ET . I . CVGERNORVM . ET . I . BAETASI
ORVM . ET . I . TVNGRORVM . MILLIARIA . ET . II . THRA
CVM . ET . III . BRACAR . AVGVSTANORVM . ET . IIII.
LINGONVM . ET . IIII . DELMATARVM . ET . SVNT
IN BRITANNIA SVB . I . NERATIO MARCELLO
QVI QVINA ET VICENA PLVRAVE STIPENDIA
MERVERVNT . QVORVM . NOMINA . SVBSCRIPTA.
SVNT IPSIS LIBERIS POSTERISQVE EORVM . CIVITA
TEM DEDIT ET CONVBIVM . CVM . VXORIBVS . QVAS .
TVNC HABVISSENT . CVM . EST . CIVITAS . IIS . DATA .
AVT . SI . QVI . COELIBES . ESSENT . CVM IIS QVAS
POSTEA . DVXISSENT . DVMTAXAT . SINGVLI . SIN
GVLAS . AD XIII K FEBR
M . LABERIO MAXIMO II
Q GLITIO ATILIO AGRICOLA II CO
ALAE . I . PANNONIORVM . TAMPIANAE . CVI PRAEEST
O VALERIVS CELSVS . DECVRIONI
REBVRRO SEVERI . F . HISPAN
DESCRIPTVM . ET . RECOGNITVM . EX TABVLA . AENEA
QVAE . FIXA . EST . ROMAE . IN MVRO . POST . TEMPLVM
DIVI AVGVSTI AD MINERVAM .
             Q . POMPEI HOMERI
             C . PAPI EVSEBETIS
             T . FLAVI SECVNDI
             P . CAVLI VITALIS
             C . VETTIENI MODESTI
             P . ATINI HEDONICI
             TI. CLAVDI MENANDRI
```

The date of this record is fixed by its internal evidence to the 20th day of January A.D. 103. The other similar monuments found in Britain are all of the same year. The example given above may be translated thus:—The emperor Cæsar, deified Nerva's son, Nerva Trajanus Augustus, the German, the Dacian, Pontifex Maximus, invested with the tribunitian power the seventh time, emperor the fourth year, consul the fifth time, father of his country, to the cavalry and infantry who serve in the four alæ and eleven cohorts, which are called the first of the Thracians, and the first of Pannonians termed the Tampian, and the second of Gauls termed the Sebosian, and the first of Spanish Vettones, Roman citizens, and the first of Spaniards, and the first of Valciones, a milliary one, and the first of Alpini, and the first of Morini, and the first of Cugerni, and the first of Bætasii, and the first of Tungrians, a milliary one, and the second of Thracians, and the third of Braccæ Augustani, and the fourth of Lingones, and the fourth of Dalmatians, and they are in Britain under Julius Neratius Marcellus, who have served twenty-five or more years, whose names are written below, to themselves, their children, and posterity, has given *civitas* and *connubium* (the rights of citizenship and marriage) with their wives, whom they might then have when citizenship was given to them, or if any of them were unmarried, with those whom they might afterwards take, that is to say, provided they have only one each. On the 13th kalends of February. To M. Laberius Maximus twice, and Q. Glitius Atilius Agricola twice consuls. To Reburrus, son of Severus, the Spaniard, decurion of the first ala of the Pannonians, termed the Tampian, which is commanded by C. Valerius Celsus. Copied and revised from the tablet of brass which is fixed at Rome on the wall behind the temple of divine Augustus near that of Minerva. Quintus Pompeius Homerus, Caius Papius Eusebes, Titus Flavius Secundus, Publius Caulus Vitalis, Caius Vettienus Modestus, Publius Atinius Hedonicus, and Titus Claudius Menander.

We have no traces of a Roman mint in Britain until the reign of Dioclesian and Maximian, on the exergue or vacant space on the reverse of some of whose coins we find the letters LON and ML, which numismatists seem agreed in interpreting *Londinium*, and *moneta Londinensis*, and in considering as an indication of the place at which they were minted. It is, however, far from certain that Roman money was not coined in the island before it was thought necessary to indicate the circumstance by such letters, and we cannot but be astonished at the extraordinary activity of the Roman mint in Britain during the usurpation of Carausius and Allectus. The great mass of their coins appear to have been struck in Britain. Those of Carausius bear in the exergues various combinations of letters, which, there can be little doubt, refer to different Roman towns in this island where they were minted. One of the more common forms is ML, which is interpreted *moneta Londinensis*, money of Londinium (*London*). In other examples there is simply an L for Londinium. Another common form is R S which is believed to signify *Rutupiis signata* (*moneta*), money coined at Rutupiæ (*Richborough*). The most common form of all is RSR, which is also supposed to mean money struck at Richborough, though the meaning of the second R has not been satisfactorily explained. The letters MRS, found on some coins of Carausius, may also signify *moneta Rutupiis signata*. Two different types of the same usurper have on the exergue the letters RSP, which are perhaps the initials of *Rutupiis signata pecunia*. The letter c is found singly on a considerable number of different types of the coinage of Carausius, and is believed to refer to Clausentum (*Bittern*), one of the great naval stations on the southern coast of Britain; and other similar inscriptions, such as MC, SC, MSC, SPC, are believed to refer to the same place, and to admit of the interpretations *moneta Clausenti, signata Clausenti, moneta signata Clausenti*, and *signata pecunia Clausenti*. The letters RSA, found in the exergue of at least one type, may refer to Rutupiæ. Other types exhibit the letters MS, or MSP, or simply M, which may possibly refer to Magna (*Kenchester*), where a remarkable quantity of the money of Carausius is constantly found. The letters may be thus interpreted, *Magnis signata, Magnis signata pecunia*, or giving merely the name of the place, *Magnis*. Many examples have numerals added to the name of the place, but their meaning is very doubtful. Thus we have many types of coins of Carausius bearing on the exergue the letters MLXXI, which seems to stand for *moneta Londinii xxi*; a combination of letters equally common is CXXI, which may stand for *Clausenti xxi*; and we have some which are marked simply with the numerals XXI. We have on other examples MLX (*moneta Londinii x*), and X by itself; LVII (*Londinii vii*); and the numerals XX and XXXX, without any indication of the name of the place. On the coinage of Allectus we find in the exergues the letters ML (*moneta Londinensis*), which is the most common; MSL (*moneta signata Londinii*); c. (*Clausenti*), which is also very common; M (*Magnis?*) CL, QL, and QC, which have not been explained. A few of the coins of Constantine the Great have in the exergue P LON (*pecunia Londinensis*), but they are far more common with the continental mint-marks. The inscription P LON is also found on the coins of Constantine's empress Fausta, of his sons Crispus and Constantine, and of his daughter-in-law (as it is supposed) Helena; but after the time of Allectus there are no indications of other towns in Britain in which money was minted; and even the simple P LON disappears after the reigns of the sons of Constantine. There may, however, have still remained a local mint, which, as far as is yet known, has left no distinguishing mark on its coinage.*

It is to be remarked that the insular coins of Carausius are not in general inferior in purity of metal and in execution to the contemporary coinage of the continent. But it is no less true that among the Roman money found in this country we find a great mass of debased or adulterated coinage, and, which is still more curious, that very extensive manufactures of spurious money have been traced. A few years ago, during the excavations for laying the foundations of King William-street, in the city of London, a considerable quantity of coins made of iron plated with silver, intended to pass as silver, were found packed up in tiers, as they had been imported into Britain, probably to pay the troops. The latest of them were of the emperor Claudius, which was perhaps the time when they were brought over hither. Most of these coins are in the cabinet of Mr Roach Smith, who also possesses a number of Roman forged coins cast in lead, found chiefly in the Thames. Amongst the numerous coins found at Maryport, in Cumberland, were a great quantity of forged denarii of Trajan and Hadrian, mostly, like those in Mr Smith's museum, cast in lead. It has been remarked that 'genuine coin must have been exceedingly scarce among the soldiers of this camp, and their credulity very great, to allow of the circulation of such base imitations.'

Extensive remains of the manufactures of spurious money under the Romans have been found in several places in this island, but more especially at Lingwell Gate, near Wakefield, in Yorkshire; at Edington, in Somersetshire; at Ruyton and Wroxeter, in Shropshire; and at Castor, in Northamptonshire. The last three places were the sites of well-known Roman towns, Rutunium, Uriconium, and Durobrivæ. The manner of casting the coins was a very simple process. A fine clay, found on the locality, was formed into small round tablets, of uniform size and thickness. A coin of one of the emperors was pressed between each two tablets, so as to leave a perfect impression, and the latter were then arranged upon one another in files or columns, the upper and lower tablets being impressed only on one side. A notch was broken into the side all the way down, which admitted the metal into each impression. Two, or three, of these columns, as the case might be, were placed side by side,

---

* It must be remarked that many of the foregoing explanations are conjectural, and they may perhaps admit of other interpretations. The c, for instance, may stand for Camulodunum, instead of Clausentum.

with the side notches joined together, and these were enclosed in a clay case, with a hole at the top, through which the melted metal ran down the opening left by the notches, by which it entered into all the impressions. The arrangement, as observed in the moulds found at Lingwell Gate, is exhibited in our woodcut, where the upper figure represents the faces of three impressed tablets as they were joined together in the columns. It was only necessary that care should be taken to place the tablets on one another so that the reverse might correspond with the head belonging to it. Their misplacement would produce those wrong reverses which are sometimes found among ancient Roman coins, and which have often puzzled the numismatist.

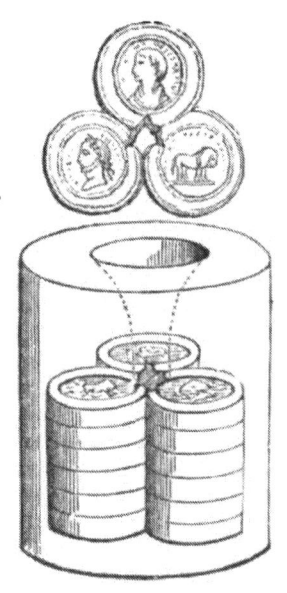

Moulds for Coining.

From the number of these moulds, which are found on the sites where they occur, we might imagine that after being used two or three times, they were thrown aside as waste, and new ones formed. In an account of those found at Edington, in Somersetshire, printed in the fourteenth volume of the 'Archæologia,' the writer informs us that 'the field in which they were found is a meadow that bears no marks of ever having been ploughed; which accounts for the moulds remaining so long undiscovered. It is situated at the north edge of Polden Hill, at about a quarter of a mile to the north of the village of Chilton. We were led to this particular spot by a person who had, some time before, cut through a bed of them in digging a drain. They were lying promiscuously scattered over a space about four feet square, and from six inches to a foot below the surface of the ground.' He adds that in the space of an hour they picked up several hundred moulds. They are found also scattered about very plentifully at Lingwell. In some instances pieces of metal have been found, and at Lingwell Gate an earthen crucible for melting it was met with. Some moulds have even been found to contain the forged coins as the metal had been poured in, which had never been taken out.

Moulds of the same kind have been found in France, especially in Lyons, and at Damery, near Epernay, in the department of the Marne. This latter place occupied the site of a Roman station. Excavations made there in the winter of 1829, brought to light, under a heap of burnt matter, the remains of extensive buildings which had evidently been destroyed by fire, and appeared to have consisted of baths and a moneyer's workshop. In some of the apartments were found vases full of coins. The first contained at least two thousand pieces of base silver, more than fifteen hundred of which bore the head of Postumus; the remainder presenting the series which is generally found from the elder Philip down to that reign. The fabric was bad, and the metal much alloyed. Another vase contained a silver coin of Antoninus; five small brass of the money of Treves, with the types of Rome and Constantinople; a hundred other small brass of the money of Treves, Lyons, Arles, Aquileia, and other towns, with the heads of Constans and Constantius, sons of Constantine; and nearly four thousand pieces in small brass of the fourth size, all of the same emperors, Constans and Constantius. All these coins were so fresh, that it seemed evident they had been made in the place where they were found, and that they had never been in circulation. This circumstance was soon explained by the discovery in an adjoining room of a manufactory of money, which, at the time the buildings were destroyed, must have been in full activity. 'There, under a heap of ashes and tiles, were found together, shears and the remains of other instruments suitable for the making of money; and several collections of moulds of baked earth, still containing the pieces which had been cast in them, and the ingot formed by the superfluous metal. These moulds were moulded from the money which they were intended to reproduce, by pressing the models between discs of worked clay of larger diameter, in order to form ledges, and were then placed one upon another, so that, with the exception of the first and last, they received on the two faces the stamp of the obverse and the reverse of a piece. The cavities and the impressions being obtained by this process, both easily and accurately, the discs composing the moulds were notched, in order to form a passage for the fused metal; they were then hardened in the fire, and replaced on one another, notch over notch, in the same order as when moulded.'

It has been a question rather learnedly and warmly discussed, whether these workshops were those of private forgers, or whether they were establishments under the direction of the imperial government. The latter supposition seems to be authorized by the fact that they are found in large towns, and apparently, in some instances, in public buildings. The moulds found at Polden Hill, in Somersetshire, were of Severus and his wife Julia, of Caracalla, Geta, Macrinus, Elagabalus, Alexander Severus, Maximinus, Maximus, Plautilla, Julia Paula, and Julia Mammæa. These, compared with other circumstances, seem to show that the forgeries were carried on after the reign of Severus, and that it was probably one scheme of the fiscal administration to raise money by the issue of debased coin, which, to protect the reigning emperor from odium, was cast from moulds of the coins of previous emperors. Of course, it does not follow necsssarily that some of the moulds which have been found in other places may not have belonged to private forgers, who thus enriched themselves by defrauding the public.

Mr Akerman has published a useful volume under the title of 'Coins of the Romans relating to Britain.' The series of Roman coins which come under this denomination have a peculiar interest connected with the history of our island. From the moment when Claudius set his foot on our shores, there was a regular series of imperial coins commemorative of victories in Britain by the emperors or by their military commanders. Those of Claudius, bearing on the reverse a triumphal arch with the inscription DE BRITTAN (over the Britons), are well known. The expedition of the emperor Hadrian was commemorated by a coin in large brass, struck in the year 121, on the reverse of which is the inscription, ADVENTVS AVG BRITANNIAE (the advent of the Augustus to Britain). The same emperor commemorated his exploits by another coin, bearing on the reverse a figure of a female seated on a rock, holding a spear on her arm, with a shield resting by her side, and the inscription BRITANNIA. There are several different coins of Hadrian with this device, from which they are usually known as the Britannia types, and similar coins were struck under Antoninus Pius; but in the latter the figure is more frequently a male than a female. It is from these Roman coins that the figure of Britannia was taken for our modern English mintage. Coins of Severus bear the inscription VICTORIAE BRITANNICAE, to commemorate the expeditions of that emperor against the Caledonians. Similar inscriptions appear on those of his sons, Caracalla and Geta. The mintage of the usurpers Carausius and Allectus furnish the most important monuments of the history of Britain during that period; while those of their successors are chiefly connected with our island by the marks of the London mint.

The great quantities of Roman coins which are found in this island, and which have been continually found for many ages, prove that there was no want of money in Roman Britain. They are usually found hoarded up in earthen vessels, each containing sometimes several thousand pieces. These had, no doubt, been concealed by the original proprietors, who were, by some accident or other, prevented from taking them from their hiding-places. The great number of pots of Roman money found in almost every part of Britain, show that this was the ordinary manner of storing up money which was not in circulation. It was no doubt buried in the ground within the limits of the residence of its proprietor, or in some spot where it was not likely to be intruded upon. Large urns of this kind are sometimes turned up by the ploughshare, and thus made to display their contents to the wondering eyes of the modern husbandman. Roman urns filled with coins have been found, in some instances—chiefly in the mining districts—concealed in crevices of rocks. The receptacle of the treasure was not always, however, an earthenware vessel. In the year 1837, a quantity of gold and silver coins of Roman emperors, from Nero to Hadrian, was found in a bronze vessel, formed like a shallow basket, and covered with a lid, concealed in the crevice of a rock at Thorngrafton, near Hexham, in Northumberland. Several instances have also occurred, where the coins had been placed in receptacles of a much more singular description. At Cirencester, in the time of Leland (under Henry VIII.), a quantity of Roman silver coin was found concealed in the shank bone of a horse, which was closed at the end with a peg;* and ten British gold coins were found by a boy tending sheep, a few years ago, near High Wycombe, in Buckinghamshire, in a hollow flint. A still more remarkable circumstance is the manner in which coins are spread over almost all Roman sites.

* 'By the town *nostris temporibus* was found a broken shank bone of a horse, the mouth closed with a pegge, the which was taken owt, a shepard founde yt fillid *nummis argenteis*.'—*Leland's Itin.*, vol. v. p. 61.

In excavating a town, or a villa, we find them scattered in the houses and courts, about the streets, and over the fields around. In the partial excavations at Lymne, where few of the usual articles of Roman antiquity were found, coins occurred everywhere. In the ploughed land on the hill round the walls of Richborough, one cannot walk long without picking up a Roman coin; and on many other long-deserted sites there is scarcely a cottager in the neighbourhood who has not a collection of coins, which he has picked up in his garden, or when at work in the adjoining fields. Any one would imagine that the Romans in Britain amused themselves with throwing their money away; and I am not aware that any probable explanation of this circumstance has yet been given.* The coins found thus scattered about are generally, as might be expected, in much worse condition than those which are found in hoards.

The mass of the Roman coins found in Britain are of very common types, and of small intrinsic value; but a few rarer specimens are generally found even in small hoards, and now and then an unique or nearly unique example occurs. This is more frequently the case with the coins of Carausius. Coins are found of all periods, from the consular series to the time when the Roman legions abandoned the island, and in collections of any extent, in whatever part of the island they are made, the proportional quantities of the coins of the different emperors are generally much the same. There are some local exceptions to this rule, more especially with regard to the coinage of Carausius and Allectus, which are found to predominate in one or two places, which were no doubt chief stations of their troops. More than eleven hundred Roman coins found of late years at Richborough, and described by Mr Roach Smith, presented the following proportional numbers for each emperor or empress:—

British	1	Brought forward	17
Consular	3	Claudius (A.D. 41—54)	15
Augustus (B.C. 27—A.D. 14)	7	Nero (A.D. 50—68)	11
Agrippa (B.C. 9—A.D. 30)	1	Vespasian (A.D. 69—79)	13
Tiberius (A.D. 14—37)	2	Titus (A.D. 69—81)	1
Antonia (wife of Drusus senior)	1	Domitian (A.D. 69—96)	10
Caligula (A.D. 37—41)	2	Nerva (A.D. 96—98)	1
	17		68

* Great quantities of Roman coins have been brought up from the bed of the river Thames at London by dredgers.

Brought forward	68	Brought forward	244
Trajan (A.D. 98—117)	7	Maximianus (A.D. 286—310)	16
Hadrian (A.D. 117—138)	5	Carausius (A.D. 287—293)	94
Sabina (wife of Hadrian)	1	Allectus (A.D. 293—296)	45
Ælius Cæsar (A.D. 136—138)	2	Constantius I. (A.D. 293—306)	4
Antoninus Pius (A.D. 138—161)	5	Helena (wife of Constantius)	8
Faustina the Elder (wife of Antoninus)	3	Theodora (second wife of Constantius)	13
Marc. Aurelius (A.D. 161—180)	4	Galerius Maximianus (A.D. 292—311)	1
Faustina the Younger (wife of M. Aurelius)	5	Maxentius (A.D. 306—312)	2
Lucius Verus (A.D. 161—169)	2	Romulus (son of Maxentius)	1
Lucilla (wife of Lucius Verus)	1	Licinius (A.D. 307—324)	12
Commodus (A.D. 166—192)	2	Licinius junior	1
Severus (A.D. 197—211)	5	Constantine the Great (A.D. 306—337)	149
Julia Domna (wife of Severus)	3	Fausta (wife of Constantine)	2
Caracalla (A.D. 196—217)	3	Crispus (A.D. 317—326)	18
Julia Mæsa (sister of Julia Domna)	1	Delmatius (nephew of Constantine)	1
Severus Alexander (A.D. 221—235)	7	Constantine II. (A.D. 317—340)	98
Gordianus (A.D. 238—244)	6	Constans (A.D. 333—350)	77
Philippus (A.D. 244—249)	4	Constantius II. (A.D. 323—361)	42
Valerianus (A.D. 254—260)	3	Urbs Roma	52
Valerianus junior	1	Constantinopolis	60
Gallienus (A.D. 253—268)	19	Magnentius (A.D. 350—353)	21
Salonina (wife of Gallienus)	4	Decentius (A.D. 351—353)	4
Postumus (A.D. 260—267)	10	Julianus II. (A.D. 355—363)	7
Victorinus (A.D. 265—267)	14	Helena (wife of Julian)	1
Marius (A.D. 267)	1	Jovianus (A.D. 363—364)	1
Tetricus (A.D. 267—272)	13	Valentinianus (A.D. 364—375)	22
Claudius Gothicus (A.D. 268—270)	15	Valens (A.D. 364—378)	39
Quintillus (A.D. 270)	2	Gratianus (A.D. 375—383)	49
Aurelianus (A.D. 270—275)	4	Theodosius (A.D. 379—395)	14
Tacitus (A.D. 275)	5	Magnus Maximus (A.D. 383—388)	6
Florianus (A.D. 276)	1	Victor (son of Maximus)	3
Probus (A.D. 276—282)	7	Eugenius (A.D. 392—395)	1
Carinus (A.D. 282—285)	1	Arcadius (A.D. 383—408)	27
Numerianus (A.D. 282—284)	2	Honorius (A.D. 393—423)	8
Diocletianus (A.D. 284—313)	8	Constantine III. (A.D. 407)	1
	244	Total	1144

Of these Richborough coins, seven (including the British coin) are of gold, fifty-six of silver, fifteen of billon or debased silver, and the rest of brass. The coins of billon, like most of the debased silver, belong to the immediate successors of Severus. Silver coins are often found in much larger proportions to the others; and the gold coins are too often carried away separately, on account of their value, and they have thus frequently found their way direct to the melting-pot. Among two hundred and sixty-eight Roman coins found at Caerleon, and described in Mr Lee's work on that ancient city, there

CHAP. XIII.] PROPORTIONAL NUMBERS OF ROMAN COINS. 439

were two of gold, forty-four of silver, eleven plated, and three of billon or debased metal. These coins belonged to the different emperors in the following proportions:—

Claudius	1	Brought forward	104
Nero	1	Gallienus	1
Vespasian	13	Salonina	2
Titus	1	Postumus	2
Domitian	5	Victorinus	4
Nerva	2	The Tetrici	7
Trajan	12	Claudius Gothicus	7
Hadrian	9	Probus	2
Antoninus Pius	11	Maximianus	5
Faustina, the elder	3	Carausius	21
Marcus Aurelius	3	Allectus	4
Faustina, the younger	1	Constantius	1
Lucius Verus	1	Helena	1
Lucilla	2	Galerius Maximianus	2
Mammæa	1	Licinius	4
Julia Soæmias	2	Constantine the Great	28
Commodus	3	Fausta	1
Severus	11	Crispus	4
Julia	2	Constantine II.	8
Caracalla	7	Constans	13
Geta	3	Constantius II.	6
Julia Mæsa	1	Urbs Roma	13
Macrinus	1	Constantinopolis	5
Severus Alexander	1	Magnentius	12
Elagabalus (Heliogabalus)	1	Decentius	1
Gordianus	3	Valens	7
Philippus	2	Gratianus	2
Valerianus	1	Arcadius	1
	104	Total	268

CHAPTER XIV.

Declining State of the Roman Empire after the age of Julian—Theodosius sent to Britain—Revolt and Career of Maximus—Stilicho—Marcus and Gratian revolt in Britain—The Usurper Constantine—Honorius—Britain independent of the Empire and harassed by the Northern Barbarians—The Britons receive assistance from Rome—The last Roman Legion withdrawn—The Angles and Saxons come in—The Angles settle in Northumbria—The Jutes in Kent—Hengest and Horsa—Ælla in Sussex—Cerdic arrives in Hampshire—Essex and the Angles—Mission of St Augustine and Conversion of the Anglo-Saxons to Christianity.

At the period when we have to resume our sketch of the history of Britain, the vast empire of the Cæsars, harassed on all sides by its outward enemies, was approaching fast towards a dissolution. It had required all the courage and vigilance of Julian to keep the Teutons at bay on the northern frontier, and the Saxons were becoming every day more formidable in the western seas. The governor or vicar of Britain, at the time when Julian ascended the imperial throne, was an officer named Alypius, who was recalled by the emperor, in order to be entrusted with the charge of directing the rebuilding of the walls of Jerusalem, which Julian had determined to restore in a feeling of hostility to the Christians. We know nothing of the state of Britain during Julian's reign, but soon after the accession of Jovian it was fearfully harassed by the joint attacks of the Picts, Scots, and Attacots from the north, and of the Saxons from the sea. They seem to have met with little resistance until the reign of his successor Valentinian, who, giving up the empire of the east to his brother Valens, employed his own energy in restoring security and order to the west. It was in the year 368, as Valentinian was on his way from Amiens to Treves, that he received intelligence from Britain of a new and terrible irruption of the barbarians, who had defeated and slain the count of the maritime district (the Saxon coast), Nectarides, while the duke Fullofaudes (no doubt the same officer called in the Notitia duke of Britain), had fallen into an ambush. In his first moment of indignation, the emperor despatched Severus, the count of the domestics, or steward of the household, to take the command in the island; but, on reflection, he recalled this appointment, and substituted in his place Jovinus, who instantly sent Provertuides to Britain to assemble the troops, that they might be ready on his arrival. Further consideration seems to have opened Valentinian's eyes still more to the gravity of the crisis, and the appointment was changed again, the command of Britain being finally entrusted to one of the ablest of the imperial generals, the celebrated Theodosius.

Theodosius hastened to Boulogne, which was at this time called Bononia, and he soon landed at Rutupiæ with a strong force, composed of the Batavii, the Eruli, the Jovii, and the Victores. We are told by the historian Ammianus Marcellinus, the brief narrator of these events, that the Picts, who at this time were divided into two great tribes (the Dicalidones and the Vecturiones), had joined with the Scots and the fierce nation of the Attacotti, in this invasion, and we can understand its grave character, when we are assured that at the time of the landing of Theodosius at Rutupiæ, the enemies were plundering the country round London, the name of which had then been changed to Augusta. The Roman commander immediately marched against them, and sub-dividing his forces, defeated their numerous predatory bands with great slaughter, and deprived them of their booty, a great part of which was restored to those from whom it had been taken. The citizens of London joyfully opened their gates to their deliverer, and he remained there a short time to give repose to his troops, and to consider the difficulties with which he had to contend. He soon learnt from deserters and captives the character of the enemy with which he had to deal, and he came to the conclusion that they might be conquered by policy as much as by arms. He issued a proclamation offering a pardon to all who would desert from their ranks, and 'on this promise a great number returned to their duty.' It is evident from this, that there was an insurrection of the subject population combined with the invasion. Theodosius next sent a report on the state of Britain to the emperor, and recommended that an officer named Civilis, distinguished for his energy and honesty, should be sent to him as governor of Britain, accompanied by a distinguished military commander, the duke Dulcitius.*

After remaining some time at London, to wait the effect of his proclamation, and the arrival of Civilis and Dulcitius with reinforcements, Theodosius left that city at the head of a brave and well-appointed army, and, by his rapid and great success, soon justified the high military character for which he was previously known. 'He always anticipated the enemy in occupying the most important positions, and gave no orders to the common soldiers which he was not himself the first to execute. In this way, discharging the duties both of an able general and brave soldier, he routed the various tribes whose insolence, prompted by security, had led them to attack the Roman province, and he re-established the cities and fortresses, which had suffered severely by their manifold losses, but which in their foundation had been calculated for preserving the island in permanent tranquillity.'† Among the auxiliary troops sent into Britain by the emperor Valentinian, and probably at this time, was a body of Germans (*numerus Allemannorum*), with a king or chief (*rex*), named Fraomarius, who received the title and office of tribune.

The first successes of a commander like Theodosius were sufficient to discourage the opponents with whom he had to deal; and he not only cleared the southern districts of their invaders, but he recovered from the Picts and Scots the country between the walls of Hadrian and Antoninus, which he found in the undisturbed possession of the enemy, and to which he now gave the name of Valentia, in honour of the emperor. He repaired and strengthened the forts and garrisons which protected the northern frontier, and the island appears to have been restored to a degree of peace and prosperity which it had not enjoyed for many years. For this Britain was probably indebted in some degree to the indulgence of Valentinian, whose constant study it is said to have been to ease the provinces by relieving them of taxes and protecting their frontiers.

* Denique edictis propositis impunitateque promissa, desertores ad procinctum vocabat, et multos alios per diversa libero commeatu dispersos. Quo monitu ut rediere plerique, incentivo percitus, retentusque anxiis curis, Civilem nomine recturum Britannias pro præfectis ad se poposcerat mitti, virum acrioris ingenii, sed justi tenacem et recti; itidemque Dulcitium ducem scientia rei militaris insignem.—*Ammianus Marcel.*, lib. xxvii. c. 9.

† In integrum restituit civitates et castra, multiplicibus quidem damnis afflicta, sed ad quietem temporis longi fundata.—*Ammianus Marcel.*, lib. xxviii. c. 3.

Indeed, when we consider the brief and imperfect account of these events given by the old historian, we become convinced that there was something more than a mere invasion of barbarians, and that these had been joined, if not called in, by a large portion of the population of the Roman province. We have seen many instances of the readiness with which the cities in Britain rose up in rebellion against the imperial authority, and it is not improbable that they looked upon the change which had turned their governor into a mere vicar under the government of Gaul as a serious diminution of their independence. Perhaps, under the new *régime*, their taxes and services had become more burthensome. It is certain, however, that Ammianus Marcellinus, in resuming briefly the character of the emperor Valentinian, blames him for an habitual inattention to the complaints of his subjects in the distant provinces, and accidentally informs us that it was this circumstance which had caused the tumults in Britain.* The people of Britain had therefore asked for a redress of grievances, and the emperor had turned a deaf ear to their complaints. Another incident mentioned by the historian shows us that there was intelligence between the insurgents and the invaders. There was, we are told, in the province a class of men employed who were entitled, according to the text of Ammianus as now printed, Areani, but which is supposed to be an error for Arcani, secret agents; for he informs us that their duty was to travel as spies among the different peoples on the frontiers of the empire, and bring early intelligence of their movements and designs. These men, we are told, in Britain, had entered into communication with the enemies, and had given them information which enabled them to make their invasions with the greater security and advantage. The Arcani had become so dangerous, that Theodosius found it necessary to deprive them of the power of doing further evil, and, as far as we can gather, the office itself appears to have been abolished.†

* In hoc tantum deerrans, quod, quum gregariorum etiam levia puniret errata, potiorum ducum flagitia progredi sinebat in majus, ad querelas in eos motas aliquoties obsurdescens; unde Britannici strepitus et Africanæ clades et vastitas emersit Illyrici.—*Ammianus Marcel.*, lib. xxx. c. 9.

† Ammianus had given a further account of these Arcani, or Areani, in a part of his book which is now lost. The manuscript which preserved his history through the destructive period which followed the fall of the empire had been much mutilated; and it happens unfortunately that, as in the case of Tacitus, the very books which would have given us important information on the history and condition of Britain were those which have perished.

Another occurrence related by the same historian gives us a passing glance of the divisions and intrigues which at this time reigned in the province of Britain. There was in Britain at this time a man named Valentinus, a native of Valeria, in Pannonia, notorious for his intrigues and ambition, who had been sent as an exile to Britain in expiation of some heavy crime. This practice of banishing political offenders to Britain appears to have been, at the time of which we are now speaking, very prevalent; for we learn from the same annalist that a citizen of Rome, named Frontinus, was at the time of the revolt just described sent into exile in Britain for a similar cause. Men like these no sooner arrived in the island than they took an active part in its divisions, and brought the talent for political intrigue which had been fostered in Italy to act upon the agitation already existing in the distant province. Such was the case with Valentinus, who, as the brother-in-law of one of the deepest agitators of Rome, the vicar Maximinus (described by Ammianus as *ille exitialis vicarius*), had no doubt been well trained for the part he was now acting. As far as we can gather from the brief notices of the historian, this individual seems, when Theodosius arrived in Britain, to have been actively engaged in some ambitious designs, which the arrival of that great and upright commander rendered hopeless. Theodosius had not been long in Londinium, when he received private information that Valentinus was engaged with the other exiles in a formidable conspiracy, and that even many of the military had been secretly corrupted by his promises.* With the vigour which characterised all his actions, Theodosius caused the arch-conspirator and his principal accomplices to be seized suddenly, at the moment when their designs were on the point of being carried into execution, and they were delivered over to duke Dulcitius, to receive the punishment due to their crimes; but, aware of the extensive ramifications of the plot in which they had been engaged, and believing that it had been sufficiently crushed, Theodosius wisely put a stop to all further inquiries, fearing lest by prosecuting them he might excite an alarm, which would only bring a renewal of the scenes of turbulence and outrage which his presence had already in a great

* Quietis impatiens malefica bestia ad res perniciosas consurgebat et novas, in Theodosium tumore quodam, quem solum resistere posse nefandis cogitationibus advertebat. Multa tamen clam palamque circumspiciens, crescente flatu cupiditatis immensæ exsules solicitabat et milites, pro temporis captu ausorum illecebrosas pollicendo mercedes.

measure appeased.* The prudence as well as the valour of Theodosius were thus united in restoring Britain to peace and tranquillity; and we are assured that when, in 359, he quitted the island, he was accompanied to the port where he embarked by crowds of grateful provincials.

The spirit of discontent and rebellion, which appears to have been so widely spread among the inhabitants of the island province, was only suppressed by Theodosius to break out a few years afterwards in a more alarming form. The emperor Valentinian died in the November of the year 375, and left the empire to his two sons, Gratian, who had already partaken in its cares, and Valentinian, a mere child. Theodosius had already fallen a victim to the jealousies of the court, but he had left a son, also named Theodosius, to inherit his greatness. The empire of the east having been made vacant by the death of Valens, Gratian chose the young Theodosius as his successor, in 379; he had already divided the empire of the west, by placing Italy and the countries bordering on the Mediterranean under his younger brother, while he retained for himself the more difficult task of governing Gaul, Spain, and Britain. The elevation of Theodosius to the imperial dignity was the signal for a general revolt in the latter province. There was at this time in Britain a young officer, a native of Spain, named Magnus Maximus, who had served in the island along with young Theodosius, and who was now a great favourite with the troops, although we are not informed what command he held. It is said that his jealous mind was profoundly wounded at the honours showered upon Theodosius, and that he was easily induced to join in a conspiracy for wresting the western division of the empire from Gratian. In the year 383, the soldiers in Britain, who are characterised by the almost contemporary historian as the most arrogant and turbulent of all the imperial troops,† rose, it appears, unanimously, and proclaimed Maximus their emperor. Maximus at once placed himself at the head of the British army, and, passing over to the continent, landed at the mouth of the Rhine. The troops in Germany immediately revolted to his standard, and the new emperor marched triumphantly into Treves, which he made his capital

* De conjuratis quæstiones agitari prohibuit, ne formidine sparsa per multos reviviscerent provinciarum turbines compositi.

† Οἷα τῶν ἄλλων ἁπάντων πλίον αὐθαδίᾳ καὶ θυμῷ νικωμένους.— Zosimus, lib. iv. c. 35.

Of the events which followed, the accounts of different writers are very contradictory; but, according to that which appears to be entitled to most credit, Gratian was residing at Paris, without any suspicion of the danger which threatened him, when he received intelligence of this dangerous revolt. Perceiving that he was deserted by the troops in Gaul, whose hostility he had provoked, and having ascertained that it was in vain to attempt to resist the usurper, he fled towards Italy, accompanied by a faithful body of cavalry. But treason seemed to beset him on all sides. The governor of the province of Lugdunum (*Lyons*) treacherously persuaded him to remain in Gaul, and amused him with deceitful stories of armies that were rising up to support his cause, until the general of the cavalry of Maximus, the unscrupulous Andragathius, arrived with a strong body of troops, to whom Gratian was delivered, to be sacrificed immediately by the hand of an assassin.

The triumph of Maximus was now complete, and having no longer any formidable rival to contend with in the west, he assumed all the insignia and attributes of empire, conferred the rank of Cæsar on his son Victor, still a child, and sent an ambassador to the court of Theodosius, instructed to represent to the eastern emperor that he had been compelled by the army to assume the purple, to express his grief for the murder of Gratian, which he pretended had been done without his knowledge, and to offer Theodosius the choice of war or peace. Theodosius, considering it prudent to temporise, chose the latter, and it was agreed that Maximus should retain Britain, Gaul, and Spain, leaving to the young emperor Valentinian the provinces which had been assigned to him by his brother. Maximus now took up his residence in Treves, where he displayed the cruelty of his disposition in persecuting some Christian heretics, with the object, it is said, of conciliating the more orthodox Christians in Italy, that they might assist him in his ultimate designs of reducing Italy to his obedience. At length, when the moment appeared favourable for this enterprise, he began by treacherously obtaining possession of the fortresses which guarded the passes of the Alps. This was no sooner effected, than the usurper, by a secret and rapid march, came unexpectedly with his formidable army before the gates of Milan. Valentinian fled with his mother, the empress Justina, and his court, and succeeded in reaching in safety the dominions of Theodosius; while Maximus, who had met with no serious opposition, entered Aquileia as emperor of the undivided west.

Theodosius was now roused to resistance and revenge by this bold usurpation, and having despatched a body of foreign auxiliaries under Arbogastes, to march along the shores of the Danube, he placed himself at the head of another army which marched through Pannonia, while a numerous fleet conducted Valentinian and his mother back to Italy. Maximus had hitherto succeeded by treason and fraud, and not by arms, and he seems to have been overcome with the consciousness of the superior military talents of the adversary with whom he had now to contend. His troops were defeated whenever they attempted to oppose the advance of the enemy, and Aquileia itself, in spite of its impregnable walls, was soon obliged to throw open its gates to Theodosius. Maximus was taken, and immediately put to death; and Arbogastes having by this time advanced into Gaul, the child Victor was also taken, and fell an innocent victim to the ambition of his father.

The expedition of Maximus has been made by the old historians of Britain a fertile source of fable. It is pretended that the island was so entirely drained of its population, that it was never again able to defend itself against its barbarian invaders; that the vast host of Britons who followed Maximus into Gaul settled in Armorica after his defeat, and caused that country to receive the name of Brittany; and that the eleven thousand virgins, who afterwards figured so prominently in the Romish martyrology, were maidens sent over from the island of Britain to serve as wives to these adventurers. Such stories have no foundation in accurate history; and we have no good reason for supposing that the usurpation of Maximus had led to any very formidable invasion of the province in which he had assumed the purple, although it is not probable that the Picts and Scots would allow such an opportunity to pass without a renewal of their predatory incursions. All that we know is, that after the death of Maximus, Theodosius marched into Gaul, where he appointed one of his eastern officers, Chrysanthus, to the government of Britain. The new vicar probably carried back with him most of the British troops, and perhaps he took reinforcements. He is said to have restored the island to a state of tranquillity. After ruling Britain for a short period, Chrysanthus returned to the east, where he was made præfect of Constantinople; and by a singular change of profession, this minister of the imperial will was subsequently made a bishop.

We are now again left in utter darkness as to the internal

condition of Roman Britain, but it seems to have been exposed to continual attacks from the Picts and Scots, or from the Saxons. The emperor Theodosius died in 395, and left his western dominions to be ruled by the feeble Honorius, while Arcadius governed the east. For a time the talents of Stilicho arrested the fate of the empire, and it appears that Britain owed to this great general some years of unusual tranquillity. In the Notitia Imperii, composed in this reign, we learn the military force which was then employed for the protection of the island.* The twentieth legion, which had been so long stationed at Deva (*Chester*), had then been entirely withdrawn; it is believed to have been taken away towards the end of the fourth century, to be employed in the Getic war. Two legions, however, still remained, with numerous bodies of auxiliaries; and as these legions were the same that had always been in Britain, they furnish evidence of the inaccuracy of the statement that the island had been exhausted of its defenders. The sixth legion remained in its old quarters at Eburacum, but the second legion had been removed from Isca to Rutupiæ, in order, no doubt, that it might be ready to act against the Saxon marauders, or, in case of need, to be transported into Gaul. The south-eastern and eastern coasts were strongly guarded, and in the latter several fortresses appear to have been newly erected, which are not mentioned at an earlier period; such as Othona, on the coast of Essex (the Saxon Ythanceaster, the site of which is supposed to be now covered by the sea), Gariannonum, in Suffolk (now Burgh Castle), and Branodunum, in Norfolk (the site of which is now called Brancaster). The cities and municipal towns no doubt retained their military organisation; and in the invasions to which the island was at this time exposed, they had to provide for their own defence.

In the beginning of the fifth century, the soldiers in Britain revolted, and conferred the title of emperor on a man named Marcus. Soon tired of his rule, they slew him in 407, and chose in his place Gratian, a burgher of one of the towns in Britain.† This shows the prominent part which the towns took in the political troubles which then prevailed. Gratian was allowed to reign four months, and then he also was slain. The lot next fell upon an obscure soldier, who is said to have

* See before, p. 418.
† Apud Britannias Gratianus, municeps ejusdem insulæ, tyrannu creatur et occiditur.—*Orosius, Hist.*, lib. vii. c. 40.

been chosen merely because his name was Constantine, which was imagined to be a good omen. It is probable, however, that he possessed other qualities, for he was no sooner invested with the purple than he showed a vigour and decision of character equal to the task he had undertaken. He at once collected his army and passed into Gaul, where he was received as a deliverer, and acknowledged as the emperor of the west. His reputation and popularity increased, when the Germans, who had harassed the country, were reduced to submission by his two præfects, Justinus and Neviogastes.

At this moment (the earlier part of the year 408), the death of the emperor Arcadius, and the elevation to the throne of the east of Theodosius II., occupied the attention of the western emperor; but, on the arrival of news of Constantine's revolt, Stilicho, who was still alive, proceeded to Rome to concert measures for suppressing it. He began by sending one of his generals, Sarus, into Gaul, who defeated the præfect Justinus in battle, and slew him and a great part of his men. He then laid siege to Valentia, where he had been informed that Constantine was holding his court. Here Neviogastes offered to negotiate, but he was entrapped by Sarus, and treacherously put to death. Constantine, not discouraged, appointed two new præfects, Edovinchus, a Frank, and Count Gerontius, a native of Britain, whose military talents were so well known, that Sarus raised the siege of Valentia, and made so hasty a retreat before Constantine's troops, that he was obliged to give up his plunder and baggage to the Bagaudi, who held the passes of the Alps.

Constantine now felt secure in his power, and he proceeded to strengthen the frontiers of his territories with garrisons and military posts. He next conferred the dignity of Cæsar on his eldest son Constans, whom, it is said, he took from a monastery to associate with him in the empire. Constans marched with a part of his father's army into Spain, and, not without some difficulty, reduced that province also to his sway, and then, leaving Count Gerontius to command it, returned to Gaul, at a moment when the death of Stilicho seemed to have relieved the usurper from all danger. Constantine now followed a policy similar to that of Maximus, in sending an embassy to Ravenna to entreat the forgiveness of Honorius for accepting an empire which he said had been forced upon him by the soldiery. Honorius, pressed by difficulties on all sides, reluctantly permitted him to retain the title he had usurped. Constantine afterwards sent Jovius, a man of learning and talent, as his envoy to the imperial court, to ask forgiveness for the murder of Didymus and Verinianus, two near relations of Honorius, who had been taken prisoners by Constans in Spain, and he succeeded in obtaining a formal recognition of his title.

The successful rebel had now to contend with a rebellion against himself. Constans returned to Spain, carrying with him a new general, named Justus, whose appointment was so offensive to Count Gerontius, that he revolted with the army under his command, and by means of his agents procured a new invasion of Gaul by the barbarians. Instead of assuming the purple himself, Gerontius conferred the dignity of emperor on a man named Maximus, and leaving him to reign in Spain, pursued Constans across the Pyrenees, and having captured him at Vienne, immediately put him to death. He then marched to besiege the father in the city of Arles. At this time (A. D. 411), occurred the death of Alaric, and Honorius, relieved from the terror which the name of the Gothic king had so long inspired, sent Count Constantius with a powerful army to assert his authority in Gaul and Spain. Constantius approached Arles at the moment when it was closely besieged by Gerontius, whose soldiers raised the siege tumultuously, and rising furiously against their commander, put him to death. Gerontius being thus disposed of, Constantius, with the troops of Honorius, continued the siege of Arles, and, after defeating a body of troops which had come to the assistance of Constantine, compelled him to surrender. He made conditions for his life, and was sent a prisoner to Italy; but he was privately put to death before he reached Ravenna.

The triumph of Constantius did not restore Gaul to obedience, and from this time its western provinces, as well as Spain and Britain, threw off all subjection to Rome, and began to rule themselves in their own way. This was not in itself a difficult task, for the cities had always been accustomed to govern themselves, while the superior government consisted principally of the fiscal department and the military command. It appears by the narrative of Zosimus, that while the usurper was establishing himself in Gaul, Britain had been again visited by the Saxon invaders, and we are assured that the British cities took up arms to defend themselves, and that they drove away their assailants.* Their freedom was acknowledged by

* Οἵτε οὖν ἐκ τῆς Βρεττανίας ὅπλα ἐνδόντες, σφῶν αὐτῶν προκινδυνεύ-

THE CITIES IN BRITAIN.

Honorius, who, in 410, sent letters to the cities of Britain exhorting them to provide for their own safety.*

We now approach a period, the real history of which is involved in profound obscurity, and to understand it at all we must glance back on what has been already said of the state of the island under Roman rule. The municipal cities, as it has been seen, were founded for the security and protection of the province, and by their constitution each was a little republic in itself, governed by itself, while they were linked together only by the superior fiscal administration which took from them certain fixed taxes, by the judicial administration which regulated the relations between them, and by the military command which held the province and defended it. During four centuries the original population of the island must have been much diminished, and perhaps, except in particular parts, consisted of little more than the servile peasantry;† the population of the cities had been recruited by the natural increase of the inhabitants and by arrivals from the continent, and we have already seen by the inscriptions and other monuments that the latter class of recruits were becoming more and more Teutonic. In fact, there can be little doubt that German blood predominated, to a great extent, in many of the Roman cities in Britain, at the time when Honorius gave them entire independence. They were thus left somewhat in the position of the free cities of the middle ages, each ruling itself internally, within its own massive walls and surrounding territory, and, in external affairs, either acting by itself or joining in confederacy with other towns.

The invasions of the Saxons resembled much that of the Danes at a later period. At first mere predatory attacks, they had gradually made their leaders acquainted with the island and its inhabitants, and these appear to have attempted soon to form permanent settlements, selecting just the same coast districts as were chosen by the Danes for the same purpose. It seems to be the received opinion that the title *littus Saxonicum*,

σαντες, ἠλευθέρωσαν τῶν ἐπικειμένων βαρβάρων τὰς πόλεις.—*Zosimus*, lib. vi. c. 6.

* Ὀνωρίου δὲ γράμμασι πρὸς τὰς ἐν Βρεττανίᾳ χρησαμένου πόλεις, φυλάττεσθαι παραγγέλλουσι.—*Zosimus*, lib. vi. c. 10.

† Some confusion has been created by misunderstanding the term Britons as used by the later historians, who apply it to the Roman population born in the island, and not to the original Celtic race. In the same way the later writers apply the term Celtic to the Romano-Gallic population of Gaul, to distinguish it from the Teutonic invaders from the other side of the Rhine.

applied to the coasts of Suffolk and Norfolk during the later Roman period, indicates that there was a Saxon population there, subject of course to the Roman government. It was perhaps also the case in other parts of the kingdom. When new invasions took place, these settlers probably often rose to join their brethren. The latter, during the divisions of the island under the later emperors, were frequently called in by one party in the island as allies, and they took part in the attempt to throw off the yoke of Rome. When, therefore, the British cities were left to themselves, it is natural that they should become more intimately connected, either as friends or foes, with the Teutons from the Rhine and the Elbe. It seems certain that in some parts, especially in some of the cities, the transition from Roman to Saxon was gradual, and that the two races mixed together. At Canterbury, Colchester, Rochester, and other places, we find Roman and Saxon interments in the same cemetery; and in the extensive Saxon burial-ground at Osengal, in the isle of Thanet, a Roman interment in a leaden coffin was met with. The result of the discoveries which have been made in the researches among the Saxon cemeteries has been to render it more and more probable that the Saxons were gradually gaining a footing in the island before the period at which the grand invasions are said to have commenced.

The Picts appear to have entered the Roman provinces, not by scaling the wall, according to the vulgar notion published under the name of Gildas, but from the Solway, where they were joined by the Scots, or Irish, and thence they spread themselves over the north-eastern parts of England. When we excavate the sites of Roman towns in this part of the country, we still meet with traces of their destructive progress. Thus, when the interior of the station at Maryport, in Cumberland, was excavated in 1766, the workmen found the arch of the gate beaten violently down and broken; and on entering the great street, they discovered evident marks of the houses having been more than once burnt to the ground and rebuilt, as though the place had been several times taken and recovered. At Ribchester, in Lancashire, the important Roman town supposed to be Coccium appears to have been destroyed in one of these later inroads. In the course of excavations made there in the earlier part of the present century, the ruins of the temple of Minerva were discovered; they presented indisputable proofs of its having been burnt, and among the *débris* were found skeletons, no doubt those of soldiers who had here made their last stand against the assailants. It was a parallel story to that of the destruction of Camulodunum by the fierce troops of Boadicea. It is also worthy of remark, that all the Roman towns on the Welsh border to the north of Gloucester were destroyed, apparently, before the period of the Saxon invasion.

Such are the slight and rather vague notions we can form of what took place in Britain after the cities were left to take care of themselves. It was not an independent state, but a number of small independent republics, which of course had a common interest against invaders, but which would most probably be soon divided into hostile confederacies amongst themselves. In these intestine wars, the prevalence of Teutonic blood in the population of so many of the towns would naturally lead them to call in Teutonic allies, and we can thus easily understand how Angles and Saxons were gradually establishing themselves on the eastern and south-eastern coasts, while the western districts were harassed by continual invasions of Picts and Scots. The only allusion to these events by a contemporary writer is found in the Chronicle of Prosper of Aquitaine, about A. D. 455, who states that in the eighteenth year of the reign of Theodosius the Younger (A. D. 441), Britain, after many slaughters and revolutions, was reduced under the rule of the Saxons.*

The period which intervened, left a blank by contemporary annalists, was at a later period filled up with fable. According to the tract which goes under the name of Gildas, when Maximus carried with him the soldiery of Britain to establish his usurpation in Gaul, he left the island not only destitute of military, but without men capable of bearing arms, and it was thus exposed in a state of helplessness to the attacks of the barbarians. The British soldiers and youths, we are told, never again returned, and 'for many years' the Britons groaned under the cruel oppressions of the Picts and Scots.† At length, their power of forbearance being exhausted, they sent an embassy to Rome, offering as suppliants to submit to the authority of the emperor if he would render them assistance. In his compassion for their sad condition, the emperor forgot their past rebellion, and sent a legion to help them, who

---

* Britanniæ usque ad hoc tempus variis cladibus eventibusque latæ, in ditionem Saxonum rediguntur.

† Exinde Britannia, omni armato milite, militaribusque copiis, rectoribus linquitur immanibus, ingenti juventute spoliata, quæ comitata vestigiis supradicti tyranni domum nunquam ultra rediit, &c.—*Gildas*, § 14.

defeated the invaders with terrible slaughter. Before the legion returned, they showed the Britons how to build a wall across the island from sea to sea, as a defence against the barbarians; but they were so unskilful as to build it of nothing but turf, and the Roman soldiers were no sooner gone than the Picts and Scots, despising such a barrier as this, spread themselves again over south Britain, and committed greater havoc than ever. 'And now again,' says the writer we are quoting, 'the Britons sent suppliant ambassadors, with their garments rent and their heads covered with ashes, imploring assistance from the Romans, and, like timorous chickens, crowding under the protecting wings of their parents, that their wretched country might not altogether be destroyed, and that the Roman name, which now was but an empty sound to fill the ear, might not become a reproach even to distant nations. Upon this, the Romans, moved with compassion, as far as human nature can be, at the relation of such horrors, send forward, like eagles in their flight, their unexpected bands of cavalry by land and mariners by sea, and, planting their terrible swords upon the shoulders of their enemies, they mow them down like leaves which fall at the destined period.' On this occasion the Romans were more generous than before, for they helped the natives to build a stone wall from sea to sea (the Wall of Hadrian); and they raised fortresses at stated intervals along the south-eastern coast. When they were gone, the Picts and Scots reappeared. Throwing up hooks, they pulled the Britons down from the top of their wall, and slew them, and then, passing the wall, they destroyed the cities and murdered the inhabitants. At length the Britons made a third appeal to Rome, and, addressing themselves to 'a powerful Roman citizen' named Ætius, in a letter entitled 'the groans of the Britons,' they implored assistance in the most piteous terms. This, however, could no longer be given, and the Britons were left to the accumulated evils of invasion and famine. After a while, however, came peace and plenty, and then the Britons fell into luxurious habits, became proud and turbulent, and quarrelled among themselves. 'Kings were annointed, not according to God's ordinance, but such as showed themselves more cruel than the rest; and soon after they were put to death by those who had elected them, without any inquiry into their merits, but because others still more cruel were chosen to succeed them.' At length rumours came of a new and terrible invasion of the Picts and Scots, and the British chiefs held a council under their proud tyrant Gurthrigern (Vortigern), and came to the fatal resolution of calling in the Saxons. These, though brought in peaceably, became worse tyrants than the Picts and Scots, until at length the Britons rose under Ambrosius Aurelianus, 'the only one of the Roman nation who had been left alive' in the island, and then followed a long struggle between the Britons and the Saxons, until the latter finally established themselves in the land.

Such is the narrative which has been usually taken for the history of Britain during the first half of the fifth century. Its composer was ignorant of the events which followed the usurpation of Maximus, as well as of the early Saxon invasions; he adopted later and vulgar legends relating to the two walls, and he evidently misunderstood and misplaced the usurpations of Marcus, Gratian, and Constantine, who were probably the cruel kings to whom he alludes. In fact, the whole story, built apparently on some slight notes in an old continental chronicler, displays the most profound ignorance of the period to which it relates. All we know relating to the book ascribed to Gildas is, that it existed before Bede—the style of its Latinity appears to me to be of the latter part of the seventh century, and these brief notices of history seem to be founded partly on Saxon traditions. This, however, is not the place to discuss the question of its authenticity.

Bede has adopted the narrative of Gildas, only adding to it some circumstances from more authentic historians, and the account of the Saxon invasion from the traditions of his own countrymen. Here he is unfortunately very brief. He tells us that the Teutonic settlers came hither under their two chiefs, Hengest and Horsa, in the year 449, and that they were received in peace, and allowed to settle in the isle of Thanet. Their success he says, induced others to follow in greater numbers, who were also received into the island as friends and allies. They consisted of three of the bravest of the Teutonic tribes—the Saxons, Angles, and Jutes. The Jutes formed the population of Kent, the Isle of Wight, and the opposite coast district. The Saxons established themselves in Essex, Middlesex, and Wessex. The Angles occupied East-Anglia, the country of the Middle-Angles, Mercia, and all the northern parts of the kingdom.

The ordinary notion, that the first settlement was that under Hengest and Horsa, has arisen from the circumstance that the Anglo-Saxon accounts of these events were founded on the traditions of Kent. It is probable, however, that they had been preceded by the Angles in the north, for when we first become acquainted with them, this tribe appears to have been long in undisputed possession of the whole country from the Humber to the wall of Antoninus, which was formed into two kingdoms, that of Bernicia and that of Deira. Eburacum, to which the Angles gave the name of Eofor-wic, afterwards corrupted into York—the important town on the wall, Pons Ælii, which was under the Saxons still a great commercial town, known by the name of Munuces-ceaster (Monk's-chester)—with others of the Roman towns in Yorkshire, appear to have passed peaceably or by treaty under the rule of the settlers; while others, more especially in Northumberland and the lowlands of Scotland, had perhaps been destroyed before their arrival. The presumption, however, is that the settlement of the Angles in the north had begun at a very early period after the island had been abandoned by the Romans, and that they had been called in to the assistance of the northern towns.

The Saxon Chronicle, composed ages afterwards, gives us the first narrative of the wars between the Saxons and the Britons in the south, after the former had gained a footing there; it is founded on the Anglo-Saxon traditions, perhaps on poems, and there are many circumstances about it which would lead us to believe that it is partly romance. Even the names of Hengest and Horsa are supposed to be mythic.* The Saxon Chronicle informs us, that in the year 455, or six years after the arrival of Hengest, a battle was fought at Ægeles-throp in Kent (*Aylesford*), between the Saxons under Hengest and Horsa, and the Britons under Vortigern, in which Horsa was slain; and according to Bede, who also mentions this battle, his tomb was still shown at a place which was called by his name—it is said to be the modern Horsted. After this, the Chronicle tells us, Hengest and Æsc, his son, obtained the Kentish kingdom. The royal race of Kent was called, after the latter, Æscingas. Next year, Hengest and Æsc defeated 'four troops' of Britons at a place called Crecganford (*Crayford*), with great slaughter. In 457 there was another battle at Crecganford, in which the Saxons slew four thousand men, 'and the Britons then forsook Kent, and in great terror fled to London.' Eight

---

* On the un-historic character of the narratives of the Saxon invasion of Britain, the reader is referred to a rather long dissertation in Lappenberg's 'England under the Anglo-Saxons' (Thorpe's Translation), and to Kemble's 'Saxons in England.'

years afterwards, in 465, Hengest and Æsc are said to have fought 'against the Welsh' at Wippedes-fleot, a place of which we are not acquainted with the modern representative, but which is said to have received that name from Wipped, a Saxon chief who was slain on this occasion. We are informed that 'twelve Welsh ealdormen,' or chiefs, were slain in this battle. After eight years again, in 473, there was another war between the Kentish Saxons and the Britons, and 'the Welsh fled from them like fire.' * After this date, we hear no more of the Kentish kingdom and its wars, except that Æsc succeeded to the kingdom in 488, until the accession of king Athelbert or Ethelbert, in 565. The principal Roman towns of Kent seem to have passed into the possession of the Saxons peacefully. Hengest and Horsa are said to have first landed at Ypwines-fleot (*Ebbs-fleet*), and the Saxons no doubt immediately received Rutupiæ (*Richborough*) into their hands. Durovernum they made their capital, and on that account it received the name of Cantwara-byrig, the city of the Kentishmen, now Canterbury; Dubræ and Regulbium retained their original names, slightly changed into Dover and Reculver; and Durobrivæ was called, it is said, from a chief who ruled over it, Hrofes-ceaster, the chester or city of Hrof, now Rochester.

Leaving the history of Kent, the Saxon Chronicle, taking up another set of traditions, tells us, that in the year 477, the Saxons, under Ælla and his three sons, Cymen, Wlencing, and Cissa, landed on the southern coast, at a place named after one of the sons, Cymenes-ora (*Keynor on Selsea*), 'and there they slew many Welsh, and some they drove in flight into the wood that is named Andredes-leah,' the Roman *Silva Anderida*. Ælla and his sons, like Hengest and Horsa, came in three ships. Here, again, eight years passed until the next great struggle between the followers of Ælla and the Britons. In

---

* The reader must bear in mind, that Britons and Welsh are merely general terms applied by the Saxons to the Romanised population of the island. The former was, of course, merely the Roman name, as they adopted it. The word Welsh (*wilisc, wælisc*) meant simply a foreigner, one who was not of Teutonic race, and was applied especially to nations using the Latin language. In the middle ages the French language, and, in fact, all those derived from Latin, and termed on that account *linguæ Romanæ*, were called in German *Welsch*. France was called by the mediæval German writers *daz welsche lant*, and when they wished to express 'in the whole world,' they said, *in allen welschen und in tiutschen richen*, in all Welsh and Teutonic kingdoms. In modern German the name *Wälsch* is used more especially for Italian. It was in its primitive sense that the Saxons applied the name to the Britons, and from them it has come gradually to its present restricted use.

485, Ælla fought against the Britons near the banks of the Mearcrædes-burna, and the battle is represented, in traditions gathered by a later writer, to have been obstinately fought, and to have had a doubtful result. For six years both parties seemed to have remained in peace; and then, in 491, in consequence, it is said, of new arrivals from the continent, the Saxons recommenced the war, and Ælla and Cissa laid siege to the ancient Roman city of Anderida, which was called by the Saxons Andredes-ceaster. It is said to have been reduced by famine, and the Saxons, irritated at its long and obstinate defence, slew all the inhabitants. The massive walls of the ancient city are still seen at Pevensey. Thus was established the kingdom of the South-Saxons, or Sussex. Here the country was evidently dependent on the Roman city, and was only conquered when that city was taken. The other Roman city, Regnum, probably submitted without a siege, and received the name of Cissan-ceaster, the chester or fortified town of Cissa, since softened down into Chichester.

The Saxon Chronicle next informs us, that in 495, another body of Saxons, under two chiefs, Cerdic and his son Cynric, landed from five ships at a place called Cerdices-ora, on the coast of Hampshire, 'and the same day they fought against the Welsh.' Six years afterwards, another Saxon chief, named Port, with his two sons, Bieda and Mægla, landed at a place named, it is pretended, from him, Portsmouth,* and there fought with the Britons, and 'slew a young British man of high nobility.' In 508, another great battle was fought by Cerdic and Cynric, in which a British king named Natan-leod and five thousand men were slain. 'After that the country was named Natan-lea, as far as Cerdices-ford (*Charford*).' In six years again (A. D. 514), Cerdic's two nephews, Stuf and Wihtgar, came with three more ship-loads of Saxons, and landed at Cerdices-ora. The Britons were still there to oppose them, but the new-comers were victorious in battle. Cerdic and Cynric are stated to have established the kingdom of the West-Saxons in 519, in which year they defeated the Britons in a great battle at Cerdices-ford. In 527 they gained another great battle at a place called Cerdices-leah. During the intervening years, Cerdic was, no doubt, occupied in strengthening and regulating his conquest; the Roman city of Venta had passed over to him, and under the

* This is most undoubtedly a legendary derivation, and should make us the more cautious in receiving the statements of the Chronicle with regard to these early events.

name of the Wintan-ceaster (*Winchester*), which, no doubt, means the chester of Venta, was made the capital of the West-Saxons. The last exploit of Cerdic and Cynric recorded in the Chronicle, is the conquest of Wight from the Jutes; Cerdic died in 534, and his son gave the Isle of Wight to Stuf and Wihtgar, who had probably been instrumental in its conquest.

Cynric soon sought to extend his kingdom. In 552 he defeated the Britons in a battle near the Roman city of Sorbiodunum, called by the Saxons Searo-byrig (now old Sarum). He died in 560, and was succeeded by his son Ceawlin, whose power extended into Surrey, and he was engaged in resisting an attack from Athelbert, king of Kent; after which he extended his conquests northwards, so far as to make himself master of some of the principal towns in the modern counties of Bedford, Buckingham, and Oxford. He next pushed his conquests westward; and, in 577, Ceawlin and his brother Cuthwine, or Cutha, defeated the Britons in a great battle at Deorham (*Derham*) in Gloucestershire, and obtained possession of the three great Roman cities of Glevum, Corinium, and Aquæ Solis, which became known to the Saxons by the name of Glev-ceaster or Gleow-ceaster (*Gloucester*), Cyren-ceaster (*Cirencester*), and Bathan-ceaster (*Bath*).

We have no information to enable us to judge on what authority the dates of the Anglo-Saxon Chronicle during this period rest; but the singular manner in which one kingdom begins to be founded, after the preceding kingdom had been established, cannot fail to arrest our attention. It seems as though the brief narrative had been abridged from some memorial poem, where the compiler mistook the order in which the establishment of the different kingdoms was told, as indicating the succession of dates at which they took place. It certainly appears more probable that the invasion of the Teutonic tribes took place nearly at the same time, or in rapid succession one after another; and we might expect them to have begun in the north.

The Saxon Chronicle, compiled in Wessex, gives little information on the progressive establishment of the kingdoms founded by the Angles. We are merely informed that, in 547, Ida began to reign in Northumbria, and that he built a town which was called, in honour of his wife Bebba, Bebban-byrig (*Bamborough*). In 560 Ida died, and was succeeded by his son Ælla. According to an obscure tradition, the Saxons first landed in Essex, under their king Æscwine or Ercenwine, as early as the year 527; they probably only came to strengthen the older settlements on what had long been known as the Saxon coast. Camulodunum and other towns seem to have been occupied without any resistance. The coasts to the north of them were seized by the Angles, who appear to have consisted of two tribes, distinguished by their positions as the North-folk and the South-folk (*Norfolk* and *Suffolk*). Their power extended over Cambridgeshire and into Lincolnshire. It was from settlements in the north of the latter county that another branch of the Angles extended themselves so rapidly through the heart of England, until they reached the borders of Wales, and intrenched upon the West-Saxons to the south. They took the name of Myrce, which has been Latinised into Mercians. The great extent of ground which the Angles occupied in Britain is quite sufficient to explain the statement of the old historians, that they had completely evacuated their native land, and left it uninhabited. From them, as the earliest settlers, and the most numerous, the island became known among foreign writers by the names of *Anglia* and *Anglorum terra*, and among the Saxons themselves it was usually called Engla-land (*England*), and the language of its inhabitants Englisc (*English*). The population of the Teutonic portion of the island is still known by no other name than that of Englishmen.

The Teutons who had come into the island at an earlier period as auxiliaries, had always, as a matter of course, conformed to the religious forms and laws of the Romans; but now they preserved their own religion and their own institutions. Saxon paganism was everywhere substituted for Roman, and it was only perhaps in a few cases—chiefly, we may suppose, in the towns—that individuals preserved for a while their respect for Roman gods, or their attachment to Roman ceremonies. The latter are sometimes traced in Saxon cemeteries, where a Roman interment is found in the midst of graves of undoubted Teutonic character. This is the only indication we have of the transition, and it would be difficult to point out an exact date when pure Saxon interments began. We have less difficulty in fixing the other limit.

The Latin language, too, continued probably for some time to be in use in the towns. I believe indeed that when the Angles and Saxons came into Britain they found the people talking not a Celtic dialect, but Latin, and hence when they formed the English language, the foreign words introduced into it were not Celtic but Latin. I think I have traced the citizens of English towns speaking Latin at a later period, and we find that it was the earlier language of our municipal records and deeds, and of the inscriptions on monuments. There was a Celtic people in modern Gaul, the Armoricans, who talk a Celtic dialect down to modern times, and who issued forth on piratical excursions on the sea about the time of the Saxon invasions; and these Armoricans invaded Cornwall and Wales apparently about the time of the Anglo-Saxon invasions of Britain, and they appear to have formed the population of the Cornish peninsula and of the principality of Wales. The remarkable similarity between the Celtic languages of Cornwall and Wales and that of the Bretons of Gaul has been frequently pointed out, and we may perhaps be justified in considering that our Welsh were really a Breton settlement from Gaul about the time of the Saxon invasions of our island, and that they by no means represent the original Celtic population of Britain, the ancient Britons, and that the Welsh language was not the British. There appear to be reasons for believing that that was similar to the modern Irish.[*]

The traffic in slaves prevailed very extensively among all the Teutonic peoples, and it is frequently mentioned or alluded to in the early historical records of Saxon England. We are told that, during the pontificate of Pelagius II., some boys from Saxon Britain, distinguished by their beauty, were exposed for sale in the slave-market at Rome. The priest Gregory, as he passed through the ancient forum, was struck with their appearance, and on being told that they were Pagans from Britain, he lamented that people having such bright countenances should remain a prey to the spirit of darkness. Continuing the conversation, with the same play upon words, he was told that they were called Angles, upon which he observed that it was a just name, for they had angelic faces, and ought to be the co-heirs of angels in heaven. He then asked the name of the province from which they came, and was told that it was the kingdom of Deira. 'It is well,' he said, 'they shall be *de ira eruti*, snatched from the wrath and brought to the mercy of Christ.' He was next told that the name of their king was Ælla. 'That,' he said, 'is Alleluiah, and it is right that the praise of God should be sung in that land.' Full of projects of conversion, Gregory hastened to the pope, and begged to be employed on this distant mission; but the citizens, with whom he

[*] See what has been said on this subject in a former chapter, at p. 219 of this volume.

was extremely popular, were unwilling to allow of his absence. Nothing further, therefore, was done towards the conversion of the Anglo-Saxons, until, in 590, Gregory himself was elected to the papal see. The Anglian children were then remembered, and Gregory despatched missionaries under the guidance of St Augustine to visit the distant island. Their zeal, however, was not equal to that of their employer; for they had proceeded no further than Provence, when they were so alarmed by the descriptions of the barbarous character of the Anglo-Saxons, that Augustine was sent back to Rome to obtain the revocation of their mission. Gregory exhorted him to persevere, gave him letters of recommendation to the Frankish kings, Theoderic and Theodebert, and to their grandmother Brunhilda, as well as to the Frankish bishops, who furnished them with interpreters. In the year 597, Augustine, with, it is said, above forty monks, landed in the isle of Thanet, no doubt in the old Roman port of Rutupiæ; from whence he sent a messenger to Ethelbert, king of Kent, to announce the object of his mission.

It happened that Ethelbert had married Berta, the daughter of Charibert, king of Paris; and it was one of the terms of the marriage contract that, as a Christian princess, she should be allowed the free exercise of her faith, and that she should retain for that purpose the Frankish bishop Liudhard, who had accompanied her to England, and who now officiated in the little church of St Martin, near Canterbury. Christianity was not thus totally unknown among the Kentish Saxons. Ethelbert received the message of the missionaries with favour, and directed that they should remain for the present in Thanet. A few days after he went to visit them, and gave audience in the open air; for, influenced by the ancient superstitions of his forefathers, he feared that if he received them in a house, they might get the better of him by magical arts. It is recorded, that when the king had patiently listened to what they had to say, he replied, 'Your words and promises are very fair, but as they are new to us, and of uncertain import, I cannot so far approve of them as to forsake that which I have so long followed with the whole English nation. But because you are come from afar into my kingdom, and, as I conceive, are desirous to impart to us those things which you believe to be true, we will not molest you, but give you favourable entertainment, and take care to supply you with your necessary sustenance; nor do we forbid you to preach and gain as many as you can to your religion.' The Roman monks marched in solemn procession to Canterbury, where they established themselves, and of which city Augustine was subsequently made the first bishop.

The new faith was ultimately accepted by king Ethelbert, and soon spread with extraordinary rapidity over Kent, and through the other kingdoms wherever that king's influence extended. The East-Saxons received baptism in 604; and in 607, the year of the battle near Chester, rendered celebrated by the slaughter of the Welsh monks, the faith of the Gospel must have been established far towards the west. With the mass of the people conversion was at first a mere change of forms, and they easily resumed their old customs; and it naturally took some years to make the change permanent. Thus Augustine had appointed Mellitus bishop of London, and he is said to have selected there the site of a ruined temple of the Roman period to build a church, no doubt because it furnished an unoccupied place and ready materials. The Saxon Chronicle informs us, that after Mellitus became bishop of Canterbury, an event which is generally placed in the year 619, 'then the men of London, where Mellitus had been formerly, became heathens again.' The example had already been set them by the East-Saxons, and even by the Kentish men, after the death of their first Christian kings.

The progress of the Christian faith among the Anglo-Saxons was, on several occasions, materially assisted by intermarriages among their chiefs. Ethelbert of Kent, before the arrival of the missionaries, had married a Christian lady, the daughter of a Frankish king. The king of Essex, who first received the Gospel, had married a daughter of king Ethelbert, who was also a Christian. Another daughter of Ethelbert, Ethelberga, was married to Edwin, king of the Northumbrians, and she no doubt paved the way for the preaching of Paulinus. The conversion of king Edwin took place in the year 626. The West-Saxons were converted by Birinus in 635; the East-Angles had embraced the new faith under their king Earpwald, about the year 632; but the Middle-Angles were not converted until the reign of Peada, the son of Penda, about the year 653. This king became a Christian on marrying a daughter of the king of the Northumbrians, and from Lincolnshire, the country of the Middle-Angles, the faith soon spread through the extensive dependencies of Mercia. At this time the faith of Christ had penetrated into every part of the island, except the small and secluded kingdom of the South-Saxons, which was cut off from the other Saxon states, and protected in its independence, by the ancient forest of Anderida, the impervious Andredes-weald. As late as the year 681, the people of Sussex remained pagans. Their condition became known to Wilfrid, archbishop of York, who, in returning from the continent was driven by stress of weather on the coast, and who subsequently founded a monastery on the little island of Selsea.

CHAPTER XV.

Anglo-Saxon Antiquities—Barrows, or Graves, and the general Character of their Contents—Arms—Personal Ornaments; Fibulæ, &c.—Anglo-Saxon Jewellery—Pottery—Glass—Other Articles found in the Barrows; Bowls, Buckets, &c.—Coins—Early Anglo-Saxon Coinage.

We derive our antiquities of the period of Anglo-Saxon paganism almost entirely from one source, the graves. It happens, however, fortunately for the study of the history of this period, that the contents of the Anglo-Saxon graves are particularly rich and interesting, and that we are enabled, from the various articles found in them, to form a tolerable estimate of the civilisation of our ancestors before the days of St Augustine. The Anglo-Saxon graves occur generally in extensive groups, and on high ground. They are found thickly scattered over the downs of Kent, Sussex, and the Isle of Wight. Extensive cemeteries have also been found in Gloucester and Oxfordshire, as well as in Leicestershire, Derbyshire, Nottinghamshire, Northamptonshire, Lincolnshire, Cambridgeshire, Suffolk, and Norfolk, and in Yorkshire. They exist, no doubt, in other counties, where they have not been explored.*

---

* The largest and most important collections of Anglo-Saxon antiquities are those of Lord Londesborough, the late Dr Faussett of Heppington near Canterbury, and the late Mr W. H. Rolfe of Sandwich, all taken from barrows in Kent. The two latter collections are now in the possession of Mr Joseph Mayer of Liverpool. Smaller private collections are found in different parts of England, and a few articles belonging to this class are met with in most local museums; but there is as yet no public collection of early Anglo-Saxon remains of any importance. The most valuable work on the subject is the 'Nenia' of Douglas, a folio volume published in 1793. An interesting volume on the Anglo-Saxon cemeteries in Gloucestershire, has been recently published by Mr W. M. Wylie, under the title of 'Fairford Graves;' and extensive materials for the archæology of this period will be found in Mr Roach Smith's 'Collectanea,' and in some of the volumes of the 'Archæologia.' We may also recommend Mr Akerman's 'Pagan Saxendom.'

An Anglo-Saxon poem belonging, no doubt, to this primitive period—the adventures of Beowulf—has been preserved; and, although it has been considerably modified in the transition, it still gives us glimpses of the manners of our forefathers before they had turned from the worship of Woden.* In this poem, but unfortunately in a part of it which is imperfect in the manuscript, we find a description of the ceremonies attendant on the burial of the hero. Beowulf's dying request was, that his people should raise a barrow ' on the place of his funeral pile,' proportionate in size to the celebrity of his deeds. They accordingly raised a mighty funeral pile to burn his corpse; it was—

> hung round with helmets,
> with boards of war (*shields*)
> and with bright byrnies (*coats of mail*),
> as he had requested.
> Then the heroes, weeping,
> laid down in the midst
> the famous chieftain,
> their dear lord.
> Then began on the hill,
> the warriors, to awake
> the mightiest of funeral fires;
> the wood-smoke rose aloft,
> dark from the fire;
> noisily it went,
> mingled with weeping.

After the burning of the body had been completed, Beowulf's people proceeded to raise—

> a mound over the sea;
> it was high and broad,
> by the sailors over the waves
> to be seen afar.
> And they built up
> during ten days
> the beacon of the war-renowned.
> They surrounded it with a wall
> in the most honourable manner
> that wise men
> could desire.
> They put into the mound
> rings and bright gems,
> all such ornaments

---

* The Anglo-Saxon poem of Beowulf was published with an English translation by my friend Mr J. M. Kemble, in 1837. An edition, in many respects more convenient, was subsequently published by Mr Thorpe, in 1855.

> as before * from the hoard
> the fierce-minded men
> had taken;
> they suffered the earth to hold
> the treasure of warriors,
> gold on the sand,
> where it yet remains
> as useless to men
> as it was of old.—*Beowulf*, line 6268.

When the mound was completed, the war-chiefs rode round it, chanting the praises of their departed king.

In England we find in the graves of the Saxon period the same mixture of the two modes of interment, cremation and the burial of the body entire, as among the Romans, but in different and varying proportions. The custom in this respect appears to have varied with the different tribes who came into the island. In the Anglo-Saxon cemeteries in Kent, cremation is the rare exception to the general rule; while it seems to have been the predominating practice among the Angles, from Norfolk into the centre of Mercia. The poem of Beowulf was perhaps derived from the Angles, and it thus describes the mode of burning the dead as it existed among them.

The Anglo-Saxon barrows in general have a character very distinct from those of the Romans or Britons. They were the prototypes of our modern graves in country churchyards. A rectangular cist, or pit, was cut in the ground, varying in depth from three or four feet to seven or eight, on the floor of which the body was laid on its back in full dress, surrounded with a variety of articles which, no doubt, the deceased had valued when alive; the grave was then filled up, and a mound of earth raised above. This mound was termed *hlæw*, a hillock, the modern word *low*, as in names like Ludlow, which is still used in Derbyshire, and *beorh*, *beorg*, or *bearw*, a word having the same signification, from which is derived our modern name of *barrow*. In Sussex they are still called *burghs*. Generally, each grave contains the remains of one body; but instances occur where more than one body has been interred in the same grave, and under circumstances which show that they must have been buried simultaneously. We can only account for this by supposing that they were members of the same family who had been carried off by an epidemic disease or slaughtered in a sudden invasion

---

* Beowulf had signalised himself by killing a dragon which guarded a hoard of treasures, of which, as a matter of course, he took possession.

of plunderers. In the Anglo-Saxon cemetery at Osengal, in the Isle of Thanet, one grave contained a male and a female skeleton, laid side by side, with their faces turned toward each other; and another contained three skeletons, a lady in the middle, a man, no doubt her husband, on her right side; and a child, apparently a little girl, on her left; they lay arm in arm. More than one instance has occurred where a grave contained all the articles usually interred with a body, but no traces of the body. A remarkable instance of this was found in a large Anglo-Saxon grave in the cemetery in Bourne Park, near Canterbury. The grave was nearly fourteen feet long, about half that width, and somewhat more than four feet deep. The floor was very smoothly cut in the chalk, and surrounded by a narrow gutter; and the grave was filled up with fine mould brought from a distance, and not, as in most other cases, with the chalky soil of the spot. At the foot of the grave, in the right-hand corner, had stood a bucket, of which the bronze hoops, in perfect preservation, occupied their position one above the other as if the wood had been there to support them. A little higher up in the grave, in the position generally occupied by the right leg of the person buried, was found a considerable heap of fragments of iron, among which were the boss of a shield of the usual Saxon form, a horse's bit, a buckle, and other fragments which appeared to have belonged to the shield, a number of nails with large ornamental heads, with smaller nails, the latter mostly of brass. From the position of the boss, it appeared that the shield had been placed with the convex (or outer) surface downwards. Not far from these articles, at the side of the grave, was found an iron ring with two smaller ones attached to it, apparently belonging to the horse's bridle, or to a belt. On the left-hand side of the grave was found a small piece of iron resembling the point of some weapon. At the head of the grave, on the right-hand side, was an elegantly-shaped bowl, about a foot in diameter, and two inches and a half deep, of very thin copper, which had been thickly gilt, and with handles of iron. It had been placed on its edge leaning against the wall of the grave, and was crushed and broken by the weight of the superincumbent earth. Two small round discs, resembling counters, about seven-eighths of an inch in diameter, were found near the head of the grave. They were flat on one side and convex on the other, the one of bone, while the other had been cut out of a piece of Samian ware. There was not the slightest trace of a body having ever been deposited in this grave; the appearances were decisive to the contrary. This may be explained by supposing that the person for whom the grave was made had been a chief killed in battle in some distant expedition, and that his friends had not been able to obtain his body. It was, in fact, an Anglo-Saxon cenotaph. This view of the case seemed to be supported by the fact that, although so many valuable articles were found in the grave, there were no traces of the long sword and the knife usually found with the bodies of male adults in the Saxon barrows. These would have been attached to the body itself as a part of the dress.

It is a singular circumstance connected with the Anglo-Saxon graves that human bones are often found among the earth at the top, sometimes in the mound above, and the unexperienced excavator is discouraged by this discovery, in the belief that the grave has been previously broken up, whereas, when he reaches the bottom, he finds that the original deposit has not been disturbed.* I can only explain this by the supposition that they are the bones of slaves or captives, slain as a propitiation to the shades of their master or mistress, and thrown upon the grave. We know that the immolation of slaves at funerals was a common practice among the Teutonic races. In the northern Edda when Brynhild, like Dido, slew herself for her faithless lover, we are told that she ordered that at her funeral pile two immolated slaves should be placed at her head, and two at her feet.

As I have said, the Anglo-Saxon barrows are generally found in large groups or cemeteries, and the mound which covers each grave is very low, but this is perhaps to be attributed to the effect of time, as they are generally placed in exposed situations. But we sometimes find isolated Anglo-Saxon barrows, which we can only appropriate by the Saxon character of the articles they contain. Several of these are found in the peak of Derbyshire; but they are met with chiefly on elevations near the sea. A bold conical hill overlooking Folkestone, in Kent, is crowned with a fine Saxon barrow. The sentiment which led to the choice of such positions may be gathered from more than one passage in the poem of Beowulf. It was the hero's dying request to his people,—

---

* In a few instances the bones in the upper part of the mound have been found so much less decomposed than those underneath, that we can hardly avoid coming to the conclusion that they belonged to some later interment.

> command the war-chiefs
> to make a mound,
> bright after the funeral fire,
> upon the nose of the promontory;
> which shall for a memorial
> to my people
> rise high aloft
> on Hronesness;
> that the sea-sailors
> may afterwards call it
> Beowulf's barrow,
> when the Brentings
> over the darkness of the floods
> shall sail afar.—*Beowulf*, line 5599.

The hill of Osengal, overlooking Pegwell Bay near Ramsgate, and furnishing a magnificent view of the Channel with the distant coast of France, is perforated like a honeycomb with the graves of an immense Saxon cemetery. Here time has entirely obliterated the barrows which once covered the graves, and the latter were only discovered accidentally in the course of the railway cutting. Many of them have been since opened by the late Mr Rolfe, of Sandwich, and have added considerably to the richness of his museum. The Anglo-Saxons generally placed their cemeteries on elevated spots, where these could be found in the neighbourhood of their settlements. People seem to have been carried for burial there from the country at a distance around; we generally also find Saxon cemeteries in the immediate neighbourhood of a Roman city or town, where it continued to be occupied in Saxon times, and it is not unfrequently placed on the site of the older Roman cemetery of the town. Such is the case at Canterbury, Colchester, and other places.

The Anglo-Saxon was buried in his full dress, with all his arms and accoutrements. By his side we often find the long iron sword, the presence of which is, in itself, an unfailing evidence of the people to whom the grave belonged. These swords are often nearly a yard long, and were evidently intended rather for cutting than for thrusting. They appear usually to have been double-edged, and the blades are plain, and nearly uniform in shape. The one represented in our plate (fig. 5), found in the cemetery at Osengal in Thanet, seems to have had but one edge, with a blunt back. The hilts appear usually to have been made of wood or some other perishable material; but sword hilts of metal have also been found, and they are then extremely ornamental. Their general

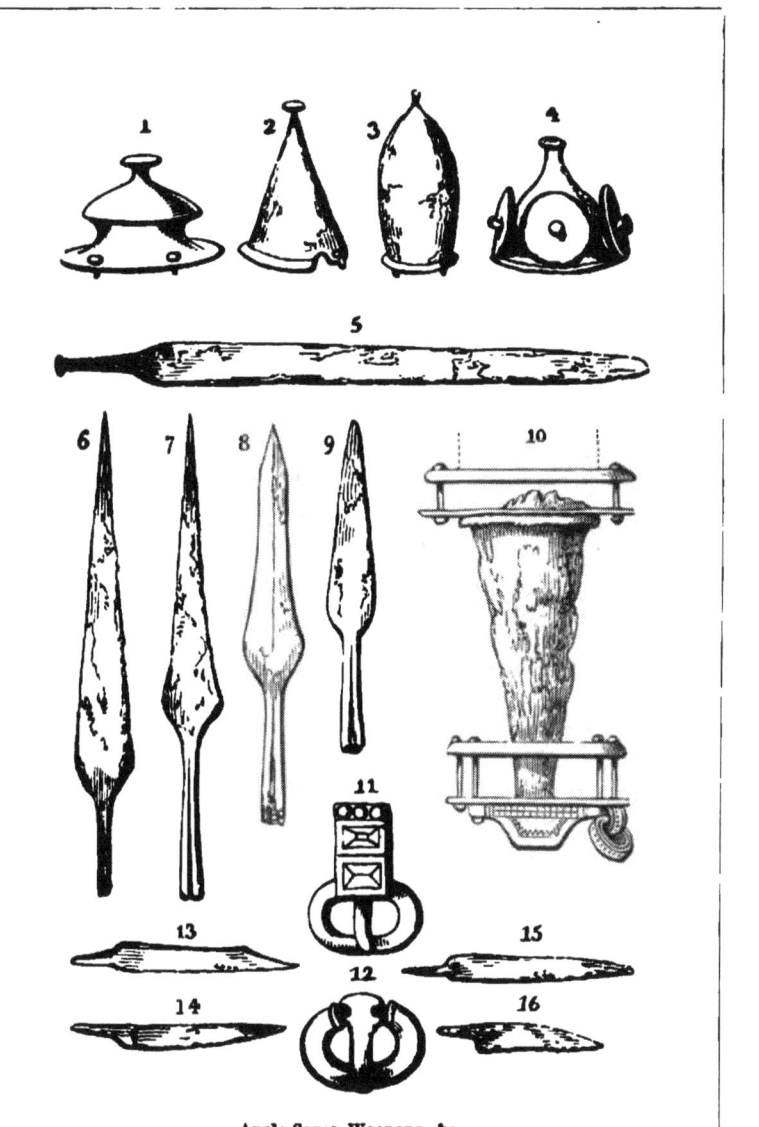

Anglo-Saxon Weapons, &c.

form may be understood by fig. 10 in our plate, which represents the hilt of a sword found in a barrow at Ash, near Canterbury, and now in the collection of Mr Rolfe. The metal appears to have been gilt or silvered. A very handsome hilt of the same description, found with the sword in the parish of Coombe, in Kent, is engraved in the second volume of Mr Roach Smith's Collectanea; the ornamental parts in this instance were of bronze gilt. Mr Rolfe also possessed the extremity of a Saxon sword-hilt of silver, ornamented, and bearing an inscription in rudely formed runes, which nobody has yet been able to decipher. This curious relic, which was found also in the parish of Ash, is engraved in the Archæological Album. In the poem of Beowulf, swords are not unfrequently described as having richly ornamented hilts. Thus one of the heroes—

> gave his ornamented sword,
> the costliest of irons,
> to his servant.—*Beowulf*, line 1338.

And in another passage it is said,—

> and with it the hilt,
> variegated with treasure.—*Beowulf*, line 3228.

And a little further on there is a description particularly interesting as illustrating the description of the sword-hilts just given, especially of the silver hilt with the runic inscription. A sword, described as follows, bore not only the name of the possessor inscribed in runes, but also an episode of the ancient Saxon mythology,—

> He looked upon the hilt,
> the old legacy,
> on which was written the origin
> of the ancient contest;
> after the flood,
> the pouring ocean
> slew the race of giants;
> daringly they behaved:
> that was a race strange
> to the eternal Lord,
> therefore to them their last reward
> through floods of water
> the ruler gave.
> So was on the surface
> of the bright gold
> with runic letters
> rightly marked,

> set and said,
> for whom that sword,
> the costliest of irons,
> was first made,
> with twisted hilt and variegated like a snake.
>
> *Beowulf*, line 3373.

The sheath appears to have been generally of wood, tipped with metal, and it was sometimes covered with, or made entirely of, leather. One found at Strood, in Kent, was covered externally with a substance resembling shagreen. A Saxon sword found at Fairford, in Gloucestershire, had its wooden scabbard partly remaining, protected at the top and bottom with bronze.

On the opposite side of the body from the shield, and similarly attached to the girdle, we usually find one or even more knives. These are usually of not very large dimensions, though they probably served the purposes of a dagger as well as those of a knife. In former days, people did not keep knives for the use of their guests, but the latter always carried their knives with them. A small knife is usually found with the other articles which appear by their position to have been suspended at the girdles of the Anglo-Saxon ladies. Mr Roach Smith has engraved an interesting collection of Anglo-Saxon knives in the second volume of his Collectanea. The four represented in our plate, figs. 13 to 16, are from the Saxon cemetery at Osengal. Some antiquaries have supposed that these knives are the *seaxas*, from which the Saxons were pretended to have derived their name.

The figures in our plate, Nos. 6 to 9, are examples of Saxon spear-heads, obtained from the cemetery of Osengal; they represent the usual forms of this weapon. The position of the shaft in the grave may generally be traced by a long line of black, decomposed wood, and a ferrule, with a knob or spike, is sometimes found at the bottom. The spear appears in some cases to have been seven, or even eight, feet long. A remarkable spear-head, with four edges, was found in the Saxon cemetery at Fairford. The spear-heads are usually from ten to fifteen inches long. Arrow-heads are occasionally found, but they are rare.

The shield was generally laid flat over the middle of the corpse. It has been traced in some instances to have been round, and not of large dimensions. It was usually formed of wood, generally of the linden tree, which was of a yellow tint.

Hence, the poem of Beowulf speaks of 'the broad shield, yellow-rimmed,' and it is sometimes called a 'war-board' (*hildebord*). In one instance we are told—

> he seized his shield,
> the yellow linden-wood.—*Beowulf*, line 5215.

The wood of the shield seems to have been sometimes covered with leather; and mention is made in Beowulf of a shield of iron. It may be suspected that the round metal shields which have been pronounced to be British, are really Saxon. The principal relic of the shield found in the graves, is the iron boss which occupied the centre externally, and which has usually attached to it all or some of the rivets which fixed it to the wood. The usual form of the boss is that of a small basin, tapering at the top to a point, and ending in a knob. Some of our old writers on antiquities have indeed taken the Saxon bosses for basins, and others have thought them to be skull-caps, so little observation was made on the circumstances of their discovery. Fig. 1, in our plate of Anglo-Saxon weapons, is also rather a common form of the boss of the shield. The three other bosses represented in the plate are unusual forms; fig. 2 was found in a barrow on the Breach downs, and was in the collection of Lord Londesborough, and fig. 3 was found at Sittingbourne, also in Kent. Fig. 4 is a very singular boss, which was found among Anglo-Saxon graves near Driffield, in the East Riding of Yorkshire; the boss itself is not of an unusual form, but it has four circular discs arranged round it, as represented in the cut.

Strips of iron, formed into different shapes, but evidently designed to be held by the hand, are often found in Saxon

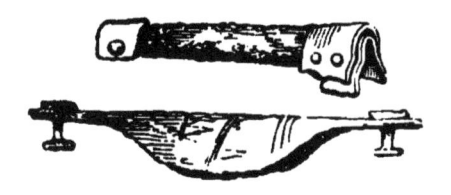

Braces of Anglo-Saxon Shields.

graves, among the remains of the shield, and were supposed by Douglas to be the braces of bows. This explanation, however, had been long doubted, when, in opening the graves at Osengal, in Thanet, a more careful observation cleared up the mystery. In every instance, the article referred to was found in the centre of the shield, just under the boss, and in such a position that there could be no longer any doubt of its having been the handle of the shield. Two of these handles, from the graves at Osengal, are represented in the annexed cut. The lower example retains the rivets by which it was fixed to the wood of the shield, in which there was, no doubt, in the middle, a hole to receive the hand, which was covered by the boss on the outside. We thus learn the importance of very careful observation, even of the minute circumstances connected with antiquarian discoveries.

The discovery of buckles of different forms shows clearly that the swords and knives were suspended to a girdle drawn tight round the body. Two such buckles, from the cemetery at Osengal, are represented in figs. 11 and 12 of our plate at p. 471. These buckles are often highly ornamented, and they are sometimes enamelled. We find very little traces of dress in the graves, though a fragment of the material found sometimes impressed in decomposed metal, seems to show that it was generally of rather coarse texture. We know from passages in the poem of Beowulf, that the early Saxons wore armour, apparently composed of rings, but no very distinct traces of it have yet been found in the graves. This may, perhaps, be accounted for by the rapid decomposition which articles made of iron undergo in the ground. Perhaps, moreover, it was not the custom to equip the body in armour and helmet when it was buried. The ribs, or framework, in bronze, of a defensive cap of some kind or other, supposed to be Saxon, were discovered on a skull dug up at Leckhampton Hill, near Cheltenham, and are preserved in the museum of that town. A framework of a helmet, not very unlike that at Cheltenham, was taken by Mr Bateman from an Anglo-Saxon barrow in Derbyshire, and his description of it is sufficiently curious to be given in his own words. It had been formed, he says, ' of ribs of iron, radiating from the crown of the head, and coated with narrow plates of horn, running in a diagonal direction from the ribs, so as to form a herring-bone pattern; the ends were secured by strips of horn, radiating in like manner as the iron ribs, to which they were riveted at intervals of about an inch and a half; all the rivets had ornamented heads of silver on the outside, and on the front rib is a small cross of the same metal. Upon the top or crown of the helmet, is an elongated oval brass plate, upon which stands the figure of an animal, carved in iron, now much rusted, but still a very good representation of a pig; it has bronze eyes. There are also many smaller decorations, abounding in rivets, all which have pertained to the helmet, but which it is impossible to assign to their proper places, as is also the case with some small iron buckles.' Mr Bateman adds, that there was found with the helmet a mass of chain-work, formed of 'a large quantity of links, of two descriptions, attached to each other by small rings, half an inch in diameter; one kind is flat and lozenge-shaped, about one inch and a half in length; those of the other sort are all of one pattern, but of different lengths, varying from four to ten inches; they are simply pieces of square rod iron, with perforated ends, through which are passed the rings connecting them with the diamond-shaped links. Along with them was a six-pronged instrument, similar to a hay-fork, with the difference that the fang, which, in a fork, is inserted into the shaft, is in this instance flattened and folded over, so as to form a small loop, as for suspension. All the iron articles, except this and the helmet, were amalgamated together from the effects of rust; they also present traces of cloth over a great part of their surface; it is therefore not improbable that they may have originally constituted some kind of defensive armour by being sewn upon or within a doublet.' Mr Roach Smith has quoted, in illustration of the swine or boar on this helmet, passages from Tacitus, and from the Anglo-Saxon poem of Beowulf, which shows that that animal was a favourite ensign on the helmets and arms of the ancient Saxons.*

Another weapon found in Anglo-Saxon graves, though it is of very rare occurrence, must not be overlooked. This is the axe, which seems to have been more common among the Franks than among the Saxons in England. The lower of the two examples given in the accompanying cut was taken from a Saxon barrow in the isle of Thanet, and is preserved in the museum of Mr Rolfe; the axe represented in the upper figure was found in a grave of this same period, from a cemetery discovered at Selzen, in Rhenish Hesse,† and is here given for the sake of

* Cuts of these helmets will be found in Mr Roach Smith's Collectanea, vol. ii. p. 238.
† A very interesting account of this cemetery, which resembled closely the Anglo-Saxon cemeteries in England, was published at Maintz, in 1848, by the brothers W. and L. Lindenschmidt.

comparison. Their identity of form is remarkable. A similarly shaped axe was found in a grave at Ash, near Canterbury; Mr Roach Smith possesses one which was obtained in Berkshire; and two or three others have been found in different parts of England.

It will be seen by what has been already said, and by the examples given, that the weapons of our Anglo-Saxon forefathers were purely Teutonic, and that so far they had borrowed nothing of the Romans. In war, they fought as Saxons: and it was only when they came in social contact with the people who had preceded them that they felt the superiority of the Romans in the arts of peace. The personal ornaments found in our Anglo-Saxon barrows are numerous, especially in Kent, where the discoveries hitherto made show a greater degree of wealth and refinement than in the other Saxon or Anglian kingdoms. Of all the articles of personal ornament found in the Anglo-Saxon interments, the fibulæ are the most remarkable, and at the same time the most characteristic; and they have a peculiar interest from the circumstance that there are several distinct varieties, and that the difference arose evidently, not from individual caprice, but from the distinctive fashions of the different races who came into the island. They help to corroborate the statements of the early Anglo-Saxon annalists of the positions of these various tribes in Britain. We have given examples of these different varieties in the accompanying plate.

The first and the richest variety of these ornaments are the circular fibulæ found in the barrows in Kent, of which some very fine examples are preserved in the museums of Lord Londesborough, Dr Faussett, Mr Rolfe (the two latter now united in the possession of Mr Mayer, of Liverpool), and other collectors. They are more usually of gold than any other material, are generally ornamented with filigree work, and are set with stones, usually garnets, or with glass or vitreous pastes, and sometimes with enamel. One of the finest examples of this class of fibulæ was found a few years ago at Sittingbourne, in Kent. The form of the ornament was that of a

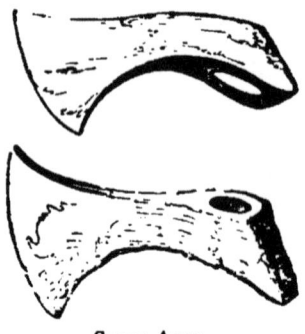

Saxon Axes.

Anglo-Saxon Fibulæ.

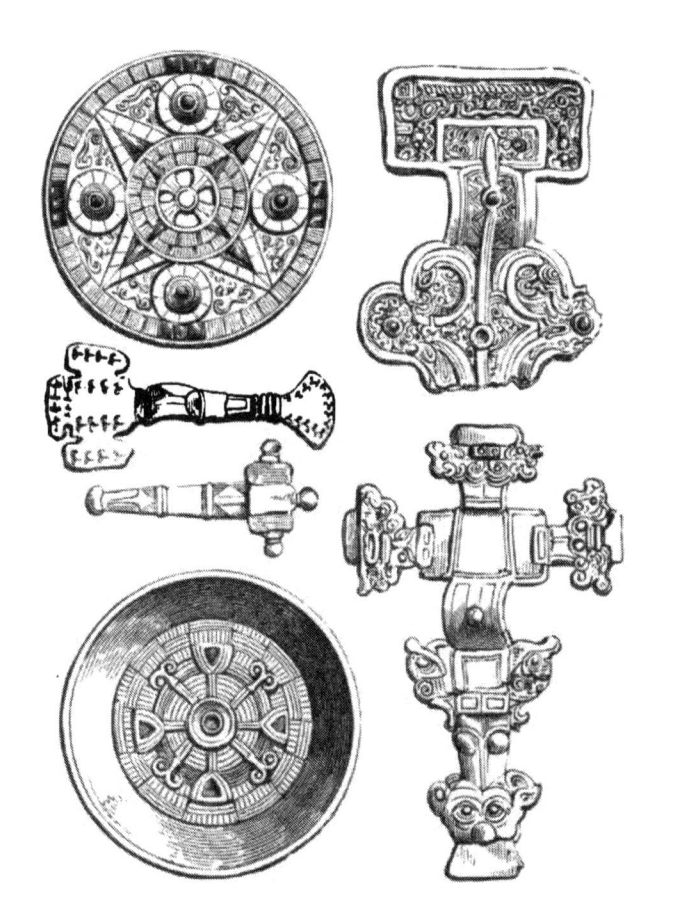

double star, set with garnets, or coloured glass, upon chequered foils of gold. The rays of the inner star were of a blue stone. Between the rays of the larger star were four studs, with a ruby in each, surrounded with a circle of garnets, the spaces between being filled up with gold filigree.

A much diminished sketch of this fibula is given in the upper figure to the left in our plate. In another very handsome round fibula in the collection of Lord Londesborough, found in a barrow at Wingham, in Kent, the outer rim is bronze, but all the rest gold, set with garnets and blue stones, as usual, over thin gold foil, which was indented with cross lines, to give greater brilliancy; the spaces between the limbs of the cross or flower formed by the stones were here also filled up with the twists of gold filigree which are so common in Anglo-Saxon jewellery. These round fibulæ appear to have been worn by ladies, and from the position in which they are found they seem to have been placed on the breast. They were evidently peculiar to the people of Kent and to the kindred inhabitants of the Isle of Wight, where examples have been found. It is very unusual to find them in other parts of England; though a very rich gold fibula of this description was found some years ago at Sutton, near Woodbridge, in Suffolk, which was covered with filigree work, and had been set with stones and enamel.*

The second class of Anglo-Saxon fibulæ present a totally different type; they are generally made of bronze or brass, though they appear in almost every instance to have been gilt. They have been usually termed cross-shaped, a term which is not always correct, and we must be careful not to imagine that the approach to the form of the cross has any connexion with Christianity, for there can be little doubt that all these barrows belonged to the pagan Saxons. Several examples of this class of fibulæ are given in our plate. The upper one to the right was found at Ingarsby, ten miles from Leicester. It has been broken, and, as will be seen by comparison with the other examples, the upper part only remains. When perfect, it must have been very large, for the part here represented is five inches in length. The figure immediately below it represents one of this class of fibulæ, of a rather different type, found at

---

* This beautiful fibula is given in colours, and of the size of the original, with several other examples of the round Kentish fibula, in a plate in the 'Archæological Album.' Other examples will be found in Douglas's 'Nenia.'

Stowe Heath, adjoining to Icklingham, in Suffolk. The original is six inches in length, and it is ornamented, like others of the same class, with attempts at representing monstrous heads. The ornamentation of the large fibulæ of this class is often very elaborate, though rude in character. The fibulæ of this form are found in large quantities in the counties of Derby, Leicester, Nottingham, Northampton, and thence through Cambridgeshire, Suffolk, and Norfolk, as well as in Yorkshire. They were evidently peculiar to the Angles, who formed the population of Mercia, East-Anglia, and Northumbria. As shown in the examples just described, some of the more ornamental ones were of very large dimensions; but others, and that by much the most numerous class, are smaller and plainer. The two examples given in our plate, between the circular fibulæ, both from Stowe Heath, in Suffolk, are types of rather a numerous class of the smaller fibulæ, found chiefly in Mercia and East-Anglia. Many similar fibulæ were found by Lord Braybrooke in the Anglo-Saxon cemetery at Wilbraham, in Cambridgeshire. Sometimes in these smaller fibulæ, the head was formed into a plain trefoil, or clover leaf, as in the example found in Yorkshire, which is given in fig. 1, in the cut below. Fibulæ of this form were found in the Anglo-Saxon cemetery at Barrow Furlong, in Northamptonshire, described in the thirty-third volume of the Archæologia. Others with square heads were found in the last-mentioned cemetery, one of which is represented in fig. 2 in our cut. This class of

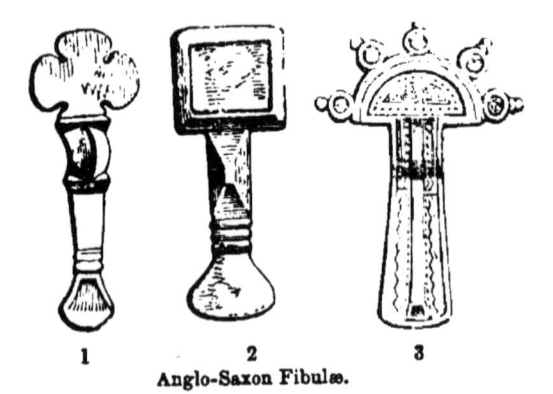

1 2 3

Anglo-Saxon Fibulæ.

fibulæ is found much more rarely out of the Anglian districts. Some have been found in Kent, differing a little in form and ornament, and by no means so common as the circular ones. We find also in Kent a fibula of this class, but of a peculiar pattern, having its head semicircular. One of these, found near the turnpike road at Folkestone-hill, between Folkestone and Dover, is represented in fig. 3 in the preceding page. The body was of bronze-gilt, the central band had been ornamented with slices of garnet, one of which still remains at the bottom in a silver rim; and the projecting buttons in the upper part had also been set with stones, or with some kind of glass. A fibula exactly similar to this was found at Osengal in Thanet, and is in the collection of Mr Rolfe. Precisely the same type has been found in Germany and in France. In fact, the class of fibulæ we are now describing is that usually found in the graves of the same period on the Continent, especially in those of the Franks in Gaul.

The third variety of Anglo-Saxon fibulæ is, as far as has yet been discovered, peculiar to the counties of Gloucester, Oxford, and Buckingham; and it can now hardly be doubted that they belonged to the West-Saxons, but comparatively little accurate observation has yet been made of Anglo-Saxon remains found in the purely Saxon districts. These fibulæ, which are also of brass or bronze, are circular, and deeply concave, or, rather, formed like a saucer. The rim, or side, is usually plain, but the flat bottom is ornamented with Saxon tracery. The example represented in our plate at p. 480, is now in the museum of Lord Braybrooke, who bought it at the sale at Stowe, in Buckinghamshire; it is said to have been found with a skeleton at Ashendon, in that county, with a smaller fibula of the same description, which is also in Lord Braybrooke's collection.* In Lord Braybrooke's example, which is, I believe, in this respect unique, the centre and the four points of the cross of the ornament are set with coloured glass on gold foil, like the circular fibulæ of Kent, from which, in other respects, it differs widely. It is much larger than the Kentish fibulæ, measuring in diameter nearly three inches and a half. Others of equal, and of smaller, dimensions have been found in the counties above mentioned. The field is always covered with ornamentation of the same class, in some instances with rude figures of faces and animals, and resembling in style

* It is a proof of the low state of antiquarian science in England till a very recent date, that, while this fibula was in the collection at Stowe, it was considered to be one of a pair of scales, and as such it was described in the sale catalogue.

and character that of the cross-shaped fibulæ. The only instance I know at present of the discovery of one of these fibulæ out of the counties mentioned, occurred in an Anglo-Saxon burial-place in Yorkshire.

Other small circular fibulæ of a much plainer and less characteristic description are also found with Saxon remains in different parts of the island. Sometimes they consist of a circular plate, at others of a mere circular rim, or flat ring, the material being generally of bronze. They are sometimes ornamented in the style of the fields of the saucer-shaped fibulæ, while in many instances they are merely marked with small circles, or lines, or are left quite plain. Fibulæ of more fanciful forms are also found with Anglo-Saxon remains, and not unfrequently shaped into the rude figure of a bird. Circular fibulæ, apparently of the early Anglo-Saxon period, made of lead, have also been found, but they are very rare, and possess many peculiarities. Of three which I have examined, one was found in Yorkshire, and the other two in London. The first is in the collection of Mr Hargrove, of York; it is a thin circular plate of lead, exactly an inch and a half in diameter, ornamented with three concentric circles, and a rude figure in the centre. The outer circle, or rim, is of a chain or cable pattern; the two inner circles are hatched in square compartments; while the central figure was intended to represent a dragon, with its tail twisted and inserted in its mouth. In one of the London specimens, the field in the centre, which is raised above the rest, bears the figure of a lion; it is surrounded with a series of concentric rings formed of ovals and circles of various sizes. The other London example, which was in the museum of Mr Roach Smith, is still more curious, from the circumstance that the ornament of the central field is made of a confused mass of letters, exactly resembling those marked on the earlier Anglo-Saxon coins.

We have no very distinct notion of the particular use of the Anglo-Saxon fibulæ in attaching the dress, though the larger and more ornamental ones were probably employed in fastening a mantle. The Kentish circular fibulæ are usually found on the breast, and the others are often in front of the body, somewhat nearer the girdle. In East-Anglia and Mercia, the cross-shaped fibulæ, and, more to the south-west, the saucer-shaped fibulæ, are often found in pairs, either over the breast, or, especially in the case of the saucer-shaped fibulæ, on the shoulders. It may be observed, that the buckle of the belt or girdle is often ornamented in the same style as the fibulæ, and sometimes it bears some resemblance in form to the cross-shaped variety. The use of other personal ornaments is more exactly defined by their form and position. Amongst these the most remarkable and numerous are rings, armlets, ear-rings, hair-pins, pendants to the neck, and beads.

Rings and bracelets are not found so abundantly as we might expect from the manner in which they are spoken of in the old Anglo-Saxon poetry, and they are seldom of better material than bronze. Finger rings of silver have been found in Kent, but, from their character, it is not improbable that they were of Roman workmanship. In the cemetery at Barrow Furlong, in Northamptonshire, only one ring was found, which was on the finger-bone of one of the skeletons; it was made simply of a bit of silver wire, bent into a circle, and tied at the two ends by twisting the wire. In the graves at Fairford, in Gloucestershire, were found several rings of bronze, all of them unornamented. A rather massive bronze spiral ring, perhaps of Roman workmanship, was found in a Saxon grave, in the same county. The Saxon ladies were evidently more anxious to adorn their heads and necks, than their hands and arms. Earrings are not very uncommon, but they are extremely varied in form. Sometimes they consist, like the finger-rings, merely of a bit of silver wire, either bent into a plain ring, or twisted in a spiral form. In the Anglo-Saxon cemetery at Chavenage, in Gloucestershire, was found a pair of ear-rings, formed of thin plates of silver, shaped like crescents, the ends drawn out fine and twisted together. Hair-pins are common, and resemble in character those of the Romans. They are usually of bronze, a metal the use of which the Saxons probably derived from the people on whose lands they came to reside. They are often ornamented, and in some cases they seem to have been enamelled. A hair-pin with the head set with jewels, was found in a barrow at Wringham, in Kent. A very highly ornamented hair-pin, of bronze gilt, found in a Saxon grave at Gilton, in East Kent, and now preserved in the Canterbury museum, is engraved in the second volume of the 'Collectanea Antiqua' of Mr Roach Smith, who considers it to be of late Roman workmanship. These pins were no doubt intended, like the Roman ones, for fastening up the hair behind the head. The greater number are mere pins of bronze, or sometimes of bone; but it is remarkable that these plain hair-pins have almost always a ring at the top, or, at least, the head pierced for one, which was, no doubt, intended for attaching some part of the head-dress with which we are unacquainted. The jewellery suspended round the neck was often rich and highly ornamented. A beautiful necklace of stones set in gold, pendent to a gold band, was found by Mr Bateman, in an Anglo-Saxon barrow in Derbyshire. Sometimes a gold ornament in the form of a cross, or a circular bulla, or, in place of these, a gold Roman or Merovingian coin, was suspended to the necklace. Examples of all these ornaments are found abundantly in the Kentish barrows, but they are rare in other parts of the kingdom. A few of these necklaces and bullæ are represented in our plate, chiefly taken from barrows in Kent. Fig. 1, from the cemetery at Sibertswold, is curious as inclosing a Roman intaglio; fig. 2, is a gold bulla from Kingston Down; 7 and 8 are examples of the bullæ from Breachdown and Wingham; 3 and 4, beads or ornaments in glass from Sibertswold and Beakesbourne; 5 and 6, the parts of a neck-ornament from Roundway Down, near Devizes, in Wiltshire. There can be no doubt of these ornaments being of native workmanship, and they show us to what a high state of perfection the art of the goldsmith was carried among our forefathers at this early period. At a later date, the Anglo-Saxons were celebrated throughout Europe for the beauty of their jewellery. A poem on the various fortunes of men, in the valuable collection of Anglo-Saxon poetry called the Exeter Book, describes the high consideration in which the Saxon goldsmith was held;—

> For one a wondrous skill
> in goldsmith's art
> is provided,
> full oft he decorates
> and well adorns
> a powerful king's nobles,
> and he to him gives broad
> land in recompense.

Beads are found in the Anglo-Saxon barrows in great variety, and they present a mixture of the common Roman types and of others which were doubtless of Saxon manufacture. Perhaps the Roman manufactories of beads continued to exist after the settlement of the Saxons; but whether this were the case or not, it is certain that almost every variety of Roman beads are found in the Saxon interments. The Roman beads are generally of glass, while of those which are purely Anglo-Saxon a large proportion are of terra-cotta or earthenware, and

Anglo-Saxon Jewellery.

these are sometimes incrusted with vitreous substances. The Saxons introduced the same kind of ornament into their earthenware beads which had been used by the Romans in beads of glass, and we find them often tastefully variegated with stripes of different colours. These colours are often very brilliant. A few examples of the glass beads are given in the plate, fig. 5. Two examples of the striated earthenware beads from the cemetery at Osengal, in Thanet, are given in the annexed cut.

Beads from Osengal.

Other substances used very extensively by the Anglo-Saxons in the manufacture of beads, were amethystine quartz, which is of a lilac colour, and amber. Beads appear to have been worn round the neck very generally by persons of both sexes; and it is probable that they were not only considered as personal ornaments, but that they were looked upon with a superstitious feeling as preservatives against danger, and especially against witchcraft. This was peculiarly the case with amber, which, according to the belief of the ancients, protected the person who bore it about him against the evil spirit. Hence we find continual instances of interments in which the deceased had merely one bead of amber attached to the neck, and sometimes it appears to have been simply placed in the grave by the side of his head. The lumps of amber were generally made into beads by drilling a hole through them, without attempting to shape them into regular form.

At the girdle of the Saxon lady was suspended a bunch of various small implements, answering to what in modern times is called a *châtelaine*, and which appears to have been usually buried with the person to whom it belonged. These articles appear to have been very numerous, but, unfortunately, from the circumstance of many of them being small, and of iron, which decomposes rapidly, they are often reduced to mere shapeless bits of rust. Sometimes, however, they are more perfect, and articles of bronze are always better preserved. We usually find among these articles a small knife—sometimes more than one—and a pair of scissors. The scissors, or rather shears, are almost always of the description represented in our cut on page 409, which were no doubt borrowed from the Romans; but one or two instances have been met with in Anglo-Saxon barrows of scissors of the same construction as those used at the present day. Scissors of this latter description were found in the Saxon burial-place at Driffield, in Yorkshire. Needles and pins, made of bronze or bone, are sometimes found; they had probably been placed in a case or sheath. Of articles of the toilet found attached to the châtelaine, if we

Anglo-Saxon Tweezers.

may adopt the word, the one of most frequent occurrence is a pair of bronze tweezers, used, no doubt, for extracting superfluous hairs from the body. This instrument is so perfectly identical in form and character with the Roman tweezers, that we might suppose it to be a mere relic of the Roman period preserved by one of the Saxon conquerors, if it were not of such common occurrence in Anglo-Saxon graves, that it must have been an article in general use. One of these bronze tweezers, from the cemetery at Osengal, is represented in our cut. A number of small implements resembling bodkins, are often found attached together by a ring; some of them seem to have been intended for tooth-picks and others for ear-picks, and they all show that the Anglo-Saxon ladies paid considerable attention to personal cleanliness. As I have before observed, it would be impossible, from the state in which they are generally found, to particularise all the various articles which the Anglo-

Anglo-Saxon Latch-keys (?)

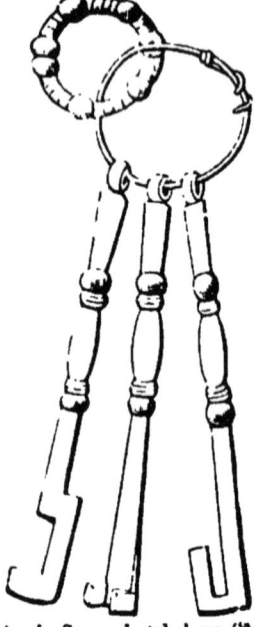

Saxon lady carried at her girdle. Some are almost inexplicable. The three implements suspended by two rings, represented in the cut on the preceding page, were found in the cemetery at Osengal, and are in the collection of Mr Rolfe. The only explanation that can be offered is, that they may have been latch-keys; but I believe that nothing exactly similar to them has been found elsewhere to assist in explaining them, though they may be compared with the Roman latch-keys, which we have given at p. 400. Another class of objects, found always with the articles hung to the lady's girdle, and invariably in pairs, has furnished a puzzle to antiquaries. Several pairs of them were found in the Anglo-Saxon cemetery at Wilbraham, in Cambridgeshire, in most cases attached together by a ring, or small frame at the top. One of these is given in our next cut, of the form which seems to have been most common. The extremities of others were of the form represented by the figure at the side. A number of other examples found at Stowe Heath, in Suffolk; near Swaffham, in Norfolk; at Scaleby, near Caistor, in Lincolnshire; and at an unascertained locality in Leicestershire; are given in the second volume of Mr Roach Smith's 'Collectanea.' They seem to be confined to the Anglian districts, and I am not aware of any example found in Kent; but, curiously enough, they are not uncommon in the Frankish cemeteries in France. They have puzzled the few antiquaries, who have observed them, extremely. They were supposed at first to be latch-keys, but their being found in pairs and the thinness of the metal (bronze) seemed to militate against this explanation, which was quite exploded when other examples were found with the ends perforated for small rings, and in some

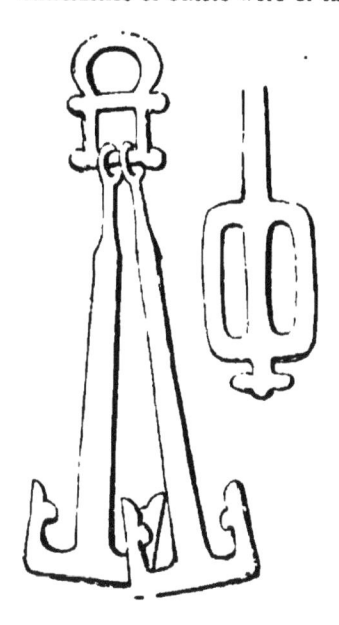

Articles from Wilbraham.

the rings were still found in the perforations. The most probable explanation seems now to be, that each pair either formed the framework of a bag or purse; or that they belonged to a frame, to which the various articles the lady carried by her side were attached. In some cases they are slightly ornamented.

Among other articles of the toilette, we must not forget to mention combs, which have been found in several instances in Anglo-Saxon graves. A double-toothed comb, of bone, with rivets of iron, was found in an urn in the cemetery at Barrow Furlong, in Northamptonshire; and a single one, of the same material, was found in a grave in Kent.

Remains of various smaller articles are found scattered about the Anglo-Saxon graves, many of which, made of perishable materials, are only indicated by decayed matter. Thus we often trace the place once occupied by a small box, or coffer, and find hinges, or clasps, or metal guards, which have belonged to it. A very remarkable small bronze coffer, or box, was found in the Anglo-Saxon cemetery at Stroud, in Kent. It was made of two thin plates of bronze, riveted together, and bound round at the lower part with a narrow band of the same metal; on one side was a ring, which appeared to have been intended for hanging it to the girdle. It was stamped with Christian figures and emblems, and was, doubtless, of foreign manufacture; perhaps obtained in barter or in war, for the interment was clearly a pagan one.* It is unnecessary to attempt an enumeration of all the small miscellaneous articles found in the Anglo-Saxon graves. In one of those at Osengal, a pair of compasses was found, and in another lay a pair of scales, the scales of which were very neatly made of thin bronze; along with them were the weights, which were formed of Roman coins, carefully adjusted by rubbing away the surface. It is not unusual to find in the Anglo-Saxon graves in Kent, sea-shells, and even snail-shells, and we sometimes meet with cowries, which must have been brought from the East. These, with the occurrence of Byzantine coins, and articles like the coffer described above, show to what extent the early Anglo-Saxon settlers held communication with foreign and even distant nations.

The larger portion of the pottery found in the Anglo-Saxon

---

* This very curious relic is engraved in Mr Roach Smith's 'Collectanea Antiqua,' vol. ii. plate 36. A somewhat similar box, ornamented with Christian subjects, has recently been found by Mr Ackerman in the Saxon cemetery of Little Wittenham, Oxfordshire.

graves in Kent, is Roman, often cups and pateræ, sometimes in fragments, of the red Samian ware. The pottery of Saxon manufacture found in this country occurs chiefly in the ceme-

Anglo-Saxon Pottery.

teries where cremation was practised, that is, in Mercia and East Anglia, and consist of burial urns. These were long classed indiscriminately as British, and it is not till lately that their distinctive characteristics have been pointed out. The cut given above presents five examples of Anglo-Saxon earthenware vessels. The two to the left, taken from a Saxon cemetery at Kingston, near Derby, are the ordinary types of burial urns found in interments of this period in England. They are usually made with the hand, without the use of the lathe, of a dark-coloured clay, and are not well baked; their colour is generally a dark brown, passing either to a black or to a dark green tint. Their distinguishing characteristics are projecting knobs or bosses at the sides, peculiar zigzag patterns, and a still more usual ornamentation of circles or squares, which have the appearance of having been stamped with the end of a notched stick. The small unornamented vessel on the right was found in the same cemetery, but without bones, and it was probably a cup for domestic purposes: it exactly resembles one found in a grave in Kent. The long-necked ampulla in the middle was found in an Anglo-Saxon grave in Kent. The vessel at the bottom, to the right, from the same cemetery at Kingston, was also used as a burial urn. An Anglo-Saxon burial urn, of a somewhat different pattern, but similar in general character, is represented in the annexed cut. It was found by Mr Bloxam, at Chertersover, in Warwickshire, filled with ashes, and accompanied with an iron sword, a spear-head, and other articles, all undoubtedly Saxon. The articles constantly found with the urns of this class, leave no room for doubt that they have been correctly appropriated to the early Saxon settlers in our island; and this appropriation is corroborated in a very remarkable manner by discoveries made on the continent. In 1848, two German antiquaries, the brothers Lindenschmit, published an account of the opening of an ancient Teutonic cemetery of the pagan period, at Selzen, in Rhenish Hesse, the articles found in which presented exactly the same character as those in our Anglo-Saxon barrows. There was a similar mixture of

Anglo-Saxon Urn.

Germano-Saxon Pottery.

the two kinds of interment, but the practice of burying the body entire seemed to prevail. The pottery was of precisely the same character; it was similar in form, and was ornamented

CHAP. XV.]   GLASS DRINKING VESSELS.   495

with the same bosses on the sides, and the same impressed notches as in the Anglo-Saxon pottery described above. For the sake of comparison, four examples of the pottery from Selzen are given in the annexed cut: the two to the left are cinerary urns, like those found in Derbyshire.

The Anglo-Saxon glass, which is not uncommon, differs from the Roman in being thinner, not so fine in texture, and more subject to that kind of decomposition, which destroys its transparency, and gives it a variegated tint. It is probable that the

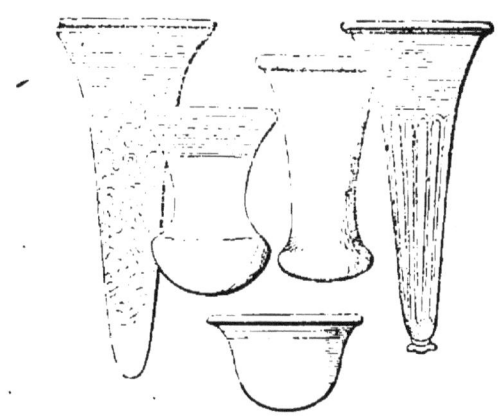

Anglo-Saxon Drinking-glasses.

Saxon glass-workers derived the art from their Roman predecessors, and they certainly possessed very great skill, although the form and ornament of their work differed entirely from Roman work. The glass vessels found in Anglo-Saxon graves are generally drinking-cups, the forms of which will be best understood by the cut above. When ornamented, they are usually ribbed or striated. The forms were evidently derived from the imitation of drinking-horns.* The examples given in our cut were all taken from barrows in East Kent, and were in the collections of Lord Londesborough and Mr Rolfe. The ornamentation answers sufficiently well to the epithet of

* It will be observed that these drinking-cups are so made that they could not stand upright; each guest was expected to drink his glass off at a draught. It is said that this custom of making drinking-cups which would not stand, in order to compel the drinkers to empty them at once, was the origin of the modern name of *tumblers*, given to glasses which are not now placed in the same predicament.

twisted, which is applied in Anglo-Saxon poetry to drinking-cups. Thus in Beowulf (line 983), we are told that—

<pre>
the thane observed his office,
he that in his hand bare
the twisted ale-cup.
</pre>

The small cup-shaped glass vessel at the bottom of our cut is also the type of a class of not uncommon occurrence in Kent. A remarkable characteristic of the early Anglo-Saxon glass

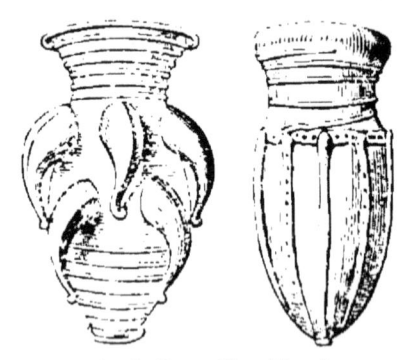

Anglo-Saxon Glass Vessels.

manufacture is an ornamentation formed by separate threads of glass twisted round the vessel after it had been formed; and sometimes of large knobs added to the glass, these latter assuming very singular shapes. It is difficult to say how far this kind of ornament was derived from the late Roman period, but there is in the little museum at Lewes, in Sussex, a glass ampulla, said to have been found among purely Roman remains, which is ornamented with the same strings twisted round the neck. I give, on this page, two examples of Anglo-Saxon glass vessels, with these singular ornamentations. The one with knobs attached was found at Reculver, in Kent, and is now preserved in the museum at Canterbury: it is about six inches high, of a colour varying from olive green to yellow (the variations perhaps caused by decomposition), the projections being of a dark green—it is also ornamented with the strings mentioned above. The other vessel represented in the cut was found at Ash, in Kent, in 1849, and is in the collection of Mr Rolfe; it is a curious specimen of the application of the thread ornament. Other examples of glass vessels, resembling the first of these, with the projecting claws, have been found in different parts of Saxon England. One is given in Mr Wylie's account of the Fairford graves, in Gloucestershire, where it was found. Another was found in a Saxon grave in Hampshire, and a fourth at Coombe, in East Kent. Another was found at Castle Eden, in Durham, and was engraved in the fifteenth volume of the Archæologia.

It is a very remarkable circumstance, and shows us the necessity of comparing the antiquities of cognate races, that one of these cups with the projecting claws, so similar to those found in England that we might suppose it had come from the same workshop, was found in a grave in the ancient cemetery at Selzen, in Rhenish Hesse.* To show the close similarity between the glass vessels found in the Selzen graves and those of the Anglo-Saxons, which is the best evidence we could have of their purely Teutonic character, I give in this page three

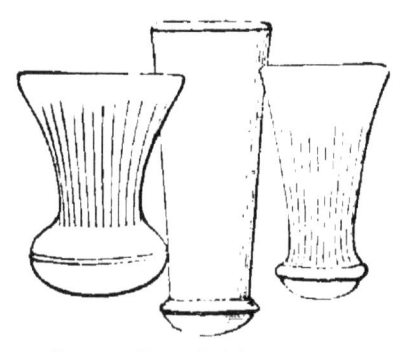

Germano-Saxon Drinking Vessels.

drinking-glasses copied from the work of the brothers Lindenschmit. One of the cup-shaped glasses, like those in our Anglo-Saxon graves, with two earthenware jugs, also from Selzen, are given in our cut on the next page. These two vessels are evidently the original type of our modern pitcher. They are not often found in Anglo-Saxon barrows, but examples have occurred, and others probably have been passed over unobserved. A good specimen is preserved in the museum of Dover; it is said to have been dug up in that neighbourhood. Mr Roach Smith

* Mr Roach Smith has given engravings of this Selzen specimen, along with the different examples found in England, in his 'Collectanea Antiqua,' vol. ii.

extracted fragments of another from a barrow on the summit of the hills behind Folkestone.

Germano-Saxon Pottery and Glass.

Although there is no doubt much of purely Teutonic character in the ornamentation of the pottery and glass, and of many of the other articles manufactured by the Anglo-Saxons, it is probable that much of it also originated in attempts, more or less rude, to imitate that which was seen on Roman work. In some of the jewellery we observe an evident design to imitate late Roman and Byzantine ornaments, and perhaps if we compared more closely the ornamental pottery, we should find it was the same. This is observable more distinctly on the Frankish pottery, which differs somewhat in character from that of the Anglo-Saxons. The accompanying cut represents a prevailing type of the Frankish burial urns, which have often, however, much more ornament. The ornament here is evidently a rude imitation of that found on the Roman red Samian wares; it may be compared with that of some late Roman pottery found in Britain, of which we have already given a cut at p. 279, and also with the ornament of a Roman altar given in p. 376. The comparison of these ex-

A Frankish Urn.

amples shows how an elegant ornament, in passing through successive imitations, degenerates into a very rude one.

There are two classes of household utensils found frequently in Anglo-Saxon interments, which are worthy of particular notice. Bowls of bronze, highly gilt, are met with in the cemeteries in Kent, and generally so elegant in form, that we can hardly

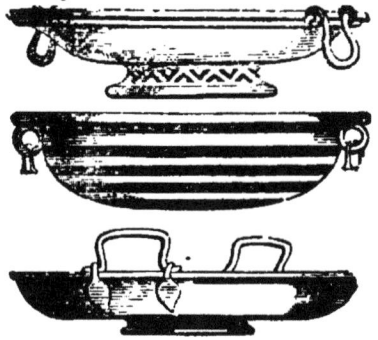

Anglo-Saxon Bowls.

hesitate in looking upon them as the work of Roman manufacturers. Three examples of these bowls are given in our cut, the first of which was found in a barrow at Wingham, in Kent; the lower example was found at Bourne Park, near Canterbury; and the one in the middle, on Barham Downs. They are of different sizes, from five or six inches to thirteen in diameter.

Another article, found very frequently in Anglo-Saxon graves, is a bucket, which generally retains sufficient proofs of having been more or less highly ornamented. These buckets are found in Anglo-Saxon cemeteries in all parts of England. Many of them have been found at different times in Kent, and traces of others, which had been formed of more perishable materials, have been met with. One found in a grave in Bourne Park, near Canterbury, had been of rather large dimensions; the hoops only remained perfect, but they were of bronze, and very elegantly formed; the lower hoop was a foot in diameter, the upper hoop

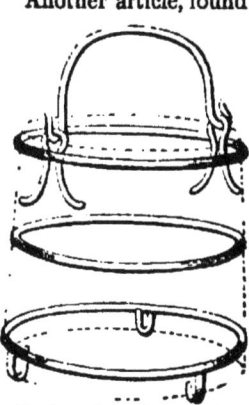

Bucket, from Bourne Park.

ten inches, and the whole height of the bucket appeared to have been about a foot. The hoops are represented in the annexed cut as they must have stood on the wood, which had perished; the hooked feet of the lower bronze hoop appear to have been intended to turn over the woodwork and hold it firm. The bucket on the right, in our next cut, was found in a grave on the Chatham lines, and is engraved in Douglas's

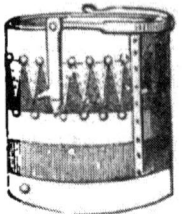

Anglo-Saxon Buckets.

'Nenia.' It was made of iron and brass, and was, therefore, better preserved. This bucket was only seven and a half inches in height, by eight inches in diameter. Buckets found in the East-Anglian cemeteries are often of still smaller dimensions. Several were found by Lord Braybrooke, at Wilbraham, in Cambridgeshire. The bucket on the left in the last cut was found in a barrow near Marlborough, in Wiltshire, opened by

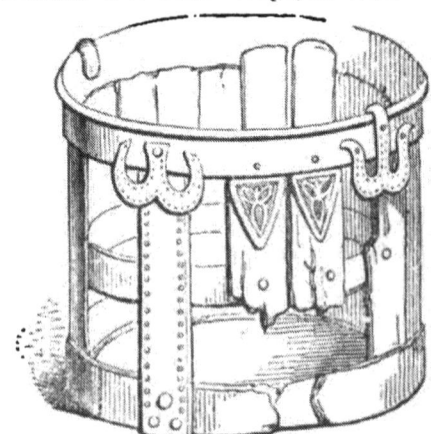

Bucket from Fairford.

Sir Richard Colt Hoare, who erroneously supposed it to be

Roman. The metal hoops, in this case, were embossed or stamped with figures of animals. Our last cut on the preceding page represents one of these bucket-formed vessels found in a grave at Fairford, in Gloucestershire, formed as usual of wood, with brass hoops, and ornaments; it was only four inches in diameter, and between three and four inches high. These buckets are, as far as I have observed, always found in the graves of men, and they were evidently vessels which served for something more than ignoble purposes. The only explanation I can suggest is, that they were for containing the ale, mead, or wine, which was to be served in the Saxon hall. They are probably the vessels (*vats*) alluded to in the words of the poem of Beowulf, which describes how

> cup-bearers gave
> the wine from wondrous vats.
> *Beowulf*, line 2316.

The Anglo-Saxon translation of the book of Judges (vii. 20), rendered *hydrias confregissent*, by 'to-bræcon þa bucas,' they broke the buckets. A common name for this vessel, which was probably called *buc*, was *æscen*, signifying literally a vessel made of ash, the favourite wood of the Anglo-Saxons.

Roman coins are not unfrequently found in Anglo-Saxon graves, and in some instances a single coin has been found, as though the deceased, or his relatives, had retained some of the older Roman customs. A few later Byzantine, and also Frankish, coins have been found, but they are much rarer than the Roman coins, which, no doubt, continued in circulation under the Saxons.[*] The earlier history of the Anglo-Saxon coinage is very obscure. On many Roman sites, especially such as are known to have been occupied down to a late period, are found very small coins in brass, which appear, from their rude character and imperfect design, to have been late imitations of the Roman coins of the size denominated third brass. These coins, from their diminutive size, are termed by numismatists *minimi*, and are supposed to have been struck during the period between the abandonment of the island by the imperial government, and the establishment of the Saxon kingdoms. It is very probable that these coins began to be struck very soon after the imperial authority was extinct, and they are of his-

---

[*] It is by no means uncommon to find coins, especially of gold, both Roman, Byzantine, and Merovingian, with loops attached to them, for the purpose of suspension as ornaments. It was a custom which prevailed among the Romans themselves.

torical interest, because they seem to show the continued existence of the municipal government in the town. These so-called *minimi* are not always of the diminutive size which gave rise to their name, as we find them sometimes as large, or nearly, as the small copper coin of the mintage of the emperors of the Constantine family, which seem in most cases to have been the types from which they were rudely copied. I give two examples from coins recently found at Wroxeter (*Uriconium*). On this site, two instances have already been met with in which, at the time the ancient city was destroyed, individuals have dropped the money with which they were attempting to make their escape, leaving us curious evidence of the class of money which was at that moment in circulation. The first of these individuals was an old man, whose skeleton was found where he had sought to conceal himself in one of the hypocausts of the public baths, and he may have been the money-taker in that establishment, for his treasure consisted almost entirely of coins of small value. They were:

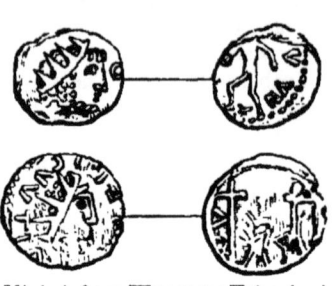

Minimi, from Wroxeter (*Uriconium*).

Tetricus (much worn) .. 1	The type URBS ROMA	24
Claudius Gothicus 1	That of CONSTANTINOPOLIS ..	34
Constantine the Elder .. 13	Valens (much worn)	1
Constans 1	Rude copies of Roman coins, or	
Constantine II. 36	*minimi*	6
Constantius II. 5	Illegible	6
Julian (a plated denarius) .. 1		
Helena 2	Total	132
Theodora 1		

The second bundle of coins alluded to, appeared to have belonged to some one who was making his escape from what is supposed to have been an enameller's workshop, and consisted of the following coins:—

Caracalla (a silver denarius) .. 1	Salonina (copper, washed with silver)	1
Severus Alexander (a plated denarius) 1	Postumus	1
Maximus (second brass) .. 1	Victorinus	8
Gallienus 2	Tetricus	3

Claudius Gothicus	..	..	2	Gratian ..	.. .. ..	1
Carausius	..	..	1	A minimus	.. .. ..	1
The Constantine family		..	12	Illegible ..	.. .. ..	2
Valentinian	..	..	1		Total	38

The *minimus* found in this second lot is the lower coin of the two engraved on the preceding page. All these coins, which are not otherwise described, are small copper; and we cannot but remark how large a proportion are those of the Constantine family. The very small comparative number of *minimi* found in circulation in so important a town, would seem to show that this coinage was quite recent when Uriconium was destroyed. On the site of some other Roman towns, which had continued to exist through the period between the Romans and the Saxons, they are found in proportionally greater numbers. In London a large quantity of these have been found; and Mr Roach Smith enumerates among the coins found of late years at Richborough (*Rutupiæ*), no less than two hundred of these *minimi*, which show that that post continued to be occupied as a place of importance during the period just mentioned. These coins were followed by a different coinage, which was undoubtedly Saxon, but which also was imitated from that of the Romans, and it is not improbable that the old minting establishments continued to exist. These early Saxon coins, for the classification of which very little has yet been done, are called *sceattas*.* It is remarkable, that while the Roman *minimi* are all in brass, the *sceattas* are invariably in silver. The devices may generally be traced to be rude imitations of Roman types, especially of the coinage of Constantine and his family, which are found in great abundance in this country. Of the two examples given in our cut, the upper has on one side a copy of a very common reverse of the coins of the Constantine period, which are usually classed under the head of *urbs Roma*, representing Romulus and Remus suckled by the wolf. The second has a head on one side, and on the other, a device which is probably copied from the altar which occurs on the coins of the Constantine family. Many are copied from the coins of Arcadius, Honorius, and others of that period. The *sceattas*

* The *sceattas* were the common coins of the Anglo-Saxons at an early period; and the name was often used as a general term for money. The word, in the singular, is *sceat* or *scæt*, and to pay your *sceat*, was literally to pay your reckoning. This has been by course of time corrupted into the modern ale-house phrase of *paying your shot*.

have been found at Richborough, Reculver, and other places in East Kent, in considerable numbers, as well as in the north of England. They are met with occasionally in the pagan Anglo-Saxon barrows or graves, which fixes the period to which they belong. The mouldering remains of what appeared to have been a small purse, with four *sceattas* of silver, were found by the side of a skeleton in a barrow on the Breach Downs, in Kent.

Anglo-Saxon Sceattas from Richborough.

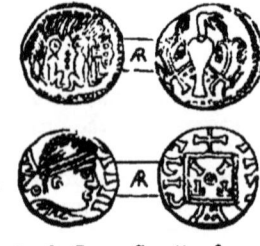

CHAPTER XVI.

Anglo-Saxon Settlement—Division of the Land—Population of the Country and of the Towns—Continuance of the Roman Municipalities—Traces of Municipal Privileges in the Anglo-Saxon Towns; Canterbury, Rochester, Dover, Exeter, London.

THE remains of our Anglo-Saxon forefathers, as described in the preceding chapter, present sufficient evidence that society then consisted of two very distinct elements: one purely Teutonic, the other derived from intercourse with the Roman population. The Teutonic settlers took possession of the land, which the various chiefs divided among themselves by lot; and it was held by a totally different tenure to that which existed under the imperial government. The characteristic of Teutonic society was a deeply implanted aristocracy, that of the heads of clans, or tribes, and there was very little tendency to the centralisation which was exhibited in the Roman imperial constitution. Each chief received his share of land, on which he settled with his household and followers, and which descended in his family as a freehold. We still trace these original allotments of land in the names of places in every part of England, which are composed of the patronymic of the family or race. Thus, when we find such a name as Birmingham, we may be sure that it was originally the *ham*, or residence, of the Beormingas, the descendants or clan of Beorm, for this was the regular form of the Teutonic patronymic—*Beorming, the son of Beorm*. And thus we have Bādlingham in Cambridgeshire, the seat of the Bædlingas; Buckingham, of the Bucingas; Warmingham, in Cheshire, of the Wearmingas; Littlington, the *tûn* or head residence of the Lytlingas; Elvington, the seat of the Elfingas; Killinghall, the hall of the Cylingas; and a vast number of similar names. The family or clan did not always take its name from the chief who obtained the allotment of land; it was often but a branch of a much older family in the land from which the settler came.

Hence we find the same patronymics in distant parts of England, which would seem to indicate that different members of the same original family had joined in various separate expeditions to Britain; and it is still more curious that this identity of name is found in districts peopled severally by the different races, Angles, or Saxons, or Jutes. This admits of two explanations: it shows the close relationship between the three races themselves; and it proves, probably, that when a great chieftain of one race, an Angle, for instance, planned an expedition to Britain, subordinate leaders from the other races, Saxons, Jutes, or others, were ready to enlist among his followers. Thus we find the Billingas at Billingham, in Durham; at Billingley, in Yorkshire; at Billinghay, in Lincolnshire; at Billington, in the counties of Bedford, Stafford, and Lancaster; as well as at other places, all within the districts occupied by the Angles. We find a settlement of the same family at Billingshurst, in Sussex; and some of them appear to have established themselves in the outskirts of London, and to have given their name to Billingsgate. The Bosingas are found at Bossingham, in Kent, and again at the two Bossingtons, in Hampshire and Somerset. The Scearingas are found at Sharrington, Sheringford, and Sharringham, in Norfolk; at Sheering, in Essex; at Scarrington, in Nottinghamshire; and at Sherrington, in Buckingham, and in Wiltshire. We have the Haningas at three places named Hannington, in Northamptonshire, Hampshire, and Wiltshire, and also probably at Hanningfield, in Essex. When we examine further we find, among these patronymics, names which belong to the great families whose history is mixed up in the earliest Teutonic mythology. The Wælsings, who are found at Walsingham, in Norfolk, at Walsingham, in Durham, and at Woolsington, in Northumberland, appear to have been offsets of the great family of the Völsungar of the Edda, the Volsungen of the old German romances. The Harlings (Herelingas), who are found at three places named Harlington, in Middlesex, Bedfordshire, and Yorkshire, as well as at Harling, in Norfolk, are also connected with the ancient Teutonic mythology, and their name is found at Harlingen, in Friesland. The Swæfas, a tribe who are known to have dwelt on the borders of the Angles, on the continent, appear to have given their name to Swaffham, in Norfolk. Mr Kemble, quoting other well-known names from the mythic and half-mythic history of the continental Teutons, points out, as further instances, that the Brentings of northern romance are found in England, at Brentingley, in Leicestershire, and at Brantingham, in Yorkshire. The Scyldings, and Scylfings, celebrated Northern races, gave their names to Skelding, and to two places named Skillington, in Northumberland and Dorset; the Ardings, who are found at Ardington, in Berkshire, and at Ardingly, in Sussex, are, he says, the Azdingi, the royal race of the Visigoths and Vandals; and the Banings of the continent, over whom, when the curious Anglo-Saxon fragment called the Traveller's Song was written, a prince named Becca ruled, are recognised in Banningham, in Norfolk. The Helsings gave name to Helsington, in Westmoreland, and to Helsingland, in Sweden; and we find the name of the Bleccingas as well in Bleckingen, in Sweden, as in Bletchington, in Oxfordshire, and Bletchingley, in Surrey. In the Gytingas, found at Guyting, in Gloucestershire, we perhaps trace the Jutungi of Germany; and another Alamannic tribe, the Scudingi, are supposed to be traced in the Scytings, who gave their name to Shuttington, in Warwickshire. In these instances, conjecture is, perhaps, carried too far, as well as in the supposition that the Wærings, who left their name in two Warringtons, in Lancashire and Buckinghamshire, and to the same number of Werringtons in Northamptonshire and Devon, belonged to the same race as the Varangians (Værinjar), so celebrated in Byzantine history; but there can be no doubt that the careful study of the Anglo-Saxon names of localities is calculated to throw a light upon the history and condition of the first settlers which we can hope to derive from no other source.* Many of these names point directly to the state of the country itself, at the time the Teutonic population came in, and we can have no doubt that then the site of Beverley was a plain so unfrequented by man, that it was occupied only by beavers, or that places with names compounded of those of wolves, boars, &c., were the usual resorts of wild beasts.

The Teutonic settlers established themselves chiefly in the country, where they retained all their old national feelings. We know that they were averse to living in towns, and, from a superstitious feeling which led them to believe that the houses built by other peoples might be rendered dangerous for them by means of charms and magic, they preferred the houses which they built for themselves. Moreover, the country villas

---

* Extensive materials on this interesting subject have been collected by Mr Kemble in the first volume of his 'Saxon in England.'

of the Romans, and the smaller and unfortified towns, had been mostly burnt or overthrown, and their plan and construction were not those to which the Saxons were accustomed. However, we do meet with instances of Roman villas occupied and altered by the Anglo-Saxon settlers, and in some instances we find that the residence of the Saxon chief did occupy a Roman site. This was the case with the two seats of the Iclings; Icklingham, in Suffolk, and Ickleton, or Icklington, in Cambridgeshire, in both which places have been found extensive traces of Roman settlement. One of them is supposed to occupy the site of the Roman station of Iciani, and it is not quite impossible that the Saxon name in this case may have arisen from mistaking the Roman name for a patronymic. The Anglo-Saxon landholders held a position totally different from that of the Romans; they were lords over their own allotment of soil and its population, and the principle of centralisation existed so little amongst them, that, rather than look up to a superior head for justice, the landlords formed associations among themselves, to manage their own affairs, and administer justice in their mutual transactions. Such mutual associations formed the groundwork of the subsequent division of the country into hundreds, shires, &c. Each landholder, nevertheless, acknowledged a certain dependence upon, or subjection to, the chief under whom he had come into the island, and the latter assumed the title of king over his chieftains and their people. These kings were soon tempted by the splendour of the old Roman rule, and they tried to establish and increase their authority by imitating Roman forms, and adopting, as far as they could, the Roman principles of administration. They were wealthy, by the extensive landed estates which they had reserved to themselves in the division of lands, and by the possession of the old Roman towns, which fell to their share; and they had a natural influence over the other chiefs who had followed their banner from the first, because they belonged to the great families of supposed divine blood, who alone commanded that sort of confidence and respect which was necessary to insure obedience.

The population of the country consisted of two elements—the chiefs and their followers, who had obtained possession and lordship of the lands, and the agriculturists and labourers, who were in the position of serfs and bondmen, and comprised chiefly the old Romano-British population, which under the Saxons was probably quite as well off as under the Romans.

The Saxons thus held the country, while the Roman citizens continued to hold the towns as tributaries of the Saxon kings, within whose bounds they stood. The country thus exhibited Teutonic rudeness, while the towns were the representatives of Roman civilisation, and though the intercourse between the two, and the gradual infusion of Saxon blood into the towns, laid the foundation of modern society, there was a feeling of hostility and rivalry between town and country, which has hardly yet disappeared. Between the aristocratic feeling of the Saxon landholders, and the republican principles that existed in the towns, arose, under the balancing influence of the crown, the modern political constitution.

We can understand best the mode and forms in which the Anglo-Saxons established themselves here, by comparing them with what took place, under similar circumstances, in other parts of Europe, where our historical accounts are more detailed and precise. There, also, the barbarian settlers seized upon the lands, while the cities were generally left in the hands of the old citizens. On a former occasion I have described briefly the internal constitution of the Roman towns, with their *curiales*, or senators, and their various municipal officers, which we know were all preserved after the Teutonic conquests in the cities in Gaul and the other Roman provinces on the continent, and which were, no doubt, also preserved in Britain.* In Italy, where, in the mixture, the spirit of the Roman institutions prevailed most over the barbarian population, the cities, relieved from the imperial power to which they had been previously subjected, became in the middle ages powerful republics, and the *curia* was the prototype of those bodies of patrician princes, whose personal feuds led in the end to their subversion. In other parts of Europe, amid the general wreck, some powerful commercial cities retained a complete independence, and became known as free cities, and some of them have continued so to the present day. In France, M. Raynouard has traced the existence of the municipal officers by their original titles, even the *defensor civitatis*, during several centuries after the fall of the Roman power. We have unfortunately few documents which throw any light on the condition of the towns in England during the Saxon period of our history; but we cannot help recognising in the Roman

* The following remarks were first published in a paper communicated to the Society of Antiquaries, and printed in the thirty-second volume of the Archæologia.

curia the origin of the elective body in our medieval towns, the *probi homines* or *boni homines* of the older records, the burgesses, who, like the *curiales* or senators, obtained their rank by birth or election. The *duumviri* answered to the two *bollivi* or bailiffs, or as the Saxons called them, *præfecti* or *reeves*, who were the chief magistrates in most of our medieval boroughs. The *principales* were the *scabini* (*échevins*) of the continental towns, in England generally known by the Saxon name of aldermen. We might go on to enumerate other minor points of resemblance between the constitutions of the *municipium* and of the medieval borough at the time when we become fully acquainted with the domestic affairs of the latter; but I will only now point out a few circumstances which tend to throw a light upon the condition of these boroughs under the Anglo-Saxons, when they have commonly been supposed by legal writers to have had no corporate existence.

It strikes us at the first glance, that the few historical facts relating to the condition of our towns during the Saxon period, preserved by the older annalists, exhibit them in a state of importance and independence, which they could hardly have reached, had it not been derived from municipal constitutions already existing when the Saxons settled in this country, and which is observed most distinctly in those places which are known to have occupied the sites of the more powerful Roman towns.* All traditions (for our history of the first Saxon invasion is nothing more than tradition, and that very vague) represent East Kent as having been occupied by the Saxons under a pacific arrangement, when they took Durovernum, or Canterbury, as their capital. Recent discoveries show that the Saxons not only continued to inter their dead on the site of the Roman burial-places around the ancient city, down to the time of their conversion, but that they afterwards erected Christian churches on the same spots; one of the strongest proofs we could have of the gradual change from Roman to Saxon in that city. We find Canterbury at an early period governed by a prefect, or reeve, who gives land to the monks; and in a later charter confirming his grant, dated in 805, there is a remarkable distinction between the *villa* or town, and the *civitas* or corporate body, such as we might naturally expect

---

* It may be observed that the destruction of Roman towns is rarely mentioned in our earlier historians. The Saxons Chronicle speaks of the destruction of Andredesceaster in 491 as though it were a remarkable occurrence.

in the transmission of the Roman principle to the Saxon people.*

Rochester (*Hrofescester*) derived its Saxon name, according to Bede, from one of its early rulers or prefects named Hrof, who, for some circumstance or other, had probably gained greater notoriety than most persons of his class and rank.† In the reign of king Ethelred (in the latter half of the tenth century), on account of some dissensions with the bishop, the king besieged this city with an army, but, being unable to take it, he in revenge laid waste the surrounding and dependent district.‡ We here find the body corporate of the city taking part with its bishop, engaged in open war with the king, and successfully resisting him. The anger of the king is said to have been finally appeased by a sum of money given by the archbishop of Canterbury (Dunstan).

Dover occupies the site of the Roman Dubræ. It is not often mentioned by our earlier historians, because Richborough (*Rutupiæ*) was the more usual port in landing from France; but an incident occurred in the reign of Edward the Confessor which throws some light on the position of its municipal body. In 1048, Eustache count of Boulogne, Edward's brother-in-law, visited the king at Gloucester, where he was then holding his court. On his return, when at a short distance from Dover, Eustache and his men put on their armour, and, entering the town in a rude manner, they proceeded to take forcible possession of the lodgings which pleased them best.§ This was a right which the feudal barons of the continent claimed under the title of the *droit de gîte*, and which was expressly provided against in the English municipal charters subsequent to the Conquest. One of Eustache's men went to the dwelling of a townsman, and wounded the householder,

---

* Hanc prænominatam terram quidam homo bonus nomine Aldhun, qui in hac regali *villa* inlustris *civitatis* præfectus fuit, pro intuitu internæ mercedis fratribus nostris ad mensam tradidit. Kemble's Codex Diplomaticus Anglo-Saxonum, vol. i. p. 231.

† Quam gens Anglorum a primario quondam illius, qui dicebatur Hrof, Hrofescestir cognominat. Bede, Hist. Eccl. lib. ii. c. 3. In another place, lib. ii. c. 6, Bede calls the city, in Latin, civitas Hrofi.

‡ Osborn's Life of Dunstan, in the Act. SS. Benedict. Sæc. V. p. 683. W. Malmsb. de Gest. Reg. p. 63. (Ed. Savile.)

§ þa hi þider comon, þa woldon hi innian hi þær heom sylfan ge-licode. Sax. Chron. From the circumstance of their arming before they came to the town, we might be led to suspect that Eustache and his men had had a previous dispute with the townsmen of Dover on this subject, perhaps when they first came to England.

because he refused to admit him. The latter seized his own weapon and slew the intruder. 'Then,' to use the words of the contemporary Saxon chronicler, 'Eustache got upon his horse, and his companions upon theirs, and they went to the householder and slew him within his own dwelling; and then went up towards the burgh, and slew, as well within as without, more than twenty men. And the townsmen slew nineteen of the count's men, and wounded they knew not how many, and Eustache escaped with only a few companions.' Eustache returned to the king, gave a partial account of the affair, and made him so 'wroth with the townsmen,' that he ordered Godwin, in whose earldom of Kent the occurrence had taken place, to proceed with an army against the men of Dover. But earl Godwin, knowing that Eustache had begun the quarrel, espoused the cause of the townsmen, and an irruption of the Welsh seems to have turned the king's attention in another direction. Four years after this, in 1052, count Eustache again visited king Edward, and on his landing at Dover the old feud was renewed. 'Then,' says the chronicler, 'went his men inconsiderately after lodgings, and slew a certain man of the town, and then another, until seven lay slain. And much harm was then done on both sides, both with horse and with weapons, until the people gathered together, and then Eustache's men fled away till they came to the king at Gloucester.' On this second occasion, Godwin more openly took part with the townsmen of Dover, and, raising a considerable army, marched towards the king, and demanded that count Eustache and his men should be delivered into his hands. We have here a town virtually claiming a very important municipal right, and defending it by force; while the king proceeds, not judicially against the individuals who had offended, but against the whole corporate body, as though it were an independent state.* We learn, also, from the Domesday Survey, that in this same reign, the burgesses of Dover had purchased certain immunities of the king, for the condition of serving him with twenty ships for fifteen days in the year.†

* The above version of the story is taken from the Saxon Chronicle as printed in the text and in the notes of the Collection of Historians edited by order of the Record Commission, which appears to be the best authority. The subsequent historians have confounded the two riots, and made only one. See Florence of Worcester, sub an. 1051; W. Malmsb. de Gest. Reg. p. 81, &c.

† Burgenses dederunt xx. naves regi una vice in anno ad xv. dies; et in unaquaque navi erant homines xx. et unus. Hoc faciebant pro eo quod eis perdonaverat sacam et socam.

We have another instance of municipal responsibility in the case of Thetford, in Norfolk. In 952, the people of that town were engaged in hostilities with the monks (probably in defence of some of their privileges), in the course of which they slew their abbot Eadhelm. King Edred appears to have taken no steps to discover the persons immediately concerned in this act of violence, but he sent an army, and caused 'a great slaughter' to be made of the townsmen.*

In 1040, king Hardacnut imposed a very heavy tribute on his English subjects. Two of the king's *huscarles* were sent to enforce its payment by the citizens of Worcester, who rose against them, and slew them in the cathedral. The king, in revenge, sent an army to ravage the neighbourhood and destroy the city, but the inhabitants had taken shelter, with their most valuable effects, in an island in the river Severn, and there they set their persecutors at defiance.† We here find a town asserting its right to exemption from extraordinary taxation; another of the municipal privileges guaranteed by the charters of a later period.

The city of Exeter affords a remarkable instance of the manner in which the Roman municipal institutions were preserved. In other towns the Romano-British population gradually disappeared; but we learn, from William of Malmsbury, that, down to the reign of Ethelstan, Exeter was inhabited by English and Welsh, who lived on an equality of rights (*æquo jure* ‡), which they could only have done by virtue of an original composition with the Saxon conquerors. It may be cited as a proof of the correctness of this view of the mode in which the Roman corporations outlived the shock of invasion, and thus became a chief instrument in the civilisation of subsequent ages, that even the Danes, in their predatory excursions, often entered into similar compositions with the Saxon towns, as with Canterbury, in 1009. It may be added, that there is no greater evidence of the independence and strength of the towns under the Saxons, than the circumstance that, while the king and his earls, with the forces of the counties, were not able to make a successful stand against the Danish invaders, it frequently happened that a town singly drove a powerful army

---

* Saxon Chron. sub an.
† Saxon Chron. Florence of Worcester.
‡ Illos [Cornewallenses] quoque impigre adorsus, ab Excestria, quam ad id temporis æquo cum Anglis jure inhabitarant, cedere compulit.—W. Malmsb. de Gest. Reg. p. 50.

from its gates, and the townsmen sometimes issued forth and defeated the enemy in a pitched battle. The Saxon Chronicle furnishes many examples. In 855, the townsmen of Rochester made a brave defence against the Danes, till they were relieved by Alfred. The inhabitants of Exeter opposed the invaders with success on several occasions; the townsmen (burgware) beat them in battle in 895. In 918, the men of Hereford and Gloucester went out, and defeated the Danes in a pitched battle. In 921, the Danes were beaten by the men of Bedford, and also by the inhabitants of Maldon in Essex. In 1001, the people of Exmouth drove away the Danish army which came to attack that town. When the Saxons began to obtain the ascendancy by the abilities of the family of Alfred, we find the towns revolting from the Danes in a manner which can hardly leave a doubt of their acting as free corporate bodies. The Saxon Chronicle, under the year 918, speaking of Ethelfleda, tells us, 'in the early part of this year, by God's help, she got into her power, by treaty, the burgh of Leicester, and the greater part of the army which owed obedience thereto (þe þær-to hyrde) became subject to her; and the people of York (Eforwicingas) had also covenanted with her, some having given a pledge, and some having bound themselves by oath, that they would be at her command.' And again, in the same year, 'Thurcytel the eorl sought king Edward to be his lord, and all the *holdas* and almost all the chief men who owed obedience to Bedford, and also many of those who owed obedience to Northampton.' In the year following, 'those who owe obedience to Bedford' are called *burgwara*, burgesses. In 921, 'the army which owed obedience to Cambridge' chose king Edward to be their lord.

We can trace the power and independence of the citizens of London from the earliest period of our annals. We have no reason for believing that this city, which was a powerful commercial port, was ever taken and ravaged by the Saxon invaders. It appears to have afforded a shelter to the people of West Kent, when that district was overrun by the Saxons in their first inroads.* At the end of the sixth century, London was considered as the capital of the East-Saxons, although Ethelbert, king of Kent, appointed Mellitus to the bishopric, and built there for him the church of St Paul.† At that

---

* See the Saxon Chron. sub an. 457.
† Bede, Hist. Eccl. lib. ii. c. 3.

period it was still a rich trading town,* and it appears to have experienced no check to its prosperity. After the relapse of the East-Saxons to idolatry, the Londoners refused to receive back their bishop, and neither the king of Kent, nor the two East-Saxon kings, had power to force him upon them.† About the year 635, Wini bought of Wulfhere, king of the Mercians, the see of the city of London, and remained bishop thereof till his death. At a subsequent period, archbishop Theodore appointed bishops of the East-Saxons 'in the city of London,' and Essex has been ever since included in the diocese. In 679, we hear of Friesland merchants in London, and it appears to have been then a great mart of slaves.‡ A comparison of these different circumstances gives us some grounds for believing that, although nominally the metropolis of the kings of the East-Saxons, London was in the fullest sense of the word a free-trading town, neutral to a certain degree between the kingdoms around, although each king exercised a greater or less degree of influence over it according as he was more or less powerful than his neighbours, and perhaps each had his officers there to look after the interests of his own subjects. This would explain in some degree an obscure law of the Kentish kings, Hlothhere and Edric (673—685), made at a time when we should expect London to have been under the power of the kings of Mercia :—' If any Kentish man buy a chattel in Lunden-wic, let him then have two or three true men to witness, or the king's *wic-reeve*. If it be afterwards claimed of the man in Kent, let him then vouch the man who sold it him to warranty, in the *wic* (town) at *the king's hall*, if he know him and can bring him to the warranty: if he cannot do that, let him prove at the altar, with one of his witnesses, or with the *king's wic-reeve*, that he bought the chattel openly in the *wic*, with his own money, and then let him be paid its worth: but if he cannot prove that by lawful averment, let him give it up, and let the owner take possession of it.'§ The *king's wic-reeve* appears to have been an officer of the king of Kent who exercised a jurisdiction over the Kentish men trading with or at London, or who was appointed to watch over their interests.

---

* Et ipsa multorum emporium populorum terra marique venientium. Bede, ib.
† Bede, Hist. Eccl. lib. ii. c. 4.
‡ Bede, Hist. Eccl. lib. iii. c. 7, and lib. iv. cc. 6, 12, 22.
§ Thorpe's Anglo-Saxon Laws, p. 14. Some antiquaries have supposed, very erroneously, that *Lunden-wic* is here another name for Sandwich.

When the different Saxon kingdoms became consolidated into one, the influence of the sole monarch over the metropolis would be of course greatly increased, but we still meet with remarkable proofs of its power and independence. Ethelstan was one of the most powerful of the Anglo-Saxon monarchs of England; yet under his reign, soon after the year 900, we find 'the bishop and reeves, who belong to London,' making in the name of the citizens laws, which were confirmed by the king (because they had reference to the whole kingdom), and are preserved in the Anglo-Saxon code. These laws prove that the body corporate of the city of London exercised an independent jurisdiction in matters which concerned themselves far beyond the limits of their own territory, and the necessity of making this power known throughout the kingdom was the cause that their laws on this subject were entered among the public laws of the land, which circumstance has led to their preservation, while every document relating to the internal government of the city at this early period has perished. These laws relate chiefly to robberies committed by strangers, to which a large commercial city was naturally exposed, and against which it could provide itself with no redress unless it could pursue the offenders to a distance. One of the clauses provides, 'if it then should happen that any kin be so strong and so great, within land or without land, whether twelve-hynde or two-hynde, that they refuse us our right, and stand up in defence of a thief, that we all of us ride thereto with the reeve within whose district (*manung*) it may be; and also send on both sides to the reeves, and desire from them aid of so many men as may seem to us adequate for so great a suit, that there may be the more fear in those culpable men for our assemblage, and that we all ride thereto, and avenge our wrong, and slay the thief, and those who fight and stand with him, unless they be willing to depart from him.' * The power of making a law like this, implies something like an understood agreement or treaty between a free commercial city and the states which surround it, whereby those states are allowed commercial privileges on condition of giving the citizens the right of pursuing offenders through their territories; and it agrees perfectly with the interpretation given to the earlier law of the kings of Kent.

This also explains to us why, at a very early period after the Norman Conquest, the privileges of the city of London are

---

* Judicia civitatis Lundoniæ, viii. § 2, 3. Thorpe, p. 100.

excepted and protected in charters given to corporate towns in far distant parts of the kingdom. In a dispute with the abbot of Bury, in the twelfth century, the citizens of London, so far from admitting (as Brady supposed) that their privileges were newly acquired from their Norman sovereigns, professed to have enjoyed them from the first foundation of their city, which they carried as far back as the time of the foundation of Rome.*

We learn from the Saxon Chronicle that, in the Danish invasion of the year 994, 'Anlaf and Swegen came to London, on the Nativity of St Mary (Sept. 8), with ninety-four ships; and they then continued fighting stoutly against the town, and would eke have set fire to it. But they there sustained more harm and evil than they ever imagined that any townsmen (*buruhwaru*) would be able to do unto them.' In 1009, the men of Canterbury bought a peace with the Danish invaders, and then, as we learn from the contemporary authority just quoted, the latter 'fought oft against the town of London; but, praise be to God, that it yet stands sound, and they there ever fared ill.' In 1013, king Ethelred sought shelter in London, which was besieged by Swegen: 'When he came to the town,' says the chronicle, 'the townsmen (seo burhwaru, *la bourgeoisie*, it is a collective noun in the singular number) would not submit, but held out against him with all·their might.' Although the Danes now overrun without opposition the rest of the kingdom, the Londoners defended the Saxon king, until at length he deserted his protectors, and then, Swegen being generally acknowledged as king of England, 'the townsmen of London submitted, and delivered hostages, because they dreaded lest he should utterly undo them.' †
When king Ethelred returned, after the death of Swegen, he was again received by the Londoners, who formed his surest defence. · In 1016, Edmund Etheling collected his forces against Cnut. 'When the forces were assembled, then would it not content them, except it so were that the king were there with them, and they might have the help of the townsmen of London.' As the townsmen would not go, Edmund's army

* Et dicebant cives Lundonienses fuisse quietos de theloneo in omni foro, et semper et ubique, per totam Angliam, a tempore quo Roma primo fundata fuit, et civitatem Lundoniæ eodem tempore fundatum. Josceline de Brakelonde, p. 56.

† Compare W. Malmsb. de Gest. Reg. Angl. p. 69, with the Saxon Chronicle.

dispersed itself. On king Ethelred's death, which occurred the same year, 'all the witan who were in London, and the townsmen (seo burhwaru, William of Malmsbury calls them the *proceres Lundoniæ*), chose Edmund to be king.' The Danes soon afterwards laid siege to London, but the citizens again defended themselves with obstinacy, until Edmund came and relieved them. They sustained a second siege the same year, but, after Edmund's defeat at Assandun, 'the men of London made a truce with the army.' *

It appears from the foregoing statements of a contemporary chronicler, that the men of London were brave and experienced warriors; but they were evidently, like the citizens of the Roman *municipium*, not liable to be called out of their own walls to fight, even when the country was on the brink of ruin by a successful invader; and the power of the monarch over them was very limited. In the course of the history I have just recited, they act in every respect as a small independent state. Another incident occurred at this period, which illustrates in a remarkable degree the extent of their power. When archbishop Elfey had been slain by the Danes in 1012, the Londoners purchased his body of the murderers, and deposited it in St Paul's cathedral. After Cnut had obtained the crown by conquest, and peace was restored, archbishop Agelnoth (Elfey's successor) applied to the king to give up the body of the martyr to the monks of Canterbury. Cnut, who was then holding his court in London, consented, but he would only undertake to get away the body by deceiving the citizens. He gave orders to his *huscarles*, or household soldiers, to disperse themselves in parties, some on the bridge and along the banks of the river, whilst others went to the gates of the city, and there raised tumults and riots.† By dint of promises and persuasions, the men who had the care of the body of Elfey were prevailed upon to assist in the plot, and, whilst the attention of the citizens was called to the disturbances at the gates, the sacred deposit was carried by stealth to the river and there placed in a boat, which was rowed in all haste beyond the limits of the capital, and then landed in Kent. The king stood on the bank of the Thames, and watched its progress with anxious

---

* Saxon Chronicle.
† Mandans omnibus familiæ suæ militibus, quos lingua Danorum *huscarles* vocant, ut alii eorum per extremas civitatis portas seditiones concitent, alii pontem et ripas fluminis armati obsideant, ne exeuntes eos cum corpore sancti Lundanus populus præpedire valeat.

eye, for *he was afraid of the citizens.** When the latter discovered the trick which had been played upon them, they sent out a party in pursuit of the fugitives, who, however, had reached a place of safety before they were overtaken.†

This anecdote gives us a curious glance at London manners at the beginning of the eleventh century. About half a century later, at the entry of the Normans, we find the citizens of London again holding the same bold position; and the conqueror of Hastings was obliged to make conditions with them before they would acknowledge him as king. It is not necessary to enter into their subsequent history; but it must be stated to their glory that, if we begin with their defence against the Danes, in the tenth century, the citizens of London have been, through at least nine centuries, the constant, powerful, and unflinching—perhaps, sometimes, turbulent—champions of the liberties of Englishmen.

To return again to the more general subject, we trace by various allusions during the Anglo-Saxon period, that in these corporate towns there was, independent of the municipal officers, an officer of the king, or king's reeve, who took certain tolls or dues which were reserved for the king on sales, manumissions, judicial executions, &c., and which the king had obtained in the transmission of the municipal system from the Roman to the Saxon government. Thus at Exeter, as we learn from the entries on the fly-leaves of the now well-known 'Codex Exoniensis,' such duties were regularly paid to an officer 'for the king's hand,' to use the phrase of the original; as, for instance, Alfric Hals took the toll in Tovie's house 'for þæs kynges hand' (fol. 6, rº); Widfet took the toll 'for þas cinges hand' (fol. 6, vº), and so forth. When we hear of a Saxon king giving a town to a queen, or to a bishop, or to an abbey, it means, of course, that the king gave to those persons merely the duties which accrued to him from the towns in question.

Although the municipal privileges were all derived directly from the Romans, it does not of course follow that such privileges were enjoyed only by towns which had been founded in Roman times. As the Saxons became established throughout the island, and adopted, to a certain degree, the manners of their Roman predecessors, they founded other towns, and they

---

* Timebat namque civium interruptiones.
† Translatio S. Elphegi, by Osborn, ap. Act. SS. Ordinis Benedict. sæc. VI. part. i. pp. 124—126. Osborn received his account from people who were present, see p. 125.

naturally imitated the forms presented to their view in the Roman models already existing. Most of these were, as the Roman towns had become, royal towns, that is, they had no superior lord but the king. But others, after the conversion of the Saxons to Christianity, gradually sprung up about, and under the protection of, episcopal sees and abbeys, and these eventually received their rights and privileges at the hands of their ecclesiastical protectors. Numerous instances of such towns might be pointed out, such as St Alban's, Bury, Beverley, &c. It was more common for the early Saxon and Frankish monarchs to give towns to bishops and abbots than to any other class of persons, or, at least, gifts to ecclesiastical dignitaries were always of a more permanent character. Hence it arises that, at a later period of mediæval history, we find so many corporate towns whose charters are derived from ecclesiastical, and not from lay, lords. On the continent, one or two towns became, in this manner, ecclesiastical principalities.

We trace in these ecclesiastical towns of the Anglo-Saxon period the existence of a municipal government, and the same jealousy of their privileges, as in the more perfect models derived from Roman times. When the Danish king Swegen, then at Gainsborough, ignorant or careless of local privileges, demanded a tax of the people of Bedricsworth, or Bury St Edmunds, the latter pleaded their exemption from royal taxes, and refused to pay. The monks of St Edmund's of course took their part, because to them the regular taxes of the town had been given. Swegen was furious, and threatened with his vengeance both the monks and the townsmen: but the ecclesiastics have recorded, exultingly, that that same night the hand of death was laid upon the proud and scornful Dane, and that the country was thus delivered from one ferocious enemy.*

In the foregoing remarks, my object has been to bring together a few historical incidents which, in the entire absence of more explicit documents, seem to show clearly that the municipal government and privileges of corporate towns, derived from Roman civilisation, had existed in this country, as on the continent, uninterruptedly from Roman times. In these incidents we trace here and there the preservation of Roman forms and Roman principles, and we trace still more distinctly almost

* An interesting account of this affair is given among the miracles of St Edmund, MS. Cotton. Tiber. B. II. fol. 25 and 26. See also W. Malmsb. de Gest. Reg. p. 71.

every municipal right and municipal power which were at a later period guaranteed by royal or other charter, and which, by comparison with the privileges and government of corporate towns in France and Italy, and elsewhere on the continent, we know to have been derived from the political constitution of the Romans. From these circumstances we are justified in concluding that our municipal corporations were not the creations of the royal will in Norman times, but that they had existed in a perfect form throughout the Saxon period. By these considerations, also, we are enabled to understand better the entries relating to the towns in Domesday Book. We find there that in many of these towns the king received *his* rates by his receiver (the *præpositus regis*), from each particular person from whom they were due individually, and in each individual case. In such towns the numbers of burgesses paying rates are enumerated, both in the time of king Edward and in that of king William. The *præpositus regis*, or king's reeve, is frequently mentioned, as at Dover, Lewes, Guildford, &c. In other instances, and these are not few, we find that the municipality, to escape the too officious interference, and sometimes oppressive conduct, of a collecting officer who was not under their own jurisdiction, had compounded for the king's taxes, by the yearly payment of a certain sum of money. Such was the case with Dorchester, Bridport, Wareham, Shaftesbury, Hertford, and other places. It was a very necessary safeguard, especially for smaller towns, whose revenue the king might let out to farm to some one who paid a certain sum, and made as much of it as he could, and would probably practise every kind of extortion to enrich himself. This was experienced more severely in Norman times; and when the towns obtained charters, they invariably bought the farm of the king's dues for ever, which was called the fee-farm of the town.

The judicial entries on the fly-leaves of the Exeter manuscript, written before and after the Conquest, show us that the municipal forms and conditions of that city underwent no change upon the transfer of the English crown to a Norman line of sovereigns; and such was probably the case in all other cities and towns then in existence. But, although their privileges and constitution were in principle untouched, in practice they were frequently trespassed upon. A new race of feudal lords had entered upon the land, who were ignorant of the customs of the people over whom they had intruded themselves, and who had little respect for any customs which stood as obstacles in the gratification of their views of aggrandisement. This must have led to continual riots and disturbances in the old Saxon towns, and to infringements of their privileges where they had little power to obtain permanent redress. After undergoing all these vexations during a few years, they saw the advantages—or we may perhaps better say the necessity—of purchasing from the king written charters, confirming their old rights, which became an effective protection in a court of law. Thus originated municipal charters, which are rather to be considered as a proof of the antiquity, than of the novelty, of the privileges they grant. They were given most abundantly under Henry II. and his sons, when it became the policy of the English monarchs to seek the support of the independent burghers against a turbulent feudal aristocracy.

Perhaps we may be thought to have wandered a little from our immediate subject in the preceding remarks; but in the absence of all contemporary information on the state of the Roman towns in Britain after they had fallen under the subjection of the Saxons, it is only by these traces of their condition at a subsequent period that we can perceive how the Roman element of civilisation was preserved in them. They hold a very important place in the history of social development, inasmuch as, while the country itself underwent so many violent revolutions—while Britons, and Saxons, and Normans, alternately gained possession of the soil—the population of the towns continued to exist without any further alteration than that gradual infusion of foreign blood which must necessarily take place in the course of ages, and to which we owe that due mixture of Saxon and Roman that forms the basis of modern civilisation.

If we possessed the necessary information on the subject, we should no doubt find that the Anglo-Saxons had adopted many of the arts and amusements of society from the Romans. Although the large potteries and such establishments in the country, having been deserted by the workmen, were no doubt left in ruin, many of the manufactories, where they existed in the towns, continued probably in activity. We know nothing of the fate of public buildings in the towns, but we have a proof that the amphitheatres continued in use, in the circumstance that long afterwards we find them the scene of performances of bears and of bull-baiting. I have stated before that the Anglo-Saxons adopted the Roman roads and bridges in every part of the island. To the former they gave the name of *streets* (*stræt*), a word no doubt derived from the Latin word *strata*, by which probably they heard them designated among the Roman population. We may still trace their course, by the continued recurrence of names of places in which the Saxon word, under such forms as *stret, strat, streat*, occurs in composition, as Stretton, Stratford, Streatham, &c. A glance at the map will show that the great Roman military roads resolved themselves into a few grand lines which traversed the island in different directions. Of these there were four principal lines, of which perhaps the most important was that which ran from Richborough or Dover, through Canterbury and London, across the island to Chester. The Saxons, who planted their own local traditions wherever they settled, connected this wonderful work with one of their own mythic traditions, and called it Wætlinga-stræt, the road of the Wætlings, or sons of Wætla,* and it was celebrated down to recent times as the Watling-street, a name still retained by the portion of it which ran through London. To the road which ran direct from Pevensey and Regnum through London, and by Lincoln and the great Yorkshire towns to the south-east of Scotland, they gave the name of Eormen-stræt, the street of Eormen, who was one of the chief Anglo-Saxon divinities, and whose name was often compounded in those of persons and things which were regarded as great or wonderful. The name at a later period was corrupted to Ermyn-street. Two other great roads which crossed the island, one from the coast of Norfolk, by Cambridge, Old Sarum, and Exeter, to the extremity of Cornwall; the other, from the mouth of the Tyne to Gloucester, and thence to St. David's; were named the Iknield-street and the Ryknield-street, but the origin of these names is very doubtful. Other roads of less importance received also their distinctive appellations. Two, originating at the great saltworks at Droitwich,

---

* The milky way was also popularly called Watling-street, and it is mentioned under this name in Chaucer's house of Fame:

   Lo there, quod he, cast up thine eye,
   So yondir, lo, the galaxie,
   The wiche men clepe the milky way,
   For it is white; and some, *par fay*,
   Y-callin it han Watlinge-strete.

Florence of Worcester, in his chronicle, under the year 1013, mentioning the British Watling-street, says, ' Omnia populis qui habitabant in septentrionali plaga Weatlingastreatæ, id est strata quam filii Weatlæ regis ab orientali mare usque ad occidentale per Angliam straverunt.' King Weatla was no doubt a personage of the Anglo-Saxon mythology.

and proceeding, one eastwardly to the coast of Lincolnshire, the other southwardly to the Hampshire coast, have been designated as the Salt-ways; and another leading from the east to Cirencester, was known as the Akeman-street, it is supposed because it was the way by which invalids travelled to Bath, one of the Saxon names of which was Akemannes-ceaster, or the city of invalids.

CHAPTER XVII.

Celtic Establishments—Strath-Cluyd, Cornwall, Wales—Early sepulchral inscriptions found in the two latter countries.

WHILE the Saxon tribes were penetrating into the island from the east and south, other races were establishing themselves on the western side, whose history is completely lost. We are assured by nearly contemporary writers that, when the Teutonic invaders began to harass Britain, the Picts and Scots, who were of course joined by the Irish, carried on their destructive inroads on the other side of Britain, which would be left in a comparatively defenceless state by the withdrawal of the legions from Deva (*Chester*) and Isca (*Caerleon*) some years before the Roman emperors relinquished the island. From this time history and tradition are equally silent, until, when we arrive again at the period when the annals of at least one part of the island become authentic, we find three distinct Celtic states in existence, that of the Strath-Cluyd Britons in the north, that of the Wealas, or Welsh, in the mountainous region to which they have given their name, and which was divided into several petty states, and that of the Cornwealas, who gave their name to Cornwall. It has been a doubted question as to whence the population of these districts came, whether they were the primitive Britons, who had arisen and taken possession of the land of their forefathers; whether they were Caledonians from the north, who, like the Saxons, at last settled down in the country which they had been accustomed to invade; or Irish from the neighbouring island; or perhaps even Armoricans, at a later period, from Gaul; but the latter appears to be the more correct explanation of the subject. We know too little of the language of the Britons before Cæsar's invasion to found any certain argument upon it; and all that we can say is, that these Celtic settlers seem to have been a barbarous people, who were much less than the Saxons capable of benefiting by the Roman civilisation with which they came in contact. We find no antiquities of this period among the Welsh, as we do among the Anglo-Saxons, and in Wales at least the Roman towns seem to have been mostly destroyed.

We can hardly doubt that it was the Caledonian Picts who, while the Angles were establishing themselves in Bernicia and Deira, got possession of the district extending on the western side of the island from Lancashire, of which they formed a kingdom, called by the Scots the kingdom of Strathcluyd, because its northern limits lay upon the Clyde. They have been called by historians Cumbrian Britons. The Cumbrian Celts preserved, we know, two Roman towns, Luguballium in the neighbourhood of the wall of Hadrian, and a strong town on the waters of the Clyde, which had been called, under the Romans, Tamea and Theodosia. The latter became the metropolis of the chieftains of the Cumbrians, and they named it, from its situation, Al-cluyd; the Irish Scots, their neighbours, called it Dun-Breton, the fortress of the Britons, a name still preserved in that of Dumbarton, by which it is known at the present day. Their southern town, Luguballium, retained its old name, corrupted, with the addition of *caer*, which, like the Saxon *ceaster*, is a mere corruption of the Roman *castrum*, and was called Caer-luel, or Caer-leol, now Carlisle. The legendary Scottish annalists give us names of the kings of Strathcluyd, and speak of their exploits; some of them pretend that Carausius granted Cumberland and Westmoreland to a Scottish king named Crathlynt, in consideration of important services which he had rendered to that usurper, and they add that Crathlynt's son was confirmed in possession. These, however, are no doubt mere fables; and all that we know with certainty is, that the Cumbrian Britons were at an early period engaged in war with the Angles, and that the southern part of the kingdom of Alcluyd, with the city of Carlisle, fell eventually under the power of the Northumbrian kings. Carlisle is celebrated in British legend as the favourite residence of king Arthur.

To judge by the tenor of these legends, the Cumbrians appear to have preserved more of Roman culture than the Welsh or Cornish. The latter seems to have had a close connection with the Irish and with the Celts of Armorica, and we can hardly help believing that invaders from the one country, and settlers from the other, helped to swell its population.

They were dependent on the important Roman town of Isca, which the Saxons called Exan-ceaster, the city on the river Exe. The Corn-wealas preserved their independence until the time of king Ethelstan.

Wales was divided under several petty chiefs, of whom those who inhabited the southern district, where the principal Roman towns stood, seem to have been the least barbarous. Here they are believed to have taken possession of the important Roman town of Maridunum, and to have preserved the memory of its ancient name in that of Caer-Marddyn, or Caermarthen, which during the middle ages was the most important town in Wales. Most of the names of Roman towns in Wales were preserved in the same manner, as in Caer-Seiont (*Segontium*), Caer-Went (*Venta*), Neath (*Nidum*), &c.; and this might certainly make us incline to believe that the Welsh race was an indigenous one, and that it consisted, at least in part, of a population which had been left there by the Romans. In memory of the second legion, which had been so long established at the Silurian Isca, they gave to the ruins of that city the name of Caer-Legion, the city of the legion, now softened to Caerleon. They gave the same name of Caer-Legion to Deva, or Chester, the head-quarters of the twentieth legion.

It is a remarkable circumstance connected with these Celtic kingdoms, that when we first become acquainted with them—about the time of St Augustine—we find that Christianity was established among them. We have no evidence, indeed, that the Cumbrian Britons were Christians, and we may perhaps presume the contrary; but there can be no doubt that the Welsh and the people of Cornwall professed the Gospel, and the former had a large establishment of monks at a place called by the Saxons Bancorna-byrig, which probably occupied the old Roman station of Bovium, which may have been called at the close of the Roman period Banchorium (a name found only in the Itinerary of Richard of Cirencester), and is supposed to be the place now called Bangor Iscoed, in the Welsh county of Flint. The origin of Christianity in Cornwall and Wales is a very obscure question, and one which it is not a part of our plan to discuss. It has been already intimated that we find no traces of Christianity among the innumerable Roman remains found in this country; and the Christian faith of the Britons seems to have been closely allied with that of Ireland. To this connection the later legends of the Welsh and Cornish saints seem distinctly to refer; and we might be induced by these legends and other circumstances to suspect that their first missionaries came from Spain or Armorica, after the period when the island was relinquished by Rome.

There is one class of antiquities found in Wales and Cornwall, but more especially in the latter county, which appears to belong to the period following immediately after that of the departure of the Roman legions. These are large, roughly-hewn stones, bearing sepulchral inscriptions, in letters nearly resembling those of the late Roman monuments. They are in Latin, but the names are apparently Celtic, and they give simply the name of the individual commemorated and his father. They differ from the Roman inscriptions in this, that usually the inscription runs the lengthway of the stone, instead of being read across. A number of examples will be found in the volumes of Lysons's Magna Britannia for Devonshire and Cornwall, and in Borlase's Antiquities of Cornwall. One of the earliest and best preserved stands in the parish of St Colomb Minor, in the latter county; it is five feet high, by twenty inches in width, and the inscription is particularly curious, as giving to the person it commemorates the Roman title of tribune:—

HONEMIMOR	Honemimorus
TRIBVN	the tribune.

Another of these stones, which is found at Lanyon, in the parish of Maddern, where it is popularly known as the *men skryfa*, or inscribed stone, has the inscription:—

RIALOBRAN	Rialobranus,
CVNOVAL FIL	son of Cunovalis

The inscription on a similar stone, at Tavistock in Devonshire, is:—

NEPRANI	Nepranius,
FILI CONDEVI	son of Condevus.

Lysons gives two others found in Devonshire, at Buckland Monachorum, and at Lastleigh. One, which had been used as the gate-post to the vicarage-house at St Clement's, near Truro, had the following inscription in one line, giving a Roman name combined with a Celtic or a Teutonic name:—

ISNIOC VITAL FILI TORRICI	Isniocus Vitalis, son of Torricus.

Sometimes the words *hic jacet* are added to the inscription. Thus the inscription on one of these monuments, standing in the road between Fowey and Castledor, and popularly called from its height (eight feet) the long stone, is:—

| CIRVSIVS HIC IACET | Cirusius lies here, |
| CVNOMORI FILIVS | the son of Cunomorus. |

At Worthyvale, not far from Camelford, in Cornwall, there is an inscribed stone, nine feet nine inches long, and two feet three inches wide, which had been formerly thrown across a small stream to serve as a bridge. The inscription is:—

| CATIN HIC IACIT | Catinus lies here, |
| FILIVS MAGARI | the son of Magarus. |

These inscriptions are usually assigned, and probably with reason, to the fifth and sixth centuries. Those found in Wales have generally a mixture of cursive letters with the capitals, and belong apparently to a later period, perhaps from the ninth to the eleventh centuries. One stone, however, which was discovered near the Roman road from Nidum (*Neath*) to the southern Bovium (*Ewenny*), is of a date as early as those found in Cornwall, and is expressed in the same form. The inscription, in one line, commemorates Cantusus, the father of Pavinus:—

HICI ACIT CANTVSVS PATER PAVINVS.

It was evidently written by one who spoke Latin corruptly; but its greatest singularity is the circumstance that the inscription is cut on the back of an older inscribed stone, dedicated to the emperor Maximinus; and although the pure Roman inscription is written in lines across the stone, the later inscription is written, like those found in Cornwall, lengthways. It remains to be stated that one or two of these stones have evidently had a cross at the top, so that there can be no doubt of the people to whom these belonged being Christians.

IX.

LISTS OF TOWNS.

...eral account of the
...entatives, as far a...
...been fixed conjec...
...n for doubt, while
...ertain, from error...
...want of a proper
...must have stood.
...ons, if we give
...with the distances

...hese is the great
...of Antoninus
...the year 320.
...tion relating to

...vallo ad port...
...ccclxxxi, si...
...lato Bulgio
...Castra Explo-
ratorum
...uvallo
...reda

BRITAIN
under the
ROMANS.

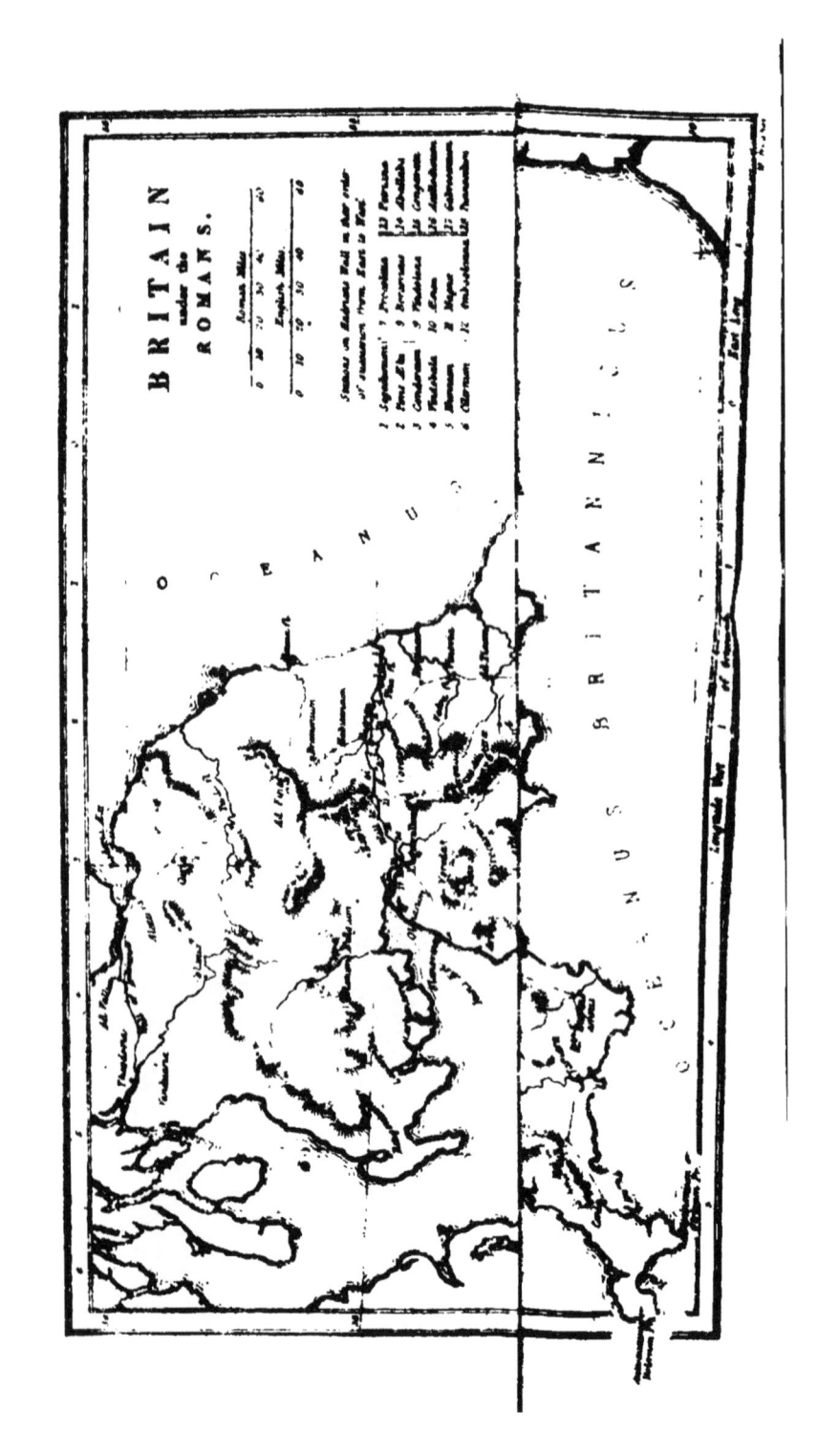

APPENDIX.

I.—THE ITINERARIES AND LISTS OF TOWNS.

In our fifth chapter we have given a general account of the Roman towns in Britain, with their modern representatives, as far as these have been ascertained, or where they have been fixed conjecturally. Many of them are identified without any room for doubt, while others (though comparatively few) remain still uncertain, from errors in the distances given in the Itineraries, or for the want of a proper investigation of the neighbourhoods in which they must have stood. It will be perhaps of use, to assist such investigations, if we give here the texts of the Itineraries relating to our island, with the distances as there given in Roman miles.

The first and most undoubtedly authentic of these is the great Itinerary of the Roman empire which goes under the name of Antoninus Augustus. It is supposed to have been composed about the year 320. The best edition is that of Wesseling, from which the portion relating to Britain is here taken.

A Gessoriaco de Galliis Ritupis in portu Britanniarum stadia numero cccl.

(1) A limite, id est a vallo, Prætorio usque . m. p. clvi.
A Bremenio Corstopitum . m. p. xx.
Vindomora . . m. p. ix.
Vinovia . . m. p. xix.
Cataractoni . . m. p. xxii.
Isurium . . m. p. xxiv.
Eburacum, leg. vi victrix . m. p. xvii.
Derventione . m. p. vii.
Delgovitia . . m. p. xiii.
Prætorio . . m. p. xxv.

(2) Iter a vallo ad portum Ritupis, m. p. cccclxxxi, sic :
A Blato Bulgio
Castra Exploratorum . m. p. xii.
Luguvallo . . m. p. xii.
Voreda . . m. p. xiv.
Brovonacis . . m. p. xiii.
Verteris . . m. p. xiii.
Lavatris . . m. p. xiv.
Cataractoni . . m. p. xiii.
Isurium . . m. p. xxiv.
Eburacum . m. p. xvii.
Calcaria . . m. p. ix.
Camboduno . . m. p. xx.
Mamucio . . m. p. xviii.
Condate . . m. p. xviii.

APPENDIX.

Deva leg. xx. vic-
trix . . . m. p. xx.
Bovio . . m. p. x.
Mediolano . . m. p. xx.
Rutunio . . m. p. xii.
Uroconio . . m. p. xi.
Uxacona . . m. p. xi.
Pennocrucio . m. p. xii.
Etoceto . . m. p. xii.
Manduessedo . m. p. xvi.
Venonis . . m. p. xii.
Bennavenna . m. p. xvii.
Lactodoro . . m. p. xii.
Magiovinto . m. p. xvii.
Durocobrivis . m. p. xii.
Verolamio . . m. p. xii.
Sulloniacis . . m. p. ix.
Londinio . . m. p. xii.
Noviomago . . m. p. x.
Vagniacis . . m. p. xviii.
Durobrivis . . m. p. ix.
Durolevo . . m. p. xiii.
Duroverno . . m. p. xii.
Ad portum Ri-
tupis . . m. p. xii.

Iter a Londinio ad portum
Dubris, m. p. lxvi, sic:
Durobrivis . . m. p. xxvii.
Duroverno . m. p. xxv.
Ad portum Du-
bris . . m. p. xiv.

Iter a Londinio ad portum
Lemanis, m. p. lxviii, sic:
Durobrivis . . m. p. xxvii.
Duroverno . m. p. xxv.
Ad portum Le-
manis . . m. p. xvi.

Iter a Londinio Luguvallio ad
vallum, m. p. ccccxliii, sic:
Cæsaromago . m. p. xxviii.
Colonia . . m. p. xxiv.
Villa Faustini . m. p. xxxv.
Icianos . . m. p. xviii.
Camborico . . m. p. xxxv.
Duroliponte . . m. p. xxv.
Durobrivas . . m. p. xxxv.
Causennis . . m. p. xxx.
Lindo . . m. p. xxvi.
Segeloci . . m. p. xiv.
Dano . . m. p. xxi.
Legeolio . . m. p. xvi.
Eburaco . . m. p. xxi.
Isubrigantum . m. p. xvii.
Cataractoni . . m. p. xxiv.

Lavatris . . m. p. xviii.
Verteris . . m p. xiii.
Brocavo . . m. p. xx.
Luguvallio . . m. p. xxii.

(6) Iter a Londinio Lindo, m. p.
clvi, sic:
Verolamio . m. p. xxi.
Durocobrivis . m. p. xii.
Magiovinio . m. p. xii.
Lactodoro . . m. p. xvi.
Isannavatia . m. p. xii.
Tripontio . . m. p. xii.
Vennonis . . m. p. ix.
Ratis . . m. p. xii.
Verometo . . m. p. xiii.
Margiduno . m. p. xiii.
Ad Pontem . . m. p. vii.
Crococalano . m. p. vii.
Lindo . . m. p. xii.

(7) Iter a Regno Londinio, m. p.
xcvi, sic:
Clausentum . m. p. xx.
Venta Belgarum m. p. x.
Calleva Attreba-
tum . . m. p. xxii.
Pontibus . . m. p. xxii.
Londinio . . m. p. xxii.

(8) Iter ab Eburaco Londinium,
m. p. ccxxvii, sic:
Lagecio . . m. p. xxi.
Dano . . m. p. xvi.
Ageloco . . m. p. xxi.
Lindo . . m. p. xiv.
Crococalane . m. p. xiv.
Margiduno . m. p. xiv
Vernemeto . . m. p. xii.
Ratis . . m. p. xii.
Vennonis . . m. p. xii.
Bannavante . m. p. xviii.
Magiovinio . m. p. xxviii.
Durocobrivis . m. p. xii.
Verolamio . m. p. xii.
Londinio . . m. p. xxi.

(9) Iter a Venta Icenorum Lon-
dinio, m. p. cxxviii, sic:
Sitomago . . m. p. xxxii.
Combretonio . m. p. xxii.
Ad Ansam . . m. p. xv.
Camuloduno . m. p. vi.
Canonio . . m. p. ix.
Cæsaromago . m. p. xii.
Durolito . . m. p. xvi.
Londinio . . m. p. xv.

(10) Iter a Glanoventa Mediolano, m. p. cl, sic :
Galava . . m. p. xviii.
Alone . . . m. p. xii.
Galacum . . m. p. xix.
Bremetonaci . m. p. xxvii.
Coccio . . m. p. xx.
Mancunio . . m. p. xvii.
Condate . . m. p. xviii.
Mediolano . . m. p. xviii.

(11) Iter a Segontio Devam, m. p. lxxiv, sic :
Conovio . . m. p. xxiv.
Varis . . . m. p. xix.
Deva . . m. p. xxxii.

(12) Iter per Muridunum Viroconium, m. p. clxxxvi, sic :
Vindomi . . m. p. xv.
Venta Belgarum m. p. xxi.
Brige . . m. p. xi.
Sorbioduni . . m. p. ix.
Vindogladia . m. p. xii.
Durnovaria . m. p. viii.
Muriduno . . m. p. xxxvi.
Isca Dumnuniorum . . m. p. xv.
Leucaro . . m. p. xv.
Nido . . m. p. xv.
Bomio . . . m. p. xv.
Iscæ, leg. ii. Augusta . . m. p. xxvii.
Burrio . . . m. p. ix.
Gobannio . . m. p. xii.
Magnis . . m. p. xxii.

Bravinio . . m. p. xxiv.
Viroconio . . m. p. xxvii.

(13) Iter ab Isca Calleva, m. p. cix, sic :
Burrio . . m. p. ix.
Blestio . . m. p. xi.
Ariconio . . m. p. xi.
Glevo . . . m. p. xv.
Durocornovio . m. p. xiv.
Spinis . . m. p. xv.
Calleva . . m. p. xv.

(14) Item alio itinere ab Isca Calleva, m. p. ciii, sic :
Venta Silurum . m. p. ix.
Abone . . m. p. ix.
Trajectus . . m. p. ix.
Aquis Solis . m. p. vi.
Verlucione . . m. p. xv.
Cunetione . m. p. xx.
Spinis . . . m. p. xv.
Calleva . . m. p. xv.

(15) Iter a Calleva Isca Dumnuniorum, m. p. cxxxvi, sic :
Vindomi . . m. p. xv.
Venta Belgarum m. p. xxi.
Brige . . m. p. xi.
Sorbioduni . . m. p. viii.
Vindogladia . m. p. xii.
Durnovaria . . m. p. viii.
Muriduno . m. p. xxxvi
Isca Dumnuniorum . . m. p. xv.

The description of Britain attributed to Richard of Cirencester has been the subject of much discussion, and appears to be made up of very discordant materials. How much was really the work of a monk of Westminster, and how much we owe to the modern editor, Bertram of Copenhagen, it is not easy to say, for the manuscript has very strangely disappeared. It is supposed, however, that the old monk may have had before him a Roman Itinerary similar to that of Antoninus, or perhaps a map, from which he extracted the part relating to Britain, which is inserted in his book under the title of Diaphragmata. I confess that the more I read this book, the more I am inclined to believe that the whole is a mere fabrication. The following is the text of Richard's Diaphragmata, which is in some parts imperfect, as stated, from the damaged state of the manuscript :—

Iter I. Rhuturis prima in Britannia insula civitas versus Galliam, apud Cantios sita, a Gessoriaco Bonnoniæ portu, unde commodissimus in supradictam insulam transitus obtingit, cccl. stadia, velut alii volunt xlvi. mille pas-

APPENDIX.

suum remota. Ab eadem civitate ducta est via Guethelinga dicta, usque in Segontium, per m. p. cccxxiiii. plus minus, sic:
Cantiopoli, quæ et
  Duroverno . . m. p. x.
  Durosevo . . . xii.
  Duroprovis . . xxv.
deinde m. p. xxvii. transit Thamesin, intrasque provinciam Flaviam et civitatem Londinium (Augustam),
  Sulomago . . m. p. ix.
  Verolamio municipio . . . xii.
Unde fuit Amphibalus et Albanus martyres.
  Foro Dianæ . . xii.
  Magiovinio . . xii.
  Lactorodo . . xii.
  Isantavaria . . xii.
  Tripontio . . xii.
  Benonis . . . ix.
Hic bisecatur via, alterutrumque ejus brachium Lindum usque, alterum versus Viriconium protenditur, sic:
  Manduessuedo . m. p. ix.
  Etoceto . . xiii.
  Pennocrucio . . xii.
  Uxaconia . . xii.
  Virioconio . . xi.
  Banchorio . . xxvi.
  Deva colonia . x.
Fines Flaviæ et Secundæ.
  Varis . . . m. p. xxx.
  Conovio . . xx.
  Seguntio . . xxiv.

Iter II. A Seguntio Virioconium usque m. p. lxxiii, sic:
  Heriri monte . m. p. xxv.
  Mediolano . . xxv.
  Rutunio . . xii.
  Virioconio . . xi.

Iter III. A Londinio Lindum coloniam usque, sic:
  Durosito . . m. p. xii.
  Cæsaromago . . xvi.
  Canonio . . xv.
  Camaloduno colonia . ix.
Ibi erat templum Claudii, arx triumphalis, et imago Victoriæ deæ.

Ad Sturium amnem . . . m. p. vi.
et finibus Trinobantum Cenimannos advenis.
  Cambretonis . m. p. xv.
  Sitomago . . xxii.
  Venta Cenom. . xxiii.
  Camborico . . xxii.
  Duraliponte . . xx.
  Durnomago . . xx.
  Isinnis . . . xx.
  Lindo . . . xx.

Iter IV. A Lindo ad vallum usque, sic:
  Argolico . . m. p. xiv.
  Dano . . . xx.
Ibi intras Maximam Cæsariensem.
  Legotio . . m. p. xvi.
  Eboraco municip. olim colonia sexta . . m. p. xxi.
  Isurio . . . xvi.
  Cattaractoni . . xxiv.
  Ad Tisam . . x.
  Vinovio . . . xii.
  Epiaco . . . xix.
  Ad Murum . . ix.
Trans Murum intras Valentiam.
  Alauna amne . m. p. xxv.
  Tueda flumine . xxx.
  Ad vallum . .

Iter V. A limite Præturiam usque, sic:
  Curia . . . m. p. . . .
  Ad Fines . . m. p. . . .
  Bremenio . . m. p. . . .
  Corstoplio . . xx.
  Vindomora . . ix.
  Vindovio . . xii.
  Cattaractoni . . . . . .
  Eboraco . . . x. .
  Derventione . . v. .
  Delgovicia . . xiii.
  Præturio . . . . . .

Iter VI. Ab Eboraco Devam usque, sic:
  Calcaria . . m. p. ix.
  Camboduno . . xxii.
  Mancunio . . xviii.
Finibus Maximæ et Flaviæ . . . xviii.
  Condate . . . xviii.
  Deva . . . xviii.

ITINERARY OF RICHARD.

Iter VII. A portu Sistuntiorum Eboracum usque, sic:
Rerigonio . . m. p. xxiii.
Ad Alpes Peninos viii.
Alicana . . . x.
Isurio . . . xviii.
Eboraco . . . xvi.

Iter VIII. Ab Eboraco Luguvalium usque, sic:
Cattaractoni . m. p. xl.
Lataris . . xvi.
Vataris . . xvi.
Brocavonacis . . xviii.
Vorreda . . xviii.
Lugubalia . . xviii.

Iter IX. A Luguballio Ptorotorum usque, sic:
Trimontio . . m. p. ...
Gadanica . . m. p. ...
Corio . . m. p. ...
Ad Vallum . . m. p. ...
Incipit Vespasiana.
Alauna . . m. p. xii.
Lindo . . . ix.
Victoria . . ix.
Ad Hiernam . . ix.
Orrea . . . xiv.
Ad Tavum . . xix.
Ad Æsicam . . xxiii.
Ad Tinam . . viii.
Devana . . xxiii.
Ad Itunam . . xxiv.
Ad montem Grampium . . m. p. ...
Ad Selinam . m. p. ...
Tuessis . . xviii.
Ptorotone . . m. p. ...

Iter X. Ab ultima Ptorotone per medium insulæ Iscam Damnonorum usque, sic:
Varis . . m. p. viii.
Ad Tuessim . . xviii.
Tamea . . . xxix.
. . . . . . m. p. xxi.
In Medio . . ix.
Orrea . . . ix.
Victoria . . xviii.
Ad Vallum . . xxxii.
Luguballia . . lxxx.
Brocavonacis . . xxii.
Ad Alaunam . m. p. ...
Coccio . . m. p. ...
Mancunio . . xviii.

Condate . . xxiii.
Mediolano . . xviii.
Etoceto . . m. p. ...
. . . .
Salinis . . m. p. ...
. . . .
Glebon colonia . m. p. ...
Corino . . . xiv.
Aquas Solis . . m. p. ...
Ad Aquas . . xviii.
Ad Uxellam amnem . . m. p. ...
Isca . . m. p. ...

Iter XI. Ab Aquis per viam Juliam Menapiam usque, sic:
Ad Abonam . m. p. vi.
Ad Sabrinam . . vi.
Unde trajectu intras in Brittaniam Secundam et stationem Trajectum m. p. iii.
Venta Silurum . viii.
Isca colonia . . ix.
Unde fuit Aaron martyr
Tibia amne . . m. p. viii.
Bovio . . . xx.
Nido . . . xv.
Leucaro . . xv.
Ad Vigesimum . xx.
Ad Menapiam . xix.
Ab hac urbe per xxx. m. p. navigas in Hyberniam.

Iter XII. Ab Aquis Londinium usque, sic:
Verlucione . . m. p. xv.
Cunetione . . xx.
Spinis . . . xv.
Calleba Attrebatum . . . xv.
Bibracte . . xx.
Londinio . . xx.

Iter XIII. Ab Isca Uriconium usque, sic:
Bultro . . m. p. viii.
Gobannio . . xii.
Magna . . . xxiii.
Branogenio . . xxiii.
Urioconio . . xxvii.

Iter XIV. Ab Isca per Glebon Lindum usque, sic:
Ballio . . m. p. viii.
Blestio . . . xii.
Sariconio . . xi.
Glebon colonia . xv.

536   APPENDIX.

Ad Antonam	m. p. xv.
Alauna	xv.

Vennonis	m. p. xii.
Ratiscorion	xii.
Venromento	xii.
Margiduno	xii.
Ad Pontem	xii.
Crococolana	
Lindum	xii.

Iter XV. A Londinio per Clausentum in Londinium, sic:

Caleba	m. p. xliv.
Vindomi	xv.
Venta Belgarum	xxi.
Ad Lapidem	vi.
Clausento	iv.
Portu Magno	x.
Regno	x.
Ad Decimum	x.
Anderida portu	m. p. ...

Ad Lemanum	m. p. xxv.
Lemaniano portu	x.
Dubris	x.
Rhutupis colonia	x.
Regulbio	x.
Contiopoli	x.
Durolevo	xviii.
Mado	xii.
Vagnaca	xviii.
Noviomago	xviii.
Londinio	xv.

Iter XVI. A Londinio Ceniam usque, sic:

Venta Belgarum	m. p. xc.
Brige	xi.
Sorbioduno	viii.
Ventageladia	xii.
Durnovaria	ix.
Moriduno	xxxiii.
Isca Damnon	xv.

Durio amne	m. p. ...

Tamara	m. p. ...

Voluba	m. p. xxviii.
Cenia	m. p. ...

Iter XVII. Ab Anderida [Eboracum] usque, sic:

Sylva Anderida	m. p. ...
Noviomago	m. p. ...
Londinio	m. p. xv.
Ad Fines	m. p. ...
Durolisponte	m. p. ...
Durnomago	m. p. xxx.
Corisennis	xxx.
Lindo	xxx.
In Medio	xv.
Ad Abum	xv.

Unde transis in Maximam.

Ad Petuariam	m. p. vi.
Deinde Eboraco, ut supra	m. p. xlvi

Iter XVIII. Ab Eboraco per medium insulæ Clausentum usque, sic:

Legiolio	m. p. xxi.
Ad Fines	xviii.
	m. p. xvi.
	m. p. xvi.

Derventione	m. p. xvi.
Ad Trivonam	xii.
Etoceto	xii.
Manduessuedo	xvi.
Benonnis	xii.
Tripontio	xi.
Isannavaria	xii.
Brinavis	vii.
Ælia castra	xvi.
Dorocina	xv.
Tamesi	vi.
Vindomi	xv.
Clausento	xlvi.

Plurima insuper habebant Romani in Britanniis castella, suis quæque muris, turribus, portis, et repagulis munita.

The work known by the title of the Cosmography of the anonymous writer of Ravenna, is a treatise on geographical science compiled in that city, apparently in the seventh century. Its writer had evidently before him large maps of the provinces of the Roman empire, from which he derived his lists of towns and rivers, but as he took them without any apparent system, paying no attention to the roads of the Itineraries, and as his names are written very corruptly, we can only identify them by similarity of sound. Two manuscripts, one in the Vatican, the other in the National Library in Paris, furnish various readings, which sometimes give assistance in explaining the printed text. I here give the part relating to Britain, placing opposite such of the names as can be made out, the parallel names from the two preceding Itineraries, or the conjectures of Horsley as to the present sites. Such of the various readings as seem important are given at the foot of the page.

In Britannia plurimas fuisse legimus civitates et castra, ex quibus aliquantas designare volumus, id est,—
  Giano
  Eltabo
  Elconio
  Nemetotacio
  Tamaris . . . (*Tamerton*)
  Durocoronavis
  Pilais
  Vernalis
  Ardua
  Ravenatone
  Devionisso
  Statio Deventia
  Stene
  Duriarno . . (Durnovaria)
  Uxelis . . (*Lostwithiel*)
  Vertevia
  Melamoni
  Scadum Namorum (Isca Dumnoniorum)
  Termonin
  Mostevia
  Milidunum
  Apaunaris
  Masona
  [1] Alongium
Item juxta suprascriptam civitatem Scadumorum est civitas quæ dicitur
  Moriduno . (Maridunum)
  Alauna silva
  Omire
  Tedertis
  [2] Londinis
  Canca
  Dolocindo
  Clavinio

Morionio
Bolvelaunio
Alauna
Coloneas
Aranus
Anicetis
[3] Moiezo
Ibernio
Bindogladia . (Vindogladia)
Noviomagno
Onna
Venta Velgarum (Venta Belgarum)
Armis
Ardaoneon . (Sorbiodunum ?)
[4] Ravimago . . (Noviomagus)
Regentium
Leucomago . (Leucarum ?)
Cunetzone . . (Cunetio)
Punctuobice . (*Cowbridge*)
Venta Silurum
Jupania
Metambala
Albinunno
Isca Augusta . (Isca Silurum)
Bannio . . . (Gobannium)
Brenna . . (*Brenbridge*)
Alabum
Cicutio
Magnis . . . . (Magna)
Branogenium . (Bravinium)
Epocessa
Ypocessa
Macatonion . . (Ariconium)
Glebon colonia . . (Glevum)
Argistillum . . (*Arwystli*)
Vertis
Salinis . . . (Salinæ)
Corinium Dobunorum
Caleba Atrebatium . (Calleva)

---

[1] Alovergium, *Vat.*   [2] Laudinis, Pr. Lindinus, *Vat.*   [3] Melezo, *Vat.*
  [4] Noviomago Regentium, i. e. Noviomagus of the Regni.

APPENDIX.

[1] Anderesio . . (Anderida ?)
Miba . . . (*Midhurst*)
[2] Mutuantonis
Lemanis . (Portus Lemanis)
Dubris . . . (Dubræ)
Duroverno Cantiacorum (Durovernum)
Rutupis . . . (Rutupiæ)
Durobrabis . (Durobrivæ)
Londini . . . (Londinium)
Tamese . . . (Tamesis)
Brinavis . . . (Brinavæ)
Alauna
Uriconium Cornovinorum
Lavobrinta
Mediomano . (Mediolanum)
Seguntio . . (Segontium)
[3] Canubio . . . (*Conway*)
Mediolano . . (*Meivod*)
Sandonio
Deva victrix
Veratino
Lutudarum
Derbentione . . (Derventio)
Salinis . . (*Nantwich*)
Condate
[4] Ratocorion . . . (Ratæ)
Eltanori
Lectoceto . . (*Litchfield*)
[5] Iacio
Dulma . . (*Dunstable*)
Virolanium . (Verulamium)
Londinium Augusta
Cæsaromagum
Camulodulo colonia (Camulodunum)
Durcinate
Duroviguto
Durobrisin . . (Durobrivæ)
Venta Cenomum (Venta Icenorum)
Lindum colonia
Banovallum . . (*Benwell*)
Navione
Aquis . . (*Aidon Castle*)
Arnemez
Zerdotalia
Mantio
Alunna . (*Allenton*, or *Whetley*)
Camulodono . (*Almonbury*)
Calunio . . . (*Coln*)
Gallunio . . (*Whaley*)

Modibogdo
Cantiumeti
Juliocenon
Gabrocentio (*Gabrosentæ*)
Alauna
Bribra
Maio
Olerica
Derventione . . (Derventio)
Ravonia . . (*Ravenglasse*)
Bresnetenati Veteranorum (*Overborough*)
Pampocalia
Lagentium
Valteris . . . (Verteræ)
Bereda . . . . (Voreda)
Lugubalum . (Luguballium)
Magnis . . . (Magna)
Babaglanda . (Amboglanna)
Vindolande
Lineojugla
Vinovia . . . (Vinovium)
Lavaris . . . (Lavatræ)
Cataractonion . (Cataracto)
Eburacum
Decuaria . . (Petuaria)
Devovicia . . (Delgovitia)
Dixio
Lugundino
Coganges . (*Cayngham*)
Corie . . . . (Corium)
Lopocarium
Iterum sunt civitates ipsa in Britannia, quæ recto tramite de una parte in alia, id est de oceano in oceano, et Sistuntiaci dividunt in tertia portione ipsam Britanniam; id est,—
Serduno . . (Segedunum)
Conderco . . (Condercum)
Vindovala . . (Vindobala)
Onno . . . (Hunnum)
Celunno . . . (Cilurnum)
Procoliti . . (Procolitia)
Volurtion . . (Borcovicus ?)
Aesica . . . . (Æsica)
Banna . . . (Banna)
Uxeludiano . (Axelodunum)
Avalaria . . (Aballaba)
Maia
[6] Fanocedi

---

[1] Andereliomiba, *Vat.* [2] Mantuantonis, *Vat.* [3] Conovio.
[4] Ratæ Coritanorum. [5] Statio Dulma, *Vat.* [6] Fanococidi, *Vat.*

THE RAVENNA LIST.

Brocara . . (Brocavonacæ)
Croucingo . . (*Crosby*)
Stodoion
Sinetriadum
Clidum . . . (*Glasgow*)
Carbantium . (Carbantorigum)
Tadoriton
Maporiton
Alitacenon . . . (*Elgin*)
Loxa . . . (*Inverlochy*)
Locatrene . (*Loch Catrine ?*)
Cambroiana
Smetri
Uxela
Lucotion . . (Lucopibia)
Corda . . (*on Lough Cure*)
Camulossesa
Præsidium . . (*Camulon*)
Brigomono . (Rerigonium)
Abisson
Ebio
Coritiotar (Curia Otadenorum ?)
[1] Celerion . (*Calendar Castle*)
Itucodon
Maremago
Duablisis . . . (*Duplin*)
Venutio . . (*Banatia*)
Trimuntium . (Trimontium)
Eburocassum
Bremenium
Cocuneda . . (*Coquet*)
Alauna . . (*Alnwick*)
Oleiclavis . (*Ogle Castle*)
Ejudensca
Rumabo . (*Drumburgh Castle*)
Iterum sunt civitates in ipsa Britannia retro (*al.* recto) tramite, una alteri connexa, ubi et ipsa Britannia plus angustissima de oceano in oceano esse dinoscitur, id est,—
Velunia
Volitanio
Pexa
Begesse
Colanica . . (Colania)
Medionemetom
Subdobiadon
Litana
Cibra
Credigone
Iterum est civitas quæ dicitur
[2] Iano
Maulion

Demerosesa . . (*Dumfries*)
Cindocellum
Cermo
Veromo
Matovion
Ugrulentum
Ranatonium
Iberran
[3] Præmatis
Tuessis . . . (*Berwick*)
Ledone . . . (*Dunbar*)
Litinomago . . (*Linlithgow*)
Devoni
Memanturum
Decha
Bograndium
Ugueato
Leviodanum . (*Livingston*)
Poreo Classis (*Forfar, or Barry*)
Levioxana . . (*Lennox*)
Cernium
Victoriæ
Marcotaxon
Tagea . . . (*Menteith*)
Voran . . .(*Caer Voram*)
Sunt autem in ipsa Britannia diversa loca, ex quibus aliquanta nominari velumus, id est,—
Maponi
Mixa
Panovius
Minox
Taba . . . . (*Tava*)
Manavi
Segloes
Daunoni
Currunt autem per ipsam Britanniam plurima flumina, ex quibus aliquanta nominare volumus, id est,—
Fraxula . . (*Ashbourne*)
Axium . . . (*Axe*)
Maina . . . (*Mintern*)
Sarva . . . (*Severne*)
Tamaris . . . (*Tamar*)
Naurum . *Nader*, Wilts)
Abona . . . (*Avon*)
Isca . . . (*Ex*)
Tamion . . (*Tavy*)
Aventio . . (*Aun*)
Leuca . . . (*Low*)
Juctius
Leugosena

---

[1] Celorion, *Vat.* [2] Lano, *Vat.* [3] Pinnatis, *Vat.*

APPENDIX.

Coantia	*(Keutzey)*	Vividin	*(Fowey)*
Dorvatium	*(Dart, or Darent)*	Durolani	*(Lenham river)*
Anava		Alauna	
Bdora		Coguvensuron	*(Soar)*
Novitia		Durbis	*(Dour, or Dover)*
Adron		Lemana	*(Lymne river)*
Certismassa		[1] Rovia	*(Rother)*
Intraum		Ractomessa	*(Racon)*
Tinea	*(Teing)*	Senua	
Liar	*(Livor)*	[2] Cimia	
Lenda		Velox	

---

[1] Rovia, *Vet.*   [2] Cania velox, *Vet.*

APPENDIX II.

ROMAN POTTERS' MARKS.

It will be useful to local antiquaries to furnish them with a list of the names of potters stamped on the red Samian ware, as mentioned at p. 275. This list is naturally incomplete, for new names are turning up daily, but it will enable those who are occupied in researches on Roman sites to judge if the names they meet with are new, or of common occurrence, and it will assist the general reader in forming a notion of the extent of the Roman power. It will be observed in this numerous list of names, that many are not Roman, and some are apparently Teutonic. The explanation of the different formulæ of the potters will be found in our text at the page just referred to. It will be seen in the list that most of the potters used the different formulæ indiscriminately.

Before these potters' marks were collected and explained, writers who had met with single instances, fell into the most ridiculous mistakes in attempting to interpret them. Dr Leigh, who published in 1699 a 'Natural History of Lancashire, Cheshire, and the Peak, with an account of the Antiquities in those parts,' obtained at Ribchester, where the Samian ware is found in great abundance, a fragment with the stamp FAB. PRO (*fabrica Probi*), which he conjectured must have been made when one of the Fabii was proconsul or procurator! A still more curious blunder was made in the county of Essex. By the road side, at Coggeshall, in that county, a sepulchral interment was found, in which, among other objects, was a vessel of Samian ware with the stamp COCCILLI. M, which will also be found in the following list. It was immediately interpreted as an abbreviation of *Coccilli manibus*, to the manes of Coccillus, and it was resolved that, from this personage, who was supposed to have been the lord of the spot, and to have been buried there, the place derived its name of Coggeshall! Such errors show us how necessary it is for the antiquary to begin by studying his science elementarily.

At the end of the list of potters' marks, I have given very imperfect lists of names stamped on mortaria and amphoræ found in this island, which have hitherto been less carefully noted than those on the Samian ware. It will be observed that the formulæ and the names are different.

The frequent use of the п, for B, will be observed in these potters' marks. See the observations on this subject at p. 233.

APPENDIX.

POTTERS' MARKS ON THE RED WARE, TERMED SAMIAN.

A.

OF. A. AN
ABALANIS
OF. ABALI
OF. ABARI
OF. ARIN
ABIANI
ABILI. M
ACCILINVS. F
OF. ACIRAP
A. C. E. R. O
ACO. M
ACRIS. O
ACVRIO. F
ACVTVS
ADIECTI. M
ADIVTORI
L. ADN. ADGENI
ADVOCISI
ADVOCISI. OF
ADVVCISI. O
AEL. XANT
AELIANI. M
AEQVIR. F
AEQVR. F
AESFIVINA
AIISFIVI. M (?)
AIISTIVI. M
AISTIVI. M
AESTIVI. M
M. INHITRA
M. AIAVCNI
AETERNI. M
AGEDILLI
AGEEDILLVS. F
AGIILITO
OFF. AGER
OF. ALBAN
OF. ALBANI
ALBANI. M
ALBILLI. M
OF. ALBIN
ALBIN. F
ALBINVS
ALBINI. MA
ALBVCI
ALBVCIANI
ALBVS
ALBVS. FE
ALBVSA
ALIVS. F.
AMABIVS
AMANDO
AMARILIS. F (? *Amabilis*)
AMATICI. OF
AMATOR
AMATORIS
AMIIEDV
AMICI. M
AMMIVS. F
AMONVS
ANDORN
ANISATVS
ANNLOS. F
ANVNI. M.
A. POL. AVSTI
APOLAVCIR
OF. APRILIS
OF. APRIS
OF. APRO
APRONIS
AQVIINVS
AQVIT
AGVIT
OF. AQVITA
OF. AQVITANI
ARACI. MA
ARDAC
ARGO. F
ARICI. M
ARICI. MA
ARRO
ASCILLI. M
ASIATICI. M
ASIATICI. OF
ATECII. M
ATEI
ATILIANI. M
ATILIANI. O
ATILIAN. OF
ATILIANVS. F
ATILLVS
ATTICI. M
ATTILLI. M
ATTILLII. M
ATTINVL
ATTIVS. FE
AVCELIA. F
AVENTI
AVENTINI. M
AVGVSTALIS
AVGVSTINVS
AVITI. M
AVITOS. OF
AVITVS
AVITVS. F
AVLIVS. F
OF. AVRAF
AVRICV. F
AVSTRI. M.
AVSTRI. OF
AVSTVS. F

B.

BALBINVS. F
BANOLVOCI
BASSI
OF. BASSI
OF. BASSICO
BELINIOCI
BELINIOCI. M
BELINICCVS. F
BELINOI. M
BELINICI
BELLIAIICI
BELSO. ARV. F
BELSO. ARVE. F
BENNIOCI. M.
BENNICI. M
BICAAICD
BIGA
BIGA. FEC
OFIC. BILICANI (?)
BILICAT
OFIC. BILICAT
BILLICI
BILLIC. OF
BIO. FECIT
BIR. ANIII
BIRANII
BIRBIIINI
BISENE . . .
BISSVN
BITVRIX
BL. AESI
BOINICCI. M
BOLDVS
BONOXVS. F
BORILL OF
BORILLI. M
BORILLI. OF
BORILLI. OFFIC
BORVSI. FE
BOVTI. M
BRACKILLO

POTTERS' MARKS. 543

BRICCI
BRICC. M
BRITARNII
BV. DO
BVCCIO
M. BVCIANI
BVRDO. F
BVRDONIS. OF
OF. BVRILINDI
BVTRIV.

C.

C. C. F
CABIAN
CABRVS
CACAS. M
CACASI. M
CACILANTRO
CADDIRON
CAI. M. S
CAIVS. F
CAIVS. OF
OF. CAI. IVI
OF. CAIVI
CAKIVFDO. FE
CALENVS. OF
CALENVS. F
CALETI. M
CALAVA
CALCIO. F
T. CALIXA
CALLI. M
CALMVA. F
CALVI. M
OF. CAL
OF. CALVI
CALVINI. M
CALVINVS
CAMBVS. F
CAMPANO
CAMTI. M
CANAI. M
CAN. PATR
C. ANPATR
CANETII. M
CANRVCATI
CAPAS
CAPELLIV. F
CAPIIRI. O
CAPRASIAS. FE
CAPRASIVS
CARANI
CARANI. F
OF. CARAN
CARANT

CARANTINI. M
CARATILLI
CARETI. M
CARBONIS. M
OF. CARI
CARINVS
CARINOS
CARITI
CARVS. F
CARO
O. CARO
CARVSSA
CASIVS. F
CASSIA. O
CASTVS
CASTVS. F
CASVRIVS. F
CATASEXTVS. ?
CATIANVS
CATVCI
CATVLII
CATVS. F
CAVPI ... FECI
OF. CL
OF. CEI
CELSIANI. F
L. C. CELSI. O
CELSINVS
CELTAS. FC
CENETLI. M
M. CENI
CENSORI
CENSORINI
OF. CEN
OF. CENSO
CENT. AI. E
OF. CERA
CEREA
CEREALIS
CERIALIS
CERIAL. M
CERESI. M
CERTVS. F
CETI
CHRESI. M
CIAMAT. F
CIMINI
CINIVS. M
CINNAMI
CINNVMI
CINTIRIO. M
CINTVAGENI
CINT. VGEN?
CIN. T. VSSA
CINTVSMI. M
CINTVSMIR
CINTVSMV

CINTVSMVS. F
CIRRI. M
CIRRVS. FEC
CIVPPI. M
CLEMENS
CLIVINTI. O
COBNERTI. M
COBNERTVS .
COCCIL. M
COCCILLI. M
OF. COCI
COCVRNV. F
COCVRO
COCVRO. F
OF. COE
OF. COELI
OF. COET
OF. COFI
COLLO. F
COLLON
COLON
COMITIALIS
COMPRIN. F
COMPRINNI. M
CONSERTI. M
CONGI. M
CONSTANS. F
CONSTAS. F
COSAXTIS. F
COSIA. F
COSI. R ...
COSIRV
COSIRVFIN
F. L. COS. V
COSMI. M
COSRV. F
COTTO. F
OF. COTTO
CRACIS. M
CRACI. S. M
CRACISA. F
CRACVNA. F
CRANI
CRAOSNA. F
CRASSIACVS. F
CRAVNA. F
CRECIRO. OFI
OF. CREM
OF. CRES
CRESCENI
CRESCENTI
OF. CRESI
CRESI. M
CRESIMI
M. CRESTI
M. CRESTI. O
OF. CRESTIO

544 APPENDIX.

CRIMVS. FE
CRISPINI. M
CROBISO M
CROBRO. F
CRVCVRO
CVCALI. M
CVCCIL
CVCCILLL. M
OF. CVEN
CVFF
CVI. M
OFI. CVIRIII
CVNI. IA. F
CVSPICI
CVTAI

D.

DACO. M
DACOIMNVS. F
DAGO
DOGODVBNVS. F
DAGOMARVS
DAGOMARVS. F
DAGOMARVS. FE
DAMIMI. M
DAMONVS
DAVICI. M
DECMI. M
DECVMINI. M
DECVMNI. M
DEM ... R. M
DESTER. F
DIGNVS
DIOGNATO
DIVICATI. M
DIVICATVS
DIVICI. M
DIVIX
DIVIX. F
DIVIXI
DIVIXTI
DIVIXTVL
DMCCIVE
DOCALI. M
DOCCIVS. F
DOIICCI
DOECA
DOLIC (?)
DOMETOS. F
DOMINAC
DOMINCI
DOMINICI
DOMITIANVS. F
DOMITVS
DONATVS

DONATVS. F
DONNA. M
DONNA. OF
DONNAV.
DONTIONI
DONV. M
DOVIICCVS
DOVIIICCVS
DRAVCVS. F
DRAVCI. M
DVPI ...
DVRINX

E.

ECVESER
ELVIL. I
OF. IIMAN
EPPA
EPPN
ERICI. M
EROR
E ∞ CVI ∞ I. M
ERRIMI
ESCVSI
ETVS. F
IIVST

F.

O. FABIN
OF. FAGE
FALENDI. O
FELIX. F
FELIXS. F
FELICIO. O
FELICIS. O
OF. FELIC
OF. FELICIF
FELICIONIS
O. FELMA
FESTVS. F
FESTVS. FO
FETI
FIR ...
O. FIRMONIF
FIVI. M
FLOI
FLORVS. I
FOVRI
FRONTINI
FRONTINVS
O. FRONTI
OF. PRONTI
O. FRONTINI

OF. FRONTINI
M. FVCA
OF. FVS
OFF. FVS

G.

GABRVS. F
GAIVS. F
GALRINVS. F
GENIALIS. FECI
GEMINI. M
GENITOR. F
G. E. N. I. T. O. R. F
GENIV.
GERMANI
GERMANI. F
GERMANI. OF
GERMANVS
OFF. GER
GERTAL. M
GLVPEI. M
GONDI. M
GRACCHVS
GRANANI
GRANI
GRANIANI
GRANIO. M
GRANIVS. F

H.

HABICNS. M
HABILIS. F
HABITIS. F
HELI ... VS. FI. FE
HELINIV
HELL ... S. FEC
HIBI ...

I.

I + OFFIC
IABI
IABVS. FE
IACOMIO. F
IANVARIVS
IANVARII
IANVARI. OF
IASSO. F
ICMCRIMO. F
IGINI. MA
ILLIANI. M
ILLIOMEN

ILLIOMRIN
IMANN
INPRINTV. F
IOENALIS
IOVANTI
ISABINI. F
ISTVRONIS
IVCANVS. F
OF. IVCVN
IVENALIS. MA
IVENIS. M
OF. IVLIA
IVLIA
IVLIA. PATR
OF. IVL. PAT
IVLII. MA
IVLIOS
IVLI. M
IVLIVS. F
IVINVMI. M
IVRONIS. OF
IVSTI. MA
OF. IVSTI
OF. IVVENAL

K.

KALENDI. O

L.

O. LAE
OF. LABIONIS
LALLI. MA
LANCIV . . .
LATINIAN. F
LATINIANVS
LATINVS
LIBERALIS
LIBERIVS
LIBER'VS
LIBERTI. M
OF. LICINI
OF. LICINIAN
LICINILVS
LICINVS
LICINVS. F
LICNVS
LILTANI. M (?)
LINIVSMIX
LITVGAMVS
LOCCO. F
LOCIRM. M
LOGIRN. M
LOLIVS. F

LOLLIVS. F
LOSSA
OF. LOVIRILO
LVCANVS
LVCANVS. F
LVCANTVS. F
M. LVCCA
OF. LVCCEI
LVGETO. FE
LVPRI. M
LVPI. M
LVPINI. M
LVPPA
LYPPA
LVTAEVS
LVTAEVS. FEC
LVTAFVS

M.

MACCAIVS. F
MACCALI. M
OF. MACCIA
MACCIVS
MACCIVS. F
MACERATI
MACI. OF
MACILLI. M
MACIRVS
MACRI. M
MACRIA
MACRINVI
MACRINVS
MACRIANI. M
MAGNVS. F
MAIANVS
OF. MAIO
MAIORI. M
MAIOR. I
MAIORIS
MAIORIS. F
MALCI. O
MALLIIDO. F
MALIVRN
MALLI. M
MALLIACI
MALLIACI. M
MALLICI. M
MALLVRO. F
MALNCNI
MAMILIANI
MANDVIL. M
OF. MANNA
MANTIIO. F
MANVS. F
Q. MAR. F

MARCELLI. M
MARCELLINI. M
MARCI
MARCI. F
MARCI. MA
MARCI. O
MARCILLI. M
MARCVS. FEC
MARINI. M
MARITVS. M
MARCILLI. M
MARTANI. M
OF. MARO
MAROI. M
MARONI. M
MARONL F
MARSL. M
MARSVS. FECI
MARTANL M
MARTI
MARTL. M
MARTIALIS. FEC
MARTIALIS. M
MARTINI
MARTINI. M
MARTINV
MARTINVS. F
MARTII. O
MARTIVS
MASCL
MASCVLVS. F
OF. MASCVL. AVERI
MASVETI
MASVRIANI
MATEMI
MATERNI
MATERNINVS
MATERNNI. M
OF. MATE
MATRIANI
MATVCRNVS
MATVCVS
MATVRI. M
MATVRN
MAXI. MA
MAXIMI
MAXMII. M
MAXMINI
OF. MEM
MEMORIS. M
MERCA
MERCAO
MERCATOR
MERCATOR. M
MERCVSSE. M
MERCVSSA. M
MEDETI. M

2 L

APPENDIX.

METHILLVS
METTI. M
MICCIO
MICCIO. F
MICCIONIS. M
MIDI. M
MILIACI
MILIANI
MILLIARII
OF. MINI
MINVLI. M
MINVS. FE
MINVS. O
MINVTIVS.
MISCIO. F
MO
OF. MO
OF. MODEST
OF. MODESTI
OF. MOE
MOM
O. MOM
MOMI. M
MON
OF. MONO
OF. MONTANI
OF. MONTECI
OF. MONTEI
OF. MONTI
OF. MONTO
MOSSI. M
MOXIVS
MVISVS. F
OF. MVRRA
OF. MVRRANI
OF. MVSERA
MVXTVLI. M
MVXTVLLI. M
MVXIVIII. M (·)

N.

NAMILI
NAMILIANI
NANII. CROES
OF. NARIS
NASSO. F
NATALIS
O. NATIVI
NEBVERI. OF
OF. NEM
NEPOTIS
NERT. M
OF. NERT
NERTVS
OF. NERI

NEQVREC
NICEPHOR
NICEPHOR. F
OF. NI
OF. NIGRI
OF. NIGRIAN
NIGRINI
NIMILIANI
OF. NITORI
NOBILIANI. M
NOBILIANVS
NVMIDI. M
IVL. NVMIDI
NVTIS

O.

OCRI. MA
ONATIVI (?)
OPPRIN (?)
OPTATI. M
OPVSIA
ORI. MAN (?)
OSBI. MA
OVIDI

P.

PANI. L. F
OF. PARI
PASSENI
PASSI. F
PASSIENI
OF. PASSIENI
OF. PASSIENVS
O. PAS. F (?)
PATER. F
PATERATI. OF
PATERCLINI. OF
PATERCLOS
PATERCLOS. FF.O
PATERCLVS. F
PATERIRANVS. FIT
PP. PATERMI
PATERNI
PATERNI. M
PATERNI. OF
PATERNVLI
PATIIRNV
PATNA. FEC
PATNI. FEC
PATRC ⊷ LINI
PATERCIINI
PATRICI. M
C. AN. PATR

OF. PATRC
OF. PATRICI
OF. PATRVCI
PAVLIANI
PAVLIVS. F
PAVLI. M
PAVLI. MA
PAVLIANI. M
PAVLLI. M
PAVLLVS. F
PAVLVS
PAZZENI
PECVLIAR
PECVLIAR. F
PECVLIARIS. F
PIINTII. MANV
PERE . . . .
PERECHILI
PEREGRIN
PERPET
PERRVS. F
PERVS
PERVS. FE
PITVRICI. M
OF. POLIO
OF. POLLIO
OF. PONTEI
OF. PONTHEI
PONTI. OFFIC
O. PONTI
POTIACI
POTITINI. M
POTITIANI. M
C. IVL. PR
PRID. FEC
PRI. IMO
PRIM
PRIMANI
PRIMI
OF. PRIM
OFIC. PRIM
OF. PRIMI
PRIMIS
PRIMITIVI
PRIMVL
PRIMVLI
PRIMVL. PATER
OF. PRIMVI.
OF. PRIMVS
PRISC. L. M
PRISCINI. M
PRIVATI. M
OF. PRM
FAB. PRO
PROBI. OF
PROBVS. F
PROTVLI

OF. PVDEN
PVONI. M
PVRINA
PVTRI. M
PYLADES

Q.

QVADRATI
QVADRATVS
QVARTVS
QVARTVS. F
QVIETVS. F
QVINNO
QVINTI. M
QVINTINI. M
QVINTINIANI
QV. C

R.

RACVNA. F
RAMVLVS
REBVRRI. OF
REBVRRIS
REBVRRVS F
RECEN. F
RECMVS
REDITI. M
REGALIS
REGALIS. F
REGENVS
REGENVS. F
REGINI. M
REGINVS
REGINVS. F
RIIGNVS
REGVILL
REGVLI. M
RIIGVLI. M
REGVLINVS
REGVLIN. F
RENECR. M
RIIOGENI. M
REVILINVS
RI. IOGENI
OF. RICIMI
RIPANI
RIVICA
ROFFVS. FRC
ROFFVS. FE
ROIPVS. F
ROLOGENI. M
ROMVLI. OF
ROPFVS. FR

ROPVSI. FE
ROPPIRVI. M
ROTTLAI. IM
OF. RVBA
RVFFI. MA
RVFFI. M
OF. RVFI
RVFIA
RVFINI
RVFINI. M
OF. RVFIN
OF. RVFNI
RVFVS. FE

S

SA. ARTI (?)
OF. SAB
SABELLVS
SABELVI
SABIANI
SABINIANVS. I
SABINVS
SABINVS. F
SABINI. M
OFF. SAB
SACERVASIII
SACERVASIFF
SACER. VASI. OF
SACERI. OF
SACEROT. M
SACIANT
SACIRAP. O
SACIRO. M
SACREM
SACRI. OF
SACRILI. M
SACROTI. M
SACROT. M. S.
SALIAPVS
SALV. F
SALVS. F
SAMACVIS
SANTINVOV. O
SANVCIVS. F
SANVILLI. M
SANVITTI. MA
SARENTIV
OF. SARRVT
SATERNVS
SATERNINI. O
SATVRNNI. OF
SATTO. F
SCOLVS
SCOPLI. F
SCOPLI. M

SCORVS
SECANDI. M
SECANDIN
SECINI
SECVNDI. OF
OF. SECVN
SECVNDINI
SECVNDVS
SECVNDVS. F
SEDATVS. F
SEDATI. M
SEDETI. M
SENI. A. M
SENICA. M
SENICI. O
SENILA. M
SENNIVS. F
SENO. M
SENONI
SENTRVS. FE
SERRVS
SERVILIS
SEVERI
SEVERI. OF
SEVERI. M
OF. SEVERI
SEVERIANVS
SEVERIANI
SEVERIANI. M
SEVERINVS. FE
OF. SEVERPVD
OF. SEVIERMI
SEXTI. O
SEXTI. M
SEXTI. MA
SIIXTI. MA
SIIXTI. MAN
SEXTVS. F
SIIXTILI. F
SHVLNI
SILDATIANI. M
SILENVS
SILVANI
SILVIIRI. M
SILVI
SILVI. PATER
SILVINI
SILVINI. F
SILVINVS. F
SILVI OF
G. SILVII
SILVI. PATRI. O
SILVIPATRICI
SILVVS
SIMVRS. O
SINTVRNV . . .
SITVSIRI. M

APPENDIX

SOIIILLL M (?)	TVRTVNN	VIRTHV
SOLIMI. OFI		VIRTHVS
SOLLEMNI. OF		VIRTHVS. FECIT
SOLLVS	**V.**	VIRTIVAS
SOLLVS. F		VIRTVTI. F
MA. SVETI	VACIR. O	OF. VIRTVTIS
SVLPICI	C. VALAB	VISI. M
OF. SVLPICI	VALERI	VITA
SVLPICIANI	VARIVS. F	OF. VITA
SVOBNI. O	VASSALI	OF. VITAL
SVODNED. OF	VAXTI	OF. VITALIS
SVRIVS	VECETI. M	OF. VITALI
SYMPHO	VEGETI. M	VITALI. OF
	VENERAND	VITALIS. FR
	VENI. M	VITALIS. M. S. F.
T.	VENICARVS F	VITALIS. M. S. FECIT
	VERECV	VITALIS. PP
TALLINI	VERECVNDI	VITINVS. F
TASCONVS. F	VEREDV. M	Q. VO
TASCIL. M	VERTECISA. F	Q. VOVO
TASCILLA	VIIRI. M	VOCEV. F
TASCILLI. M	VERVS	VOSIICVNNVS
TAVRI	VESPO. F	VNICVS. F
TAVRIANVS	VESPONC	VRNINI
TAVRICVS. F	VEST. M	VRSVLVS. FR
TEBBIL	VESTRI. OF	VSTI. MA
TEDDI	VETERNIV	VXMLINI
TENEV. M	OF. VIA	VXOPILLI. M
TERRVS	VICARVS. F	
TEROII. M	VICTORI. M	
TERT. M	VICTORINVS	**X.**
TERTI. MA	VIDVCOS. F	
TERTIVS	VIDVCVS. F	XANTHI
TESTVS, FO	VIMPVS	XIVI
TETTVR	VINN	XVNX
TETTVR. O	VIRIL	
TETVR. O	O. VIRILI	
TITTICI	VIRILIS. F	**Z.**
TITTILI	OF. VIRILLI	
TITTIVS	OF. L. COS. VIRIL	ZAPEPIDIV
TITVRI. M	OF. L. C. VIRIL	ZOIL
TITVRONIS	OF. L. Q. VIRIL	ZOLVS
TITVRONIS. OF	VIRONI. OF	. . RVIL LV. F
TVLLVS. F	VIRT	OIVNV
TVLLVS. FE		

POTTERS' MARKS ON MORTARIA.

ALBINVS	CAS . . .	EOAB
ALBINVS. FECIT	CATVLVS. F	ESVNERT
APRILIS	CIREKOFNS	Q. VALERI
ANDON	CRICIR. OF	GATTIVS
P. ARVA	DEVA . . .	MANSINVS
ANDID. FECIT	DVBITATVS	LICINILVS
AMMIVS	DOINV	LITVCENI
RRIXSA	DO . . .	LVGVDI. F

POTTERS' MARKS.

LVGVDVS. FACTVS	P. R. R	L. CAN. SEC
LVGVDV	POTATICVS. FE	SECVNDVS
F. LVGVDV	Q. S. D	SOLLVS
LVGVDV. FACTV	RIDANVS	SOLLVS. F
L. E. ECIT	RIDANVS. M	TANIO
MARINVS. FECIT	RIPANI	SEX. VAL
MARTINVS. F	RIPANVS TIBER. P	Q. VALC. F
MATVCENVS	A. TEREN	VERANI. F
MATVSENS. F	RIPANI	Q. VALERI.
MAXI	RVCCVS	ESVNERTI
PRASSO. OF	SAVRANVS	Q. VALERIVS
PRIMVS. F	SATVRNINVS	VERANIVS
L. LVRIVS. PRISCVS	SATVRNINVS. FEC	T . . . S. VALEN
P. P. R	Q. VA. SE	VIALLA

POTTERS' MARKS ON THE HANDLES OF AMPHORÆ.

A. A. F	GMT.	CANTON. QV. ET
AERI	G. S. A.	CANT. QVESI (?)
C. F. AI	HILARI	QIMPN
C. AZ.	L. A. GE	ROMANI
AXII	L. C. F. P. C. O	L. V. ROPI. M
BELLVCI	IIVN. (?) MELISSAE	RVFSANI
L. VI. BR	MELISSE	SAENVS
C.	L. IVNI (?)	OF. SANI
C. IV. R	MELISSI	SCALENS
C. V. H	MAMILI (?)	L. SER SENC
L. CES	MELISSI	C. SEMPOL
C. AP. F	M. P. R	L. S. SEX
CRADOS	MCC	L. C. SOL
CARTVNIT. M (?)	MIM	C. MARI. STIL
CORI	NYMPH	S. VENNR
F. C. CVFIA	P. S. A	VALERI
L. F. CRESCIV. FE (?)	POR. L. AN	VENVSTI
EIPC	Q. S. P	VIBIOR
EROV. IF	CAT. QVIE	S. YENNR
FAVSTI. MANIB	CANTON. QV	

INDEX.

A.

Aballaba (*Watch-cross*), 158
Abona (*Bitton*), 169
Acus, 393
Ad Abonam (*Bitton*), 169
Ad Abum (*Winterton*), 152
Ad Alaunam (*Lancaster*) 164
Ad Alpes Penninos, 164
Ad Ansam (*Stratford*), 160
Ad Antonam, 165
Ad Aquas (*Wells*), 168
Ad Decimum, 169
Ad Fines, (*Broughing*), 150
Ad Lapidem (*Stoneham*), 167
Ad Lemanum (*on the Lymne*), 170
Ad Petuariam (*Brough*), 153
Ad Pontem (*Farndon*), 152
Ad Sabrinam (*Sea Mills*), 169
Ad Tisam, 154
Ad Trajectum (*Severn side*), 169
Ad Trivonam (*Bury*), 165
Ad Uxellam (*Bridgewater*), 168
Ad Vigesimum (*Castle Flemish*), 162
Adminius, a British prince, 41, 43
Æratus, 18
Æs, 18, 19
Ælia Castra (*Alcester*), 166
Ælla, the leader of the West Saxons, 457
Æquipondium, 413
Æsc, king of Kent, 456
Æsculapius, worship of, 325
Æscwine, king of the East Saxons, 459
Æsica (*Great Chesters*), 153, 214
Ætius, letter of the Britons to, 454
Age, average of the Romans in Britain, 385
Agelocum (*Littleborough*), 152
Agger, 222
Agminales, 223
Agricola, Julius, 57—60
Agriculture, state of, under the Romans, 255—257
Akeman-street, 524
Akemannes-ceaster (*Bath*), 524
Alauna (*Alcester*), 165
Alauna (*Lancaster*), 164
Alauna (*Kier*), 123, 155
Albani (*Scottish tribe*), 63
Albinus, Decimus Clodius, 128—131
Alcluyd (*Dumbarton*), 526
Aldermen, 510
Aliona (*Whitley Castle*), 158
Allectus, his usurpation, 142
Alonæ (*Ambleside*), 164
Altars, Roman, 316—320
Amber, use of, and superstitions connected with, among the Anglo-Saxons, 489
Amboglanna (*Birdoswald*), 158
Ambrosius Aurelianus, 455
Amphitheatres, Roman, 212
Amphoræ, 280, 403, used for coffins, 365
Ampulla, 363, 403
Ancalites (*People of Berkshire?*), 34

Ancasta, a goddess worshipped in Roman Britain, 351
Anderida (*Pevensey*), 169
Andredes-ceaster (*Pevensey*), 458
Andredes-leah (*Silva Anderida*), 457
Angles, 455
Anglo-Saxons, their mode of settling on the conquered lands, 505, prejudiced against settling in towns, 507
Animal remains found near Roman sites, 405
Ansa, 413
Antivestæum (*the Land's End*), 61
Antoninus Pius, 126
Antoninus, Itinerary of, 146, 531—533
Antoninus's wall, 127, 133
Apollo, worship of, 322, 324
Aquæ Calidæ, Aquæ Solis (*Bath*), 68, 121, 210
Arcani, agents employed in Britain, 443
Arciaconus, a deity worshipped in Roman Britain, 351
Ariconium (*Weston*), 161
Armillæ, 393
Armour, Roman, 414, Anglo-Saxon, 470, 471
Arrow-heads of stone, 96; Anglo-Saxon, 474
Astarte, worship of, 325
Athelbert becomes king of Kent, 457; converted to Christianity, 462, 463
Attacotti (*Scottish tribe*), 63, 139, 441
Attrebates (*Berkshire*), 62
Augustine, St., the apostle of the Anglo-Saxons, 462
Auteri (*Irish tribe*), 64
Avebury, British circles at, 83
Avisford, in Sussex, remarkable Roman tomb found there, 364, 387
Axe, Anglo-Saxon war-axe, 477
Axelodunum (*Bowness*), 158

B.

Banatia (*Bonness*), 123

Banchorium (*Bangor*), 163
Bancorna-byrig (*Bangor Iscoed*), 527
Banna, a Roman town near Hadrian's Wall, 257
Barrows, or sepulchral mounds, 70, 71, 86; Roman, 377, 378; Anglo-Saxon, 467, 469
Bartlow hills, 377
Basilica, Roman, 211
Bathan-ceaster (*Bath*) 459
Baths, in Roman houses, 199, 200; public, 211, 212, 414
Beads, Roman, 287, 288; Anglo-Saxon, 486, 489
Debban-byrig (*Bamborough*), built, 459
Belatucadrus, a god worshipped in Roman Britain, 349
Belgæ (*Hants, Wilts,* and *Somerset*), 25, 43, 61
Bells, Roman, 405
Bennaventa (*Burrow Hill*), 149
Benonæ (*High Cross*), 149
Beorh, beorg, bearw, 467
Beowulf, the Anglo-Saxon poem of, 466
Bericus, a British prince, 40, 42
Bernicia, kingdom of, 456
Bibracte, 161
Bibroci (*People of Sussex*), 34
Bignor, Roman villa at, 243
Bilanx, 413
Blanii (*Irish tribe*), 64
Blatum Bulgium (*Middleby*), 156
Blestium (*Monmouth*), 161
Boadicea, 51—55
Bolanus, Vettius, 56
Bolerium (*the Land's End*), 61
Bollivi, 510
Boni homines, 510
Bonus Eventus worshipped, 233, 337
Borcovicus (*Housesteads*), 158, 316
Bos longifrons, 404
Bovium (*Bangor*), 163
Bovium (*Ewenny*), 162
Bowls, Anglo-Saxon, 499
Box, branches and leaves of, buried with the dead by the Romans, 387, 388
Braccæ, 65

INDEX

Braciaca, an epithet of Mars, 319
Brannogenium (*Leintwardine*), 122
Bravinium (*Leintwardine*), 163
Bremenium (*High Rochester*), 123, 155
Bremetenracum (*Brampton*), 158
Bremetonacæ (*Overborough*), 164
Bricks or tiles, Roman, 183, 184
Bridges, Roman, 225
Brigantes (*North of England*), 45, 62, 126
Brigantes (*Irish tribe*), 64
Brigantia, the goddess, 351
Brigis, or Brige (*Broughton*), 167
Brinavæ (*Black-ground*), 166
Britain, description of, by Cæsar, 36; by Strabo and Diodorus, 37
Britannia, the goddess, 333
Britons, their condition and manners, 37, 65; serving as auxiliaries abroad, 139
Brocavium (*Brougham*), 155
Bronze, age, 2; swords, 5—18, 101; coins, 14, 16; spearheads, 15; daggers, 15, 103; primary origin of, 16; armour, 18; weapons, 19; Celts, 20; instruments made of, 95; Roman manufactures in, 9, 19, 22, 297
Bronzes, Roman, 408
Brovonacæ (*Kirby Thore*), 155
Buckets, Anglo-Saxon, 499
Bullæum, *see* Burrium
Burgwara, 314, 517
Burrium (*Usk*), 122, 161, 169
Bustum, 388

C.

Caer, 526
Caer-Legion (*Caerlon*), 527
Caer-Luel (*Carlisle*) 526
Caer-Marddyn (*Caermarthen*), 527
Caer-Seiont, 527
Caer-Went, 527
Cæsar, Julius, invades Britain, 28; his second invasion, 30
Cæsaromagus (*Chelmsford*), 159
Cairns, 77
Calcaria (*Tadcaster*), 152, 213
Calceus, calceamentum, 398

Caledonia Sylva, 63
Caledonii (*Scottish tribe*), 18, 59, 63, 131
Caliga, 396
Caligula marches to the coast of Gaul, 41
Calleva (*Silchester*), 122, 161
Cambodunum (*Slack*), 122, 164
Camboricum (*Cambridge*), 160
Camulodunum (*Colchester*), 41, 43, 45, 52, 122, 159
Camulodunum, *see* Cambodunum.
Candelabrum, 407
Cangi, 45, 62
Canonium (*Kelvedon*), 159
Cantæ (*Scottish tribe*), 63
Canterbury, its municipal condition under the Anglo-Saxon, 510
Cantii (*tribe inhabiting Kent*), 37, 61
Cantwara-byrig (*Canterbury*), 457
Capulus, 409
Caput stateræ, 413
Caracalla, 11, 133, 137
Caractacus, 40, 45
Carausius assumes the empire, 139; his coins, 140; murdered, 142
Carbantorigum (*Kirkcudbright*), 123
Carnabii (*Scottish tribe*), 63
Carnonacæ (*Scottish tribe*), 63
Carnydd, 77
Cartismandua, 47, 48, 57
Cassi (*Hertfordshire*), 34, 62
Cassivellaunus, 31, 34
Castra Exploratorum (*Netherby*), 156
Cataracto, or Cataractonium (*Catterick*), 122, 154
Catini (*Scottish tribe*), 63
Catus Decianus, 52
Catyeuchlani (*Buckingham, Bedford*, and *Hertford*), 62
Cauci (*Irish tribe*), 64
Cauponæ, caupones, 223
Causennæ (*Ancaster*), 151
Caves, habitations in, 115, 118
Ceajius, a deity worshipped in Roman Britain, 351
Censter, 526

INDEX. 553

Ceawlin, king of the West Saxons, 459
Celtic tribes, their origin and movement, 23
Celtis, 10
Celts, instruments so called, 8, 10, 16, 20, 98
Cemeteries, Roman, 213
Cenia (*the Fal*), 168
Cenimagni (*the people of Suffolk*), 39
Cenotaph, Anglo-Saxon, 367, 368, 469
Centrum stateræ, 413
Centurial stones, 418, 420
Cerdic, king of the West Saxons, 458
Cerealis, Petilius, 53, 57
Ceres, worship of, 321
Cerones (*Scottish tribe*), 63
Châtelaine of the Anglo-Saxon ladies, 489
Christianity, its establishment in Roman Britain questioned, 353, 356; among the Welsh, 527
Cilurnum (*Chesters*), 137, 157, 210, 328, 338, 418
Circinus, 413
Circles of stones, 79, 83
Cissan-ceaster (*Chichester*), 458
Cities of Britain, their condition when the Roman legions left the island, 451
Civitas, 426, 427, 428, 510
Classicianus, Julius, 56
Claudius, his expedition to Britain, 42
Clausentum (*Bittern*), 167, 351, 422, 431
Cnut, king, deceives the citizens of London, 518
Coal, Kimmeridge, 290, mineral, used as fuel by the Romans, 292
Coccium (*Ribchester*), 164, 210, 336
Cochlear, 410
Cocidius, a god worshipped in Roman Britain, 350
Cogidubnus, or Cogidunus, 51
Coinage, Roman, 14, 15; British, 40

Coins, British, 109, 112; Roman plated, 431; forged, 432; coins relating to Britain, 435; modes in which they were hoarded up, 436, 437; proportional numbers in which Roman coins are found, 438, 439; Anglo-Saxon, 501
Colania (*Carstairs*, or *Lanark*), 123, 156
Collegia, 427
Coloniæ, 426
Colonies, Roman, 296
Colum, cola nivaria, 402
Combretonium (*Burgh*), 160
Combs, Roman, 398; Anglo-Saxon, 492
Comius, a British prince, 40
Commius, the Attrebatian, 27, 29, 30, 35
Commodus, 128
Compasses, Roman, 412
Condate (*Kinderton*), 163
Condercum, (*Benwell*), 210, 335, 348
Congavata, 158
Connubium, 428
Conovium (*Caer hûn*), 163
Constans visits Britain, 143
Constantine the Great, 143
Constantine, the usurper, his history, 449, 450
Constantius, marches against Carausius and Allectus, 142
Copper, found in Britain, 22
Corbridge lanx, 326
Corda (*Birrenswork*), 123
Coria, 123
Corinium (*Cirencester*), 122, 161, 168
Coriondi (*Irish tribe*), 64
Coritavi (*Northampton, Leicester, Rutland, Derby, Nottingham, Lincoln*), 61
Cornabii (*Warwick, Worcester, Stafford, Salop, Cheshire*), 62
Corn-wealas, 525
Corstopitum (*Corchester, Corbridge*), 154, 325
Costume of the Romans, 391
Cowey Stakes, 36
Cowries found in Anglo-Saxon graves, 492

INDEX.

Crassus, Publius, 24
Creones (*Scottish tribe*), 63
Crococolana (*Brough*), 152
Cromlechs, 72—77; their position, 83—86; age of, 106, 107
Cryptoporticus, in Roman villas, 240, 243
Culinary utensils, Roman, 401, 403
Culter, 314, 409
Cumbria, kingdom of, 526
Cunetio (*Folly Farm*), 169
Cunobeline, 40, 41
Curator viarum, 223
Curia (*Currie*), 123, 155
Curia, 426, 509
Curiales, 426, 509
Cynric, king of the West Saxons, 459
Cyren-ceaster (*Cirencester*), 459

D.

Daggers, early bronze, 15, 16
Damnii (*a Scottish tribe*), 63, 123
Damnonii (*Devon* and *Cornwall*), 43, 63
Danum (*Doncaster*), 152
Darini (*Irish tribe*), 64
Decianus, Catus, 52
Decuriones, 426
Defensor civitatis, 427, 509
Deira, kingdom of, 456
Delgovitia (*site uncertain*), 153
Demetæ (*Welsh tribe*), 62
Derventio (*Old Malton*), 153
Derventio (*Little Chester*), 165
Deva (*Chester*), 123, 163
Devana (*Old Aberdeen*), 123
Diana, worship of, 320
Dicalidones (*a Scottish tribe*), 441
Didius Gallus, Avitus, 47
Diplomata, 223
Diversoria, diversores, 223
Dobuni (*Gloucester* and *Oxford*), 42, 62
Dogs, British, 38, 257, 558
Dolichene, Jupiter, 316
Dolmen, 72
Dorocina (*Dorchester*, Oxf.), 166
Dover, its municipal privileges under the Anglo-Saxons, 511
Drift, geological formation, 1

Drinking-glasses, Anglo-Saxon, 495
Droit de gite, 511
Druids, their political faction in Gaul, 27; retire to Anglesea, 49; their system and worship, 66—69
Druids' circles, 79
Druids' beads, 288
Dubræ (*Dover*), 146, 170, 184
Dunium (*Dorchester*), 121
Durius (*the Dart*), 167
Durnovaria (*Dorchester*), 121, 167
Durotriges (*Dorset*), 61, 121
Durobrivæ (*Rochester*), 146, 360
Durobrivæ (*Castor*), 151, 210
Durocobrivæ (*Dunstable*), 148
Durolevum (*Davington*), 146
Durolipons (*Godmanchester*), 150, 160
Durolitum, or Durositum (*Romford*), 159
Durovernum (*Canterbury*), 121, 146, 457
Duumviri, 426, 510

E.

East-Anglia, kingdom of, founded, 459; the East-Angles converted to Christianity, 463
Eastlow hill, in Suffolk, a remarkable barrow opened by Professor Henslow, 377
East-Saxons converted to Christianity, 463
Eblani (*Irish tribe*), 64
Eburacum (*York*), 122, 133, 136, 152, 153, 456
Echevins, 510
Elauna, the goddess, 352
Ellebri (*Irish tribe*), 64
Ensis, 19
Eofor-wic (*York*), 456
Epiacum (*Lanchester*), 122, 154, 293
Epidii (*Scottish tribe*), 63
Epistomium, 404
Epona, the goddess, 338
Eppillus, a British prince, 40
Erdini (*Irish tribe*) 64
Ermyn Street, 523

INDEX.

Erpeditani (*Irish tribe*) 64
Eteocetum (*Wall*), 149, 164
Eustache, Count of Boulogne, his quarrel with the burghers of Dover, 511
Exeter, its position under the Anglo-Saxons, 513
Exan-ceaster (*Exeter*), 527

F.

Fanum Cocidis (*near Bankshead*), 350
Ferrum, 19, 21
Fibulæ, Roman, 392; Anglo-Saxon, 478, 484
Fire-dogs, Roman, found in Britain, 401
Fire-places, Roman, 401
Flint implements, 1
Flora, coin representing the goddess, 14
Focus, 314, 401
Forfex, 408
Forgeries of Roman coins, 432, 434
Forks, Roman, 410
Fortune, worship of, 336, 337
Forum Dianæ (*Dunstable*), 148
Frontinus, Julius, 57
Fulgur divom, 389

G.

Gabrosentæ (*Burgh-upon-Sands*), 158
Gadeni (*Cumberland* and *Scottish hordes*), 64, 351
Gagates, or jet, 289, 290
Galacum (*near Kendal*), 122, 164
Galava (*Keswick*), 164
Galgacus, 17, 60
Galgal, 77
Gallus, Avitus Didius, 47
Gangani (*Irish tribe*), 64
Gariannonum (*Burgh Castle*), 448
Genii, worship of the, 329, 331, 333
Gerontius, Count, 449
Gessoriacum (*Boulogne*), 28, 139, 142

Gildas, his legendary history, 452—455
Gladius, 19
Glanovanta, 159
Glass, Roman, 282; manufactured at Brighton, 283; different articles made of it, 284, 287; Anglo-Saxon glass, 495; German-Saxon glass, 497
Glass windows in Roman houses, 205
Gleow-ceaster (*Gloucester*), 459
Glevum (*Gloucester*), 161
Gobannium (*Abergavenny*), 163, 169
Gold found in Britain, 296
Goldsmiths, skill of the Anglo-Saxon, 486
Goldsmith's sign at Old Malton, 304
Government, Roman, in Britain, 416
Governors of Roman Britain—
Proprætors:
  Aulus Plautius, 42, 424
  Ostorius Scapula, 44
  Avitus Didius Gallus, 47
  Veranius, 49
  Caius Suetonius Paullinus, 49
  Petronius Turpilianus, 56
  Trebellius Maximus, 56
  Vettius Bolanus, 56
  Petilius Cerealis, 57
  Julius Frontinus, 57
  Julius Agricola, 57—60
  Sallustius Lucullus, 124
  Julius Severus, 126
  Priscus Licinius, 126, 424
  Lollius Urbicus, 126, 424
  Platorius Nepos, 424
  Aufidius Victorinus, 127
  C. Valerius Pansa, 424
  Ulpius Marcellus, 127
  Perennis, 127
  Publius Helvius Pertinax, 128
  Decimus Clodius Albinus, 128
  Virius Lupus, 131, 336, 424
  Claudius Xenophon, 425
  Marius Valerianus, 137, 425
  Mæcelius Fuscus, 425
  Gnæus Lucilianus, 425
  Claudius Paulinus, 425
  Nonnius Philippus, 137, 425

Governors (*continued*)—
  Vicarii:
    Martin, 144
    Alypius, 440
    Civilis, 441, 442
    Chrysanthus, 447
Gratian, a British usurper, 448
Gregory, Pope, undertakes the conversion of the Anglo-Saxons, 461

H.

Habitancum (*Risingham*), 154, 337, 420
Hadrian in Britain. 124
Hadrian's wall, 125, 156, 157, 210
Hair-pins, Roman, 393; Anglo-Saxon, 485
Ham, 505
Hammia, a goddess worshipped in Roman Britain, 352
Harimella, a goddess, 352
Hengest and Horsa arrive in Kent, 455—457
Herculentus, the god, 352
Hercules, worship of, 325
Heriri Mons (*Snowdon*), 150
Hibernia (*Ireland*), invaded by the Romans, 61: description of, by Ptolemy, 64
Himilco, the Carthaginian, 25
Holy Promontory (*Carnsore Point*), 64
Honorius, the emperor, gives liberty to the cities of Britain, 451
Horestii (*Scottish tribe*), 63
Household gods of the Romans, 407
Houses, Roman, 187—199
Hrofes-ceaster,(*Rochester*),457, 511
Hunnum (*Halton-chesters*), 157, 213, 389, 419
Huscarles, 513, 518
Hypocausts in Roman houses, 196, 199

I.

Iceni (*Suffolk, Norfolk, Cambridge, and Huntingdon*), 44, 61

Iciani (*Icklingham*), 160, 508
Ictis (*the Isle of Wight*), 25
Ida, king of Northumbria, 459
Ierne, 25
Iknield Street, 523
Imanuentius, king of the Trinobantes, 31
In Medio, 153
Inscriptions, on Roman coins, 14; in Roman villas, 245, 254; on drinking vessels, 286; on a Roman pig of copper, 291; on pigs of lead, 294, 295; on silver, 296; on medicine stamps, 299, 303; on signs, 304; on roundels at Colchester, 312; on altars, 314—352; sepulchral inscriptions, 378—387; centurial stones, 418, 419; early inscriptions to the emperors, 420—423; to municipal officers, 427; sepulchral inscriptions found in Cornwall and Wales, 528, 529
Iron, swords, 7, 19; early use of, 17, 22; procured in Britain, 37; manufacture under the Romans, 291—294
Isannavaria (*Burnt Walls*), 149
Isca Dumnoniorum (*Exeter*), 121, 167
Isca Silurum (*Caerleon*), 48, 122, 162, 169
Ischalis (*Ilchester*), 121, 168
Isinnae (*Ancaster*), 151
Isurium (*Aldborough*), 122, 154, 213, 225, 404
Itininaries, Roman, 145, 162, 166, 527, 528
Ituna (*Solway Firth*), 158
Iverni (*Irish tribe*), 64

J.

Jewellery, Anglo-Saxon, 485, 486
Jugantes, 61
Julianus, Didius, 128
Jupiter, worship of, 315—318
Jutes, 455, 506

K.

Kent, kingdom of, founded, 456

INDEX.

Keys, Roman, 399; Anglo-Saxon, 490, 491
Kimmeridge coal, ornaments made of, 288
Kist-vaen, 72
Knives, Roman, 409; Anglo-Saxon, 474, 489

L.

Lachrymatories, 284
Laconicum, 236
Lactodorum (*Towcester*), 151
Lamps, Roman, 406, 407
Lamps placed in Roman graves, 363
Lancula, 413
Lares, 407
Lavatræ (*Bowes*), 155, 336, 425
Lead, manufactures in, in Roman Britain, 294; leaden coffins found in Roman cemeteries, 368
Legions, Roman, in Britain, 123, 448
Legiolium (*Castleford*), 152
Lemanis Portus (*Lymne*), 146, 170
Leucarum (*Llychwr*), 162
Libra, 413
Lichavens, 74
Licinius Priscus, 126
Ligula, 410, 411
Lightning, people killed by, buried on the spot, 389
Lindum (*Lincoln*), 122, 151
Lindum (*Ardoch*), 123, 155
Locks, Roman, 399, 400
Logi (*Scottish tribe*), 63
Londinium (*London*), 53, 121, 147, 148; the residence of the proprætor, 185
London, its municipal history under the Anglo-Saxons, 514—517
Low, 70, 79, 467
Lucerna, 406
Lucius, king, a fabulous personage, 354, 355
Lucopibia (*Whithern*), 122
Lucullus, Sallustius, 124
Luentinum (*Llanio*), 122, 169
Luguballium, Luguvallium (*Carlisle*), 155, 158
Lundenwic (*London*), 515
Lupicinus, 144
Lupus, Virius, 131
Lutudarum (*Chesterfield*), 166

M.

Mæatæ (*a northern tribe*), 131
Madus (*Medway*), 146
Magiovintum (*Fenny Stratford*), 151
Magna (*Kenchester*), 163, 299
Magna (*Carvoran*), 158, 321, 349
Magnatæ (*Irish tribe*), 64
Magnentius, 144
Mais, a town near Hadrian's wall, 257
Mancipes, 223
Mancunium (*Manchester*), 164
Mandubratius, chief of the Trinobantes, 31, 33
Manduessedum (*Mancetter*), 149
Mansiones, 223
Maponus, a god worshipped in Roman Britain, 352
Marcellus, Ulpius, 127
Marcus, a British usurper, 448
Margidunum (*Bridgeford*), 152
Maridunum (*Caermarthen*), 122, 162
Mars, worship of, 318
Martin, governor of Britain, 144
Masonry, Roman, characteristics of, 179—191
Matres deæ, worship of the, 338; traces of, in the middle ages, 338—345; Roman altars in Britain dedicated to, 345—347
Matunus, a god worshipped in Roman Britain, 352
Maurusius, Victorinus, 138
Maximus, Magnus, his revolt and usurpation, 445; his death, 447; fables connected with him, 447
Medicine stamps, Roman, 299, 304
Mediolanum (*Chesterton*), 164
Mediolanum (*on the Tanad*), 122, 150
Menapia (*St. David's*), 162
Menapii (*Irish tribe*), 64

INDEX.

Menhir, 74, 82
Mercia, kingdom of, 460, 463
Mercury, worship of, 322
Mertæ (*Scottish tribe*), 63
Middle Angles converted to Christianity, 463
Mile-stones, Roman, 224; length of the Roman mile, 225
Military force in Britain under the Romans, 418
Milliarium, 223, 421
Minerva, worship of, 320
Minimi, 115, 501—503
Mint, Roman, in Britain, 430
Mirrors, Roman, 398
Missio, 428
Mistletoe, a sacred plant among the Druids, 69
Mithras, worship of, 326—329
Mogontis, a god worshipped in Britain, 350
Mona (*Anglesea*) 49, 62
Money, *see* Coins.
Mons Heriri (*Snowdon*), 150
Morbium (*Temple-borough*), 166
Moridunum (*Honiton ?*), 167
Mortar, Roman, 189
Mortaria, Roman, 280, 403
Mucrones, 17
Municipia, 425, 426, 510
Munuces-ceaster (*Newcastle*), 456
Mutationes, 223

N.

Nails in the Roman sandals, 397
Nasica, Cæsius, 48
Needles, Roman, 408
Nidum (*Neath*), 162, 527
Niger, Pescennius, 128
Northumbrians converted to Christianity, 463
Notitia Imperii, 416
Novantes (*a Scottish tribe*), 63
Noviomagus (*Holwood hill*), 121, 147
Nucleus, 221
Numen, numina, 311, 335
Nymphs, worship of the, 330

O.

Octopitarum Promontorium, 163

Oculists' stamps, Roman, 300—303
Officials, Roman, in Britain, 417, 418
Olenacum (*Old Carlisle*), 159
Olicana (*Ilkley*), 122, 164
Olla, 403
Ordovices (*North Wales*), 45, 57, 62
Orestii, *see* Horestii.
Orrea (*Bertha*), 123, 155
Ostorius Scapula, 44
Otadeni (*Northumberland and South of Scotland*), 62
Othona (*Ythanceaster*), 448
Oysters, British, 120
Oyster-shells found on Roman sites, 404

P.

Parisii (*Yorkshire*), 61
Patera, 314
Paullinus, Caius Suetonius, 49, 56
Paulus Catena, 144
Pavements, tesselated, 230, 246—254
Pavimentum, 221
Pecten, 398
Penates, 407
Pennocrucium (*on the Penk*), 149
Perennis, 127
Periods, division of pre-historic times into, 2, 5
Pertinax, 128
Petriana (*Cambeck Fort*), 158, 210
Petronius Turpilianus, 56
Petuaria, 122, 153, 316
Peulvan, 74, 82
Philippus, Nonnius, 137
Picts and Scots, 139, 441, 454
Planets, deities of the, 322
Plautius, Aulus, 42, 44
Plebs, 427
Polybius, anecdote by, 17
Polycletus, 56
Pons Ælii (*Newcastle*), 155, 157
Pontes (*Staines*), 161
Population of Roman Britain, its character, 306
Portus Lemanis (*Lymne*), 146, 170, 404

INDEX.

Portus Magnus (*Portchester*), 169
Portus Sistuntiorum (*Freckleton*), 164
Potters' marks, 275, 541—549
Pottery, British, 93; Roman, made in the Upchurch marshes, 260; at Durobrivæ, 263; potters' kilns, 264; Samian ware, 269—276; other varieties of Roman potteries, 277; Anglo-Saxon, 493, 494; German-Saxon, 494, 498; Frankish, 498
Præfecti, 510
Præfericulum, 314
Præpositus regis, 521
Prætorium (*Flamborough Head ?*), 153
Prasutagus, 51
Principales, 426, 510
Probi homines, 510
Procolitia (*Carrawburgh*), 158
Proprætors of Britain, *see* Governors.
Province, Roman, its constitution and divisions, 416
Pteroton Castrum (*Burghead*), 143
Ptolemy's account of Britain, 61
Puncta stateræ, 413
Puticuli, 389
Pyra, 358

Q.

Querns, for grinding corn, 404

R.

Ratæ (*Leicester*), 122, 151
Ravenna, anonymous geographer of, 145; his list of Roman towns in Britain, 257, 537
Reeves, 510, 515, 521
Regni (*Sussex* and *Surrey*), 61
Regnum (*Chichester*), 51, 210
Regulbium (*Reculver*), 146, 410
Retigonium (*Stranraer*), 122
Ricagm . . ., a goddess worshipped in Roman Britain, 352
Richard of Cirencester, 145, 533; his Itinerary, 527

Rigodunum (*Coccium*), 122
Rings, Roman, 393
Roads, Roman, construction of, 221—223; adopted by the Anglo-Saxons, 522—524
Robogdii (*Irish tribe*), 64
Rochester, its municipal privileges under the Anglo-Saxons, 511
Rocking-stones, 84
Rogus, 358
Roofs of Roman houses, 206
Roundels, inscribed, found at Colchester, 311
Rubbish pits attached to Roman towns, 215
Rudge cup, 257
Rudus, ruderatio, 221
Rutunium (*Rowton*), 150, 163
Rutupiæ (*Richborough*), 120, 121, 146
Ryknield Street, 523

S.

Salinæ (*Droitwich*), 164
Salinæ of Ptolemy, 122, 165
Salt-ways, the roads so called, 524
Samian ware, 269—275
Sandals, Roman, 396, 397
Sarabus sinus, Neptune so called, 352
Sarcophagi of stone at York, 363
Saxonicum littus, 451
Saxons, invasion of the, 452, 455—459
Scabini, 510
Scales, Roman, 413
Scapula, Ostorius, 44
Sceat, sceattas, 503
Scissors, Roman, 408; Anglo-Saxon, 490
Scopus stateræ, 413
Scots, 139
Scowles, 292
Sculptures on stone, 12, 13
Searo-byrig (*Old Sarum*), 459
Seaxas, 474
Securis, 314
Segedunum (*Wallsend*), 157
Segelocum (*Littleborough*), 152
Segontiaci (*Hampshire* and *Berks*), 34

INDEX.

Segontium (*Caer Seiont*), 150, 163
Selgovæ (*a Scottish tribe*), 63
Sepulchre, modes of, among the Romans, 357—360; articles buried with the dead, 363; rites of, among the Anglo-Saxons, 466
Sera pensilis, 401
Serapis, worship of, 329
Sestuntii (*Westmoreland* and *Cumberland*), 62
Setlocenia, a goddess worshipped in Roman Britain, 352
Severus, the emperor, 129; proceeds to Britain, 133; establishes his court at Eburacum, 133; his campaigns against the Caledonians, 134; dies at York, 136
Severus, Julius, 126
Severus, Junius, 128
Shields, Anglo-Saxon, 475
Signa, 322
Silures (*border of Wales*), 45, 47, 57, 62, 65
Silvanus, worship of, 257, 324
Silver, found in Britain, 295
Sitomagus (*Dunwich*), 160
Slaves, traffic in, among the Saxons, 461; sold in London, 515
Slaves, immolated at the burial of their chiefs by the Anglo-Saxons, 469
Sorbiodunum (*Old Sarum*), 167
South-Saxons, kingdom of the, founded, 458
Snails found on Roman sites, 404; snail shells found in Anglo-Saxon barrows, 492
Spears, Anglo-Saxon, 21, 474
Speculum, 398
Spinæ (*Speen*), 161, 168
Spoons, Roman, 410
Spurs, Roman and Saxon, 415
Standard, Roman, found near Stoney-Stratford, 415
Statera, 412, 413
Statores, 223
Statumen, 221, 223
Steel for sharpening knives, Roman, 410
Steelyards, Roman, 413
Stependiariæ civitates, 426
Stone, early use of, 4, 5; sculptures, 12, 13; implements, 95—98
Stonehenge, 79, 83, 85, 108
Strathcluyd, kingdom of, 526
Street, 523
Strigils, 413
Sturius (*the Stour*), 160
Stylus, 411
Suetonius Paullinus, Caius, 49, 56
Sulloniacæ (*Brockley Hill*), 148
Summum dorsum, summa crusta, 222
Superstitions connected with ancient monuments, 85, 86, 105
Swegen, king, his death, 520
Swords, bronze, 5, 20; iron, 7, 19; characteristics of Roman, 7—14; on coins, 14; used by the Gauls, Romans and Britons, 17; British or Roman, 101, 102; Anglo-Saxon, 21, 470—474
Syria dea, worship of the, 322

T.

Tabernæ, diversoriæ 223
Tabula, 411
Tabulæ honestæ missionis, 429
Taixali (*Scottish tribe*), 63
Tamara (*on the Tamar*), 121, 168
Tamesis (*Sinodun Hill?*), 166
Tamia (*Braemar Castle*), 123
Tasciovanus, 40
Tegula, 363
Terra-cottas, Roman, 281
Tertianæ deæ, 338
Testudo, 30
Tetricus, 138
Theatres, Roman, 212
Theodosia (*Dumbarton*), 156
Theodosius takes the command in Britain, 441
Thetford, the townsmen of, kill their abbot, 513
Tibia (*the Taaf*), 162
Tiles, Roman, 183
Tin, procured from Britain, 24, 25
Tinc . . . , a British prince, 40
Tintinnabulum, 405
Tisa (*the Tees*), 154
Titus, the emperor, 42

Togodumnus, a British prince, 40, 43
Tombs, Roman, made of tiles, 360
Torques, torquis, 394; torquis brachialis, 395
Town, Roman, description of a, 171; its walls, 172; gates, 174; houses, 187; streets, 207; public buildings, 210; suburbs, 212; drainage, 213
Towns, municipal, under the Romans, 425; preserved under the Anglo-Saxons, 508; examples, Canterbury, 510; Rochester and Dover, 511; Thetford, Worcester, Exeter, 513; London, 514—519; charters granted to towns, 520
Trebellius Maximus, 56
Trebonius, Caius, 32
Triliths, 74
Trimontium (*Eildon*), 123, 155
Trinobantes (*the people of Essex*), 31, 61
Tripontium (*Dove Bridge*), 149, 151
Trua, or *trulla*, 403
Trutina, 413
Tuesis (*Cromdale*), 123
Tumblers (origin of the word), 495
Tumulus, 71
Tun, 505
Tunnocelum (*Drumburgh*), 158
Turpilianus, Petronius, 56
Tweezers, Roman, 399; Anglo-Saxon, 490

U.

Urbicus, Lollius, 126, 127
Uriconium (*Wroxeter*), 122, 149, 163, 212, 301
Urns, sepulchral, Roman, 359; Anglo-Saxon, 493
Usdiæ (*Irish tribe*), 64
Ustrinum, 358
Uxaconium (*Red-hill, or Oakengates*), 149
Uxela (*Bridgewater*), 121
Uxelum (*Raeburnfoot*, or *Castleover*), 123, 156

V.

Vacomagi (*Scottish tribe*), 62
Vagniacæ (*Southfleet*), 147
Valentinus, his intrigues against Theodosius, 444
Valerianus, Marius, 137
Vanduara (*Paisley*), 123, 156
Varæ (*Bodfari*), 163
Vectis (*Wight*), 44, 167
Vecturiones (*Scottish tribe*), 441
Velibori (*Irish tribe*), 60
Vellocatus, 57
Veniconii (*Irish tribe*), 64
Venonæ, 151
Venricones (*Scottish tribe*), 63
Venta Belgarum (*Winchester*), 121, 167
Venta Icenorum (*Caistor*), 122, 160
Venta Silurum (*Caerwent*), 169
Venusius, chief of the Brigantes, 48, 57
Veranius, 49
Verbeia, a goddess worshipped in Roman Britain, 352
Veredarii, 223
Veric, a British prince, 40, 42
Verlucio (*Highfield*), 169
Verometum (*near Willoughby*), 152
Verteræ (*Brough*), 155
Verulamium (*near St. Alban's*), 36, 41, 53, 122, 148, 212
Vespasian, the emperor, 42
Veteres, Vetires, or Vetiris, a god worshipped in Roman Britain, 349
Vettius Bolanus, 57
Viæ vicinales, privatæ, agrariæ, deviæ. 22
Vicarii of Britain, *see* Governors.
Victoria (*Dealgin Ross*), 123, 155
Victorinus, Aufidius, 127
Victorinus, Maurusius, 138
Victory, worship of, 336
Villa, 510
Villa Faustini, 160
Villas, Roman, 227—255; occupied by the Anglo-Saxons, 508
Villages, British and Roman, 113—115, 255

Vindobala (*Rutchester*), 157
Vindogladia (*Gussages*), 167
Vindolana (*Chesterholm*), 158
Vindomis (*Whitechurch*), 167
Vindomora (*Ebchester*), 154
Vinovium or Vinnovium (*Binchester*), 122, 154
Viradesthi, a goddess worshipped in Roman Britain, 353
Viroconium, *see* Uriconium.
Virosidum (*Maryport* and *Ellenborough*), 159
Vodiæ (*Irish tribe*), 64
Voliba (*on the Fowey*), 121
Volsellæ, 399
Voluba (*the Fowey*), 168
Voluntii (*Lancashire*), 62
Voluntii (*Irish tribe*), 64
Vortigern, king of the Britons, 455, 456

W.

Walls, Roman, character of, 172—177; Hadrian's, *see* Hadrian.
Water-cock, Roman, 404
Watling Street, 523
Weapons, Roman, 414
Week, gods of the days of the, 322, 323
Welsh, origin and meaning of the word, 457; the Welsh settlement in England, 525—527; Christianity introduced among them, 527
Wessex, kingdom of, founded, 459
West-Saxons, kingdom of the, founded, 458; converted to Christianity, 463
Wintan-ceaster (*Winchester*), 459
Woodchester, Roman villa there described, 229—240

THE END.

Printed by BALLANTYNE, HANSON & CO.
Edinburgh & London

Lightning Source UK Ltd.
Milton Keynes UK
UKHW022037280219
338222UK00007B/118/P